Reading Authentic English Picture Books
in the Primary School EFL Classroom

FREMDSPRACHENDIDAKTIK
INHALTS- UND LERNERORIENTIERT

Herausgegeben von Carmen Becker, Gabriele Blell und Rita Kupetz
Mitbegründet von Karlheinz Hellwig

BAND 37

Zu Qualitätssicherung und Peer Review der vorliegenden Publikation

Die Qualität der in dieser Reihe erscheinenden Arbeiten wird vor der Publikation durch drei Herausgeberinnen der Reihe geprüft.

Notes on the quality assurance and peer review of this publication

Prior to publication, the quality of the work published in this series is reviewed by both editors of the series.

Julia Reckermann

Reading Authentic English Picture Books in the Primary School EFL Classroom

A Study of Reading Comprehension, Reading Strategies and FL Development

PETER LANG

Bibliografische Information der Deutschen Nationalbibliothek
Die Deutsche Nationalbibliothek verzeichnet diese Publikation
in der Deutschen Nationalbibliografie; detaillierte bibliografische
Daten sind im Internet über http://dnb.d-nb.de abrufbar.

Library of Congress Cataloging-in-Publication Data
A CIP catalog record for this book has been applied for
at the Library of Congress.

Zugl.: Bielefeld, Univ., Diss., 2017

Die Grafik auf dem Cover wurde gestaltet von: Leonie Borgmann

Gedruckt auf alterungsbeständigem, säurefreiem Papier
Druck und Bindung: CPI books GmbH, Leck

D 361
ISSN 1430-8150
ISBN 978-3-631-75646-1 (Print)
E-ISBN 978-3-631-76115-1 (E-PDF)
E-ISBN 978-3-631-76116-8 (EPUB)
E-ISBN 978-3-631-76117-5 (MOBI)
DOI 10.3726/b14360

© Peter Lang GmbH
Internationaler Verlag der Wissenschaften
Berlin 2018
Alle Rechte vorbehalten.

Peter Lang – Berlin · Bern · Bruxelles ·
New York · Oxford · Warszawa · Wien

Diese Publikation wurde begutachtet.

www.peterlang.com

Acknowledgements

This book is the final result of a long journey and I would like to take the opportunity to thank all those who supported and encouraged me along the way. In the following I would like to highlight some of the people that have contributed to my project in special ways.

First of all, I am indebted to Prof. Dr. Paul Lennon for employing me at Bielefeld University and by doing so making my PhD project possible. Paul's professional supervision, helpful advice, endless patience, constructive feedback and words of encouragement were invaluable throughout the whole process. Without him, I would not have been able to conduct my research and write my thesis. Also, many thanks go to Prof. Dr. Petra Josting for her interest in my project and spontaneous willingness to be part of the examination committee. Thank you also to Prof. Dr. Ralf Schneider, who was the third member of this committee. I would like as well to thank Prof. Dr. Henning Rossa, who enabled me to work at the Technical University of Dortmund in the last two years of this project. This gave me fresh motivation and valuable research time that contributed to the completion of this book.

A number of fantastic colleagues from Bielefeld as well as other universities, many of whom have become friends over time, were always willing to discuss my project with me, never hesitated to provide critical feedback, corrected my language mistakes and encouraged me in many different ways until the end of this project. All of them have contributed to this project's quality and kept me motivated throughout. Special thanks goes to Dr. Tanja Freudenau, Dr. Patricia Skorge, Prof. Dr. Dominik Rumlich, Dr. Peter Schildhauer and Dr. Nathan Devos. I value your support and friendship and very much look forward to future cooperations.

Thank you also to Prof. Dr. Bärbel Diehr, Prof. Dr. Eva Wilden and Prof. Dr. Andreas Rohde for helpful advice during their research colloquia. More invaluable feedback came from the DGFF summer school in Riezlern, Austria, in 2014. I would like to thank the DGFF for this unique opportunity.

Without the primary school where I collected my data, this project could never have come into being. Therefore, great thanks goes to the teachers, pupils and parents at this school, particularly to Jessica W. and the learners in her English classes 4a and 4b. Jessica's support and patience allowed me to collect all the data I needed and I owe her cookies for the rest of her life.

A number of friends and student assistants supported me in this project as well. I am particularly grateful to Stewart for support with academic writing in English, to Edi and Jessi for helping out whenever possible in the earlier stages, to Vanessa for helping out in the last steps of this project and to Sandra for her help with transcribing. A special thanks also goes to Leonie who was a great support in creating pictures and designing the cover of this book.

Lastly, I would like to thank my family, particularly my parents, who always trusted and supported my decisions and career choices. Their endless encouragement kept me motivated and greatly contributed to the success of this project. Last but not least, Chris, I am so grateful to you for being so supportive and understanding when I was working late at night or all weekend long. You are an irreplaceable friend and incredible support.

Thank you all very much!

Table of Contents

Part B: Research Design

7. Introducing the Empirical Study: Research Questions, Setting and Participants, Research Design

This book contains an online appendix. This can be downloaded
from our website. Please go to the last page of this publication for
the activation code.

List of Figures

List of Tables

List of Pictures

List of Abbreviations

BIG	*Beratung Information Gespräch Stiftung Lernen* [consultation information communication foundation learning]
BSFU	*Bilingualer (Sachfach)Unterricht* [bilingual content subject teaching (Rumlich, 2016: 28)]
CEFR	Common European Framework of References for Languages
CHILITEX	Children's literature and experiments
CLIL	Content and language integrated learning
CLT	Communicative language teaching
DESI	Deutsch Englisch Schülerleistungen International [German English learner achievement internationally]
df	Degree of freedom (statistical measurement)
EFL	English as a foreign language
ELLiE	Early language learning in Europe
e.g.	for example [the abbreviation 'e.g.' is only used in brackets and figures]
EU	European Union
EVENING	*Evaluation Englisch in der Grundschule* [evaluation of English in the primary school]
FL	Foreign language
FLL	Foreign language learning
FMKS	*Verein für frühe Mehrsprachigkeit an Kindertageseinrichtungen und Schulen e.V.* [association for early multillingualism at kindergarden and schools]
GDR	German Democratic Republic
i.e.	that is [the abbreviation 'i.e.' is only used in brackets and figures]
IEA	The international association for the evaluation of educational achievement
JuLE	*Junge Lerner lesen Englisch* [young learners reading in English]
KMK	*Kultusministerkonferenz* [The Standing Conference of the Ministers of Education and Cultural Affairs of the Länder in the Federal Republic of Germany]
LiPs	*Lesen im Englischunterricht auf der Primarstufe* [reading in the primary school English classroom]
L1	First language

L2	Second language
MSW NRW	*Ministerium für Schule und Weiterbildung des Landes Nordrhein-Westfalens* [Ministry of School and Further Education North Rhine-Westphalia]
MuViT	Multilingual virtual talking books
NRW	*Nordrhein-Westfalen* [North-Rhine Westphalia]
MKJS BW	*Ministerium für Kultus, Jugend und Sport Baden-Württemberg* [Ministry of Education, Cultural Affairs, Youth and Sport of Baden-Württemberg]
PIRLS	Progress in international reading literacy study
Qual	Qualitative
Quan	Quantitative
RG 1	Reading group 1
RG 2	Reading group 2
RG 3	Reading group 3
R:	Researcher (only used when direct quotations from the transcripts are displayed)
SLA	Second language acquisition
TBLL	Task-based language learning
TEFL	Teaching English as a foreign language
TIMSS	Trends in international mathematics and science
YLE test	The 'Cambridge young learners English movers' test
ZPD	Zone of proximal development

See Appendix D.1.2 for an explanation of the abbreviated references made to the transcripts on reading comprehension and reading strategies.

Definition and Clarification of Terms

English as a foreign language (EFL): When referring to foreign language learning in the primary school, this book will mean learning English as a foreign language, unless stated otherwise. In fact, the choice of a FL depends on different factors, such as the location of the school or the history of a state (see Hermann-Brennecke, 1994; Klippel, 2000: 11ff; Meyer, 1992). In Germany, mostly English and French are taught as modern FLs at the primary school level. However, some schools also include regional languages (like Low German) or languages from border countries (e.g., Dutch) in their curriculum. Still, English in primary schools greatly dominates over other languages. One good reason for that is that English has long since become a global language and gained the status of a lingua franca and is by far the most common L2 in the world (see Crystal, 2003; Seidlhofer, 2011; Saville-Troike, 2012: 9). Also in Europe, English is the most widely used foreign language (European Commission, 2012: 5) and two thirds of all Europeans believe English to be the most useful foreign language for them (European Commission, 2012: 7).

Foreign language (FL) and second language (L2): The terms foreign language and second language will be used interchangeably in this book. The book refers to a foreign or second language when referring to any additional target language which language learners learn in addition to their mother tongue(s), irrespective of whether this takes place in an environment where the language is spoken naturally or in an environment where this is not the case. In other works, second and foreign language do not necessarily refer to the same idea. According to Saville-Troike (2012), a second language is in its general sense a term that refers to any language acquired after the first language. However, in a more specific sense it contrasts with foreign language, as a second language would be learnt within a context where it is socially dominant and needed for, for example, education or employment, whereas a foreign language would be a new language that is not widely used in the learner's immediate social context. It is often hard to provide a clear-cut distinction between foreign or second language contexts, however. For instance, Phillipson (2007) points out that particularly across Europe, English is gradually becoming an L2 and no longer has the status of a FL. Thus, the two terms will be used interchangeably unless explicitly stated otherwise.

German as a first language (L1): In order to refer to German school learners' L1, 'German as L1' will be used. Clearly, this also includes learners whose L1 might be different to German or who grew up with German and one or more additional languages. However, because the language of schooling is German, this will for reasons of simplicity be taken as the learners' L1, in the full knowledge that multilingualism prevails in classrooms.

Primary school (level) (learner): Primary school will be defined as the school that provides children with a fundamental school education from the ages of five or six to ten or eleven (see also Doyé, 1993: 49). In Germany this mostly includes Years 1 to 4 (see 'young language learner').

Reading: The term 'reading' is used in this book to express that the learners read texts on their own. 'Reading' does not imply that the teacher reads out a text to the learners, as is often done in the primary school with the method of storytelling. Thus, unless stated otherwise, 'reading' in the context of this book means that the learners read a text independently and by themselves.

Secondary school types – *Gymnasium, Realschule, Hauptschule, Volksschule* (see KMK, 2010): The German school system is divided into different school types at secondary school level. Traditionally, the different school types were *Gymnasium, Realschule* and *Hauptschule*; other school types such as *Gesamtschule* or *Sekundarschule* exist as well, but are not important for this book and study. The *Gymnasium* covers lower and upper secondary level (Year 5 to 12 or 13) and provides an in-depth general education that aims at a general higher education entrance qualification. The *Realschule* is a type of school at lower secondary level (Year 5 to 10) that provides pupils with a more extensive general education and the opportunity to go on to courses of education at upper secondary level that lead to vocational or higher education entrance qualifications. The *Hauptschule* is a type of school at lower secondary level that provides a basic and compulsory school education (Year 5 to 9 or 10). This division into different school types is only important for secondary school level, because there is no such division at the primary school level. The *Volksschule* does not exist any longer but is the former name for compulsory school, today known as primary school and *Hauptschule*.

Storytelling: Storytelling, in the literal meaning of the word, implies that somebody tells a story. In the context of this book it refers to a method that is commonly used in teaching English to young learners. In this method, the English teacher reads out a story, often an English picture book, to the learners (see Böttger, 2005: 85f; Cameron, 2001: 160; Schmid-Schönbein, 2008: 85ff). Whilst reading to the learners, the teacher uses special techniques that support comprehension of the story (see Böttger, 2005: 87f; Brewster & Ellis, 2002: 196f).

Young language learner: By this term, this book denotes learners at the primary school level, that is Years 1 to 4, when the learners are aged about six to ten. In some federal states in Germany, primary school lasts six instead of four years and thus the learners would be up to about 12 years old. In North Rhine-Westphalia, which is the federal state that the current empirical study was conducted in, Years 1 to 4 are the primary school years.

1. Introduction

Abstract: This chapter introduces the core topic of this book, reading in the primary school English classroom, and embeds it into the broader context of teaching FLs to young learners. It briefly elucidates on the current state of research, provides an overview of the study which is the major focus of this book and outlines this book's structure.

There is a rising interest in early foreign language learning (FLL) around the globe. Learning and teaching modern languages to young learners is a worldwide phenomenon nowadays and is becoming a central issue in today's globalised society. In Europe, the European Union's (EU) policy supports language learning and encourages "all citizens to learn and speak more languages" (European Commission, 2012: 2). Europe thus calls for the support of multilingualism (European Commission, 2008) and has established the long-term objective that "all EU citizens should speak two languages in addition to their mother tongue" (European Commission, 2006: 9). This interest in early FLL at schools is not a novelty: "Europe [...] has a long history of early FLL at primary and pre-primary levels, stretching back over 40 years in some regions" (Enever, 2011a: 10). Today, teaching modern languages early has been extensively implemented across the EU (Johnstone, 2000: 123) and the majority of European countries start language learning at the primary school level (Enever, 2011b: 24). Hence, the number of children learning English as a foreign language (EFL) at primary school increases from year to year (Copland & Garton, 2014: 223). The most prominent reason for such an early start is the belief that early FLL creates a basis for life-long language learning (Klippel, 2000: 15; Piepho, 2003: 33).

By 2006, all federal states in Germany had introduced English at the primary school level (Schmid-Schönbein, 2008: 19). In North-Rhine Westphalia (NRW), which is the German federal state where the present study was conducted, two lessons of English were taught in Years 3 and 4 between 2003 and 2008. This implementation was evaluated in the EVENING study (see Engel et al., 2009) and led to a revision of the curriculum: English was introduced in Year 1 (second term) in the school year 2008/09 with two lessons per week.[1] Thus, nowadays primary school learners in NRW learn English for three and a half years with two lessons per week. The same holds true for four other German federal states: Baden-Württemberg,

---

1   See http://www.schulentwicklung.nrw.de/cms/angebote/egs/angebot-home/englisch-in-der-grundschule.ht ml (last access: 15.05.2017).

Brandenburg, Hamburg and Rhineland-Palatinate (see Kultusministerkonferenz[2] (KMK), 2013). All other German federal states start with FLs in Year 3. Mostly the FL is English, but in parts French is also chosen (KMK, 2013).

With regard to FL skills development in the primary school, the focus is on listening and speaking, whilst reading and writing are only ascribed a supportive function (Elsner, 2010: 40; Pinter, 2006: 45). However, the importance of reading should not be underestimated. Literacy is a key qualification and an invaluable skill in a society that is very much based on literary language (Schulz, 2010: 7).[3] In the context of school education, literacy is important in any subject. Being able to read and understand texts is a key competence for learners and forms the basis for autonomous learning in all classes (Steck, 2009: 3). As such, reading and writing abilities form the basis of the successful acquisition of content matter and therefore influence a learner's career and existence in society (Ehlers, 2007: 107). Reading is not only important in the learners' first language (L1), but also in their second language (L2) (Lázaro Ibarrola, 2010: 95), in that reading is a necessary and important means for successful FLL (Gorsuch & Taguchi, 2010: 27; Henseler & Surkamp, 2010: 87).

Therefore, Frisch (2014d: 34) strongly suggests moving reading more into the centre of attention in primary school English teaching in order to allow learners access to English texts and underline the communicative function of reading. Freudenau (2012: 100) explains that "everyone who has taught English in a German primary school has experienced how many children have a great interest in seeing and reading English words." Likewise, Bland (2013a: 34) notes that "most young learners are ambitious to read for themselves [...]; usually they are enthused by their recent success in learning to read in their mother tongue." However, Bland (2013a: 35) criticises the fact that the "motivational leap forwards due to their newly acquired reading skills is often under-utilised in early second language learning." In fact, reading and particularly reading comprehension of FL texts is by no means in the foreground of teaching in the primary school EFL classroom in Germany (BIG-Kreis[4], 2015: 28). This book addresses this desideratum and focuses on EFL reading with young learners.

---

2   Original German term for 'The Standing Conference of the Ministers of Education and Cultural Affairs of the Länder in the Federal Republic of Germany.'
3   Also see Kennedy (2013) for a more detailed definition of literacy that goes beyond the scope of being able to read and write.
4   The 'BIG-Kreis' (Beratung Information Gespräch Stiftung Lernen (BIG) [consultation information communication foundation learning]) is an association founded by Prof. Piepho in 1999 and consistes of ten professors of TEFL in different German federal states (see BIG-Kreis, 2015: 5).

EFL reading with young learners has been neglected as a skill for a long time and has only gradually gained more importance in teaching practice and EFL research in recent years. Based on curricular decisions and classroom observations, researchers and teachers now pay increasing attention to EFL reading (Diehr & Rymarczyk, 2010: 9). Nevertheless, Frisch (2015: 15) points out that statements about FL reading at the primary school level are often still based on teachers' experiences and opinions, but too seldom on empirical evidence and structured reflections of classroom practice. Thus, she concludes that empirical studies on reading-related issues in the primary school EFL classroom have been rare and more research is needed (Frisch, 2010: 107). So far, research has been conducted on the general idea of integrating written language in the primary school English classroom (particularly Duscha, 2007; Reichart-Wallrabenstein, 2004), on teaching reading in the primary school English classroom (particularly, Frisch, 2013; Jöckel, 2016), on reading aloud with a focus on pronunciation abilities (particularly, Diehr, 2010; Diehr & Frisch, 2010b), on reading comprehension of words and sentences (particularly, BIG-Kreis, 2015; Engel, Groot-Wilken & Thürmann, 2009) and on cooperatively reading picture books and strategies used for doing so (Kolb, 2013; Reichart-Wallrabenstein, 2004). Still, many questions remain unanswered, many aspects have not been researched yet and the foci already investigated need further research to back up the results.

With regard to reading comprehension and reading materials, an issue that is still under debate is the extent to which reading at text level should be used in class and how difficult and complex reading materials and tasks should be. The BIG study has recently shown that English teachers in Germany ask pupils to read at the word and short sentence level regularly, but that stories or books are only seldom used for reading tasks (BIG-Kreis, 2015: 28). BIG-Kreis (2015) tested the EFL competence of about 2,100 pupils in Germany at the end of Year 4. The results revealed that the participants' reading comprehension was very good and that the tasks at the word and sentence level were too easy for the learners. Further studies on reading competence in the primary school EFL classroom include the EVENING[5] study (Engel et al., 2009; Paulick & Groot-Wilken, 2009) and a study by Wilden, Porsch and Ritter (2013). Central results of both studies suggest that the reading tests they used, testing reading at word and sentence level, were too easy for the learners and that the learners' reading performance was above everyone's expectations. Thus, researchers suggest that

---

5   Evaluation Englisch in der Grundschule [Evaluation of English in the primary school] (EVENING).

reading comprehension should be assessed at the text level and not just at the word and sentence level (Paulick & Groot-Wilken, 2009: 195). Consequently, Frisch (2014c) has stressed that research is needed concerning the comprehension of short English texts.

This issue will be addressed in this book, which will focus on reading texts in the primary school EFL classroom. As such, the EFL classroom's focus on oral skills (see, e.g., Klippel, 2000: 22) will not be contested, but reading will simply be brought more into the centre of attention and the potential and possibilities of reading will be explored in more depth. In particular, authentic English picture books will be explored as reading material for young EFL learners. Such books offer authentic English language input as well as meaningful stories (Bleyhl, 2000: 26). As such, they are possibly suitable reading materials for the primary school EFL classroom. With regard to picture books, Bland (2013a: 36) notes that their inherent motivational power could help to initiate the positive habit of extensive reading for pleasure.

However, reading English children's books or other such fairly unknown texts hardly ever takes place in primary school EFL lessons (see, e.g., Kolb, 2013: 33). Kolb (2013: 33) points out that it is almost exclusively the teacher who reads out the story of picture books to the children in storytelling phases and that "hardly ever do the children get the chance to explore an unknown text on their own or to read a picturebook [sic] by themselves." However, Waas (2016: 36) has just recently suggested that teachers should try reading picture books with Year 4 learners.

To date, research about reading authentic English picture books in the primary school EFL classroom is rare, as only four, partly small-scale, studies have been conducted. A small-scale study by Kolb (2013) provides the first evidence that young EFL learners are not overtaxed with the task of extensive reading of authentic English picture books in cooperative reading settings and that young learners are on the contrary interested in these books and highly motivated to read them. Furthermore, she found that they used a number of different FL reading strategies. Reichart-Wallrabenstein (2004) investigated the use of written language in a Year 3 EFL classroom and amongst other aspects found that picture books are well-suited for reading at that level, with a focus on comprehension in cooperative reading settings. With regard to reading comprehension, Frisch's (2013) study has shown that young EFL learners can read phonic readers[6] in English after phases of

---

6   Phonic readers are not authentic picture books but were designed for the purpose of teaching English literacy (see Chapter 5.1.4).

explicit teaching of reading. With a focus on reading aloud in a reading competition, Diehr and Frisch (2010b) found that Year 4 learners are generally interested in reading authentic picture books and that they showed good reading aloud abilities after explicit practice of this task. Therefore, some initial insights have been provided concerning picture books as reading materials, young learners' reading strategies in cooperative reading settings, young learners' reading aloud abilities and teaching reading with the help of phonic readers. The results are promising and suggest exploring the notion of reading picture books with young EFL learners in more depth.

This book aims at further exploring the possibility and potential of reading these books with young learners and investigates the three foci reading comprehension, reading strategies and FL performance. In order to explore these aspects with regard to reading authentic English picture books with young EFL learners, the study presented in this book pursues the following three research questions:

I. To what extent are Year 4 EFL learners capable of reading and understanding authentic English picture books?
II. Which reading strategies do young EFL learners apply when reading authentic English picture books for understanding?
III. To what extent does the reading of authentic English picture books influence the FL performance of EFL learners in Year 4?

To answer the research questions, a longitudinal reading study was conducted over five months with a group of eleven Year 4 learners at a German primary school. In weekly reading sessions, these learners read six different authentic English picture books and were involved in various activities that provided data about their comprehension of the books and their strategies used during reading (research questions I and II). During reading, supportive devices were provided and their potential helpfulness was investigated as well. In order to research whether regular reading had an influence on the learners' FL performance, their FL competence was tested against that of a control group ($N = 12$) at three points in time over the five months. This comparison provided data for research question III.

The study's aim was therefore to explore whether primary school EFL learners are capable of reading authentic English books, what levels of comprehension they reach, what means of support they effectively use, what reading strategies they apply and which strategies prove useful for successful comprehension, the extent to which the learners are aware of their strategy use, a possible development of comprehension and strategy use and the extent to which reading might have an influence on FL competence.

To explore these issues, Part A of this book will provide a theoretical foundation for reading, with a focus on reading in the primary school EFL classroom, including reading materials, research results, reading processes and an outline of practices in EFL teaching to young learners. Firstly, Chapter 2 will give a more general insight into the developments and current practices of teaching FLs at the primary school level and outline current trends and developments in (early) FL teaching. Based on that, Chapter 3 will show the extent to which the skill of reading is integrated into teaching English in the German primary school and elaborate on the development and current status of reading as well as the question of a reading methodology. Next, Chapter 4 will explore the skill of reading, especially FL reading, and offer details about reading processes and reading strategies. Chapter 5 will then look at potential reading materials and particularly focus on the use of authentic English picture books. Since reading such authentic FL texts is challenging, Chapter 6 will then outline the balance between challenge and support and explore ideas of supporting reading in the primary school EFL classroom.

The theoretical part will show that there is a lack of research concerning various aspects of FL reading in the primary school; in particular with a focus on reading at the text level, reading authentic picture books, FL development through reading and young learners' use and awareness of reading strategies. The two main aspects, reading in the primary school and authentic English picture books, will be brought together since reading authentic English picture books in the primary school was investigated in the empirical study presented in this book. Research desiderata, concepts of teaching English in the primary school, details about reading, explanations of support in reading and choosing reading materials will provide the basis for this study.

Part B then provides details about the empirical study of this book. Firstly, Chapter 7 describes the mixed methods research design, which integrates a longitudinal reading study that investigates research questions I and II with a quasi-experimental study that yields data on research question III. The research questions will be explained in detail and the data collection procedure for each research aspect will be outlined. Information about the study's setting and participants, a primary school in Bielefeld that follows a bilingual programme to a certain extent, will be given. In addition, my role as researcher as well as quality criteria will be reflected on. Subsequently, Chapter 8 will explain the research instruments used in this study, together with a detailed description of the research materials and instruments as well as the methods used for analysing the data.

In Part C, the results of the study will then be presented, interpreted and discussed. Chapters 9 to 11 will present and interpret the results of the three foci of the study; each chapter is dedicated to one of the three foci. Finally, Chapter 12 will bring the central results of the empirical study into connection with each other and offer a final conclusion and discussion. Based on the results, practical implications for future teaching as well as ideas for further research will be provided, also taking into consideration the limitations of the study and an outlook on future research.

Part A: Theoretical Foundations

Abstract: Part A is concerned with the theoretical foundations of the study. It outlines developments and teaching practices with young FL learners and examines reading processes and FL reading in the primary school. The chapter discusses authentic English picture books as reading materials and elucidates on supporting learners in FL reading.

2. Teaching English in the Primary School: Developments and Current Practice

Abstract: Looking back at roughly 60 years of teaching FLs to young learners, this chapter touches on the most important developments and gives an overview of current practices. This includes the history of implementing FLs in primary schools, the notion of CLIL, the principle of topic-based instruction and an overview of FL skills development.

Introducing FLL at the primary school level has been one of the major developments with regard to FLL at German schools over recent decades. Another important development is the increasing implementation of bilingual education at both the secondary as well as the primary school level. This approach of using English in other subjects outside of the EFL classroom will be dealt with next. After that, the notion of using meaningful content for FLL, which underlies the idea of bilingual education, will be explained. Such topic-based teaching forms a basic principle of learning and teaching FLs at the primary school level. Moreover, the basic principles of FL skills integration and FL skills development with young learners will be outlined.

2.1 The History of Implementing FLs in German Primary Schools

This chapter will briefly trace the historical development of teaching FLs at primary school level in Germany from its early beginnings in the private school sector around the 1920s to the pilot phase of the 1960s and 70s, to a gradual move towards establishing FLs for young learners around the 1990s and to its final implementation in all German federal states in 2006 (Schmidt-Schönbein, 2008: 11f).

In the beginnings of the 20th century, the first attempts at early FL teaching in Germany took place in the private school sector (Böttger, 2005: 14). Waldorf Schools in Germany, which are private schools that follow alternative pedagogical approaches, have been teaching FLs at the primary school level in Germany since 1920 (Schmid-Schönbein, 2001: 11). Another historical landmark took place in the German Democratic Republic (GDR) about 30 years later. In the GDR, Russian was introduced in primary school curricula as a FL in 1952 and was taught in so-called R-classes with selected and usually very proficient pupils from Year 3 onwards (Bahls, 1992: 11).

An international milestone in early FLL was the so-called Sputnik crisis, which mainly influenced the United States of America, but also had implications for other nations (Schmid-Schönbein, 2008: 12). This Sputnik shock was caused by the Soviet Union, which managed to send the first satellite into space in 1957 and successfully transmitted radio signals back to Earth. The consequent shock resulted in initiatives to improve education and defence in America, so that they could remain internationally competitive (Schmid-Schönbein, 2001: 12). One reform that aimed at keeping up to date with development and internationalisation was a revolution of the US education system, which included the introduction of FLs at primary school level (Kloth, 2007; Sauer, 2000: 7).

In Germany, too, the implementation of early FLL was dependent on political and economic development (Sauer, 2000: 5). Technical innovations and the growing mobility of people worldwide coupled with the demand for English as a lingua franca led to a call for 'English for all'[7] during the 1950s and 1960s (Sauer, 2000: 7). Hence, English had become a mandatory subject in all German secondary schools[8] by 1964. Subsequently, the debate about introducing teaching English as a foreign language (TEFL) as early as in primary school continued, because all pupils would carry on learning English at secondary level anyway (Doyé & Lüttge, 1977: 7). Other initial reasons for starting FLL early included the optimum age or critical period hypothesis, which provided the first evidence that due to a child's advantage in brain plasticity language learning was best between the ages of two and 12 (Schmid-Schönbein, 2001: 13). Early research on this issue within the field of L1 acquisition assumed that the benefits of starting language learning early could be transferred to L2 learning (Sauer, 2000: 7). Consequently, the belief of "the earlier the better" was spread and initiated a number of pilot projects that explored an early start of TEFL in German primary schools (Sauer, 2000: 7).

As a result of the points mentioned above, a wave of projects started in the 1960s and 70s in Germany that aimed at introducing FLs at the primary school level (Leopold-Mudrack, 1998: 11).[9] The very first of these pilot projects started in Hesse in 1961, where English was introduced in Year 3 of primary school (Meyer, 1992: 62). In NRW, the first projects to implement English in primary

---

7   Author's translation for '*Englisch für alle*'.

8   Before 1964, only the *Gymnasium* and *Realschule* taught FLs. In 1964, it then became a mandatory subject in all secondary schools, including the *Volksschule* (see explanation of terms for the school types).

9   Sauer (2000) provides a detailed overview of all pilot projects.

schools started in the school year 1969/1970 (Sauer, 2000: 8). In 1973, NRW even published a new curriculum for primary schools that also included English and French as FLs.

Extensive research was conducted during this wave of early FLL and the results generally supported an early start. One of the best-known projects was conducted by Doyé and Lüttge (1977).[10] With very positive research results, including better FL competences in the long run, no negative effect on other curricular areas and popularity among all parties involved, Doyé and Lüttge (1977: 117f) concluded that starting English in the primary school was highly desirable. Hellwig conducted another research study which showed that after one year of English in the primary school the learners successfully managed to complete an English language test (Fay & Hellwig, 1971: 93ff). Lastly, Sauer (2000: 18, 22) reports on a large-scale study which found that almost 4,000 primary school learners displayed a positive attitude towards learning English in the primary school.[11]

The pilot projects conducted in the 1960s and 70s were discussed for a long period of time, but despite their positive overall results did not lead to an introduction of early FLL in Germany. Some reasons for this were that many teachers and educationalists remained sceptical, that there was no well-founded concept for teaching FLs to young learners, that primary school teachers could not qualify as FL teachers due to a reform in teacher training, a lack of awareness of the importance of FLs and a lack of coordination between primary and secondary schools (Leopold-Mudrack, 1998: 11; Hellwig, 1995: 19; Sauer, 2000: 10). Consequently, in 1982, the German Ministry of Education and Cultural Affairs[12] decided against FLs at the primary school level and in 1983 all pilot projects came to an end (Sauer, 2000: 10ff; Schmid-Schönbein, 2008: 14f).

---

10 In a quasi-experimental study with over 1,000 participants over five years, Doyé and Lüttge found that the English competences of the early starters in Year 3 were at all times of data collection significantly better than those of the late starters in Year 5 (Doyé & Lüttge, 1977: 109). Moreover, L1 reading and writing competences as well as mathematical competences were comparable amongst both groups, so that introducing English early had no significant (negative) effect on other areas of the curriculum (Doyé & Lüttge, 1977: 109). The pupils themselves as well as their parents believed that starting English early was beneficial and the teachers also supported the early start (Doyé & Lüttge, 1977: 110).

11 Sauer (2000) is not clear about both the research team and the authors of the study and also does not refer to any other publications. His text, however, indicates that he himself was part of the research team.

12 Official translation for 'Kultusministerium' (see KMK, 2010: 8).

Despite this setback, many researchers and teachers did not give up on the idea of early FL teaching. With a growing awareness of the importance of FLs in an increasingly globalised world, debates and discussions about early FLL continued during the early 1990s (Leopold-Mudrack, 1998: 11). Overall, this became known as the reform of the 1990s, which was characterised by various initiatives to implement FLs in German primary schools. A well-known initiative came from Gompf, who in 1989 started the association *Kinder lernen europäische Sprachen* [children learn European languages].[13] This association has been advocating the introduction of FLs in the primary school since it was founded. Their aim was to finally achieve a reform of FL teaching and they tried to achieve this aim through publications, research projects, conferences and workshops (see Gompf, 1992: 5f).

Moreover, several convinced researchers and teachers presented the so-called *Begegnungssprachenkonzept* [a concept of encountering languages] in 1985 (Sauer, 2000: 12). Through this concept, children at primary school level were supposed to experience multilingualism and several different FLs already at a young age (Sauer, 2000: 13; Schmid-Schönbein, 2001: 19). In primary school, an increased awareness of FLs should be encouraged, raising children's interest in other languages (Schmid-Schönbein, 2001: 19). This concept was not limited to English, but should give children an insight into several FLs, but without explicitly teaching or learning them. NRW implemented this concept in its curriculum in 1992 with the edict that became known as the *Begegnungssprachen-Erlass* [language encounter edict] (Beckmann, 2006: 19). The concept was supposed to enhance intercultural education and language awareness, but was not supposed to be understood as the explicit teaching and learning of FLs (Doyé, 1993: 59f; Klippel, 2000: 12; Sauer, 2000: 14, 33). Overall, although the idea of integrating FLs into the primary classroom was welcomed, this concept met with heavy criticism and the debates started to turn in favour of teaching FLs explicitly but in a child-friendly way instead (Klippel, 2000: 11; Sauer, 2000: 15).

Towards the end of the 1990s and around the start of the new millennium, early FLL experienced a change. The discussions and moves towards implementing FL teaching continued to be encouraged and eventually a change in policy was announced in 1999 at a conference about language teaching in Germany (Mindt & Schlüter, 2007: 6; Sauer, 2000: 15). Finally, the usefulness

---

13 See http://www.kles.org/frameset.html?mainFrame=http://www.kles.org/rueckblick_1. html (last access 15.05.2017) for more information.

and importance of learning English in the primary school had ceased to be a contested issue (Klippel, 2000: 13). As early as in 1992 and 1993, Saarland and Saxony were the first federal states to introduce FLs in their primary school curricula (see Gompf, 2002a: 108; Leopold-Mudrack, 1998: 11). By 2006, all federal states in Germany had introduced English at the primary school level (Schmid-Schönbein, 2008: 18f).[14] Nowadays, five federal states, including NRW, start teaching English as early as Year 1, the others start in Year 3 (see Chapter 1).

2.2 English beyond the EFL Classroom: The Idea of Bilingual Education

In addition to learning FLs at the primary school level, another aspect of learning and teaching FLs that has developed over the past few decades is bilingual education. Hamers and Blanc (2000: 321) broadly define bilingual education as a cover term for "any system of school education in which, at a given moment in time and for a varying amount of time simultaneously or consecutively, instruction is planned and given in at least two languages." In schools, the main idea of bilingual education is to use the FL alongside or instead of the L1[15] to teach content subjects such as science or physical education (Elsner & Keßler, 2013b: 1). This is in accordance with the widely accepted premise that using meaningful content in purposeful ways (also see Chapter 2.3) facilitates successful language learning and content subjects potentially offer authentic and relevant themes for FLL.

Bilingual education is gradually increasing in importance, recognition and implementation and is becoming increasingly popular in primary as well as secondary education throughout Europe (Elsner & Keßler, 2013b: 2; Schwab, Keßler & Hollm, 2014: 3). As the primary school where the empirical study that is presented in this book was conducted is one with a bilingual programme, the following subchapters will briefly explore what bilingual education and the related terms 'immersion' and 'content and language integrated learning (CLIL)' are and will provide information about current practices in German primary schools.

---

14 Alternatively, another FL was introduced; particularly French in the border region of the Saarland.
15 See Diehr (2012) for details on language use, particularly L1 and FL, in (true) bilingual teaching settings.

2.2.1 Immersion, CLIL and the German Approach to Bilingual Education

Over the last few decades, several different programmes with various labels have evolved, all of which are based on the principle of bilingual education (Krüger, 2011: 345). The actual term 'bilingual education' has its roots in America (Genesee, 1987: vii), bilingual education in Germany became known as '*bilingualer (Sachfach)Unterricht (BSFU)*'[16], the well-known Canadian programme is that of 'immersion' and in the European context 'CLIL'[17] has gained currency (see Klippel & Doff, 2007: 26). In the German school context, CLIL and immersion are terms that are used alongside *BSFU*, and will therefore briefly be explained in terms of their origins, definition and major characteristics.

Immersion has its roots in Canada and has proven to be an effective approach to L2 learning and teaching there. The idea behind immersion is to provide an effective L2 learning model by immersing speakers in a new language without neglecting the support of L1 development. Genesee (1987: vii) defines an immersion programme as

> a form of bilingual education designed for majority language students, that is, students who speak the dominant language of society upon entry to school. In immersion programmes, a second language, along with the students' home language, is used to teach regular school subjects such as mathematics and science as well as language arts. A major objective of immersion programs[18] is bilingual proficiency.

Canadian immersion programmes were initially designed for native speakers of English (majority language) who were immersed in French (minority language) in order to gain profound L2 competences. Immersion programmes started as early as 1965 in a primary school in St. Lambert (Quebec) and have been well-established in numerous Canadian schools up until today to support the learners' proficiency in French (see, e.g., Genesee, 1987; Mehisto, Marsh & Frigols, 2008; Wode, 2009).

A lot of research has been conducted in these Canadian immersion programmes. Despite very positive results concerning second language acquisition (SLA), researchers also found that students failed to achieve high levels of performance in some aspects of grammar and continued to have numerous errors

---

16 Literally translates to 'bilingual content subject teaching'.
17 Also known as 'EMILE' in France, as 'AICLE' in Spain and as 'AILC' in Italy (Wolff, 2013: 20).
18 In direct quotations the original orthography, grammar and punctuation has been preserved.

in their language production (Swain, 2000: 99; Lightbown & Spada, 2013: 177). This phenomenon was also referred to as "immersion interlanguage" (Lyster, 1987: 714) and Mehisto et al. (2008: 18) blame it on the greater emphasis which immersion programmes place on fluency before accuracy. Lightbown and Spada (2013: 173) mention that it was thus increasingly suggested that "subject matter instruction needed to be complemented by instruction that focused on language form" (also see Snow, Met & Genesee, 1989: 201).

This problem of 'immersion interlanguage' lead to the development of the European concept of CLIL. The term CLIL was coined in Europe in 1994 (Mehisto et al., 2008: 9). CLIL is used as a "generic term to describe all types of provision in which a second language is used to teach certain subjects" Eurydice (2006: 8). This broad definition overlaps with other approaches (e.g., immersion), but several authors clearly distinguish CLIL from those. They emphasise that CLIL is focused not just on content but on language as well: CLIL is a "dual-focused educational approach in which an additional language is used for the learning and teaching of both content *and* language" (Coyle, Hood & Marsh, 2010: 1; italics in original). As such, CLIL is not only about learning content-matter through a FL, but it also includes explicit L2 learning. According to Wolff (2007: 15), the CLIL approach should comprise language and subject matter to an equal extent.

It is difficult to clearly identify if forms of bilingual education in Germany follow the CLIL approach, the immersion approach, neither of them or a mixture of both. Bach (2005: 14) explains that the German term *BSFU* refers to school subjects which are taught through an L2 as the language of instruction. This understanding of *BSFU* is not congruent to the dual-focus of CLIL, because the understanding of *BSFU* hardly provides any details about a particular and integrated focus on the FL next to subject matter. In fact, *BSFU* in Germany focuses more on content than on language learning, mostly because bilingual classes in Germany have to follow the regular content curricula.[19] *BSFU* is also not congruent to the Canadian immersion approach, because learners mostly have only one or two content subjects in a FL and as such learners are only partially immersed in the FL.

---

19 See, for example, https://www.schulministerium.nrw.de/docs/Schulsystem/Unterricht/Lernbereiche-und-Faecher/Fremdsprachen/Bilingualer-Unterricht/index.html (last access: 15.05.2017) for NRW.

Regardless of (inconsistent and confusing) terminology, schools generally organise and implement their own specific bilingual programmes. Each school can make its own choice about aspects such as the onset of bilingual education, the amount of tuition time in the FL, the question whether a programme is permanent or temporary, the choice of a FL and the choice of subjects.[20]

Because of the school's partial freedom in setting up their individual bilingual programmes, terminology around the phenomenon of bilingual education becomes even more difficult and varied. Overall, there is no clear-cut terminology for the type of bilingual programme(s) as found in Germany. Depending on school, researcher and programme, the terms described so far are often used interchangeably. Instead of finding a clear-cut definition of the German concept of bilingual education it thus seems more important to carefully describe a school's bilingual programme in detail in order to fully understand such a setting.

However, one striking aspect that holds true for many bilingual classes is that the composition of such classes may be atypical in comparison to regular classes. Schools often undertake a selection process so that the bilingual classes are often positively selected (see, e.g., Lasagabaster & Sierra, 2010: 373; Schwab et al., 2014: 4; Rumlich, 2016: 80ff).[21] Selection criteria range from the learners' intelligence,

---

20 Bilingual programmes can be full/total or partial programmes, which refers to the extent to which the L2 is used (see Genesee, 1987; Mehisto et al., 2008; Möller, 2009). Apart from that, a bilingual programme can be temporary or permanent. So-called bilingual modules are temporary and thus usually topic-specific and limited in time (see Elsner & Keßler, 2013a; Krechel, 2003). In permanent, longer-lasting bilingual streams or branches, at least one subject is taught bilingually over at least one year (Otten & Wildhage, 2003: 14f; Werner, 2007: 20). Moreover, any bilingual programme can take place in a second, foreign, regional or minority language (Ruiz de Zarobe, 2011: 130), but there is a drive towards using English (Copland & Garton, 2014: 228; Lasagabaster & Sierra, 2010: 371), which also holds true for bilingual primary and secondary schools in Germany.

Particularly German primary schools have few clear-cut regulations to follow when implementing a bilingual programme, although permanent programmes of course need official permission. Guidelines for the secondary school are more elaborate; see https://www.schulministerium.nrw.de/docs/Schulsystem/Unterricht/Lern bereiche-und-Faecher/Fremdsprachen/Bilingualer-Unterricht/index.html (last access: 15.05.2017) for NRW.

21 In contrast to the practice of many schools, bilingual programmes are actually suitable for a wide range of learners and not just for high achieving ones (see Bach, 2005: 15; Schmidt, 2016; Schwab et al., 2014).

marks and motivation to their parents' ambitions. Therefore, learners attending a bilingual programme might be exceptionally intelligent, highly motivated and from a supportive social background. Such a possible positive selection of pupils should always be critically taken into consideration when investigating and evaluating bilingual programmes.

2.2.2 Bilingual Education in German Primary Schools: Spread, Issues and Research Results

Bilingual education in (German) primary schools as well as research in that field is still in its infancy (Rittersbacher, 2009: 75).[22] The first public bilingual primary school in Germany opened in 1996 in Altenholz; private primary schools had already been working bilingually earlier than that (see, e.g., Werner, 2007: 24). Currently, bilingual education in German primary schools is more or less a trend that is just about to gain widespread acknowledgement. In August 2014, there were 287 bilingual primary schools in Germany, which is triple the number of such schools compared to 2003 but only 1.8 % of all primary schools in Germany (FMKS[23], 2014).[24]

One of the reasons why bilingual teaching is still a grassroots movement in German primary schools is the lack of trained teachers, teaching materials and systematisation. Teachers should be specially trained in bilingual teaching, as they need to know about methodological aspects which are important in bilingual programmes and should have exceptional FL competences (see Egger, 2012). However, there is currently no special qualification for bilingual teachers at primary school level in Germany. In addition, only a very limited pool of teaching materials for bilingual teaching at the primary school level is available (Steiert, 2010: 119). Because of the lack of teaching materials, teachers are burdened with a lot of additional work as they have to find, adapt, design and evaluate their own teaching materials. Additionally, there is no curriculum for

---

22 See a list of bilingual primary schools in Germany at http://www.fmks-online.de/bili schulen.html (last access: 15.05.2017); also see Rumlich (2016: 60) for the secondary school.

23 Verein für frühe Mehrsprachigkeit an Kindertageseinrichtungen und Schulen e.V. [association for early multilingualism at kindergarten and schools] (FMKS). See www. fmks.eu (last access 15.05.2017).

24 Germany has 15,749 primary schools (see https://www.destatis.de/DE/ZahlenFakten/ GesellschaftStaat/BildungForschungKultur/Schulen/Tabellen/AllgemeinBildendeBe ruflicheSchulenSchularten.html;jsessionid=492914634B228354538BD7D35C1A723A. cae2 (last access: 15.05.2017)) so that 287 bilingual ones make up 1.8 %.

planning, teaching and evaluating CLIL lessons at primary school level in Germany up to the present.[25]

Nevertheless, a number of studies have provided research results on bilingual education in primary school that are quite promising. Firstly, researchers have found that bilingual programmes are valuable for FL development (see studies from Burmeister & Piske, 2008; Jiménez Catalán et al., 2006; Navés, 2011; Swain & Lapkin, 1982). Secondly, despite common doubts, the learning of subject matter is not negatively affected by bilingual teaching and even seems to partly benefit from it (see Genesee, 1987; Massler & Steiert, 2010; Wode, 2009: 53; Zaunbauer & Möller, 2007). Lastly, bilingual programmes have been found to also have no negative impact on L1 development (see Gebauer, Zaunbauer & Möller, 2012; Swain & Lapkin, 1982).

2.3 The Principle of Content- or Topic-Based Instruction

The notion of teaching a language through meaningful content and teaching meaningful content through a FL, which underlies the idea of bilingual education, complies with a topic-based approach to language teaching. Topic-based or content-based language learning refers to "an approach to L2 teaching in which teaching is organized around the content [...] rather than around a linguistic or other type of syllabus" (Richards & Rodgers, 2014: 116). According to the current understanding of FLL in Germany, FLs are learnt through meaningful content based on a thematic thread that serves for continuity. Any FL activities are planned around this topic. This idea of topic-orientation in language teaching is notably fulfilled in the topic-based approach to teaching FLs at primary school level in Germany (Böttger, 2012: 100; Dines, 2000), which is why topic-based language teaching in the primary school EFL classroom has even been compared to CLIL (see Böttger, 2012: 100; Rittersbacher, 2009: 78). In practice, unit planning for the EFL classroom generally starts with choosing a content-based topic; various media, methods, tasks and activities are then selected and created on the basis of the respective topic (Dausend, 2014a: 182; Meyer, 2010: 23).

The topic-based approach to FLL developed in the context of the communicative language teaching (CLT) approach. Chapter 3.1.1 will outline the developments in FL teaching from the classic grammar-translation method to

---

25 First attempts, however, have been made, for example, by Coyle et al. (2010), Meyer (2010), Massler and Burmeister (2010), Elsner and Keßler (2013b) and Dausend (2014a).

CLT and task-based language learning (TBLL) in more detail. In short, though, during the 1970s the idea of CLT and therefore a shift towards a focus on FL communication arose (see Richards & Rodgers, 2014: 84f). With a focus on meaningful communication instead of on grammatical correctness, teaching according to communicative principles is planned around interesting topics that could act as meaningful situations for language use (Dines, 2000: 72f).[26] The focus of language teaching was thus shifted from rule learning to meaning and content.[27]

There are multiple reasons for applying topic-based teaching approaches in language teaching. The overall idea is that FL knowledge can better be acquired through meaningful content:

> There is growing awareness that language learning is much more effective when the content and contexts are related closely to target language acquisition rather than taught in isolation. Language learning linked to meaningful content [...] has proven to be highly successful" (Egger, Lechner & Ward, 2012: 11).

Moreover, topic-based approaches should extend the scope of language learning as well as subject learning (Dausend, 2014b: 31). Pupils will enhance their knowledge not only of the target language but of content matter as well. Particularly for young learners, structure-based approaches that include complex grammar rules are too abstract, so that a more child-friendly approach is needed (Dines, 2000: 72). According to Massler (2012b: 39), it is content-based approaches and therefore topic-based instruction that make FLL more accessible to them. Children find orientation and understand the world through situations and through concrete content aspects (Dines, 2000: 72); a precondition that is central in topic-based approaches to FLL. As such, topic-based language teaching meets the needs of young language learners and is, more generally speaking, connected to contemporary ideas of effective and successful FLL through meaningful content.

Because of this idea of planning teaching and learning around a topic, specific subject borders are often broken down and topic-based approaches often imply

---

26 This holds true for the (primary school) EFL classroom in Germany as well as many other countries. However, in some parts of the world, particularly in less economically well-developed countries, the grammar-translation method is still widely used in teaching FLs (Richards & Rodgers, 2014: 7).

27 As will also be outlined in Chapter 3.1.1, grammar is not entirely neglected in current approaches but is understood as to serve language acquisition rather than guide it.

working across the curriculum.[28] Activities from different subjects can be inter-linked by focusing on a common topic. That is, "different areas of the curriculum can be taught in an integrated way" (Cameron, 2001: 181). In fact, choosing a topic and then dealing with it in either one or in several subjects is the usual procedure of planning units in German primary schools (Finck & Schulz, 2008: 36; Peterßen, 2000)[29] and said to "better suit the way that young children naturally learn" (Cameron, 2001: 181). In fact, topic areas of FL curricula often overlap with those from other subjects (Aristov & Haudeck, 2013: 46; Mindt & Schlüter, 2007: 49), so that topics dealt with in the EFL classroom can derive from different subjects across the curriculum.

2.4 Skills Development

As seen in the previous chapter (Chapter 2.3), units in the primary school EFL classroom are topic-based, in that the topic serves as a basis and a common thread for language learning activities. Building upon that, this chapter outlines the different skills and components of a language in order to give an overview of what elements of a FL are actually learnt and taught in FL classrooms. As such, this subchapter brings 'reading' into the broader context of TEFL. After a more general outline of skills and components in FLL, this section provides an overview of how language skills and components are integrated and worked on in the primary school EFL classroom.

2.4.1 Integration of Language Skills and Components in Language Learning

Language can be broken down into different elements. Depending on who does the classification, certain elements prevail. In linguists' breakdowns of language, the following components are habitually found: phonetics, phonology, morphology, syntax, lexis, semantics (see Hecht & Waas, 1980: 11; Müller, 2002; Yule, 2006). With a stronger emphasis on language use in communication, pragmatics

---

28 This idea of combining different subjects because of their shared topics has most often been referred to as theme-based teaching: "Many different activities are linked together by their content; the theme or topic runs through everything that happens in the classroom and acts as a connecting thread for pupils and teacher" (Cameron, 2001: 180).

29 Also see, for example, the curriculum of NRW (Ministerium für Schule und Weiterbildung des Landes Nordrhein-Westfalen (MSW NRW), 2008b: 12) or the English curriculum of Baden-Württemberg (Ministerium für Kultus, Jugend und Sport Baden-Württemberg (MKJS BW), 2004: 99).

and discourse/interaction analysis are also added (Kindt, 2002; Müller, 2002; Yule, 2006). Although the components are not perfectly distinct, the linguist's view of language is mostly concerned with "knowledge of the language itself" (Hedge, 2000: 46).

Hedge (2000: 45) objects that this linguistic view is "a too narrow focus on language as a formal system" and thus he emphasises that language learners need to learn how to use the language and hence develop communicative competence. He argues that grammar rules are useless without also knowing about the rules of language use (Hedge, 2000: 45). This view of encompassing not only linguistic knowledge but also the ability to put this knowledge into practice in communication underlies approaches to language that focus on language teaching. In the area of FL teaching, a language is hence often described in terms of communicative skills. These are usually the four skills listening, speaking, reading and writing. More recently, researchers and curricula also list mediation as a FL skill (e.g., Klippel & Doff, 2007: 72; MSW NRW, 2008b: 79), which refers to translating FL extracts by content as to convey their overall message instead of giving a word by word translation.

Attempting to summarise the linguists' as well as the language teaching perspective on different elements of language, Figure 1 provides on overview of language components and skills:

Figure 1: The interplay between components and skills of language (based on Hecht & Waas, 1980: 11; Kindt, 2002; Klippel & Doff, 2007: 43, 72; Müller, 2002; Yule, 2006).

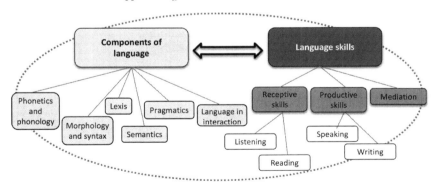

Although differentiated in this model, the skills and components of a language do in fact not stand in isolation but are intricately interwoven and connected to each other. For example, a word as a lexical item is pronounced in a certain way (phonology), can be listened to, read, spoken or written, can be translated into another language, takes certain grammatical markers, might have different meanings in different contexts and is used in interaction in manifold ways. This intricate interplay between the skills and components of a language and also between the skills itself is referred to as 'language skill integration' or 'integrated skills' (Stork, 2010: 100f).

In FLL, the skills and components are gradually developed. The model in Figure 1 does not account for this development, but only displays the different elements of a language that can and need to be developed. How FL competence progresses by developing the elements displayed in Figure 1 has not been mutually agreed on. Different concepts of FL development and acquisition have evolved over time; see Brown (2007), Lennon (2008) or Lightbown and Spada (2013) for overviews.

For the sake of brevity, just one model of acquiring FL communicative competence will be displayed here: Hecht and Waas' (1980; also Waas, 2014a) multi-layered competence model,[30] which takes into consideration most of the components and skills of a language as outlined above (see Figure 2).

Figure 2: Multi-layered competence model for learning languages (adapted from Waas, 2014a: 35).

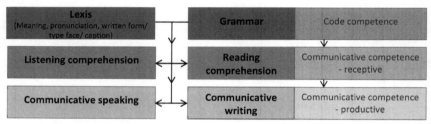

According to this model, language teaching combines the linguistic components (code competence) with communicative competence in the four different skills and shows the interplay of all elements. Code competence is said to be a prerequisite for communication in the four skills (Hecht & Waas, 1980: 11). Thus, lexis (including meaning, pronunciation and spelling) as well as grammar (including morphology and syntax) are paramount and form the basis for the productive as well as receptive communicative skills listening, speaking, reading and writing (Waas, 2014a: 35). Mediation, as explained above, is missing in this model, but could be added as an element of communicative competence which is receptive

---

30 Author's translation for '*Mehrschichtiges Kompetenzmodell*' (Hecht & Waas, 1980: 15).

as well as productive. Pragmatics, too, is missing, but could be implied in the element of productive communicative competence.

Overall, this model complies with the principle ideas of information processing, in that declarative knowledge of the language (code-competence) gradually becomes procedural knowledge (knowledge of how to use the language) that leads to automatised FL use (DeKeyser, 1998, 2001; Lightbown & Spada, 2013: 109). This view of processing new information and acquiring new skills is not uncontested in FLL. Krashen (1981; 1989), for example, states that language is for the most part acquired unconsciously, which means that the stage of learning about linguistic elements of a language is only of minor importance.[31] Generally, though, FLL in the primary school seems to follow the model presented in Figure 2, as will be outlined in the following subchapter.

2.4.2 Principles of Teaching FL Skills and Components in Primary School

In the primary school EFL classroom, the communicative skills are implicitly integrated with the linguistic components of the FL. The overall teaching perspective is holistic and skills or components of a language are not taught in isolation (see Harmer, 2007: 265). How this works at the practical level is exemplarily shown in Figure 3 and will briefly be discussed in the following paragraphs.

---

31 In his acquisition-learning hypothesis, Krashen (1981: 1; italics in original) states that L2 learners develop two interrelated systems in an L2, which are "subconscious language *acquisition* and conscious language *learning*." Acquisition is said to happen through comprehensible input and therefore competence develops without instruction (Krashen, 1989: 443). Although opposed to it, Krashen (1989: 454) admits that conscious learning appears to have at least some impact and can lead to consciously learnt competence. Hence, acquisition and learning coexist, whereas acquisition appears stronger and more important for language mastery, as through learning only "a limited amount of 'language-like' competence can be developed" (Krashen, 1989: 454).

Figure 3: The integration of language skills and components in the primary school EFL classroom.

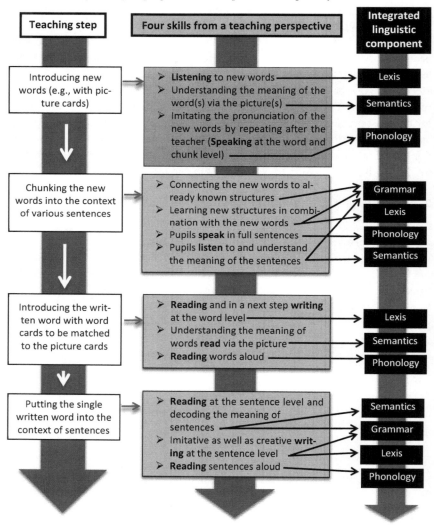

Figure 3 provides an overview of how units in the primary school EFL classroom are usually built up in terms of implicitly integrating FL skills and linguistic components. The red arrows show that the different linguistic components of language are interwoven into the practical teaching steps. However, the arrows can only display the most prominent connections; more connections between the teaching steps as well as language skills and linguistic components are conceivable.

This overview, however, only serves as a basis for EFL units with young learners and only displays how EFL is quintessentially taught in the primary school. Clearly, the teaching steps and activities can vary (see Brewster & Ellis, 2002: 85ff). Figure 3 shows how teaching English in the primary school is generally organised and how reading comes into play, but this does not mean that units cannot be organised differently. For instance, a unit can also be based on a storybook (see, e.g., Cameron, 2001: 169ff). In addition, alternative and more modern teaching approaches such as project work (see, e.g., Kamitz, 2015) or open tasks (see, e.g., Lauströer, 2013; Reckermann, 2017) break up the systematic structure that is delineated in Figure 3. Therefore, the following paragraphs will refrain from explaining the steps as shown in Figure 3 in detail, but will instead shed light on more general principles of teaching FL skills and components in the primary school EFL classroom.

Units in the primary school EFL classroom usually start with what Hecht and Waas (1980; also Waas, 2014a) described as code competence, in that the learners are introduced to new lexical items. By using visualisations such as picture cards, picture books or realia for this introduction, meaning is established on the iconic level. All lexical items to be introduced are based on the topic which was chosen according to the topic-based approach to FL teaching (see Chapter 2.3).

Generally, new as well as already known words should not be taught and used in isolation, but in the context of a chunk, sentence or story. This ensures that lexical items are embedded into a larger context (Decke-Cornill & Küster, 2010: 169). At the primary school level, the EVENING study found that single words without context are not enough to learn a FL, which is why words should be put into a context from the very beginning (Keßler, 2009: 175). Not only the teacher uses words in context, but also the learners should be encouraged to use the FL in chunks and full sentences. With new words chunked up in sentences, the learners already encounter an implicit introduction of grammar in the form of chunks (Cameron, 2001: 98). Therefore, grammar is also implicitly introduced as a component of code-competence in the course of a unit.

As already indicated in the practical teaching steps in Figure 3, the order of skills development, though not always clearly separable, goes from listening to speaking and then from reading to writing (Klippel & Doff, 2007: 72; Legutke, Müller-Hartmann & Schocker-v. Ditfurth, 2009: 51; Mindt & Schlüter, 2007: 52; Piske, 2010: 38), analogous to L1 development. There is more or less consensus that the written form of a word should only be offered after learners are familiar with the word's meaning and pronunciation (Legutke et al., 2009: 58). Given the complex grapheme-phoneme correspondence of English, this is deemed important to ensure that learners can read words with their correct pronunciation. The learners' familiarity with the words at the oral/aural level should prevent them from decoding the written words letter by letter.[32]

However, not all words that are read or written can be introduced beforehand. This is impossible in a teaching approach that includes challenging, meaningful and holistic tasks. While usually the most prominent words of a unit are used in reading and writing only after they have been introduced orally, other words might be encountered in written form without the children knowing their pronunciation and meaning.

In general, Figure 3 might evoke the impression that learning EFL in primary school only consists of the introduction and intentional practice of new words and chunks in listening, speaking, reading and writing. However, this is clearly not the case. The process of acquiring new lexical items is supported in context, in that new knowledge builds on and is integrated into already existing knowledge (Timm, 2013: 43, 45). In addition, creative language use is encouraged. Legutke et al. (2009: 54f) explain that young learners' FL use goes from imitation to reproduction to production. Only the first two steps are displayed in Figure 3. However, the latter forms an important part of successful FLL, because 'production' supports learners in using and understanding new language items in different situations and contexts (Klippel, 2000: 38). In practice, production phases can consist of more creative tasks such as 'describe your dream house' or 'present your favourite animal'. In such open tasks, the learners try to use the language themselves, and in creative ways, but might need individual vocabulary that was not introduced by the teacher beforehand. Therefore, supportive techniques such as using picture dictionaries need to be applied (see Reckermann, 2016b: 17).

Despite the notion that words should not be taught in isolation, communicative skills generally progress from word to sentence to text level. Figure 3 partly indicates this, in that new words are first used and practised by the learners in listening, speaking, reading and writing individually or in short chunks, but are eventually used in the context of sentences and longer units. Due to the focus of

---

32 However, Frisch (2013) has shown that explicitly introducing a phonics approach to reading can be more beneficial than this holistic approach. Analysing the grapheme-phoneme correspondence of words in bottom-up processes could help young learners to read them (see Chapters 3.4 and 5.5.2).

this book on reading, this will be elaborated on in more detail taking the development of reading skills as an example. Mindt and Schlüter (2007: 57) outline seven stages that children go through in the process of acquiring FL reading skills, which serve as a basis for suitable and stage-appropriate reading tasks and activities with young learners (see Table 1).[33]

Table 1: Stages in learning and teaching reading in the primary EFL classroom (based on Mindt & Schlüter, 2007: 57).

Stage 1	Silently read single words; match a single word to the corresponding picture
Stage 2	Read single words aloud
Stage 3	Put a few words into order to form a full short sentence
Stage 4	Silently read a short sentence and match it to the corresponding picture
Stage 5	Read a short sentence aloud
Stage 6	Silently read short sentences and put them in order to form a short text
Stage 7	Read a short text aloud

One can see that these stages gradually progress from word to sentence to text level. This order of progressively developing FL skills through increasingly larger units of to a certain extent also holds true for the other skills.

As such, skills development in the primary school EFL classroom can be quite different to what teachers and researchers know from secondary schools. Not only is the introduction and practice of new vocabulary as well as the amount of grammar different (see Decke-Cornill & Küster, 2010: 174), but reading and writing also play a slightly altered role at the primary school level. In the secondary school, it is common to read and write whole texts. However, the role of written language in the primary school has long been questioned (see Chapter 3.1.2), and until today the written skills are mostly only ascribed a supportive function. In primary school, written language is usually introduced at the word level and (unfortunately) many teachers never manage to leave that stage (see Chapter 3.2.2). Generally, however, listening, speaking, reading and writing in English in the primary school should not only be concerned with single words, but the

---

33 Partly, opposing opinions are found in this respect. Cameron (2001: 143), for example, suggests that particularly learning to read in the L2 can begin at any level: the letter, word, sentence or even text level: The whole language approach (see Richards & Rodgers, 2014), for instance, strongly supports reading at the text level from the very beginning.

acquisition process should proceed from single words to chunks to sentences and lastly to texts. The mere word-level can be left quickly. In fact, the text-stage can already be reached in Years 1 and 2 and there is no need to procrastinate about introducing longer and coherent units of language until later.

This description of important factors in FL skills development in primary school has not yet provided much detail about elements that go beyond lexis and grammar, namely other components such as discourse competence, fluency or pragmatics (see Hedge, 2000: 56). Clearly, they are not ignored in the primary school, but interwoven into various classroom activities. This, however, goes beyond the scope of this book and hence will not be touched on further for now. The same goes for language awareness as well as mediation skills.

2.5 Summary of Chapter 2

Chapter 2 has shown how EFL teaching developed in German primary schools over the past century, with a particular focus on its final implementation during the last 20 years.[34] Only since 2006 has English become a mandatory subject in all German primary schools. Therefore, its methodology is still rather young and teachers and researchers are in the process of establishing successful practices for teaching FLs to young learners. One highly debated issue is that of the introduction of written language, as will further be explored in Chapter 3. This book, with its focus on FL reading at primary school level, aims to contribute to developing classroom practices that support young learners in acquiring EFL.

A recent development with regard to teaching FLs at school is the increasing implementation of bilingual teaching in secondary as well as primary schools, worldwide as well as in Germany. Particularly the primary school, however, still faces difficulties with regard to the implementation of bilingual programmes, although initial research results are promising. The study that underlies this book was conducted at a German primary school with a bilingual programme, which is one rare example of a bilingual primary school in Germany. This study's results can hence contribute to the research on bilingual teaching in the primary school. At the same time, the results of this study might also be applicable to schools without a bilingual programme; but this still needs investigation and further research. Reasons for why a school with a bilingual programme was purposely chosen for the study that is described in this book are found in Chapter 7.2.

---

34 In all chapter summaries that are found at the end of each chapter, sources and references are left out for reasons of readability because they had already been given within the text of the chapter.

Chapter 2 has also shown that the topic-based approach to FL teaching that underlies the idea of bilingual education in that it organises FLL around meaningful content, is commonly used in primary school EFL teaching. The study presented in this book respects this in that picture books based on the topics dealt with in the learners' EFL classroom were chosen for reading. More details will be provided in Chapter 8.1.1.

Lastly, the skill of FL reading, which this book focuses on, was described as integrated into an interplay of language skills and components and an overview of FL skills and components taught holistically in the primary school was provided. This overview already indicates that the focus of FL teaching at the primary school level is on listening and speaking, while reading and writing are mostly given a supportive function. This notion will be deepened in the following chapter (Chapter 3), which will outline the status of reading and related issues in primary EFL learning.

3. Reading in the Primary School EFL Classroom: Its Developing Role, Curricular Demands, Current Research and Practices

Abstract: This chapter focuses on reading in the primary school EFL classroom. It examines the developing status of reading as well as current curricula and practices, discusses the question of an EFL reading methodology and elaborates on previous studies that investigated young learners' FL reading.

Based on the above mentioned history and teaching principles, the development, role and current status of written skills, particularly reading, will be outlined in this chapter. The chapter will start by outlining the varying status of reading firstly across different teaching approaches and secondly in the primary school EFL classroom. This brief historical overview will demonstrate that against the backdrop of a debate on early biliteracy, reading and writing have gradually gained acceptance at the primary school level in recent years. As such, the current role of reading will be explained next. Moreover, the prevailing question of a reading methodology will be detailed. The last subchapter will then elaborate on previous research on reading competences in the primary school EFL classroom.

3.1 The Developing Status of Reading

As could be seen in Chapter 2.4, reading is integrated into skills development in the primary school EFL classroom in today's approach to teaching FL to young learners, but in fact the status of written language and the role of reading have been a matter of debate for a long time. Therefore, this subchapter will start by describing the changing status of reading across different teaching approaches and provide insights into the influence of SLA research thereupon. Then, based on the history of introducing English in the primary school (see Chapter 2.1), the gradual acceptance of reading in the primary school EFL classroom in Germany will be elaborated on. As will become apparent in the historical outline, a debate around early biliteracy has dominated the last few decades in TEFL at the primary school level; therefore, the last section details central arguments of this debate.

3.1.1 Towards a Communicative Function of Reading: The Status of Reading across Different Teaching Approaches and the Influence of SLA Research

Reading has played varying roles in the development of the major approaches to teaching FLs, moving from the traditional grammar-translation method to the more recent approach of CLT and emerging approaches such as CLIL. Because of the limited scope of this book, only these three major approaches will be taken into consideration with regard to their emphasis on the different language skills, paying particular attention to the role of reading across these approaches.

Historically, reading and writing were at the centre of language teaching for a long time. Until about two centuries ago, ancient languages such as Greek or Latin were studied at the secondary school level and beyond in order to read and understand FL texts (Roche, 2008: 13). In the 18th century, learners aimed at acquiring reading knowledge of FLs and did so by studying the grammar and vocabulary of the FL in order to understand and interpret traditional FL texts (Howatt, 1984: 131). The common assumption underlying this comprehension-based approach to L2 acquisition was that learners acquire language abilities through reading and working with FL texts. With the grammar-translation method, the major focus of learning and teaching FLs was hence on reading and writing while only little attention was paid to speaking and listening (Richards & Rodgers, 2014: 6). However, this method soon proved to be unsuccessful with younger school pupils[35] (Howatt, 1984: 131) and also proved ineffective for the acquisition of oral communication skills (Richards & Rodgers, 2014: 8). Thus, during the 19th century, the need for speaking proficiency was recognised and challenged the initial focus on reading comprehension and grammar (Richards & Rodgers, 2014: 9).

With a more communicative approach to FLL, teaching approaches have changed in favour of the development of oral skills. In the late 19th century, the reform movement of language teaching brought into focus the absolute priority of an oral methodology (Howatt, 1984: 171). Languages should not only be learnt for reading comprehension and the translation of texts, but for actively being able to communicate in these languages and using the languages in everyday situations. Various approaches to focusing on oral skills eventually led to a shift towards more emphasis on communication during the 1970s and 80s and resulted

---

35 With younger learners Howatt refers to lower secondary school level, as FLs had not yet been extensively introduced at the primary school level.

in the emergence of CLT (Richards & Rodgers, 2014: 83).[36] CLT brought about a major change in orientation. In a communicative classroom, the use of language in meaningful contexts and for meaningful purposes as well as the notion of fluency before accuracy were moved into the foreground of teaching (Brown, 2007: 241). As already explained in Chapter 2.3, communicative FL classes were organised around meaningful content and a topic served as the common thread. For secondary school, CLT meant a change in methodology. In fact, secondary schools in Germany hesitated and procrastinated before acquiescing to a focus on oral communication (see Decke-Cornill & Küster, 2010: 174f). By contrast, teaching English in primary school had followed the communicative ideas from the beginnings: From its onset, the key focus of teaching FLs in primary school was set on communication (Doyé & Lüttge, 1977: 16).

TBLL is closely tied to CLT and can be seen as the more practical tool of this rather broad approach (Richard & Rodgers, 2014: 174). TBLL aims at designing tasks which are suitable for implementing the idea of CLT in the classroom (Müller Hartmann & Schocker-v. Ditfurth, 2014: 39). In TBLL, teachers attempt to make use of tasks which focus on meaning and allow the learners to use the FL for (close to) real-life communicative situations in preparation for the challenges they will face when using the FL outside the classroom (Kolb, 2008: 61; Legutke et al., 2009: 32). This describes exactly what the goal of CLT was, namely communicative competence (Brown, 2007: 241). Communicative competence is still the aim of teaching FLs in primary as well as secondary schools today and is explicitly mentioned in the curricula (see, e.g., MSW NRW, 2008b: 71).

Although the focus on oral language is paramount, written language is not altogether ignored in CLT and TBLL. Hedge (2000: 45) emphasises that communicative competence does not only refer to oral communication, but it also encompasses the written language skills reading and writing, as meaningful communication can also take place when these skills are used. Spada (2007: 279) clearly points out that reading as a comprehension skill and writing as a production skill have "always been part of the fundamental principles and practices of CLT." She adds that written skills naturally belong to a holistic teaching concept and naturally contribute to and are a fundamental part of learning FLs (Spada, 2007: 279). With regard to FL reading in particular, Klippel and Doff (2007: 79) explain that preparing FL learners to eventually be able to autonomously use the FL includes, amongst other aspects, independent reading comprehension.

---

36 The ideas of CLT had already been appealing to teachers a long time before the 1970s and were known as the 'natural method' or the 'direct method' (Howatt, 1984: 192).

Particularly in the more recent approach of CLIL (see Chapter 2.2) written FL competence is indispensable. In CLIL classrooms, reading and writing are essential skills for the learners, as they receive instruction and information through oral as well as written input. As such, literacy serves as a basis for gathering and understanding information (Burmeister & Piske, 2008: 187). For instance, the learners have to understand FL texts and teachers rely "on the [pupils'] ability to process texts of all kinds" (Bosenius, 2009: 18; also see Thürmann, 2005: 80). Therefore, it is critical for CLIL learners to acquire L2 reading and writing skills in order to be able to participate successfully in various classroom activities.

To recapitulate, reading has played varying roles in the major teaching approaches of the last decades and centuries, but its status in TEFL is uncontested nowadays. Moreover, a certain focus on literacy is also supported by SLA research.

Today's EFL classroom's attention to written FL skills is linked to a revised focus on language form, as researchers have gradually realised over the past two decades that a pure focus on (mainly oral) communicative competence does not necessarily lead to successful FL acquisition: Since the 1990s there has been "a re-emphasis on the formal aspects of language in classroom teaching" (Lennon, 2008: 102). This "renewed focus on form" (Müller-Hartmann & Schocker-v. Ditfurth, 2014: 101) implies that learners' attention should be drawn to form and accuracy from time to time in that the focus on meaning and fluency should be supplemented with occasional phases of FL instruction and a focus on formal correctness (Lightbown & Spada, 2013: 182f). Ideas on teaching grammar have gradually become more important again, not in the traditional sense of the grammar-translation method or of explicitly teaching grammar, but rather with current ideas about focusing on form (Cameron, 2001: 105).[37]

This emphasis on fluency and communication with an embedded focus on form naturally includes the communicative function of reading and writing (see Brown, 2007: 241). Hulstijn (2001: 283) explains that learners can encounter new elements of a language, such as new grammatical structures, by reading texts. Cook (2008: 125) distinguishes between 'decoding', which refers to the ability to understand the meaning of a sentence, and 'codebreaking', referring to discovering the linguistic system which carries the meaning and therefore allows learners to deduce rules from language input. Codebreaking is likely to happen when encountering new language structures via reading; for instance, Harmer (2007:

---

37 For more information on focusing on form in the primary school EFL classroom see Cameron (2001), Kuhn (2006) and Pinter (2006).

212f) presents an example in which pupils encounter the irregular past tense of certain verbs while reading a text.

In theorising how language acquisition can be supported, Krashen underlines the significance of comprehensible input and stresses the essential role of reading for L2 acquisition. In his comprehensible input hypothesis, he states that "we acquire language by understanding messages" (Krashen, 1989: 440). Therefore, comprehension-based instruction is the key to language acquisition in his view (Skehan, 1998: 12).[38] Emphasising the importance of reading, Krashen (1982: 60) argues that an L2 is acquired via understanding input from listening and reading (also see Chapter 5.4).

In contrast to previous ideas of acquiring a language unconsciously (e.g., Krashen, 1982: 89), Schmidt (2001) argues that nothing is learnt unless it has been noticed. For Schmidt, attention and awareness are crucial to learn target language features. He claims that "SLA is largely driven by what learners pay attention to and notice in target language input" (Schmidt, 2001: 3f). This suggests that input plays a very important role when it is noticeable (Schmidt, 2001: 10), as "noticing is the first step in the acquisition of a language aspect" (Schmidt, 2001: 31). Input can, for instance, be made noticeable in texts (see Sharwood Smith, 1993). However, the extent to which input enhancement really draws learners' attention to L2 features has been discussed critically (see Lightbown & Spada, 2013: 163 and Chapter 5.4).

The concept of learning styles has also influenced FLL approaches during the last couple of decades. Learning styles "refer to the different ways in which learners perceive, absorb, process and recall new information and skills" (VanPatten & Benati, 2010: 102).[39] Language learners all have different learning styles and some learning styles are supported by written input. Classical distinctions are, for example, made between visual, auditory and kinaesthetic learners. Research on learning styles attributes a supportive function of written language for visual learners in particular, as they take up and process information mainly through their eyes (Brewster & Ellis, 2002: 34). Brown (2007: 129) explains that visual learners tend to prefer reading or other types of visualised information as a

---

38 Opposing opinions are found about this statement. Swain (2000), for example, states that output is essential for successful FL acquisition. This will not further be taken into consideration, as Krashen's argument is only introduced here to show that reading can be important, regardless of other crucial factors for successful FLL.

39 For more information on learning styles, including a critical view on them, and more detailed distinctions between different styles that go beyond the ones mentioned in this section, see Brown (2007).

means of input. Klippel (2000: 23) argues that the written language should therefore not be withheld from young learners, as some need it as a crucial learning aid. Therefore, whilst not all language learners prefer a visual way to encounter new language features, the ones who do should profit from written language as it provides a central source of input for them. Hence, research on learning styles also supports the importance of reading for FL development.

To sum up the information provided in this subchapter, viewed historically, the role of reading has varied across different teaching approaches, from a prominent focus on it during the grammar-translation era to a gradual shift to oral communication with the advent of CLT and its predecessors. However, nowadays, written language is seen as a set part of FL classrooms that focus on communication, thanks to its potential for a focus on form, its potential for comprehensible input and its benefits for visual learners.

3.1.2 From Neglect to Acceptance: The Status of FL Reading with Young Learners from the 1960s to the Present

The previous subchapter has established the role of reading in different approaches to FLL and outlined perspectives from SLA research. This subchapter will outline how the status of written language, particularly reading, has changed over the last about 50 years of English instruction in the primary school in Germany, and is based on the historical overview provided in Chapter 2.1. The following sections will show that from the beginning of primary school EFL teaching in Germany around the 1960s, reading and writing have mostly been ignored, but that recently they have come to be generally accepted as part of the curriculum (Mindt, 2007: 12). A detailed analysis of the reasons for neglecting FL literacy is found in the following subchapter (Chapter 3.1.3).

During the first waves of TEFL pilot projects in primary schools in the 1960s and 70s, written language was for the most part neglected and primary school EFL methodology mainly focused on oral competences. Doyé, (1993: 67) provides an overview of methodological approaches to FLL at the primary school level from its onset up to the 1990s and shows that the FL classroom focused on oral skills and that these took priority over reading and writing. Few researchers approved of a careful use of written language due to its supportive function, while other researchers fully excluded FL literacy (Doyé, 1993: 67; Doyé & Lüttge, 1977: 21f). In other words, during the first years of FLL in the primary school reading and writing were mostly avoided.

Hellwig was one of the very few supporters of the early introduction of written language in teaching FLs around that time. In contrast to many others, he had already outlined the importance of written language as early as 1971 (Fay & Hellwig, 1971). Although Hellwig and Fay (1971: 19f) argued that written skills should only play an indirect role in early FLL, while the focus should remain on oral skills, they still advocated introducing written skills before learners advance to secondary schools and even provided suggestions on how to integrate reading and writing into early FLL (Fay & Hellwig, 1971: 60ff). Support for this approach was provided by Hellwig's study dating from 1966/67, in which short adapted reading texts were successfully used in a Year 4 (Fay & Hellwig, 1971: 88f). Further support came from the 1976 study that Sauer reported about[40] (see Chapter 2.1), which showed that three quarters of the participating pupils reported that they liked to read in English (Sauer, 2000: 24).

When NRW first implemented FLs in primary schools in 1969/70, a draft for the guidelines to teach English pointed out that it should take place in a playful and child-friendly way, merely focusing on listening and speaking; reading and writing were excluded (Sauer, 2000: 8f). In contrast, Hesse was one of the few federal states which allowed written language in the FL classroom already in its early stages (1970 to 1986) in that Hesse's methodological concept suggested that reading and writing be incorporated in FLL with young learners (Gompf, 2002b: 43).

During the reform movement of the 1990s, the status of written language gained increasing acknowledgement, but remained a highly debated issue. Kubanek-German (1999: 159) writes that the debate centred on whether reading and writing should be postponed until secondary school or whether the written skills should already be introduced at the primary school level. For example, in 1991, Rhineland-Palatinate started a pilot project and introduced English (in some schools French) in Year 3 (see Helfrich, 1992). This project followed the standard methodological principles of teaching FLs to young learners (Helfrich, 1992: 32f). However, the use of written language was completely ignored in these principles, but a special emphasis was placed on oral language. Similarly, in his article on the principles of communicative progression in the primary FL classroom, Alig (1992: 8) took the position that the main focus of EFL lessons with young learners should be on listening and speaking; he did not mention written skills at all. Sarter[41] (1997: 51) also maintained that teaching FLs at primary school level for the most part refrains from using written language. Nevertheless,

---

40 See Footnote 11 on the research team and authors of that study, which both somehow remain unclear.
41 Sarter focuses on learning and teaching French as a FL at primary school level. However, many aspects she mentions can be transferred to the EFL classroom.

she also provided reasons for at least using the written form of already known words and short sentences, as this was, based on her experience, not too demanding for young FL learners (Sarter, 1997: 51, 115).

However, there were also supporters of written language during the 1990s. Towards the beginning of the decade, Hellwig (1992, 1995) again strongly supported the use of written language in primary FL lessons. Based on a small research project with 30 learners from five different primary schools, Hellwig and his team found that the use of written language, to a limited extent, could be useful for making progress in FLL (Hellwig, 1992: 39). Hence, he concluded that despite a focus on oral language, written language should be implemented as a learning aid in the context of a holistic approach to a FL (Hellwig, 1992: 46). He also explicitly mentioned that children should also read at the sentence instead of only at the word level, as sentence-level reading helps them to fully understand FL structures (Hellwig, 1992: 46). Hellwig reinforced his argument in his 13 principles for early FLL (Hellwig, 1995: 76). In a similar vein, Kubanek-German's (1999: 159) position was that a holistic approach to FLL does not justify any kind of order amongst the different skills. She raised doubts whether a focus on speaking was actually beneficial for all learners, or whether only those children who are extroverted and enjoy speaking and communicating profited from this methodology and hence argued for a greater appreciation of reading comprehension as well as including the use of narrative texts (Kubanek-German, 1994: 27f).

It was only towards the end of the 20th century that written language gradually gained more wide-spread acceptance and a trend towards implementing literacy in early FLL became clear. Teaching oral skills exclusively had meanwhile been recognised as dogmatic and one-sided (see Edelhoff, 2003: 146), so that the discussion slowly but relentlessly experienced a change. Reading and writing became more and more accepted for young FL learners, and teachers as well as researchers increasingly saw how written language could foster FLL.[42] Cameron (2001: 18), for example, claimed that the young language learner should "experience literacy development as integrated within spoken language development" and that despite a primary focus on oral skills, the written skills

---

42 Some opponents to written language could still be found. In sharp contrast to many others, Fröhlich-Ward (1999: 57f) stated that there is more or less consensus that young children should be taught FLs by "avoiding the use of the written language as far as possible." She even argued that teachers should "not waste time" on making learners read and copy FL words (Fröhlich-Ward, 1999: 66). But for the time being, she was one of the very last challengers of including written language skills.

should not be completely neglected. In 2002, Gompf found that all German federal states prominently focused on oral skills in the primary FL classroom, but reading and writing were used in a supportive function (Gompf, 2002a: 100). Klippel (2000: 23) proposed that written language should be used to support the learning process, without explicitly introducing reading and writing. Bleyhl (2003: 18) further pointed out that as soon as young learners have established a basic vocabulary of about 400 to 500 words, they should and will start to move from the oral skills to reading and writing.

In spite of ongoing oppositions in some quarters (see Footnote 42), the move towards implementing written language did not stop and eventually led to a general acceptance of literacy in early FL teaching that has continued up to the present. Today, written language is widely accepted as an integral part of FLL in the primary school and is now a clearly established part of the curricula (Becker & Roos, 2014: 37; also see Chapter 3.2.2). In addition, primary school English teachers are more open to introducing more reading and writing activities, partly because pupils seem to enjoy and request them (Diehr & Frisch, 2011: 42).

Lastly, increasing attempts have been made to bridge the gap between primary and secondary school in recent years, in that a break between the methodology of learning and teaching English at two different school types should be kept at a minimum (Schmid-Schönbein, 2008: 123). This entails on the one hand that the secondary schools should carefully consider the communicative and playful approach to FLL which is employed to teach primary school EFL learners. On the other hand, a smooth transition means that primary schools should pay more attention to what is required of learners when they switch into secondary school and should carefully prepare them for it. One of the major complaints of secondary school teachers, in fact, is the lack of EFL reading and writing competences of primary school children (Doms, 2010: 8; Fuchs & Tippelt, 2012: 84; Wagner, 2009: 21, 23), which is not surprising given the long debate of the implementation thereof. Course books and publishers have recently been reacting to this by offering materials with enhanced reading and writing activities for pupils in Year 4.[43]

In sum, this chapter has shown that over the last few decades the implementation of written language in early FL teaching has gradually become accepted and is an established part of early FL teaching today. Common arguments in this debate, which is also known as the 'early biliteracy' debate, will be outlined in the

---

43 Examples include "Ginger – Fit for Five" from Cornelsen (Gehring, 2013) or "Let's Read and Write… That's it!" from Mildenberger (McCafferty & Kresse, 2011).

following subchapter, to support understanding as to why the introduction of written skills has been such a controversially discussed issue.

3.1.3 Pros and Cons of Early Biliteracy

A debate on early biliteracy has accompanied the gradual introduction of early FLL in Germany. Early biliteracy in this context refers to explicitly making use of written language in the EFL classroom and thus is understood in this book as the more or less simultaneous introduction of reading and writing in German (L1) and English (L2). However, it is not necessarily concerned with explicitly teaching young EFL learners how to read and write in English. The general debate and common arguments put forward in the discussion around early biliteracy are summarised in Table 2 and will be detailed in the course of this subchapter, allowing for a preliminary conclusion that will form the basis for further discussions in this book.

Table 2: Summary of pros and cons in the debate on early biliteracy.

Cons of early biliteracy	Pros of early biliteracy
→ Fear of overtaxing learners → FL literacy is too demanding for learners who are still learning to read and write in their L1 → Negative influence with L1 literacy; interlingual mistakes → Too much emphasis on written language (particularly in assessment and as a selection criterion at the end of Year 4)	→ Children desire FL literacy and ask for written forms → A pure focus on oral communication might eventually lead to a lack of variety in teaching methods → Young learners naturally encounter written English in their surroundings → Including all skills complies with a holistic way of teaching → Invented spelling occurs when learners are not introduced to literacy; danger of fossilisation of mistakes → Literacy supports language awareness → Research has proven that learners are not overtaxed by early biliteracy and that early biliteracy has no negative influence on L1 development → Including FL reading and writing does not negatively influence FL speaking and listening competences → Early biliteracy can positively influence FL pronunciation and the recognition of word boundaries → Literacy supports learner autonomy → Visual learners benefit from literacy

To begin with the cons, opponents of early biliteracy advance a number of arguments that are mostly concerned with a fear of overtaxing young FL learners. They worry that literacy in English "would put excessive demands on learners" (Legutke et al., 2009: 57) while they still have to cope with learning to read and write in their L1. Opponents therefore discuss firstly whether and secondly when written language should be introduced in English, and favour leaving English literacy until later while learners are still in the process of acquiring their L1 literacy (Kierepka, 2010; Piske, 2007: 46). As a result, the primary school EFL curriculum in Baden-Württemberg (MKJS BW, 2004: 69ff) only required teachers to introduce reading and writing in Year 3, but not in Years 1 and 2, until 2016. This has changed just recently with the new curriculum of 2016 (MKJS BW, 2016: 15).

Another common argument is that early biliteracy in German and English might negatively influence the learners' literacy in their L1 (Kierepka, 2010: 93f). Different orthographies, for instance, could possibly confuse children and lead to interference between both systems (Zaunbauer, 2007: 46). Because of such interferences, literacy in the L2 should be postponed in favour of L1 literacy.

According to Bleyhl (2007: 47), some critics also fear that teachers might put too much emphasis on the written language, especially with regard to assessment. This would go against the principle that the primary focus of teaching is supposed to be on oral and aural skills. Kierepka (2010: 92f) goes one step further and discusses the apprehension that development of L2 literacy would be used as a selection criterion at the end of Year 4 to assign individual learners to different school types.

In contrast to regarding the early introduction of FL literacy critically or even negatively, there are also strong arguments that support the use of FL reading and writing in the early stages of primary education. These arguments offer answers to the prejudices and reservations outlined above and also suggest many further advantages of an early and simultaneous introduction of literacy in German and English.

Firstly, children want to learn the written form of EFL. According to Diehr & Rymarczyk (2010: 9), "young learners explicitly ask for written forms" and Diehr (2010: 53) adds that "children as early as in Year 1 show a keen interest in written English." Rymarczyk (2008: 170) reports the example of a little girl who was just about to start school and pointed out with delight how eager she was to learn to read in EFL in order to be able to read English books and street signs. Similar desires have been elaborated on by Bleyhl (2003: 18), who said that learners will want to read a FL text once they realise that they might have enough knowledge to do so. Böttger (2014b: 7) further adds that not integrating literacy into the primary school English classroom would sooner or later lead to boredom and a lack of variety in the English lessons. Additionally, Zaunbauer (2007: 46) outlines how neglecting the written skills would be contrary to what children naturally experience in their everyday life, as children obviously encounter English words such as 'airport' or 'shop' in writing. It would thus be artificial to separate the four skills and falsely isolate listening and speaking from reading and writing.

A further consideration is that if the teacher does not introduce learners to written words, so-called 'invented spelling' (see Scharer & Zutell, 2013: 470f) is likely to occur. Prompted by their desire to write English words, "learners invent their own spelling rules" (Diehr & Rymarczyk, 2008: 9). They simply use the rules they know from writing in German as their L1 and incorrectly transfer these rules onto the spelling of words in English; this is so-called rule-based invented spelling (Rymarczyk & Musall, 2010: 70). Because of the complex grapheme-phoneme correspondence of English, which contrasts with a simpler relationship in German, this leads to countless spelling mistakes. In the long run, it might even result in "fossilisation of inaccuracies" (Diehr & Rymarczyk, 2010: 9). Thus, to prevent invented spelling and its consequences, children should be introduced to the written form of English words by the teacher.

In addition, a reflection on the writing system of a FL can support language awareness, even for young language learners. Diehr (2010: 54) found that experience with written English helps to raise language awareness as it draws the primary school learners' attention to differences between German as their L1 and English as their L2. Generally, instead of just omitting written language, it is crucial and supportive in FLL to reflect on difficulties with English literacy, such as the complex grapheme-phoneme correspondence (Waas, 2014a: 35).

Zaunbauer (2007: 46) further argues that research in various immersion contexts has shown that simultaneous biliteracy does not have negative consequences for young learners. Young learners were neither overtaxed nor confused by its introduction; instead, they were able to separate between the two different language systems. Whilst interferences between the L1 and the L2 possibly occur, they only do so rarely and have no longer lasting negative effect (Piske, 2010: 42f). Several researchers (Diehr & Rymarczyk, 2008: 8; Rymarczyk & Musall, 2010: 69) have found in empirical studies that the simultaneous introduction of German and English literacy does not have negative effects on the development of literacy in German as an L1. In fact, it is actually the German language that influences the reading and writing in English and not vice versa (Rymarczyk &

Musall, 2010: 69). Piske (2010: 37) concludes that early contact with two languages in written form positively influences the development of literacy in the L2 in the long run without negatively influencing L1 literacy.

Moreover, introducing FL reading and writing early does not negatively influence other FL competence areas. Duscha (2007: 309) found that introducing and working with written language in English from the very beginning has a positive influence and effect on EFL development with regard to communicative competence, and that no other areas of English, such as speaking or listening, were negatively influenced.

Furthermore, early literacy in EFL can positively support pronunciation in English (Diehr & Frisch, 2011: 43). Learners find it helpful to actually see how a word is spelled in order to then be able to correctly pronounce it (Bassetti, 2009: 192f). This concurs with Schmid-Schönbein's (2008: 54) argument concerning English chunks and sentences: She states that written input helps children to identify word boundaries and that particularly weaker learners can benefit from this. Written language helps learners to decode the segmentation of sound sequences into single words (Diehr, 2010: 54). Thus, the written form of English words and sentences should be used naturally to support what learners learn orally.

Reading and writing also foster learner autonomy. To a certain extent, being able to read a text on their own enables learners to take over responsibility for their learning (Little, 1999: 11), because reading allows them to independently seek and understand information. For example, working with a picture dictionary supports learner autonomy (see Freudenau, 2012), but is only possible when learners are acquainted with FL reading and writing. Therefore, the use of the written language allows the teacher a greater variety and more options for meaningful tasks and activities.

Another advantage of using the written form as early as possible becomes obvious when taking different learning styles into consideration (also see Chapter 3.1.1). Visual learners are likely to benefit from the written form of words as this corresponds to their preferred way of learning (see Brown, 2007: 129). Not only for visual learners but for all learners, however, it has been amply demonstrated that a multisensory approach to learning helps to retain information – hence not only hearing a word but also seeing its orthographic representation helps learners to remember it more easily (Schmid-Schönbein, 2008: 54f).

To recapitulate, the arguments supporting the early introduction of literacy seem stronger than the arguments against it. Many arguments against early biliteracy have been proven to be misleading and erroneous by research. Today, "there is a tendency to argue for integrating these [written] skills" and also "current curricula emphasise the supportive function of reading and writing" (Legutke et al., 2009: 57). Frisch (2010: 108) argues along the same lines when noting that recently more and more researchers as well as teachers have been calling for the supportive function of literacy in the primary school EFL classroom to be recognised. Reviewing several studies on this issue in primary immersion classrooms in Germany, Piske (2010: 46) concludes that arguments against early biliteracy are rather weak and that hence the question should not be whether and when the written form should be introduced, but how literacy should be taught. Chapter 3.3 will come back to this issue, after the next subchapter has provided detailed information about the current status of reading in the primary school EFL classroom in Germany.

3.2 The Current Status of Reading

The previous subchapters have shown that written language is accepted as part of the primary school English classroom by now and that arguments against early biliteracy have lost their justification. Still, the focus on spoken rather than written language in classroom practice remains untouched. This primacy of oral skills will be outlined first, before curricular expectations and current classroom practice with regard to FL reading is elaborated on.

3.2.1 The Primacy of Spoken over Written Language

Despite the fact that written language is accepted as a part of the primary school EFL classroom today, the focus is still on the oral skills listening and speaking. This focus on oral communication is found in all EFL curricula in Germany and has also been advocated by many researchers (see, e.g., Elsner, 2010: 40; Klippel, 2000: 22; Pinter, 2006: 45; see also MSW NRW, 2008b: 71).

There are several reasons for focusing mainly on oral skills at the primary school level. Legutke et al. (2009: 51) argue that due to the learners' competence level, a focus on oral skills is necessary. Beginners need some time to get used to the sound and the speech flow of a new language (Elsner, 2010: 41), which is best done by listening and speaking. Opportunities to listen to rich input are very important (Pinter, 2006: 45), as listening comprehension forms the basis for L1 development as well as for FLL (Schmid-Schönbein, 2008: 52). Trying the language out in speaking happens either parallel or a bit later (Klippel, 2000: 22; Pinter, 2006: 45). The young learners thereby get used to the FL in listening and speaking before written language is manageable for them. This seems particularly important in a language with a complex grapheme-phoneme correspondence, such as English. Additionally, listening and speaking potentially have priority over reading and writing for children, in L1 but probably also in early L2 development. Younger learners are more likely to find themselves in situations in which they use the oral language rather than the written one.[44]

The primacy of spoken over written language in the primary school EFL classroom is not bound to the German context. In Norway, too, teaching priorities in the primary school EFL classroom are set on oral skills more than on reading and writing (Drew, 2009: 103f). The same holds true for the Netherlands (Drew, 2009: 107). Nevertheless, this primacy of spoken over written language is not a general or global one in FLL, but one that is to a certain extent unique to the primary school EFL classroom. For instance, German secondary schools hesitated and procrastinated over putting more emphasis on oral skills for a long time after the introduction of a more communicative approach to language teaching (also see Chapter 3.1.1). Countries that still work according to the principles of the grammar-translation method, mostly less economically developed countries (Richards & Rodgers, 2014: 7), also place more emphasis on written language whilst spoken language comes second.

Nevertheless, there seems to be a general agreement that in early stages of L2 learning, reading and writing should have a "supportive function" (Legutke et al., 2009: 57) in promoting successful FL learning and maintaining motivation (Mindt & Schlüter, 2007: 56). As outlined in Chapter 3.1, the written skills are important in the process of FLL, which is why they have gained acceptance also for beginner language learners nowadays. Still, written language should by no means be in the centre of early EFL teaching and the focus on oral skills remains uncontested.

3.2.2 Curricula and Classroom Practice

Reading has made its way into primary school EFL curricula and classrooms, even if it is not in the foreground of teaching. Chapter 2.4 has already provided an overview of how reading is quintessentially integrated into skills development. This subchapter will present results of a cursory qualitative content analysis of German

---

44 In other contexts and more generally speaking, oral language is not necessarily more important than written language. This is highly dependent on the individual users and contexts. In some contexts, for instance new media, written language is potentially more important than speaking and listening.

EFL curricula in that it summarises curricular expectations with regard to reading and compares these to current classroom practices.

After a long time of uncertainty and trial and error with regard to including literacy in the primary school English classroom, written language is finally being paid attention to in research, methodology and educational policy (Diehr, 2010: 51; Diehr & Frisch, 2010a: 26). Still, the current status of reading activities does not always mirror what research as well as curricula reveal. Moreover, the extent to which FL reading and writing is supposed to made use of in German primary school EFL classrooms varies greatly amongst different schools and federal states (Frisch, 2014d: 33).

Taking a look at German curricula for teaching English in primary school, with a particular focus on the curriculum for NRW, one finds that reading has a fixed place in them today. With NRW's new curriculum of 2008 (MSW NRW, 2008b; also see Chapter 1) in particular, a stronger emphasis was placed on literacy, highlighting the supportive function of FL reading and writing from the very beginning (MSW NRW, 2008b: 73). Reading as well as writing outcomes are clearly defined and for reading these go as far as the global comprehension of short texts at the end of Year 4 (MSW NRW, 2008b: 78). The curriculum mentions authentic materials, such as picture books, as possible reading materials and outlines that these are important for young FL learners (MSW NRW, 2008b: 74). Other German curricula put less emphasis on reading. For instance, the curriculum for English in Saxony, a state that introduces English in Year 3, notes that young EFL learners should merely be able to recognise written words which they already know (Sächsisches Staatsministerium für Kultus [Saxonian State Ministry for Culture and Education], 2009: 2). However, the tendency is towards gradually supporting and including more reading and writing. For example, Baden-Württemberg, whose initial curriculum from 2004 omitted literacy in Years 1 and 2 (MKJS BW, 2004), now implements it at these levels with its new curriculum of 2016, even if only carefully (MKJS BW, 2016: 15).

Despite the curricular demands, reading activities are limited with regard to their frequency and level of difficulty in the primary school EFL classroom, and Kolb (2013: 33) notes critically that "reading activities are often restricted to isolated phrases and short sentences and mainly consist in understanding task instruction." Common reading activities include reading short task instructions supplemented by pictograms, playing games such as bingo, labelling the classroom with classroom words and looking at written versions of songs or rhymes which are read together with the teacher (see, e.g., Bebermeier & Stoll, 2008: 83; Meendermann, 2014: 147f).

The BIG study (BIG-Kreis, 2015) underlines what has already been stated and reveals information about the extent to which teachers at 80 different schools in Germany use reading tasks in the EFL classroom. The study's results show that single words and short sentences are read regularly, but that teachers scarcely ever use stories, books or coherent texts for reading (BIG-Kreis, 2015: 38). The BIG-Kreis concludes that teachers overall still underestimate the importance of FL literacy as well as the learners' cognitive potential to read FL texts.

Similarly, primary school course books are also very limited with regard to reading tasks. Frisch (2014a: 14) found that the selection of reading texts is restricted and there are only very few activities that go beyond matching words and pictures. Vollmuth (2004: 121) underscores this statement. In a detailed course book analysis, she found that reading is a neglected skill in course books for the primary school EFL classroom, as reading was addressed regularly in only one out of the seven analysed books and virtually ignored in some of them. A more recent analysis cannot be found, but with the gradual acknowledgement of the importance of reading and writing for young EFL learners, this finding might change in the near future.

As one can imagine from the limited use of reading activities and their low degrees of difficulty, the reading activities conducted are mostly restricted to reading words which the learners are already familiar with orally. Chapter 2.4.2 has shown that the order of teaching FL skills goes from listening to speaking and then from reading to writing and that every word that is read should be known to the children orally in that they are familiar with its meaning and pronunciation. In Piske's (2010: 40) view, children are likely to mispronounce words they encounter in written form if they have not encountered them orally before. Of course, learners cannot possibly know all the words in advance when engaging with more challenging reading tasks, such as reading authentic books, as these as well as other short texts inevitably contain words which the children are not familiar with yet. This book, however, argues that given support children can still read such books or texts, even if they do not know all the words (orally) yet (also see Chapter 6.2).

One of the reasons why teachers do not engage their young EFL learners in more demanding reading activities appears to be a lack of time. Elsner (2010: 43) states that FL teachers in the primary school EFL classroom in Germany – who only have two lessons per week – do not have enough time to offer children sufficient support to enable them to read and understand longer English texts. Kierepka (2010: 91) underlines this notion and argues that there is not enough time to introduce English literacy when lessons are offered only twice a week, and hence the limited time is often dedicated to the spoken skills.

Despite the restricted amount of reading in regular classroom activities and in course books, several researchers are calling for engaging learners in more challenging and demanding reading activities (see also Chapter 3.4). The same holds true for the present book. Frisch (2014d: 34) believes that from a research perspective reading is not too challenging for young EFL learners but can by contrast positively influence other areas of learning as well as enhance learners' motivation. Therefore, Frisch (2013) as well as Jöckel (2016) both suggest explicit teaching of reading competence in the primary school EFL classroom (see Chapter 3.3.2). Diehr (2010: 55), moreover, hypothesises that children can exceed current curricular expectations.[45] In practical terms, Gehring (2004: 75), for example, suggests reading and working with texts which the pupils have to work hard on in order to understand them instead of just using simple reading activities. Another supporter of literacy in the primary school EFL classroom, Böttger (2014b: 9), also suggests including different activities that support and practise reading comprehension, encompassing the independent reading of unknown texts of different lengths. The notion of reading longer texts such as picture books will further be elaborated on in Chapter 5.5.1 and an overview of previous research as well as an outlook on reading competence will be provided in Chapter 3.4. Beforehand, Chapter 3.3 explores the question of an EFL reading methodology with young learners.

3.3 The Prevailing Question of an EFL Reading Methodology

Despite the fact that reading has its place in primary school EFL curricula nowadays and that it is, at least to a certain extent, also applied in current classroom practices, there is a prevailing lack of a clear reading methodology (Diehr, 2010: 52). Thus, the question of an EFL reading methodology will be dealt with in this subchapter. Two common approaches to teaching reading will firstly be outlined in order to subsequently explain current practices and the actual lack of a methodology for teaching reading in the primary school EFL classroom in Germany.

---

45 Diehr refers to the curriculum of NRW. This curriculum is one of the most elaborate ones in terms of reading and places high reading demands on young EFL learners. Thus, other curricula with less ambition with regard to reading could clearly be made more challenging in Diehr's view.

3.3.1 Common Approaches to Learning and Teaching Literacy

Several methods for teaching literacy skills have been established in German and English primary schools;[46] usually concerned with literacy in the learners' L1. On a broad scale, the phonological and the whole language method are distinguished (Lázaro Ibarrola, 2010: 95). The major aspects of both will now briefly be touched on.

The whole language method is based on the direct access to the meaning of a word via its visual image without paying attention to individual letters (Lázaro Ibarrola, 2010: 95). Learners are introduced to core vocabulary with the help of word cards (Diehr, 2010: 62) and the sequence of letters is supposed to be recognised as a whole picture and not as single letters; hence, it has also been referred to as the whole word approach (Diehr, 2010: 62). In this approach, learners recognise the form-meaning correspondence of words without analysing them via (decoding) their constitute graphemes (Frisch, 2013: 83). Such "sight-vocabulary" develops through practising the "fast recognition of whole words" (Cameron, 2001: 149). The child is supposed to holistically understand the meaning of words or phrases without explicitly decoding them. This holistic approach to written words attempts to build up a vocabulary store of key words, in which the words are stored as a holistic picture and learnt by heart (Reichart-Wallrabenstein, 2004: 261). Frith (1985: 308) criticises this rather top-down approach, as he says that the pictorial lexicon soon reaches a critical limit in that visually similar words become confused. Cameron (2001: 148) says that this approach is already inefficient after about 50 words because it rapidly becomes difficult to remember each word as a separate picture. Thus, other approaches of decoding the words, possibly in a more bottom-up way, are needed. Therefore, at a certain point a phonological approach that analyses the grapheme-phoneme correspondence of words is needed (Frith, 1985: 307).

Phonological approaches offer explicit instruction in decoding words via their grapheme-phoneme correspondence and focus on the identification of letters with their corresponding sounds (Cameron, 2001: 149). The pupils systematically learn the correspondence between letters and sounds and learn how to decode words on that basis: Children "construct the sound of a word, recognise it and link it to its meaning" (Lázaro Ibarrola, 2010: 95). In contrast to the whole word approach, the phonological approach requires bottom-up skills (Frisch, 2010: 113).

In German, the grapheme-phoneme correspondence is relatively simple and thus the alphabetic principle of a phonological approach works well (Eisenberg

---

46 For a detailed overview and a comparison of approaches used in Germany and English-speaking countries, see Frisch (2013: 81ff).

& Fuhrhop, 2007: 37). Methods like 'reading through writing' (Reichen, 1988) suggest that children read and write on the basis of the phonetisation of a word, which presupposes that children know which phoneme corresponds to which grapheme with the help of initial sound tables.[47] A phonological approach that is commonly applied in teaching literacy in English as an L1 in English-speaking countries is phonics.[48] It slightly differs from the German approach, because phonics does not only focus on letters but also takes the phonetics of groups of letters into consideration (Frisch, 2010: 108; Lázaro Ibarrola, 2010: 89). This is due to the complex grapheme-phoneme correspondence of English, for which the phonetisation of words based on single letters is impractical.

In successful practice, often a method-integrated approach is used, amalgamating the holistic capturing of whole words (top-down) and the analysis of the grapheme-phoneme correspondence of the language (bottom-up) (Cameron, 2001: 124; Dehaene, 2010: 251; Hall, 2013: 535). Cameron (2001: 124) points out that learners need both skills in order to become effective readers and that therefore a combination of the whole word and the phonological approach needs to be used. As will be seen in Chapter 4.1, the holistic capturing of words and automatisation in word decoding becomes especially important for advanced readers and for developing reading fluency, when bottom-up decoding is not practical any longer.

With regard to simultaneously teaching literacy skills in two languages, for example English and German, two different practices are conceivable. Teaching literacy can either follow the same methodological principles in both languages, or two different methodological principles can be used with one approach for each language. Both practices have advantages and disadvantages and so far there are no empirical results in favour of one or the other.[49]

---

47 Author's translation for '*Anlauttabelle*'.

48 See Frisch (2010) or Johnston and Watson (2007) for details.

49 Using similar approaches for both languages allows for contrasting the two languages and their written system as well as benefiting from similarities. The comparison, however, also entails the potential for incorrect transfer of aspects which are not transferable, and thus might lead to confusion and interlingual errors. Using different approaches for both languages might prevent wrong transfer and the confusion between the two languages; however, it might be more complicated for children to learn two different systems. So far, no research has been published with regard to this question. However, Claire from the 'KIBS International Primary School Hanover' reported that in their year-long bilingual teaching experience, the practice of using the same method for both languages has proven to be suited best at their school (Claire, 2013).

3.3.2 A Lack of Methodology for Teaching FL Reading in the Primary School in Germany

Despite long-established approaches to teaching literacy in German or English as L1s, there is no coherent methodology for teaching FL reading in the primary school EFL classroom in Germany: "A consistent scheme for the introduction of written language in primary EFL is lacking" (Kolb, 2013: 33). EFL curricula for the primary school level do not provide teachers with guidelines how to teach reading, but only provide the desired outcome (see Chapter 3.2.2). Curricula do not explicitly determine whether children are supposed to remember words as a whole, holistically, or if learners are supposed to learn to decode the words' grapheme-phoneme-correspondences (Frisch, 2010: 109).

Therefore, to date, the introduction of written language to young language learners has been characterised by disorganisation and randomness with regard to the methods chosen (Diehr, 2010: 52). Nevertheless, the holistic approach seems to prevail in classroom practice. Frisch (2010: 110) found that primary school EFL teachers tend to apply a more holistic approach to reading and writing in English, that is, the whole word method (see Chapter 3.3.1). The same approach holds true for most course books, which mostly focus on whole word reading (Frisch, 2013: 95).

However, if teachers (and curricula) expect young learners to develop FL reading and writing skills, literacy in English needs a methodology and needs to be integrated systematically: "Written language constitutes a means of communication in its own right and thus requires clear objectives as well as explicit instruction" (Diehr, 2010: 54). One proposal for teaching reading in the primary school EFL classroom comes from Diehr (2010: 55ff). She suggests the so-called 'LiPs[50] scheme', which is a structured teaching method to implicitly as well as explicitly teach reading to young EFL learners. It consists of a total of six phases and provides guidelines for teachers to introduce reading (Diehr, 2010; Diehr & Frisch, 2011). The phases include raising phonological awareness by drawing the learners' attention to the rules and analogies of the English grapheme-phoneme correspondence by making use of the phonics approach. The phonics approach itself has then been paid attention to in two empirical studies conducted by Frisch (2013) and Jöckel (2016).

---

50 Lesen im Englischunterricht auf der Primarstufe [reading in the primary school English classroom] (LiPS).

Based on the aforementioned LiPs scheme, Frisch (2013) conducted a study in which she investigated the explicit teaching of EFL reading at primary school level in Germany and compared the two different methods 'whole word' and 'phonics'. She tried both approaches with two Year 2 classes over a period of 18 months. Frisch (2013: 209ff) found that overall, reading does not overtax young learners and outlines the advantages of the two different approaches she investigated, whereby the phonics approach seemed to be generally more promising. Therefore, Frisch (2013: 215) suggests implementing more reading, including explicitly teaching reading, in the primary school EFL classroom. She concludes that both methods showed advantages and that is does not matter so much how teachers teach reading, but that they teach reading and initiate as well as maintain reading motivation (Frisch, 2013: 215).[51]

The second study was conducted by Jöckel (2016), who investigated how current course books can be supplemented with materials to explicitly teach reading competences in the primary school EFL classroom. She based her study on Frisch's (2013) finding that phonic-based approaches to reading seem to benefit young language learners (Jöckel, 2016: 134). For her research, Jöckel developed a workshop as well as a handbook including materials for teachers and asked them to implement activities based on the phonics approach in Years 3 and 4 of their primary school EFL classrooms (Jöckel, 2016: 138f). Via different questionnaires she found that on the one hand, many teachers found it difficult to implement the phonics approach; on the other hand, they evaluated the approach and the materials as very useful and expressed their intention to implement phonics-based activities on a regular basis (Jöckel, 2016: 140).

Based on both studies, the phonics approach seems promising for young EFL learners in Germany, but at the same time seems difficult to implement. Thus, addressing the skill of reading in teacher training and creating clear guidelines for teachers seem necessary to move forward in establishing a successful reading methodology. Additionally, more research is needed in order to establish a well-grounded basis for suggestions on how to teach reading.

---

51 Despite some criticism about the whole language approach (see Chapter 3.3.1), it has actually proven to be successful in acquiring reading competences in English as well, at least for L1 speakers of English (see Coles, 2013). Except for Frisch's (2013) study, which only partly applied the whole language approach, no empirical data on its potential for (young) EFL learners is available at present.

3.4 Previous Research and Outlook on Reading Competence in the Primary School EFL Classroom

Because reading in the primary school EFL classroom is still in its early stages, not much research on young learners' EFL reading competence has been conducted so far. The few studies that have been conducted are the EVENING study (Engel et al., 2009), the BIG study (BIG-Kreis, 2015) and studies conducted by Wilden et al. (2013), Kolb (2013), Frisch (2013), Jöckel (2016) and Reichart-Wallrabenstein (2004). The latter four studies were concerned with reading instruction, reading strategies and reading books; hence, their results with regard to reading competence either have already been given or will still be presented later in Chapters 4.6.4 and 5.5. The results of the BIG study, the EVENING study as well as Wilden et al.'s study will be presented here, as these were directly concerned with reading competences. In addition, two studies from the European context as well as one well-known study from the secondary school level will be taken into consideration.

The EVENING study (see Börner, Engel & Groot-Wilken, 2013; Engel et al., 2009) investigated the first implementation of teaching English in primary schools in NRW between 2005 and 2007. Specifically, it looked at the learners' EFL competences after two years of English in the primary school at the end of Year 4. Amongst many other aspects, the reading comprehension of the learners was investigated. This was tested via a pen and paper test that consisted of two parts: The first part was a multiple choice task and the second part matching sentences to pictures (see Groot-Wilken & Husfeldt, 2013: 127ff). Both tested reading comprehension at the word and sentence level. The test was based on the Common European Framework of References (CEFR) and on the German curricula for EFL at the primary school level and complied with standardised quality criteria after repeated piloting (Groot-Wilken, 2009: 139; Thürmann, 2013: 19). About 3,000 pupils took two slightly different versions of this test in the school years 2006 and 2007 (Paulick & Groot-Wilken, 2009: 180).[52] The overall results with regard to reading competence indicate that teachers as well as researchers had underestimated the learners' competences and that the tasks were mostly too easy (Paulick & Groot-Wilken, 2009: 189). On average, the pupils scored 14.7 out of a maximum of 22 points, with 74 % of the pupils reaching more than 50 % and thus a score higher than 11 points (Paulick & Groot-Wilken, 2009: 189). Almost 32 % of the learners scored very high between 18 to 22 points and only 4 % scored very low with 0 to 4 points (Paulick & Groot-Wilken, 2009: 189). Overall, these results corresponded

---

52   See Paulick & Groot-Wilken (2009: 180f) for the exact changes that were made between test version 2006 and test version 2007.

to and partly also exceeded the curricular requirements (Paulick & Groot-Wilken, 2009: 194f). Therefore, the research team suggests testing reading comprehension at the text level and not only at the word and sentence level in follow-up studies (Paulick & Groot-Wilken, 2009: 195). Such testing could avoid the ceiling effect that probably occurred in the EVENING study. One practical consequence of this study was that literacy gained more importance in the new curriculum for primary school EFL teaching in NRW, which was revised based on the results of the EVEN-ING study (Engel, 2009: 202; also see Chapter 3.2.2).

A recent study on learning English at the primary school level was conducted by the BIG-Kreis in 2013 (see BIG-Kreis, 2015: 8). For the main part, the researchers used the same instruments as the EVENING study, which had already been proven to meet quality criteria, to test the English language competence of about 2,100 children all over Germany at the end of Year 4. With regard to reading, they used an adapted version of the EVENING study's reading test, which focused on read-ing comprehension. Although the tasks of the EVENING study had partly proven to be too easy for the learners, no information about a possible enhancement in task difficulty is mentioned for the BIG study. Overall the research team found that the learners' reading comprehension was very good: 60 % of all participants reached a very high score of 15, 16, or 17 points (max. 17 points), while 33 % of all participants reached the maximum score of 17 points (BIG-Kreis, 2015: 43). Only about 9 % of the learners reached a score of only 8 points or less, which equals a score of less than 50 %; thus, about 90 % of all participants scored more than 50 % of the points, with a tendency towards higher rather than lower scores (BIG-Kreis, 2015: 43). These results are very promising and indicate that Year 4 pupils have good EFL reading comprehension skills. However, the results also display a ceiling effect: The tested pupils' reading competences in English were very high and the tasks that were used were too easy for them (BIG-Kreis, 2015: 43, 68). As in the EVENING study, it would have made sense to test reading comprehension at the text level and not only at the word and sentence levels.

A contrastive study was conducted by Wilden et al. (2013), which measured, among other aspects, the reading competences of a total of 6,500 pupils at the end of Year 4. The study compared two groups of Year 4 pupils, the first of which had been taught English for two years and the second for 3.5 years at the point of data collection.[53] They found that the children who had learnt English for

---

53 These two groups were found at primary schools in NRW, where English was taught in Year 3 and 4 from 2003 to 2008, and since 2008 English has been taught from Year 1 (second term) on (see Chapter 1).

3.5 years showed significantly better results with regard to reading comprehension (with a low effect size). In an earlier study by Böttger (2009: 4), secondary school teachers had claimed that by the end of Year 5 there was no difference in EFL competence between learners who started learning English in Year 3 and those who started in Year 5. Thus, Wilden et al.'s study was able to provide initial counterevidence to these teacher views and to show that more years of learning English do make a difference to the EFL competence of young learners, at least at the end of Year 4. However, Wilden et al.'s (2013) study did not investigate the extent to which the later starters might catch up with the earlier starters in the long run, for example at the end of Year 5, and can therefore only very carefully be compared to Böttger's investigation.

So far, the studies presented have focused on early EFL learning in Germany. Further studies have been conducted in the European context and two selected studies that focused on reading will be presented here. In the ELLiE[54] project (Enever, 2011a), a well-known large-scale research project that investigated TEFL at the primary school level in a number of European countries, a reading comprehension test was conducted at the end of Year 4 with 1,400 pupils in several primary schools across Europe (Germany was not part of the study). Children were asked to match short sentences to the speech bubbles of a comic strip. This test was based on the researchers' observation of classroom practices, but it was not standardised. The results show that in two of the eight items, the children displayed a success-rate of over 75 % (Szpotowicz & Lindgren, 2011: 134). These two items were syntactically simple and overall not complex. Other items that were more complex and required world knowledge as well as vocabulary that went beyond the context of the comic were more difficult and could only be solved with a success rate of 32 to 60 % (Szpotowicz & Lindgren, 2011: 134). Further results were not presented. Because of a lack of information about the test's quality and no clear-cut results a further interpretation of this study's results is difficult. However, the initial impression is that many learners succeeded in solving the easier parts of the comic, but that the learners partly struggled with the more difficult ones.

In Switzerland, Husfeld and Bader-Lehmann (2009) investigated almost 800 primary school pupils after two years of English in primary school. To test reading comprehension, a slightly adapted version of the already well-trialled test used in the EVENING study was used. The results showed a normal distribution with only a few children that showed exceptionally positive or negative results.

---

54 Early language learning in Europe (ELLiE).

90 % of the learners displayed good reading competences at the word level, whilst only one third showed good competences at the short text level (Husfeld & Bader-Lehmann, 2009: 7). However, the results were still better than the research team had expected them to be and they interpreted this as evidence for a relatively high level of reading comprehension (Husfeld & Bader-Lehmann, 2009: 7).

The overall impression from these research results at the primary school level is that young FL learners' reading abilities have been constantly underestimated and that despite many prejudices against reading from previous decades, young learners are quite able to take on FL reading tasks. Therefore, more challenging reading activities might be supportive for young learners in order to allow them to display and develop their full potential with regard to FL reading.

Interestingly, the reading results of FL learners at the secondary school level are not as promising as the ones from the primary school. This was found, for example, by the DESI[55] study and will briefly be outlined here. The DESI study is a well-known study that investigated the English and German competences of Year 9 learners in Germany in 2003/04 (Klieme, 2008: 1). Amongst other aspects, reading comprehension in English was tested with a number of different tasks at different levels. The research team distinguished between four different competence levels, which will further be outlined in Chapter 4.5.2. The study found that almost half of the learners did not reach the minimum curricular standards with regard to reading comprehension in English: The learners only proved to have very basic reading competences (equal to level A1 in the CEFR), which is not sufficient for Year 9 learners (Nold, Rossa & Chatzivassiliadou, 2008: 134). Out of the other 56 % that reached the curricular reading standards, only 22 % reached the higher CEFR competence levels B and C, whilst 34 % could only reach level A, indicating that they reached the minimal curricular standards (Nold et al., 2008: 135). Overall, the DESI study found that the EFL reading comprehension of German Year 9 learners was below average and a large number of pupils only had basic reading competences that were below the curricular expectations (Nold et al., 2008: 137).

Against this backdrop, it is reasonable to assume that increased reading activities at the primary school level could possibly help learners in the acquisition of FL reading skills in the long run. Primary school might be able to lay a solid basis for the more challenging reading activities of secondary school. Certainly, the gap between primary and secondary school, particularly with a focus on written

---

55 *Deutsch Englisch Schülerleistungen International* [German English learner achievement internationally] (DESI).

skills, might be bridged by enhanced FL reading at the primary school level (also see Chapter 12.3). Whether this positively affects FL reading competences in later years remains for future research to ascertain.

3.5 Summary of Chapter 3

The beginning of Chapter 3 has shown that reading and writing had varying roles across different teaching approaches, but that in today's communicative EFL classrooms written language has a set place. The importance of FL reading is not as such contested, but the status of FL reading with young learners has been an issue of controversial discussions since the start of early FLL around the 1960s and 70s. Reflecting on arguments in the debate around early biliteracy, it becomes clear that arguments that support an early and more or less simultaneous introduction of FL literacy seem to outweigh those of critics and opponents. Nowadays, there is for the most part consensus that including written language in the primary school EFL classroom is beneficial for young FL learners and in accordance with a holistic and supportive FLL environment. The present book concurs with the current status, as it foregrounds reading and supports its use in the primary school EFL classroom. As the empirical study that is presented in this book has a bilingual primary school as its setting, this study also supports the importance of reading skills in the emerging approach of CLIL and provides research in this area.

Still, with young learners, the focus remains on the oral skills listening and speaking, and the written skills are given a subordinate role and a supportive function. The necessity for this focus on spoken language is by no means contested in this book; rather the book attempts to raise the visibility of written language in the primary EFL classroom and explore the extent to which the skill of reading can be used in that context. This is based on the current consensus that young FL learners benefit from a certain degree of exposure to written language and should have the opportunity to develop written language skills.

Despite this approval of reading, there is still no coherent EFL reading methodology for young learners. Two different approaches, the whole word and a phonetic approach, dominate the teaching of literacy, but no clear-cut recommendations for either of the two are found in primary EFL curricula. Initial research results suggest that a phonics approach is beneficial for young EFL learners, but this has not yet let to an implementation of such activities in curricula or classroom practice. The current book more or less ignores the debate on methods of teaching EFL reading however, but rather investigates the reading comprehension and strategies of young learners as found without an explicit teaching approach. This might shed light on areas where young EFL learners possibly need some more explicit instruction in FL reading.

This book is concerned with reading at the text level and makes proposals for including the reading of picture books in the primary school EFL classroom. This logically follows upon current research results. Studies that have so far been conducted with regard to EFL reading at the primary school level suggest that children can and should be engaged in more challenging reading activities than is currently done. Chapter 3.2.2 indicated that despite curricular demands, an unknown but probably large number of teachers seldom assign EFL reading tasks, let alone challenging ones. The young learners' abilities seem to be constantly underestimated. Therefore, more challenging reading tasks, including reading at the text level, seem to logically link to what is known about EFL reading with young learners by now. Initial projects focusing on the reading of EFL texts will be presented in Chapter 5.5.2, and this book will contribute to the discussion as well.

4. FL Reading Competence: Theoretical Foundation, Definition, Reading Processes and Reading Strategies

Abstract: This chapter is concerned with reading competence and discusses a definition of the latter. Based on a number of different processes involved in L1 and FL reading, the chapter provides details about reading styles and strategies and elaborates on text difficulty as well as varying levels of reading comprehension.

Reading, particularly FL reading, is a complex and highly interactive task in which various cognitive processes as well as eye movement are in a constant interplay. Reading is a receptive skill (Goodman, 1988, 12; Haß, 2006: 74), but by no means passive. On the contrary, reading is a highly active process, in that it can be seen as an interaction between reader, text and context, and the reader is involved in an active process of making meaning and immersed in a dynamic relationship with the text at all times (Biebricher, 2008: 9; Carrell, 1988: 1; Hedge, 2000: 188; Westphal Irwin, 2007: 16). Readers bring in their individual attitudes, interests, expectations, skills and prior knowledge in order to interpret and actively infer the writer's message (Westphal Irwin, 2007: 8).

Generally, reading starts with the linguistic surface representation in the form of written words and ends with the reader actively constructing meaning out of it (Goodman, 1988: 12). What happens 'in between' will be the focus of this chapter. To this end, firstly the basic mechanics of reading, namely the role of the eyes, will briefly be explained. With a focus on FL reading, differences and similarities between L1 and L2 reading are outlined next, and common hypotheses about L2 reading are examined. What reading competence actually means will be defined in Chapter 4.3, and it will become clear that in the context of this book that reading competence means reading comprehension. Going into more detail with the latter, processes that are involved in reading comprehension will then be outlined with the help of a model of FL reading and factors that can influence comprehension will be explored. Lastly, reading strategies will be detailed, as these play a major role in the process of reading.

It is important to mention at this point that the process of reading with a focus on reading comprehension, as outlined in this chapter, is usually concerned with reading at the text level. Reading at the word level, which takes place particularly at the very beginning of FLL (see Chapter 2.4.2), is of minor importance when looking at general approaches to and theories of reading competence.

4.1 The Eye's Role in Reading: Reading Rate and Fluency

Eye movement plays a crucial role in reading, as all textual elements are first and foremost recognised visually. Readers basically look at a written word and cannot help but read it (Dehaene, 2010: 23). By doing so, they possibly grasp a word's sound and meaning successfully or are unsuccessful in decoding it. Reading thus starts with the eyes, and what was picked up by the eyes is then processed in the reader's brain; a highly complex process that can only briefly be explained here.

To begin with, only 15 degrees of a person's field of vision can be used for reading, and this field of vision is asymmetric, depending on the reading direction (Dehaene, 2010: 27). The direction of reading in English is from left to right, so that the recognition of letters is shifted to the right-hand side where readers recognise about double the amount of letters that they do on the left. To grasp a reading text, the eyes have to move ceaselessly (Dehaene, 2010: 23) and glide over the lines of a text. However, the eyes do not glide evenly and smoothly, but jerkily and in so-called saccades (Haß, 2006: 84). Saccades are defined as "rapid movements of the eyes" (Rayner, 1998: 2). Essentially, the eyes jump from one fixed point to the next in order to focus on a certain amount of letters for a short time. Between the saccades, the eyes remain relatively still during so-called "fixations" (Rayner, 1998: 2). During this short break, referred to as the "fixation duration" (Rayner, 1998: 5), the brain works at full capacity in order to decode and save the letters that the eye recognises on the left and right hand side of the fixation. Figure 4 visualises this process.

Figure 4: Saccades and fixations involved in eye movement in reading.

The length of a saccade depends on the reader's reading competence. Good EFL readers' saccades are rather long (up to 31 letters), whereas weaker readers show noticeably shorter saccades (Haß, 2006: 84). Böttger (2014b: 6) notes that young and beginner EFL readers only have short saccades of about four letters. As such, saccades do not necessarily consist of one word, but can also consist of several words or only parts of a word. Generally, fixations can be at the beginning, in the middle or at the end of a word, while readers tend to aim at word centres for fixations during reading (Krügel, 2014: 5).

However, a learner's saccades do not always have the same length but are adjusted to the level of difficulty of a text or section thereof. Readers adapt their visual analysis to the density of characters; the denser the characters, the shorter the saccades (Dehaene, 2010: 28). The more difficult a sequence of letters is, the shorter the saccade. Saccade length is also partly dependent on how familiar a reader is with a word and how frequently a word occurs in a text (Biebricher, 2008: 32).

Once a fixed part has been understood, the eye jumps to the next fixation; in the negative case of not understanding what was read, the eye has to jump back to re-fix a previous point (Haß, 2006: 84). This is referred to as 'regression' and usually occurs because the reader made too long a saccade and thus a short saccade back is necessary for reading to proceed efficiently (Rayner, 1998: 4). Also, longer regressions of, for example, whole paragraphs occur when readers have to re-read a certain part of the text that was not understood (Rayner, 1998: 4).

A reader's reading rate, or reading speed, depends on the eye movements, particularly on the length of the saccades. To a limited extent, this can be practised and also improved through practice (Dehaene, 2010: 29). Particularly young and beginner readers of English with saccades of only about four letters can advance their reading competence through practice in that they gradually enlarge their saccades and therefore their reading rate. However, good readers, with approximately 400 to 500 words per minute, have most likely reached the limits of their visual sensor (Dehaene, 2010: 29).[56] Nevertheless, even good and proficient readers slow down their reading pace when they come across complex parts of a text (Ehlers, 2007: 117). In fact, it is a sign of proficient reading skills to flexibly and appropriately adjust the reading pace for different parts of a text and for different purposes of reading (Ehlers, 2007: 119).

Another central aspect of reading, one which is paramount for good comprehension and overall reading proficiency, is fluency (Rasinski, Rupley, Paige & Nicholas, 2016: 163). Fluency is seen as the "bridge between decoding and comprehension" (Garbe, 2010: 18), in that fluent readers are those who skilfully decode words and sentences and as such successfully comprehend a reading text. Fluent readers "read with adequate speed and word recognition automaticity" (Rasinski et al., 2016: 164), and therefore reading fluency is dependent on the reading rate and is hence influenced by the learners' ability to decode FL words quickly. Hence, fluency develops from an automatisation of basal

---

56 The reading rate usually differs between the L1 and the L2, with a faster reading rate in the L1. Ehlers (1998: 166) points out that even very talented, proficient and advanced learners read more slowly in their L2 than in their L1.

reading skills, in particular the decoding of words as well as the pace of reading (Garbe, 2010: 18).

This implies that fluency is influenced by how readers decode the lexical items of a text. Readers need to develop the ability to quickly and automatically recognise words accurately to become fluent readers (Rasinski et al., 2016: 164). Slow readers spend a lot of time and energy on decoding words and thus only have limited mental capacity available for comprehension (Frisch, 2013: 49; Nampaktai, Kaebsombut, Akwaree, Wongwayrote & Sameepet, 2013: 35). Decoding every word based on its grapheme-phoneme correspondence reduces the reading rate and pulls away the reader's attention from text comprehension (Rasinski et al., 2016: 164). Therefore, EFL learners have to practise word decoding, because enhanced automatisation and accuracy in decoding words allows readers longer saccades and shorter fixation length and as such frees up mental capacity for comprehension beyond the word level. At first, accuracy in word decoding needs to be developed (Rasinski et al., 2016: 165), which requires bottom-up skills and provides learners with the ability to precisely decode FL words (see Chapter 3.3). At the second stage, learners then develop automaticity in word recognition, which allows them to decode a word quickly and with relative ease, so that they eventually become more fluent readers (Rasinski et al., 2016: 165).

Overall, fluency is important for effective reading and successful reading comprehension and should be developed through frequent practice (Gorsuch & Taguchi, 2010: 27; Skehan, 1998: 18). Continuous reading practice can positively influence the reading rate in that word recognition becomes more accurate and automatic, so that saccades gradually become longer and fixation lengths become shorter. Thus, reading fluency is supported in that automatisation in word recognition is trained. Taken these processes together, the learners should eventually become fluent readers and good comprehenders with a relatively fast reading pace.

4.2 First and FL Reading: Challenges for German Learners of English

FL reading is in many aspects similar to L1 reading, but also differs in some respects. Two major theoretical positions can be found, one of which argues that reading in a FL is a language problem (threshold hypothesis), the other one arguing that it is a reading problem (interdependence hypothesis) (Müller-Hartmann & Schocker-v. Ditfurth, 2014: 88). Both hypotheses will be explained in this subchapter, including related aspects that are relevant for the differences and similarities between L1 and L2 reading. Thereby, the focus will be on the foreign language 'English' as learnt by learners in German schools.

Generally, reading in a FL is more difficult than reading in the L1. This has already been indicated in Chapter 4.1, where it was noted that a learner's L1 reading rate is better than his/her L2 reading rate, no matter how proficient he/she is. When reading in one's L1, written text has to be transferred into language and decoded for its meaning. In FL reading, yet another variable comes into play, which is the FL. This dual-language involvement makes L2 reading more complex (Koda, 2007: 1), because a learner refers to at least two language systems when reading in the L2, while in L1 reading only one language system is needed (Frisch, 2013: 50).

The involvement of the L2 in FL reading is one of the major points of the threshold hypothesis (Laufer, 2013; Park, 2013). This hypothesis argues that FL reading depends on competence in the FL, and particularly on lexical L2 knowledge. This means that the FL itself needs to be known and understood to a certain extent, and in particular L2 vocabulary knowledge is crucially important (Cameron, 2001: 137). In order to establish meaning from a word that is read, that word needs to be stored in the learner's mental (L2) lexicon so that the learner actually knows the word in the L2. In L2 reading, however, a certain number of words will probably be unknown to the learner and therefore he/she needs coping strategies (see Chapter 6.6) that are not necessarily needed in L1 reading. As will be detailed in Chapter 6.6.1, several researchers hence argue that reading competence in a FL develops once a certain threshold of L2 competence is reached; but up to the present no clear threshold could be defined.

The interdependence hypothesis (Cummins, 1979), which, in contrast to the aforementioned threshold hypothesis, states that FL reading is a reading issue and not a language issue, is concerned rather with the transfer of reading skills. Proponents of the interdependence hypothesis point out that children transfer L1 skills to L2 skills (for example, Möller, 2013: 24; Swain & Lapkin, 2005: 181). The hypothesis argues that FL reading is dependent on L1 reading and that reading strategies are transferred from L1 to L2 reading (Cummins, 1979). As such, a high premium is placed on L1 reading competence. Tarone, Bigelow and Hansen (2009: 3) summed up several studies done in this area and came to the overall conclusion that a good command of reading and writing in the learner's L1 has a positive and beneficial influence on developing L2 literacy.

However, a successful transfer is influenced by the extent to which the L1 and L2 are apart. There is a difference in acquiring reading skills across different languages, which is mostly based on the varying complexity of the grapheme-phoneme correspondence. English has a particularly difficult grapheme-phoneme correspondence, while the German one is rather simple. In German, a phoneme on average is represented by only 3.7 graphemes, while in English a phoneme corresponds to 12.8 graphemes on average (Bleyhl, 2000a: 86). For example, the German phoneme /i/ can be represented by four different graphemes. In contrast to that, there are 21 possible graphemes in English that can be pronounced as /i/ (Bleyhl, 2000a: 86). Hence, some languages are easier than others with regard to reading. For instance, Dehaene (2010: 262) underlines how difficult it is to learn to read in English, saying that even English children need several years to become efficient readers in English.[57] Therefore, Frisch (2013: 65) points out that especially for EFL learning it is crucial to be able to decode a written word by understanding the relatively complex grapheme-phoneme relation of the English language. German learners acquiring English literacy thus need an understanding of the differences in the grapheme-phoneme correspondences of both languages and also need knowledge about the relation of letters (or their combinations) and corresponding sounds. Only then can L1 reading skills be effectively transferred to FL reading.

The alphabet as well as the reading direction of a language also play a role in successfully transferring reading skills (Cameron, 2001: 136). English and German share the same alphabet (apart from a few additional graphemes in German) and also share the reading direction from left to right. These similarities make the transfer of reading skills easier.

Returning now to the threshold and the interdependence hypotheses, it has been debated whether one of the two hypotheses or whether both of them explain and predict FL reading competence. Laufer (2013: 868) argues there is an interplay between the processes postulated in both hypotheses, since readers need to possess a critical mass of lexical and grammatical L2 knowledge in order to be able to apply general reading skills which might be based on L1 reading competence. Frisch (2015) underlines this by asserting that learners effectively transfer L1 reading skills to reading in the L2, but only when a certain threshold of FL competence is reached. Park's (2013: 44) study supports the interplay of both hypotheses, as the study found evidence that "L2 reading comprehension was a function of L1 reading and L2 knowledge." Overall, this distinction comes down to the question whether FL reading is a language issue or a reading issue or both. Except for the argumentation presented here, namely that both hypotheses hold true and influence FL reading to a certain extent, no clear-cut answer can be found.

---

57 For example, an English child needs at least two more years of additional teaching to reach the reading level of a French child (Dehaene, 2010: 262f), who experiences an easier grapheme-phoneme correspondence in French. Unfortunately, no such comparison between English and German can be found.

Ultimately, it is indisputable that learning to read (and write) in English is complex for German learners of English, but by no means impossible. Similarities between reading in the two languages as well as the transfer of certain reading skills should skilfully be used. At the same time, the differences between the two languages and thus potential difficulties in transfer need to be known and made explicit in order to counter them with methods that enable learners to overcome them and develop strategies for reading and writing in English. Clearly, knowledge of the FL is also beneficial in decoding a FL reading text and should be supported as well (also see Chapter 6.6).

4.3 Reading Competence: Reading Comprehension vs. Reading Aloud

Regardless of potential differences between L1 and L2 reading, this chapter will outline what reading competence means and entails. Reading competence can be understood in broadly two ways: on the one hand as reading comprehension and on the other hand as reading aloud abilities. Both notions will be elaborated on in the following subchapters, which will demonstrate why reading comprehension is the favourable reading outcome, but affirm the importance of reading aloud abilities as well. For the latter, particularly the factor of semi-vocalisation will be explained.

4.3.1 A Definition of Reading Competence and Reading Comprehension

This subchapter will argue that reading competence is mostly understood as reading comprehension, and provide a definition of the latter; it is this definition which underlies this book's understanding of reading competence. Nampaktai et al. (2013: 35) state that it "is generally acknowledged that reading comprehension is […] the preferred reading outcome […]." In other words, reading is all about constructing and understanding text meaning and as such reading comprehension is understood as the main and overriding purpose of reading (Koda, 2007: 1). In this sense, reading competence means decoding the information presented through text and being able to understand the content and message of it.

Reading comprehension is a crucial basic skill in contemporary industrialised and globalised societies. Reading with and for understanding is of existential importance and a basic prerequisite for the successful participation in work as well as social life and for finding one's way through a modern world of new media (Haß, 2006: 83; Klippel & Doff, 2007: 75; Steck, 2009: 1). Thus, as Böttger (2014b: 8) points out, teaching children the importance of reading comprehension is of paramount importance. Learners should experience reading as a meaningful activity, implying that they should be enabled to decode texts for meaning and comprehension.

Reading comprehension refers to the active engagement of readers with texts, aiming at the complex process of constructing meaning and understanding at the letter, word, sentence and text level (Steck, 2009: 22). The learners need to understand the relationship between words and chunks used in a specific context and grasp the overall structure of phrases and sentences. This enables them to make sense of the whole text. With regard to FL reading competence, another variable, the FL, comes into play (see Chapter 4.2). Thus, reading comprehension in a FL is the competence to actively retrieve information and construct meaning from a text written in the FL (see Steck, 2009: 22; Wilden & Porsch, 2015: 62).

In a model of FL reading competence for the upper secondary school level, Burwitz-Melzer (2007: 137f) describes FL reading competence as consisting of five sub-skills: motivational competence, cognitive and affective competence, intercultural competence, communicative competence and reflective competence. For these sub-skills, she describes different levels that should be reached by the EFL learners (see Burwitz-Melzer, 2007: 140ff). For the primary school, however, only parts of those are applicable. Still, it is important to note from Burwitz-Melzer's complex description that other aspects such as motivation or cognition also play a crucial role in the development of reading competence, while reading comprehension is seen as its overriding aim. Particularly for teaching reading competence at the secondary school level, the different parts of this model can be taken as a basis for developing in-depth reading competences and initiate literary learning (see Spinner, 2006).

4.3.2 Distinguishing Reading Comprehension from Reading Aloud

As seen in the definition provided in the previous subchapter, reading should be concerned with reading for meaning and understanding a message, and this is the view inherent in this book as well. However, teachers in particular often view reading as an opportunity to practise pronunciation, fluency and expressive speaking (Nuttall, 2005: 2). As such, reading competence is sometimes taken as reading aloud abilities. Because of this frequent misinterpretation, this subchapter will briefly distinguish between reading comprehension and reading aloud.

The importance of silent reading for one's own comprehension and reading aloud to some kind of audience has been discussed controversially. According to Haß (2006: 83), silent reading is the norm, whereas other forms, such as reading aloud, are of less importance. He states that silent reading is the natural way of reading, including, for example, reading a newspaper or a novel for pleasure (Haß: 2006: 88). However, Rasinski (2010: 27) points out many situations in which people make use of oral reading, for example, singing songs, reading stories to someone or reporting news. He sees reading aloud as the connector between spoken and written language (Rasinski, 2010: 29). Indeed, Meendermann (2014: 144f) goes so far as to maintain that reading aloud does not have much to do with reading but actually belongs to the competence of speaking.

Clearly, reading aloud differs from silently reading for comprehension (Brewster & Ellis, 2002: 111) and one does not entail the other. Reading aloud does not necessarily imply comprehension, and neither does comprehension imply reading aloud competence (Klippel & Doff, 2007: 89). In their research in primary school, Rymarczyk and Musall (2010: 82f) found very interesting results when testing on the one hand Year 1 pupils' abilities to read single English words aloud and on the other hand the comprehension of these words in a word-picture matching test. The results showed that most children sounded out the majority of words incorrectly, but that they could recognise the meaning of almost all the words when reading silently. Hence, the children showed poor oral reading but good reading comprehension abilities.

Generally, reading comprehension precedes reading aloud. Klippel and Doff (2007: 89) recommend that learners should only be engaged in oral reading when a text is already understood content-wise. Only when learners have understood a text's meaning can they focus on the actual reading aloud with correct pronunciation, expressive intonation and overall continuity (Wright, 1995: 19). Knowing the content enables the pupils to concentrate on the process of reading aloud.

Beginners in particular cannot manage both reading comprehension and reading aloud at the same time. A basic assumption of information processing, a model of learning from cognitive psychology that is applied to SLA (Saville-Troike, 2012), is that there is "a limit to the amount of focused mental activity we can engage in at one time" (Lightbown & Spada, 2013: 108). That is, learners only possess limited mental space to process new information and can thus only engage with one aspect of language at one time (McLaughlin, 1987: 136). This idea implies that new language features have to be processed in small units and with a great deal of cognitive effort until they become automatised to free mental space for new information (DeKeyser, 1998, 2001; Segalowitz, 2003). For reading, this means that as long as the skill of reading has not become automatised, young learners can only focus on one aspect of processing at a time, either reading a text silently for comprehension or reading a text aloud to an audience. In fact, reading aloud, without a previous phase of reading comprehension, can hinder reading for understanding, as pupils focus too much on the articulation of words (Gehring, 2004: 76). Conversely, having already grasped the content of a story frees processing capacity to concentrate on reading fluently and correctly pronouncing words in a reading aloud situation.

Overall, there are arguments for both silent reading for comprehension as well as reading aloud. With regard to reading comprehension, it is important to convey to learners the actual sense of reading and ensure that they experience reading as a pleasant activity (Brewster & Ellis, 2002: 112). As outlined in Chapter 4.3.1, this is done by supporting them in developing reading comprehension skills. Dehaene (2010: 260) underlines that children have to understand that reading is about meaning and understanding and not about just reading letters and words out loud without any sense. Hence, teachers should foster purposeful text comprehension rather than repetitive and meaningless sounding out of words.

Nevertheless, there are also arguments and methods that support reading aloud and emphasise that it is not irrelevant.[58] This notion is also supported by German curricula (e.g., MSW NRW, 2008b: 32), which focus on reading for understanding but also mention that children should learn how to present a text to an audience. Reading aloud can, for instance, help to build fluency (Rasinski, 2010: 15), because it supports and provides practice in the correct pronunciation and intonation of words and sentences (Böttger, 2014b: 8). Additionally, Diehr (2010: 53) says that oral reading "is a technique for raising language awareness, especially phonological awareness, and [...] [supports] the development of a second language inner voice." She explains that oral reading needs to be practised in order to gradually develop the habit of semi-vocalisation and sub-vocalisation in FL reading (Diehr, 2010: 61; see Chapter 4.3.3).

In sum, reading comprehension and reading aloud are different activities which both have a legitimate role in FLL. However, this book is based on the assumption that FL reading comprehension is more important for learners than reading aloud abilities, also considering that it precedes reading aloud competence. As such, reading competence is clearly understood as reading comprehension in this book.

4.3.3 The Role of Semi-Vocalisation and Sub-Vocalisation

In silent reading for comprehension, the vocalisation of language still plays a role. Readers vocalise some or all of the words that they read, either aloud to themselves or without an audible articulation (Dehaene, 2010: 39). The former

---

58   Spinner (2010: 55) provides an overview of the potential and also the methodology of reading aloud.

notion of reading to oneself, aloud or in a whisper, is referred to as semi-vocal-isation; the latter one of a silent vocalisation is referred to as sub-vocalisation.

To begin with sub-vocalisation, readers experience an "inner speech" as they read, in that they (silently) pronounce printed words (Daneman & Newson, 1992: 55). This process of "translating print to sound has been called *speech recording* or *sub-vocalization*" (Daneman & Newson, 1992: 55; italics in original). It refers to the inner voice in reading that is not audible and not meant for an audience. The role of sub-vocalisation is two-fold. Firstly, readers gain access to the meaning of lexical items as stored in the mental lexicon through recoding printed words into speech. Dehaene (2010: 21, 39) explains that in reading two kinds of processing work in parallel: The lexical and the phonological way. Phonological processing makes it possible to decode the letters into sounds, and lexical processing opens up the mental lexicon to retrieve the meaning of a word which was read.[59] The second role of sub-vocalisation is that rendering text as speech helps readers to retain the information from a text in their working memory and allows the brain to integrate a sequence of words during the text comprehension process (Dane-man & Newson, 1992: 56; Diehr, 2010: 60f); and it is for this reason that sub-vocalisation is important in the process of reading and reading comprehension.

Sounding out words to oneself is called semi-vocalisation and refers to an au-dible and active articulation of words while reading. Such reading or whispering aloud is not meant for an audience, but for the reader him/herself (Diehr, 2010: 58). Semi-vocalisation can support reading comprehension in that an audible articulation of a text can help to decode the words (Diehr, 2010: 58). The process is the same as explained for sub-vocalisation, only that semi-vocalising readers need the audible vocalisation of words in order to decode them and access them via their mental lexicon.

Beginner readers in particular need the stage of semi-vocalisation, while good readers usually make use of sub-vocalisation in order to connect the lexical and phonological processes in reading (Dehaene, 2010: 39). Diehr (2010: 61) explains that an inner voice in reading develops through practice and passes through the stages of reading aloud (to oneself) to semi-vocalisation to sub-vocalisation. Therefore, as readers advance, they gradually leave the stage of semi-vocalisation and develop an inner voice in reading.

Especially new, difficult and unknown words are often semi-vocalised, even by advanced readers. Readers make use of the phonological strategy of semi-vocalising

---

59 For more information about how the meaning of a word is retrieved from the mental lexicon and how the process of phonology is involved see Dehaene (2010).

unknown words in audible sounds in order to access the mental lexicon and possibly establish word meaning (Dehaene, 2010: 39). While beginner readers decode many words through vocalisation, advanced readers only vocalise unknown and difficult words in order to decode their meaning (Diehr, 2010: 60).

However, decoding words via vocalisation implies that readers are able to decode the words' correct pronunciation. With the complex grapheme-phoneme correspondence of English, vocalisation can be difficult and misleading, particularly for beginner FL learners (Diehr, 2010: 53). With those learners, Diehr and Frisch (2010a: 27) describe a phenomenon they term "invented phonation". It means that beginner EFL readers derive the rules of the German grapheme-phoneme correspondence to pronounce English words as soon as they encounter an English word that they cannot read. Establishing an incorrect pronunciation of an English word based on the German rules of phonetisation, however, implies that learners cannot effectively access word meaning from their lexical word storage, even if they actually know the word. An incorrect phonation of a known word cannot necessarily be brought into accordance with the word that is stored and thus hinders comprehension, as word meaning cannot be retrieved. Again, the importance of EFL learners having knowledge about decoding the English grapheme-phoneme correspondence is underlined; or at the very least they need to develop an awareness of the differences in grapheme-phoneme correspondences between German and English.

For successful reading comprehension, the reading process should be arranged and defined individually with regard to a possible vocalisation of the text. Individualised reading implies that children have a choice about how they read; whether they choose to read a text aloud to themselves in that they use semi-vocalisation or prefer to read it silently with sub-vocalisation. Indeed, a mixture of both is common, depending on different parts of the text and varying difficulty of different words.

4.4 Processes Involved in Reading for Comprehension

When reading a text for comprehension, several processes are applied by the reader in order to construct text meaning. Broadly, two different processes are involved: bottom-up and top-down (Müller Hartmann & Schocker-v. Ditfurth, 2014: 87), and these two will be elaborated on first. However, further processes play a role when readers go about reading a text and establish text meaning, moving from words to sentences to the whole text. These processes will be described subsequently, based on a model of FL reading, adapted from Diehr and Frisch (2010a).

4.4.1 Bottom-Up and Top-Down Reading Processes

Processes involved in reading are often divided into bottom-up and top-down processes. This was partly already elaborated on in Chapter 3.3.1, which distinguished between bottom-up and top-down reading skills during the acquisition of literacy.

Bottom-up models of reading emphasise the decoding of words and sentences to understand a written message. Learners make use of their knowledge about the language itself to construct text meaning (Müller-Hartmann & Schocker-von Ditfurth, 2014: 73). As such, bottom-up processing refers to the actual decoding of letters, words and other language features (Hedge, 2000: 189). Bottom-up processing hence draws on linguistic or systematic FL knowledge; knowledge which helps the reader to decode the language, such as syntactic or morphological knowledge as well as knowledge about the grapheme-phoneme correspondence of a language (Hedge, 2000: 189). On a broader level, bottom-up reading processes are also concerned with processing the discourse organisation of a text (Müller-Hartmann & Schocker-von Ditfurth, 2014: 87). Awareness about different types of texts and their particular discourse patterns and text organisation thus support reading comprehension (Müller-Hartmann & Schocker-v. Ditfurth, 2014: 87).

By contrast, top-down models concentrate on a holistic reading approach and the construction of overall coherence. Top-down processing describes the application of previous knowledge in order to make meaning of a text (Hedge, 2000: 189). Such models thus focus on the reader and his/her existing knowledge, which is employed in reading while confirming or rejecting expectations of a text (Müller-Hartmann & Schocker-v. Ditfurth, 2014: 87). Accordingly, top-down processes draw on schematic knowledge: knowledge which enables the reader to interpret the meaning of a text, such as topic or general world knowledge (Hedge, 2000: 189). Schema theory, too, emphasises the importance of previous knowledge, for comprehension. This theory relies on top-down processes and explains that schemata are pre-existing knowledge structures stored in the mind, and that comprehension is a process of mapping the information from a reading text onto the pre-existing knowledge (Nassaji, 2007: 83; Nuttall, 2005: 7).

Nowadays, both processes, bottom-up and top-down, are said to be interconnected and to work interactively and more or less simultaneously in reading (Biebricher, 2008: 31; Hedge, 2000: 190). Different types of knowledge and various processes are in a constant interplay, which integrates bottom-up and top-down processes and thus combines a focus on the FL as well as on the readers' previous knowledge. According to Nuttall (2005: 17), both processes can even be mobilised by conscious choice. For example, a complex word can purposefully be decoded via its grapheme-phoneme correspondence (bottom-up) in order to make sense of it, or previous knowledge of the text can be used in order to deduce its meaning from the larger context of the story (top-down).

4.4.2 A Model of (FL) Reading Comprehension

The distinction into bottom-up and top-down processes in reading is rather broad and does not capture all processes involved in reading for comprehension. Ehlers (2007: 116) even states that this distinction is slightly outdated. Therefore, to explain reading comprehension processes in more detail, a model of FL reading comprehension will be presented in this section. This model is based on Diehr and Frisch's (2010a: 27) model of FL reading competence and supplemented with processes as described by Westphal Irwin (2007) and an explanation of reading provided by Ehlers (2007). The model is displayed in Figure 5 and contains bottom-up as well as top-down processes (see Chapter 4.2) and also includes the processes of reading at the word, sentence and text level as described in Chapter 2.4.2. The model presented here is meant for FL reading comprehension, but can also be transferred to L1 reading, since many processes overlap or are the same.

Figure 5: A model for the process of FL reading (mainly based on Diehr & Frisch, 2010a: 27; including ideas of Ehlers, 2007) and Westphal Irwin, 2007).

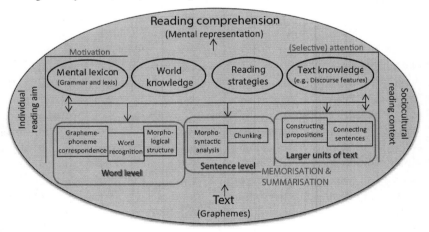

The model is based on the assumption that reading is a purposeful activity and happens consciously (Diehr & Frisch, 2010a: 26); that is the reader has a reading aim which is related in one way or another to the comprehension of the text (see Chapter 4.6.2 on reading purposes). The reading process of any individual with his/her specific reading aims takes place in a broader context of a reading situation. Westphal Irwin (2007: 9) explains that any reading and comprehension process is "embedded in a complex sociocultural context," in that cultural as well as world knowledge and the overall context of reading, for example a classroom situation, play an important role in decoding a written message. With regard to this, Börner and Frisch (2013: 75) also emphasise that a learner's reading socialisation and previous experiences with reading play a crucial role in FL reading. To reiterate, then, reading happens with a certain reading aim and in a particular reading context, both of which influence the reading process in some way; for example, pupils who want to meet the teacher's expectations of detailed understanding will tailor their reading process to this aim.

Within this reading context, reading motivation and directing attention to reading are also factors that influence reading comprehension. Both factors are interwoven with each other, in that motivation dictates the level of concentration, attention and cognitive effort that a learner invests in the reading task (Ehlers, 2007: 117). Paying attention to reading also includes paying selective attention to aspects that readers deem as important or not. As such, text comprehension differs from reader to reader, amongst other factors, because it is based on individual processes of directing attention to individually relevant factors (Ehlers, 2007: 116).

Based on the overall reading context that is characterised by the reading aim and the reader's motivation as well as selected attention, the actual reading process of a text consists of various types of different processes. These happen at the word, sentence and text level and are presented in the seven squared boxed in the middle of the figure. All these processes more or less work in parallel and simultaneously during reading (Börner & Frisch, 2013: 75; Westphal Irwin, 2007: 2); readers do not gradually proceed from one step to the next.

At the word level, firstly the process of decoding words is of crucial importance (Westphal Irwin, 2007: 7). The reader recognises graphical representations as words and decodes these for meaning (Biebricher, 2008: 30). Three different ways of decoding a word are distinguished and used interchangeably, depending on the word and the reader's level of competence (Diehr & Frisch, 2010a: 27; Frisch, 2013: 47f; Steck, 2009: 31f). As already outlined in Chapter 4.4.1, a word can be decoded via its grapheme-phoneme correspondence (bottom-up) or holistically via automatisation of word recognition through previous word and context knowledge (top-down). This depends on the extent to which the word is already known to the reader. Moreover, words can be decoded via their morphological structure (e.g., pre- and suffixes).

In a subsequent step, comprehension at sentence level is established by analysing a sequence of words morphologically as well as syntactically (Diehr & Frisch, 2010a: 27). Knowledge stored in the mental lexicon is called upon in order to, for instance, establish that an action took place in the past and was conducted by the subject of the sentence. Understanding sentences includes "chunking" (Westphal Irwin, 2007: 2), that is, grouping words together logically in order to construct meaning. It further implies remembering selected bits of information which are of importance for the further course of the text (Westphal Irwin, 2007: 3). Such information is not remembered verbatim, but reduced by the reader to a summary of its most important parts.

Beyond the sentence level, several sentences have to be placed in a broader context in order to grasp the meaning of larger units of text. Information from one sentence has to be related to the information of others. Westphal Irwin (2007: 3) refers to this as "connecting sentences". It means that individual ideas are connected into a coherent whole, that is, the relationship between sentences is understood (Westphal Irwin, 2007: 3). At the latest at this stage, information that was retrieved and constructed earlier is not stored at the linguistic level or even verbatim any longer, but is summarised and stored semantically by transferring it into propositions (Börner & Frisch, 2013: 76).

Ultimately, "understanding the whole" as the final outcome of the whole reading process refers to the ongoing process of summarisation, which includes retaining summed up information and central topics in short-term memory as one reads on (Westphal Irwin, 2007: 4). The learners construct a mental representation of the text's meaning (Börner & Frisch, 2013: 77). Diehr and Frisch (2010a: 27) explain that learners form propositions and chunk them together to larger units of meaning. The meaning of the text is stored semantically, in summarised and chunked-up units of information. This mental representation includes the text base, which is neither verbatim nor complete or necessarily veridical, plus varying amounts of the reader's own interpretation based on previous knowledge (Kintsch, 1998: 50). The representation can also, at least partially, be pictorial, in that the reader forms a mental image of what was described (Briner, Virtue & Schutzenhofer, 2014: 96). Text comprehension and meaning is therefore constructed through processes that gradually proceed from word, to sentence, to text level, while at the same time processes at each level interact and work in parallel. Taken together, this leads to comprehension at the text level.

All the steps and processes involved are based on a constant interplay with the mental lexicon, with reading strategies, with world knowledge and with text knowledge (see four black circles in the figure). Firstly, FL knowledge from the mental lexicon is used and referred to during reading at all times. Such knowledge enables readers to understand the text's vocabulary and structures, as the mental lexicon stores vocabulary as well as phonological and grammatical information (Diehr & Frisch, 2010a: 26). Likewise, more general world knowledge is utilised in order to understand a reading text; for example, facts, values or cultural knowledge (Diehr & Frisch, 2010a: 26). The role of world knowledge has already been explained as a top-down process involved in reading (Chapter 4.2). All along, reading strategies are applied during reading and play an important role in all processes involved. As Chapter 4.6 is dedicated to such reading strategies, this will not be elaborated on further at this point.

Lastly, text knowledge and particularly the knowledge of written discourse features is drawn upon during processes of reading comprehension. According to Diehr and Frisch (2010a: 27), detecting the discourse form of a text helps comprehension in that it is helpful for the learners to know whether a text is a letter or a fairy tale or another type of text. Knowing about the text type enables learners to set up expectations about what is about to come in the text and to align the text's meaning with the type of text. With regard to young EFL learners, however, the significance of discourse form or text type in reading is questionable, as they might not yet have enough experience with reading and literature to detect features they could ascribe to particular discourse forms. Still, very obvious text features such as the introductory sentence 'once upon a time' can already be detected at a young age.

The complexity of the reading process becomes clear when taking all the steps and processes involved into consideration. Up to the present, there is no model that describes the development of reading competence based on these processes (Frisch, 2013: 70). However, the development of reading comprehension is dependent on all the factors included in the model presented here as well as the components of reading competence outlined in Chapter 4.3.1 and can therefore be deduced from both to a certain extent.

4.5 Text Difficulty and Levels of Comprehension

The process of reading and its outcome, reading comprehension, can be influenced by several factors, including factors related to the context of the reading process as well as factors at the text level. Such factors will be outlined in this subchapter. With texts of varying degrees of difficulty and with learners of varying competences, different reading comprehension levels, which indicate the extent to which a reader has understood a text, are achieved; these will be discussed subsequently.

4.5.1 Factors that Influence Reading Comprehension and Text Difficulty

As already indicated in Chapter 4.4.2, contextual factors have an influence on the reading process and thus also on reading comprehension. There is a multifaceted connection and interaction between the reader, the text and the author, which are all embedded into the context of the EFL classroom, which is again embedded into the context of a school and society (Westphal Irwin, 2007: 9). All these elements play a role in comprehending a text (Steck, 2009: 22f). These contextual factors, however, cannot easily be influenced, apart from attempting to create a reader-friendly environment and a relaxed reading atmosphere. Thus, this aspect will not be elaborated on further in this chapter.

Figure 5 has also shown that factors at the level of the learners' emotions and motivation can influence reading comprehension (Steck, 2009: 23). Gailberger (2011: 18ff) points out that reading competence is influenced at the level of the individual readers themselves; their emotions, motivation, knowledge and interests. Also the factors of intelligence, general language abilities, previous knowledge and intake capacity influence a reader's perception of text difficulty (Geisler, 1985: 122). With regard to the FL classroom it is hence important for teachers to support a reading-friendly setting by selecting texts which are of interest to children and can be understood on the basis of their existing knowledge, while at the same time embedding the reading process into a meaningful context. But even so, individual learner factors are hard to control. The same holds true for how the reader perceives the difficulty of a text: Each reader has his/her own opinion and perception of the difficulty of a reading text, which is dependent on many factors including the aforementioned emotions and motivation (see Rosenzweig & Wigfield, 2017). As perceived difficulty is also very hard to influence, this aspect will also not be elaborated on further here.

Influential factors and characteristics of texts at the actual text level will be examined instead, as these influence the level of reading comprehension and can be measured to a certain extent. Text difficulty can be controlled in that a reading text can be carefully chosen based on certain factors. Geisler (1985) distinguishes between linguistic and typographic factors, which influence the learners' comprehension of a text. Parts of her classification is shown in Figure 6.[60]

---

60   Further aspects mentioned by Geisler (1985) are irrelevant in reading picture books. More details of factors listed in Figure 6 will be provided inline.

Figure 6: Factors that determine text difficulty and influence reading comprehension (adapted from Geisler, 1985: 122).

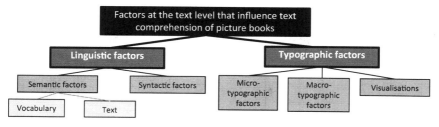

Linguistic factors that influence the difficulty of a text are divided into semantic and syntactic factors. Semantic factors include aspects of vocabulary and text. Vocabulary-related factors that influence the degree of difficulty of a text include the familiarity of words, the frequency of words and the length of words (Geisler, 1985: 122). Semantic factors that influence the text's difficulty include the structure of the text and the occurrence of repetition (Geisler, 1985: 122). Syntactic factors include the length, type and depth of sentences (Geisler, 1985: 122).

Typographic factors are divided into microtypographic as well as macrotypographic factors and visualisations. Microtypographic factors are concerned with the font of the text and include the font size, boldness of print, the font itself and possible capitalisation of letters (Geisler, 1985: 122). Macrotypographic factors are concerned with the layout of the text and include the division of text into sections, the distribution of text over a page and special textual elements (Geisler, 1985: 122). Finally, visualisations are mostly found in children's literature, particularly in picture books, and they can also influence the comprehension of a text (Geisler, 1985: 122; also see Chapter 6.5). Characteristics of the visualisations that influence text comprehension include the size of visuals, the type of visuals and the relation between visuals and text (Geisler, 1985: 122).

Roschlaub (2012) lists further factors which determine text difficulty. Looking at Geisler's factors, Roschlaub (2012: 8ff) adds the logical order of events as well as continuity in the text, the length of the whole text and whether explanations of difficult terms are available.

Finally, some broader aspects of text difficulty should be taken into consideration. These include topic familiarity and the complexity of the text's message (Nuttall, 2005: 6). Concerns about topic familiarity will be outlined in Chapter 6.5. With regard to complexity of a text's message one can assume that children's books and in particular picture books, which were written for a young audience, do not convey an overall message that is of high complexity and potentially too difficult for children. Therefore, there is no need for further concern about this factor here.

4.5.2 Levels of Reading Comprehension

The actual level of a learners' reading comprehension can be measured based on different levels of understanding, as have been described in various previous projects and will be outlined in the following sections. In the end, a synthesis of previously described levels will be provided.

For FL reading, Westphal Irwin (2007: 194) suggests four different competence levels that describe the learner's level of reading comprehension of a FL text, based on what learners are able to ascertain about a text. These levels range from identifying incoherent and unorganised details which might be inaccurate (level 1) to exposing coherent, organised and accurate major points supported by important details (level 4). These competence levels are determined by five different aspects which include accuracy, coherence and organisation of the account of what was understood. As further factors to evaluate a learner's comprehension level, Westphal Irwin (2007: 195) suggests also analysing whether the learner's recall follows the organisation patterns of the author, whether the learner recalls most important details, whether the learner infers implicit information from the text and whether the learner includes the explicitly stated main points of the text.

Another system for describing FL reading comprehension levels was developed by Nold and Rossa (2007). In the DESI study, Nold and Rossa (2007: 199f) used descriptors for the assessment of reading comprehension. They distinguished between global and detailed understanding, implicitly and explicitly stated information, recognition, interference and interpretation of information, connecting information to world knowledge and the grasp of coherence. Different types of information were also distinguished between: events, emotions and opinions (Nold & Rossa, 2007: 200). The authors further defined four different task-specific competence levels for each of the reading tasks that were used in the DESI study (see Nold & Rossa, 2007: 207f), which will not be elaborated on further here, because they are largely context- and task-specific.

Steck (2009) offers a differentiation of reading comprehension levels with specific reference to young learners. Although concerned with L1 reading, her categories can easily be transferred to L2 reading comprehension. Steck (2009: 72) describes three different levels of competence with regard to the quality of answers to questions to a text. Her first level is concerned with finding out single pieces of information, her second level describes drawing connections between sentences and facts from parts of the text and her third level describes understanding at the text level in terms of grasping implicitly presented information in order to draw conclusions.

Steck's (2009) classification is very similar to a general distinction of competence levels made by an addition to the NRW curriculum for primary schools (MSW NRW, 2008a: 17f). This addition describes three different competence levels which should be applied globally to every task in each subject. Level one is the lowest and concerned with the reproduction of already acquired knowledge, level two is concerned with drawing connections between already acquired knowledge and new information and level three is about the reflection on tasks and the transfer of knowledge to more general conclusions (MSW NRW, 2008a: 16).

These different elaborations can be synthesised to five different comprehension levels, with one being the lowest and five the highest and best. The factor of visualisations was added to what has been outlined so far, because visualisations are unique features of children's literature (see Chapters 4.5.1 and 5.3.3). Table 3 shows this synthesis and displays five differentiated levels of reading comprehension, with level 1 being the lowest and level 5 the highest possible level.

Table 3: Five competence levels of reading comprehension concerning picture books; Level 1 being the lowest and level 5 the highest and most proficient level.

Level	Description of characteristics of each level of reading comprehension
1	• (Almost) no comprehension • Only single, redundant details which are isolated statements and out of context • What was understood is mostly understandable from the pictures • Includes irrelevant, redundant and inaccurate elaborations • No coherence, information is presented in isolated pieces
2	• Comprehension of simple details which are mostly not contextualised • Integration of only a few major ideas which are found in a limited part of the text • What was understood is explicitly presented in the text by means of simple language and/or the pictures (no interpretation) • May include irrelevant elaborations • Does not really show coherence and information is presented in isolated pieces • Purely reproductive • May contain inaccurate elaborations

Level	Description of characteristics of each level of reading comprehension
3	• Comprehension of mostly simple but also some more complex details, even if partly presented through more complex language • Integration of some information to show a more global understanding • What was understood was mostly presented in the text and deduced by the reader • Shows acceptable coherence and organisation • Shows logical connections • For the most part accurate elaborations
4	• Comprehension of complex details, presented mostly through language and only partly understandable from the pictures • Integration of information shows global understanding • Displays logical connections between events • No redundant details are presented • Details presented support comprehension • Shows coherence and logical organisation • All elaborations are accurate
5	• Comprehension of complex details presented exclusively through language • Integration of various aspects spread over the whole text to show thorough global understanding • Contains implicit information • Presents major points as well as supporting details • What was revealed comes from deducing and interpreting information from the text • Different parts of the text are logically combined to show coherence • Overall more general and reflective

4.6 Reading Styles and Reading Strategies

While each individual text will have its own inherent difficulties, each individual learner will also approach a text differently – using a different reading style and applying different reading strategies that are specific to the task and given context. The following sections firstly explain reading styles and outline how reading styles, text genre and the individual reading purpose suggest reading strategies. The following subchapters will then focus on reading strategies, defining and categorising them as well as providing an insight into the idea of teaching strategies with a focus on young learners.

4.6.1 Reading Styles

Reading styles refer to the different ways in which learners read (Gehring, 2004: 72), that is, encounter and go about decoding a text. Based on the type of text and the learner's individual reading intention, a specific reading style is chosen to approach the text. The most prominent reading styles are skimming and scanning, as well as intensive and extensive reading. Further reading styles, which are more task- or text-specific, include receptive reading, analytical/critical reading, flexible reading and reflective reading (Hedge, 2000: 195; Müller-Hartmann & Schocker-v. Ditfurth, 2014: 90; Otten & Wildhage, 2003: 36). Only the four most prominent ones will be described here.

Skimming, also referred to as reading for gist, is used to grasp the overall and global meaning of a text: The reader roughly reads over the text to get an idea of its overall content and determine its gist (Klippel, 2000: 108; Nuttall, 2005: 49). The aim is to get a global impression and a brief overview of what the text is about (Haß, 2006: 86; Müller-Hartmann & Schocker-v. Ditfurth, 2014: 89). The reader thus seeks for orientation in the text and wants to establish the topic as well as the central action(s) and characters (Gehring, 2004: 76).

In contrast to skimming, the aim of scanning a text is to quickly find a certain piece of information (Haß, 2006: 86). The reader explicitly and selectively looks for that specific information to find answers or information on specific aspects (Müller-Hartmann & Schocker-v. Ditfurth, 2014: 89). Hence, when scanning a text, the reader does usually not read the whole text, but only focuses on finding what he/she is looking for (Gehring, 2004: 76). The text as a whole is of minor importance. For example, a learner scans a picture book in order to find the name of a certain character or scans a dictionary to find the translation equivalent of a specific German word. This can also be referred to as selective reading.

Intensive reading, also referred to as reading for detail, requires very careful reading in order to identify details of a text that go beyond the overall gist of it (Gehring, 2004: 76). The aim of intensive reading is finding details in a text and grasp all the information it provides (Haß, 2006: 86; Müller-Hartmann & Schocker-v. Ditfurth, 2014: 89). Intensively reading a picture book means taking time to read it and closely studying the whole text to get a detailed understanding of the story. Intensive reading for details is often contrasted with skimming, where only global understanding or understanding for gist is needed. As such, reading for gist and reading for detail are often distinguished in EFL classroom practice, in that texts are usually read at least twice: The first reading is for gist and the second (and following ones) for detail (Böttger, 2005: 89).[61]

Finally, extensive reading is characterised as reading of a large quantity of reading material on a regular basis and over a longer period of time, for pleasure

---

61 This refers to storytelling where the teacher reads a story to the learners (see Chapter 5.5.1). However, it can be transferred to the pupil's own reading as well.

and personal interest, in class as well as at home (Hedge, 2000: 202). Krashen (2013: 15) also refers to it as free reading or voluntary/self-selected reading. A defining feature of extensive reading is that learners choose their reading texts themselves in order to read them for pleasure and individual language improvement (Harmer, 2007: 283). In order to support extensive reading, an extensive reading programme can be offered to the pupils in school (for more information see Harmer, 2007: 283ff; Biebricher, 2008).

4.6.2 How Genre, Reading Purpose and Reading Style Suggest Reading Strategies

The reading strategies which a learner applies to reading a text depend on several different factors, including the aforementioned reading style, but also the genre of the text and the purpose of reading. Figure 7 provides an overview:

Figure 7: How text genre, purpose of reading and reading style suggest reading strategies.

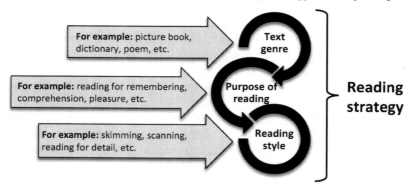

Nuttall explains that first of all readers need to know what they want from reading and thus establish their reading purpose (Nuttall, 2005: 46). A certain type of text can dictate a certain reading purpose which will again suggest a certain reading style. If, for example, the text is a dictionary (genre) and the purpose of reading is to find out the translation of a lexical item, the reader usually reads selectively (reading style) and only reads those parts which are of importance at that particular moment (Spinner, 2010: 55). A novel, in contrast to that, would be read from cover to cover, often with the purpose of pleasure and comprehension, using a combination of reading for gist and detail as a reading style. Therefore, the genre of the text first and foremost serves as a basis for reading purpose, style and strategies. However, in some cases, the purpose will dictate the genre. If a learner's purpose is to find the L1 equivalent to an L2 word, the learner chooses a dictionary rather than any other kind of book (genre).

As noted above, the reading purpose dictates a certain reading style. Henseler and Surkamp (2010: 9) show the interdependence of reading purpose and style and, for example, explain that reading for orientation suggests skimming as a reading style, and reading to understand details suggests intensive reading. Further reading purposes include reading for pleasure and enjoyment, learning something through reading, reading for remembering or reading for communication (see, e.g., Spinner, 2010; Westphal Irwin, 2007). When one takes a closer look at reading for overall comprehension, for example, this interdependence between reading purpose and reading style becomes clear. When reading for comprehension it is important to make clear to the readers what kind of comprehension and what level of understanding of the text are expected from them: "If learners know [...] that they are [...] reading something to get a general picture they will [...] read in a slightly different way than if they are expected to [...] read in detail for specific parts of a message" (Brewster & Ellis, 2002: 113). Hence, reading purpose dictates reading style.

Lastly, Hedge (2000: 195) as well as Biebricher (2008: 32) both point out how different reading purposes determine different strategies, in that reading purposes presuppose the way that the information in a text is processed. This includes both reading style and strategy. Thus, reading purpose suggests not only reading styles but also reading strategies.

To sum this up, reading strategies depend on an interplay of text genre, reading purpose and reading style. The yet unanswered question of what reading strategies actually are will be addressed in the following subchapters.

4.6.3 Defining Reading Strategies

Strategies are not only applied in FLL, but also in all other domains of learning, and in conducting any tasks or activities. This section will therefore firstly define strategies in general, to then narrow down to language learning strategies and subsequently to (FL) reading strategies. Also, the term 'strategy' will be distinguished from various other terms with which it is often confused.

Strategies in general describe the mental plan which underlies a learner's actions. According to Brown (2007: 119), "strategies are specific methods of approaching a problem or task, modes of operation for achieving a particular end, planned designs for controlling and manipulating certain information." In other words, they are "specific attacks" that learners make on a given problem (Brown, 2007: 132). As such, they are target-oriented actions taken by the learners to facilitate their own learning and the accomplishment of tasks (Chamot, 2005: 112; Oxford, 1990: 8). In learning, the use of strategies helps learners to comprehend, learn and retain new information (O'Malley & Chamot, 1990: 1) and thus through strategies learning becomes "easier, faster, more enjoyable, more self-directed, more effective and more transferable to new situations" (Oxford, 1990: 8).

Naturally, strategies are also applied in language learning. FLL strategies are described by Gehring (2004: 63) as the purposeful and target-oriented use of competencies in order to learn a FL. Wolff (1998: 72) goes into further detail and explains that FLL strategies refer to strategic behaviour which the learner makes use of when using as well as when acquiring or learning a FL. In other words, FLL strategies guide the process as well as the behaviour during FL interaction and guide the acquisition of the FL.

To focus now on reading, reading strategies are those which learners apply during all types of reading tasks; in L1 as well as in FL reading.[62] Westphal Irwin (2007: 10) defines reading strategies as the conscious selection of a comprehension process for a specific purpose while reading. A certain reading strategy or a set of reading strategies is chosen in order to approach a reading text and/or a reading task. Which reading strategies exist and can be used for (FL) reading will be addressed in Chapter 4.6.5; firstly, some more detailed information on strategy use itself will be provided.

As already indicated above, strategies are always specific to a certain context and depend on the learner, the setting and particularly the task given (Finkbeiner, 2013: 247). Brown (2007: 119) notes further that strategies vary from moment to moment, from one situation to the next, from one culture to another and also within an individual. A strategy that might be helpful in one context to achieve a certain goal may not be as useful for another goal or context (Chamot, 2005: 113). Therefore, the strategies which learners use to solve a problem or accomplish a task depend to a large degree on a number of different factors which all vary. This also holds true for reading strategies, which, according to Finkbeiner (2013: 247), vary individually, over time and according to the purpose of reading (also see Chapter 4.6.6).

The term 'strategy' has sometimes been confused with 'techniques, and in fact it is difficult to distinguish strategies from techniques, as there are constant overlaps in the accounts found in the literature (Finkbeiner, 2013: 233; Steck, 2009:

---

62 As already described in the interdependence hypothesis in Chapter 4.2, FL reading strategies might differ from L1 reading strategies but at the same time L1 reading strategies might be transferred to L2 reading.

96). Steck (2009: 96) states that a strategy consists of various different techniques. Finkbeiner (2013: 233f) makes this hierarchy more explicit, noting that strategies are referred to nowadays as superordinate, with techniques being applied within a strategy. Often, it is possible to observe techniques, but not possible to directly observe strategies, as a technique is only applied on the basis of individual mental plans, which are referred to as the underlying strategies (Finkbeiner, 2013: 234f). Therefore, strategies are operationalised through techniques (Haudeck, 2011: 271). This, however, presupposes that strategies are not observable and are merely internal, cognitive operations. Because the borders of the two are blurry, in this book only the term 'reading strategies' will be used and might overlap with what other researchers termed 'techniques'.

Afflerbach, Pearson and Paris (2008: 364) also point out that there is a lack of consistency in using the terms 'reading skills' and 'reading strategies'. What they define as skills was partly referred to as techniques by Finkbeiner (2013) and Steck (2009). According to Afflerbach et al. (2008: 368), reading skills are automatic actions which usually occur without the reader being aware of them, in that they are used from habit and automatically. Strategies, in contrast, are deliberate and goal-directed attempts to control and modify the reading process (Afflerbach et al., 2008: 368). So to them the key difference is the distinction between acting either automatically or under deliberate control. This has not been supported by everyone, as will be seen in Chapter 4.6.6, in which awareness of strategy use will be discussed. Therefore, the term 'skill' will also not be used in this book in the context of reading strategies.

However, strategies can easily and more clearly be distinguished from learning styles. Learning styles are described as more general attributes or traits inherent in each individual person (Schnaitmann, 1996: 131), which reflect the individual's preferred way(s) of perceiving, absorbing, processing, recalling and retaining new information and skills (VanPatten & Benati, 2010: 102). For example, a learner might be more visually than aurally oriented (Brown, 2007: 119). Learning styles are thus an underlying and much broader trait than strategies are, as strategies are far more context- and task-specific.

Reading strategies are also clearly distinct from reading styles (see Chapter 4.6.1), as a reading style is a broader approach, such as overall manner, of approaching a particular reading text (see Chapter 4.6.1), while reading strategies are specifically applied to a specific problem while reading, for example, decoding an unknown word.

4.6.4 Research on FL Reading Strategies

Historically, the overall idea behind researching strategies was to find out to what extent the strategies of efficient language learners can be identified and in return be taught to less efficient learners (Brown, 2007: 132f). In the context of FL reading, identifying successful reading strategies implies that these could be taught to less effective readers in order to help them to become more proficient.

While there is a considerable body of research on the reading strategies of older and more advanced FL learners (e.g., Finkbeiner, 2005; Gorsuch & Taguchi, 2010; Young, 1993),[63] very little research on young and beginner learners' FL reading strategies can be found. There seems to be a rather simple reason for this: Research on strategies was done over the past 40 years (Chamot, 2005: 112). But only for a relatively short time has the role of reading in teaching FLs to young learners been acknowledged in the primary school EFL classroom in Germany (see Chapter 3.1). Thus, research on young FL learners' reading strategies could hardly have been conducted extensively so far.

Nevertheless, two reading strategy studies were conducted in the context of the German primary school EFL classroom. Kolb (2013) conducted a small qualitative study and examined the comprehension strategies of Year 4 learners when reading English picture books of their own choice in pairs or small groups. Another study was done by Reichart-Wallrabenstein (2004), who examined comprehension strategies of Year 3 pupils in Germany within the setting of a reading conference where English picture books where read in cooperation. The core results of these two studies will be part of the categorisation of reading strategies in Chapter 4.6.5 and will also be returned to in Chapter 4.6.7 in the section on young learners' awareness of strategy use. Overall, Chamot (2005: 126) points out the lack of research and highlights the importance of further research into young learners' reading strategies.

4.6.5 Categorising Reading Strategies

Despite only limited research on young learners' FL (reading) strategies, the latter have still been identified in previous studies; less so with beginner EFL learners, but more so with older and more advanced ones. After a few early descriptive attempts (see O'Malley & Chamot, 1990: 3ff), the first prominent and detailed classification of FLL strategies was presented by Oxford (1990). She distinguished between direct

---

63 Also see Chamot (2005: 119), Finkbeiner (2005: 109ff) and Macaro (2001: 83ff) for an overview.

strategies, including memory, cognitive and compensation strategies, as well as indirect strategies, including meta-cognitive, affective and social strategies, with all of them being interrelated (Oxford, 1990: 15).[64] Wolff (1998: 72f) described FLL strategies from a more practical standpoint of language use in that he distinguished strategies to acquire linguistic means, strategies that refer to language competences, strategies to communicate in the FL, strategies to reflect about the language on a meta-level, strategies to learn the language and social strategies. Macaro (2001: 116) adds reception strategies to communication strategies, and puts them both under the umbrella term of interaction strategies, encompassing input as well as output. Pinter (2006: 100), who focuses on young language learners, distinguishes between social and affective strategies, awareness-raising strategies focusing on what language learning is, meta-cognitive strategies and direct or cognitive strategies. One can see that many of these FLL strategy classifications overlap to a certain extent, depending on the angle that one looks at FLL from and the focus that one places.

The strategies of a specific field of L2 learning or L2 knowledge, for example reading strategies, are included in several of these more general classifications. Hence, the categorisation of reading strategies overlaps with what has already been described for FLL strategies and categories of reading strategies are in various ways embedded in these general classifications. For example, one finds reading strategies in strategies that refer to language competences as well as in strategies to communicate in the FL. Finkbeiner (2013: 233), who investigated the reading strategies of EFL learners at the secondary school level in Germany, distinguished between cognitive and meta-cognitive as well as between social and affective strategies. This classification goes back to O'Malley and Chamot (1990: 46), who were one of the first researchers to explicitly categorise and describe FL strategies.

For the purpose of this book, the following categorisation will underlie the classification of reading strategies into categories. It is mainly based on O'Malley and Chamot's (1990) distinction, but also linked to Finkbeiner's (2005, 2013), Oxford's (1990) and Pinter's (2006) categorisation:

- Meta-cognitive strategies
- Cognitive strategies
- Social strategies
- Affective strategies

---

64 She specifies each category further with two to four sets (Oxford, 1990: 17), which are again specified by displaying up to eight very practical strategies each (Oxford, 1990: 18ff). These she divides into more subcategories and explains them with a special focus on FLL in a classroom context.

Meta-cognitive strategies are concerned with organising the reading process. They belong to the category of indirect strategies which are used for "general management of learning" (Oxford, 1990: 135). Meta-cognitive strategies "allow learners to control their own cognition – this is, to coordinate the learning process" (Oxford, 1990: 135). With regard to reading, they enable learners to organise and coordinate their reading process.

In contrast to that, "cognitive strategies [...] enable learners to understand and produce new language by many different means" (Oxford, 1990: 37). These are crucial in language learning and, in the context of reading, help learners to comprehend FL texts by means that are directly related to the FL, since, as Oxford (1990: 37) puts it, cognitive strategies are direct strategies which "directly involve the target language [and] [...] require mental processing of the language."

Social strategies are those which "help students learn through interaction with others" (Oxford, 1990: 135). They can be used in peer learning activities such as co-operative reading sessions. For instance, learners can solve a vocabulary problem that they come across in a reading text cooperatively and supplement each other's knowledge or hypotheses when discussing the potential meanings of a lexical item.

Lastly, affective strategies "help to regulate emotions, motivations [sic], and attitudes" (Oxford, 1990: 135). Such strategies, then, allow learners to gain control over their reading at an affective level. For example, affective strategies can create a positive attitude towards a text and keep learners motivated while reading a difficult text.

Oxford (1990) also included compensation strategies and memory strategies, neither of which were used as analytical categories in the research presented here. Compensation strategies, to clarify, "enable learners to use the new language for either comprehension or production despite limitations in knowledge" (Oxford, 1990: 47). They thus make up for a gap in FL knowledge and allow learners to understand a FL text despite the limitations of their interlanguage. Looking at reading comprehension strategies, however, almost all strategies are to a certain extent compensation strategies in that they help learners to overcome problems in understanding parts of a text that go beyond their FL knowledge. Therefore, compensation strategies are implicit in most of the strategies outlined below and will not be categorised as such explicitly. Oxford's memory strategies were left out as well, as this book is concerned primarily with the actual process of reading and the strategies applied to comprehend a text, and less so with the storing and retrieving of new language information (see Oxford, 1990: 37).

In the four main categories of meta-cognitive, cognitive, social and affective strategies, many different reading strategies have been identified in previous theory and research in the field of FL reading strategies so far. Table 4 provides a synthesised overview.

Table 4: Classification of reading strategies (based on Böttger, 2005: 148; Böttger, 2014a: 13; Brown, 2007: 134ff; Finkbeiner, 2005: XIVff; Hedge, 2000: 222; Kolb, 2013: 36ff; Macaro, 2001: 14f; Macaro & Erler, 2008: 105, 109; Nuttall, 2005: 58f; O'Malley & Chamot, 1990: 45ff; O'Malley, Chamot, Stewner-Marzanares, Kupper & Russo, 1985: 32ff; Oxford, 1990; Reichart-Wallrabenstein, 2004: 443f; Steck, 2009: 97ff; Westphal Irwin, 2007: 130, 178f; Young, 1993).[65]

	Strategy	Explanation
Meta-cognitive reading strategies	• Turning the pages backwards and forwards to re-read or read ahead	The learners flip through the pages of the book in order to - skim the text and get an initial impression. - read ahead to see what comes next and what is to be expected. - check something on a previous page.
	• Concentrating and paying attention	The learners consciously focus on the task of reading comprehension and concentrate in that they direct their attention and ignore irrelevant distractions.
	• Seeking orientation via a pointing finger[65]	The learners follow the text with a pointing finger in order not to get lost in the text while reading and to find orientation in longer parts of texts.
	• Tolerating ambiguity	The learners tolerate the fact that a word/ phrase/ sentence/ section of the text was not fully understood.
	• Continuing with reading	The learners continue reading even if they did not understand parts of the text.
	• Monitoring and self-questioning	The learners ask themselves to what extent they have understood what was read and are concerned about their own comprehension.
	• Adjusting the reading rate	The learners adjust the reading rate by slowing down or speeding up, depending on the part of the text.
	• Deciding on importance	The learners decide on the importance of a word or part of the text if they did not fully understand it.
	• Recognising and ordering importance of information	The learners recognise the structure of the text and can distinguish between important and unimportant parts of the text.
	• Omitting and skipping	The learners consciously omit or skip words or parts of the text.
	• Planning the reading process	The learners plan their reading process and consider the task, what steps to take, what supportive devices might be needed, etc.

---

65 The meta-cognitive strategy of putting a pointing finger under the text is a reading strategy that has not been described in studies with older learners. Putting a finger under the text so as to not get lost is a well-known and widely-used approach with young learners (Nuttall, 2005: 58f). Such reading marks help children to organise their reading and to maintain the overview of the text (Braun, 2010: 182). As such, finger-pointing focuses the young reader's attention. However, this strategy has been criticised and can be a sign of poor reading, because finger-pointing word by word, in order to decipher each word individually, slows down the reading and thus hinders fluency and comprehension (Nuttall, 2005: 58f). Still, finger-pointing will be considered a regular reading strategy in this context, as young learners often make use of it.

	Strategy	Explanation
Cognitive strategies	• Expecting and hypothesising	The learners have expectations of what will come next in a story based on what has already been understood.
	• Elaboration	The learners integrate and link ideas contained in new information with already known information.
	• Re-reading and repeating	The learners start again and re-read a confusing or difficult word, phrase, sentence or longer part.
	• Dividing the text into sections	The learners break up the reading process and divide the text into sections instead of reading straight through. (Doing so in advance and in planning the reading process would be a meta-cognitive strategy)
	• Highlighting and note-taking	The learners highlight or underline certain parts and/or take notes while reading to structure the input and make it easier to retain.
	• Summarising	The learners intermittently synthesise what was read to ensure that the information is retained.
	• Repeating in own thoughts	The learners repeat what they have read in their thoughts.
	• Speculating beyond the text	The learners speculate about implications or inferences in the text that go beyond the explicit information found in it.
	• Imagery and visualising mentally	The learners mentally visualise the content of the text in their inner eye or use actual images for comprehension.
	• Translation	The learners translate parts of the text or even translate the whole text word by word.
	• Vocalisation	Learners vocalise words, phrases or parts of the text; this includes lip-movement and whispering and aims at establishing grapheme-phoneme associations.
	• Imagining the text as a listening text	The learners imagine the text as a listening text while reading it and imagine the sound of the text.
	• Use of an audio-recording	Learners listen to an audio-recording and read along.
	• Thinking hard	The learners think hard about words they do not understand.
	• Inventing meaning	The learners invent meaning and use their imagination to understand parts that they are uncertain about.
	• Using deduction processes	The learners use a process of deduction in order to eliminate possible meanings to approach the actual meaning.
	• Inferencing	The learners use available information to guess the meaning of unknown words or fill in missing information.
	• Resourcing	The learners use resources: e.g., a dictionary to look up an unknown lexical item.

	Strategy	Explanation
Social strategies	• Working cooperatively	The learners read together with a partner or in a small group.
	• Asking others	The learners ask others (e.g., the teacher or peers) for clarification, verification, confirmation or correction.
	• Expressing need for help	The learners state explicitly that they need help.
	• Express misunderstanding	The learners share the fact that a certain part of the text was not understood.
	• Expressing and comparing understanding	The learners express their understanding of the text (can be in their L1) and compare it to the comprehension of their peers.
Affective strategies	• Being confident	The learners approach a reading text confidently and with feelings of self-assurance and confidence about their own skills; they at least try to be confident about it.
	• Positive attitude	The learners encounter the text with a positive attitude that encourages them to read on.
	• Self-motivation	The learners motivate themselves to understand the text and attribute their own understanding to their own efforts.
	• Dealing with anxiety	The learners skilfully deal with potential anxiety and do not let it hinder their reading process.
	• Being persistent	The learners do not give up easily.
	• Setting realistic goals	The learners set themselves realistic goals with regard to the level of comprehension of the text.
	• Reacting emotionally	The learners react to the text emotionally, for instance with laughter.
	• Having an opinion	The learners have and express an opinion on the text.
	• Being emphatic	The learners feel empathy and/or identify with a character in the text or the author.
	• Acknowledging a lack of understanding	The learners acknowledge a lack of comprehension or lack of familiarity with the text and its content.

As the main focus of the project presented in this book is reading comprehension, this classification is concerned only with reading comprehension strategies. However, strategies such as writing summaries, summarising the most important aspects of a text or any other strategies that involve free FL writing have been left out, as they are clearly too complex for young EFL learners.

4.6.6 Strategies on a Continuum: Awareness, Observability and Success

In various perspectives, reading strategies can be found on a continuum. Particularly with regard to research on strategies, the question of awareness as well as the question of observability dominates. With regard to reading comprehension, there is also a continuum between successful and unsuccessful strategies as well as strategies that display competence versus those that display problems. The following paragraphs will discuss these aspects.

As already indicated in Chapter 4.6.3, some strategies are applied consciously and the learner is aware of using them, whereas other strategies are used without the learner being aware of using them. Strategy awareness is an issue that has received a good deal of attention in research on young language learners, which is why this is treated in a separate section (Chapter 4.6.7). Readers in general should have conscious as well as automatised reading strategies available, which they can then call on according to the situation or task (Steck, 2009: 96). Finkbeiner (2005: 91f) explains that strategies can be used on a continuum from conscious to unconscious use and that there might even be movement on this continuum for a certain strategy during the reading process or with experience. With experience, for instance, strategy use can become automatised and hence the learner applies these strategies unconsciously without paying attention to them. Chamot (2005: 112) points out that especially in the beginning learners often use strategies consciously, whereas once a learner becomes familiar with a strategy it becomes more automatic and hence less conscious. This process, however, is sometimes difficult to measure, as it is possible that highly-proficient language learners in particular unconsciously make use of internalised strategies in approaching tasks, while it is also conceivable that they consciously plan and conduct their steps (Finkbeiner, 2013: 233). Moreover, strategies which the learner was not aware of using might become available to consciousness in retrospect, when the learner is asked about using certain strategies (Wendt, 1997: 77). Chamot (2005: 112) explains that often, even if a strategy was used automatically and unconsciously, one would in most cases still be able to recall it to conscious awareness.

With regard to researching reading strategies, a distinction between observable and unobservable strategies also needs to be made. For example, it is not observable whether a learner guesses the meaning of an unknown word or whether he/she just skips it. Also, whether a learner re-reads a sentence cannot necessarily be observed, unless eye movement tracking is involved in the research procedure (see Duchowski, 2007). In contrast to that, it is easily observable when a learner quickly skims through the whole book before starting the actual reading process. Oxford (1990: 12) sums up that "some strategies are hard to observe even with the help of videotape."

Strategies, regardless of awareness and observability, should optimise the learning process; however, not every strategy is an effective strategy and the use of a strategy or set of strategies does not necessarily lead to successful task completion (Finkbeiner, 2013: 246). A strategy should be task-appropriate in order to improve the learning or working process (Finkbeiner, Ludwig, Wilden & Knierim, 2006: 260). In this regard, Finkbeiner, Knierim, Smasal and Ludwig (2012: 61) distinguish between the two dimensions of situation-adequate and learner-adequate reading strategies. A strategy that relates well to the L2 task is situation-adequate, whereas a strategy that leads the individual learner to successful completion of a task is learner-adequate, and only those strategies that were employed effectively are labelled as successful (Finkbeiner et al., 2012: 61). For example, successfully guessing the meaning of an unknown word by its context in a reading text would be a successful strategy. Getting stuck at that word and searching for it in a dictionary for a long time without success would not be an adequate or effective strategy.

As such, the use of certain strategies, successful or not, can also reveal a readers' competence. The effective use of strategies for profound reading comprehension usually displays competence, while an ineffective use of strategies displays problems with reading. As outlined in Chapter 4.6.4, research on strategy use was initiated through the question of the good language learner. Good learners potentially use successful strategies, can draw on a pool of different strategies and can compensate for problems through their strategy use (see Brown, 2007: 136). Hence, such learners usually use strategies which display competence. By contrast, permanent or frequent semi-vocalisation and finger-pointing are strategies which are usually applied when learners face problems. Moreover, learners may use a large number of strategies, but this does not necessarily imply that their strategy use is successful (Finkbeiner et al., 2012: 60). Hence, Finkbeiner et al. (2012: 60f) state that it is the appropriateness and success of strategies, and not only their frequency, that is important in the use of strategies.

To recapitulate, the use of reading strategies is complex and determined by various different factors. A strategy can be used consciously or unconsciously, can later be brought to conscious awareness, can be observable or not, can be successful and/or adequate or not and might reveal either competence or difficulties. Research on reading strategies evidently has to take these factors into consideration and shed light on strategy use from these perspectives.

4.6.7 Young Learners' Awareness and Understanding of Strategies

As already indicated in the previous paragraph, researchers and teachers debate whether young learners are cognitively mature enough to reflect on their learning and working process on a meta-level and whether or not they can actually report on their strategy use. Haudeck (2011: 282), for example, states that talking about and attempting to teach FL strategies is most likely to be effective with experienced FL learners, and she doubts that younger learners are already able to reflect on and talk about the ways they learn. While young language learners certainly use strategies, they might not yet be aware of using them and lack the cognitive maturity to talk about and reflect on them.

However, a number of researchers do not agree with these reservations. At primary school level, the discussion about strategies and strategy learning has often been referred to as 'learning to learn' and "this process needs to start as early as possible" (Pinter, 2006: 99). Pinter (2006: 99) points out that raising children's awareness about their FLL process is a fundamental part of language teaching in primary school. She says that even young language learners are able to work and reflect on a meta-level and can hence make their strategies explicit to a certain extent (Pinter, 2006: 104).

Doms (2012: 71) also states that children can, with increasing experience, become aware of strategies and can consciously decide for one or another. However, reflecting on strategies on a fairly regular basis is a pre-condition for this development (Doms, 2012: 72). Schmid-Schönbein (2008: 111), too, argues that learning strategies should be made explicit to young learners in the primary school EFL classroom, by explicitly talking about them as well as supporting and encouraging the learners to make use of them. In order to prepare children for a life-long language learning career, it is crucial to already start making strategies and techniques explicit at primary level, so that pupils can find out early on what supports their FLL process (Elsner, 2010: 108).

In addition, Böttger (2014a: 12) points out that children simply want to know 'how it works', but that teaching and addressing this question in class has to be done in a child-friendly way. He lists some principles for introducing learning strategies in the primary school EFL classroom, which include the recommendation that teachers should briefly provide a reason for why strategies are needed, that the teacher should demonstrate and explain a strategy understandably, that the teacher should allow sufficient time to try it out and practise it and that the teacher helps as well as advises the pupils (Böttger, 2014a: 12f). Macaro & Erler (2008: 105f) support this view and point out that pupils need to be made aware of and reminded of strategies which they either use already or which they could use.

In a study with a specific focus on the reading strategies of young learners, Kolb (2013: 41) found that the Year 4 pupils in her picture book project demonstrated they were "very able to reflect on their learning experiences and to describe the procedures they used when working with the books." This is a skill which, as Kolb (2013: 41) states, is often underestimated.

Therefore, while children might not be as adept at reflecting and reporting on strategy use as older and more proficient learners are, there is no reason to assume that they are entirely incapable of reflecting on their FL reading on a meta-level. Finding out about young learners' reading strategies might simply require other research instruments, different questions and a mixed-methods approach in order to achieve more reliable results.

4.6.8 The Idea of Teaching Successful Strategies

The previous section has already indicated that the point of teaching strategies is to enable learners to apply them so as to have greater success in FLL. The overall aim of teaching strategies to FL learners is to make a successful, autonomous and life-long learning process possible for them (Finkbeiner, 2013: 254). Indeed, being aware of learning strategies and purposefully using them and trying them out is a crucial part of learner autonomy (Jäger, 2012: 210). Finkbeiner (2013: 235) points out the importance of dealing with supportive reading strategies in class. Making reading strategies explicit to learners should reinforce helpful ones and assist the learners in becoming more consciously aware of such supportive strategies. Given this, it seems desirable to be able to teach reading strategies.

But as already implied in Chapter 4.6.7, it is not clear whether strategies should and can be taught. Finkbeiner (2013: 231) states that practising suitable strategies is highly important and that learners should be supported in the process of activating and using helpful strategies. Gehring (2004: 64) agrees and suggests that strategies should systematically be taught and also be repeated on a regular basis. Chamot (2005: 122) is more cautious and outlines that one can be "cautiously optimistic about the effectiveness of learning strategy instruction, given that is has been well established in L1 contexts and shows promise in second language learning." With a specific focus on young learners, Macaro and Erler (2008: 105) argue that reminding children of supportive strategies is necessary for them to internalise these and to actually apply them to reading texts. In fact, Schick (2016) has shown that young language learners benefit from strategy instruction with regard to the acquisition of FL words. Overall, then, there seems to be broad consensus that strategies should be taught, even to young learners.

However, one problem in teaching strategies is that some strategies that are helpful to certain learners are not helpful to others (Oxford, 2011: 246). The success of applying a certain strategy is therefore not inherit in the strategy itself but also depends on the context and particularly on the individual learner (also see Chapter 4.6.3 and 4.6.6). Thus, it is hard to establish which strategies are successful and should be taught. This problem gives reason to suggest that a range of possible strategies needs to be (made) available to learners and the learners have to establish which of the strategies are useful to them in certain situations and for certain tasks.

As far as reading is concerned, Gehring (2004: 76) states that teaching reading strategies and using them for specific purposes is one of the most important aims of working with texts. Also Ortlieb (2013: 145) notes that already at elementary level, learners should be equipped with comprehension strategies for reading which are transferable to any content area and thus a large number of different reading texts. He postulates that reading strategies should be taught explicitly and not just explained theoretically (Ortlieb, 2013: 136). This means that they should be actively practised by applying them in reading situations. Similarly, Böttger (2005: 147) suggests that teachers should offer a range of strategies to young learners, allow them enough time to practise them and find out which strategies are the most useful for them as individuals. However, the acquisition of reading strategies is a long-term process and strategies are not learnt in one lesson (Ortlieb, 2013: 156).

Two recent studies that focus on teaching reading strategies to young EFL learners arrive at somewhat divergent conclusions. Firstly, Ruiz de Zarobe and Zenotz (2015; also Ruiz de Zarobe, 2015) applied a strategy training cycle that was developed by Macaro (2001: 176) to teach reading strategies to Year 5 learners at a CLIL primary school in Spain. They compared an experimental group (N = 25) that received instruction on reading strategies over two years to a control group (N = 25) that did not receive any strategy training. Their result was that after one year of instruction the strategy training in the experimental group made a difference in reading performance in comparison to the control group (Ruiz de Zarobe & Zenotz, 2015: 326). However, this effect disappeared after a two-year intervention: The control group caught up with the experimental group, despite not having received reading strategy training (Ruiz de Zarobe, 2015).

In contrast to that, the results of Macaro and Erler's study (2008) are more promising. Macaro and Erler (2008: 90) compared two groups of eleven to twelve-year-old English learners of French with regard to reading comprehension; the intervention group (N = 62) received a reading strategy training, the control group (N = 54) did not. They found that strategy instruction improved comprehension of simple as well as more elaborate texts and that the experimental group outperformed the control group with regard to reading comprehension (Macaro & Erler, 2008). In particular, low-input[66] combined with high-scaffolding[67] over a longer

---

66 'Low input' means that the intervention only took place for 10 minutes per week and later on for only 20–30 minutes every second or third week (Macaro & Erler, 2008: 106).
67 'High-scaffolding' means that pupils are reminded to try strategy combinations while reading and receive feedback about their strategy use after reading (Macaro & Erler, 2008: 111).

period of time proved to be an effective form of strategy instruction (Macaro & Erler, 2008: 115f). In conclusion, more research is needed in this area to complement
to the results of the two studies presented here.

However, reading strategies are not the only key to becoming a successful
reader. Schulz (2010: 7f) outlines the importance of reading motivation, interest
and a solid self-concept as the basis for active reading behaviour, which in turn
results in reading competence. Hence it is important that any attempts to develop reading competence, for example by explicitly focusing on reading strategies,
do not result in a lack of reading motivation (Garbe, 2010: 16). However, one
does not necessarily exclude the other, as acquiring a range of supportive reading strategies can enable learners to skilfully read a text and thus enjoy reading,
which can in return enhance their reading motivation (also see Chapter 9.1.2 on
Nuttall's (2005) virtuous circle of reading).

4.7 Summary of Chapter 4

Chapter 4 provided information about the processes of reading, with a focus on
FL reading. Firstly, the role of the eyes in reading was determined. Their saccades
and fixations are an important factor during the reading of a text and influence
aspects of reading rate and reading fluency, both of which are crucial for successful reading competence.

The importance of eye movement is central in L1 as well as L2 reading. Other
processes are also the same for reading in different languages, but there are differences as well. The differences between L1 and L2 reading were mostly explained by the threshold and the interdependence hypothesis, which question
whether FL reading is a language or a reading issue. Nowadays, there is more
or less consensus that both hypotheses play a role in FL reading and that a good
basis of FL knowledge, particularly vocabulary knowledge, as well as the basics
of L1 reading competences are needed for successful L2 reading. Both aspects
are important for this book because young learners at the primary school level
do not yet possess profound FL abilities and have thus possibly not yet reached
a critical threshold of FL knowledge, while they have already acquired the basics
of L1 literacy and might hence be able to transfer certain strategies to FL reading.

Following this, reading competence was defined as reading comprehension.
Particularly in a school context, this distinction is not always clear because
teachers tend to focus on reading aloud as much as or even more than on reading comprehension. Still, the latter is the main goal of FL reading and also underlies the understanding of reading competence in this book. Nevertheless,
vocalisation is not irrelevant in reading, in that on the one hand reading aloud

activities can be beneficial for FLL and on the other hand the notion of semi- and sub-vocalisation are important practices in reading, particularly for young and beginner FL learners. Chapter 10.1.3 will show that also in the current study semi-vocalisation played a central role in reading picture books.

In Chapter 4.4 it was then shown that a number of different processes are involved in reading and that hence reading is a highly complex activity. It involves bottom-up as well as top-down processes at the word, sentence and text level, brings in world knowledge, reading strategies, text knowledge and the mental lexicon, is concerned with summarisation and memorisation and is embedded into a reading context and the readers' individual reading aims, motivation and attention. These processes help to understand how reading works and thus how reading can be supported.

The reading process itself is influenced by text difficulty. The level of difficulty of a text depends on various factors, while mostly those at the actual text-level can be controlled for. These include, for example, the lengths of sentences, the amount and quality of visualisations or the number of (unknown) words. The factors of text difficulty that were established in Chapter 4.5.1 will be used as a basis to analyse the difficulty of the picture books that were used for the current study (see Chapter 8.1.2). Also, the five different levels of reading comprehension that readers can achieve when reading a text, as outlined in Table 3, will be used in this study in order to determine each participants' comprehension level of each picture book (see Chapters 8.2.2.2 and 9.2.2).

Finally, detailed information was provided about reading strategies. Firstly, reading strategies were defined as specific approaches and actions related to how learners go about a reading task and problems they face therein, and the term strategy was distinguished from other related terms. A set of previously found reading strategies was presented and classified into the categorisation of meta-cognitive, cognitive, social and affective reading strategies. The extent to which these strategies (Table 4) were also used by the young learners in the study of this book will be explored in Chapter 10.1. However, particularly young learners do not always use reading strategies consciously and learners also use strategies that are not observable. Lastly, not all strategies used lead to success or display competence. Overall, this goes to show how hard it is to research (reading) strategies and suggests using various research instruments and a mixed methods approach in order to get a detailed picture of strategy use. Chapter 8.3 will illustrate that this was done in the present study.

5. Reading Material: Authentic English Picture Books

Abstract: This chapter explores the use of English picture books as reading materials. Based on a discussion of the principle of authenticity, it explores characteristics of authentic English picture books, delineates their potential for supporting learners' development and provides details on research as well as current practices in this area.

Considering the extent to which reading can and should be used in the primary school EFL classroom in Germany, this chapter will take a closer look at reading material in learning and teaching EFL, in particular the use of authentic English picture books. The educational value of picture books is undeniable in EFL contexts, as authentic English picture books provide FL learners with meaningful input and relevant topics (Bleyhl, 2002).

Thus, this chapter will first elaborate on the principle of authenticity that underlies the use of books not primarily intended for teaching purposes; authentic books will be distinguished from graded readers and a reform in the selection of reading material in favour of authentic materials will be outlined. Second, the chapter will examine the concept of children's literature and identify picture books as belonging to this genre. Subsequently, a working definition of authentic English picture books will be provided and the suitability of these books for young language learners will be discussed. Having established their appropriacy, reasons for reading authentic (picture) books in the primary school EFL classroom will be provided, outlining learning aims with regard to learners' emotional and cognitive development, content and culture. A detailed account will be given of the potential that reading (picture books) has for FLL. The chapter concludes with a review of the current use of books in the primary school EFL classroom and provides an overview of pioneer projects that have focussed on reading these books with young and beginner EFL learners.

5.1 The Principle of Authenticity

Observing the principle of authenticity is a desired aim in the (primary school) EFL classroom and authenticity is one of the core principles of FL pedagogy and language education (Böttger, 2005: 69; Legutke et al., 2009: 17; Van Lier, 1996: 123).

Reasons for a desire for authenticity in language teaching are manifold. First and foremost, authenticity is said to increase learners' motivation. Reisener

(1999: 17) lists "the authentic" as one of the core features to foster motivation in the classroom. In language teaching, authentic and meaningful language, content and materials are used to create motivating and challenging tasks (Meyer, 2010: 19). In addition, Roche (2008: 82) argues that retrieval of what was learnt is most likely to take place when language learning happened in the frame of an authentic context with real communication purposes. Apart from that, authenticity is "attractive to the learners" (Haines, 1995: 62). Its importance has been underscored by a study in which Pinner (2013: 50) found that a lack of authenticity was one of the main reasons for dissatisfaction about EFL teaching amongst Japanese students. For the primary school EFL context, no empirical study is available. Still, there is a strong consensus that FLL is supported through authenticity.

Demands for authenticity in the FL classroom date back to the beginnings of CLT in the 1970s,[68] as it became clear how important an increased use of authentic materials, and the principle of authenticity in general, were in fostering FL communication (Hedge, 2000: 67). In the context of a shift to CLT, Widdowson (1978: 79) stated that "it is precisely the ability to cope with genuine discourse that we are aiming to develop in the learner." The learner needs to learn "to cope with real-world language" (Haines, 1995: 64). This still holds true for language teaching today and provides a basis for defining the principle of authenticity. Such a definition will be attempted in the following section. After that, the degree of authenticity that is viable in the context of FL teaching will be critically discussed.

5.1.1 Defining Authenticity

Authenticity is a very complex phenomenon which is somewhat difficult to define due to its multi-layered nature (Pinner, 2013: 44). 'Real-world language' is the key expression that surfaces in many attempts at defining authenticity in language teaching. Heckt (2010: cover), for instance, defines authenticity as anything that is "real English". In other words, anything that is authentic and is representative of the English language and culture usually has its origins in a country or place where English is a, or the, dominant language.[69] Authenticity has accordingly also been referred to as naturalness or genuineness (Taylor, 1994: 4).

---

68 For more information on CLT, see Chapter 3.1.1.
69 Besides English-speaking countries and regions such as Great Britain or America, this includes countries such as Kenya or India where English is an official language, as well as any other places/sources where English has, for whatever reason, a dominant status.

In the context of the EFL classroom, it is widely accepted that anything that is authentic has not been created, adapted or changed for teaching purposes and was not created especially for FL learners (see, e.g., Haines, 1995: 60; Meyer, 2010: 15). An English picture book is hence taken as authentic, because it was not especially written for an audience of EFL learners. As such, authenticity in language teaching is often limited to authentic materials and texts (Van Lier, 1996: 123) and further dimensions of authenticity, such as task authenticity, are often not taken into consideration. The actual use of an authentic picture book in class is not by definition authentic, but depends on the interaction with the book in terms of, for example, reading purpose and reading tasks.

In this context, Widdowson (1978: 80) makes a distinction between authentic and genuine:

> Extracts [meaning extracts of real dialogues which are presented in written form] are, by definition, *genuine* instances of language use, but if the learner is required to deal with them in a way which does not correspond to his normal communicative activities, then they cannot be said to be *authentic* instances of use. Genuineness is a characteristic of the passage itself and is an absolute quality. Authenticity is a characteristic of the relationship between the passage and the reader and it has to do with appropriate response.

In other words, introducing an authentic English children's book into the EFL classroom means to bring an item that is 'genuine'; but depending on classroom activities around that book, its use might not be authentic. This will further be elaborated on in Chapters 5.1.2 and 5.1.3.

In sum, authenticity is a multifaceted phenomenon with a lot more to it than just authentic materials and texts. Instead of attempting to find a definition or working definition of authenticity – which seems to be almost impossible because of its complexity – the dimensions of authenticity in EFL learning and teaching will be explored in the following subchapter to shed some light on this seemingly difficult principle.

5.1.2 Dimensions of Authenticity in the FL Classroom

The notion of authenticity is multi-layered and encompasses various facets. The following dimensions of authenticity can be identified for the language classroom, based on recent literature on the phenomenon and also taking older publications into account:[70]

---

70 This list displays a synthesis of discussions on authenticity by Appel (2010), Böttger (2005), Breen (1985), Haines (1995), Haß (2006), Hedge (2000), Mishan (2005), Pinner (2013), Taylor (1994) and Van Lier (1996).

- Authenticity of classroom and context
- Authenticity of language and interaction
- Authenticity of materials and texts
- Authenticity and authentication of tasks and activities
- Authenticity of purposes and aims

Figure 8 puts the dimensions into the complex context of a language classroom:

Figure 8: Dimensions of Authenticity and their interplay in the language classroom.

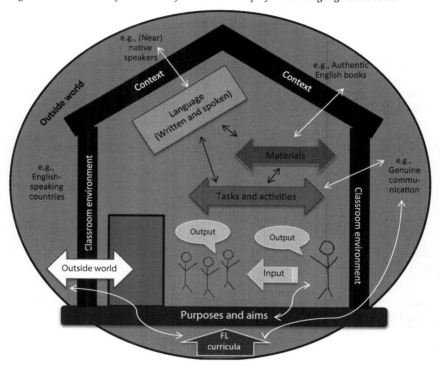

The different aspects that determine authenticity determine one another and overlaps within the dimensions are inevitable.[71] The following sections will elaborate on the different dimensions in more detail. Thereby it will become apparent that the dimensions of authenticity are reciprocally related and closely interwoven with each other, as already indicated in Figure 8.

Authenticity of classroom and context

An overarching dimension of authenticity in EFL learning and teaching is concerned with the authenticity of classroom and context. Van Lier (1996: 138) maintains that context authenticity consists of the four aspects setting, participants, topics and activities and thus describes the major factors at play in the FL classroom.

In EFL teaching, the setting is usually the language classroom with learners and teachers as its participants. One could easily get the impression that what happens in the L2 classroom is almost by definition artificial and not authentic. However, Taylor (1994: 1, 7ff) argues that a "classroom has its own authenticity" in that also in class learners can recognise the communicative value of a FL which the classroom enables them to practise. Van Lier (1996: 124) explains that classroom learners themselves are authentic when they know what they are doing and when they are responsible for their actions. Hereby, he views authenticity as closely related to autonomy and outlines that the learners' personal commitment, genuine interest in and identification with the goals and procedures of the classroom can make it an authentic FLL place for them (Van Lier, 1996: 143f).[72] Therefore, teachers can strive towards authenticity of classroom and context by enabling learners to recognise the communicational value of the FL by choosing communicative and meaningful tasks and allowing them space to practise the FL in close to real-life situations during class.

An authentic FL classroom hence includes the use of authentic topics and content. Pinner (2013: 51) found that learners stated that it is first and foremost

71 For example, teachers, learners, language and materials have an influence on which tasks and activities are used, as they work together to build the foundation for any action in the classroom. There is a constant interplay between the participants in a classroom, the language and interaction in class and the tasks and activities taking place. Moreover, any purposes and aims that build the framework for all ongoing processes in the classroom are determined by the teacher and based on the outer context such as, for example, the curriculum. These, in return, are based on the needs of language learners in every-day life communication.

72 However, such an "authentic person [...] is an ideal which we rarely see embodied" (Van Lier, 1996: 144).

the content that makes a FL class authentic. As such, context authenticity can be achieved when the classroom deals with language and content from outside the classroom (Van Lier, 1996: 139). In practical terms, this entails choosing topics which the learners are interested in, which derive from their everyday lives and spheres of experience and which create a meaningful context for them (Böttger, 2005: 69). Thereby, the authentic world outside the classroom should be brought into the classroom itself. Excursions such as field trip or exchange programmes can serve for yet more authentic experiences, in that the actual classroom context is left behind (see, e.g., Haß, 2006; Gehring & Stinshoff, 2010).

Authenticity of language and interaction

The account of authenticity of context already indicated the importance of authenticity of language and interaction, another dimension of authenticity in FLL. Language and interaction in the FL classroom are authentic when one finds genuine instances of language use (including genuine questions and dialogues) which resemble the learners' normal communicative activities and are hence natural (Taylor, 1994: 4f). According to Guariento and Morley (2001: 347), the skilful use of authentic language can bridge the gap between the classroom and the real world, in order to develop skills for the world outside the classroom.

Traditional L2 classroom interaction in particular is almost by definition unnatural as it is often easily distinguishable from language use elsewhere (Van Lier, 1996: 123). The common question 'How old are you?' is by no means authentic when a teacher has known a class for a while and obviously only wants to practise English question formation. Hence, Van Lier (1996: 123) argues that the classroom should try to be less classroom-like and more natural with regard to language use. To achieve this, both the language itself and classroom interaction, should be as authentic as possible (Appel, 2010: 5). There are a number of factors that determine and influence the authenticity of interactions such as the equality and symmetry with regard to the interlocutors or the purpose of instructional conversation in contrast to genuine communication (Van Lier, 1996: 140ff). That is why Mishan (2005: 74) proposes that classroom communication should be "meaningful in that it has a genuine purpose" and should not only reflect pedagogical purposes. This can, for instance, be achieved by fostering learner-learner interactions in cooperative working situations (Appel, 2010: 5; Roche, 2008: 213).

Moreover, it is important to expose language learners to authentic language right from the beginning (Haß, 2006: 97). One source of authentic FL input is the EFL teacher. Authentic language used to be referred to as "language produced by 'native speakers'" (Pinner, 2013: 45). This, however, is somewhat problematic, taking into consideration that there are far more L2 than L1 speakers of English (Saville-Troike, 2012: 9) and that most EFL teachers speak English as their L2 and not their L1. Thus, this definition is increasingly falling out of favour. However, even if EFL teachers are not native speakers, their input can still be authentic if they are able to use the target language accurately (Böttger, 2005: 71f); a notion that is gaining importance due to the increasing use of English as a lingua franca (see Decke-Cornill, 2003). Language teachers should have an excellent command of the L2 and know about aspects of native-like language (Haß, 2006: 97), but they do not have to be native speakers.

Still, teachers modify their input depending on the proficiency level of their learners in order to make it comprehensible. Van Lier (1996: 133) argues that so-called "audience design" is a natural feature of language use and hence complies with the principle of authenticity. However, Harmer (2007: 273f) points out that modified teacher language can only be authentic if it is not unnatural or altered in a way that makes it unrecognisable as the language of a competent speaker. Therefore, teachers need to be skilled in modified input in order to make it less pedagogical and more authentic.

Besides spoken language input from different types of media, written FL input should be authentic as well. Authentic written language and interaction is found in authentic texts such as books, online sources or songs, as well as in authentic means of written communication, such as e-mails. Whenever pupils communicate with a real person, for example other learners, in writing, and when the pupils have a real purpose for writing, for instance, writing an e-mail to a pen pal in another country, written communication becomes authentic. Taylor (1994: 5) refers to this as a "real writer", that is any person who writes to a "real audience" with a "real message being conveyed."

Authenticity of materials and texts

As outlined in the previous section, authentic texts are a source of authentic FL input. In fact, authentic texts and materials are potentially the most prominent and best-known dimension of authenticity in language teaching. Haines (1995: 60) defines authentic materials as "written or spoken language which has been produced for native speakers rather than for foreign learners of a language" and which is available on some sort of medium (e.g., a CD). It includes any materials to which no concessions were made to FL learners and that contains normal and natural language used by native or competent speakers of a language (Harmer, 2007: 273). The creator of the materials will not have had the needs of FL learners in mind either (Meyer, 2010: 15). In other words, authentic materials in the FL classroom are those that were not created for FL teaching or learning purposes. Therefore, one of the greatest advantages of authentic materials is that they are not aimed at FL learners and hence do not patronise learners nor makes any assumptions about their proficiency or knowledge (Haines, 1995: 62).

Resources that can serve as authentic materials in the EFL classroom include books, films and songs in English, realia from the English-speaking world, pictures that display the English-speaking world or English websites. While traditional authentic media were usually available in print form or in recorded form, authentic written or audio materials are also available nowadays in the online world. As Mishan (2005: 19) puts it, "today's learners can reach out and touch 'real life' at the tap of the keyboard." Roche (2008: 21) notes that new media, and especially the Internet, play a crucial role with regard to the notion of authenticity in FLL, as they authentically represent genuine and real-life situations and can serve as authentic tools in the context of FLL.

Authentic books, the focus of this work, are a subcategory of authentic materials. Any book or text is considered as authentic when it was originally written for non-classroom purposes to serve genuine communicative aims and represent a sample of the target culture (Deana & Rumlich, 2013: 183; Mishan, 2005: 1; Pinner, 2013: 45). Such authentic books are also referred to as 'real books' (Cameron, 2001: 167). Authentic texts provide readers with rich FL input and give learners the feeling that they are "learning the 'real' language" (Guariento & Morley, 2001: 347) and thereby potentially maintain and increase the learners' motivation (Guariento & Morley, 2001: 347).

As already indicated in Chapter 5.1.1, though, using authentic texts and materials for teaching purposes and FLL activities can limit their authenticity (Coyle et al., 2010: 11; Mishan, 2005: 18; Taylor, 1994: 5). Although this factor is often ignored in discussions of authenticity in EFL learning and teaching, it will be further explained in Chapter 5.1.3 in order to show its implications.

Authenticity and authentication of tasks and activities

The previous sections have already indicated that authenticity is to a great extent dependent on EFL classroom tasks and activities (also see Guariento & Morley, 2001: 349).[73] According to Westphal Irwin (2007: 18), tasks are authentic if they are interesting and relevant to the learners and if the task's purpose goes beyond satisfying school requirements. Therefore, authentic tasks have a genuine purpose

---

73 This chapter relies on Cameron's (2001: 31) definition of tasks and activities, with activities being any kind of events that children and teachers participate in in the classroom. Activities are actual tasks if they fulfil certain criteria based on the notion of TBLL, as found in Cameron (2001: 31f), Mishan (2005: 65ff) or Nunan (2004).

and real communication has to take place to achieve this purpose (Guariento & Morley, 2001: 349ff): Any authentic task is related to "something we usually do in the 'real world'" (Westphal Irwin, 2007: 18). That is why authentic tasks are also referred to as "real-world tasks" (Nunan, 2004: 1ff) and are described as a task "as it is performed for one-to-one use outside the classroom" (Legutke et al., 2009: 117). Such tasks should have a clear relationship to the learners' needs and learners perform communicative situations in the same way they would also do in real situations. Learners are encouraged to interact naturally (Willis, 1996: 18) and, in fact, "in the classroom must speak and write as if they were somewhere else" (Van Lier, 1996: 123). Such tasks obviously make the language and interaction in the FL classroom more authentic, as outlined earlier in this chapter.

Mishan (2005: 62) adds that a task is authentic if it is appropriate for the learners' proficiency levels and hence challenges learners without being too demanding. Matching a task to the learner's ability belongs to classroom authenticity, as "simple pedagogic tasks used with low-level students can still be described as authentic" (Guariento & Morley, 2001: 352) as long as genuine communication can take place, even if on a low proficiency level. Cameron (2001: 30) sees the authenticity of tasks for young children in the "real-ness [sic] in outcome", focusing more on the process of solving the task and its end product than on the task itself. Cameron (2001: 30f) argues that real and authentic language use raises problems with young learners and one should aim for "dynamic congruence", which means choosing activities and content appropriate for the learners' age and experience; only then can the learners develop context authenticity (see earlier in this chapter).

Another perspective of task authenticity is authentication (Mishan, 1996). According to Mishan (1996: 70f), task authenticity "is a factor of the learner's involvement with the task" and hence is highly dependent on what the learners actually do with a task given to them. The process of authentication thus takes place through the learners, who can "authenticate their learning environment and activities" (Van Lier, 1996: 135). However, conditions for authentication are somewhat hard to pinpoint (Van Lier, 1996: 126, 139). Nevertheless, Külekci (2014) states that materials and tasks can be authenticated when a connection to real life and communication is made. One example he found in an EFL classroom is the following: While practising if-clauses the teacher started a sentence with 'If I went to Syria'. The learner's response authenticated this rather artificial practice of a grammatical feature by spontaneously responding 'No! I wouldn't go there! There's a war!'. Hence, instead of finishing the if-clause with the use of the correct tense, the learner gave an impulsive answer which was unquestionably appropriate and reflected his real-world opinion. This spontaneous output is an example of authentication in the EFL classroom and should by all means be supported by the teacher, as it authenticates originally non-authentic tasks. Therefore, (task) authenticity can also be the result of a process of authentication (Van Lier, 1996: 133).

Authenticity of purposes and aims

The dimension of authenticity of purposes and aims is closely related to task authenticity as outlined in the previous section. For Van Lier (1996: 139), purpose relates to the "intended outcome of a speech event." An authentic purpose means that the teacher as well as the learner should know the aim of an activity. Thus, it is also possible to "'authenticate' a task to learners" through a careful explanation of its purpose and its rationale (Guariento & Morley, 2001: 351). In this sense, authenticity is related to the pupils' immediate learning goals, which might go beyond the interaction in the classroom and their curricular learning outcomes (Pinner, 2013: 47). This already suggests that one should also see aims and purposes on a broader scale, taking into consideration why learners actually learn the FL and hence work on its relevance for the world outside the classroom.

In content-based approaches to FLL, for example CLIL, the language is used to reach content aims; hence, CLIL is said to achieve its "authenticity through authenticity of purpose" (Coyle et al., 2010: 5) and apparently "the word content in CLIL is almost synonymous with authenticity" (Pinner, 2013: 46). This suggests that topic-based approaches to language teaching (see Chapter 2.3), as found in ClIL or in German primary schools, also to a certain extent fulfil authenticity of purpose as the FL should be taught via topics that are meaningful to the children.

5.1.3 Factors Influencing the Degree of Authenticity

As already indicated in the different dimensions of authenticity, authenticity in its various dimensions can be present or absent in varying degrees. The degree of authenticity is inseparable from the question of for whom something is authentic, in which context and for which purpose (Breen, 1985: 61). Figure 9 displays these three factors which rate and determine the actual degree of authenticity and go back to ideas of Breen (1985) and Widdowson (1978). The authentic dimension/aspect in the middle circle refers to the dimensions explained in Chapter 5.1.2.

Figure 9: Determining factors for the degree of authenticity (based on Breen, 1985 and Widdowson, 1978).

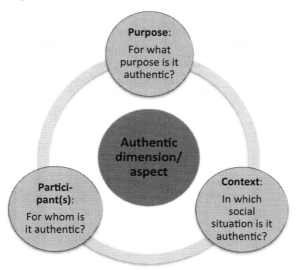

The way to which the degree of authenticity can be determined will be explained with the example-sentence "What time is it?", as it is used in spoken discourse. It is certainly a linguistically correct sentence of English which is used in everyday life contexts and hence can be referred to as genuine. Its degree of authenticity, however, only becomes clear when taking a closer look at the overall context. If this question is asked on the streets by someone without a watch, it is a genuine question with the real or authentic purpose of finding out the actual time. For the asker and also the person asked, this is an authentic question. This already reveals an important aspect which was also pointed out by Van Lier (1996: 125): Authenticity depends on both the speaker's intention and on the listener's interpretation as well as on the relevance of the language used. One can say that context, purpose and also participants make it authentic. On the other hand, if the L2 teacher asked this question in the EFL classroom, where usually a clock hangs on the wall, this question is not authentic and simply a display question which requires the learners to display their EFL knowledge about saying the time in English.[74] Hence, it is not authentic to the participants and also

---

74 For more information on the distinction between genuine and display questions see Nunan & Lamb (1996: 88) and Lightbown & Spada (2013: 145).

takes place in an unreal context. The purpose of asking the question is triggering the learner to produce the correct answer in English, so it has a clear language learning purpose and does not have the purpose of a real conversation. In sum, the context, the participants and to some extent the purpose limit the degree of authenticity in this case. Therefore, the decisive factors in determining the degree of authenticity in FL classrooms are not only the authentic dimensions, but also what is actually done with seemingly authentic factors in the broader context of the FL classroom.

5.1.4 Semi- and Quasi-Authenticity

What can be referred to as authentic materials was already established in the previous sections, but further nuances of authenticity are found on a scale from authentic to inauthentic. Such a range is particularly important with regard to materials and texts as used in EFL classrooms. Figure 10 provides an overview:

Figure 10: A scale from authentic to inauthentic.

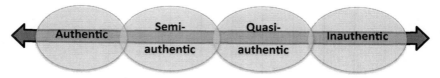

Haines (1995: 60) refers to semi-authenticity as authentic materials which have been doctored either to exclude difficult language or to include correct examples of specific language points. Widdowson (1978: 88) refers to texts as "simplified versions" when they are derived from genuine instances and simplified by a process of lexical and syntactic substitution, so that they do not display genuine instances of language use any longer. In other words, something authentic was taken as a basis but has been changed or adapted to fit the needs or proficiency levels of the FL learners. This has also been referred to as edited input (Young, 1993). Further discussions of adapting authentic texts are found in Chapter 5.2.3.

In contrast to semi-authentic materials, nothing authentic was taken as a basis for quasi-authentic materials. Quasi-authentic materials are those that were specifically designed for the learner and for teaching purposes, but are made to appear authentic (Haines, 1995: 60; Haß, 2006: 148). In other words, a letter, for instance, is written specifically for FLL, but by giving it the layout of an actual letter, it is designed to look authentic. Other than with semi-authentic materials, no authentic text is taken as a basis, but the quasi-authentic text is entirely made up to suit teaching purposes. In its extreme form, these creations or simplifications produce texts which are strictly controlled or graded with regard to grammar and vocabulary (Haines, 1995: 60). They include input which is simplified on the morphological, syntactic, semantic and also phonological level (Mishan, 2005: 23). EFL school books and materials for all different proficiency levels generally make use of quasi-authenticity, for example, by displaying letters or weather forecasts which were simplified and created simply for teaching purposes. Especially at the primary school level, songs are used which are not real English songs but those created especially for L2 teaching, apparently to best fit the beginner learners. All these creations that are supposed to look authentic, but are not, can be referred to as 'fake' or, as Pinner (2013: 52) would say, as contrived materials or tasks.

Inauthenticity, also referred to as artifice or artificiality, is said to be the opposite pole of authenticity (Mishan, 2005: x[75]; Taylor, 1994: 2). It refers to anything which was specifically designed for the learner and for teaching purposes (Haß, 2006: 148) and does not even claim to appear or be authentic or real. A classic example would be a fill-in-the-gap text to practise a grammar rule.

As indicated by the overlapping circles in Figure 10, these four parts of the scale are not always fully separable. There are overlaps between the four categories and one can, for instance, not always be sure if something is supposed to appear authentic (quasi-authentic) or if something authentic was taken as a basis for simplification (semi-authentic). These overlaps are further influenced by the notion of authentication (see Chapter 5.1.2).

5.2 Authentic Books vs. Graded Readers: A Reform in the Selection of Reading Materials

Chapter 5.1 has shown that not only authentic books, but also quasi- and semi-authentic ones, exist for FL teaching. As both are used in teaching practice (see Haines, 1995: 94), this subchapter will firstly provide a definition of authentic books as well as of graded readers based on the notion of authenticity as described in Chapter 5.1 and distinguish the two. In a next step, reasons for choosing one or the other will be provided and the current trend of choosing authentic books rather than graded readers will be explained (see Ellis &

---

75 'x' is the Latin page number of the preface of her book.

Brewster, 2014: 14; Haß, 2006: 147f). Lastly, arguments related to adapting authentic reading materials will be presented.

5.2.1 Defining Authentic Books and Distinguishing them from Graded Readers

Authentic books are distinguished from graded readers by their degree of authenticity as outlined in Chapter 5.1. Authentic books are real books that were written with native speakers in mind and were not created for language teaching purposes (see Chapter 5.1.2). An authentic text is not edited, by the publisher or by the teacher, to meet the language learners' limited proficiency level (Meister, 2012: 274). Authentic English children's books were "written by 'real' authors for parents to buy for children" (Cameron, 2001: 167) and "written for children whose L1 is English" (Brewster & Ellis, 2002: 188). Dunn (2006: 118) adds that authentic books are published by children's publishers who print what is known as trade books for recreational reading and these books are sold in a regular book store and not by educational publishers. An authentic book, that is, is not in any sense adapted to or written for FL teaching purposes.

Further dimensions of authenticity that go beyond the dimension of authentic materials and texts (see Chapter 5.1.2) depend to a significant degree on the actual use of reading materials in class. The material 'authentic book' can in itself be truly authentic, but depending on reading purpose, reading context and readings tasks in the classroom, the actual degree of authenticity can vary (see Chapters 5.1.2 and 5.1.3). Since these factors, however, are highly individual across different classes, they cannot be taken into consideration when defining authentic English books as such. This leads to the following working definition of authentic books that will be used in this work:

> Authentic books are trade books as sold in a regular book store that were written by 'real' authors for recreational reading with native-speakers in mind and not created for or adapted to FL teaching purposes and language learners' proficiency levels.

As such, authentic books are distinguished from graded readers, also referred to as 'readers', which are adapted and simplified books that were especially written and designed for the L2 classroom and FL teaching purposes (Cameron, 2001: 167). Such graded readers are either semi-authentic, when they are adapted or simplified versions of authentic stories, or quasi-authentic, when they consist of a text that was merely written for language teaching purposes and made to appear authentic although no authentic text served as a basis (see Chapter 5.1.4).

5.2.2 The Trend towards Selecting Authentic Books

For a long time, graded readers and adapted texts were mainly or even exclusively used for FL reading at the secondary school level in Germany. Haß (2006: 89) states that in the FL classroom pupils have always read FL texts; however, these were simplified versions of authentic English texts. For instance, Brusch (1994) conducted a library project and provided some secondary schools with 100 English books each, all of them graded readers. Today, a large variety of graded readers is available on the German market for EFL teaching materials for secondary schools.[76] For primary school, considerably fewer graded readers are available.[77] A simple reason for this is that the demand for reading materials was and still is limited, because written skills are only gradually finding their way into teaching young EFL learners in the German context (see Chapter 3.1.2).

At first glance, graded readers seem easier and better suited for FL learners, especially for beginners. For them, authentic language can be very demanding, so that carefully graded and selected books with seemingly suitable language appear to be more appropriate. However, this has proved to be a misconception and graded readers have often been criticised in recent years (e.g., Bland, 2013a: 293f). Many teachers and researchers perceive readers as boring and not motivating, since such texts provide artificial language and only a limited selection of words (Frisch, 2013: 131). The language in graded readers is carefully selected, aims at not overtaxing the learners and attempts to introduce and encourage the practising of certain vocabulary and certain structures; but this makes the language artificial and unnatural (Frisch, 2014a: 16). Furthermore, graded readers often just present characters that merely move through a sequence of activities instead of setting up a problem and working towards its solution as real stories would do (Cameron, 2001: 162). This, in return, can dampen learners' interest in the books, because they are less attention-grabbing (Young, 1993: 459). Overall, graded readers lack authenticity and all advantages that rich and authentic texts entail.

With a growing awareness of the notion of authenticity and the disadvantages of graded readers in FL teaching, also the importance as well as the advantages of authentic materials and texts became apparent. This has led to a trend in favour of authentic reading texts over the past two decades or so. Haß (2006: 147f), for

---

76 For instance, the educational publisher Klett (2014) publishes a 120-page magazine annually which lists a large number of graded readers for the EFL classroom at all proficiency levels.

77 One example would be Mildenberger's 'Time for Stories' (Mildenberger, 2006).

instance, points out that the use of authentic texts in the (secondary school) EFL classroom is increasing noticeably at all (secondary school) levels in comparison to the previous use of adapted and simplified texts. This even holds true for the lower-level classes in the secondary school context (Haß, 2006: 147f) as well as for the primary school: Ellis and Brewster (2014: 14) note that since the 1990s, many teachers have begun using authentic storybooks to offer a rich source of authentic input and to challenge learners in a positive sense. In fact, a number of researchers propose that even for young and low-proficient EFL learners, well-crafted and first-rate authentic children's texts are more suitable than edited texts (see, e.g., Bland, 2013a: 293f; Young, 1993: 459). From a practical perspective, only a limited selection of graded readers is available for the primary school EFL classroom anyway, so that teachers usually had and still have to use authentic English children's books (see Chapter 5.5.1; also see Bechler & Reckermann, 2018).

This trend towards choosing authentic books is supported by current EFL curricula for all school types. The current curriculum for English at the NRW *Hauptschule* and also at the NRW *Gymnasium*, representing the lowest and highest secondary school type,[78] both place a high premium on authenticity (MSW NRW, 2007: 19). Both curricula require the learners in Years 5 and 6 and even more so in Years 9 and 10 to work with authentic English texts (MSW NRW, 2007: 23, 28, 35 and MSW NRW, 2011: 16, 27f). As already outlined in Chapter 3.2.2, also the NRW curriculum for TEFL at primary school level includes authentic materials such as picture books (MSW NRW, 2008b: 74).

Generally, there are good reasons for favouring authentic texts instead of graded readers as they offer several advantages. Firstly, authentic texts provide rich and varied authentic input (Mishan, 2005: 41), which is known to support language acquisition (e.g., Böttger, 2005: 79; Cameron, 2001: 20). Cameron (2001: 159), for example, points out that stories are "holistic approaches to language teaching and learning that place a high premium on [...] rich, authentic uses of the foreign language." Haines (1995: 94) explains that it is sensible to use authentic materials from the earliest stages on in order to ensure that learners get used to authentic language and do not get "brain-washed by simplified material." As such, authentic texts can be a positive challenge for the learners (Mishan, 2005: 44) and comprehension of authentic texts can build up learners' confidence in their ability "to tackle apparently 'impossible' material" (Haines, 1995: 63). Because of the potential difficulties of authentic reading texts, such

---

78 See 'Explanation of Terms' for *Hauptschule* and *Gymnasium*.

texts can also support the development of reading strategies which are needed to successfully read these texts (Haines, 1995: 63; Young: 1993: 459f).

Besides rich language input, authentic texts also offer rich and authentic cultural material, in that they contain and represent the culture of the target language. Authentic stories originate in real-world contexts and can therefore bring the world outside into the EFL class (Cameron, 2001: 159). This also ensures the currency and topicality of the reading material (Mishan, 2005: 44) so that learners' interests in contemporary issues can be catered for.

Apart from that, authentic texts can have a positive impact on the affective aspects of learning, including motivation and emotional involvement (Mishan, 2005: 41), and engage learners more than graded readers: "Texts drawn from the culture of the target language tend to be more involving to the learner" (Mishan, 2005: 29). Authentic texts may be more motivating to the extent that they often address the learners' interests more convincingly (Mishan, 2005: 26f). Motivation, in return, correlates positively with success in L2 learning (Brown, 2007: 168). Motivated learners are said to stick to tasks and are willing to keep learning (Lightbown & Spada, 2013: 87). When learners are affectively engaged through authentic texts, their affective filter can be lowered and put them in a positive mind-set (Mishan, 2005: 28). Consequently, the resulting positive mood and emotionally comfortable learning atmosphere can have a positive influence on FLL (Hermann-Brennecke, 1998).

In addition, Böttger (2013: 43) emphasises that the language proficiency of FL learners improves faster and better through the use of authentic and interesting materials. Young (1993: 451) found in an empirical study that all of the learners of her research project (adult students of Spanish at three different proficiency levels) understood significantly more from authentic passages than they did from edited ones. Also, the learners responded more favourably to authentic texts. No such study is available for young learners' FL reading. However, as will be detailed in Chapter 5.2.3, a small-scale classroom research project suggested that for storytelling in primary school an adapted text is understood better and in more detail than the original one (see Gerngroß & Diekmann, 2003). Clearly, more research is needed to come to more conclusive findings for young learners, as one study alone that is concerned primarily with storytelling cannot offer representative results.

Looking at teaching approaches, the advantages of using authentic reading materials is underscored by the whole language approach to L2 teaching, which is devoted to helping young language learners learn to read and focuses on the use of authentic literature and the reading of real texts (Richards & Rodgers,

2014: 142). From the very beginning, in this method, FLL is organised around the use of authentic FL texts.

Despite the arguments in favour of authentic texts, one should not neglect the difficulties that authentic texts can pose for learners, particularly for young (and other) beginners. Some authentic texts are bound to be too difficult for young EFL learners and as such "it goes without saying that some authentic texts are unsuitable for lower-level learners" (Haines, 1995: 63). In fact, it is essential to give learners reading material that they can comprehend and that is not too difficult for them (Westphal Irwin, 2007: 171). In this regard, Westphal Irwin (2007: 170) lists two main criteria that enable learners to comprehend texts: interest and readability. To ensure both, primary school teachers apply well-established criteria when selecting authentic picture books for storytelling (see Chapter 5.2.3), which can be transferred to selecting reading texts for young learners.

In support of the use of authentic texts it is important to mention that teachers need not choose very simple texts, but rather need to have realistic expectations with regard to the depth of understanding (Guariento & Morley, 2001: 349). When teachers adapt their expectations with regard to the level of comprehension of a text, also more challenging texts can be used. When reading these, young EFL learners maybe do not understand every single detail; but when reading for pleasure and out of interest, the comprehension of the gist of the story can also be motivating in that it shows beginner learners that they can successfully read an authentic text and globally understand it. Therefore, realistic teacher expectations are an important factor in the choice of reading materials.

As a final note, there might also be reasons for using adapted texts which go beyond the notion that such texts are seemingly easier. Haines (1995: 64), for instance, explains that pupils also need contextualised examples of certain structures or features of the language which are unlikely to be found in authentic materials. Therefore, he states that "it is sensible to use both kinds of material from the earliest stages" (Haines, 1995: 94). Whether this is truly necessary cannot be further elaborated on here, because the issue is essentially one of the acquisition of language structures and would need a thorough investigation as a topic in itself.

5.2.3 Criteria for Carefully Choosing Authentic Books

Chapter 5.2.2 has shown that the learners' interest in a text as well as the text's readability and suitability in terms of level of complexity are crucial factors that determine the success of a reading text in class. Therefore, teachers need to carefully choose reading materials which meet the learners' proficiency levels as well as their interests. Criteria for selecting such texts can be transferred from those that teachers use when selecting books for storytelling, a method in which teachers read or tell a story to the class (see Chapter 5.5.1).

The first important criterion for the selection of an authentic book is the language used in it. Aspects that teachers consider when evaluating the difficulty of the language in authentic English children's books include: both known was well as unknown words are used, the lexical load should not be too high, there is a clearly separable use of narratives and dialogues, the text is written in simple past, simple present or present continuous tenses, rhyme and rhythm are present, the text contains onomatopoeia, repetitive patterns are used and the sentences are neither too long nor too complex (see Cameron, 2001: 163f; Brewster & Ellis, 2002: 190f; Böttger, 2005: 85f; Haines, 1995: 63; Westphal Irwin, 2007: 168f; Willgerodt, 2003: 51).

Further aspects for evaluation include the topic and content (which should be relevant and interesting for the learners), the clarity of the sequence of events (which should not be too complex), the book's layout (which should be appealing and not too small) and the book's length (which should neither be too long nor too short) (see Böttger, 2005: 85f; Brewster & Ellis, 2002: 189ff; Cameron, 2001: 167ff; Haines, 1995: 63).

In addition, the visualisations in children's books need a careful analysis, in that teachers should carefully examine the aspect of congruency between textual and visual elements (also see Chapter 5.3.3). According to Reichart-Wallraben-stein (2004: 444), young learners believe that picture and text are congruent in picture books. This belief implies that "the words echo, or shadow, the pictures and vice versa" (Lewis, 2001: 42). For many picture books this holds true, but for others (e.g., 'Handa's Surprise' (Browne, 1994)) it does not. Therefore, congruency or symmetry as well as possible contradictions of text and pictures should be analysed by the teacher, and possible asymmetries should be discussed with the learners.

All the criteria listed above derive from numerous publications on selecting suitable books for young learners and are to date mostly used to select books for storytelling. However, the criteria can also be used for choosing suitable reading texts for young EFL learners. Clearly, not all criteria can be fulfilled in one text, but still teachers can use the criteria as an orientation to evaluate and select authentic books.

5.2.4 The Question of Adapting an Authentic Book

Despite awareness of the advantages of authentic English books and numerous criteria which help to carefully select them, a common reservation about them is that the authentic language might be too hard for early learners of English to understand (see, e.g., Appel, 2010; Cameron, 2001). Rich input as provided through authentic texts is likely to contain lexical items that the learners are not familiar with. Therefore, teachers on the one hand carefully choose the books (see Chapter 5.2.3) and on the other hand they partly make adaptations to them.[79]

If primary EFL teachers deem it necessary to adapt a book, such adaptations can be made to the medium of presentation (e.g., copy small pages of a book onto larger ones), to the content (e.g., leaving out certain details) and to the language. Possible adaptations to the language include substituting difficult words/phrases with seemingly easier ones or with words/phrases the pupils already know, changing the tense, leaving out sentences that are redundant for understanding the gist of the story or shortening sentences and reducing sentence complexity. If adaptations are made to an authentic book, its authenticity cannot fully be preserved and it ultimately turns into semi-authentic material. As a rule of thumb, Klippel and Doff (2007: 90) therefore suggest keeping the text as authentic as possible and only simplifying what is really necessary.

If adaptations are made, these should always be done seamlessly and without taking away the actual appeal and attraction of the text (Guariento & Morley, 2001: 348). For example, in the story 'The Gruffalo' (Donaldson & Scheffler, 1999), teachers should not simplify the text at the expense of the rhyme scheme, as this is what makes the text attractive, allows it to flow smoothly and ensures that it is easy to remember. Also, rhyme, for example, helps understanding and is a means to easily relate and recall language patterns (Todtenhaupt-Duscha & Duscha, 2008: 18). The same holds true for words that somehow sound funny, are particularly difficult or are very uncommon: Children tend to like these words (Decke-Cornill & Küster, 2010: 170) and want to remember them, because "children pick up words that they enjoy" (Cameron, 2001: 163). In addition, learners lose their fear of unknown words and structures when they are exposed to them regularly in authentic texts (Meyer, 2010: 15); a factor that is of crucial importance for communication outside the FL classroom. All these aspects suggest that words and phrases that appear difficult should not necessarily be replaced by seemingly easier ones.

---

79 This holds true for storytelling (see Chapter 5.5.1), but the aspects can be transferred to reading as well.

With regard to actual benefits of adapting an original text, Mishan (2005: 23) found that only elaborative changes can improve comprehensibility and stimulate acquisition. They involve adding conversational-like features such as repetition, paraphrases, clues and topic-saliency to the text. Young (1993: 458) found in her study that adapted texts can only enhance reading comprehension as long as features of authentic texts, such as the organisation structure, are preserved.

In the context of the primary school EFL classroom, one study that was already briefly mentioned in Chapter 5.2.2 provides tentative and initial evidence that adapting authentic texts used for storytelling can be beneficial for learners' comprehension. Gerngroß and Diekmann (2003) conducted a small-scale action research project in which they did a storytelling session with the picture book 'The Gruffalo' (Donaldson & Scheffler, 1999) in two parallel Year 4 classes; one class was read to the original story, the other class an adapted and simplified version of it.[80] By means of analysing a free oral and written recall after the storytelling phase the researchers found that the class which was read the simplified story could better understand a number of global aspects of the story (Gerngroß & Diekmann, 2003: 22f). This led the research team to the careful conclusion that it might be better to adapt some stories for storytelling and that teachers need to carefully check the extent to which their learners truly understood a book (Gerngroß & Diekmann, 2003: 23). Clearly, more research is needed, because the study was on the one hand conducted in 2003, when English had only just been introduced at the primary school level, and its methodology was not yet as developed as it is today. On the other hand, it is only a single study with just two classes and with just one book. Also, only data about comprehension was provided, but no other factors such as motivation or interest in the text were considered.

As already outlined in Chapter 5.2.2, a final argument against adapting authentic texts, is that it is not necessarily the text that should be adapted, but rather the teachers' expectations and the tasks provided with the text (Guariento & Morley, 2001: 349; Harmer, 2007: 274; Mishan, 2005: 62). In other words, realistic expectations and suitable tasks can make an adaptation of the authentic text unnecessary. This appears preferable, because adapting elements of a book means that it loses its authenticity and the advantages that authenticity brings

---

80 The simplifications which were made to the story should be regarded very critically, as the adapted text is very simple, written in present instead of past tense and the rhythm of the verse, which is such a defining feature of the original, is lost (for the adapted text see Gerngroß & Diekmann, 2003: 23).

with. Nuttall (2005: 178) sums up the major downside of adapting a text: "However good a simplification is, something is always lost."

5.3 Defining and Categorising Authentic English Children's Books

Because of their advantages outlined in the previous subchapter, the following subchapter will focus on authentic books only. Firstly, different types and characteristics of authentic children's books will be outlined. Picture books constitute one subtype thereof. The subsequent section will elaborate on story grammars and the idea of telling a story in children's books. Based on both sections, Chapter 5.3.3 will give a working definition of authentic English picture books, which also takes into consideration the notion of authenticity (Chapter 5.1) and the definition of an authentic book (Chapter 5.2.1). Lastly, the appropriateness of authentic picture books at the primary school level will be discussed.

5.3.1　Identifying Different Types of Children's Books

Children's books are one part of children's literature. Children's literature is a part of children's culture and defined by Bland (2013b: 1) as "all literature for children and adolescents, including oral literature, such as fairy tales and nursery rhymes, graphic narratives and young adult literature, reflecting the eclectic interests of children." Generally, literature entails oral, audio-visual and written literature (Meyer, 2005: 8) and does hence not only include books, but also any artefacts of a culture which are captured in oral or written form. Despite these various facets of literature, however, this book focuses on written literature only with a particular focus on children's books. In accordance with the principle of authenticity (Chapter 5.1), only authentic books are taken into consideration (see Chapter 5.2.1). More so, in view of the EFL classroom, only books whose language is English are considered; which includes all books in English that were written in a context where English is in some sense a dominant language.[81]

81　This, for example, includes American and British authors, authors from Canada, New Zealand or Australia, and authors from former British colonies such as South Africa or India. This also includes authors that wrote in a context in which English for whatever reason is a dominant language.

A number of different types of authentic children's books can be classified. These include storybooks, picture books, graphic novels, comics, factual books, folk and fairy tales, rhyme and poetry books.[82] Table 5 provides an overview:

Table 5: Classification of authentic English children's books (partly based on Albers, 2014; Belgrad & Pfaff, 2010; Burwitz-Melzer, 2013; Dunn, 2006; Haß, 2006; Legutke et al., 2009; Meyer, 2005; Nampaktai et al., 2013).

Authentic English children's books					
Literary/narrative texts (Fiction or (partly) non-fiction)				Factual texts (Non-fiction)	
Storybook	Picture book	Graphic novel	Comic	Topic-based fact books	Children's encyclopaedia
Books mainly containing textual elements	Books containing an intricate combination of visual and textual elements that complement each other	The same as picture books, but more complex and difficult because of more textual elements	Books that are separated into panels on each page and mostly contain text in speech that complement the pictures	Books that contain facts and information on one topic (also referred to as science books when dealing with scientific content)	Books that contain facts and information on several topics, often ordered alphabetically
These books include anthologies (e.g., of fairy tales or poems) or tell an ongoing story. Stories in storybooks, graphic novels or comics are sometimes divided into chapters (chapter books), whilst picture books are usually not chaptered.					

The first distinction made in this classification is between literary/narrative and factual texts. The latter are non-fiction and contain facts and factual information (Belgrad & Pfaff, 2010: 63f). Typical non-fiction texts for children include children's encyclopaedias or books that focus on facts in a field such as science. On the other hand, texts which tell a story, either fiction or non-fiction, are literary texts (Belgrad & Pfaff, 2010: 63f). Such texts belong to the narrative genre (Meyer, 2005: 7).[83] Narrative texts are those which tell a story and contain a

---

82 This list is based on Albers (2014), Bland (2013b), Böttger (2005), Brewster & Ellis (2002), Burwitz-Melzer (2013), Deane and Rumlich (2013), Dunn (2006) and Legutke et al. (2009).

83 The concept of genre is often used to classify different sorts of texts. A well-known distinction is the differentiation into the three genres of poetry, drama and narrative (Meyer, 2005: 7). However, only narratives will be taken into further consideration in this book.

combination of narrative text and other discourse forms (Nampaktai et al., 2013: 35f; Meyer, 2005: 56).

While factual texts are always non-fiction texts, literary or narrative texts can either be fiction or non-fiction. This distinction is basically determined by the way in which literature imitates reality (Meyer, 2005: 5). A fictional children's books consists of elements that were made up by the author's imagination and creativity, whereas a non-fictional children's book discusses the real world and deals with real facts and stories. Whilst most picture books are fictional texts, the boundaries are often not clear-cut, as a fictional picture book might also contain realistic elements and all sorts of fictional children's books might also contain factual information to a certain extent (Dunn, 2006: 188). A good example of this is Well's (1993) picture book 'Is a blue whale the biggest thing there is?'. The title already suggests that this picture book, although it tells a fictional story, also contains factual information such as the size of a whale (non-fiction). Moreover, children's books may be based on real-life stories, which makes them non-fiction to a certain extent as well. In sum, all literary children's books can be fiction, non-fiction or a combination of both, while factual texts are, by definition, non-fiction.

Four types of literary/narrative children's books can be identified: storybooks, picture books, graphic novels and comics. Legutke et al. (2009: 78) describe storybooks as children's books which contain textual elements only.[84] Some storybooks might include single pictures on selected pages. Such pictures are often just sketches in black and white, have more of a decorative function and usually do not carry meaning that is necessary to understand the story.

In contrast, picture books consist of textual and visual elements that complement each other. Picture books contain an "intricate relationship between visual and textual elements" (Legutke et al., 2009: 78) in which text and pictures are "intricately linked and work together" (Burwitz-Melzer, 2013: 58). This connection creates a multi-layered meaning (Mourão, 2013: 71) and implies that picture books are only understandable through the connection of text and pictures and cannot be understood without either of the two. Text and visual elements complement each other.[85]

---

84 The term storybook is also used as a generic term to refer to any authentic book that is suitable for children, for example, by Brewster & Ellis (2002: 188), Böttger (2005: 85) or Dunn (2006: 118). However, in this book the term 'storybook' will only be used to talk about children's books that contain mainly textual elements.

85 Bland (2013b: 1) even purposefully writes 'picturebook' as one word, in order to "emphasize the word/image interdependency."

Graphic novels are also characterised by a connection of visuals and text and, similar to picture books, present one ongoing story or closely related stories (Burwitz-Melzer, 2013: 58). However, they are more sophisticated than picture books and more suitable for older learners (Albers, 2014: 7f), as the text load of graphic novels is denser, texts' font size is smaller and the themes are invariably more suited to older readers.

Like picture books and graphic novels, comics are also identified by the interplay of visual and textual elements, but are distinguished from picture books and graphic novels by their layout. They also consist of text and pictures which are highly dependent on each other, but comics are presented in panels. A comic has up to ten panels per page, which can vary in size and shape and are usually framed (Burwitz-Melzer, 2013: 60). The reader reads through the sequence of the panels. Verbal text is typically almost exclusively direct speech written in speech bubbles (Burwitz-Melzer, 2013: 61). What is more, comics often visualise spoken language, for example, by means of font type and size, bold print and capitalisation (Deane & Rumlich, 2013: 187). Visualisation of languages is a feature that is sometimes also found in picture books, but not as extensively. Generally, the boundaries of picture books, graphic novels and comics are blurred, as they share a number of characteristics.

There are other types of texts that are found in storybooks, picture books, graphic novels or comics. These include anthologies of, for example, poems, rhymes or fairy tales. Dunn (2006: 118) explains that rhyme or poetry books contain a collection of children's rhymes or poems. These books represent just a collection of short individual texts that do not tell an ongoing story but are little stories in themselves. Folk and fairy tales are a lot longer than that and have been adapted from universal folk tales and fixed in written form (Legutke et al., 2009: 77).

As already mentioned above, factual texts are non-fiction, as they present matter-of-fact information. Factual books can either be topic-based, explaining, for instance, the life cycle of a bee, or they can be encyclopaedias containing a list of explanations on various terms and topics. Most importantly, such factual books always convey subject-related information (Haß, 2006: 147).

Lastly, although they do not appear in the classification above and are not relevant for this book, hypertexts will be given a brief mention (also see Chapter 12.2). Hypertexts are becoming increasingly important in the present media age as they are texts made available through the help of new media (e.g., computers). They are usually not as linear texts as books are, but are better described as a branched network (Spinner, 2010: 55).[86] Apart from that, texts and books are nowadays available on e-readers. However, this work focuses on printed books only.

5.3.2 Story Grammars in Children's Books

The books outlined in the previous chapter all tell some kind of story; a term that is well-known and very broad. According to Meyer (2005: 55), a story is "about characters in a sequence of actions and events in particular circumstances." Hence, all literary books can be understood as stories.

The way in which characters and events are brought into the context of a story is described by story grammars. Put simply, 'story grammar' is the way a story is constructed or built (Nikolajeva, 2005: 99, 110). Story grammars look closely at the structures and operations of narrative texts and analyses their patterns (Holle, 2010: 142). As such, story grammars are concerned with coherence and the logic in the events of a story's plot. The plot of a children's book, which is "the sequence of events in a story" (Nikolajeva, 2005: 100), is usually built up as shown in Figure 11. The storyline as seen in Figure 11 is rather simple and allows for the coherent and logical order of events that is often found in picture books.

Figure 11: Building blocks of a plot in children's literature (Nikolajeva, 2005: 102).

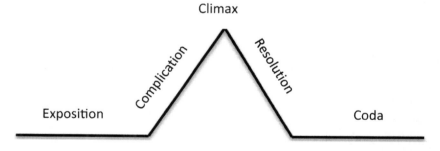

Holle (2010: 165) and Nampaktai et al. (2013: 36) explain that there is a connection between story grammars and reading comprehension in that learners benefit from knowledge about basic elements of a story because it enables them

---

86 For an idea of how to use (adapted) hypertexts in the primary EFL classroom see, for example, the MuViT project by Elsner to be retrieved from: https://www.uni-frankfurt. de/44712109/MuViT_Elsner (last access 15.05.2017).

to identify and comprehend different parts of the story and to remember the story chronologically better. Therefore, particularly beginner EFL learners might benefit from stories which follow a simple storyline, in that this might help them with comprehension.

The literary books defined in Chapter 5.3.1 were all characterised as books that tell a story and to some degree follow the building blocks shown in Figure 11 and described by story grammars. However, very easy children's books do not really tell a coherent story but are more so a display of disjointed events or very easy facts. They lack the plot that is outlined by story grammars. Backes (2014) refers to these books as 'board books' or 'concept books', which, for example, teach easy concepts such as colours or names of animals and are sometimes even wordless. Examples of English picture books that are concept books in that they lack a plot are 'Brown Bear, Brown Bear What Do You See?' (Martin & Carle, 1999) or 'Mrs. Pirate' (Sharatt, 1994). Such books are certainly authentic children's books as well, but are not taken into further consideration in this book. Only books that tell an actual story will be considered.

5.3.3 A Working Definition of Authentic English Picture Books

Based on the considerations in the previous chapters, the following working definition of authentic English picture books will be used throughout the remainder of this book:

> Authentic English picture books are real children's books that were written in a context in which English is a dominant language and not created for language teaching purposes. They tell a story which follows a storyline through an intricate interrelation of visual and textual elements, both of which are essential for full comprehension by creating multi-layered meaning.

This definition is in accord with the features that denote authenticity of materials and texts as outlined in Chapter 5.1.2, ensuring that genuinely authentic books and not graded readers are meant. However, the definition does not consider the various further dimensions and degrees of authenticity (see Chapter 5.1), which come into play in the specific context of classroom procedures. Reasons for this were already provided in Chapter 5.2.1. With regard to the authenticity of picture books it should be added that "authenticity means that nothing of the original text is changed and also that its presentation and layout are retained" (Grellet, 1986: 8). So called purists argue that materials are not truly authentic unless presented to the learners in their original form (Haines, 1995: 63). This purist stance suggests that when authentic English children's books are used, the original books should be given to the learners instead of copies or the like. Also, possible adaptations, as elaborated on in Chapter 5.2.3, are not undertaken if the authenticity is to be preserved.

Coming back to the definition of authentic English picture books, it does comply with Legutke et al.'s (2009) definition of picture books as books that contain visuals and text that both tell a story which is not understandable if one or the other were missing (see Chapter 5.3.1). The visual as well as the textual elements are essential for full comprehension (Nikolajeva & Scott, 2000: 226), but their interaction is complex, ranging from symmetry to contradiction (for more details see Lewis, 2001: 31ff and Nikolajeva & Scott, 2001). Lastly, based on the notion of story grammars, picture books as defined and referred to throughout this book follow a coherent storyline.

5.3.4 Are Authentic Picture Books too Childish for Primary School EFL Learners?

One criticism with regard to using authentic picture books in the German primary school EFL classroom is that the content might be too simplistic for pupils of school-going age, because such books are often originally aimed at children from a lower age group. For example, Häuptle-Barceló and Willerich-Tocha (2008: 103) warn that the content of children's books might not mentally challenge pupils as such books often address topics which are relevant for younger children. In fact, in Diehr and Frisch's (2010b: 156) reading study, some Year 4 pupils deemed the picture books that were used as not age-appropriate and too boring. This criticism should certainly be taken into consideration by researchers and teachers.

Still, many researchers and teachers have found that primary school children actually truly like authentic English picture books and their inherent challenges. Brewster and Ellis (2002: 188) state that in a FL, children are often very happy to accept stories which they may reject when written in their L1, because working with an authentic book is "very motivating for a child as they experience a strong sense of achievement." They are simply proud of being able to understand a real English story which children in English-speaking countries would also read. This view was confirmed by Kolb (2013: 42), who used picture books for a reading project in a Year 4 and found that the linguistic challenge of these books was part of the experience and the learners were not at all concerned about the more or less simple content. Burwitz-Melzer (2013: 56) and Rymarczyk (2010: 33) support this view and explain that picture books can be demanding as well as interesting and can involve readers at all competence levels until the end of primary school. Picture books often contain content which is still funny and appealing for an older age group.[87]

Indeed, not all but many picture books are content- and topic-wise in congruence with primary-school-aged children's interests (Bland, 2013a: 40; Häuptle-Barceló & Willerich-Tocha, 2008: 104). Hence, it is particularly important that teachers carefully select picture books which are not too simplistic. A possible way to overcome this potential pitfall is to provide a collection of different picture books in the language classroom so as to ensure that the variety of books can address different preferences and interests.

5.4 Reasons for Reading (Picture) Books in the EFL Classroom: The Potential for Learners' Development

There are several reasons why books and stories are used in education and in FLL in particular. The following sections will outline the major reasons and explore such books' potential for the (primary) EFL classroom. A focus will be on reading these books, but overlaps with storytelling (see Chapter 5.5.1) will occur because the rational for both reading and storytelling are partly the same. Firstly, more general ideas of the educational value of books and stories will be provided. With a stronger emphasis on FLL, the subsequent three subchapters will then focus on the content and cultural aims of reading books as well as the widely-perceived potential of FL development through reading.

5.4.1 The Educational Value of Books and Stories

The educational value of using storybooks and the importance of stories for the development of children is undisputed throughout the world (Aristov & Haudeck, 2013: 47; Bland, 2013b: 2; Brewster & Ellis, 2002: 186). Children need stories to understand the past, present and future (Häuptle-Barceló & Willerich-Tocha, 2008: 103). Wright (1995: 3) explains that:

> We all need stories for our minds as much as we need food for our bodies. [...] Stories are particularly important in the lives of our children: Stories help children to understand their world and to share it with others. Children's hunger for stories is constant.

---

87 In fact, Nikolajeva and Scott (2001) repeatedly elaborate on the adult co-reader and note that thus picture books often contain wry, ironic or even snarky subtexts.

As this quote points out, the major advantage of storybooks is that they can help satisfy young learners' hunger for stories, as they love books and stories. Stories that are specifically written for children are motivating for them as they deal with topics that cater to their interests and thus provide them with meaningful input (Wright 1995: 3). This activates learners' interest and participation.

Additionally, Traverso (2013: 183) points out that children's emotional development can be positively influenced through the use of children's literature, especially with regard to self-esteem and positive attitudes. Children easily identify with the characters of a story and become emotionally attached to a book. Thereby, the social and emotional development of readers in particular is supported through the examination of and engagement with characters in a story (Steck, 2009: 2). This is an advantage for the classroom, as emotional attachment and motivation are desirable for effective learning. Moreover, through children's literature, topics such as diversity, tolerance, self-acceptance and self-confidence can be brought into the focus of discussion and reflection (see, e.g., Lütge, 2013).

Besides more general learning objectives such as emotional and social development, reading can also contribute to children's cognitive development (Steck, 2009:1). For instance, Krashen (2013: 17) has highlighted the positive long-term effect of reading on cognitive skills. It plays an important role in developing cognitive thinking processes (Steck, 2009: 2), which is unsurprising in view of the complex processes that are involved in reading (see Chapters 4.1 and 4.4). Therefore, a number of different cognitive processes which are not exclusively needed for reading but also in other areas of (FL) competence can be trained through reading.

With regard to school education, reading can also support autonomous learning. Bland (2013b: 3) notes that extensive reading supports the development of learner autonomy. The more learners read and the more advanced their reading skills are, the better and more easily they can retrieve information from written sources such as books or the internet. In turn, knowing how to independently seek information and construct meaning from written texts enables learners to organise their own learning and to thereby become more autonomous.

The positive educational value of books as outlined in this subchapter does not only hold true for stories in the learners' native language, but also for the FL classroom; it applies to all (language) learners regardless of age and level (Appel & Wilson, 2010; Bleyhl, 2002; Burwitz-Melzer, 2013: 56). According to Kobela (2008: 113), the advantages of using books and stories in primary EFL teaching are sufficiently well-known and undebated; books and stories can be seen as one of the most efficient learning opportunities (Häuptle-Barceló & Willerich-Tocha,

2008: 103). They can foster "holistic learning of a new language while offering excitement, fun and many new ideas to young people" (Burwitz-Melzer, 2013: 56).

5.4.2 Content and Cultural Aims through Integrating Language and Content

In addition to the more general benefits of reading in education, books can make for a skilful integration of language and content in the EFL classroom. Books are advantageous because "content is inseparably woven into the language" (Bland, 2013b: 4) and hence content and language are naturally accessible in an integrated way. Thus, the use of topic-related books in EFL units offers a good opportunity to integrate content and language and support the acquisition of both. After all, content is conveyed through language and in return language is conveyed via meaningful content. This natural dual-focus of books is in accord with the topic-based approach to language teaching as explained in Chapter 2.3: Topics provide meaningful content to the learners and FLL appears more natural, as the content and FL are learnt simultaneously. As such, learners can acquire content knowledge almost as a side-effect in reading books and stories. The topics of picture books are usually interesting for young learners, which potentially enhances their desire to learn about them.

By naturally integrating content and language, books can also serve the teaching approach of CLIL (see Chapter 2.2.1), whose most distinctive feature is its dual-focus on content and language. In this approach, both subject matter and the FL should be learnt simultaneously and in an integrated fashion. However, integrating the two can be challenging for CLIL teachers and there are still "limited methodological resources and practical guidance to enable teachers to plan and teach with a multiple focus that is vital for the successful integration of content and language" (Meyer, 2010: 12). Hence, one of the major issues in CLIL resolves around the questions of what learning and teaching materials must be like in order to support language as well as content learning (Elsner & Keßler, 2013: 3; Klippel & Doff, 2007: 27). The use of authentic books and stories, and in the primary school particularly the use of picture books, could be one possible answer, since the nature of texts can serve the double-focus of CLIL.

For instance, English books can be used for the integration of language and content in subjects such as science. In their CHILITEX[88] project, Aristov, Haudeck and McCafferty (2015) have demonstrated that English picture books can be used in German bilingual science classes at the primary level for learning

---

88 Children's literature and experiments (CHILITEX).

about science. In their project they sought to demonstrate the extent to which the use of English picture books can enhance science lessons and support both subject and language learning (see Aristov & Haudeck, 2013; Aristov et al., 2015). Selected books, such as Well's (1993) picture book 'Is a blue whale the biggest thing there is?', can provide information about a theme dealt with in science and can thus serve the integrated learning of content and FL. As such, English books and stories can also provide cross-curricular teaching opportunities (Wright, 1995: 5), as they might contain content that is relevant for more classes than just the FL classroom. These aspects make picture books a promising source of teaching material in CLIL classes.

Another, unavoidable content element of authentic books is the cultural aspect (Mishan, 2005: 44). Any linguistic product of a culture, including books, is representative of the culture (Mishan, 2005: 45). Of course, cultural elements in books or stories are not always explicit; this depends on the content of a book. For instance, cultural aspects are easily identifiable in the picture book 'Handa's Surprise' (Browne, 1994),[89] but less so in 'The Gruffalo' (Donaldson & Scheffler, 1999). According to Bland (2013b: 1), children's literature offers manifold opportunities to develop learners' intercultural communicative competence, in that cultural aspects such as cultural values can be approached through children's literature. Stories can, for example, support the learner's understanding of self and otherness (Lütge, 2013), which is part of developing intercultural competence and cultural awareness. For a detailed exploration of the potential that picture books provide for intercultural learning, Alter (2013), Bland (2013a) and Reichl (2013) provide an overview.

5.4.3 FL Development through Reading: Vocabulary and Beyond

As outlined earlier, books offer holistic approaches to language teaching and provide learners with interesting and authentic FL encounters. Stories can thus offer learners rich FL input and can serve as a major source of language experience (Wright, 1995: 3). The potential of reading for FL development is manifold. Reading books can support communicative skills, but also linguistic components of language such as vocabulary knowledge, grammar and orthography. All these aspects will be touched on in the following paragraphs, but particularly the effects of reading on vocabulary growth, as one of the most prominent and well-researched areas, will be outlined.

---

89 However, this book should be regarded critically in terms of its cultural aspects, because these are highly stereotypical.

Firstly, communicative skills can benefit from using English books in the EFL classroom. In particular, the skills of FL listening and reading can be improved through contact with stories (Aristov & Haudeck, 2013: 47). It has always been undisputed that comprehension practice, for example through reading texts, is beneficial, if not crucial for FLL (Trofimovich, Lightbown, Halter & Song, 2009: 611). Additionally, stories can offer a basis for further communicative tasks such as speaking or writing tasks (Wright, 1995: 4f). With a focus on written skills, stories are an essential element in the development of language learners' literacy, in that children learn to read and write with the help of stories: "The use of children's literature in L1 literacy development is a well-accepted practice" (Ma, 2014: 352); a statement that can be transferred to FL literacy development.

Secondly, it is widely believed that vocabulary is broadened through reading: "the learner learns new vocabulary through reading words that have not been met elsewhere" (Hu Hsueh-chao & Nation, 2000: 403). Lightbown and Spada (2013: 162) state that "reading is a particularly valuable source of new vocabulary" and that "the best source of vocabulary growth is reading for pleasure" (Lightbown & Spada, 2013: 61). They base their arguments on Krashen, who states that "vocabulary is most efficiently attained by comprehensible input in the form of reading" (Krashen, 1989: 440) and thus "more comprehensible input, in the form of reading, is associated with greater competence in vocabulary" (Krashen, 1989: 441). Although Krashen's research on reading examined L1 acquisition, he states that vocabulary growth through reading also holds true for FLL (Krashen, 1989: 447, 454).

However, research has produced contradictory evidence regarding vocabulary growth through reading. Biebricher (2008: 9) reviewed several studies on the acquisition of vocabulary through extensive reading and found that results vary greatly. In contrast to Krashen's findings, studies conducted by Jenkins, Stein and Wysocky (1984) or Waring and Takaki (2003), for instance, suggest that reading only leads to a very low rate of vocabulary growth, which was much lower than previously anticipated. In Waring and Takaki's (2003: 150f) study, for instance, only one new word was learnt in a one-hour reading session.

Based on these findings, many researchers have come to the conclusion that vocabulary growth through reading is influenced by many factors, which will be elaborated on in the following sections. Firstly, the role of consciousness for vocabulary growth through reading has been discussed controversially. As already indicated in Chapter 3.1.1, Krashen has argued that learners acquire vocabulary even when they read for meaning and do not explicitly focus on words or on form (Krashen, 1989: 445); unconscious language acquisition happens as a side effect while the learner consciously pays attention to meaning (Krashen, 1989: 440). The opposite was postulated by Schmidt (1990; 2001; also see Chapter 3.1.1), who claimed that noticing is crucial to FLL. He believes that nothing is learnt unless it has been noticed: "noticing is the first step in the acquisition of a language aspect" (Schmidt, 2001: 31). The extent of conscious or unconscious noticing, however, has not yet been agreed on. Ellis (2005) has come to an intermediate position and states that explicit and implicit processes are dynamically interwoven in language learning, so that consciousness appears to at least partly play a role in vocabulary acquisition through reading.

Pulido (2007: 157) elaborates further on the role of noticing and consciousness and outlines preconditions for the acquisition of lexical items while reading. She believes that readers must first and foremost notice that a particular word is unfamiliar and that there is a gap in their knowledge. After that, the meaning of this lexical item has to be established. Finally, this new item then has to be integrated into the developing L2 system, which involves some elaborative rehearsal of it. This process entails the conscious noticing of a lexical gap. If the learner does not notice that gap because he/she, for example, does not deem an unknown word important, then the word cannot be acquired. Hence, noticing an unknown word is a pre-requisite for it to possibly be acquired.

Moreover, establishing word meaning also plays a role in vocabulary growth. The reader has to be able to establish the meaning of an unknown word in order to acquire it. This presupposes that the reader has noticed an unknown word and finds it important enough to try and decode the word's meaning. Words might only be treated on a superficial level and not processed deeply. Pulido (2007: 157) explains that if there are too many constraints on the individual's capacity to process a text or if an unfamiliar word is not deemed important or relevant, it is not likely to be retrieved from memory at a later time as it was only processed at a superficial level. Thus, a learner needs sufficient time, willingness and mental capacity in order to pay closer attention to a word. It is the "*quality* of processing during reading [that] is crucial for lexical development to occur" (Pulido, 2007: 158; italics in original). Pulido's findings appear to support Jenkins et al's (1984: 782) redundancy hypothesis, which suggests that redundant information in a text, such as unknown words which are not seen as important for understanding the text, are not attended to selectively. This holds particularly true if unknown words are accompanied by further aids to text comprehension, such as visualisations as found in picture books. As a final point, the acquisition of new vocabulary might be hindered by the simple fact that the reader might be unsuccessful in figuring out the meaning of an unknown word.

When it comes to remembering new vocabulary from a text, the frequency of a word occurring in a text is another important factor (Biebricher, 2008: 37; Lightbown & Spada, 2013: 162). Laufer (2013: 870) points out that words need to appear in texts often enough in order for learners to have a chance to remember them. So far, however, it has been hard to establish an actual benchmark of how often a word should occur. Waring and Takaki (2003: 150f) found that for long-term retention, an occurrence of at least five times, if not more, is necessary. In another study with Year 5 pupils, Jenkins et al. (1984: 782) found that a word must be read at least six to ten times in a text in order for it to be remembered.

Another aspect that deserves consideration is text comprehension. Pulido (2007: 181), for example, has found that the better the comprehension of a passage of text, the likelier vocabulary from that passage will be retained. She also reports from other L2 studies that found similar results (Pulido, 2007: 159f). This finding is linked to another result: The better the readers, the more likely they are to acquire word meaning (Jenkins et al., 1984: 781). Good readers usually are also good at comprehension. Hence when someone has good reading abilities, that person is also likely to understand a text better than someone with poor reading skills. Hence, the reader's reading competence as well as the comprehension level of a text influences the likelihood of vocabulary acquisition.

Apart from the comprehension of a text, the choice of the text itself can also influence vocabulary growth. Biebricher (2008: 37) states that very simple texts can support word recognition and reading fluency, but cannot foster vocabulary growth; this can only be achieved through more complex texts. This statement concurs with Krashen's ideas of comprehensible input as stated above, to which he just recently added that particularly authentic texts offer great potential for vocabulary growth through reading, as these texts are a rich source of vocabulary (Krashen, 2013: 20).

Overall, learners might need special learning activities and task involvement in order to pay attention to vocabulary acquisition and potentially broaden their vocabulary through reading (Laufer 2013: 870). This argument supports the notion of consciousness as outlined earlier. When desired, carefully selected while-reading activities should promote vocabulary learning and make strategies explicit to the learners at the same time. Hulstijn and Laufer's (2001) involvement load hypothesis supports this notion. This hypothesis claims that the "retention of unfamiliar words is, generally, conditional upon the degree of involvement in processing these words" (Hulstijn & Laufer, 2001: 545). In other words, vocabulary is best retained when pupils are deeply involved in tasks that process the new words. Therefore, tasks with a higher involvement load[90] are more effective for vocabulary learning (Hulstijn & Laufer, 2001: 545).

With respect to young FL learners, it is difficult to obtain an accurate assessment of the effect of reading on vocabulary growth, because most of the research has been conducted with older FL learners and no study on vocabulary acquisition through reading can be found for young EFL beginners. The only vague result found for the primary school is bound to the CHILITEX project. In regard to their research, Aristov and Haudeck (2013: 46f) state that during purposeful reading of task instructions in English, children learn words and phrases incidentally and occasionally use these during peer interactions. However, no empirical data is presented in support of this. Thus, research is needed with regard to young EFL learners' vocabulary growth through reading.

In sum, the factors that seem to determine possible vocabulary growth through reading are: The frequency of words in texts, the level of reading comprehension and the reader's individual reading abilities, the choice of texts, the successful establishment of word meaning during the reading process and the learners' involvement in while-reading activities that focus on vocabulary. Similar conditions hold true for acquiring other areas of FL apart from vocabulary, as will briefly be outlined in the following sections.

Grammar and spelling in particular are, like vocabulary, sometimes said to benefit from FL reading. As in the case with vocabulary acquisition, however, this is debated among researchers. For example, Chomsky (1972) states that grammatical competence builds up through reading over a long period of time. Krashen (1989: 441) claims that the correct spelling of words is acquired and practised through reading: "more comprehensible input, in the form of reading, is associated with greater competence in [...] spelling." In contrast, Sharwood Smith (1993) notes that even "enhanced input," that is, input that is altered through typographical enhancement or exaggerated stress in speaking (Lightbown & Spada, 2013: 217), does not lead learners to notice particular forms. Lightbown, Halter, White and Horst (2002: 452) have found evidence that pupils simply overlook other features of the target language, such as function words, grammatical markers or spelling, while reading. They hence imply that grammatical rules and spelling do not improve or maybe even cannot be acquired through reading. The authors believe that some "pedagogical guidance" is necessary in order to use the language accurately and to improve significantly

---

90 Involvement consists of three components: need, search and evaluation. For more detailed information, see Hulstijn and Laufer (2001: 543f).

(Lightbown et al., 2002: 452f). They argue that reading allows pupils to decode language, but it does not allow codebreaking (see Chapter 3.1.1). With regard to the acquisition of any FL feature by means of reading, learners need to read on a regular basis in order for it to show an effect on FL development. For example, Biebricher (2008: 36) found in her study with Year 8 learners that FL reading for 15 minutes per week is too short a time for FL development to take place. However, it can be difficult to trace a specific FL development and to clearly ascribe an improvement in FL competence to reading (also see Chapter 12.2).

5.5 Authentic Books in the Primary School EFL Classroom

As seen above, there are several reasons for using authentic English picture books in the primary school and also good reasons for using these for reading. However, this has scarcely been done so far. Therefore, the following sections will first present the current practice and the curricular requirements relating to the use of authentic English picture books in the EFL classroom. Secondly, some pioneer projects using authentic English picture books in more challenging contexts will be presented and an outlook on their future usage will be given.

5.5.1 Curricula and Current Practice

Generally, primary schools in Germany attempt to create a book-friendly and literate environment through various measures, including school and class libraries (Holderried, Lücke & Müller, 2012: 11). The potential of school libraries has been supported by research that has repeatedly found that more access to books results in more and better reading (Krashen, 2013: 20). Also the NRW curriculum, for instance, declares that there should be a number of books found in every primary school so as to foster a book-friendly environment, encourage and inspire the learners to deal with books and develop good reading habits through reading for pleasure (MSW NRW, 2008b: 31).

Although desirable, such efforts are mostly concerned with German children's books and not with English ones. School and class libraries usually only contain a small number of English books, if any. Sometimes, EFL teachers set up English corners or book corners and include English books in them (Brewster & Ellis, 2002: 199; Johannsen, 2014). Because German pupils usually also do not have many English children's books at home,[91] they only have limited access to English children's books and the most probable potential encounter with them is the EFL classroom.

Thus, it is the English teacher's responsibility to provide English children's books, the use of which is prescribed by EFL curricula (see, e.g., MSW NRW, 2008b; also see Chapter 3.3.2). The NRW curriculum for English in primary school requires that teachers use authentic books in the EFL classroom so as to ensure authenticity and allow for cultural learning (MSW NRW, 2008b: 74). More so, the learners should become familiar with some authentic English children's books (MSW NRW, 2008b: 80) and should listen to and understand English stories (MSW NRW, 2008b: 73). The curriculum also notes that authentic materials such as English children's books should be used to support reading competence (MSW NRW, 2008b: 74). However, the curriculum is not very specific as to what extent or how reading competence should be supported through authentic stories. In comparison to curricula from other federal states in Germany, the requirements of the NRW curriculum with regard to reading and the use of authentic books seem very high. In addition, not all the demands of the curriculum are mirrored in current classroom practice (also see Chapter 3.2.2.)

Commonly, authentic children's books are used for storytelling, but not for reading activities. Storytelling is an oral activity in which the teacher reads out or tells a story to the learners (Cameron, 2001: 160) and is a well-established method in the primary school EFL classroom.[92] Authentic English picture books are both advocated and frequently chosen for storytelling (Böttger, 2005: 85f; Schmid-Schönbein, 2008: 85ff). They are easily available, inexpensive, observe the desired principle of authenticity, when carefully selected comply with the learners' interests and can foster their motivation (Appel, 2010; Böttger, 2005: 69; Wright, 1995: 3; also see Chapter 5.3.4). The methodology of storytelling has been well-described and elaborated on, including techniques of storytelling that are used to ensure the learners' comprehension of authentic stories (see, e.g., Böttger, 2005: 87f; Brewster & Ellis, 2002: 196f). By contrast, the primary school EFL classroom still lacks a clear reading methodology (see Chapter 3.3.2), so that suggestions about the learners' reading of authentic stories are rare.

---

91 The learner questionnaire that was conducted in the empirical study presented in this book supports this statement (see Chapter 7.2): of the 23 participants, eight stated that they had no English children's books, two learners said that they only had one and the rest said that they had one to ten at home.

92 For reasons why teachers use stories and storytelling see, for example, Brewster and Ellis (2002: 186f) and Legutke et al. (2009: 72f).

Hence, English children's books or other fairly unknown texts are very seldom used for reading at the primary school level. As already indicated in Chapter 1, Kolb (2013: 33) reports that teachers usually read out and present stories to young EFL learners, but that the latter hardly ever explore or read such texts by themselves. The BIG study also supports this claim in that it found that teachers seldom use stories, books or coherent texts for reading but far more often use reading activities at the word and sentence level (BIG-Kreis, 2015: 38). This phenomenon is not unique to the German context. A study conducted in Norway found that most pupils never or hardly ever read an English book by themselves in the primary school EFL classroom (Drew, 2009: 105).

There are two major reasons for why picture books are so rarely used for reading activities. Firstly, Kolb argues that "many primary teachers still have reservations about the role of written language in the EFL classroom" (Kolb, 2013: 33). Chapters 3.2.2 and 3.4 have already shown that reading itself is still not routinely done with learners and that their abilities with regard to written language are constantly underestimated. The second argument is provided by Elsner (2010: 43), who explains that teachers do not have enough time to offer the necessary support and teach the learners the basic skills needed for reading picture books (see Chapter 3.2.2). Therefore, uncertainty and reservations about reading in general as well as time constraints seem to be the main two reasons why picture books are hardly ever used for reading activities but often for storytelling.

By contrast, the role of reading and the use of literature for reading have never been contested for EFL teaching at the secondary school level. The use of literature plays a significant role in the secondary school EFL classroom and is a long-lasting tradition in teaching English (Haß, 2006: 147; Klippel & Doff, 2007: 128f). Also, reading and working with texts is a major part of the secondary school EFL curriculum (Klippel & Doff, 2007: 129). Right from the beginning of secondary education, pupils have to read texts and books in the EFL classroom (Haß, 2006: 89; Beyer-Kessling, Decke-Cornill, MacDevitt & Wandel, 1998). English novels or chapter books, both graded readers and authentic texts, are read in class from cover to cover and dealt with extensively in terms of pre-, while- and post-reading activities (Haß, 2006: 148). Drew (2009: 106) argues that this routine of using English books in the secondary school should also be applied to the primary school EFL classroom. He thus advocates including a variety of reading materials in EFL teaching with young learners in order to support meaningful and challenging reading activities also in the early beginning of FLL. Authentic English picture books, as already used for storytelling, can provide a basis for this. Some pioneer projects that concur with this claim will be outlined in the following subchapter.

5.5.2 Pioneer Projects, Previous Research and Outlook

In spite of the fact that challenging reading tasks are mostly avoided with young learners (see Chapter 3.2), some small-scale pioneer projects have been undertaken that support the early introduction of reading stories in primary EFL learning. A number of educators and researchers have been calling for the number of reading activities with children's books to be increased (e.g., Reisener, 2008: 156) and thus individual teachers and researchers have made attempts to use (authentic) books for reading instead of storytelling. These empirical studies and practical projects will briefly be presented and discussed in this subchapter.

Firstly, an empirical study conducted by Frisch (2013) was concerned with the alternative use of picture books. Frisch (2013) used phonic readers[93] to explicitly teach EFL reading in a Year 2 and 3 at primary school level (see Chapter3.4). In her study, Frisch could show that the learners could read and understand these readers after explicitly being taught how to read in English either through the phonics approach or through the whole word approach (Frisch, 2013: 83ff). Her results indicate, however, that the phonics approach leads to a better reading comprehension of the books than the whole word approach (Frisch, 2013: 209ff). At a more general level Frisch (2013: 214f) also found that the learners were not overtaxed by the task of reading the books.

Kolb (2013) used authentic English picture books for extensive reading activities in the primary school EFL classroom and also provided some initial evidence that young EFL learners are not overtaxed by reading authentic picture books in small cooperative reading settings. Kolb (2013) conducted a small qualitative study over a period of three weeks with a class of Year 4 pupils in Germany on extensive reading, focusing on reading strategies and the effect of extensive reading on reading competence. Her participants were provided with a total of nine different English picture books of different degrees of difficulty and on different topics, which they could choose from in small groups and read freely. For support, they could work cooperatively and also had access to an audio-recording for some of the books. There were no follow-up activities on the reading, as the focus was on real-world extensive reading. Also, reading comprehension was not clearly investigated. The project aimed at improving the learners' reading motivation and confidence, the learners' reading competence and the learners' language competence. The focus of research was on the way the pupils coped with the

---

93 By the definition provided in Chapter 5.3.3, phonic readers are not understood as authentic children's books, as they were originally created for teaching purposes; however, for L1 rather than L2 learners of English.

books, the use and development of strategies for understanding and the effects on learners' reading competence. Data were collected through interviews with selected learners and the teacher, the learners' reading logs, video recordings and pre/post learners' self-assessment questionnaires on reading competence. The results indicate that the learners could work with English picture books on their own, made use of a variety of comprehension strategies and their awareness of strategy use increased over time (Kolb, 2013: 41). Also, a rise in reading motivation, confidence and competence could be observed (Kolb, 2013: 41).

Reichart-Wallrabenstein (2004) used authentic English picture books for a reading conference with Year 3 learners in order to examine the children's comprehension strategies when faced with so-called 'words in context'. She asked the children to get into groups of two or three and choose one out of six different English picture books. In collaboration, the children had to read and globally understand the story, following a four step procedure which she developed (Reichart-Wallrabenstein, 2004: 434ff). The comprehension strategies she found were included in Chapter 4.6.5; however, except for the general message that the learners coped well with the authentic books, no further research on reading competence was conducted.

Another picture book project was done by Börner and Brusch (2004), who provided 58 primary schools in Hamburg with 65 authentic English picture books each. A survey revealed that many teachers used them for storytelling, some teachers presented selected books to their EFL classes to raise their interest in them, several teachers encouraged the children to look at and read through the books during autonomous working phases and a few schools made the books available in reading corners. More detailed data of that project is unfortunately not available, as it first and foremost aimed at an enhanced use of English books in the primary school; an aim which was clearly fulfilled.

Diehr and Frisch (2010b) report on a questionnaire with Year 4 pupils ($N =$ 328) about reading picture books in English based on the preparation for an English reading competition. The results indicate that learners at primary school level are in fact not overtaxed by reading authentic English texts and are actually interested in them. Reasons the learners provided for their pleasure in reading the books included that they liked the language, that they simply enjoyed reading in English and that they deemed reading books as supportive for their learning progress (Diehr & Frisch, 2010b: 156ff).

In addition, some practical teaching ideas have been published in selected EFL teaching magazines. For example, Krüsmann (2003) published a practical idea that includes reading an adapted English text and working on various tasks around that text with young EFL learners. Also, Johannsen (2014: 26) strongly suggests supporting free voluntary reading in English by providing an English reading box that contains authentic English magazines, books and texts. Furthermore, Mayer (2013) as well as Albers (2014) have both developed a teaching idea that consists of reading authentic English comics and graphic novels in the primary school EFL classroom. Lastly, Frisch and Holberg (2015) describe a reading competition in which Year 4 learners took part in an English reading competition and read out authentic English picture books to an audience.

All these research projects as well as practical suggestions indicate and propose that authentic English children's books can and should be used for other activities than storytelling in the primary English classroom. First and foremost, these activities imply that learners read such texts themselves.

5.6 Summary of Chapter 5

The beginning of Chapter 5 provided detail about the notion of authenticity in the FL classroom. While classroom practice mostly focuses on the authenticity of materials and texts, the actual construct of authenticity is a lot more complex, characterised by various dimensions and influenced by many factors. Using an authentic text in class, that is, in short, a text that was not designed or adapted for FLL purposes, can be reduced in its authenticity by the purpose of reading, the tasks conducted with the text and the context of reading. Therefore, for reading FL texts to maintain authenticity, texts should not only be read for FLL purposes.

For young learners, authentic materials can be difficult, so their competences need to be taken into consideration when striving for authenticity. The study presented in this book will investigate to what extent young learners can cope with authentic English picture books, despite the authenticity of the text. To what extent further dimensions of task and context authenticity were fulfilled during the data collection process is questionable due to the structure needed for an empirical study (see Chapters 7 and 8). Authenticity in the current context is thus rather limited to authentic materials and texts; a focus that complies with how the term is often used in the realm of EFL teaching.

Based on this discussion on authenticity, a working definition of authentic books is arrived at, and clearly distinguishes them from graded readers. In short, authentic books are, in contrast to graded readers, understood as books that were not written for language teaching purposes or with the needs of FL learners in mind. Although graded readers have been and partly still are prominent in FLL, the last decades slowly experienced a change in favour of using authentic texts instead of carefully created ones. In fact, authentic texts offer various advantages, also for beginner EFL learners, particularly when carefully chosen and possibly skilfully adapted. In weighing the evidence for and against authentic texts and for and against adapting the text, this book follows the position of generally not adapting texts but sticking to authentic English picture books for the present study.

In the study described in this book, authentic English picture books were thus used for reading at the primary school level. They are one type of children's books and were defined, in short, as authentic books that follow a storyline with an intricate interrelation of visual and textual elements, both of which crucial for understanding. The concept of story grammars was taken into consideration for this definition, as simple concept books are excluded from the study. The notion that also more complex picture books might still be too childish for primary school EFL learners was discussed critically, but based on previous research experiences with picture books in the primary school EFL classroom there is good reason to assume that these are, when carefully selected, still suitable for the respective age group.

With a focus on reading, there are numerous reasons, for the most part based on empirical data, for reading (picture) books in the EFL classroom. On the one hand, they support learners' social and emotional development and skilfully integrate language and content as well as cultural aspects. On the other hand, readers' FL development can benefit from regular reading, although claims regarding gains such as vocabulary growth and the acquisition of grammar or spelling competence are controversial and depend on a number of factors.

Despite these advantages, books and texts are rarely used for reading in the primary school EFL classroom, mostly for fears of overtaxing the learners or time constraints. Although curricula require that authentic texts like picture books should be utilised in reading activities, teachers for the most part only use them for storytelling. Hence, there is currently a desideratum with regard to using authentic English picture books for reading tasks in the primary school EFL classroom. However, some pioneer projects have been conducted and results provide the first and tentative evidence that young and beginner EFL learners show a keen interest in reading such English texts and are equal to this task. The present study thus complies with the current wish that more challenging reading activities should be introduced in the primary school EFL classroom, including the use of picture books for reading. Therefore, this book provides further insights into and evidence about reading authentic English picture books at the primary school level.

6. Supporting the Reading of Authentic English Picture Books in the Primary School EFL Classroom

Abstract: Based on the notions of challenge and support in teaching, this chapter provides an overview of how (young) learners can be supported in FL reading tasks. Different supportive techniques are presented, brought into the broader context of reading demands and then discussed critically with regard to their benefits for (young) FL learners.

Reading a long and coherent EFL text is a challenge for young learners (Frisch, 2014a: 14), especially because they have just mastered or are still in the process of mastering learning to read and write in their L1. Thus, Chapter 6.1 will firstly outline the notions of challenge and support in learning and based on that on the one hand explain why it is justified to confront pupils with demanding reading tasks but on the other hand consider the necessity of scaffolding to bridge the gap between the demands of a reading text and the learners' current competence. With particular emphasis on the importance of task support, Chapter 6.2 will then provide an overview of supportive measures that can help young learners to read authentic English picture books. All the scaffolding devices mentioned will be further explained in the subsequent subchapters.

Because of a lack of experience with reading in the primary school EFL classroom in teaching practice as well as in research, no clear-cut recommendations have yet been made with regard to which scaffolds support young learners most effectively. The explanations in this chapter hence rely on well-established concepts from SLA research as well as on initial research results from various studies, also with older learners; but the supportive devices' relevance for reading with young EFL learners still needs to be thoroughly investigated.[94]

6.1 The Notions of Challenge and Support

As was outlined in Chapter 5.5, authentic English picture books are currently only rarely used for reading in the primary school EFL classroom. Thus, this section will discuss arguments that support the idea of challenging young EFL learners by reading such demanding texts. With a view to supporting learners in

---

94 See Chapters 6.9, 8.1.3 and 9.3 for more detail on how the use of supportive devices was integrated into the empirical study of this book.

this task, additionally the notion of scaffolding will be explained in the context of balancing task demand and task support.

6.1.1 The Argument for Challenging Young EFL Learners through Reading

Learners' abilities are often underestimated by adults; a phenomenon that is repeatedly found in education (Spiegel & Selter, 2003: 19; Young, 1993: 453) and also holds true for EFL reading at the primary school level. As seen in Chapter 3.4, this tendency was, for example, shown in the EVENING study (Engel et al., 2009) as well as in the BIG study (BIG-Kreis, 2015). For instance, the teachers who were involved in the EVENING study expressed some major reservations about the reading test that was used, anticipating that it would be too hard and too complex for their pupils. However, the study showed that these reservations were unsubstantiated and not supported by the research results (Paulick & Groot-Wilken, 2009: 180). In other words, the young EFL learners' reading competences were underestimated by their EFL teachers. Consequently, the researchers suggested that reading comprehension should not only be tested at the word and sentence level, as done in the EVENING study, but should also be assessed at the text level (Paulick & Groot-Wilken, 2009: 195). However, as Chapters 3.4 and 5.5 have shown, this has seldom been done to the present.

Rather than underestimating learners' abilities and being afraid of overtaxing them, it is in fact important and justifiable that teachers challenge learners and confront them with tasks that draw them out of their comfort zone. A contemporary concept relating to the question of challenging children is Bartnitzky's (2009: 320f) notion of 'support through challenge'.[95] In brief, this concept entails supporting pupils at their individual level by challenging them at just that level. Bartnitzky (2009: 322) argues that all children should be deliberately confronted with complex tasks in order to activate their strengths. He further claims that learning means overcoming difficulties and that learners only face difficulties when they are pushed to their limits through appropriate challenges (Bartnitzky, 2010: 10). Hence, challenging tasks should be used in order to opening up learners' opportunities for development and gauge how far they can be pushed.

Along the same lines as Bartnitzky's (2009) argument, a number of different authors have also suggested challenging young EFL learners more than is currently being done. Böttger (2013: 44), for example, states that children are capable of, can and want to do more than what is asked of them. In particular, he

---

95 Author's translation for '*Fördern durch Fordern*'.

supports the idea of early biliteracy and states that this contributes to challenging learners sufficiently. Börner (1997: 81f) supports this point in arguing that young EFL learners want to be challenged, want to be confronted with challenging tasks, and that one can usually expect them to be capable of doing more than one would assume on the basis of their FL production abilities. In other words, their receptive skills, that is listening and reading competence, go beyond their speaking and writing skills and should thus be supported at a level that exceeds their actual FL production. Likewise, Wright (1995: 3) indicates that "children can be helped to understand quite complex stories in language well above their own active command." Thus, all three researchers from the field of TEFL suggest using challenging reading (and writing) tasks with young EFL learners. This notion complies with what Meyer (2010: 13) outlined about EFL classroom materials: He states that one of three main criteria for selecting appropriate classroom materials is that it should be challenging.

On the subject of challenging reading tasks, Bleyhl (2000a: 85) points out that the process of learning to read and write in a FL proceeds more smoothly and easily when the learning environment is rich and challenging. To support his argument he quotes from Smith (1978 in Bleyhl, 2000a: 87): "It is so easy to make learning to read difficult." Bleyhl (2000c: 15) explains that pupils who are in the process of acquiring FL reading competences need an arrangement of activities and reading tasks that are challenging and help them to develop their capability and potential. It is the teacher's role to challenge learners by providing them with "extensive meaningful comprehensible input" (Piepho, 2000: 55) as, for example, found in authentic children's books.

With regard to input, Meyer (2010: 13) argues that "challenging input is one of the main pillars of foreign language acquisition" (Meyer, 2010: 13). This was already established by Krashen in the 1980s. Krashen (1982) explains L2 learning through his monitor model, which consists of five different hypotheses. One of them is the input hypothesis, which states that "we acquire by understanding language that contains structure a bit beyond our current level of competence (i+1)" (Krashen, 1982: 21; italics in original). This implies that learners acquire language only when they understand the language they are exposed to and when this language contains structures that are slightly beyond their actual competence (Krashen, 1982: 21). Input should be comprehensible for the learner and contain i+1; 'i' being the learner's current proficiency level and '+1' being just one step above that. According to Krashen (1989: 441), "more comprehensible input, aural and written, results in more language acquisition" (also see Chapter 5.4.3). Therefore, the input hypothesis is a strong argument for providing young

EFL learners with many opportunities to read EFL texts that they can understand but are just slightly above their level. Potentially, authentic English picture books fulfil this demand. According to Mishan (2005: 22), Krashen's input hypothesis justifies the use of authentic texts in the EFL classroom, as long as they are, to a certain extent, comprehensible.

Challenging young EFL learners through reading authentic English picture books can support FLL in that it can mean that learners work in their zone of proximal development (ZPD) (Vygotsky, 1978), a well-established concept of learning and development. Vygotsky (1978) states that children develop and learn when working in their ZPD. The basis of this concept is that learning should match the child's current level, referred to as the 'actual developmental level', which describes what learners can do independently and on their own (Vygotsky, 1978: 84). However, children can outperform their actual developmental level with support from others and are capable of mastering slightly more complex tasks. The difference between what children can do independently and what children can achieve with assistance is referred to as the ZPD. It is defined as *"the distance between the actual developmental level as determined by independent problem solving and the level of potential development as determined through problem solving under adult guidance or in collaboration with more capable peers"* (Vygotsky, 1978: 86; italics in original). In other words, what learners can do alone is what they can achieve at their actual performance level, while what they can achieve with help is their potential developmental level.

The ZPD defines what is in the process of development (Vygotsky, 1978: 86). As Vygotsky (1978: 87) puts it, "what a child can do with assistance today she will be able to do by herself tomorrow." Hence, the teacher should pay special attention to those functions that are about to develop or are just in the process of developing, as those are the functions open to instructional intervention and offer great learning potential (Lantolf & Poehner, 2014: 150). In the context of FL reading at the primary school level, this could be reading at text level. When learners are capable of reading at the word and sentence levels (actual performance level), the next step would be to read at the text level (potential performance level); for example picture books.

However, reading demands should be realistic and not overtax learners. Any task solved within the ZPD is a task "within reach" (Lantolf & Poehner, 2014: 149), meaning that it can realistically be accomplished when the learner is provided with support and assistance. In support of this point, Garbe (2010: 12) elaborates on the importance of conveying a positive self-concept and self-efficacy with regard to reading to the learners, so that they develop the belief of 'I can read' instead of

'I cannot read'; an attitude that contributes greatly to the reading competence of children. Teachers thus have to be careful to not demand too much from the learners and to ensure that the learners become confident and competent readers of authentic English picture books.

In sum, learners need challenging but manageable tasks in order to be able to develop their full potential and advance in their process of acquiring skills and competences. Considering the many positive aspects of providing young EFL learners with challenging tasks, it seems to be justifiable to assume that they can be beneficially challenged by reading authentic English picture books. However, appropriate task support is necessary, and this will be elaborated on in the following sections.

6.1.2 Scaffolding and the Balance between Task Demand and Task Support

Even if it is acceptable and appropriate to challenge young EFL learners, as outlined in the previous subchapter, they should not be overtaxed. When young FL learners are asked to read an authentic FL text, such as a picture book, they might need support for doing so. Therefore, this subchapter seeks to explore the balance between task demand and necessary task support.

Generally speaking, tasks should not be too simple, so as not to bore the learner and risk a loss of interest and motivation; however, at the same time they should not be too hard, in order to avoid frustrating the learner and cause continuous feelings of failure, disappointment, discouragement and a loss of motivation (Cameron, 2001: 26). Good tasks should hence challenge every individual learner at their current level and allow the learner to complete the task based on his/her individual abilities (MSW NRW, 2008a: 13f). According to Bartnitzky (2010: 10), the teacher has to create a learning environment in which children find the support they need in order to overcome difficulties when confronted with challenging tasks. Still, it is important to find a "dynamic relationship between demands and support" (Cameron, 2001: 26) to achieve the right balance between challenge and support. Cameron stresses that "if a task provides too much support, then learners will not be 'stretched." Therefore, not too much but just enough support should be provided.

The idea of supporting learners appropriately is congruent with Vygotsky's notion of the ZPD, which was already outlined in the previous subchapter. In order to reach their assisted performance levels and hence work in the ZPD, learners need assistance (Vygotsky, 1978: 87). Learners are capable of reaching their potential developmental level when assisted by someone or something, like a more knowledgeable other or a supportive device (Swain, Kinnear & Steinmann, 2011). Lantolf (2000: 17) explains this phenomenon as follows: "The ZPD is the difference between what a person can achieve when acting alone and what the same person can accomplish when acting with support from someone else and/or cultural artifacts."

This idea of assistance has often been brought into context with Wood, Bruner and Ross' (1976) concept of scaffolding. Scaffolding is a process that supports learners in solving a problem or carrying out a task. In FLL, scaffolding includes supporting the production as well as the comprehension of language (VanPatten & Benati, 2010: 144f). Vygotsky's original idea was that an expert or more capable other provides assistance, whilst recent work suggests that it can also be a peer of equal ability (Saville-Troike, 2012: 119f; Swain et al., 2011: 26). Further, the scope of who provides support has been extended in more recent works. While Vygotsky explained that assistance is provided by a more knowledgeable other person, Swain et al. (2011: 21) and Lantolf (2000: 17) state that the (expert) other does not necessarily need to be animate but could also be a symbolic or material cultural artefact (also see Chapter 6.1.1). With regard to FL reading, collaborative reading among peers can assist the reading process just as well as help from a teacher (=expert) can. Likewise, a dictionary that provides learners with the translation of an unknown word can also function as a scaffold (Swain et al., 2011: 21). Thus, support in reading can derive from the teacher or other learners, but can also derive from inanimate supportive devices such as dictionaries (see Chapters 6.2 and following for more details).

Within the co-construction of knowledge in the ZPD, assistance (=scaffolding) is given when needed and withdrawn systematically to enable self-regulation (Swain et al., 2011: 26). That means that support is provided for the learners as long as they need support, but as soon as they are capable of solving a task independently, the assistance is carefully withdrawn. This conforms to the idea of appropriately balancing task demand and task support. With regard to reading picture books, this implies that learners are likely to develop the competence to read these books independently over time. They might need support for reading the first books, but might not need the same amount of support for reading further ones. As Wood et al. (1976: 90) point out, the scaffolding process not only enables the learners to successfully complete a task beyond their capacity, but it may also result in development of task competence.

Massler and Ioannou-Georgiou (2010: 63) distinguish between input-oriented scaffolding, which are techniques that focus on making input comprehensible for learners, and output-oriented scaffolding, which are techniques that focus on the active participation in and production of the target language in class. Concerning reading, particularly the comprehension of written language is important. Hence, written input as found in authentic texts needs to be made comprehensible by means of input-oriented scaffolding. Scaffolding in reading "reduces the cognitive and linguistic load of the content/input" and thus makes the written input accessible and understandable (Meyer, 2010: 15). The process of reading should thus be supported in order to help the learners to understand the written text, but without providing them with the full comprehension of it (Meyer, 2010: 15).

Generally, individual learners will need individual support. They will use and prefer different devices to support their individual learning processes. This is based on individual differences in learners with regard to their learning styles, their levels of competence and their individual needs.[96] Catering for individual learners and enabling individual learners to read authentic texts therefore involves providing differentiated reading tasks with regards to task demand and task support. In order to create a differentiated reading environment, firstly teachers should adjust their expectations to the competences of individual learners, and secondly teachers should provide a range of supportive means to allow differentiated support based on the learners' needs and preferences (Doms, 2012: 61).

In sum, young learners need various individual scaffolds to master the task of reading authentic picture books. However, these scaffolds should balance task demand and task support in order to ensure that "learners can do the task" (Cameron, 2001: 26) but at the same time challenge the learners at exactly their current level of competence. Still, despite support, reading demands should be realistic and not overtax learners.

6.2 An Overview of Support for Reading

As outlined above, young EFL learners need support for reading authentic English books: "To make sure that students successfully deal with authentic materials [...] it is essential for students to receive ample support" (Meyer, 2010: 15). As young EFL learners in Germany have not explicitly learnt how to read in English, there is reason to assume that their limited reading abilities have to be

---

96 Individual differences that are important with regard to FL reading include, for example, reading motivation, L1 reading competence, reading behaviour, L2 competence, knowledge and transfer of reading strategies (for more information see Artelt, Stanat, Scheider & Schiefele, 2001; Chiu, Hong & Hu, 2015; Diehr & Frisch, 2010b: 146; Frisch, 2013: 215; Koda, 2004: 20f; Lightbown et al., 2002: 453; Steck, 2009: 104).

supplemented by supportive devices in order to enable them to cope with reading in EFL (Aristov & Haudeck, 2013: 50).

Until now, research has hardly established what kind of support helps primary school EFL learners in Germany to read authentic picture books. Only two studies have been conducted on reading picture books at the primary school level, and these provide initial ideas for support: Kolb (2013) reports the effective use of an audio-recording; and Kolb (2013) as well as Reichart-Wallrabenstein (2004) report on support through cooperative reading settings (Reichart-Wallrabenstein, 2004). However, support in reading can derive from various further sources, as already indicated in Chapter 6.1.2. Figure 12 therefore provides an overview of possibilities for supporting FL reading:

Figure 12: An overview of possibilities for supporting reading.

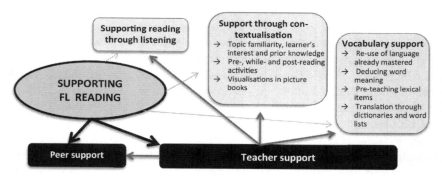

First and foremost, teachers are responsible for organising and initiating support. They can either encourage peer support in that cooperative reading settings are initiated, or provide support in the form of different supportive devices (see grey boxes in Figure 12). Such supportive devices include different means of vocabulary support, different means of support through contextualisation and the option of supporting reading through listening. The following subchapters will elaborate on these.

6.3 Teacher Support in Reading: Autonomy versus Guidance

Teachers can scaffold and support learners in reading and are a major source of support for them. However, with the aim of educating independent readers, finding the correct balance between teacher guidance and learner autonomy can be difficult and will thus be discussed in this section.

The notion of autonomy in learning has its roots in the constructivist approach to learning and teaching (Ushioda, 2011: 11). Learners should construct knowledge themselves through interaction with their environment and are said to learn best by doing so. Learner autonomy includes the assumption that the learners understand what they learn, why they are learning it, how they are learning and to what extent they are successful in learning (Little, 1999: 13). Learner autonomy in language learning and teaching emerged in the wake of CLT (Mishan, 2005: 36), where it became increasingly important that FL learners got to know how to effectively use the FL for communicative purposes. As such, learner autonomy in language learning means that learners "assume responsibility for their own language learning progress" (Lennon, 2012a: 9).

In teaching, learner autonomy implies a shift from teacher-centred forms of teaching to more open forms of learning (Klippel & Doff, 2007: 289). More open forms of learning naturally entail different roles for both teachers and learners.[97] While the teacher has to take a step back and be more the initiator and guide of learning processes, the learners are at the centre of attention and more responsible for organising their learning.[98] Corresponding with these roles, more open learning settings support learner autonomy (Waschk, 2008: 46).

However, English teaching in the primary school is often very much determined by teacher-centeredness (Waschk, 2008: 13). This is due to the fact that the learners need a role model who provides them with language input before they can implement and practise the language more independently. Nevertheless, the autonomy of young language learners can already be fostered in the primary school EFL classroom (Lennon, 2012b: 42ff) and ways of opening up the primary school EFL classroom have been suggested by several researchers and teachers (see, e.g., Elsner, 2010; Leeck, 2012; Reckermann, 2017; Waschk, 2008). As such, learners are made responsible for their FLL step by step. This can, for example, include giving them a choice of reading material or a ragne of supportive devices to choose from.

Thus, supporting autonomy in the primary school EFL classroom also includes a shift from storytelling to reading books independently. Through storytelling, the young learners get an idea about strategies to understand a children's book (i.e., using the pictures for support, tolerating ambiguity in comprehension, primarily focusing on reading for gist, etc.). These strategies can also be

---

97 For a detailed discussion see Waschk (2008: 33ff).
98 Still, phases of teacher-centeredness are not fully redundant (see MSW NRW, 2008b: 14).

applied in reading, where children are made responsible for making sense of an authentic text themselves.

In general, the ability to read is a key to being an autonomous learner. For example, the educational curriculum of Baden-Württemberg states that reading skills are the most important competence for autonomous learning in all school areas (MKJS BW, 2004: 44). Being able to read and understand texts is not only the basis for autonomous learning in school, but outside the school context as well (Steck, 2009: 17). Doing a search on the Internet, for example, only works successfully when the searcher possesses sufficient reading skills. That is why Westphal Irwin (2007: 16) states that teaching FL reading should aim at educating "active rather than passive readers." Hence, the goal of effective reading programmes is to create independent readers (Gorsuch & Taguchi, 2010: 31). Young learners should learn how to find, read and understand texts independently and how to autonomously seek help when they encounter problems.

Independent readers can autonomously read and understand texts that match their current level of competence and can autonomously seek support when needed in order to improve their reading comprehension. This implies that independent readers know how to enhance their own reading comprehension and know about the range of supportive devices that can be helpful. Autonomy in reading also involves choosing a reading text that learners are interested in and reading it out of their personal interest. All these skills and sub-skills of autonomous reading need to be practised. Learning to learn is the paramount aim of learner autonomy (Haudeck, 2011: 270f). To foster its attainment, learner autonomy should be practised as early as possible (Pinter, 2006: 113; Reichart-Wallrabenstein, 2004: 559). In short, EFL reading should be supported early in the process of FLL in order to eventually become independent readers.

However, as indicated above, this process needs teacher guidance and the teacher plays a crucial role for learners in becoming independent EFL readers. The teacher is the initiator of a language learning environment that supports autonomy in that he/she acts as a "facilitator, supporter and guide" (Lennon, 2012a: 9). The teacher's role is hence to arrange the learning environment (Meyer, 2004: 120ff) in that he/she provides meaningful texts and reading tasks. To this end, teachers can pre-select a collection of suitable books and provide a range of supportive devices as discussed below. More so, it is the teacher's task to be present during the reading process and provide help "in the form of guided reading and explicit process instruction when needed" (Westphal Irwin, 2007: 17). The teacher is available for questions and acts as an advisor or as a guide while the children are independently working on their reading tasks. This presence of the teacher is very important, even if learners work more autonomously. Although they are given freedom of choice and responsibility whenever possible, fostering autonomy does not mean leaving the learners alone and letting them figure out their own learning. Still, learners should learn to help themselves (Pinter, 2006: 99) and not turn to the teacher whenever a minor problem or question arises. Lastly, it is also the teacher's role to include reflection phases, which reflect on the reading process and, for example, aim at explaining certain reading strategies. Such phases guide the learners in becoming independent readers through developing a range of successful strategies for the task of reading. In brief, with the supportive guidance of the teacher and with continuous practice, FL learners can ultimately become independent FL readers.

6.4 Peer Support in Reading: Cooperative Reading Settings

As outlined at the end of Chapter 6.1.2, not only experts but also peers of equal ability levels can support learners. This implies that in cooperative reading settings learners can scaffold each other in order to reach text comprehension.

The notion of cooperative (FL) learning has long been established in the primary school (EFL) classroom and the supportive notion of cooperation is generally acknowledged by teachers and researchers (see, e.g., Brüning & Saum, 2009; Green & Green, 2005; Wysocki, 2010). A cooperative teaching approach makes maximum use of cooperative activities involving peer support or coaching and emphasises cooperative activities in pair and small group work (Richards & Rodgers, 2014: 244). Green and Green (2005: 12) explain that when working cooperatively, learners can solve more difficult tasks and their overall performance level is higher (also see ZPD in Chapter 6.1.1). As such, cooperation with other learners can lead to collaborative performance that surpasses performance based on individual competence alone.

With regard to reading, Westphal Irwin (2007: 16) suggests that learners should work together cooperatively and be engaged in meaningful interaction with other readers in order to share constructed meaning as well as reading strategies. Cooperating with another learner can result in better reading comprehension because learners can mutually help each other in constructing and discussing the meaning of a FL text. This implies that learners read the same reading text (see Coelho, 1992: 132). As a general feature of cooperative learning, one important aspect is sharing material in order to encourage cooperation (Green & Green, 2005: 88). Thus, learners might have to share a reading text to be able to read cooperatively.

In spite of the many benefits cooperative learning offers, Brüning and Saum (2009: 16) point out that cooperative learning should be alternated from time to time with individual working phases for pupils to first get the chance to deal with the materials by themselves so they can have enough time to become familiar with them before working together with others. This is supported by one of the most prominent techniques of cooperative learning: "think-pair-share" (Brüning & Saum, 2009: 17).[99] According to this principle, pupils work individually in the phase of thinking, before sharing information with others. Brüning and Saum (2009: 16) argue that working together constructively cannot work unless there has been preceding individual work.

When applied to reading, they suggest that learners should first of all read the text individually (and also with their own copy of it) before discussing it with a peer (Brüning & Saum, 2009: 104). This is linked to individual differences in reading and the need for differentiated reading tasks. Frisch (2014b: 31) points out that when children read silently and for themselves, they are allowed their reading pace, reading strategies, pauses and own imagination. Thus, reading alone allows for the reader's own reading processes and permits individualised reading. Such processes could be hindered in cooperative reading settings. Thus, cooperation in reading should be organised with care and a possible phase of individual reading might be beneficial for a follow-up phase of cooperation.

As a final note, it appears that not all learners can and want to work in cooperation with others. This raises the question whether all learners benefit from cooperative learning (Richards & Rodgers, 2014: 255). Therefore, teachers as well as researchers sometimes leave it up to the learners to choose whether or not to work cooperatively or on their own (see, e.g., Kolb, 2013: 34; Reichart-Wallrabenstein, 2004: 567).

6.5 Support through Contextualisation of Reading Picture Books

In addition to the broader concept of teacher and peer support, support in FLL settings can also derive from "the contextualisation of language" (Cameron, 2001: 27). With regard to reading authentic books in a FL, this suggests that the reading process as well as the book itself should be put into a context for

---

99 The principle of 'think-pair-share' was not originally coined by Brüning and Saum but is a lot older than their book. They state that Frank Lyman from the University of Maryland was the first to talk about it, while it was later on picked up by several others (Brüning & Saum, 2009: 16).

the children. In practice, this can be done by ensuring the learners' familiarity with the topic and the content of the books, by choosing books that the learning group would find interesting and by means of the visuals in picture books which provide a context for the text. Moreover, embedding the reading process into the context of pre-, while- and post-reading activities serves for orientation. These four aspects will be detailed in the following sections.

6.5.1 Topic Familiarity, Learners' Interests and Prior Knowledge

Generally, reading in the EFL classroom should be embedded into the context of a topic, because familiar topics and content serve as a form of support through contextualisation (Cameron, 2001: 27). As outlined in Chapter 2.3, units in the primary school EFL classroom are based on topics, so that any books chosen should be embedded into the context of that topic. Legutke et al. (2009: 83) stress how important it is to make literary texts accessible to the learners by framing them in a thematic unit. When, for example, a teaching unit deals with the topic 'animals', a book that fits this context would be 'The Gruffalo' (Donaldson & Scheffler, 1999). This ensures topic familiarity as well as knowledge about the book's basic vocabulary.

Additionally, reading comprehension is enhanced when pupils are already familiar with the topic of a book and possess previous knowledge about it (Hu Hsueh-chao & Nation, 2000: 404). Using prior knowledge, including world as well as subject-specific knowledge, is a well-known reading strategy (see Chapter 4.6.5) and helps readers to extract the meaning from a text. Previous knowledge and topic familiarity facilitate and allow top-down reading processes which are needed to read and understand a reading text (see Chapter 4.4.1). For obvious reasons it is difficult to read about a topic such as astrophysics if one does not know anything about it; so prior knowledge reduces the cognitive load of the complex reading process. Moreover, background knowledge of or even personal experience with a topic allow learners to make guesses about the course of the story and anticipate the plot of the book. Pulido (2007: 161) has reviewed the findings of several studies and concludes that there is "ample empirical support for the positive effects of background knowledge on L2 text comprehension, namely that comprehension is enhanced when readers possess prior knowledge of the topic."

Furthermore, Carell (1988: 2) points out that cultural knowledge is important to fully understand an L2 text. Erten and Razi (2009: 62) have reviewed several studies which provide evidence that cultural familiarity has positive effects on reading comprehension. Also in their own study (Erten & Razi: 2009: 70) they found a strong positive correlation between cultural background knowledge and reading comprehension. The picture book 'Santa's Secret' (Dumbleton & Jellett, 2013), for instance, can only be fully understood if the children know about Australian Christmas traditions.

A controversial idea for providing topic familiarity and previous knowledge is to use equivalent books in the learners' L1. Whilst teachers in the English classroom should use as much English as possible at all levels, some selected situations allow a careful use of the L1 (Klippel, 2000: 29; Schmid-Schönbein, 2008: 65ff; Wessel, 2012: 57f). With regard to reading authentic English picture books in the primary school EFL classroom, Appel and Wilson (2010: 8) suggest that using the L1 German is a resource for understanding authentic English texts. One suggestion is that learners should first read a text in German to become familiar with its content before reading it in English (Appel & Wilson, 2010: 8). According to Butzkamm and Caldwell (2009: 184), re-reading a book in a FL is the best opportunity to bridge the gap between the highly demanding nature of authentic texts and a beginner learner's competence level. Another suggestion is that teachers give a short summary of a book's content in the L1 before the pupils read the FL text (Appel & Wilson, 2010: 8). However, this approach should be regarded critically, as already knowing the overall plot or even the whole content of a book might reduce the learners' reading motivation and interest in the book; an important factor in reading as will be seen below. Worse still, the appeal of the authentic book can get lost. So ultimately, L1 book equivalents do not appear necessary to achieve previous knowledge; other more interest-raising techniques exist for this.

Besides prior knowledge about the book's topic, it is of crucial importance that reading texts comply with the learners' interests. The learners' interest in the topic and text and also the learners' reading motivation are important factors for successful reading comprehension. Cameron (2001: 27) argues that support through contextualisation derives from content that the learners can engage with and link to their interests. Likewise, Westphal Irwin (2007: 160) argues that "comprehension is improved when students are motivated and interested." She points out that one way of enhancing the reader's motivation is choosing books that deal with topics that the readers can relate to and that are of interest to them. This enables the learners to identify with the story and attach to it emotionally, but at the same time ensures topic familiarity.

In sum, being familiar with a book's topic in terms of previous world, subject-specific and cultural knowledge eases the reading process and leads to better reading comprehension. At the same time, the learners' interests should not be neglected in the choice of reading texts.

6.5.2 Pre-, While-, and Post-Reading Activities

As outlined in the previous subchapter, previous knowledge is a prerequisite for effective reading processes, and should thus be activated before reading. This is usually done by means of carefully selected pre-reading activities. In the pre-reading stage, teachers prepare the learners for reading the text (see, e.g., Gehring, 2004: 74; Haß, 2006: 88; Hedge, 2000: 192), and activating prior knowledge in this phase can in turn support the activation of top-down processing in reading compression (see Chapters 4.4.1 and 6.5.1). This is the first of in total three stages of reading.

The well-known principle of embedding and sequencing activities into the context of pre-, while- and post-task activities also applies to reading activities (see Brewster & Ellis, 2002: 113; Haß, 2006: 87; Klippel & Doff, 2007: 83). Embedding the reading process into such a meaningful framework can support the reading process and thus the reading of any FL text should be approached by following these three stages (Aristov & Haudeck, 2013: 48).

For contextualisation of reading, the pre-reading phase is most important, but also while- and post-reading tasks serve for orientation and thus support reading. The while-reading phase is used to accompany the actual reading process of the pupils and purposeful while-reading activities help learners in understanding a text (Klippel & Doff, 2007: 84; Krüsmann, 2003: 49). Post-reading or follow-up activities are conducted after the actual reading process in order to creatively deal with the content and/or the language of a story (Müller-Hartmann & Schocker-v. Ditfurth, 2014: 82).

6.5.3 Visualisations

The visualisations found in picture books play a further important role in providing contextualisation, since picture books, by definition, offer textual as well as visual elements that complement each other to establish meaning (see Chapter 5.3.3). Deane and Rumlich (2013: 190) see great potential in this combination of visual and verbal context, because it develops the pupils' ability to deduce meaning from both areas.

The supportive function of visuals for FL reading has often been highlighted. With regard to the young learners' limited FL competence, "the interplay between text and pictures can help overcome linguistic difficulties" (Kolb, 2013: 35). Chapter 5.2.3 has already shown that the authentic language of authentic English children's books may, in places, be too difficult and complex; hence, the support offered by pictures might alleviate this problem to a certain extent. Meyer (2010: 14) points out that visuals in a text "serve to illustrate and clarify complex matters presented in a foreign language." Likewise, Böttger (2005: 77) says that storybook visuals can support the learners' understanding of the story even if the language is sometimes too difficult. According to Legutke et al. (2009: 78), the visuals provide or add information that the reader cannot extract from the text.

Kolb (2013: 36) also investigated the use of visuals in reading picture books in the primary school EFL classroom and found that young FL learners indeed used the pictures extensively for support and that the pictures turned out to be a great help. She also established that the learners focused predominantly on the text and did not try to understand the story by only looking at the pictures (Kolb, 2013: 36). The latter strategy is nevertheless a factor that EFL teachers need to guard against in order to ensure that the learners are indeed engaging with the FL.

Picture books also offer the advantage that they foster the learners' visual literacy (Aristov & Haudeck, 2013: 46), which is the "skill of comprehending visual representations" (Westphal Irwin, 2007: 99). The notion of visual literacy when reading picture books implies making meaning out of reading the pictures (Bland, 2013a: 32). Children partly learn to read and understand the pictures in order to understand a story. While reading picture books, in which both language and text are crucial for understanding, learners have to carry out the complex procedure of decoding the verbal and visual mode and their interaction in a text (Burwitz-Melzer, 2013: 63). As such, picture books are an example of multimodal input.

Cameron (2001: 169), however, adds that the comprehensibility of a story sometimes depends on "how well the pictures [...] support the meaning of the words." Therefore, any visuals in a picture book should correspond to the story's content if they are supposed to serve for support in reading comprehension. Given that "you read what you expect to read" (Haß, 2006: 84), it is clear that pictures which match the text can enhance comprehension and at the same time help learners to build up an expectation of what they are about to read.[100]

6.6 Vocabulary Support

While reading a text in the L2, the learners will inevitably encounter some unfamiliar words and phrases. Young EFL learners in particular only have a limited command of English vocabulary, and some words in authentic books will be unknown

---

100   See Lewis (2001) and Nikolajeva and Scott (2000) for more information about the congruence of visual and textual elements in picture books, reaching from symmetry at the one end and contradiction at the other.

to them. Thus, many teachers and researchers see vocabulary knowledge as a major prerequisite as well as a causative factor in reading comprehension (Hu Hsueh-chao & Nation, 2000: 403f). This is exactly the point of the threshold hypothesis in FL reading, as outlined in Chapter 4.2, which makes FL reading a language problem and seeks to define a threshold of FL knowledge without which successful FL reading comprehension cannot be attained. There are certain means that can provide vocabulary support to young EFL readers. These include the re-use of language that has already been mastered, strategies to deduce the meaning of unknown words, pre-teaching of lexical items and the availability of translations through dictionaries or word lists. The following subchapters will provide more information on these means.

6.6.1 Re-Use of Language Already Mastered and a Threshold of Unknown Lexical Items

According to Cameron, language support in a FL comes from the "re-use of language already mastered" (Cameron: 2001: 27). With regard to reading books this means that it is important that they contain words and phrases which the pupils already know and can recognise. A study on FL reading comprehension showed that learners' comprehension scores in a text increase as the coverage of known words increases – the more words learners know, the more they understand (Hu Hsueh-chao & Nation, 2000: 419).

Young EFL learners will already know a certain number of words in a picture book, especially when the book corresponds to the topic or topics dealt with in class. Hu Hsueh-chao and Nation (2000: 406) point out that more than 90 % of the words in novels for young readers of English derive from the 2,000 most common English words, with almost 85 % deriving from the 1,000 most common words. Young EFL learners should already know at least some of these very frequently encountered words and are certainly familiar with a number of simple structural words which are used in almost every lesson and in almost every book (e.g., 'is', 'it', 'and' or 'the'). They will also be familiar with words they have learnt in their English lessons. It is important that books selected for reading refer to a topic dealt with in the classroom, and to ensure that a certain number of words are already familiar to the pupils, in addition to some common words that are familiar to them anyway.

The re-use of already known language is in line with the principle of a spiral curriculum, a notion which implies that skills (including vocabulary) are gradually built up, always constructing new knowledge on the basis of what is already known (Börner, 2000: 99; Böttger, 2005: 23). Books contain words that are already known and also introduce learners to unknown vocabulary. Thus, the activity of reading picture books is also in accord with Krashen's comprehensible input hypothesis, which postulates that input should contain i+1 (see Chapter 6.1.1).

Still, the extent to which young FL learners should be familiar with the vocabulary of a given authentic picture book has not been clearly established thus far by research. As a rule of thumb, Cameron (2001: 169) indicates that a story can only be understood if it does not contain too much new language and the overall total of new words should not be too high. The number of words that need to be known depends on the type of text (Laufer, 2013: 867). Several researchers have attempted to define a threshold with a minimum score of words necessary for understanding. These thresholds range from 65 % to 98 %, leading Hu Hsueh-chao and Nation (2000: 410) to conclude that research "so far has not been able to provide a clear guideline about the optimal density of unknown words." However, they also explain that any threshold is always influenced by other factors such as overall reading skills, background knowledge or other supportive factors that also contribute to comprehension (Hu Hsueh-chao & Nation, 2000: 419).

A unique feature of a picture book is the presence of visuals which certainly reduce the necessity to understand each word and enhance the possibility of ignoring unknown words without risking significant comprehension difficulties. Until now, however, no study has been conducted to provide evidence for a vocabulary threshold for picture books, in which the visualisations potentially limit the threshold for unknown words. Nevertheless, the strong visual support they provide should not be underestimated in terms of comprehension (Nation, 2006: 76).

In sum, the comprehension of a reading text is supported through the re-use of language already mastered, and therefore teachers should ensure that learners are already familiar with a certain number of words in a picture book before having to read the book for understanding.

6.6.2 Pre-Teaching Lexical Items

As just outlined, learners should know a certain number of words in a reading text. Mihara (2011: 51) as well as Krashen (1989: 442) thus suggest pre-teaching and the deliberate study of relevant vocabulary as a technique effective for text comprehension; and generally, pre-teaching crucial vocabulary is a common pre-reading activity (see Chapter 6.5.2).

In the EFL classroom, it is advisable to take a close look at the book and its topic in order to explicitly pre-teach selected words that are important for the story. As nouns tend to be overtaught at the primary school level (Engel, 2009: 199; Reckermann, 2014: 29), it is important to embrace other word classes as well, particularly prepositions, verbs and adjectives. Which words exactly and also how many words should be pre-taught largely depends on the individual books and it is very difficult to make any general statements about this.[101] The pool of pre-taught words should certainly include unknown words which are crucial for understanding the meaning of the whole book and are at the same time difficult to decipher, even with the help of decoding strategies (see Chapter 6.6.3).

In addition to words and phrases, some grammatical structures found in a book can also be taught before reading. Rymarczyk (2010) points out that pre-teaching and dealing with certain grammatical structures in a book can support comprehension. Raising the pupils' awareness for typical structures in the book, which are usually found in repetitive chunks, helps pupils to predict what comes next and to make sense of the content of the story. In any case, lexis and grammar are not separable, but are tightly interwoven in that one influences and determines the other (Cameron, 2001: 72). Especially with young learners, this highlights the role of chunks which combine lexis and grammar and are accessible with a relatively low command of the FL.

That said, not all words, chunks and structures in an authentic book can be pre-taught, and should not be, either. Haß (2006: 86) cautions that pre-teaching too many words might give pupils the impression that the text is only being read for the sake of learning the words, phrases and lexical structures in it. As a result, the authentic book might lose its appeal. Also, there is a limit to the number of words and phrases that can be taught at a time. And last but not least, it might be more important to raise awareness of the importance of ambiguity tolerance (see Chapter 6.8); an aspect that might be lost sight of when focusing too much on the pre-teaching of vocabulary.

6.6.3 Deducing Word Meaning

As it is unavoidable that learners encounter unknown words in a book, they need strategies to deduce their meaning. There are various strategies with whose help the meaning of unknown words can be decoded and teachers should encourage learners to develop a number of these.

---

101 Brewster and Ellis (2002: 80ff) suggest important factors to think of when considering vocabulary size and selection. They also provide guidance on how to teach new words (also see Chapter 2.4 on this issue).

Learners can, for example, guess or deduce the meaning of an unknown word from the context of the story and contextual clues such as words and phrases around an unknown word (Cameron, 2001: 27; Hedge, 2000: 193). In addition, visualisations in picture books provide contextual clues. Moreover, background knowledge, which consists of language knowledge as well as more general knowledge, can help to deduce the meaning of an unknown word (Hedge, 2000: 193). Language knowledge can include knowledge of similar words in another language, understanding parts of the unknown word (e.g., its stem or word family) and decoding parts of the word (e.g., prefix, suffix or composite). For decoding unknown or difficult words, an audible articulation, also referred to as a semi-vocalisation, may help as well (Biebricher, 2008: 31; Diehr, 2010, 58; also see Chapter 4.3.2). Lastly, a further strategy to decode an unfamiliar word is to look up its meaning in some sort of reference work such as a dictionary (see Chapter 6.6.4).

Figure 13 provides an example from the picture book 'The Gruffalo' (Donaldson & Scheffler, 1999) of how a sentence that contains a number of unknown words can be decoded with the help of various strategies.

Figure 13: Decoding a sentence with unknown words (sentence taken from Donaldson & Scheffler, 1999).

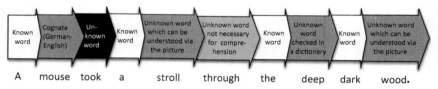

As in the example, known or decodable words in a text usually alternate with unknown ones. However, the likelihood of learners figuring out the meaning of unknown words increases when they only encounter a reasonable number of them (Lightbown & Spada, 2013: 162). Chapters 4.2 and 6.6.1 have already discussed this threshold. Depending on this threshold, Hedge (2000: 193) states that learners are "capable of guessing 60 to 80 % of unknown words in a text, if the density of new words is not too high."

Regardless of all strategies, some words will simply remain unknown. On the whole, this should not interfere with understanding at least the gist of a text, but at the most make some details incomprehensible. The primary school EFL teacher should bear that in mind and set realistic expectations with regard to comprehension.

6.6.4 Seeking Translation: Dictionaries, Word Lists and L1 Books

As indicated in the example in Figure 13, unknown words can also be looked up in a dictionary. Dictionaries offer the advantage that children can, at least theoretically, look up every word they would like to look up when reading an English book. The Ministry of School and Further Education North Rhine-Westphalia[102] (LSW NRW, 2001: 5) says that using dictionaries is one of the fundamental strategies that learners need to acquire in order to read and understand FL texts and that dictionaries gain in importance with regard to reading authentic texts. The importance of starting to work with a dictionary as early as in the primary school EFL classroom is commonly acknowledged, as this lays the foundation for its use in later stages (Bezirksregierung Detmold, 2008: 18; LSW NRW, 2001: 9).

There are various dictionaries on the market, such as online dictionaries, multimedia dictionaries (CD-ROM), picture dictionaries, monolingual dictionaries, bilingual dictionaries, etc. (see Freudenau (2012) for a more detailed description). The primary school English classroom usually works with picture dictionaries, which should be available in every EFL classroom in NRW (Bezirksregierung Detmold, 2008: 19). Picture dictionaries usually offer either topic-based or alphabetically ordered English words, which are translated into German and also described via or supplemented by a picture. However, picture dictionaries for primary schools only offer a limited range of about 700 to 2000 words (Freudenau, 2012: 103) and therefore restrict the number of words that can be looked up. It is hence probable that an unknown word in an authentic book cannot be found in the picture dictionary. Therefore, with regard to reading authentic books in the primary school EFL classroom, one could consider introducing bilingual dictionaries which provide the German translation of a much wider range of English words. However, these dictionaries are more complex than picture dictionaries, because they contain considerably more words in a smaller font-size, significantly more pages and no visualisations. Thus, the process of looking up a word is more difficult and potentially too demanding for young learners.

A downside of all print dictionaries is that they do not provide the young learner with the correct pronunciation of the word. A solution to this problem may be computer-based dictionaries, such as multimedia or online dictionaries, as they generally have an audio function and allow the children to listen to the correct pronunciation of a word. This enables learners to look up the meaning

---

102 Translation for '*Ministerium für Schule und Weiterbildung des Landes Nordrhein-Westfalen*', which was still called '*Schulministerium*' in 2001.

of an unknown word and also listen to its correct pronunciation, which prevents learners from learning the wrong pronunciation of a word through invented phonation (see Chapter 4.3.3). Teaching young learners to use phonetic transcriptions is a further method suggested by a handful of researchers, for example Marschollek (2005); for many teachers and researchers, however, this seems to be far too complex and difficult for young EFL learners.

Nevertheless, as Freudenau (2012: 103) argues, "it is important that pupils know how to use a dictionary to find search words successfully." Irrespective of the type of dictionary, it is of paramount importance that the pupils know how to use it effectively. Learners should thus be introduced to a dictionary before reading and should become accustomed to using it as a learning aid. And although dictionaries are undeniably a valuable instrument in reading authentic texts, their usefulness for young learners' reading of FL texts still needs to be investigated.

Word lists can offer an alternative to dictionaries, as they are tailored to the lexical load of a particular book. A word list contains explanations of words that are crucial for understanding the content of a particular book. As such, they need to be especially created for each book. Graded readers (see Chapter 5.2.1) work with such lists and provide a glossary with vocabulary support, usually at the end of the book or on every page. In readers suitable for the primary school, three different glossaries are found. The easiest is built up like a picture dictionary, displaying words, mostly nouns, with the corresponding picture. The other two are more complicated as they give a list of vocabulary and then the corresponding explanation of the words in English, only partly supported by pictures. No glossary with a translation into L1 was found in graded readers for the primary school. However, Krüsmann (2003: 50) used such a list with English-German translations for a reading text in the context of the primary school EFL classroom.

It is striking that all three word lists as found in graded readers restrict their explanations to nouns and hardly display any other word classes. As already outlined above, nouns often dominate the primary EFL classroom for reasons of demonstrability and opportunism (Brewster & Ellis, 2002: 81f). This is an unfortunate deficit in these three examples, as especially for understanding a story, other content words and also function words may be important for comprehension as well.

Currently, no word lists exist that have been especially made for authentic English picture books. Consequently, the following criteria have been developed in the scope of the present study, based on the ideas for word lists in graded readers and on common picture dictionaries, and can be used as criteria to create word lists to be used with authentic picture books.[103] The criteria are that the word list

- consists of one laminated page that is made available during reading by placing it next to the book.
- mainly contains nouns but also other word classes as well as short phrases that are crucial for understanding.
- is well structured and provides a clear overview, including only a limited number of selected lexical items.
- lists the words according to the sequence they appear in the book.
- gives explanations through pictures, short English explanations or synonyms whenever possible; alternatively, German translations are used in exceptional cases.

Such a word list enables the learners to look up the meaning of selected unknown words which are crucial for full text comprehension. An example of such a list is found in Appendix B.

Apart from word lists and dictionaries, the L1 equivalent of a book can also be used to allow translation of unfamiliar and difficult words and phrases. This idea was already outlined in Chapter 6.5.1, but whilst there the focus was on the successive reading of a book first in the L1 and then in the L2 to ensure topic familiarity, the suggestion at hand is to work with both versions simultaneously (see Häuptle-Barceló & Willerich-Tocha, 2008). The comparison with the L1 book should make the English book accessible to the learners and also foster language awareness. For example, the learners could use the German book if they do not understand an event in English or if they want to look up or double-check the meaning of a phrase or sentence. The notion of providing a story in different languages, including the learners' L1, is the underlying idea of the MuViT-project, in which children can choose between different languages to listen to a story on a computer.

In sum, dictionaries as well as word lists can provide useful support to learners when reading an authentic FL text with a number of unknown lexical items. Still, for all these different options for seeking the translation of words as outlined in this subchapter, one issue needs to be taken into consideration: such devices should be used skilfully and with care. The skilful use of means of

---

103   For more information on the principles of working with vocabulary that partly underlie the ideas listed here, see Böttger (2005: 82f) and Pinter (2006: 86f).

translation includes not trying to look up every single unfamiliar word, as this hinders learners from developing both a global understanding of a text and a tolerance of ambiguity in comprehension; it might also lead the learners to translate the text into their L1 word by word. All such techniques are not desirable with regard to enhancing the development of L2 reading strategies. Thus, as outlined earlier, the skilful use of these means needs to be practised and critically reflected on in class.

6.7 Supporting Reading through Listening

Another supportive factor in reading is providing an audio-recording of the book that the learners listen to while they are reading. This method is a form of assisted reading[104] and means that the learner reads and follows a text while somebody else reads it aloud. The text of the recording should perfectly match the text in the book and be read out clearly, preferably by a (near-) native speaker of English. If possible, readers should have their own recording that they can listen to via earphones in order to allow individual reading paces. The technical equipment should allow readers to stop the audio-recording if and when necessary and to rehearse parts of the text.

Various researchers suggest that assisted reading is a beneficial method in FL reading, for a number of reasons. Firstly, in addition to a reading text audio-recordings enable learners to listen to the correct pronunciation of written words and allow the learners to gain an implicit insight into the grapheme-phoneme correspondence of the English language (Bezirksregierung Detmold, 2008: 17f). Secondly, Brusch (2000: 41) points out that reading and simultaneously listening to the same text enhances the contact time in the FL. Thirdly, audio-recordings can be especially beneficial for weaker readers when reading an English book (Frisch, 2014b: 31). Gailberger (2011: 74ff) argues that assisted reading helps even very weak readers to develop a positive attitude towards reading, and that the technique can support the understanding of a reading text and is well-liked by pupils.

Numerous previous studies and projects have used audio-recordings as a supplement to reading and provide evidence that it benefits reading comprehension as well as other FL competences. For example, audio-recordings were used in Kolb's (2013: 34) picture book project where children had the opportunity to listen to an audio-recording while they were reading a picture book. The research

---

104 Author's translation for '*Mitleseverfahren*'.

team gave the learners the option of listening to the recording should they feel it was needed. Kolb (2013: 37) found that the learners used the recordings and followed them closely either before or while reading the text and that, according the learners' feedback, both helped them to better understand the texts; for example, a learner mentioned that the audio-recording helped him in understanding many of the words. Results of parts of the JuLE[105] project (Diehr, 2010) showed that Year 4 pupils could read authentic English children's books aloud expressively and with only very few pronunciation mistakes after they had listened to an audio-recording of the text a couple of times. These results have led the LiPs research group to include assisted audio reading as one of their six stages to approaching reading in the primary EFL classroom (Diehr & Frisch, 2010a: 28). In another study, Brusch (2000: 41) investigated classroom libraries in secondary schools in Germany, where all the books were supplemented with a cassette to introduce reading step by step and support this process by listening to the cassette while reading. He found that over 90 % of the young learners welcomed the idea, found it very motivating and enjoyed reading the texts while listening (Brusch, 2000: 41). At the international level, several studies on comprehension-based language programmes, an approach to FLL where the learners read a text in the FL and simultaneously listen to an audio-recording of it, found that both reading and listening comprehension, as well as some aspects of speaking, benefit from this approach (e.g., Lightbown et al., 2002; Trofimovich et al., 2009).

Assisted reading with the help of audio-recordings has thus been convincingly shown to entail many advantages. It supports the reading process as well as the comprehension of FL texts and enhances language learning opportunities. However, for more independent reading Metzger (2010: 79f) suggests only using the audio-recordings for parts of a book and alternate assisted reading with independent reading, particularly once learners have gained experience with assisted FL reading. This is a good chance for low-proficiency readers to not completely lose track of the gist of the text but to still move in the direction of reading independently in that support is gradually reduced (also see Chapter 6.1.2).

There is one downside to assisted reading, though, which is related to investigating a learner's reading comprehension in empirical research. With assisted reading, it is impossible to test reading comprehension on its own; what is tested is necessarily a combination of reading and listening comprehension with a certain degree of uncertainty regarding which of the two led to what level of comprehension (see Chapter 8.1.3 for a critical discussion).

---

105   Junge Lerner lesen Englisch [young learners reading in English] (JuLE).

6.8 Tolerating Ambiguity in Comprehension

Despite all the means and attempts to provide support that were outlined in the previous sections, learners also need to experience as well as learn that a certain degree of ambiguity in comprehension sometimes needs to be tolerated when reading authentic books in a FL. According to Whittaker (2003: 183), "tolerating vagueness" is a skill which learners have to apply when reading FL texts with a rich and authentic lexical load. As already indicated in the previous subchapters, this implies that not all words of a text have to be fully understood, not all words can be pre-taught and that looking up a large number of unknown words is not a supportive strategy in reading.

Haß (2006: 86) stresses that it is essential for pupils to understand that they should not be dismayed or discouraged if they do not understand a specific word here or there. Pupils should get used to the experience of not understanding every word in a text and develop tolerance towards unknown lexical items. As such, the learners also need to learn to aim at reading for global understanding. Meyer (2010: 15) points out that "students can easily understand the gist of what is being said even though they do not have complete understanding of the text." This, however, is challenging and requires a willingness to take risks (Mishan, 2005: 61); that is, being willing to accept that not every word or sentence is understood, guessing meaning, guessing meaning out of a broader context or simply skipping incomprehensible details in order to reach global understanding instead.

Willingness to take such risks and to accept ambiguity in comprehension can indeed even have a positive impact. Deane and Rumlich (2013: 190) point out that "a particular degree of uncertainty, excitement, provocation, ambiguity or conflict [...] also contributes to a favourable level of activation." Risk and ambiguity can therefore be intriguing and motivating for the learners, assuming that the teacher's expectations allow a certain level of uncertainty. However, risk-taking is only positive to a certain extent; it should be calculated and not be mere carelessness (Mishan, 2005: 61).

Hence, ambiguity tolerance needs to be practised and guided in the language classroom. In storytelling, a first step has already been made in the primary school EFL classroom. Young EFL learners are used to globally understanding stories and authentic picture books that have been read out to them by the teacher. Also, following the classroom discourse, which is for the most part in English, supports learners in developing ambiguity tolerance in comprehension from the very beginning. Similarly, and building up on previous experience with it, ambiguity tolerance also needs to be gradually developed for FL reading.

6.9 Summary of Chapter 6

This chapter has provided information about the notions of challenge and support in reading. Firstly, a firm basis for the idea of challenging (young) learners has been provided by elaborating on current ideas of 'support through challenge' (Bartnitzky, 2009) as well as more traditional ideas of the ZPD (Vygotsky, 1978) and comprehensible input that contains i+1 (Krashen, 1989). Several researchers have outlined the importance of challenging young EFL learners, also with regard to FL literacy, and emphasised that EFL learners' abilities should not be underestimated.

Given the potential benefits of challenging young language learners, independently reading an authentic English book is clearly a worthwhile challenge to pose. It is of course important to balance task demand and task support, so that the learners are not overtaxed by reading; finding this balance, however, can be difficult because learners should neither be overtaxed nor bored by the task. Consequently, individual learners need different means of support in reading, which cater to their individual needs and support their reading at exactly their level of competence. This idea of scaffolding entails supporting learners right at the point where they need help. The support can be provided either by more expert others or equal-ability peers, or by inanimate artefacts.

Chapter 6.2 has provided an overview of support in reading. First and foremost, the teacher is responsible for providing a supportive reading environment, while at the same time being aware of the notion and importance of learner autonomy. Peers can also provide support in cooperative reading settings. For such settings to be supportive, teachers might want to contemplate whether it is necessary that learners share a reading text, whether an initial phase of individual reading might cater more to individual reading pace and strategies and whether cooperative reading is beneficial for all learners.

Further support for reading derives from the contextualisation of the reading text, which can primarily be ensured through topic familiarity, the learner's prior knowledge about the text's content and topic and learners' interests in the text. Prior knowledge should be activated in the pre-reading phase to enhance top-down comprehension processes during reading. Generally, the reading process should always be contextualised by a cycle of pre-, while- and post-reading activities, which serve for orientation and embed reading into a meaningful context of activities. When reading picture books, the visualisations support the learners by offering a visual context for the textual elements.

Because of possible linguistic difficulties, vocabulary support is also important in FL reading. According to the threshold hypothesis, learners should be familiar with a certain number of lexical items of a text prior to reading; such a threshold, however, has not yet been defined for reading picture books. Still, teachers should ensure that learners are familiar with a certain number of words and phrases in a text, which can be done by using a book that contains a good amount of already known vocabulary and also by pre-teaching selected lexical items. Moreover, strategies to deduce word meaning are crucial and should thus be practised and reflected on. Lastly, translation aids such as dictionaries or word lists can also offer a source of vocabulary support in reading.

As a final source of support, assisted reading, meaning that learners listen to an audio-recording of the text while reading it, has been proven useful in previous projects. The combination of listening and reading can particularly support beginner or weaker readers; on the one hand to not lose track of a reading text and on the other hand to support decoding language phonemically.

Despite the clear benefits of all these supportive factors, the gradual development of ambiguity tolerance should not be forgotten. Ambiguity tolerance is an important factor in developing communicative FL skills and should be trained from the very beginnings of FLL.

A number of the techniques and tools outlined in this chapter will be tested for their supportive function in FL reading with young learners in the empirical study described in this book. As Chapter 8.1.3 will show, support during reading was provided to the study's participants via the following: cooperative reading, topic-familiarity, re-use of language already mastered, visualisations found in the picture books, a bilingual dictionary, a picture-dictionary, a word-list and an audio-recording of the texts. Bearing in mind that learners all read at individual competence levels, they also need individual support; thus they were allowed to freely choose from a range of supportive aids during their reading tasks in this study.

Part B: Research Design

Abstract: Part B is concerned with the research design of the study presented in this book. It details the research questions, the study's setting and participants, the data collection procedure and the study's research materials and instruments. The role of the researcher and the study's quality are also critically discussed.

7. Introducing the Empirical Study: Research Questions, Setting and Participants, Research Design

Abstract: This chapter is concerned with the research design. Based on details of the research foci, questions and aims, it gives insights into the setting and participants as well as the data collection procedure of this mixed methods study. It also discusses the extent to which the study complies with quality criteria.

As outlined in the theoretical part of this book, reading authentic English picture books independently is a relatively new phenomenon in the primary school EFL classroom and hence needs to be investigated from various perspectives. Therefore, a mixed methods research design has been chosen and developed, the specifics of which will be presented in this chapter. First, the research questions and the aim of the empirical study will be outlined, followed by an explanation of the setting and participants. Next, the research design and the data collection procedure will be elaborated on in detail. The chapter concludes with an examination of the mixed methods approach used in this study and then provides a brief discussion of research quality criteria in this approach.[106]

7.1 Research Foci, Questions and Aims

This study examines the use of authentic English picture books in the primary school EFL classroom. Overall, three foci, each with its own research question, underlie this study: The main focus is on (I) reading comprehension with a second on (II) reading strategies; a minor focus lies on (III) FL performance. Figure 14 summarises the study's foci and their varying weights.

---

106 Although the research instruments are part of the empirical study and its design, they will be presented in a separate chapter (Chapter 8); due to the complexity of the research design, which is outlined first, a number of instruments were used and these need extended explanations. For the sake of readability and structure, the chapter on research instruments is hence separated from the introduction of the study's design.

Figure 14: Three foci of the empirical study.

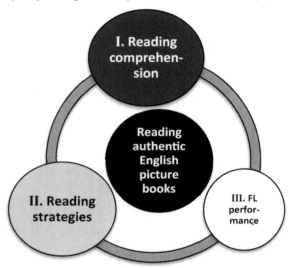

Each of the three foci is investigated through one main research question. These are:

I.   To what extent are Year 4 EFL learners capable of reading and understanding authentic English picture books?
II.   Which reading strategies do young EFL learners apply when reading authentic English picture books for understanding?
III. To what extent does the reading of authentic English picture books influence the FL performance of EFL learners in Year 4?

The first two questions, which concern reading comprehension and reading strategies, are the main questions of this study. The third is treated as a subsidiary research question to provide some initial insight into the potential influence of FL reading on young learners' FL performance. The following subchapters will provide more detailed information about the three foci and questions, which were investigated with an emphasis on various key aspects.

7.1.1 Details of Research Question I (Reading Comprehension)

The first research question focuses on reading comprehension and reads as follows:

> (I) To what extent are Year 4 EFL learners capable of reading and understanding authentic English picture books?

Reading authentic English picture books is challenging (see Chapter 6.1) and there has been very little research that has explored whether it is possible with young EFL learners. There are hardly any empirical research results that answer the question whether young EFL learners are overtaxed by reading authentic English picture books on their own or not (see Chapter 5.5.2). As outlined in Chapter 4.3, being able to read a book implies being able to understand it – that is, it implies reading it for comprehension. So far, no research is available on how well young language learners understand authentic picture books when they read them on their own. Additionally, various authors have suggested the use of supportive devices to foster reading comprehension (see Chapter 6.2). However, empirical evidence on the types of devices that are useful for young EFL learners does not yet exist. Thus, key aspects investigated in research question I are:

a) **The task of reading and the learners' reading competence:** The first key aspect refers to the question of whether Year 4 EFL learners can read authentic English picture books by themselves or whether they are overtaxed by the task. As the participants in the study read six different books over a period of five months, also a potential development of reading competence will be looked at.

b) **The level of reading comprehension:** In a next step, the level of comprehension of these books is investigated in order to ascertain the extent to which the participants understand authentic English picture books when reading them on their own.

c) **The use of supportive devices:** While reading, the participants were free to select from a range of different supportive devices (see Chapter 6.2 and 8.1.3). The study seeks to explore which supportive devices young EFL learners choose for reading authentic English picture books and which of the chosen devices they deem useful.[107]

---

107 The use of devices overlaps with research question II on reading strategies, as, for example, a possible cognitive strategy for understanding an unknown word is to look it up in a dictionary (supportive device). Still, the supportive devices are very much concerned with the actual process of reading, so that they will be dealt with under research question I, being aware of the overlap with research question II.

7.1.2 Details of Research Question II (Reading Strategies)

Research question II on reading strategies reads as follows:

> (II) Which reading strategies do young EFL learners apply when reading authentic English picture books for understanding?

As mentioned in Chapter 4.6, there is currently only very little research on young EFL learners' reading strategies when reading authentic English picture books. Although two small-scale studies have described reading strategies that young EFL learners used in mostly cooperative reading settings, they barely touched on the learners' awareness of strategy use. Moreover, the development of reading strategies over a longer period of time has not yet been explored so far, nor has a possible connection between the use of strategies and the comprehension of picture books been researched yet. Thus, key aspects investigated in research question II are:

a) **The description and categorisation of reading strategies:** This part of the research on reading strategies first of all explores, describes and categorises the reading strategies used by the learners in the study.

b) **The development of strategy use:** As the reading sessions took place over a period of five months, a possible development or change in the use of strategies over this period is investigated next.

c) **The awareness of strategy use:** Whether young learners are aware of strategies and able to talk about them on a meta-level has often been debated (see Chapter 4.6.7). Hence, the learners' awareness of their strategy use is researched.

d) **The connection of reading strategies and the level of comprehension:** The last key aspect draws the connection between the level of reading comprehension (research question I) and the use of strategies (research question II), and explores whether there is a potential correlation between the children's strategy use and their level of reading comprehension.

7.1.3 Details of Research Question III (FL Performance)

Research question III on FL performance reads as follows:

> (III) To what extent does the reading of authentic English picture books influence the FL performance of EFL learners in Year 4?

This subordinate question provides some initial insight into the FL performance of the pupils that were engaged in reading picture books over the five months of the study. It is based on research which attributes positive learning effects to FL reading (see Chapter 5.4). There is currently no research which investigates positive FLL effects of a long term reading programme at primary school level. Therefore, this study explores whether there is a difference in language skills between children who were regularly engaged in FL reading (reading group) compared to children who were taught according to the regular concept (control group). The emphasis is on FL semantic, orthographic and syntactic morphemic knowledge.

7.1.4 Summary of Foci, Questions and Aims of the Study

Table 6 sums up the information provided in the previous subchapters on the three foci with their research questions and key aspects investigated:

Table 6: Summary of research foci, research questions and key aspects investigated.

Focus	Research question	Key aspects investigated
I Reading comprehension	(I) To what extent are Year 4 EFL learners capable of reading and understanding authentic English picture books?	→ The task of reading and the learners' reading competence → The level of reading comprehension → The use of supportive devices
II Reading strategies	(II) Which reading strategies do young EFL learners apply when reading authentic English picture books for understanding?	→ The description and categorisation of reading strategies → The development of strategy use → The awareness of strategy use → The connection of reading strategies and the level of comprehension
III FL performance	(III) To what extent does the reading of authentic English picture books influence the FL performance of EFL learners in Year 4?	→ FL performance of the reading group compared to that of the control group

In view of the lack of research in all three foci, the aim of this study is to shed light on the use of authentic English picture books with young learners in the area of reading comprehension, reading strategies and FL performance. The study aims to show whether young EFL learners can read authentic English picture books and which supportive devices potentially enable them to do so. The level of comprehension of the books is supposed to show the extent to which the learners can understand the books when they read them on their own. This study also seeks to find out whether comprehension develops, changes and improves over a longer period of time, as well as whether general reading competence or confidence develops. Furthermore, the study aims at discovering whether young learners use common reading strategies, and, if so, identifying which ones prove to be relevant. The study also investigates if these strategies develop over time and to what extent the children are aware of the strategies they use. In addition, the study attempts to show whether some strategies are more successful than others with regard to reading comprehension and might hence be worth dealing with in class. Finally, the study will provide some insight into a potential FLL effect through reading authentic English picture books.

To achieve this aim, all three foci of the study as outlined in Table 6 are integrated into one broad reading study. In order to investigate (I) reading comprehension and (II) reading strategies, weekly reading sessions were conducted with a reading group of eleven Year 4 EFL learners over a period of five months. For the subsidiary question on FL performance (III), the achievement of the reading group was compared with that of a control group at three points in time over the five-month period. The following subchapter will firstly provide information about the setting and participants and Chapter 7.3 will then outline details of the study's design and procedure of data collection.

7.2 Setting and Participants

The study was conducted with Year 4 pupils at a primary school in NRW. Before conducting the study, all parties involved gave their consent to participate. Firstly, the school's head teacher gave her permission after an oral discussion of the project between her, the vice head and myself as the researcher. Secondly, the teachers that were affected by the data collection were informed about the study and gave their consent. Thirdly, the participants' parents signed a written consent based on a detailed information letter before their children were involved in the study. Also, the children were asked and enlightened about their voluntary participation in the project.

The following subchapters firstly outline why the respective school and classes were chosen and provide insights into the reasons for selecting a Year 4 at a school with a bilingual programme. After that, details about the school, the class the participants were chosen from and the participants themselves are provided. Chapter 7.2.4 will also discuss the selection of participants for the reading and control groups. The information about the school and parts of the information about the participants were collected in two semi-structured interviews with the English teacher, who was also the vice head of the school, as well as a short questionnaire with the learners' class teachers. Additionally, data about the participants were collected via a learners' and a parents' questionnaire (see Appendix C.1 and C.2).

7.2.1 Reasons for Choosing Year 4 Pupils at a Primary School with a Bilingual Programme

There are several reasons for choosing Year 4 pupils for the study. Firstly, the learners in Year 4 had already been learning English for about three years prior to the onset of the study and therefore already had some previous FL knowledge. Secondly, the debate about early biliteracy was taken into consideration (see Chapter 3.1.3): It has long been a matter of discussion whether learners in lower years, who are still learning to read in their L1, should be confronted with too many reading demands in the L2. By Year 4, however, learners should have gained reading skills at the text level in their L1 (Klippel, 2000: 107) and it seemed reasonable, therefore, to confront them with reading texts in their L2.[108] A similar decision was made within the ELLiE project (Enever, 2011a; see Chapter 3.4).[109]

Moreover, the primary school where the present study was conducted has a bilingual programme (see Chapter 7.2.2 for details) through which the children received additional EFL input from Year 1 on. Although this limits the generalisability of the study, a school with a bilingual programme was chosen for the following reason. Additional input in English might be of benefit for the children when reading, particularly with regard to the threshold hypothesis (see Chapter 4.2). As research has so far hardly produced any evidence regarding the extent to which young EFL learners in Germany are able to work with authentic English

---

108   As outlined in Chapters 3.1.3, 3.2.2, 3.4, 5.5.2 and 6.1, there are very good reasons to use challenging reading activities earlier than Year 4. Also, according to the German curricula, children are expected to have gained basic L1 reading competences by the end of Year 2 (see, for example, MSW NRW, 2008b: 31f). Still, Year 4 learners were chosen to counterbalance possible doubts about overtaxing the study's participants.

109   For the ELLiE project, a reading test was only conducted in Year 3 and 4, after at least two years of previous teaching in English. The research team intentionally left out Years 1 and 2, as the ELLiE project group did not want to put any reading demands on the learners until they had had at least two years of experience with EFL.

picture books on their own at all, this project is mostly explorative and therefore conducted with learners who were in an enhanced English programme.

If Year 4 learners in a bilingual programme are not overtaxed by the reading sessions, the same study can in future be conducted at a primary school without a bilingual programme. Conversely, if the participants selected for this study cannot successfully handle the tasks given to them, trying the task out at a regular school with no bilingual programme seems redundant. Reading authentic picture books is thus firstly investigated with Year 4 learners at a bilingual school in this study, with the idea of possibly conducting the same study with other learners at different schools in future.

Last but not least, this study's results can contribute to the pool of research on CLIL in German primary schools and offer insights into using authentic English picture books as potential learning materials; aspects that have only marginally been investigated so far (see Chapter 5.4.2). Additionally, research on CLIL learners' reading skills can likewise contribute to future developments of primary CLIL classrooms, because reading is an indispensable skill for CLIL learners (see Chapter 3.1.2).

7.2.2 The Bilingual Primary School

The school where the study was conducted is a public primary school with a bilingual programme in NRW. In the school year 2014/2015, in which the present study was conducted, 209 pupils were taught by 14 teachers in two parallel classes per year. The school is close to the centre of a larger city, and has a very mixed catchment area. Both families of high and low social as well as educational status live close by and send their children to that school. Hence, the school has a very heterogeneous group of learners, including many children with a migrant background.[110]

Since 2011, the school's special focus has been its bilingual programme. Since the school year 2014/15, all the pupils participate in the bilingual programme and all monolingual classes have been phased out. In this bilingual programme,

---

110 Despite its bilingual programme, the school is therefore anything but an elite school. In bilingual schools researchers often mention the danger of these schools being elite schools with carefully selected, highly motivated, very talented pupils whose parents have a high economic and social status (see Chapter 2.2.2). The school in question, however, started its bilingual programme in order to motivate more parents to send their children to the school, as an increasingly low number of pupils would have meant that it might have had to close down in the school year 2010/2011.

all the pupils get enhanced English lessons from the very beginning. They already start with English in the first week of Year 1 and have three instead of two regular English lessons per week. Additionally, two subjects per year are taught bilingually. These vary and can be physical education, music, arts or science. Especially in the first two years, the bilingual subjects are partly taught through team-teaching with two teachers present in class, one of whom speaks German while the other speaks English.

In total, the school had three bilingual teachers that spoke only English to all the children at all times during the school year in which the data were collected. One of these teachers was the vice head of the school, and she coordinated the bilingual programme. With regard to materials for the bilingual subjects and also for the English lessons, the school is building up its own pool. Teachers regularly work with the course book 'Playway' (Gerngross & Puchta, 2009) in English, but this is often too easy for the pupils.

7.2.3 Relevant Information about Year 4

The study was conducted with children from both Year 4 classes in the school year 2014/2015. The pupils were the first cohort that had been in the bilingual programme. In Year 1, they had two English lessons in the first term and then three English lessons in the second term. Additionally, physical education and music were taught bilingually in Year 1. In both bilingually taught subjects, team-teaching with a German-speaking and English-speaking teacher was conducted. In Year 2, the pupils still had three English lessons per week plus physical education and arts taught bilingually. Team-teaching, as explained earlier, was occasionally still applied in physical education. In Year 3, the three English lessons remained, plus physical education fully taught bilingually and parts of their science class taught bilingually. One science lesson was taught in German, while two science lessons were taught in team-teaching using mostly German, but also English. In Year 4, physical education was still taught in English, one of three science lessons was taught in English and the regular three English lessons remained. Over the years, that makes a total of about seven English or bilingual lessons of team-teaching with English and German per week. In comparison to the two English lessons per week at regular primary schools, this adds up to about double and even partially triple the standard amount of input in English.

Ms. Scott[111] had been the English teacher and teacher of all bilingual subjects in both classes since Year 1. She taught in both parallel classes, so that both classes

---

111 The teacher's name was changed to ensure anonymity.

received the same input and instructions in all subjects taught in English.[112] At the time the study was conducted, Ms. Scott had been a qualified primary school teacher of English for 5 years. She had been working at the that school since 2011 and had since then coordinated the bilingual programme, which started off the same year. Since 2013, she had also been the vice head of the school.

According to Ms. Scott, reading and writing activities in English increased in Year 3, for the most part in connection with the regular course book. The children were not explicitly taught how to read and write in English, and reading strategies, she said, had also never been discussed or taught in class. The groups did not usually read longer English texts, but were only asked to read at the word and phrase levels. Sometimes, they read very short texts. Frequent activities were matching pictures with short sentences or reading short rhymes. Only rarely did they read short and adapted factual texts, for example about the water cycle in the science class. These were usually supported by a short word list, which provided the German translation for important terms. Infrequently, the teacher read out short texts from the course book and the class read in chorus with her. From time to time, read-aloud activities were conducted to practise pronunciation. On one occasion, the children also read parts of a picture book aloud with one of the children's parents in small-group situations. Occasionally, the children could look at (and read) English picture books during phases of free work. This reading activity was voluntary and was also not talked about in class. Neither the content of the books nor strategies for reading them were discussed. The teacher believed that many children just looked at the pictures and did not read the text. Furthermore, right before the onset of the data collection, the children had just started to get used to working with the picture dictionary 'FindeFix' (Elsner, Kühl, Leonhardt-Holoh, Spangenberg & Wolfram, 2004). Against this background, it can be concluded that the children were not used to reading longer and/or authentic texts in English prior to the empirical study.

As for the availability of authentic picture books in English, the school was poorly equipped. Merely a small collection, which all the classes had to share, was available. Hence, there were no English picture books available to the children in class, as all the books were kept in the teachers' room. According to Ms. Scott, the children in Year 4 knew some classic English picture books such as 'Winnie the Witch' (Thomas & Paul, 1987), 'Froggy Goes to School' (London &

---

112   In one of the classes the English lessons were partly conducted in team-teaching with a trainee teacher for about one year. The regular teacher was still in charge of that class and was present in all lessons, either observing or helping out. Still, both classes covered the same content during that time.

Remkiewicz, 1996), 'Snore' (Rosen & Langley, 1998) and 'Peace at Last' (Murphy, 2007) from storytelling in Years 1 to 3.

7.2.4 Selection of Participants for the Reading and Control Groups

The reading and control groups for the study were chosen from the two Year 4 classes described in the previous subchapter. The reading group was selected from one of the classes and the control group selected from the other one.[113] Only those children who had been given their parents' consent were selected (38 out of 49 pupils received the consent of their parents). Of the 38 pupils permitted to participate, only 34 filled in the learners' and the parents' questionnaires (see Appendix C.1 and C.2). Of these 34 pupils, five had to be excluded because they had not attended the classes from Year 1 onwards (either because they came from another school or had repeated a year). In addition, two German-English bilingual children who regularly spoke English at home were excluded.

Of the remaining 27 pupils in both classes, the reading and the control group were then carefully selected through convenience sampling (Davidson, 2006a: 196).[114] The aim of sampling was to create groups that were as similar as possible. Of course, this was only possible to a certain extent as two groups of children can never be fully alike. Hence, while selecting the groups, those variables were taken into consideration that were likely to influence the outcome of the study and which seemed to be of particular importance with regard to reading. The selection criteria were:[115]

- The gender of the learners
- The age of the learners
- The learners' strongest language
- Mono- or bilingual upbringing of the learners at home

113　The two groups could not be taken from one class as there were not enough pupils in a single class to form two large enough groups that were allowed to participate in the study.

114　In convenience sampling, participants are selected on the basis of practical criteria and the possession of certain key characteristics that are related to the purpose of the investigation (Dörnyei, 2007: 99). According to Dörnyei (2007: 98), this is the most common sample type in applied linguistics research. As this study demanded a purposeful and limited number of participants (McKay, 2006: 7), random or probability sampling (Davidson, 2006b: 271) was not possible.

115　See Artelt et al. (2001), Chiu et al. (2015), Diehr & Frisch (2010b), Frisch (2013), Koda (2004), Krashen (1989), Lightbown et al. (2002), McElvany, Becker and Lüdtke (2009), Mishan (2005) and Steck (2009) for individual differences between readers.

- Migrant background of the learners (learners were first generation migrants)
- Migrant background of the parents (learners were second generation migrants)
- Socio-economic status of the learners' families
- L1 (German) reading behaviour and background of the learners
- EFL reading behaviour and background of the learners
- L1 (German) reading skills of the learners
- EFL proficiency level of the learners
- EFL reading and writing skills of the learners
- The learners' overall and more general school performance

Information about these aspects was mainly gathered via the learners' as well as the parents' questionnaire (both questionnaires can be found in the Appendix C.1 and C.2).[116] Additional information was collected by means of two semi-structured interviews with the English teacher and also one short questionnaire filled in by the class teachers and the participants' English teacher.

Finally, twelve children from one class were selected for the reading group and another twelve children from the other class for the control group. As one girl from the reading group moved to another city half way through the data collection phase and hence could no longer take part in the study, this girl was excluded from the group and not taken into consideration for the analysis of the data. Thus, there were ultimately eleven participants in the reading group. This makes a total of 23 participants. A table with detailed information about each participant can be found in Appendix A. Table 7 provides an overview of the two groups.

---

116 Both questionnaires were based on Chomsky's (1972) first proposals to assess children's backgrounds, the learners' as well as the parents' questionnaire used in the PIRLS study (progress in international reading literacy study) and TIMSS-study (trends in international mathematics and science) (The International Association for the Evaluation of Educational Achievement – TIMSS & PIRLS International Study Center (IEA), 2011a; IEA, 2011b), questionnaires from the supportive reading programme of the Austrian Ministry of Education (Bundesministerium für Unterricht, Kunst und Kultur, Stadtschulrat für Wien, Pädagogisches Institut der Stadt Wien, 2008), various questionnaires used by Finkbeiner (2005) and the learner questionnaire used in the ELLiE project (Mihaljević Djigunović & Lopriore, 2011). Both questionnaires were shown to and approved of by the head teacher as well as vice head teacher of the school. The language of all the questionnaires was German in order to ensure comprehension.

Table 7: Overview of the participants in the reading and control groups.

Variable	Reading group ($N = 11$)	Control group ($N = 12$)
Gender	5 female, 6 male	6 female, 6 male
Age[117]	on average 112.9 months	on average 112.5 months
Strongest language	11 x German	12 x German
Mono- or bilingual upbringing	1 x bilingual, 10 x monolingual	2 x bilingual, 10 x monolingual
Migrant background (1st or 2nd generation migrant background)	7 x no migrant background 4 x migrant background	10 x no migrant background 2 x migrant background
Socio-economic status (on a scale from 1 to 9, with 1 being the lowest and 9 being the highest possible status)	$M = 7.2$	$M = 7.5$
L1 (German) reading behaviour and background (on a scale from 21 to 63, with 21 being the lowest and 63 the highest/best reading behaviour and background)[118]	$M = 51.6$	$M = 48.6$
EFL reading behaviour and background (on a scale from 9 to 27, with 9 being the lowest and 27 the highest/best reading behaviour and background)	$M = 16.1$	$M = 15.1$
L1 (German) reading skills (in marks from 1 to 6, with 1 being the best and 6 the worst possible mark)	$M = 1.8$	$M = 1.8$

117 This number displays the children's age at the beginning of data collection in September 2014, which for the children was the beginning of Year 4.

118 The scales for EFL and L1 reading behaviour begin at 21 or else 9, because points from one to three were given to the questionnaire items which provided information about reading behaviour. Because zero points were not allocated to any answer to any of the items, the scales do not begin at zero or one.

Variable	Reading group ($N = 11$)	Control group ($N = 12$)
EFL proficiency level (in marks from 1 to 6, with 1 being the best and 6 the worst possible mark)	$M = 2.1$	$M = 2.1$
EFL reading and writing skills (on an adapted Cambridge young learners English movers text (YLE test), max. score 40 points)	$M = 21.9$	$M = 18$
Overall and general school performance (on a scale from 1 to 5, with 1 being the lowest and 5 the highest/best possible overall performance)	$M = 3.2$	$M = 3.2$

All 23 children stated that German as an L1 is their best and strongest language. One child from the reading group grew up bilingually with German and French and two children from the control group grew up bilingually with German and French and German and Greek. To ascertain if a child was monolingual or bilingual, the children were asked in the learners' questionnaire which languages they spoke, which language was their strongest language, and which languages, other than German, were spoken at home. In a few cases, short follow-up interviews were conducted with selected children, in order to obtain a more detailed picture of the children's language environment. A child was regarded as bilingual if it used more than one language on a regular basis and if a language other than German was used at home on a regular basis. This follows Gramley's (2008: 303)[119] definition of "bilinguals as people who use two languages in their everyday life."

Whether the children had a migrant background was determined by asking in which country the child was born and also in which country one or both parents were born. None of the 23 participants had a direct migrant background, as all the children were born in Germany. However, some children's parents were born outside Germany and hence these children had a migrant background. In the reading group, four children had one parent each that was born in Israel, Barbados, France or India. In the control group, two children had one parent each that was born in France. A migrant background beyond the second generation was not taken into consideration as it was not considered important for

---

119   Gramley partly refers to Grosjean (1992).

this study. Ultimately, there were two more participants with an indirect migrant background in the reading than in the control group.

On average, both groups of participants had a rather high socio-economic status of 7.2 (reading group) and 7.5 (control group) on a scale from 1 (lowest) to 9 (highest). In order to assess the children's socio-economic status, the parents' occupation was determined, which is said to be "an intervening variable between education and income" (Ganzeboom, DeGraaf, Treimann & DeLeeuw, 1992: 2). Ascertaining the socio-economic status of a family via the parents' occupation is a procedure also used by Frisch (2013) in the LiPs study. The occupational status, from which the socio-economic status was deduced, was determined using Hollingshead's (2011: 26ff) occupational scale; a nine-step scale encompassing an extended list of occupations on every level, with 9 being the highest and 1 being the lowest possible status. The occupation of both parents was ascertained and the higher one was then taken to define the family's socio-economic status. Overall, the socio-economic status of the control group was slightly higher (0.3 points) than that of the reading group.

The L1 and the L2 reading backgrounds of the children were determined via a number of items in the form of questions on the learners' and parents' questionnaires. These questions aimed at finding out about each child's reading habits, reading environment and their parents' reading habits. All the answers were rated on a three-point scale, with 3 describing a very high literate reading background and 1 describing a very low or even non-literate background. This three-point scale was developed for the research presented in this book to help interpret some of the items on the questionnaires. For example, possessing many books and reading on a very regular basis would be a highly literate background (3 points), whereas possessing no or only a few books and never reading for pleasure would be a low or non-literate background (1 point). The same procedure was followed to investigate the children's reading background with regard to English books. The L1 reading background was measured with a score of minimum 21 points and maximum 63 points and deduced from the information provided in several questions from both questionnaires. On average, the L1 reading background of the reading group is 51.6 and of the control group 48.6. Therefore, the L1 reading background of the reading group is slightly higher (3 points). The same holds true for the L2 reading background with a maximum score of 27 and a minimum score of 9. The average of the reading group is 16.1 and thereby 1 point higher than that of the control group, whose average is 15.1. The differences of 3 out of 63 and 1 out of 27 points, however, are not marked enough to be likely to influence any results of the study.

Furthermore, the proficiency level of the pupils in reading skills as well as in EFL skills was taken into consideration. This was done first of all via the pupils' marks from the last report card (end of Year 3).[120] The average mark for L1 reading proficiency was 1.8 in both groups. The average English mark was 2.1 in each group. Both average marks are the same and seem to be rather high. This does not necessarily indicate that the participants were exceptionally talented. School marks are merely subjective evaluations by the individual teacher and can differ greatly amongst teachers or schools. In sum, with regard to their mark in L1 reading and in English, both groups are comparable and the marks for each group were given by the same teacher. Also, no extreme outliers that perform a lot better or a lot worse than the average of the group were found.

To get a better insight into the participants' EFL reading and writing competence, a standardised test was conducted with both groups: The 'Cambridge young learners English movers' test (YLE test). It should be noted, however, that it was impossible to use Cambridge English's official examination procedure, in which the test is conducted by approved examination institutions and evaluated by Cambridge itself. This would have proved impractical, not only because of the high costs it would have incurred, but also because only the reading and writing parts of the exam were relevant to the study. In agreement with the School of English in Cologne,[121] an official examination institution for Cambridge Certificates in NRW, a sample test was used, which was made available through them (University of Cambridge, n.d.). This test is said to fully meet the quality criteria of the original tests.[122] The YLE movers test is located on the A1 level of the CEFR.[123] A piloting of the test with a strong and a weak pupil of the classes, who were not members of the reading and control groups, ensured that the level of difficulty of this test was appropriate. The only obstacle for the children was

---

120 The German marking system ranges from 1 to 6, with 1 indicating 'very good' and 6 'insufficient. As marks are found on a ordinal and not on a metric scale, actually a mean should not be calculated. However, other measures such as a median or mode do not provide an insight into the average performance of a small group of learners. Therefore, the mean was calculated, although the ordinal scale of marks would ususally require other statistical calculations.

121 See http://englisches-institut-koeln.de/cambridge-examinations/ (last access: 15.05.2017).

122 Confirmed by the School of English in Cologne in a personal conversation on June 13, 2014 (Mrs. Dupont).

123 See diagram on http://www.cambridgeenglish.org/images/126130-cefr-diagram.pdf (last access 15.05. 2017).

the rather complicated task instructions in English. Hence, these were translated into German and added to the test. This ensured that possible mistakes or failure at tasks were not due to a misunderstanding of the task instructions but due to actual problems with reading and writing. The test was analysed quantitatively by scoring the different tasks based on the analysis and scoring rubrics used by Cambridge English (maximum score = 40 points). One aspect, however, was dealt with differently: With regard to writing, the analysis of the test was done in accordance with the curriculum for English in primary school of NRW (MSW NRW, 2008b: 82), which does not require that children write English words in an orthographically correct way (see Chapter 8.2.3 for more details). Hence, incorrectly spelled words were taken as a correct answer as long as one could phonemically understand which word the pupil meant.

The results show that the performance of both groups on the YLE test is more or less comparable. The reading group's mean was $M = 21.9$ points with a standard deviation of $SD = 7.1$. The control group's mean was $M = 18$ points with a standard deviation of $SD = 5.8$. Although the reading group seems to be slightly better than the control group, this difference is not significant. A t-test analysis of the difference between means yielded a $t(21) = 1.45$, which is not significant at the $p < .05$ level (with $df = 21$). Even if not significant, which is not surprising with such a small sample, the difference of almost four points in means might still be relevant and should not fully be ignored. Matloff (n.d.: 311) points out that an important difference can be missed in a t-test analysis if the sample is too small. For instance, nuances of language performances might be masked (Brown & Abeywickrama, 2010: 5), which could firstly not clearly be shown on the test and then secondly their significance could not be shown by statistical measures. Therefore, there might potentially be a slight difference in EFL reading and writing proficiency between the two groups, in favour of the reading group, which the YLE test could not clearly show.

To gain insight into the overall school performance and the participants' overall learning achievements, their English teacher as well as their two class teachers were asked to rate each child's performance on a scale from 1 to 5. On the scale, 3 meant that the child is average (according to the teachers' many years of experience), 5 that the child is far above average and 1 that the child is far below average. For the control group, this scale was filled in by three teachers (their class teacher, English teacher and maths teacher) and for each child the mean of the three evaluations was calculated. In a next step, the children's means were added up and divided by the number of children, to calculate the control groups' overall mean. The same procedure was followed for the reading group, with the only difference being that only two instead of three teachers provided their evaluation (the class teacher, who also was the maths teacher and the English teacher). The result was that both groups were evaluated with a mean of 3.2 with regard to overall school achievement and performance, showing that both groups were overall the same in this regard.

Further information which the teachers revealed about the participants was that in the reading group one child had problems with orthography and two children had problems with concentration and tactile perception. In the control group, one child had dyslexia as well as problems with auditory perception. Another child from the control group had behavioural problems.

In summary, apart from minor differences which can hardly be avoided in research with children, both groups were comparable with respect to the variables which might influence the outcomes of the study. It is hence unlikely that any differences in the results pertaining to FL performance can be attributed to differences between the reading and the control group. However, possible differences would only be significant for research question III (FL performance) anyway, as the control group is irrelevant for research questions I and II and only the description of the reading group is relevant for these two main foci.

7.2.5 My Role as Researcher

As I, as the researcher, conducted the reading sessions and all other research procedures with the learners, I was a participant of this study as well and will reflect on my role in this section. My researcher's role in the present study was twofold, as I inherited the double function of researcher and teacher in one person. From the school teachers' perspective, I was the researcher they communicated and cooperated with, whereas from the pupils' perspective I was some kind of teacher.

In my role as a researcher, I conducted the study and organised the whole research process, including all communication and cooperation with the teachers. As recommended by Aguado (2000: 124), I strove to maintain a positive and relaxed relationship to the teachers, as I wanted to communicate with them as equals and peer professionals and keep them motivated to participate in my research project. The relationship was supported by engaging in regular consultations and conversations with all the teachers involved, providing transparency about all the steps of my project, being flexible with regard to school practice and writing a summary of my study for the school's portfolio.

In addition to my role as researcher, I partly took over the role of the teacher for the time when the children were taken out of class to take part in the reading sessions with me. The learners knew that I was a university-based researcher, but at the same time they felt they were in a regular small group teaching situation. This is due to the fact that the learners were used to being taught in small groups from time to time for individual support or extra activities. It is common that teachers, student teachers, assistant teachers or social workers take children out of classes at this school. Indeed, for primary school children, all adults working in a school and involved in any kind of teaching or learning situation with them tend to be viewed as teachers to a certain extent; thus, the children appeared to see me as a teacher, or at least a person who works for the school. It was important for me to convey to the children that I did not give them marks and hence they should just show their normal performance; at the same time, I emphasised that it was important that they performed just as they would do if their regular teachers were working with them. This was intended to reduce the pressure of the small group situations in which the children probably felt observed by me and the camera, but, at the same time, to create a certain degree of discipline that the children would also have experienced in a regular teaching situation. In sum, considerable emphasis was placed on creating a comfortable atmosphere in which the children felt at ease and did not experience pressure. In this regard, I, for example, allowed the children to get used to the camera by explaining its purpose and assuring them that nobody would watch the videos but me.

One problem that should be taken into consideration when a researcher takes over a teacher-like role is the possible influence of the presence of the researcher on the behaviour of the learners and thus on the results of the study. This refers to the so-called 'Hawthorne effect', which indicates that participants perform differently once they know that they are being studied (Dörnyei, 2007: 53). Wilden (2008: 81) points out the danger of interfering in a project in a way that influences the participants in favour of the research interests. Thus, it is important that the researcher is both aware of and takes account of these possible effects, in order to be able to reduce a potential impact (Swann, 2001: 325).

In this study, this influence could have manifested itself in several ways. On the one hand, the children could have invested extra effort into the tasks given to them in order to meet my expectations and to appear as competent individuals (even if expectations in the direction of high performance were never communicated). On the other hand, the children might have felt more constrained in a small group situation than they would have in a classroom. Special attention was therefore paid to avoiding leading questions, selecting balanced groups of children which included both low and high performers and to constantly reflecting on my own role(s). In any case, as I did not explicitly teach the learners any content, there was little danger that I would greatly influence them.

The constant presence of and observation by a researcher, sometimes supplemented by a video camera, is of course not a natural situation, even if the person is taken as some kind of teacher. Similar to the effect and researcher's influence outlined above, Labov (1972: 209) refers to this as the observer's paradox: "The aim of linguistic research in the community must be to find out how people talk when they are not being systematically observed; yet we can only obtain these data by systematic observation." Although Labov refers to natural speech data in his remarks on data collection, this paradox can easily be transferred to other research contexts in which observation and the presence of a researcher or camera play a role. The researcher aims at obtaining a natural and realistic picture of learning processes and situations. For the observation, the researcher takes part in the learning or teaching situation, which is likely to influence the natural situation and hence might lead to different results. To overcome this paradox, Labov (1972: 61f) argues that a researcher should use at least two devices to address one and the same research object from different directions and see the extent to which they generate the same or similar results. This is in line with the idea of methodological triangulation and also the present study's mixed methods research approach. While, for example, reading strategies were investigated by means of observation and video analysis by me as the researcher, they were also researched via small group interviews and a questionnaire. Labov (1972: 209) further suggests creating situations in which the participants do not feel observed. He suggested this for the recording of speech data, but it can again be transferred to other research contexts. By creating a relaxed and comfortable atmosphere, as described above, the pressure to perform and also the feeling of being observed can be reduced. Moreover, by explaining the reason for the observation and the processes and procedures of data collection to the participants, the study was made transparent to them, which also reduced the pressure and unnaturalness of an observation situation. Aguado (2000: 127) explains the importance of not degrading a study's participants to mere deliverers of data, but of acknowledging their (expert) roles in learning and teaching FLs and of enlightening them about the research project and its procedures. A final aspect that reduces a possible effect of the teacher/ researcher as observer is familiarisation. With the passage of time, children generally get used to unusual or new procedures. Leeck (2014: 131) reports on this so-called familiarisation effect from her regular observations in primary school English lessons. As will become apparent in the presentation of results in Chapters 9 to 11, the same was also observed during the data collection phase of the the current study.

In observation research, a general distinction is made between the participant observer, who takes part in the events he/she is observing, and the non-participant observer, who does not take part (Swann, 2001: 324). Non-participant observers are seen as the ideal type, as they probably have minimal influence on the participants. In classroom research, however, this is rarely possible, as any observer in the classroom is not completely isolated from the events and people in the class but will always be included to a certain extent (Swann, 2001: 324). As outlined above, it can even be difficult to strictly distinguish between the role of teacher and the role of researcher. However, it is not always necessary for the observer to be a non-participant, as the subjectivity of the observer should not necessarily be seen as a regrettable disturbance but as a natural element of human interaction in general and in classroom learning and teaching situations in particular. It is normal for learners at school to be observed. The role of the researcher in this study was that of a researcher as participant, but due to the role of 'teacher' a different sort of participant than the learners of the study.

In sum, the issues mentioned above are inherent in the nature of classroom research and cannot be fully controlled for. Aguado (2000: 123) explains that researchers in EFL classroom research can never play the role of an objective observer, but might always influence processes based on their subjective expectations and concepts to a certain extent. Hence, reflecting on the role as researcher in classroom situations is of utmost importance (Aguado, 2000: 124). This subchapter provides insights into (parts of) my reflection process regarding my role as researcher.

7.3 Research Design and Data Collection Procedure

A unique mixed methods research design was developed for the study, to investigate young EFL learners' reading of authentic English picture books. This design as well as the data collection procedure, embedding the three foci as outlined in Chapter 7.1, will be part of this subchapter.

To investigate research questions I (reading comprehension) and II (reading strategies), a five-month reading study was conducted that consisted of weekly reading sessions with the reading group. This reading study will be described in Chapter 7.3.1. After that, the collection of data on these two foci will be outlined. For research question III (FL performance), a quasi-experimental part was embedded into the reading study to test the FL performance of the reading group against that of the control group. This embedded quasi-experimental study will be explained in Chapter 7.3.3. Subsequently, the collection of data on FL performance will be detailed. In fact, the data collection process on all three foci was tightly interwoven, and so Chapter 7.3.5 will provide a summary and overview of the whole data collection procedure.

7.3.1 A Longitudinal Reading Study to Investigate Reading Comprehension and Reading Strategies

In this section, information will be given about the longitudinal reading study that constitutes the basis for the empirical research in this project. In this reading study, the reading group took part in weekly reading sessions from September 2014 to January 2015. For these reading sessions, the reading group was taken out of their English class once a week and participated in a reading session for one lesson instead (see Chapters 7.3.2 and 8 for more details about the reading sessions). During these sessions, data were collected with the help of various research instruments (see Chapter 8) that shed light on the children's reading comprehension and reading strategies (research questions I and II). Figure 15 shows a graphic representation of the reading study:

Figure 15: Overview of the reading study on reading comprehension and reading strategies.

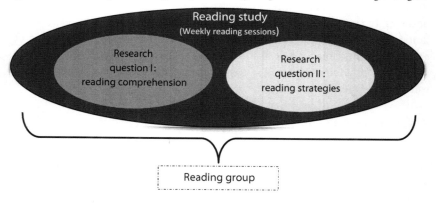

The overall approach of this reading study is explorative, as the study gathered data about aspects which have not been well investigated before (Bortz & Döring, 2006: 354f; see Chapter 7.1). As such, the study is "preliminarily concerned with discovery" (Davies, 2006: 110). For this reason, the manageable number of eleven participants (in the reading group) in a small-scale setting were chosen (Sumner, 2006: 249; see Chapter 7.2).

Essentially, the reading study is longitudinal in nature. Bynner (2006: 164) defines a longitudinal study as one that involves the collection of data from the same group of individuals across time. Thus, information on a certain aspect is gathered at a series of points in time (Dörnyei: 2007: 79). The present study collected data on the reading comprehension and reading strategies of the reading group over a period of five months. Although longitudinal studies are often understood as studies which last for a longer period of time and include a large number of participants (see Bortz & Döring, 2006; Bynner, 2006), the nature of classroom research as well as the explorative approach of the present study did not allow for a larger sample, nor require a significantly longer time span. Hence, while the study is longitudinal in terms of the definitions given above, it does not necessarily display all the distinctive features of this approach.

As the study followed the same participants at different points in time over a specific period, it is a so-called 'panel study' or 'prospective longitudinal study' (Dörnyei, 2007: 82). Bynner (2006: 164) points out that working with one group over a longer period of time enables researchers to look at change or the development of aspects such as reading comprehension and strategies based on the temporal sequencing that is involved. However, examining one group of participants with the same or similar research instruments across time runs the risk of a familiarisation effect, a memory effect and a training effect (Bortz & Döring, 2006: 566). Such effects might have occurred in the present study, as several procedures and research instruments were used repeatedly (see Chapter 8). However, if aware of possible effects, the researcher can keep them in mind and consider them during the analysis and interpretation of the data.

In fact, a familiarisation effect can also be regarded positively, and there are good reasons why the study was conducted over a period of five months and why the children were involved in the reading sessions on a weekly basis. Generally speaking, learning is a long-term process and learning new competences means that learners have to become acquainted with them and practise them in various contexts (Brown, 2007: 1). For the primary school EFL classroom, Frisch (2014d: 34) points out the importance of continuity and frequency in FL reading and writing in order to achieve sound results. As the participants in the present study were not used to EFL reading prior to the study, the longitudinal approach in the form of weekly sessions gave them the chance to get accustomed to this task. Furthermore, possible effects of the out-of-the-ordinary, such as, for instance, an initial enhanced motivation due to the unusual situation of being taken out of class as well as excitement at being video-taped, are likely to be reduced over time. Lastly, it was possible to read six different books over the five months so that a possible effect that might have resulted from varying interests in certain books or topics could be counterbalanced.

To recapitulate, the reading study was based on weekly reading sessions with the reading group. The study was explorative and followed a longitudinal design so as to investigate the participants' reading comprehension and the reading strategies they used while reading English picture books.

7.3.2 Collecting Data on Reading Comprehension and Reading Strategies in Weekly Reading Sessions

Data on reading comprehension and reading strategies were collected during the weekly reading sessions; details of these as well as the actual data collection procedure are provided in this section.

Firstly, the reading group of eleven learners was divided into three smaller groups of three to four pupils (3-4-4 respectively; see Appendix A), which are referred to as reading group 1 (RG 1), reading group 2 (RG 2) and reading group 3 (RG 3). Apart from having an equal number of boys and girls[124], the small groups were selected randomly and remained the same over the five months of data collection.

Three small groups were formed because there were three English lessons per week.[125] This allowed taking out one small reading group per English lesson and made it possible to conduct highly focused reading sessions with the small number of three or four participants. The content of the reading sessions was the same for all three small groups. The order in which the small reading groups were taken out of their English lessons varied, so that no group missed every English lesson on a particular day. Matching the number of small groups to the number of English lessons per week also ensured that the reading study did not interfere with further school subjects or activities.

The reading sessions were based on authentic English picture books. In total, six different picture books on three different topics were dealt with in the reading sessions (see Chapter 8.1 for more detail). This relatively wide selection of books ensured that the results were not influenced by preferences for or dislikes of certain books or topics. For each of the three topics that were dealt with in

---

124 In the group of three pupils there were two boys and one girl. The second girl in that group had moved away half way through the data collection process (see Chapter 7.2.4).

125 In the rare case of public holidays or illness of the teacher/researcher, the next English lessons were chosen.

class during the five months, two different picture books were chosen. For each book, then, two reading sessions were conducted in two consecutive weeks. This is illustrated in Figure 16:

Figure 16: Overview of the procedure of data collection on reading comprehension and reading strategies.

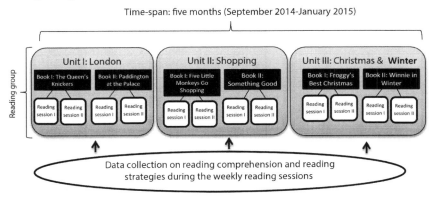

The reading sessions consisted of reading picture books and working on tasks concerned with the books; a procedure that was uniquely developed for the present study (Bortz & Döring, 2006: 102; Dörnyei, 2007: 116). For each book, the two reading sessions followed the same procedure. In reading session I, the children first of all encountered a new book of which they received one original copy each that they then read independently. They were given the time they needed for reading and could choose from a range of supportive devices while reading (see Chapter 8.1.3). While they were reading, I as the researcher observed them and took field notes on their reading strategies. Immediately after the reading, each child individually rated his/her perceived level of understanding. After that, the small reading group was engaged in an oral recall of the book's content and answered questions on the book orally.[126] Finally, a short semi-structured interview was conducted on the learners' use of reading strategies. In reading session II, which usually took place one week after reading session I, the children each received the same book again and individually worked on written comprehension tasks related to the content of the book.

---

126 The group procedure, which potentially has an influence on the learners' comprehension, will be critically discussed in Chapter 8.2.2.

These sessions served to produce data for research questions I and II. More details on the instruments and the analysis of the data will be given in Chapters 7.3.5 and 8. Beforehand, Figure 17 sums up the major characteristics of the reading sessions based on the information provided in this chapter:

Figure 17: Overview of the weekly reading sessions of the reading study.

Characteristics of the weekly reading sessions:

➔ Took place over a five-month period (September 2014 to January 2015)

➔ Participants: eleven Year 4 pupils (reading group) that were subdivided into three smaller groups (RG 1, RG 2, RG 3)

➔ About the reading sessions themselves:
  o One session per week per small group
  o Each small group's reading session replaced one of their three regular English lessons per week
  o Duration: 30 to 45 minutes per session
  o Reading sessions were conducted by me as the researcher
  o All sessions utilised authentic English picture books and were based on these
  o Two sessions in two consecutive weeks were conducted for each of the six books

➔ Data on reading comprehension and reading strategies were collected through various measures during the reading sessions

---

As a final note about the reading sessions, the practice of taking learners out of their English class on a regular basis will be discussed.[127] Taking the participants out of the English classroom once a week meant that they missed one in three regular English lessons; in sum, each participant missed 12 English lessons in the five months. As units usually build up logically and follow a certain structure, this can be a disruption for the children. Hence, although they were being taken out of class regularly, the participants were not supposed to miss out on too much of the regular class content. Therefore, various measures were implemented to keep possible

---

127 The alternative of conducting the reading sessions in addition to the regular English lessons was considered unfeasible because it would have been too difficult to coordinate with daily school practice over such a long time. Moreover, such an approach would have prevented the comparison with the control group.

negative effects at a minimum. Firstly, the books chosen for the study matched the topics dealt with in the English classroom. Secondly, all lessons missed in class, including their content, were documented to maintain an overview of what might have been missed out on. Thirdly, there were regular consultations with the English teacher, and in fact she reported in these that the children did not have any deficits with respect to class work or their grasp of the current topics.

7.3.3 Implementing a Quasi-Experimental Design to Research FL Performance

To investigate research question III, three language tests on FL performance were conducted with the reading group as well as the control group (see Chapters 7.3.4 and 8.4). The reading groups' results in this test were compared to those of the control group to investigate whether the reading study, that is, the regular reading sessions, had an influence on the reading groups' FL performance.

This part of the research, with a comparison of two groups, followed a quasi-experimental design.[128] A quasi-experimental study is characterised by a treatment group which receives an experimental treatment in the form of some new approach and a control group which receives a control treatment (Brown & Rodgers, 2002: 211). The experimental treatment in the present study was provided by the weekly reading sessions of the reading study; the control treatment consisted of the regular English lessons. The impact of the reading sessions on FL performance was investigated by comparing the reading group to the control group that did not receive any reading sessions (DeVaus, 2006: 106). A control group was necessary so to be able to attribute a possible effect on FL performance to the reading sessions (Bortz & Döring, 2006: 113). Hence, the results of the language tests offer some initial insights into a possible enhancement, decrease or stability in FL performance for both groups.

The control group was comparable to the reading group with respect to all other relevant factors that could be controlled for except for the reading sessions (Dörnyei, 2007: 116; see Chapter 7.2.4). Thus, the reading study, that

---

128 True experimental designs are usually laboratory studies that are characterised by random sampling and the elimination of all possible variables that might potentially influence the outcome of the experiment (Bortz & Döring, 2006: 58). Hopkins (2008: 40f) as well as Dörnyei (2007: 117) point out that in educational contexts true experiments are rarely feasible or possible. The field 'school' is a natural setting and not a laboratory situation. This makes the experiment "less-than-perfect" and is accordingly referred to as a quasi-experimental design (Dörnyei, 2007: 117).

is the reading sessions, is the one variable that distinguishes the reading group from the control group for the quasi-experimental study. As such, the reading study is seen as one variable, even though the sessions contained several different activities and materials. Hence, the analysis of a possible effect of the reading sessions on FL performance can only be attributed to the whole reading study. The variable 'reading study' cannot be split up into its different component parts. Accordingly, the findings of this study do not give any details about what parts of the reading sessions might have had an influence on the results as reflected in FL performance (also see Chapter 12.1).

Because the reading sessions served as the variable in the quasi-experimental part, the quasi-experimental study did not stand on its own but was closely related to and integrated into the reading study. Figure 18 shows how the quasi-experimental study was integrated into the reading study:

Figure 18: Overview of the integration of a quasi-experimental study into the reading study.

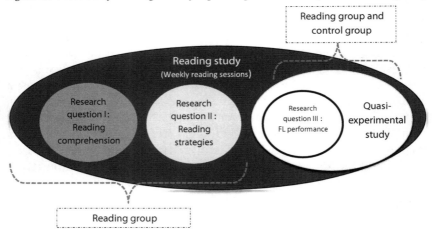

7.3.4 Collecting Data on FL Performance

As already mentioned in the previous section, data on FL performance were collected by means of three language tests (see Chapter 8.4). These tests were conducted with both groups after each of the three thematic units outlined in Chapter 7.3.2 (also see Chapter 8.1.1) and based upon the respective topics 'London', 'Shopping' and 'Christmas and Winter'. At the point when the participants took the tests, the reading group had had two regular English lessons per week on the respective topic and had also worked with two different picture books about it during the reading sessions once a week. The control group had received three regular English lessons per week on that topic. For the tests, both the reading and the control group were taken out of their English class and took the test in a separate room.[129] This collection of data on FL performance is summarised in Figure 19:

Figure 19: Overview of the procedure of data collection on FL performance.

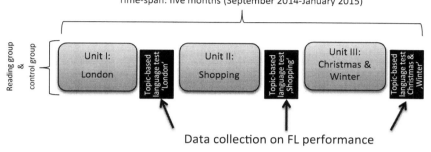

Data collection on FL performance

A possible psychological effect that the reading sessions might have had on the reading group's performance on the tests was considered with regard to research question III. Taking children out of class implies paying special attention to them and this can have a positive and motivating effect on their achievement. Therefore, the reading group might have had an advantage over the control group with regard to motivation, which might have positively influenced their results on the language tests, reflecting the psychological effect out of their out-of-the-ordinary experience rather than actual advances in FL performance. This effect was counterbalanced and minimised in several ways during the study. First of all, the children were used to being taken out of class from time to time (see Chapter 7.4), so that hardly any effect was attributable to the out-of-the-ordinary in general. The reading group also quickly got used to me as a teacher/researcher and already knew me from previous visits to the school. Thus, myself as the researcher limited too rather than fostered a possible effect. In addition, the room where the reading sessions took place was a regular room in the school that the teachers also used for small-group teaching. Thus, the setting was familiar to the reading group and there was nothing special about it. In fact, although the reading group showed some excitement during the first two sessions, that quickly ceased as the familiarisation effect set in

---

129   Depending on school practice, the whole reading group and the whole control group were taken out for the test; no subdivision into smaller groups took place. Still, both groups took the test separately, depending on when their regular English lesson was scheduled.

(also see Chapters 7.2.5 and 7.3.1). Last but not least, it is safe to assume that any psychological effect would not last over a period of five months, as children tend to become accustomed to new procedures. Overall, one can assume that only a minimal, if any, psychological effect at all occurred in the reading group, and that the study's results were thus almost certainly not influenced by it.

7.3.5 Overview of the Overall Research Process

As outlined above, the studies to answer the three research questions cannot be treated separately, but are tightly interwoven. Table 8 provides an overview of the process of data collection for the whole study. The instruments mentioned in this table are further described in Chapter 8.

Table 8: Summary of the data collection procedure, including all instruments as well as reading and control group.

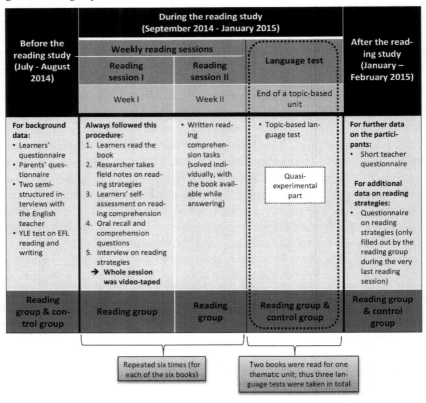

The data collection process started in July 2014 by gathering background information about the participants. This involved a learners' and parents' questionnaire, two short semi-structured interviews with the English teacher and the YLE test on EFL reading and writing competence. As detailed in Chapter 7.2, the reading and control groups were formed on the basis of these sources. To gather more information about the participants and to back up the sampling, a short questionnaire was filled out by the English teacher as well as the class teachers of the two groups after the data collection phase. This questionnaire provided information about the participants' general school performance (see Chapter 7.2.4).

The reading study then started at the beginning of September 2014 and lasted until the middle of January 2015. During this time, the reading group worked with a total of six authentic English picture books during the weekly reading sessions. Two reading sessions (= two weeks) were allocated for each book.[130] The sequence of activities in the reading sessions was established beforehand and always followed the same structure as outlined in Chapter 7.3.2 and summarised in the second and third column of Table 8. Only reading session I on the last book ('Winnie in Winter) was slightly changed in that a questionnaire on reading strategies was filled out by the learners right after the reading. This served to supplement some of the previously collected data on reading strategies.

After the English teacher finished a topic-based unit in the EFL class, which was planned such that the reading group had read and worked with two books in the reading sessions, both the control and reading groups took a topic-based language test. As three topics were dealt with in the English classroom in total, three topic-based language tests were administered. This quasi-experimental part of the study, which included the control group, is highlighted via the dotted box in the table.

As a final note to this summary, a possible effect of classroom reading which might have influenced the results of the study was controlled for in cooperation with the EFL teacher. All participants were taught by the same teacher, Ms. Scott, so that all learners executed the same reading tasks in class. As extensive reading

---

130 Six books with two weeks each plus three further weeks for the topic-based language tests after each thematic unit equals 15 weeks of data collection. This seems shorter than the time-span of five months, but had to be organised according to school practice. Factors such as a class trip, the autumn and winter school holidays, public holidays and illness of the teacher or researcher had to be taken into consideration, so that in some weeks during the five months no data could be collected and also no reading sessions could take place (see 'Data Collection Calendar' in Appendix A.

activities as well as reading authentic picture books had not been common class-room occurrences before the study (see Chapter 7.2.3), it was easy for the teacher not to assign these kinds of activities during the study. Hence, in class only the regular reading of sentences or short adapted texts in the course book was con-ducted. Thus, it can be assumed that the regular classroom procedures did not have any influence on reading performance or on performance on the language tests; even if they had had any influence, it would have been the same in both classes.

7.4 Identifying the Mixed Methods Design of this Study

This subchapter shows how the qualitative as well as quantitative elements that provide various perspectives on the three research questions are tightly inter-woven in the study and hence constitute a mixed methods research design. A combination of both qualitative and quantitative data, as found in mixed meth-ods studies, is believed to offer a more holistic approach to solving problems and answering research questions (Kuckartz, 2014: 17).

A commonly cited definition (see, e.g., Creswell & Plano Clark, 2011) is that of Johnson, Onwuegbuzie and Turner (2007: 123), who define mixed method research as follows:

> Mixed methods research is the type of research in which a researcher or team of research-ers combines elements of qualitative and quantitative research approaches (i.e., use of qualitative and quantitative viewpoints, data collection, analysis, inference techniques) for the broad purposes of breadth and depth of understanding and corroboration.

This definition not only incorporates the idea of mixing different research meth-ods (qualitative and quantitative), but in a more holistic view embraces the whole research methodology. Whilst the term research methodology embraces the whole research project and its components, the method refers to the specific method employed in the data collection process, which of course is partly prede-termined by the methodology (Bitchener, 2010: 141). Johnson et al.'s (2007) defi-nition attempts to find a consensus based on 19 different definitions (Creswell & Plano Clark, 2011: 3) and encompasses a holistic view of the multiple steps of the research process. However, one minor point needs to be added. As mentioned by Kuckartz (2014: 33), the combination and integration of qualitative and quan-titative methodologies can happen in all the phases of a research project and should take place in one and the same research project in order for it to be mixed methods research. In the current study, then, mixed methods in the area of EFL classroom research is defined as follows:

Mixed methods research refers to the purposeful and target-oriented combination and integration of various elements of qualitative and quantitative research approaches in some or all phases of a research project in order to arrive at a holistic picture of FLL and teaching.

Because of the integration of qualitative and quantitative approaches, mixed methods research is sometimes understood as a distinct methodological field that offers an alternative to the two traditional dichotomies of qualitative and quantitative research (Teddlie & Tashakkori, 2010: 2).

The skilful combination and integration of qualitative and quantitative approaches is central in mixed methods research, while researchers traditionally distinguished between qualitative and quantitative research. According to Kuckartz (2014: 28), quantitative research is associated with standardised research instruments and works with numerical data. A representative sample is chosen in order to allow statistical inferences about a larger population. Qualitative methods, in brief, do not work with numerical data but with words (Kuckartz, 2014: 28). In classroom research, qualitative research is typically based on the assumption that classroom procedures must be studied holistically and cannot be broken down into single parts or into numbers (McKay, 2006: 6). Qualitative research by no means replaces quantitative methods, but presents an alternative methodology.

Mixed methods research assumes the compatibility of qualitative and quantitative approaches.[131] That is why researchers in mixed methods research focus more on the research question and the practical issue of "what works" instead of attempting to combine the philosophies and world views of both methods (Kuckartz, 2014: 20, 35f). This makes mixed methods very practical, as the researcher is "free to use all methods possible to address a research problem" (Creswell & Plano Clark, 2011: 13). The present study also follows this practical approach, as will become clear in the following discussion about research paradigms.

Mixed methods research allows for a wide range of different designs, as the researcher has a wide array of options from which to choose. Over the past 30 years, a large number of different mixed methods designs have been classified (see Creswell & Plano Clark, 2011: 56ff for an overview). However, instead of

---

131 In the traditional debate about qualitative and quantitative approaches there are purists who argue that both methods (and methodologies) cannot be mixed (see, e.g., Kuckartz, 2014: 34; Teddlie & Tashakkori, 2010: 8). The combination of the two different world views, philosophies and theoretical foundations which underlie qualitative and quantitative research is deemed impossible (see Creswell & Plano Clark, 2011: 19ff; Johnson & Gray, 2010).

using one of the predetermined designs, the current study made use of the dynamic approach to creating its own design (Creswell & Plano Clark, 2011: 55ff). The design of the study is a fixed and not an emergent one, as all its elements, except for the questionnaire on reading strategies, were planned and organised from the beginning (Creswell & Plano Clark, 2011: 54). Moreover, it involves mixing at the level of only one single study (Johnson et al., 2007: 123). A further key component of a mixed methods design is the way in which qualitative and quantitative strands[132] of the study relate to each other. According to Creswell and Plano Clark (2011: 64), four decisions need to be made about the strands: (1) the level of interaction between the strands, (2) the priority of the strands, (3) the timing of the strands and (4) the procedures for mixing the strands.[133] The design of the present study is a fully mixed design, following an interactive level of interaction [sic] with equal priority given to qualitative and quantitative elements in a multiphase combination timing (see Cresswell & Plano Clark, 2011: 64). In other words, the design mixes at all levels of the research project, the qualitative and quantitative strands are not kept independent but interact with each other, equal importance is given to qualitative and quantitative methods and there are multiple phases of sequential and concurrent timing involved. Qualitative and quantitative elements are tightly interwoven and neither strand can be separated from the other, both with regard to the level of interaction and to timing. Finally, the three research questions were not investigated separately because the data collection process integrated all three foci (see Chapters 7.3.3 and 7.3.5).

Moreover, the research instruments used for the data collection contained qualitative as well as quantitative instruments. Table 9 shows which instrument collected qualitative or quantitative data and also shows how the collected data were ultimately analysed. The last column shows the priority of either the qualitative or the quantitative element from the data collected with each instrument.

---

132 These strands are also referred to as research phases by Nastasi, Hitchcock and Brown (2010: 315).

133 Other design typologies or decisions have been described by Nastasi et al. (2010) and Morse (2010). However, all these designs can principally also be described with the four components outlined by Creswell and Plano Clark (2011). Hence, only that one will be referred to here.

Table 9: Qualitative and quantitative instruments and their analysis (a number '1' or '2' after a cross indicates the priority of either the qualitative or the quantitative analysis of the data provided by one instrument).

Instrument		Collection of qualitative data	Collection of quantitative data	Qualitative analysis	Quantitative analysis	Summary[134]
Reading comprehension	Self-assessment of reading comprehension		x		x	QUAN
	Oral reading recall and comprehension questions	x		x^1	x^2	QUAL→quan
	Written comprehension tasks		x		x	QUAN
Reading strategies	Semi-structured group interview	x		x		QUAL
	Field notes	x		x	x^2 (Category system is subsequently quantified)	QUAL →quan
	Observation and analysis of video-recording	x		x		QUAL
FL perfor-mance	Questionnaire on reading strategies		x		x	QUAN
	Topic-based language tests		x		x	QUAN

134 The notation system with lower-case and capital letters displays the emphasis on either the qualitative or the quantitative approach and the arrow indicates which approach is followed by which. This system was, for example, explained by Morse (2010).

As seen in Table 9, the amount of qualitative and quantitative data was about the same. Priority was given to neither of the two. This is partly based on the fact that mixing did not only take place at the level of data collection and design, but it occurred during the analysis and the interpretation of the data as well. Particularly the data provided by a qualitative instrument is firstly analysed qualitatively, but can often be quantified in a following step.

In the present study, mixed methods were used as the overall approach to researching, whilst some aspects of triangulation[135] were embedded in the design as well. Triangulation is sometimes carelessly used as a synonym for mixed methods, but is not the same.[136] Brown and Rodgers (2002: 244) summarise seven different types of triangulation:[137] Data, investigator, theory, methodological, interdisciplinary, time and location triangulation. Only methodological triangulation refers to mixing different research methods.[138]

---

135 Triangulation is a term borrowed from seafaring and land measurement; in social research it essentially refers to the investigation of the research issue as well as the attempt at understanding an aspect from more than one standpoint (Brown & Rodgers, 2002: 243; Flick, 2006: 305).

136 'Mixed methods' is understood as a much broader concept, even as a research paradigm, whereas triangulation is taken rather as a means of validation and a way of enriching perspectives (Greene, Caracelli & Graham, 1989: 256). In contrast to the detailed descriptions of mixed methods research designs found in literature on research methods (e.g., Creswell & Plano Clark, 2011), the literature on triangulation does not offer concrete suggestions for research designs or other guidance for practical implication. In his original conceptualisation of triangulation, Denzin (1970: 301) includes between-method as well as within-method triangulation. The latter denotes combining methods within either a qualitative or a quantitative approach, for example by using a closed questionnaire as well as standardised FL tests to gather two sets of quantitative data. In this sense, triangulation has a broader scope than mixed methods, as mixed methods always includes the combination of qualitative and quantitative data and is, hence, only concerned with between-methods triangulation.

137 Brown and Rodger's (2002) synthesis is based on Brown (2001), Denzin (1978), Freeman (1998) and Janesick (1994).

138 Methodological triangulation is the most common form of triangulation, which is why the term triangulation is often taken to denote methodological triangulation only (Flick, 2011: 27).

242

Three of these types were used within the mixed methods design of the current study. First of all, methodological triangulation was applied because of the integration of different research methods. Following Denzin's (1970) more detailed explanation of methodological triangulation, between-method triangulation was used because both qualitative as well as quantitative methods were utilised. Moreover, the study made use of data triangulation, because data were collected from multiple sources, namely from the children in the reading and the control group as well as from their parents and teachers. Furthermore, data were collected via various different instruments. This was done to counteract possible biases of individuals and to get a more realistic impression on the participants' reading competences (Brown & Rodgers, 2002: 244). Finally, time triangulation was also applied. Over the period of five months, data were collected on multiple occasions in order to generate a data pool that could be used as the basis for a thorough analysis (Brown & Rodgers, 2002: 244).

Generally speaking, there are various reasons for choosing a mixed methods research design that included different types of triangulation for the present study. FL reading is a multifaceted phenomenon that needs to be investigated from various different angles. Thus, the study did not address only one but three research questions; and the different research questions required different research instruments and methods. Mixed methods offered an ideal approach to investigate the research questions thoroughly and gain a holistic picture of the affordances of reading authentic English picture books at primary school level (Kuckartz, 2014: 51). Various instruments were chosen so that more data and evidence could be collected to illuminate the phenomenon of FL reading from a variety of angles and perspectives and provide a rich and detailed account (Creswell & Plano Clark, 2011: 12). Additionally, several sources of data can supplement each other and shed light on aspects which other instruments or methods may not reveal. In sum, the mixed methods approach served to enhance the credibility of the findings because it investigated young learners' FL reading from different perspectives.

7.5 Meeting Quality Criteria with the Mixed Methods Design

As previously stated, the mixed methods design has been implemented to enhance the study's credibility. This subchapter will extent this point and offer insight into the efforts undertaken to meet quality criteria in the study.

At the present time, there is no consensus on quality criteria in mixed methods research and the discussion about them is still in its infancy (Ludwig, 2012; Mayring, 2012; Creswell & Plano Clark, 2011). Mayring's (2012) suggestion of ten steps which every mixed methods project should follow and O'Cathain's (2010) very similar quality framework for mixed methods research are currently the only two guidelines to standards found in mixed methods research. The present study followed and acted upon Mayring's (2012: 291ff) suggestions of undertaking ten relevant steps when creating a high-quality mixed methods research design. This included formulating a practice-relevant and user-oriented research question (see Chapter 7.1), elaborating on the current status of research (see Chapter 2 to 6 and 7.1) and developing a suitable research design with a clear description of the research methods (see Chapter 7.3) and a clear selection and description of the sample (see Chapter 7.2). Outlining significant consequences for teaching practice is also part of these steps (see Chapter 12.3). However, these steps should not only be followed in mixed methods studies, but in any studies concerned with classroom research and as such these standards might not be sufficient to ensure the quality of a study. Therefore, further criteria were taken into consideration for the present study.

Generally, (quantitative) studies make use of two common and well-established quality criteria: validity and reliability. However, these standards cannot and need not be held to in mixed methods studies with an explorative approach and a number of qualitative elements. While validity and reliability usually play a key role in quantitative research, concepts for enhancing both criteria in more explorative studies were proposed in that both criteria find counterparts that correspond to them in qualitative research. According to Lincoln and Guba (1985), trustworthiness is the qualitative concept of validity and reliability; in turn, credibility, transferability as well as dependability are said to make a research project trustworthy. The following table provides an overview:

Table 10: Quality criteria in quantitative and qualitative research (based on Dörnyei, 2007; Hopkins, 2008; Lincoln & Guba, 1985).

Common research criteria in quantitative research		Qualitative descriptions of research criteria		
		Qualitative equivalent according to Lincoln and Guba (1985)	Qualitative counterpart according to Lincoln & Guba (1985)	Selected techniques to enhance validity and reliability based on Hopkins (2008)
Validity	Internal validity	Trustworthiness	Credibility	– Collect data at different points in time – Be clear and rigorous throughout all stages of analysis – Triangulation
	External validity		Transferability	– Collect data from more than one site
	Construct validity		/	– Use multiple sources of evidence – Have key informants review drafts – Establish a chain of evidence – Use tactics for verifying conclusions
Reliability	Internal reliability		Dependability	– Protocol
	External reliability			

The following sections will elaborate on these standards and make an attempt to apply them to the current study.

First of all, validity generally refers to "the extent to which conclusions drawn from research provide an accurate description [...] or a correct explanation of what happens and why" (Jupp, 2006: 311) and is usually divided into internal, external and construct validity. As outlined in Chapter 7.4 and as can also be seen in Table 10, using mixed methods and data triangulation supports the internal validity of the present study because it elucidates research objects from various different perspectives so that a holistic and realistic result can be reached. The study also achieves a certain degree of internal validity through careful sampling, because it controls for variables that might influence the results of the study (Mc-Kay, 2006: 12). Internal validity is said to correlate with credibility (see Table

10). A detailed description of the research project, its results and the analysis of these results, as found in Chapters 7 to 11, demonstrates how the techniques mentioned in the right column in Table 10 were implemented to increase the present study's credibility.

The detailed description also underscores the transferability (Brown & Rodgers, 2002: 242). According to Dörnyei (2007: 57), transferability is the "'applicability' of the results to other contexts and the equivalent to external validity." Through the careful description of the study, the reader gets a clear picture of the study's context and can thus decide on the extent to which it might be transferred to other contexts, as "the degree of transferability depends to a large degree on the similarity of the learning contexts being examined" (McKay, 2006: 13). In principle, the present study could be conducted at any other primary school in Germany, but a primary school with a bilingual programme would of course make the setting more similar. Generally, 'school' is such a unique setting that it is very difficult to find a markedly similar one. This becomes clear when taking heterogeneous classrooms and schools with different foci and in various catchment areas into consideration. Also, critically speaking, transferability in classroom research is not necessarily desirable, as in explorative classroom research projects the researcher aims primarily at getting a clear picture of the specific context to formulate implications for exactly that context (McKay, 2006: 7). There is not always a need to transfer and generalise the results of an explorative study to a different or larger sample.

Another aspect of validity which the present study tried to ensure is construct validity. Construct validity refers to "the degree to which the instruments used in a study measure the construct that is being examined" (McKay, 2006: 12). With regard to the current study, the instruments and methods chosen to collect data on reading comprehension, reading strategies and FL performance must appear to an outsider to actually test what should be tested.[139] This is on the one hand ensured through mostly choosing instruments and measurements which were used before, but in slightly different contexts. On the other hand, some instruments were designed according to what was dealt with in class as well as during the reading sessions. Following this procedure in creating instruments ensures that what was done in class or during the reading sessions was also tested; for example in the topic-based language tests (see Chapter 8.4). This corresponds to content validity, which Dörynei (2007: 50) describes as one aspect of construct validity.

---

139 In quantitative research, the validity of test instruments can be measured by numerical means; however, this is not possible with qualitative instruments and a small sample size.

Reliability, the "degree to which the results of a study are consistent" (Brown & Rodgers, 2002: 241), is also approached in the current study to a certain extent. Reliability can be broken down into two types, internal and external reliability. Internal reliability refers to the consistency of results when data are analysed by another researcher (Brown & Rodgers, 2002: 241). However, this presupposes that the resources of a project are sufficient to engage more than one researcher. For the reason of very limited resources of the present project, no other researcher could be called in. Still, given the detailed explanation of how the data were analysed and the fact that several quantitative instruments were scored with an answer key and thus did not allow any scope for speculation (see Chapter 8 for details), one can cautiously assume that another researcher would have come to similar results when analysing the data of the current study.

External reliability refers to the degree to which results are consistent if the study were to be repeated by another researcher (Brown & Rodgers, 2002: 241). A similar outcome would be probable if the study were repeated in exactly the same setting, but questionable if another researcher conducted the study in a different setting (also see external validity). Even if a study were to be repeated in the same setting, the researcher is likely to have a particular influence in some way (see Chapter 7.4). However, it is questionable to what extent the same results would be desirable, because, as already outlined above, explorative research with qualitative elements does not necessarily aim at transferability of the results.

With regard to qualitative research standards, reliability is more or less analogous to dependability, which is the degree to which the findings can be trusted (Brown & Rodgers, 2002: 242; Dörnyei, 2007: 57). In this study, triangulation and the use of mixed methods support the trustworthiness of the results (Brown & Rodgers, 2002: 242), as well as the detailed report or protocol of them (McKay, 2006: 14) as noted previously.

Independent of standard quality criteria as outlined in the previous sections, Henrici (2001: 33) points out the importance of the internal and external acceptability of a research project in the field of EFL research. Firstly, internal acceptability refers to the acceptance of the research object itself, the research design and the study's results within the research community (Henrici, 2001: 34). For the present study, internal acceptability is achieved through the presentation of the study or parts of it at a number of conferences, including a discussion of the research project with various experts.[140] Secondly, external acceptability refers to the importance and the practical relevance of the research in learning and teaching FLs, that is whether the research objects, methods and results are relevant and acceptable for teachers in the practice of teaching FLs (Henrici, 2001: 34f). The practical relevance of the present study became apparent in various discussions with in-practice teachers and experts in EFL teaching practice; that is, at conferences as mentioned in Footnote 140, in teacher workshops where practical ideas from the project were presented (e.g., *Grundschultag Englisch* [workshop day for English in primary school], Bielefeld, 2014) and in regular discussions with the teachers at the school the study took place at. Moreover, some of the practical ideas and materials are being and will be published in practice-oriented magazines on teaching English in primary school in Germany, specifically *'Grundschule Englisch'* [English in primary school] and *'Grundschulmagazin Englisch'* [magazine about the teaching of English in primary school].[141]

In summary, one can see that as many measurements and reflections as possible relating to the quality of the study were considered in order to ensure the quality of this explorative mixed methods project. While the study has some shortcomings with regard to quantitative research standards (though it is questionable whether such standards can and need to be reached with explorative studies), it also has some major advantages and strong points in terms of quality criteria from other perspectives. The limitations of the current study will critically be discussed in Chapter 12.2, reflecting upon possible downsides of the chosen design and instruments and outlining alternatives.

7.6 Summary of Chapter 7

Chapter 7 provided detailed information about the design of the study, which investigated reading authentic English picture books in the primary school

---

140 The conferences and expert meetings include, among others: the summer school of the *Deutsche Gesellschaft für Fremdsprachenforschung* (DGFF) [German Society for Foreign (and Second) Language Research] in August 2014 in Riezlern (Austria), three research colloquia in the area of EFL learning and teaching research in May 2015 (University of Wuppertal and University of Vechta) and June 2016 (University of Cologne), the interdisciplinary *Bielefelder Frühjahrstagung* in May 2015, the *Language in Focus* conference in Turkey in 2014 and 2015, the *DGFF Nachwuchstagung* in February 2015 (Münster) and September 2016 (Frankfurt), the *DGFF Jahrestagung* in October 2015 and the MATSDA conferene in Tilburg in June 2017.

141 See Reckermann (2016a) for an article on the book 'The Queen's Knickers'.

EFL classroom from various perspectives. Firstly, the three research foci on (I) reading comprehension, (II) reading strategies and (III) FL performance were outlined and explained, and three corresponding research questions that included a number of key aspects to be investigated were formulated and explicated. In brief, the aim of this study is to find out about young learners' competence to read and understand authentic English picture books by focusing on reading comprehension, reading strategies and a possible effect of reading on FL performance.

Chapter 7.2 then provided details about the participants and setting of the study. The study was conducted in a Year 4 at a NRW primary school with a bilingual programme. Two groups of participants, a so-called 'reading group' that was involved in reading picture books and a 'control group' that was not involved in reading, were selected. The reading group consisted of eleven learners from one Year 4 class, and the control group of 12 learners from the parallel class (in total $N = 23$). Both groups were comparable in all aspects that were deemed relevant for a potential influence on the study's results.

Subsequently, the study's design with its different research methods as well as the procedure of data collection were outlined. Firstly, a longitudinal reading study was conducted over a period of five months during which the reading group (subdivided into RG 1, RG 2 and RG 3) was involved in weekly reading sessions that were concerned with reading picture books and various tasks related to this activity. These reading sessions provided data on the reading groups' reading comprehension (research question I) and reading strategies (research question II). For research question III, the control group came into play, in that a quasi-experimental design was embedded into the reading study that tested both groups' FL performance via a language test at three points during the five months. This allowed a comparison of FL performance between those learners that were involved in the reading sessions and those that only took part in the regular classroom activities.

Because of the integration of different research elements, qualitative as well as quantitative, the study's overall design is a mixed methods study. This was elaborated on in Chapter 7.4, which outlined to what extent qualitative and quantitative research elements were integrated. Also, methodological, data and time triangulation as used in the present study were explained.

Finally, a reflection on meeting quality criteria in this study was provided in Chapter 7.5. As such criteria hardly exist at all for mixed methods research, familiar criteria from quantitative research (validity and reliability) were discussed together with their qualitative counterpart of trustworthiness and its component elements. The extent to which these criteria can and should be met in explorative classroom research are debatable, but the subchapter still provided an insight into attempts to comply with quality standards in this study. Finally, also details of the internal and external acceptability of the current project in the area of learning and teaching FLs in research and practice were elaborated on.

8. Research Materials, Instruments and Methods of Data Analysis

Abstract: This chapter rounds off the presentation of the research design by describing the research instruments and materials used in the study. It provides explanations of the materials and instruments that were used, as well as a description of the analysis of data collected via the different instruments.

To begin with, Table 11 provides an overview of the research materials and instruments that were used in this study:

Table 11: Overview of research materials and research instruments; divided by research foci.

Research materials	Research instruments			
	Collecting information about setting and participants (reading and control group)	(I) Reading comprehension (reading group)	(II) Reading Strategies (reading group)	(III) FL performance (reading and control group)
→ Six authentic English picture books → Posters for reading session transparency Supportive devices: → Picture dictionaries → Dictionaries → Word lists → MP3-players with audio-recordings of the books	→ Learners' questionnaire → Parents' questionnaire → YLE test on EFL reading and writing competence → Two semi-structured teacher interviews → Short teacher questionnaire	→ Self-assessment of reading comprehension → Oral reading recall and comprehension questions → Written reading comprehension tasks	→ Observation: field notes and analysis of video-recordings → Semi-structured group interviews → Question-naire on reading strategies	→ Topic-based language tests
Will be explained in Chapter 8.1	**Was already explained in Chapter 7.2**	**Will be explained in Chapter 8.2**	**Will be explained in Chapter 8.3**	**Will be explained in Chapter 8.4**

The first column shows the research materials that were used during the reading sessions, including the picture books and the supportive devices. Detailed information about the research materials will be provided in Chapter 8.1. The second column summarises the instruments that were used to gather information about the setting and participants as already explained in Chapter 7.2. The remaining three columns on the right list the research instruments that were used to investigate the three research foci of the study. The instruments for the main foci 'reading comprehension' and 'reading strategies' were used solely with the reading group during the reading sessions. The control group was only relevant for the subsidiary focus on FL performance. In the course of this chapter, a subchapter each is dedicated to each of the three foci and will describe the instruments in detail as well as elaborate on how data were collected and analysed.

All the instruments listed in Table 11 were piloted, but they were piloted individually and not in an actual pilot study. The piloting took place with several different participants from different schools at different points in time. In the following chapters, the piloting will only be mentioned if any changes or decisions of interest resulted from it.

8.1 Selection of Topics, Books and Supportive Devices for the Reading Sessions

This chapter will elaborate on the materials that were used in this study. As already indicated in Chapter 7.3.2, a total of six different authentic English picture books on three different topics were worked with during the reading sessions. They were carefully chosen and then analysed with regard to their degree of difficulty, which will be outlined in Chapters 8.1.1 and 8.1.2. After that, selected supportive devices that were available to the children while they were reading will be detailed in Chapter 8.1.3.

8.1.1 Choice of Topic-Based Books for the Reading Sessions

The books for the reading sessions were initially chosen based on the following criteria:

- They were authentic English picture books as outlined in Chapter 5.3.3.
- All the books were previously unknown to the pupils. This was established by asking both the teacher and the pupils.[142]

---

142   Max stated that he knew the book 'Froggy's Best Christmas' from his home. His data on this book were hence taken out of the data pool so as to not skew the results.

- Each book dealt with the same topic that the English class was covering at that time. These topics were determined by the English teacher and books were selected by me for the reading sessions on that basis.[143]

Table 12 presents the topics that were covered, including the books as well as the time frame in which they were read.[144]

Table 12: Topics and books for the reading study.

Time	Topic	Picture books dealt with
September – October 2014	London	• The Queen's Knickers (Allan, 1993) • Paddington at the Palace (Bond, 2010)
October – November 2014	Shopping	• Five Little Monkeys Go Shopping[145] (Christelow, 2007) • Something Good (Munsch, 1990)
December 2014 – January 2015	Christmas and Winter	• Froggy's Best Christmas (London & Remkiewicz, 2000) • Winnie in Winter (Thomas & Paul, 1996)

Four original copies of each book were provided, so that in the small reading groups (see Chapter 7.3.2) each child had his/her own copy of the book. This ensured that the learners could read according to their individual pace and reading strategies. Also, choosing original books, instead of copies, for example, complied with the principle of authenticity and maintained the appealing character of a real book (see Chapter 5.1).

During the selection process, the criticism that these books were written for a younger age group (see Chapter 5.3.4) was considered. However, drawing on the experience of other researchers (Brewster & Ellis, 2002; Burwitz-Melzer, 2013; Kolb, 2013) and primary school EFL teacher colleagues, using carefully selected picture books in a Year 4 still seemed reasonable. During the reading sessions this decision was confirmed as the children in most cases said that they had liked the books.

---

143 As outlined in Chapter 7.3.2, this ensured that the reading group did not miss out on too much class content. Not only that, but topic congruence between the EFL class and the books selected also ensured that the reading group had some previous topic knowledge (see Chapter 6.5.1).

144 The authors of the respective picture books will only be given in this table and be listed in detail in the list of references. In the following course of this book, only the picture books' titles will be given for reasons of readability.

145 This book will henceforth be referred to as 'Five Little Monkeys' for reasons of readability.

8.1.2 Analysing and Comparing the Degree of Difficulty of the Books

This chapter takes a closer look at the degree of difficulty of the books chosen for the reading study and analyses the extent to which the books are comparable. This analysis is based on the multidimensional factors that determine the comprehension of a text that were outlined in Chapter 4.5.

All six books have many features in common. They are all authentic English picture books that tell a story based on a storyline and are not just a list of disjointed facts or topics (Nikolajeva, 2005: 100ff). Continuity is found throughout all texts and all stories follow a logical and chronological order of events (Roschlaub, 2012: 9). In all six books, the textual and visual elements are for the most part symmetrical and congruent and no contradictions between the text and the pictures are found (see Chapters 5.2.3 and 5.3.3). In the stories, each book has a limited number of up to three main characters. Moreover, all the books contain a combination of narrative and dialogue (see Cameron, 2001: 165). As for the layout of the books, they all have a minimum of one coloured picture on each double page as well as at least one sentence on each double page (Geisler, 1985: 122). Hence, every page displays a mixture of text and picture(s), the relation of which will be further elaborated on below. Moreover, the font size – a typographic factor that determines text difficulty (Geisler, 1985: 122) – of all the books is comparable, ranging from 4 to 6 millimetres[146] with an average of 4.5 millimetres. The actual length of a book or text is a further important aspect with regard to its degree of difficulty (Roschlaub, 2012: 10). Indicated by the number of pages, the length of a book is heavily dependent on the actual size of a page as well as the relation between the text and the pictures, but all the books used range from ten to 16 pages[147] with an average length of 13.5 pages.

In spite of all similarities, these books also differ to a certain extent. Factors of text difficulty are determined on the one hand by the text itself and on the other hand by the recipient of the text (see Chapter 4.5.1). However, as researchers have little to no influence on the reader, the focus for analysing the degree of difficulty of the books was directed towards the text itself. Based on the considerations outlined in Chapter 4.5.1, a number of linguistic factors, two factors on the text level as well as the relation of textual and visual elements were taken into consideration for the analysis of the books. Table 13 displays an overview of the analysis of the books' degrees of difficulty. The factors mentioned will further be elaborated on in the following sections.

---

146   The capital letter 'T' was taken as a measurement in each book.

147   Only the pages which contained the story were counted. A double page was always counted as one page, as in picture books double pages usually constitute a coherent unit.

Table 13: Analysis of the degree of difficulty of the books.

	Linguistic factors						Factors at the text level		Visuals
	Number of words (tokens)	Number of different words (types)	Token-type ratio	Frequency analysis (percentage of infrequent types)	Average number of words per page	Average length of sentences (in words)	Supportive language patterns (repetition, onomatopoeia, rhyme) + frequent o occasionally - not at all	Tenses used (Main tense in bold plus occasional additional tenses)	Average relation of texts and visuals
The Queen's Knickers	385	207	1.86	Infrequent types: 13.2 %	25.6	7.1	-	**Simple present** Simple past Past perfect	79 % visuals 21 % text
Paddington at the Palace	666	258	2.58	Infrequent types: 2.9 %	70	13.2	-	**Simple past** Simple present Will future Present continuous	66 % visuals 34 % text
Five Little Monkeys	571	166	3.44	Infrequent types: 2.1 %	35.7	6.4	+ (repetition and onomatopoeia)	**Simple present** Present continuous Present perfect	81 % visuals 19 % text

	Linguistic factors				Average number of words per page	Average length of sentences (in words)	Factors at the text level		Visuals
	Number of words (tokens)	Number of different words (types)	Token–type ratio	Frequency analysis (percentage of infrequent types)	Average number of words per page	Average length of sentences (in words)	Supportive language patterns (repetition, onomatopoeia, rhyme) + frequent o occasionally - not at all	Tenses used (Main tense in bold plus occasional additional tenses)	Average relation of texts and visuals
Something Good	654	206	3.17	Infrequent types: 1.9 %	54.5	7.8	O (repetition and onomatopoeia)	**Simple past** Simple present Present continuous Will future Going-to future Present perfect	69 % visuals 31 % text
Froggy's Best Christmas	679	259	2.62	Infrequent types: 6 %	45.2	4.4	O (onomatopoeia)	**Simple past** Past continuous Simple present Present continuous	75 % visuals 25 % text
Winnie in Winter	594	219	2.71	Infrequent types: 4 %	49.5	7.3	O (repetition and onomatopoeia)	**Simple past** Simple present Past perfect Past perfect continuous Past continuous	84 % visuals 16 % text

The number of tokens, types and the resulting token-type ratio are semantic factors that influence the comprehension of a text (Geisler, 1985: 122; Roschlaub, 2012: 8f). The more types there are and the more complex the token-type ratio is, the higher the lexical density of a text (McCarthy, 1990: 72). In order to establish the number of words (tokens) and different words (types), an online analysis tool[148] was used, which Paulick and Groot-Wilken (2009: 185) also made use of in the EVENING study. In order to determine lexical variation and the lexical density of the text, the ratio between tokens and types was calculated (McCarthy, 1990: 73), using McCarthy's equation of tokens divided by types. The lower the result, the more difficult, dense or complex the token-type ratio is.[149] In sum, the lower the token-type ratio is, the higher is the lexical variation of a text.

At the word level, not only lexical density but also the familiarity of words is important for understanding. Words that children are familiar with are easier to read and understand than those they are not familiar with (Böttger, 2005: 85; Geisler, 1985: 122). Hence a frequency analysis of the words in the text was conducted in order to find out if the words used in the text belong to a child's basic vocabulary or whether they occur infrequently in children's speech. This was done on the basis of an online tool for vocabulary profiles (Lextutor)[150], which draws on corpora of word lists that were generated from children's oral productions.[151] Hence, this tool provides information regarding the extent to which the words used in the text are frequently used by children and belong to children's basic vocabulary in English. The tool draws on types and not on tokens for calculation. An oral corpus had to be used, as there is no written corpus of children's vocabulary available to German researchers.[152] Moreover, no corpus for EFL learners is available so that data of native speakers as provided by the corpus had to be adhered to. The number of words that occurred infrequently in children's language was then calculated as a percentage

---

148   To be found as freeware on http://www.usingenglish.com/resources/text-statistics. php (last access 15.05.2017).

149   McCarthy (1990: 73) refers to it as token-type ratio, which is hence used for this book as well. Generally, also a calculation of the type-token ratio is common.

150   To be found as freeware on http://www.lextutor.ca/vp/kids/ (last access 15.05.2017).

151   This is the information provided by the website about the corpus they work with: "VP-Kids matches children's texts against 10 modified 250-word lists generalised from several empirical studies of children's oral productions (Murphy 1957; Johnson 1971; Hopkins 1979; Moe et al. 1982) by Stemach & Williams."

152   Oxford University Press has a written corpus based on English children's books, but it was impossible to go through the application procedure of at least one year in a timely manner. Only a few applications are granted and, if so, researchers are only given limited access.

value using the aforementioned online tool. Words were deemed 'infrequent' when they were not found in the children's corpus and are hence assumed to be infrequent in children's language. The higher the number of infrequent words (in types), the higher is the level of difficulty of the text.

Looking at the next criterion, the average number of words per page provides information about the text independent of the font size and actual length of the book. The average number of words per page was calculated by dividing the number of words by the number of pages. One page was always defined as one double page (see Footnote 147).

The average length of a sentence is a syntactic factor that also influences the difficulty of a text (Geisler, 1985: 122). One can assume that on average the shorter the sentences, the easier they are to read. However, this also depends on other aspects such as the structural complexity of the sentence. The average length of sentences was calculated by dividing the number of words (tokens) by the number of sentences. The number of sentences was established by the online analysing tool also used to count the types and tokens (see Footnote 148).

At the text level, the occurrence of supportive language patterns such as repetition, onomatopoeia and rhyme are frequently listed as factors that ease the comprehension of a storytelling book for young EFL learners (Böttger, 2005: 85; Brewster & Ellis, 2002: 190; Willgerodt, 2003: 51). These are typical features of children's books, especially picture books. Each book was scanned for patterns such as these that might support the children's understanding and memorisation of a text. The focus was on repetitive patterns, onomatopoeia and rhyme. For each aspect the analysis determined whether some or all of these elements were present frequently, occasionally or not at all.

Another aspect at the text level is the (main) tense of the text, as tense is a grammatical feature that can reflect the difficulty of a text (Frisch, 2013: 127). Children's books are usually written in the simple past, simple present and present continuous, which are all said to be understandable to young EFL learners (Cameron, 2001: 166). In each book of the present study, every sentence was checked for the tense or tenses used in it to first establish the main tense of the book and second determine possible further tenses which were only used occasionally.

Finally, the relationship between the text and the visuals was determined, as this is a factor of text difficulty especially found in picture books (Geisler, 1985: 122). The relationship between text and visuals in each book was calculated by first determining the relationship of text and visuals on every page.[153] The average

---

153 A double page was as usual taken as one page.

relationship was then calculated by adding up the percentages and dividing them by the number of pages. Depending on the quality of the visuals, the more visuals a book has, the more these visualisations potentially support comprehension. The relationship, however, also depends on the font size of the text, the number of words per page (two factors also analysed) and the page-size of the book. For example, in the book 'Winnie in Winter' the page-size is very big (A4), whereas the font size is rather small (4 millimetres). The relation of 84 % visuals to 16 % text at a first glance suggests that the book is very easy with a very light text load. But this is relativised when one looks at the number of words per page.

With the help of Table 13, it was possible to compare the books with respect to various factors that determine their levels of difficulty. However, in order to determine the degree of difficulty of a book, one always has to consider and carefully look at all the relevant factors: A book may score high on one factor but then low on another one. Seemingly difficult features of one book often seem to be counterbalanced by another factor which makes it easier. This makes a clear-cut distinction between the easiest and hardest book or a ranking of difficulty of the books nearly impossible. However, a careful analysis of Table 13 shows that all the books are more or less comparable as they all have a mixture of seemingly easy and difficult features. In sum one can assume that, because of the books' many similarities and the careful analysis of a number of different factors in each individual book, the books are comparable with regard to their degree of difficulty.

8.1.3 Support Provided for Reading the Books

In reading session I (see Chapter 7.3.2), supportive devices were provided to help the children with reading the books. These were based on the considerations in Chapter 6 on how reading can be supported. A number of supportive devices were made available so as to establish in the course of the study which of them the children actually used and which of them were truly helpful for comprehension. The learners were already familiar with some of these devices from their regular English classes; these were supplemented with other devices that were partly specifically designed for each book.

Four different supportive devices were made available while the children were reading the books: a picture dictionary, a dictionary, a word list and an audio-recording of the book. As picture dictionaries are (or at least should be) regularly available in primary English classrooms, they were chosen as the first device. The *FindeFix Englisch* picture dictionary (Elsner et al., 2004) was used, as the pupils were already familiar with it to a limited extent from their EFL classroom.

Because of the limitations of a picture dictionary (it only contains a very limited number of words, see Chapter 6.6), a regular bilingual dictionary (Langenscheidt Collins, 2007) was also provided. However, the children were neither used to nor had they been introduced to working with such a dictionary prior to the study. Therefore, a word list that was directly related to the book was provided in addition to the dictionaries. This was designed according to the criteria outlined in Chapter 6.6.4 and a new word list was specifically created for each book. An example can be found in Appendix B.

Apart from vocabulary support by means of dictionaries and word lists, an audio-recording of each book was also provided. The recording was read by a native speaker of English and made available to the children on MP3-players. Chapter 6.7 has shown that audio-recordings had successfully been utilised in several previous reading projects and therefore seemed a viable supportive device for FL reading. However, the use of such a supportive device still needed thorough investigation with regard to its use for young EFL learners' reading. In an attempt to explore the potentially challenging task of reading authentic texts in the primary school, some learners might profit from the listening function, in that the audio-recording might make reading texts accessible to them.[154] The decision to provide an audio-recording was thus mostly of a methodological nature with regard to feasible classroom practices. However, it makes researching reading comprehension slightly difficult. Listening to a recording requires listening comprehension, while reading a book requires reading comprehension. Both combined lead to a combination of reading and listening comprehension, while it is impossible to control to what extent which content aspects of a book were understood from listening, reading or a combination of both. Thus, the extent to which those learners who read the books while listening to the audio-recording understood aspects from listening and/or from reading remains unclear. This problem cannot be solved, but will be critically considered for the presentation and interpretation of results in the respective chapters.

The devices were placed in front of the children (see Picture 1) so they could use them freely. Four copies/items of each device were available so that the children did not have to share or wait but could theoretically use all the devices at any time during the reading process. Independently seeking support when needed is said to support learner autonomy and is a common procedure in the

---

154 As will be seen in Chapter 9.3, the present study has shown that including the audio-recordings made reading feasible and manageable for all the participants in the current reading project.

primary school EFL classroom (Böttger, 2005: 140). It also serves for individual working processes and caters to individual differences amongst the children.

Support was also provided by peers as well as by myself as the researcher. First of all, the children were allowed to choose if they wanted to read in cooperation with a partner or by themselves (see Chapter 6.4). During their reading they were also allowed to ask their peers questions. In primary school, this is a regular procedure of methodological differentiation (see Klippert, 2010: 53). Teacher support was also provided for the children by me as the researcher when necessary. Whenever the children had a question, I supported them just as any other teacher would support them in class.[155] As long as my support did not reveal the answer to a test-item, I would sometimes give the children hints or encouragement with respect to what they were doing or saying. This was done to ensure a relaxed atmosphere that was as close to a regular teaching situation as possible (see Chapter 7.2.5 and 7.4). With regard to teacher support, Steck (2009: 69) points out the importance of the researcher not being taken for a person who wants to test the children but as a person that is willing to support them and offers help where needed.

Picture 1: A small reading group during reading session I of the reading study (permission to print this picture was kindly given by the learners and written consent was given by the learners' parents).

To comply with the principle of transparency in teaching (Meyer, 2004: 25f; Standardsicherung Englisch NRW, 2010: 2), two posters were provided. One

---

155 As I am a professionally trained primary school teacher with three years of teaching experience, I could realistically estimate when and how to do so.

poster gave an overview of the steps and phases during the reading sessions. The other one provided the basic rules of the reading session, including the choice of language and the free choice of supportive devices.

8.2 Research Instruments for Research Question I: Reading Comprehension

This subchapter will outline the research instruments that were used to measure the participants' (level of) reading comprehension of the six books. Many previous studies have only included one measurement to investigate reading comprehension; in particular, multiple choice questions and/or written comprehension tests seem widely used, also with young learners (e.g., Frisch, 2013; Groot-Wilken & Husfeld, 2013). As this seems insufficient to thoroughly investigate reading comprehension, Westphal Irwin (2007: 193) suggests a more qualitative approach to testing reading comprehension in that she recommends a free recall. Additionally, Kolb (2013: 41) used the young EFL learners' self-assessment to investigate their competence with regard to reading picture books (also see Steck, 2009: 78). In the present study, all three of these instruments were used in order to get a holistic picture of the young learners' reading comprehension and to counterbalance possible disadvantages of certain instruments with other measurements. Following the idea of mixed methods an, the instruments include qualitative as well as quantitative measurements to investigate reading comprehension from different perspectives.

8.2.1 Self-Assessment of Reading Comprehension

Directly after reading each picture book, the participants were asked to self-asses their comprehension level. Steck (2009: 78) points out the importance of children's self-assessment for diagnosing children's reading comprehension, as it provides the teacher/researcher with useful information about the learners' reading competence. Following Young (1993: 454), a metric five-point scale, ranging from 'understood all of it' to 'understood none of it', with only the two extremes of the scale labelled, was used (see Table 14). The question and answer extremes were in German to ensure comprehension.

This scale was presented to the children on a laminated Din A4-sized sheet. The children were asked to rate their individually perceived comprehension by putting a small object onto the point of the scale that best described their understanding. So that the children were not influenced by their peers when it was their turn to rate their performance, their classmates had to close their eyes, as seen in Picture 2. A potential influence by me as the researcher could not fully be controlled for (also see Chapter 7.2.5). However, as some children also pointed at low levels of comprehension, an influence by me in the direction of acceptability is unlikely.

Picture 2: The girl on the left displays her perceived comprehension level by indicating it on the scale while the other children close their eyes (permission to print this picture was kindly given by the learners and written consent was given by the learners' parents).

For the analysis, the five-option-scale was coded into numbers as follows:

Table 14: Scale for self-assessment of reading comprehension and coding of the answers for analysis.

Layout of the instrument:	**Wie viel hast du von dem Buch verstanden?** *How much of the book did you understand?*				
	Alles *All of it*				**Gar nichts** *None of it*
	O-------------O-------------O-------------O-------------O				
Coding of the answers:	5	4	3	2	1

This allowed a quantitative analysis of the results. These will be presented and discussed in Chapter 9.2.1, which will also include a general discussion and critical view on how realistic young learners' self-assessment is.

8.2.2 Oral Reading Recall and Oral Comprehension Questions

After self-assessing their level of comprehension of the book, the children were asked to freely recall what they understood and then to answer questions related to the book. As overlaps between the reading recall and the oral comprehension questions are unavoidable, the two parts will be explained and also analysed together in the study.

8.2.2.1 An Explanation of the Two Instruments

In the oral reading recall, the children were asked to freely reveal what they had understood and what the book was about after reading the book and giving their self-assessment. Westphal Irwin (2007: 193) describes the oral reading recall technique as a way to examine what a learner has comprehended and refers to it as "free recall". Young (1993: 455) points out that it is important to prompt the recall directly after the reading to ensure that the readers still remember everything. The recall was initiated by me as the researcher through one or two guiding questions such as "What did you understand?" (see Appendix C.3). On the one hand, a recall provides insights into the reader's ability so summarise a text; on the other it examines the reader's ability to select important details (Westphal Irwin, 2007: 193). Before reading the respective book, it was made transparent to the children that they would be asked to freely recall what they had read and that they should focus on understanding the book's content.

The free recall phase was immediately followed by comprehension questions on the book, as "asking questions can be an effective way of assessing student comprehension" (Westphal Irwin, 2007: 193). Answering specific questions related to a text is a common classroom procedure in primary schools and serves well to diagnose reading comprehension (Steck, 2009: 72). The oral questioning procedure was conducted with the help of a prepared set of eight guiding questions for each book. An example can be found in Appendix C.4. These, however, just guided the conversation and were not followed rigidly. Sometimes, the young learners came up with their own questions, other questions were derived from the context and some questions from the guide had already been answered during the free recall phase. Hence, the questioning phase was handled flexibly, partly integrated into the recall phase and adapted to the situation at hand. Still, all the small groups were asked the same guiding questions, whereas further questions varied from group to group.

The oral recall and questioning phase took place in German and the questions, too, were asked in German. At the participants' level of language competence, retelling a story and answering questions about it in English would have been very demanding and would not have revealed the actual understanding of the story; instead, it would have tested their L2 speaking proficiency, their vocabulary knowledge and their ability to understand English questions. Another reason for using German for this phase was the fact that the children were already used to retelling an English story in German from storytelling phases in class (see Chapter 5.5.1). Of course, using English or using a mixture of both languages was also acceptable on the part of the learners.

The oral recall and questioning phase was conducted in the small reading groups and not individually. This could have some implications on the data that were collected. What is said in a group discussion is influenced by the other participants and particularly influenced by what others have said before. That means that once a child has revealed some content matter, the researcher can no longer tell who else might have or have not understood this prior to the statement being made. Moreover, if a learner repeats an aspect that has already been mentioned by another child, the researcher cannot know if the learner would have known this by himself/herself or if it was a mere repetition of the previous statement. Although this is certainly a drawback of the group procedure, it was taken into consideration in the analysis of the data (see Chapter 8.2.2.2).

8.2.2.2 Analysing Oral Recall and Questioning with an Analysis Scheme

The oral recall and questioning was video-recorded for each book and group and then transcribed for the later analysis. The transcription conventions as well as an example of a transcript of the oral recall and questioning can be found in Appendix D.1.1 and D.1.3.

The transcriptions were then analysed with the help of an analysis scheme that I developed for the purpose of this study. The scheme was mostly developed deductively, based on ideas on the level of reading comprehension found in research by Westphal Irwin (2007), Nold and Rossa (2007), Steck (2009) as well as the curriculum for primary schools in NRW (MSW NRW, 2008a) (also see Chapter 4.5.2). Furthermore, concepts from story grammars, which were based on features identified by Nikolajeva (2005) and Holle (2010) and outlined in Chapter 5.3.2, were considered. In addition, inherent factors of the study's data collection procedure were inductively taken into consideration as well, such as the support of visualisations in the picture books or the retelling procedure in groups. An overview of the analysis scheme is found in Picture 3, a readable analysis scheme is found in Appendix D.2.1. Examples of completed analysis schemes can be found in Appendix D.2.2.

Picture 3: Analysis scheme to analyse the oral recall and questioning for each book and each child. See Appendix E.3 for a readable version.

Child: ___ **Book:** ___ **Date:** ___

Analysis of single utterances

(part 1)

Utterance	Accurate: Yes	Accurate: Partly	Accurate: No	Mentioned before by someone else: Yes	Mentioned before by someone else: Partly	Mentioned before by someone else: No	Level of information: Global understanding (main message)	Detail: Put into context	Detail: Out of context	Detail: Important	Detail: Redundant	What type of information is it? Fact	Event	Character	Emotion	Opinion	How was the information presented? Explicitly presented information: Only in the picture	In the picture and pictures text	Only in the text	Implicitly presented information (Between the lines / own interpretation)	What was done with the information? Recognised	Linked to another aspect from the book	Interpreted	Combined with/ deviated from world knowledge	Own opinion/ reaction provided
Utterance 1																									
Utterance 2																									
...																									

Analysis of coherence

(part 2)

Follows the storyline/ organisational pattern of the book: O Yes O Partly O No

Overall impression

(part 3)

Level of compre-hension	1	2	3	4	5

1
- (Almost) no comprehension
- Only single, redundant details which are isolated statements and out of context
- What was understood is mostly understandable from the pictures
- Includes irrelevant, redundant and inaccurate elaborations
- No coherence, information is presented in isolated pieces

2
- Comprehension of simple details which are mostly not contextualised
- Integration of only a few major ideas which are found in a limited part of the text
- What was understood is explicitly presented in the text by means of simple language and/or the pictures (no interpretation)
- May include irrelevant elaborations
- Does not really show coherence and information is presented in isolated pieces
- Purely reproductive
- May contain inaccurate elaborations

3
- Comprehension of mostly simple details but also some more complex details, even if partly presented through more complex language
- Integration of some information to show a more global understanding
- What was understood was mostly presented in the text and deduced by the reader
- Shows acceptable coherence and organisation
- Shows logical connections
- For the most part accurate elaborations

4
- Comprehension of complex details, presented mostly through language and only partly understandable from the pictures
- Integration of information shows global understanding
- Displays logical connections between events
- No redundant details are presented
- Details presented support comprehension
- Shows coherence and logical organisation
- All elaborations are accurate

5
- Comprehension of complex details presented exclusively through language
- Integration of various aspects spread over the whole text to show thorough global understanding
- Contains implicit information
- Presents major points as well as supporting details
- What was revealed comes from deducing and interpreting information from the text
- Different parts of the text are logically combined to show coherence
- Overall more general and reflective

Notes: ___

(part 4)

One sheet was used per participant per book. The oral recall and questioning were conducted for five books in total,[156] which resulted in a total of five filled-in sheets per participant. As the study had eleven participants, this made 55 filled-in analysis sheets in total. These provided a detailed analysis of each participant's comprehension of each of the books.

The analysis scheme consists of four parts:

Part 1: Analysis of single utterances
Part 2: Analysis of coherence
Part 3: Overall impression in terms of rating the level of comprehension from 1 to 5
Part 4: Further notes

In part 1, each utterance a participant made about a book was analysed in detail. For this, all the utterances a child made about a book were taken from the transcriptions and put into the analysis scheme one by one (one utterance per line). An utterance was defined as one content element, including its context. Each utterance was then analysed with regard to several parameters. First, the extent to which the utterance was accurate was determined. After that, I established whether the utterance had already (partly) been mentioned by another participant from that group before; a factor that derived from the data collection in a group situation. Anything that was either incorrect or had already been revealed by another child was not taken into consideration and not analysed further. For each utterance that could be analysed further, the actual level of the information presented was determined by firstly deciding whether the information was on a global or detail level. If it was a detail, it was decided whether it was an important or redundant detail and whether it was put into the context of a broader action and the book's whole content, or if it was out of context and more of an isolated or unrelated statement. Secondly, the type of information that was revealed was analysed. Types of information include, for example, events that took place or a character that was mentioned. Thirdly, I established whether the information was presented explicitly or implicitly in the book. This distinguishes between information which was explicitly presented through text and/or through the pictures and information that

---

156   The last book, 'Winnie in Winter', was used to fill in the questionnaire on reading strategies (see Chapter 8.3.3). This had to be done right after the reading, as otherwise the children would not have remembered their strategies. Hence, the recall and questioning were skipped in favour of the questionnaire.

had to be deduced by 'reading between the lines'. It is a unique feature of picture books that information can also be presented through pictures; therefore, the information value of pictures was considered in the analysis, too. Finally, what the pupil did with the information was examined. Information might only be recognised, but it might also be interpreted or linked to another piece of information and hence put into a broader context.

Part 2 examined whether and to what extent the learners' utterances followed the organisational patterns of the book and thus coherently shadowed the book's storyline. This was done by reading through the single utterances of part 1. However, in many cases this could only realistically be analysed for the first child of the group speaking, as that child usually summarised the plot of the book and the other children only supplemented this with further bits of information.

In part 3, an overall level of comprehension of the book on a scale of 1 to 5 was determined. The five different levels were explained and presented in Chapter 4.5.2 and are closely related to the aspects of analysis in part 1 of the analysis scheme and, for the most part, build on them. Any utterance that was mentioned by another group member before was left out when establishing the overall comprehension level of a learner.

Lastly, part 4 allowed for taking notes that could not be covered in the previous sections. This part is more open than the others and should cater for unexpected or interesting behaviour, a remark about the learner's mood or a comment about the researcher's impression of the learner's overall performance.[157]

With this analysis scheme, a holistic and more qualitative approach to evaluating the retellings and responses to the questions was used that intentionally avoided merely counting the number of ideas and answers. A holistic approach avoids a predetermined system focusing only on content aspects as well as a system that relies on counting the quantity of ideas (Westphal Irwin, 2007: 193). The reason for choosing such a holistic approach is that the participants' answers were highly individual and that not every participant had the chance

---

157 Because the recall and questioning was video-recorded, the data would have also allowed an analysis of gestures, mime and facial expressions. For instance, non-verbal expressions of confusion, consent or disagreement could have been analysed thereby. However, this was deliberately not done, because I could hardly detect facial expressions in a group of four learners and then clearly ascribe them to an utterance of another learner. Including this into the analysis scheme thus seemed too complex and not trustworthy. Instead, notes were taken in part 4, as explained above, and striking expressions, verbal or non-verbal, were included there.

to contribute everything he/she had understood due to the group-format of the data collection. Taking all four parts of the analysis scheme together provides a holistic picture of each participant's reading comprehension of each book.

8.2.3 Written Reading Comprehension Tasks

In reading session II, which usually took place one week after the reading group had first encountered the book in reading session I, the participants individually worked on written reading comprehension tasks on that book. In contrast to the recall and questioning in small groups, these tasks were completed individually in order to get a picture of each individual learner's performance. Of course, a possible effect of the oral group discussion on the content of the book that took place a week earlier cannot be excluded. However, it is deemed to be unlikely because of the time gap.

The written comprehension tasks consisted of four worksheets that included six different tasks. An example is found in Appendix C.5. For each book the tasks followed exactly the same structure, which will be outlined below. As no (standardised) written comprehension tests were available for the six books, the study had to rely on tasks that I as the researcher created; these were developed on the basis of well-established and frequently-suggested activities for young learners of English. The same procedure was followed in Frisch's (2013) reading study. The tasks used for the present study, however, are more extensive and vary more with regard to choice of tasks.

All the task instructions were provided in English as well as in German in order to ensure the pupils' understanding, though the tasks themselves were all in English. Except for task three, the pupils had to answer the tasks in English. With regard to writing in English, the analysis of the test was done in accordance with the curriculum for English in primary school of NRW (MSW NRW, 2008b). The curriculum states that children are expected to be able to write down words phonetically more or less correctly at the end of Year 4 (MSW NRW, 2008b: 82). Hence, any answer which might be erroneous with regard to grammar, spelling or lexis was regarded as valid as long as the mistakes did not interfere with meaning (also see Finkbeiner, 2005: 269).

Following Krüsmann's recommendations (2003), the children were allowed to use the book while they were working on the tasks. The tasks were thus not used so much to establish whether information and comprehension had been retained in the learners' memory after reading, but rather to ascertain what information the learners can derive from the books via reading comprehension processes.

A variety of different tasks totalling six in all were chosen. As some tasks could theoretically have been completed correctly by chance (e.g., in multiple choice tasks), these were supplemented by tasks of a different nature which eliminated the chance of lucky guesses. In addition, some tasks allowed the learners to demonstrate knowledge on a rather basic level (e.g., numbering pictures in task 6), whereas other tasks were more demanding and went beyond the mere reproduction level (e.g., short answer questions in task 3). Therefore, different tasks catered to individual pupils' preferences and performance levels.

Task one required the pupils to match a sentence and a picture. The pictures were taken from the book and the sentences used were similar to the corresponding ones in the book, but not exactly the same. There were a total of four sentences and eight pictures. Frisch (2011: 79) used a similar task (single words instead of sentences) in order to test the reading comprehension of a text with Year 2 pupils. For Year 4 pupils, sentences appeared more suitable and were also used in the EVENING study (Börner & Frisch, 2013: 86). Following Rymarcyk and Musall's (2010: 82) suggestion, more pictures than sentences were used in order to ensure that the children actually read all the sentences. The pictures and sentences were chosen carefully to guarantee that only one picture corresponded with one sentence.

Task two was a cloze task where pupils had to fill in gaps in sentences. There were six sentences, similar but not the same as the sentences in the books, with one or two gaps each. The gaps had to be filled in using single words or set expressions (e.g., 'at home'). Enever (2011a: 16) used the same task for checking reading comprehension in the ELLiE project. Following common practice in EFL course books for primary schools, the children could choose words to fill the gaps from a box below the gapped sentences. As in task one, there were more words than gaps (twelve words for seven gaps).

The third task, a short-answer question task, was more open than the first tasks. The pupils were asked to provide short answers (a word, phrase or short sentence) to two questions related to the content of the book. The answer could be found in the book, either through the identification of a single piece of information or through the combination of various pieces of information in the text (see Finkbeiner, 2005: 267). The more open-ended nature of the task allowed for a number of possible answers which could be classified as correct, partly correct or incorrect. The learners were allowed to answer in English, German or a mixture of both, as comprehension and not language competence was being tested. In her study, Finkbeiner (2005: 269) even allowed to pupils at upper secondary level to answer in such a way.

Task four consisted of three multiple choice items with three possible answers each, one of which was correct. Again the wording was not exactly the same as in the book. Multiple choice questions are a popular method to test reading comprehension and are suggested and/or used by a large number of researchers (e.g., Lipka & Siegel, 2011; Krüsmann, 2003; Frisch, 2013).

Task five consisted of six statements which the participants had to mark as true or false in a box next to the statement. Again the wording of the statements was not exactly the same as in the book. This task was suggested by Böttger (2005: 153) and Haß (2006: 91) and also used in other projects in a similar way (e.g., Krüsmann, 2003: 50; Frisch, 2011: 78f).

The sixth and final task required the children to put parts of the story into the correct order. Six boxes presented parts of the story in one or two sentences and the corresponding picture, and these boxed had to be numbered in the correct order. As suggested by Böttger (2005: 155) and Elsner (2010: 157), this task is particularly suitable for primary school learners. Erten and Razi (2009) made use of such a task in their study on reading comprehension as well. One has to take into consideration that it might be possible to correctly order the sentences by looking at the pictures carefully and only to a certain extent by reading the sentences. This would still, however, reveal a certain degree of comprehension of the book, as the pictures themselves normally cannot be put into the correct order without understanding the content of the story at least to a certain extent.

One possible objection to this selection of tasks might be the extent to which FL reading competence as opposed to actual comprehension of the book is tested. In order to test actual reading comprehension of the book, researchers often test participants in their L1 to avoid testing L2 reading comprehension skills. The idea of transfer-appropriate processing (Morris, Bransford & Franks, 1977: 528) is a counter-argument to this, as it states that knowledge is best retrieved in the same or a similar context in which it was gained. However, the question of whether task-appropriate processing produces more reliable L2 reading comprehension results cannot fully be answered here. As it is common classroom practice, the FL was chosen for the tasks to get results that offer relevant implications for the EFL classroom. To counterbalance a possible problematic effect that the use of the FL in the tasks might have had, I sometimes translated words for the participants if they asked me to or read words/phrases aloud to them. Translations were particularly often requested for in task three (short answer question) and reading aloud was sometimes required in task five (true or false). Moreover, the tasks to a limited extent also tested L1 and/or L2 writing skills. This, however, cannot be avoided when going beyond the level of ticking answers.

The reading tasks used in the study were not a standardised test but rather tasks which are commonly used in the (primary school) EFL classroom. As such, they can shed light on the extent to which such post-reading tasks can be used in EFL lessons. As Alderson (2005: 212) points out, the design of classroom activities often does not differ much from the design of test items. Thus, the written comprehension tasks in the present study should not only be understood as instruments to investigate reading comprehension, but also as possible classroom activities.

The tasks were analysed quantitatively, with scores attributed to each task. A maximum score of 30 points could be attained with the six tasks.

8.3 Research Instruments for Research Question II: Reading Strategies

Data on the reading strategies that the pupils used for reading the books were collected via observations, group interviews and a questionnaire.[158] This use of different instruments should provide a detailed picture of the reading strategies the participants used. The three different instruments will firstly be explained in detail in the following sections, after which an outline of how the data pool on reading strategies was organised and how the data were subsequently analysed with the help of qualitative content analysis can be found.

8.3.1 Observation of Reading Strategies: Field Notes and Video Analysis

First of all, I as the researcher looked for reading strategies while observing the learners during the actual reading process. Macaro (2001: 36) recommends observing language learners while they work on language tasks such as reading to gather date on strategy use. While observing, I took field notes on the learners' reading strategy use. Appendix C.6 show the rather open observation scheme that was used to take the field notes.

Researchers often suggest detailed and usually quantitative observation schemes to collect data on strategy use (e.g., Ortlieb, 2013; Westphal Irwin, 2007). This was handled differently in the current study because of the lack of extensive data on L2

---

158   Using a think-aloud procedure was contemplated firstly, because it is commonly applied to find out about reading strategies with older FL learners (for example, Young, 1993). This procedure requires readers to voice their thoughts while they are reading (Westphal Irwin, 2007: 195f) and reading strategies are identified by analysing these utterances. In the piloting phase, this turned out to be very difficult and not very productive with young EFL learners. The children found it confusing to read in English and at the same time switch back to German to express their thoughts. Also, the children could not simultaneously (and consciously) focus on the reading process and FL reading comprehension at the same time. For these reasons, the think-aloud procedure was not included in the present study.

reading strategies of young learners prior this study (see Chapter 4.6.4). Also, children often display unexpected behaviour that is better investigated when the researcher stays open-minded towards strategies which might not have been described before. Accordingly, the study used a more qualitative and open observation scheme which allowed me as the researcher to freely fill in all the strategies which were directly observable; this was partly of course based on my prior knowledge about reading strategies.

The pilot phase showed that video-taping the reading procedure was absolutely indispensable, as it was too difficult for one person to spot all the minor details while simultaneously observing the reading process of all learners. For that reason, the data on reading strategies were also collected by video-taping the reading procedure and later observing and analysing the video with regard to strategy use. Notes were then taken with the help of the same observation scheme. All the notes were subsequently typed up for each child and then summarised and synthesised (see Chapter 8.3.4).

8.3.2 Interviews on Reading Strategies

As outlined in Chapters 4.6.6, not all strategies are observable. Therefore, group interviews in which the learners reported on their strategies were also used to collect data on the participants' reading strategies. At the end of each reading session I, a semi-structured group interview on reading strategies was conducted with the small reading groups. According to Chamot (2005: 113), an interview is one option to "generate insights into the unobservable mental learning strategies of learners." She describes this type of interview on learners' strategies as a retrospective interview, as "learners are prompted to recall a recently completed learning task and describe what they did to complete it." In this sense, the interview is a way to identify strategies in a self-reporting procedure. The interviews were conducted in German (as in the ELLiE project; found in Enever, 2011a: 17), because young FL learners are not yet capable of supplying information on a meta-level in the FL.

The semi-structured interviews were framed by an interview guideline. According to Macaro (2001: 56) this is a

semi-structured list [that] has a number of general questions you want answered but if the diverging route looks like a useful one to follow, you allow the respondent to proceed down it, perhaps bringing him/her back to your own line of questioning.

The interview guideline used for this study is found in Appendix C.7. As a stimulus to elicit strategies, questions such as "What helped you to understand the book?" or "What was difficult to understand and what did you do about that?" were asked by me as the researcher. However, I tried to avoid leading questions such as "Was the dictionary helpful?" in order to prevent the learners from answering in a way that would appear more socially acceptable or pleasing to an observer. Moreover, the learners still had their picture books in front of them during the interviews, which served as a 'prompt' to remind the children of the reading process and allowed them to demonstrate something they attempted to explain.

These interviews were conducted five times with each small reading group; thus, there are a total of 15 short group interviews on reading strategies. All the interviews were video-taped and the videos were then transcribed (the conventions were the same as for the oral recall and questioning, see Appendix D.1.1).

8.3.3 Questionnaire on Reading Strategies

As a final instrument, a questionnaire was also used to investigate the young learners' reading strategies. It was conducted at the end of the data collection phase; thus after the learners had read the last book: 'Winnie in Winter'.

Many researchers have suggested and also used questionnaires in order to investigate reading strategies (e.g., Macaro, 2001: 36). At first, this seemed to be too demanding and difficult for young EFL learners, but as the interviews in the reading sessions turned out to not reveal a lot about the pupils awareness of their strategy use,[159] I decided to compile a questionnaire suitable for young learners on their use of reading strategies (see Appendix C.8). A pilot test with children of the same age and various proficiency levels indicated that this questionnaire would not be too demanding for the participants and that despite previous reservations they could well understand the answer scale. Ruiz de Zarobe and Zenotz (2015) have successfully used a questionnaire, too, to investigate young learners' reading strategies, but unfortunately did not publish it.

The questionnaire used in the present study is based on a questionnaire which Finkbeiner (2005) used with secondary school learners in order to find out about their L2 reading strategies. Finkbeiner's structure was used as a basis, but many of her statements were left out because they seemed too difficult for primary school children or did not apply to picture books. Additional statements were included into the questionnaire of the present study which were based on the literature review on reading strategies (see Chapter 4.6)[160] and in parts on the previously collected data from the

---

159 One possible reason might be that the children, despite the guiding questions, did not know what to say and what possible strategies might be. Prompts and discussions on reading strategies might have helped here to a certain extent, but would have influenced the results of the study.

160 These items are based on research and discussions by Böttger (2014), Finkbeiner (2005), Hedge (2000), Macaro (2001), Macaro & Erler (2008), Steck (2009), Westphal Irwin (2007) and Young (1993).

interviews and observations. The order of the statements was mixed to avoid a possible effect of a logical order of the items (see Finkbeiner, 2005: 261). Also, for internal reliability and consistency, internal contradictions were used within the statements; for instance, 'Do you like to read aloud?' vs. 'Do you like to read silently?'.

The scale that was used to select the items was the same as that used by Finkbeiner (2005) and consisted of four options that ranged from 'fully applies' to 'does not apply at all'. A fifth option was added for the present study ('do not know'), which allowed the children to state that they did not know whether they used a strategy or not. This was done so as not to overtax the children and give them the feeling that it did not matter if they were unsure about their strategy use.

To analyse the questionnaire, the first and the latter two items from the scale were combined so that there were two instead of four options for strategy use left (see Table 15). Taken together, the first two indicate that the strategy was used (either often or sometimes), whereas the last two indicate that the strategy was not (really) used. When the last option was chosen, that answer could not be analysed because the learner did not know about his/her use of the respective strategy.

Table 15: Analysis of the questionnaire items based on a simplification of the original scale.

Original scale:	*Trifft voll und ganz zu* [fully applies]	*Trifft eher zu* [partly applies]	*Trifft eher nicht zu* [does not really apply]	*Trifft gar nicht zu* [does not apply at all]	*Weiß nicht* [do not know]
Combined scale for an easier analysis:	YES, the strategy was used either often or sometimes.		NO, the strategy was not (really) used.		No answer that could be analysed

8.3.4 Organisation and Analysis of the Data on Reading Strategies

As outlined, data on reading strategies were collected via three different instruments and yielded notes from the observation and video analysis, interview transcriptions and questionnaire data. To organise this data pool, all the data were synthesised and summarised in case summaries for each participant (see Kuckartz, Desing, Rädiker & Stefer, 2008: 34).[161] An example for the participant 'Ina' is found in Appendix D.3. Subsequently, qualitative content analysis was used for a classification of the reading strategies into categories.

---

161   In this chapter, Ina's strategies will be used exemplarily to illustrate how the case summaries were created.

For the case summaries, initially the strategies of each child discernible from the qualitative observation data (field notes plus notes from the video analysis) were synthesised (see Figure 20). This was done by compiling a table for each learner that contained the data from both types of notes. These notes were summed up for each book to avoid doublings (right column in Figure 20). Subsequently, the summaries of all six books were synthesised to an overall summary (dark grey box at the bottom of Figure 20). Hence, the table provided an overall summary of all the strategies for each learner that were observable and noted as field notes while the learner was reading the books. The overall summary was divided into two sections: strategies that were used regularly and strategies that were only used sometimes. Regularly used strategies were defined as those strategies that were used at least twice by that learner and in at least two different reading sessions. Strategies that were only used sometimes are those that were used only once or twice and in not more than one reading session.

Figure 20: Summarisation process of the data of each participant on strategies from the field notes and the video observation.

Learner: Ina			
Book	**Field notes from the observation during reading**	**Field notes from the video analysis**	**Summary of the field notes**
The Queen's Knickers	- Strategy a - Strategy b - Strategy d	- Strategy a - Strategy b - Strategy c	- Strategy a - Strategy b - Strategy c - Strategy d
Paddington at the Palace	...	...	...
Five Little Monkeys go Shopping	...	...	...
Something Good	...	...	...
Froggy's Best Christmas	...	...	...
Winnie in Winter	...	...	...
Overall summary: Strategies used regularly: .... Strategies used sometimes: ...			

After that, the transcription data of the 15 group-interviews was taken into consideration.[162] The transcripts were analysed for each child, in that anything that one learner had said during the interviews was extracted for that one learner

---

162 An example of the transcriptions can be found in Appendix E.2.4.

and subsequently summarised and synthesised. All learner statements that might have been based on biased questions (e.g., "Did you use the word list?") were left out in this synthesis. The summary of each child's interview data indicated how often and in which interview the learner mentioned each strategy. It was supplemented with selected quotations from that learner. An example of the summary of Ina's interview data can be found in Appendix D.3.

As a final instrument, the questionnaire provided quantitative data on reading strategies and information on those strategies that the learners had either used or not used.[163] The strategies that each learner stated he/she used were then summarised for each learner. An example for Ina is found in Appendix D.3.

Finally, case summaries that consisted of the overall summary of the notes from observation and video data, the analysis of the interviews and the analysis of the questionnaire were compiled for each learner. The case summaries thus consist of all the strategies that each child used or claimed to have used and also indicate which instrument provided data on each strategy; thus, they synthesise each learner's data on reading strategies. Table 16 provides an overview of such a case summary and an example of Ina's case summary is found in Appendix D.3.

Table 16: Overview of a case summary for one learner in order to summarise and synthesise that learner's reading strategies.

Learner: Ina			
Instrument:	**Field notes and video observation**	**Interviews**	**Questionnaire**
Reading strategies	…	…	…

All the learners' case summaries formed the pool of all the reading strategies that were identified in this study. For a final synthesis of all strategies, the case summaries were analysed with the help of qualitative content analysis (Kuckartz, 2012). This procedure allows the creation of categories and sub-categories of reading strategies so that all the strategies found in the study could be synthesised, structured and classified. The study used structured qualitative content analysis (Kuckartz, 2012: 77ff),[164] which is one of the main types of a qualitative content analysis, as this type

---

163   As outlined in Chapter 8.3.3, the scale of the questionnaire was summed up into 'used' and 'not used'.

164   Author's translation for '*inhaltlich strukturierende qualitative Inhaltsanalyse*' (Kuckartz, 2012: 77).

allows the researcher to structure the data in categories on a continuum from fully deductive to fully inductive. For this study, the categories were developed deductively based on previous research on reading strategies (see Chapter 4.6) as well as inductively based on the data from the present study as found in the case summaries (Kuckartz, 2012: 77). Chapter 10 will present the results of this analysis.

8.4 Research Instrument for Research Question III: FL Performance

As Chapter 5.4 has shown, some studies attributed a positive FLL effect to reading. The FL performance of the reading group was therefore compared to that of the control group, which did not take part in the reading sessions. This was done with the help of topic-based language tests, which I as the researcher developed for this study. As there are no standardised tests available to research topic-based FL knowledge at primary school level, these tests had to be developed from scratch.[165] These made it possible to measure what was actually dealt with in class and in the books, and – although the tests were not standardised – to gain some insight into the pupils' FL performance. An example is found in Appendix C.9.

In total, three tests were conducted on three different topics (these topics were 'London', 'Shopping' and 'Christmas & Winter'). The tests investigated the extent to which the children gained topic-based orthographic, semantic and syntactic morphemic FL knowledge. They did not focus on all aspects of language development, but on those which were likely to develop through reading (see Chapter 5.4) and also on those which can be tested with young learners of English.

All task instructions were provided in German as well as in English to prevent difficulties arising from simply not understanding the task. However, the tasks themselves were in English. The same task format was used for all three language tests, which made these tests comparable to a certain degree.

The tests were analysed quantitatively, with scores attributed to each task. A maximum score of 44 points could be attained in each test. The language tested in the tests was chosen with the help of a multi-layered procedure, which will be outlined in Chapter 8.4.1 before the tasks are explained in Chapter 8.4.2.

---

165 Course books offer suggestions for class tests based on the course book's topics. However, these tests could not be used as they are specifically created for the course book's specific content and vocabulary and can therefore not cover a wider range of FL knowledge about a topic.

8.4.1 Language Chosen for the Tests

As this test was completed by both the control group as well as by the reading group, the language used and tested could not be taken exclusively from the picture books, as the control group had not read them. Hence, the following procedure was followed in order to allow all participating children to complete the test successfully, but to still allow those who read the books to demonstrate their potential additional FL knowledge. The language chosen was categorised into three word categories, A, B and C, which are explained in Table 17:

Table 17: Sources for language chosen for the topic-based language tests.

Category	Source for language	Words and phrases derive from:	Comment on how the words and phrases for the category were found:
A	Topic	A **synthesis** of: a) Words which **teachers** introduce in primary schools in Germany with that topic b) Words which **course books** for teaching English in German primary schools introduce with that topic c) Words which **children's picture dictionaries** which are organised by topic display for that topic	About a) Nine primary school teachers, all of whom are qualified English teachers and had been teaching English in primary schools for at least four years, were asked to write down 10 words which they found most important for the respective topics. About b) Three different teacher guides for course books for teaching English in NRW in Year 3 and 4 (Discovery (Westermann, 2008; 2009); Sally (Oldenbourg, 2009a; 2009b); Ginger (Cornelsen, 2009a; 2009b))[166] were analysed to find out which words they introduced for the topics. About c) Three picture dictionaries *FindeFix Englisch* (Elsner et al., 2004), *ELI Illustrierter Wortschatz* (Ernst Klett Sprachen GmbH, 2007a), *PONS Englischwörterbuch für Grundschulkinder* (Ernst Klett Sprachen GmbH, 2007b) were analysed with regard to the words they displayed for the topics. For a), b) and c), a list ordered by frequency was compiled for each topic. Out of this list, a synthesis ordered by frequency was created for each topic. Words for each topic's language test were then chosen from the final list.

---

166   See the list of teaching materials in the reference-section for the detailed references.

Category	Source for language	Words and phrases derive from:	Comment on how the words and phrases for the category were found:
B	General words	a) List of 100 most frequent words in English b) List of 100 most frequent words in authentic English children's picture books	About a) This list displays the 100 most frequently used/found English words from written English, in particular in literature, as published by the Oxford Dictionary.[167] It does not contain children's books. About b) Eight primary school teachers, all of whom are qualified English teachers and had been teaching English in primary school for at least four years, were asked to write down ten English picture books which they felt were used most often in German primary schools. The texts[168] of all the books listed were then entered into TextStat[169] in order to find the 100 most frequently used words in English picture books as used in primary schools in Germany. Words from both lists a) and b) were chosen for the tests to equal numbers.
C	Books	Specific terms and most frequently used words from the study's picture books	With the help of TextStat (see Footnote 169), a frequency list of words used in each book dealt with was created. From this list, words specific to the books and occurring with a certain frequency were chosen for the tests.

In each language test, every task was constructed so that it contained words from all three categories. If, for example, a task contained six sub-tasks, then two of

---

167   The list can be retrieved from https://en.oxforddictionaries.com/explore/what-can-corpus-tell-us-about-language (last access 15.05.2017).

168   The texts were lemmatised before they were entered into the programme. Lemmatisation is "the process whereby related individual word-form instantiations are subsumed under the lemma they instantiate in language use (for example, the lemma GIVE subsumes the word forms give, gives, given, giving)" (Bartsch, 2014: 110; capitalisations in original). The following lemmatisations were made: nouns were entered in their singular form; verbs were entered in their infinitive form; capitalisation was ignored.

169   TextStat is a freeware computer programme which generates word-frequency lists from a corpus of text that is entered (it is to be found for downloading, e.g., at http://textstat.soft112.com/ (last access 15.05.2017)).

them contained words/phrases from category A, two contained words/phrases from category B and another two contained words/phrases from category C. From the maximum score of 44 points, 15 points came from category A and 14.5 each came from categories B and C.

8.4.2 Tasks for the Language Tests

The test was divided into three parts: orthographic, semantic and syntactic morphemic knowledge. The first part consisted of three tasks which examined the area of orthography. Orthography is part of the English curriculum in NRW (see MSW NRW, 2008b: 82), but is only regarded as a minor aspect: While teachers aim at a correct spelling of words, orthographic factors must not influence the children's marks. The second part of the test aimed at examining the learner's semantic knowledge. It also consisted of a total of three tasks. The last part, made up of two tasks, sought to explore the children's syntactic and morphemic knowledge. See appendix C.9 for an example.

The first task on orthography was an oral word dictation at the word level. The children had to recognise six spoken words and write them down. The first three words stood on their own, whereas the other three words were embedded into the context of a short sentence. Following August's (2011) procedure, the full sentence was read out loud to the children while they read along with a blank line for the target word. The whole task aimed at examining productive orthography at the word level as well as the children's association of sound and orthography. During the piloting of this task, the children had no problem with the task format; therefore, although correct orthography is only a minor part of the curriculum (see MSW NRW, 2008: 82b), the task was still used.

The second task was on brick words. The children were given a word with a gap or two in it, which was symbolised by a line (or two). Each line stood for a missing letter and the children were asked to fill in this letter. This task aimed at testing productive orthography on the letter level. This type of task is regularly used in course books for the primary school EFL classroom and was thus included in the test administered for the purpose of the study.

The third task was concerned with recognising the correct spelling of a word. The children were provided with three different options of a word's spelling and had to decide which one was correct. A total of six words were tested. For each word, the children got either a picture or the German equivalent of the target word to make sure that possible mistakes were not based on a misunderstanding. This task aimed at testing receptive orthography at the word level.

Task four was the first task that focused on semantic knowledge. It required the learners to match six words and three short phrases with the correct picture. There were nine semantic items but eleven visuals so that the children actually had to know the words/phrases they matched. This is important to see how many vocabulary items the children actually know (Rymarczyk & Musall, 2010: 82). A similar word recognition test was also used in the EVENING study (Börner & Frisch, 2013: 88). This task aimed at examining the children's recognition of vocabulary meaning at the word or phrase level and their ability to associate a picture with a word/phrase.

In the fifth task, the learners were first asked to translate from German into English and then from English into German. The English words written down by the children were considered correct if they could be recognised as the right English word, even if the spelling was incorrect (see MSW NRW, 2008: 82). Translating from German into English is not a common practice in the primary school EFL classroom. Still, several considerations underlay the decision to use this type of task. First, the children did not have any problems with this task during the piloting phase and actually seemed to have enjoyed it. Second, the same procedure was effectively applied by Freudenau (2017: 202ff). Third, it is congruent with the skill of 'mediation' as found in German curricula for teaching English at all levels (see, e.g., MSW NRW, 2008b: 79). The aim of this task is to examine the children's association of an L1 word with an L2 word and also of an L2 word with an L1 word. It hence examines access to words in both directions. Following Freudenau's (2017) example, the children were further asked to state where they knew the English word from. This part, however, was optional, as it might have been too difficult for the learners to remember.

Task six was a fill in the gap task. The children were provided with an English sentence with a gap of one word (which is symbolised by a blank line). They were asked to choose the correct word from a choice of three options. This gap-fill activity is a task-type suggested for young learners of English in the federal state of NRW (Bezirksregierung Detmold, 2008: 23). A total of three sentences had to be completed with the correct word. The children were provided with a picture for each sentence in order to prevent a misunderstanding of the whole sentence. All word options given were in the grammatically appropriate form so that actual word knowledge and not grammatical knowledge was tested. This task aimed at examining the children's productive ability to use a word correctly in the context of a sentence.

The last two tasks aimed at testing syntactic morphemic FL knowledge. Task seven consisted of jumbled sentences. Three sentences were given in a mixed-up word order. The children were asked to sequence the words into a grammatically correct sentence. As the only clue provided, the first letter of the first word of the sentence was capitalised. This type of sequencing task has been recommended by, for example, Brewster and Ellis (2002: 115). The purpose of the task was to examine the learners' knowledge of syntax and, implicitly, morphology.

Task eight asked the children to match the beginning of a sentence to the grammatically correct ending. The beginning always consisted of a noun-phrase plus verb-phrase, which allowed a noun, an adverb, an infinitive, a gerund or an adjective as possible endings. The correct type of ending depended on the type of verb-phrase. This easy sentence structure was deliberately chosen, as the children's level of language control is still quite limited. Such a matching activity was also used in the EVENING study (Börner & Frisch, 2013: 88); however, in the tasks at hand the overall structure of the sentences was consistent. The children were provided with three sentences and had to choose between two different endings; one of which was grammatically correct. This task aimed at examining the children's receptive syntactic and morphemic knowledge at the sentence level.

The overall test seemed to be quite long for young learners. In the pilot phase, the pupils at the end of Year 3 needed 30–40 minutes to complete it. Three tasks, which were not described above, were removed from the piloted test, as they were unsuccessful or unfeasible during the piloting phase. Thus, it was assumed that the pupils in Year 4 would need less than 30 minutes on the final test and that the test would not be too demanding for them. This assumption was confirmed during the data collection phase.

8.5 Summary of Chapter 8

Chapter 8 has provided the final part of the account of the research design: the research materials and instruments. Firstly, an overview of all the materials and instruments used was given and the latter were assigned to the three research foci.

To begin with, the research materials consisted of six different authentic English picture books that were carefully selected for this study. This selection process was based on the EFL classroom's topics during the research period and also included an analysis of the books' degrees of difficulty to ensure a certain degree of comparability across them. Also, the range of supportive devices that the learners could use independently while reading the books was presented. These were picture dictionaries, bilingual dictionaries, word lists and MP3-players that contained an audio-recording of the respective stories. Also, peer support and, to a limited extent, teacher/researcher support were available. As such, Chapter 8.1 has provided insights into how the reading sessions were organised.

Chapters 8.2 to 8.4 have given detailed information about the instruments used. Firstly, Chapter 8.2 explained the instruments that collected data on research question I (reading comprehension). These included the learners' self-assessment of their reading comprehension, an oral recall and questioning phase as well as written comprehension tasks. After that, Chapter 8.3 outlined the three different instruments that were used to collect data on research question II (reading strategies): field notes on an open observation scheme based on the observation of the learners while they were reading the book, including a video-recording of this process; a total of 15 semi-structured group interviews in the small reading groups; a questionnaire on reading strategies that was conducted after the learners had read the very last book. Subsequently, Chapter 8.4 elaborated on the topic-based language tests that were used to investigate the orthographic, semantic and syntactic morphemic FL knowledge of the reading and the control group (research question III on FL performance). Within all these subchapters, the analysis of the respective data was also elaborated on.

Part C: Presentation and Interpretation of Results

Abstract: Part C presents and interprets the results of the study and summarises the discussions and findings that conclude this book. In accordance with the three foci of the empirical study, this part is firstly divided into three chapters that are each concerned with the results of the respective foci. At the end, Chapter 12 offers a conclusion.

When reading about the results the reader should keep in mind that the study was concerned with explorative research and a small sample-size. There is no claim or requirement for a generalisation of the findings or for general transferability. This will not be mentioned for each finding but will be discussed in the final conclusions and remarks on the limitations of the study in Chapter 12.2.

9. Reading Comprehension: Presentation, Interpretation and Discussion of Results for Research Question I

Abstract: This chapter presents, interprets and discusses the study's results for focus I: reading comprehension. It firstly outlines the results on comprehension obtained with the three different instruments and then summarises these results. After that the chapter provides details of the participants' use of supportive devices while reading.

One of the three foci of this study was on reading comprehension and investigated the research question with four key aspects as presented in Table 18.

Table 18: Reiteration of research question I including investigated key aspects.

Focus	Research question	Key aspects investigated
I Reading comprehension	(I) To what extent are Year 4 EFL learners capable of reading and understanding authentic English picture books?	→ The task of reading and the learners' reading competence → The level of reading comprehension → The use of supportive devices

In this chapter, firstly an overview of the actual task of reading will be given, providing data on the question whether reading authentic books was too challenging for the participants and how they coped with the task of reading in general. In a next step, the reading comprehension levels of the children will be presented as investigated by the three different instruments outlined in Chapter 8.2: the children's self-assessment of comprehension, an oral recall as well as oral comprehension questions and written comprehension tasks. It will also be investigated to what extent a development of comprehension over time could be found and which factors possibly influenced comprehension. After that, the use of supportive devices (see Chapter 8.1.3) while reading will be elaborated on and it will be shown which of these devices proved useful and which did not. Finally, Chapter 9.4 provides a summary of the results as well as an answer to the research question.

9.1 The Task of Reading and Development of Reading Competence

As reading authentic picture books at the primary school level has scarcely been investigated so far and is a challenging task for young EFL learners, the issue was whether the participants in the reading study could cope with the task of reading and whether their (FL) reading competence was sufficient to read the authentic English picture books on their own. The results that are relevant to these questions are based on my observation of the learners during their reading and the learners' comments about reading the books. A final answer on the success of the reading process can of course only be provided based on the actual comprehension of the books as dealt with in Chapter 9.2.

9.1.1 Presentation of Results

To begin with, most of the children indicated that they liked the books and that they enjoyed reading them. Firstly, they were looking forward to encountering new books and were eager to look at them and read them. Jonas,[170] for example, asked whether he could start reading 'Paddington at the Palace' right after he saw the book (#4:54).[171] Also, some children asked in advance of a session which book would be dealt with and were happy to hear a new book being announced. Additionally, most learners stated that they liked the books after they had read them. Reasons included mostly that they found the books funny and that overall the books were appealing to them. Jonas explained, *"Hmm (...), dass da ähm ganz oft nicht so viel Text stand. Und ähm da waren auch ähm manchmal so lustige Sachen"*[172] (Transcript RS QK2 05.09.2014 #36:24).[173]

---

170 To ensure the children's privacy and anonymity, pseudonyms are used in this book that do not allow the drawing of any connections to the actual children.

171 The hashtag plus time marker in brackets indicates at what point of the video on that reading session the utterance or action can be found. This is only provided when the utterance was not part of the transcriptions that were compiled for the oral recall and questioning ('Transcript RC') and for the interviews on reading strategies ('Transcript RS'). In the latter case, the reference to the transcript is provided (see Footnote 173).

172 Any German citation taken from the data and found in Chapters 9 and 10 are not translated into English to preserve their authenticity. Instead, all German quotations are summarised in English either before or after the German quote.

173 All transcriptions derive from the video-recording of the oral recall and questioning as well as of the interviews on reading strategies (see Chapters 8.2.2 and 8.3). The transcript information in brackets indicates in which transcript and at what exact point of it that utterance can be found. An explanation of the abbreviation for the

A few children, however, were not as keen on reading the books and were sometimes unmotivated and unhappy about being taken out of class. Lara and Ali in particular, who were both in RG 1, expressed their discontent. They neither showed much interest in reading nor in the books. Both of them, as will be seen in the following chapters, encountered some problems with reading and needed additional support. When provided with support, particularly through an audio-recording, they were more contented.

During the reading process no child gave the impression of being completely overtaxed. Instead, they all seemed to be able to cope with the task to a certain extent. When I occasionally asked about the difficulty of a book, the answers ranged from easy to difficult, but the learners never stated that they found it too hard. For example, after reading the book 'The Queen's Knickers' Jonas said that he found it easy, but not too easy, and Dani stated that she found it of medium difficulty, partly easy and partly difficult (see Transcript RS QK2 05.09.2014 #36:01 and #36:46). Overall, all the books were read by all children from cover to cover. While reading, no child ever stated that he/she could not read the text at all and also no child ever gave up on a book. Some children, however, needed support (see Chapter 9.3) or had to be encouraged to read.

Also, the children seemed to actually read the text and not just look at the pictures. This can, for example, be seen in the videos. In the videos, the reading process can be followed to a certain extent because the children sometimes put a finger under the text, because the children's eye movement is to a certain extent trackable and also because the children's pace of turning the pages can be followed. Moreover, the analysis of the learners' reading comprehension (see Chapter 9.2) shows that the children's understanding of the books included information that could only be obtained from the textual elements or a mixture of textual and visual elements, rather than simply from the visual elements.

In the course of the five months, most learners' reading confidence seemed to improve. This could be observed through a decrease in questions and insecurity while working with the books and the corresponding tasks. Jonas, for example, asked for confirmation and clarification a lot during the first sessions, but he did not do so any longer with the later books. The same was also noticeable for Simone and Ali. Ali in particular learnt how to use the supportive devices

---

reference to a certain transcript can be found in Appendix E.2.2. The excerpt above 'Transcript RS QK2 05.09.2014 #36:24' refers to the transcript of the interview on reading strategies (RS) after reading the book 'The Queen's Knickers' with RG 2 (QK2), which was conducted on 5th September, 2014 (05.09.2014). In this transcript, the utterance is found at time marker '#36:24'.

and knew after the first two books that the audio-recording could help him with reading. Furthermore, Dani explicitly mentioned that previous reading experience with some of the books helped her in reading other books (Transcript RS PP2 30.09.2014 #39:13):

> **Dani:** *Und ich glaube das hat auch geholfen von dem letzten Buch was wir gelesen haben.*
> **R:** *Ah Ok.*
> **Dani:** *Da habe ich nämlich wesentlich weniger verstanden als da.*

Therefore, as the children became familiar with reading, their reading confidence also increased.

Naturally, some children needed more time for reading a book than others.[174] The time they needed was measured via the videos, where the exact reading time could be calculated by the exact starting and finishing point of each learner's reading.[175] Looking at the first book, 'The Queen's Knickers', the fastest child was Emil, who only needed 2 minutes and 56 seconds, and the slowest reader was Simone, who needed 8 minutes and 18 seconds; about triple the amount of time Emil needed. Similar figures hold true for the other books. Figure 21 shows the reading time every child needed for each book. The black bar indicates the reading time that each child needed on average.

Figure 21: Reading time of each child on each book (in seconds).

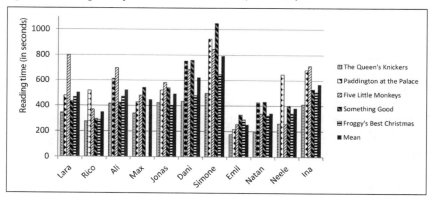

---

174 Children that finished earlier were given simple tasks, like drawing a picture about the book, in order to prevent them from disturbing the others during their reading process.

175 This could only be done for the first five books. To accommodate the questionnaire on reading strategies, there is no video-recording of the reading session on the last book, 'Winnie in Winter'.

One can see that Emil was overall the fastest reader. Also Rico, Natan and Neele seem quite fast, at least on most of the books. Emil and Rico needed only between around two to five minutes for a book. The slowest reader was Simone. She needed between about eight to seventeen minutes for a book. Also Dani seemed to need a lot of time for reading. Overall, there is a broad range with regard to reading time, which shows that the individual reading time needed for a book varies greatly amongst different children.

For an individual child the reading time also seems dependent on the books. Looking at Figure 21 this can be seen in the varying lengths of different bars for a child. Neele, for example, needed more than double the amount of time for 'Paddington at the Palace' than she needed for 'The Queen's Knickers'. With regard to the reading time of individual children, no clear decrease or increase can be detected across the different books, but rather the bars seem to rise and fall randomly.

Figure 22 displays the average reading time that was needed for each book, in order to show if there are noticeable differences across the books.

Figure 22: Reading time needed on average for each book.

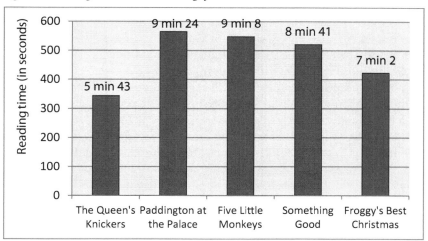

The participants on average needed the least amount of reading time for 'The Queen's Knickers' and the longest reading time for 'Paddington at the Palace', closely followed however by 'Five Little Monkeys'. The latter four books suggest a slight decrease in time needed for reading, whereas the first book is the one for which the least reading time was needed. Thus, reading time did not truly decrease gradually.

9.1.2 Interpretation and Discussion of Results

Overall, the task of reading appeared to have matched the learners' competence levels. Reading the books was clearly not too easy for them, but also not too demanding. This conclusion is supported by the fact that most of the children gave the impression that they liked reading the books, were interested in them and wanted to know more about them. Therefore, most of the children encountered the reading of authentic picture books with a positive attitude, feelings of success and a high reading motivation. For those children, this lasted over the period of five months and six different books.

Many learners also improved their FL reading confidence over time, which shows that they became accustomed to the task and learnt to cope with it over the five months. An increase in reading confidence was also found by Kolb (2013: 39) in her three weeks reading programme. One can assume a familiarisation effect here: The more familiar learners are with reading authentic English picture books, the more confident they get. They simply need to get used to the task of reading and gradually learn how to cope with it. An increase in confidence, however, probably only occurs through positive reading experiences. This is supported by Nuttall's (2005: 127) notion of a virtuous circle of the good reader, which proposes that good readers enjoy reading, read faster, understand better and overall read more. Such a cycle of growth is desirable and should be attained by FL readers, particularly by those that are caught in the vicious circle of the weak reader (Nuttall, 2005: 127). Therefore, positive reading experiences should be ensured through various means of support and realistic teacher expectations in order to allow readers to reach the virtuous circle of reading (also see Chapter 9.2.1.2).

However, not all the learners in the present study enjoyed reading. This is not surprising, as all the learners are individuals who all prefer different types of learning and might thus not enjoy reading or might simply not be good readers. Biebricher (2008: 198ff) lists possible factors which might decrease reading motivation. These factors include a lack of personal interest in the topics of the texts, a reduction of attractiveness of reading due to routine (the effect of the new and unknown may fade quickly) and the fact that FL reading can be a challenging activity that can lead to frustration, failure and disappointment. The latter point might hold true for Lara, as she encountered reading difficulties in terms of a very low level of ambiguity tolerance in the beginning (see Chapter 10.1.1). This might have led to frustration and subsequently to demotivation. Such learners might quickly be caught in the aforementioned vicious circle of reading (Nuttall, 2005: 127).

Taking into account the individual differences of the participants, individual reading times that differ across the learners and the books are not unexpected.

The fact that the average time needed for each book varies considerably (see Figure 22), indicates that reading time for a book to a certain extent depends on the book itself. The varying average times might indicate that the books' levels of difficulty could vary with regard to certain aspects, especially with regard to perceived difficulty, which cannot be calculated or analysed in advance. Particularly the book 'The Queen's Knickers', for which the children on average only needed a reading time of 5 minutes and 43 seconds, might be easier to read than other books, for example 'Paddington at the Palace', for which the children needed 9 minutes and 24 seconds on average. This might be connected to how long a book actually is, how many words it contains and how complex its sentences are (e.g., lengths of sentence). When looking at Table 13, one can see that the book 'Paddington at the Palace' has the highest number of words per page as well as by far the longest sentences. In addition, the visual elements in 'Paddington at the Palace' are more complex than in other books, in that they contain multiple events in one picture, show crowd scenes and contain unfamiliar street scenes that are full of architecture; features which make the pictures difficult to read and "trigger more careful and intensive processing" (Skorge, 226: 68).[176] All these factors might have an influence on reading time and reading pace. Varying reading times for different books, however, do not only depend on the books, but also on individual differences amongst learners. On the one hand, their overall L1 and L2 reading competence plays a role; on the other hand, also interest in a book as well as previous language and topic knowledge can influence the reading rate.

With regard to classroom teaching, the results on reading time are interesting in that they underline the importance of giving different learners the time that they individually need to finish a reading task. When teachers differentiate reading tasks, not only might the tasks themselves need differentiation, but also the time allocated for the actual reading process.

Given the fact that there is no clear decrease or increase in reading time, although the books are, at least to a certain extent, comparable in their degrees of difficulty, the indication is that reading picture books once a week does not necessarily improve reading pace, but indicates instead that reading pace is on the one hand dependent on the actual reading text and on the other hand might need more continuous practice in order to develop. Although fluency

---

176 In fact, the complexity of the pictures is a factor which had not been analysed prior to the study, as at a surface level it seems that pictures in picture books are all similar. However, a closer analysis shows that actually they are not, so that this might be a point worth adding to the analysis of a book's degree of difficulty.

and reading competence are said to develop through regular practice (see Chapter 4.1), reading only one book per week in the FL with no further reading instruction seems not enough to improve FL reading fluency and reading rate. Differences between the books and the readers seem to have a greater effect on the reading rate as long as only a little reading is conducted. For an improvement of the FL reading rate of young FL learners, more continuous reading activities seem necessary, maybe including some explicit instruction in reading techniques and strategies. For true comparisons of reading time, however, very similar if not the same reading texts would be needed.

Overall, the results relating to the participants' reading competence convey the impression that the children were not overtaxed by the task of reading, but that on the contrary most of the children seemed to enjoy reading the books and could cope well. The challenge seemed to be just right for them and meet their current levels of competence while at the same time stimulating them just above their independent performance levels. By reading on a regular basis the children had the chance to get used to reading authentic picture books on their own, could familiarise themselves with the task and were able to enhance their reading confidence. The data also provide evidence that reading pace is dependent on many different factors, including the books' levels of difficulty as well as individual factors such as L2 competence, availability of successful reading strategies or topic interest, and that for an improvement of reading pace more continuous practice appears necessary. For a better picture of the learners' reading competence and a potential development of it, the next chapter will examine the participants' levels of reading comprehension more closely.

9.2 The Participants' Levels of Reading Comprehension

As outlined in Chapter 8.2, three different measures were used to investigate the participants' reading comprehension. Thus, this chapter is divided into three subchapters, which each present the results on reading comprehension as investigated through the different instruments. The children's perceived comprehension levels will be presented in Chapter 9.2.1. Chapter 9.2.2 will then outline the results of the oral recall and oral comprehension questions. After that, Chapter 9.2.3 will present the results of the written comprehension tasks. The results on reading comprehension will subsequently be summarised and compared to each other in Chapter 9.2.4.

9.2.1 Self-Assessment of Reading Comprehension

This chapter will present the learners' perceived levels of comprehension of the picture books as rated by them individually after reading each book.[177] The procedure of rating and analysing their self-assessment with a five-point scale was outlined in Chapter 8.2.1.

9.2.1.1 Presentation of Results

Table 19 shows the indicated level of comprehension on the first five books[178] as given by all the participants:

Table 19: Overview of the results on self-assessment of reading comprehension, including the average comprehension level by book and by participant. Numbers shaded in grey indicate that that book was read with the audio-recording.

	The Queen's Kickers	Paddington at the Palace	Five Little Monkeys	Something Good	Froggy's Best Christmas	Average perceived comprehension level of each learner
Lara	4	2	3	3	4	M = 3.2 SD = 0.84
Rico	4	3	4	5	5	M = 4.2 SD = 0.84
Ali	3	2	4	3	3	M = 3.0 SD = 0.71
Max	5	5	5	4	– – –[179]	M = 4.75 SD = 0.5
Jonas	5	4	5	5	5	M = 4.8 SD = 0.45
Dani	2	3	4	4	3	M = 3.2 SD = 0.84

---

177 Whenever results are presented according the six books that were read, the books are arranged in the chronological order in which they were read.

178 The sixth book, 'Winnie in Winter', was used to fill in the questionnaire on reading comprehension right after reading and therefore no self-assessment could be conducted right after the reading process.

179 There is no self-assessment of the book 'Froggy's Best Christmas' by Max, who was not included in the reading of that book because he was already familiar with it (see Chapter 8.1.1).

	The Queen's Kickers	Paddington at the Palace	Five Little Monkeys	Something Good	Froggy's Best Christmas	Average perceived comprehension level of each learner
Simone	2	2	2	3	2	M = 2.2 SD = 0.45
Emil	5	5	5	4	5	M = 4.8 SD = 0.45
Natan	3	2	3	3	3	M = 2.8 SD = 0.45
Neele	4	4	4	4	4	M = 4.0 SD = 0.0
Ina	4	3	4	4	4	M = 3.8 SD = 0.45
Average perceived comprehension level of each book	M = 3.73 SD = 1.1	M = 3.18 SD = 1.17	M = 3.91 SD = 0.95	M = 3.82 SD = 0.75	M = 3.8 SD = 1.03	

The results presented in Table 19 will be detailed in the following sections. Firstly, for each book, the average perceived comprehension level was calculated via the mean (see bottom line of the table). For a better overview, Figure 23 shows the average self-assessment on all books.

Figure 23: Average self-assessment of the level of reading comprehension, ordered by books.

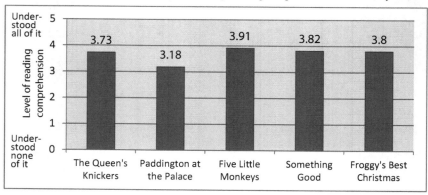

The average comprehension levels of the books range from M = 3.18 for the book 'Paddington at the Palace' to M = 3.91 for the book 'Five Little Monkeys'. While the average comprehension levels all seem very similar, 'Paddington at the Palace' displays the lowest comprehension level, while the other four books range only from M = 3.73 to M = 3.91. As such, the difference between the latter four books is only 0.18, while the difference to 'Paddington at the Palace' is 0.55. Therefore, 'Paddington at the Palace' is perceived as being least well understood by the children, while all other books are perceived similarly, but all noticeably higher than 'Paddington at the Palace'.

As can be seen in Table 19, the standard deviation of the average understanding of all the books is quite high, ranging from SD = 0.75 to SD = 1.17. This indicates that the comprehension levels of one book are very different across individual participants. Therefore, Figure 24 shows the children's perceived levels of comprehension of each book, ordered by children.

Figure 24: Self-assessment of the level of reading comprehension of each book by participants.

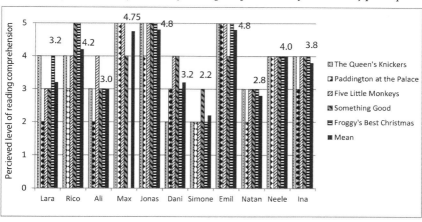

The grey bars indicate the comprehension levels of the individual books and the black bar displays the average comprehension of each child taking all five books together. These means have to be regarded with caution, though, because the books might slightly vary in their degrees of difficulty despite the comparison that was outlined in Chapter 8.1.1. Therefore, the means of each child only serve for an overview of their overall perceived comprehension levels, without revealing anything about the potentially varying difficulties of the books.

Nevertheless, one can see that the participants' average levels of perceived comprehension vary from 2.2 to 4.8 (black bars) and thus show a very high range, that is the average extent of comprehension differs considerably across individual participants. Some learners rated their comprehension continually around the same level: Max, Jonas, Emil, Neele and Ina rated their comprehension continually as fairly high (level 4 or 5; except for Ina who rated the book 'Paddington at the Palace' at level 3) and Ali, Simone and Natan rated theirs continually as fairly low (level 2 or 3). Lara, Rico and Dani show a wider range of possible ratings. Therefore, their standard deviation as seen in Table 19 is higher than that of those children with more continuous ratings.

However, one can see that most of the learners rated their understanding of the books differently, depending on the books. As the books are displayed in the order that they were used during the reading sessions, one would see if there was a decrease or increase in the perceived comprehension levels. Such a trend in comprehension, however, cannot be identified. Over the five books, neither an increase nor a decrease in perceived comprehension can be detected.

Focusing on the levels of self-assessment that are shaded in grey in Table 19, which show those books that were read with the audio-recording,[180] one can see that there does not seem to be a big difference between the comprehension levels of books read with and without the recording. Some learners' perceived comprehension seems to be even worse with the recording, in particular Natan's and Ina's. This can, of course, also be based on the book's difficulty. Neele's comprehension level of the book 'Paddington at the Palace', which is the only book that she read with the recording, is just the same as the perceived level of the other four books. Looking at Lara and Ali, who read four of the five books displayed in the table with the recording, a comparison is not really possible since not enough books were read without it.

9.2.1.2 Interpretation and Discussion of Results

Looking at the means of self-assessment of each book (see Figure 23), all average comprehension levels are above 'three'. With 'one' meaning 'understood none of it' and 'five' meaning 'understood all of it', 'three' would roughly mean 'understood half of it' whilst 'four' would roughly mean 'understood most of it'. Therefore, the average perceived comprehension of all books ranged between understanding about half to most of the books. In sum, this indicates that the

---

180 See Chapter 8.1.3 for why the audio-recording was used and for a critical discussion on its use.

participants on average self-assessed their comprehension as being quite good, demonstrating that they had on average understood something between half and most of the books. This clearly shows that overall the learners did not perceive reading authentic books as too demanding but rather felt that they could cope well with this task in terms of reading comprehension.

It is interesting to see that some children have a high standard deviation, indicating that their ratings vary considerably across the books. This may have several reasons. Firstly, it is possible that they perceived the books' levels of difficulty as quite different. This could result from several factors, such as varying previous knowledge of the books' topics, the degree of previous knowledge of the language found in a book or simply interest in the books' topics. The differences in perceived comprehension could also be due to personal factors such as daily moods and the actual reading motivation. Particularly with young learners, the factor of 'mood' is hard to control in empirical research and could partly influence the reading performance and thus the perceived comprehension level of a particular book. Other learners rated their comprehension more continually across the different books. Thus, they might not be influenced to the same extent by the various factors mentioned above and thus show a more stable level of comprehension of different books. This suggests that young learners' reading comprehension and their own perception of it can depend on a number of different factors across different books. These should be taken into consideration with regard to choosing reading texts, setting reading tasks and defining realistic aims for reading comprehension.

The mean values for perceived level of reading comprehension for each book also display a high standard deviation. This indicates that the eleven learners said that they had understood the same book on very different levels. This goes to show how different (perceived) reading competences are in heterogeneous classrooms and how important it is to cater for individual needs by providing differentiated reading tasks. As already mentioned in the previous paragraph, it is thus essential to take individual competences into account and provide individualised reading tasks and goals when reading authentic books in the setting of the EFL classroom.

Kolb (2013: 40) found that in her picture book project of three weeks, the children's self-assessment of reading competence increased. However, such an increase in comprehension cannot be seen in the data presented above. The learners appear rather to have been influenced by other factors, such as the book's difficulty, in their ratings and do not seem to have perceived a gradual increase in comprehension over time. For such an increase, more reading might be needed and a stronger focus on self-assessment might be necessary.

Interestingly, the audio-recording does not seem to improve the perceived level of reading comprehension. There does not appear to be a big difference between books read with and books read without the recording, at least with those children that only used the recording once. Natan and Ina even perceived their comprehension level of the one book that they read with the recording as lower than their comprehension of the books they read without it. This can, of course, be due to the difficulty of the book – they might have simply found that book most difficult – but it can also show that the recording was not of much benefit for them and that they found that they could just as well read the books without the recording. This is different for Ali and Lara, who used the recording for almost all books and rated their perceived comprehension levels based on reading while listening.[181] It would be interesting to see how they would rate their comprehension of a book that they read without the recording after reading with it for a couple of books.[182] In follow-up studies it would be instructive to investigate whether the perceived level of comprehension is in some way dependent on or developed through an audio-recording and whether this supportive mean can gradually be reduced again.

Overall, all the children stated that they had understood at least some of each book, if not all of it. Therefore, reading these books seems to have been worthwhile for all the learners, low and high performing ones, as they all practised their reading competences and were able to understand at least some aspects of the books. The learners seem to have perceived the task as appropriate and manageable. Such learners' self-assessments provide insight into how they perceived the reading process and how they perceived their comprehension level. If they had continually indicated that they understood either nothing or everything of a book, one might have had to consider whether the books were either too difficult or too easy for the learners. However, this was not the case, so that the assumption that authentic picture books are suitable reading material for the primary school EFL classroom is supported.

One final aspect, however, should critically be taken into consideration, and that is the extent to which (young) learners' self-assessment is realistic and mirrors their actual level of competence. Whenever it comes to (young) learners' self-assessment, researchers and teachers have to keep in mind that it is not

---

181   See Chapter 8.1.3 for a discussion on the difficulty that a combination of reading and listening places on researching reading comprehension.

182   Lara read the last book, 'Winnie in Winter', without listening to the audio-recording, but unfortunately no self-assessment of reading comprehension was conducted for that book (see Footnote 179).

always accurate and has to be practised in a long-term process (see, e.g., Leeck, 2014: 109). Children find it difficult to self-assess their own performance and often assess themselves unrealistically. Only when children are encouraged to reflect regularly on their self-assessment compared to their actual level of achievement, can their self-assessment become more realistic (see, e.g., Leeck (2014) and Kolb (2007) for related studies in the primary school EFL classroom). Within the scope of the present study, no reflection of the perceived levels of comprehension took place with the children and therefore the extent to which the levels presented here are realistic remains unclear. Nevertheless, as most children rated their comprehension levels differently for each book, one can assume that they thought about the rating and at least tried to display a level of self-assessment that they deemed realistic for themselves. Besides, apart from self-assessment, two further instruments were used to measure comprehension, the results of which will be presented in the following subchapters. A comparison between these results and those on self-assessment will be drawn in Chapter 9.2.4 and allows a distinction between those children that potentially over-assessed or under-assessed their reading abilities.

9.2.2 Comprehension Levels as Indicated by the Oral Recall and Questioning

The second instrument used to investigate reading comprehension was the procedure of oral recall and questioning explained in Chapter 8.2.2. In this procedure, all the learners orally expressed what they had understood of a book right after reading each one, starting with a free recall and ending with guided questions. This was video-recorded, transcribed and then analysed with the help of the analysis scheme explicated in Chapter 8.2.2.2 (also see Appendix D.2).

9.2.2.1 Presentation of Results

To begin with, the different levels of comprehension ranging from 1 to 5 will be discussed (see Chapter 4.5.2); level 1 is the lowest and level 5 the highest possible level of comprehension. To illustrate how the performance of a learner was attributed to a certain comprehension level with the help of the transcriptions and the analysis scheme, an example for each level will be given here for the book 'Five Little Monkeys'. These examples will show the differences in comprehension between the five levels and gives transparency about how the data were analysed. The completed analysis schemes of the selected learners (Simone, Ali, Jonas, Ina, Emil), which the following paragraphs are based on, are found in Appendix D.2.2.

Level 1: Simone

Simone reached level 1 of reading comprehension for the book 'Five Little Monkeys'. During the recall and questioning phase, Simone listened very carefully but only contributed one utterance. While the other learners participated actively and mentioned many more aspects, my impression was that Simone was contented to listen and concentrate on what the others had understood. This one utterance she gave was triggered by a question that I directed at her and she might have said nothing at all without this direct request. The utterance was accurate and had not been mentioned by another learner before. It was contextualised by the question that I had asked her and that could be retrieved from the text as well as from the pictures. Simone had understood the information in the book and gave a short one-word answer to the question that focused on it. Thus, her utterance could not reveal anything about her understanding of the coherence or the logical order of events of the story. Because of her general passivity during the recall and questioning phase, there is reason to assume that she did not understand much more than single details on her own. Therefore, her performance complies with level 1 of the reading comprehension levels.

Level 2: Ali

Ali reached level 2 of reading comprehension with his utterances about the book 'Five Little Monkeys'. Ali contributed five utterances during the recall and questioning, but two of them were wrong or not appropriate. The remaining three utterances could be analysed for comprehension. All three utterances were related to details of the story; Ali did not say anything that revealed a more global understanding of it. Overall, he did not follow the storyline of the book in his remarks, as his contributions were either isolated statements or answers to my questions. Ali mentioned facts and events from the story that were all presented in the book's visual as well as textual elements, and he did not refer to anything that could only be understood from the text. What Ali did understand was accurate, but not dealt with any further in terms of linking it to other aspects of the book or interpreting it. Overall, it was difficult to establish a comprehension level based on only three utterances, but what he revealed content-wise allowed the conclusion that there must have been more that he had understood. For example, he could not have understood that there were fourteen monkey children in total (his first utterance) without grasping the gist of the story and at least partly understanding where these monkeys came from. Therefore, his total utterances were attributed to level 2 of reading comprehension.[183]

Level 3: Jonas

Jonas' comprehension of the book 'Five Little Monkeys' was at level 3 of reading comprehension. Overall, Jonas contributed 15 utterances. Two of them were not accurate and another two aspects had already been mentioned by another learner, so that a total of eleven utterances remained for the analysis of his comprehension. Two of the eleven utterances revealed a more global understanding, in that they contained aspects that recurred throughout the whole story. His other utterances revealed details of the story, of which all but one were put into the broader context of the story. The information that Jonas presented consisted of facts, events and characters from the story. These were mostly presented in the textual as well as in the visual elements of the book, while two aspects could only be understood from the text. Moreover, Jonas provided several aspects that were not explicitly presented in the book but were rather implicit information that he read between the lines and combined with his own interpretation. Generally, Jonas did not only correctly understand content aspects of the book, but often interpreted them. Usually, he used his world knowledge to do so. Moreover, he consistently gave his own opinion on the story.[184] Overall, Jonas attempted to compensate for a lack of comprehension by providing comments, interpretations and his own opinion of the text, and moreover by making guesses about certain details. For instance, he correctly said that an announcement that the saleslady made implied that all the monkeys should come back and come to the counter. The counter was not mentioned in the text, but the monkeys were supposed to come to the "children's clothing department" (Christelow, 2007: 29). As Jonas obviously did not understand this detail, he probably just guessed that the counter would be a reasonable spot to meet again. Coming back to Jonas' overall recall, it partly followed the storyline and organisational patterns of the book. In sum, the analysis of his utterances complies with the description of level 3.

---

183 The fact that Ali read the book with the audio-recording and that thus his comprehension level is based on reading as well as listening comprehension, was already critically discussed in Chapters 8.1.3 and 9.2.1.

184 For example, he stated that it was the monkey mother's own fault that she lost her monkey children in the store. His explanation for this statement indicated that his view was probably based on his own experience.

Level 4: Ina

Ina's utterances about the book 'Five Little Monkeys' were analysed as comprehension at level 4. Overall, she made 12 utterances, all of which could be analysed for comprehension as they were all accurate and had not been mentioned by another learner before. Her first two utterances revealed a more global understanding of the whole story, which she then supported through mostly important details that were for the most part put into the context of the whole story. During her recall she followed the storyline and stuck to the organisational patterns of the story. The information she provided consisted of facts, events and characters. These were presented mostly in the textual as well as in the visual elements of the book, while some aspects could only be understood from the text. For example, Ina could list the items which the monkey family bought at the store and could point to the correct text passage. This information could not be retrieved from the pictures. Not only that, but she translated the content of a more complex sentence which was part of an announcement that the saleslady made in the book. All 12 aspects Ina mentioned were recounted correctly and often also linked to other parts of the book. Overall, the analysis of Ina's utterances complies with the description of level 4 of reading comprehension.

Level 5: Emil

Emil's utterances about 'Five Little Monkeys' were analysed as overall comprehension at level 5. Firstly, he contributed 18 different utterances. All of these utterances were accurate, while two had been mentioned before. Thus, 16 utterances remained for analysis. Emil's remarks revealed global comprehension of the book as well as supporting details. All the details he mentioned were important ones that were put into the broader context of the story. The information he offered consisted of facts, events and characters. All the content aspects were correctly recognised and he was able to link the great majority of his utterances to other aspects from the book or topic. Once, he also interpreted a situation from the book, whereby he probably used his world knowledge. What he had understood was often presented in the pictures as well as in the text, with a tendency towards more textual than visual elements. Several utterances could only be understood from the text and not retrieved from the pictures. These textual parts he was able to understand were sometimes rather complex, for instance the utterance of the monkey mother when she directed her monkey children to stay with her: "Stick with me [...] and don't go wandering off" (Christelow, 2007: 7). Overall, Emil's recall was coherent and followed the storyline and organisational patterns of the book. In sum, his comprehension was very elaborate and the analysis of his utterances complies with the description of level 5 of reading comprehension.

The details for each comprehension level show that there is a positive trend with regard to different aspects of comprehension when gradually proceeding from level 1 to 5. This trend is supported when looking at all the learners' analysis schemes of all books. Progressively rising from level 1 to level 5, more utterances were made and an increasing number of these were accurate. Also, more global aspects could be depicted and details that were mentioned were increasingly contextualised in that they were put into the larger context of the book. On the medium and higher levels, usually no redundant details were presented any more. With regard to the types of information that were depicted one can clearly see that mostly facts and events were described. Sometimes characters were mentioned implicitly or explicitly, but only very seldom were emotions or opinions as found in the book commented on by the learners. When this did occur, it was those learners that reached a fairly high comprehension level who did so. With regard to the way that the information was presented in the book, a gradual trend from recalling information from pictures to recounting information that could only be retrieved from the text is found, accompanying a corresponding rise in comprehension level. Implicitly presented information, however, was not only mentioned by learners with a high comprehension level, but in fact more so by those who generally interpreted more and used the strategy of guessing and interpreting regularly (particularly Natan and Jonas). The same holds true with regard to what the learners did with understood pieces of information, that is whether they just recognised it or linked it to their world knowledge or provided their own opinion. Some learners tended to interpret more and provide their own opinion more than other learners, but this appeared to be independent of the level of comprehension. Still, weak comprehenders did not do so as often as the average and stronger ones. The same holds true for deriving content aspects from previous world knowledge. For example, Emil, Max and Rico (all good comprehenders) used their knowledge of a trip to London to explain parts of 'Paddington at the Palace' (also see Chapter 10.1.1). However, Ali (weaker reader) also used his world knowledge for comprehension; for example, he explained that he knew 'ginger ale' (Munsch, 1990) from the book 'Something Good', because he had tasted it before. By contrast, a difference between weaker and stronger comprehenders is seen with regard to linking the information they were able to gain from the text to other aspects of the book. The higher the comprehension level, the more the information could be linked to the overall book's content or to related content aspects.

The procedure of attributing a comprehension level to each learner via the analysis schemes was followed for every book[185] and every learner. Table 20 provides an overview:

Table 20: Comprehension levels as revealed by the oral recall and questioning, analysed by means of the analysis scheme (see Appendix D.2). Grey numbers indicate that the level of comprehension listed here might not reveal the actual comprehension level of that child; numbers shaded in light grey indicate that that book was read with the audio-recording.

	The Queen's Kickers	Padding-ton at the Palace	Five Little Monkeys	Some-thing Good	Froggy's Best Christ-mas	Average comprehension level of each child	
						Including grey numbers	Excluding grey numbers
Lara	3	2	4	4	4	M = 3.4 SD = 0.9	/
Rico	4	4	2	3	5	M = 3.6 SD = 1.14	M = 4 SD = 0.82
Ali	1	2	2	2	2	M = 1.8 SD = 0.45	M = 1.75 SD = 0.5
Max	4	3	5	3	– – – [186]	M = 3.75 SD = 0.96	M = 4.5 SD = 0.71
Jonas	3	3	3	3	3	M = 3.0 SD = 0.0	M = 3.0 SD = 0.0
Dani	4	4	5	4	4	M = 4.2 SD = 0.45	M = 4.25 SD = 0.5
Simone	1	1	1	2	2	M = 1.4 SD = 0.55	/
Emil	5	5	5	4	5	M = 4.8 SD = 0.45	/
Natan	3	3	3	2	3	M = 2.8 SD = 0.45	/

185 The oral recall of the last book, 'Winnie in Winter', was only conducted briefly after the questionnaire on reading strategies was filled in, therefore the recall was not video-recorded and could not be analysed. Thus, the following table only contains data on the first five books.

186 Max was left out on this book because he knew it already (see Chapter 8.1.1).

	The Queen's Kickers	Paddington at the Palace	Five Little Monkeys	Something Good	Froggy's Best Christmas	Average comprehension level of each child	
						Including grey numbers	Excluding grey numbers
Neele	4	4	2	3	3	M = 3.2 SD = 0.84	M = 3.5 SD = 0.58
Ina	2	2	4	4	4	M = 3.2 SD = 1.1	M = 3.5 SD = 1.0
Average comprehension level of each book (including grey numbers)	M = 3.09 SD = 1.3	M = 3.0 SD = 1.18	M = 3.27 SD = 1.42	M = 3.09 SD = 0.83	M = 3.5 SD = 1.08		
Average comprehension level of each book (excluding grey numbers)	M = 3.1 SD = 1.3	M = 3.11 SD = 1.27	M = 3.56 SD = 1.42	M = 3.22 SD = 0.83	M = 3.5 SD = 1.2		

Table 20 shows the comprehension level of each learner on each book and also displays the average comprehension of the books and of the learners. The average results of the learners can only be used as an indicator and have to be taken with care, as the mean does not reflect possible differences in the books' degrees of difficulty (see discussion in Chapter 9.2.1.1). The numbers in Table 20 that are shaded in grey again indicate that the learners read these particular books while listening to the audio-recording of it (see Chapters 8.1.3 and 9.2.1).

Moreover, some numbers in Table 20 are written in a grey font. These numbers indicate that this comprehension level might not mirror a realistic picture of the learner's actual comprehension of that book. The reasons for this are manifold. One reason is that some learners had already revealed so much content before it was another learner's turn, that the latter could only repeat what had been said before and did not get the chance to display his/her own comprehension. During the recall and questions on the book 'Five Little Monkeys', for example, Neele hardly had a chance to recount what she had understood, as almost everything had already been said by Emil, Ina and Natan before it was her turn. This is due to the nature of the data collection that was conducted in small groups instead of individually. Another reason why the results may not be an accurate reflection of the true comprehension levels is that sometimes some learners simply did not say and contribute much during the recall and questioning phase. During the discussion on the book 'Paddington at the Palace', for example, the other participants hardly gave Ina any chance to speak, so that she could not contribute very much. Grey numbers, however, were only given for this instance when there was reason to assume that the learners had actually understood more than they did reveal. This assumption was based on the few utterances the learners made, which partly indicated that there must be a deeper comprehension behind what they revealed. Also, some learners sometimes simply did not want to participate a lot. This was mostly due to their moods. In the reading session on 'Five Little Monkeys', for example, Rico was in such a bad mood that he did not want to participate in the discussion. The same holds true for Max for the books 'Paddington at the Palace' and 'Something Good'. Lastly, the reading session of RG 2 on the book 'Froggy's Best Christmas' was interrupted by another teacher who needed the room, so that there was hardly any time for the regular recall and questioning phase. Thus, Jonas and Dani could not say everything that they had wanted to say.

Therefore, the average comprehension for each learner and each book was calculated twice, once including and once excluding possible unrealistic results (grey numbers). For the following presentation and interpretation of results only the latter results, which exclude possible mistakes, will be used. Although this is partly incomplete, these results provide a more realistic picture of the learners' actual comprehension levels and exclude variables that might distort the results.[187]

To take a closer look at the results, firstly an overview of the average comprehension levels for each book is given in Figure 25:

---

187   The fact that possibly not all learners revealed a realistic picture of their actual comprehension level partly mirrors daily classroom practice when working with young learners. Children are easily influenced by their emotions and cannot always control them for the sake of school work. This is not a circumstance that can or should be controlled for, but is a factor that researchers have to deal with when working with and investigating young learners. Therefore, it seemed most feasible to just exclude these results from the overall presentation and interpretation of results on reading comprehension.

Figure 25: Average levels of reading comprehension for each book as indicated by the oral recall and comprehension questions (on a scale from 1 to 5; 1 being the lowest and 5 the highest possible level).

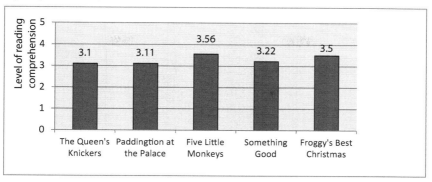

The average comprehension levels for each book as seen in Figure 25 range from $M = 3.1$ to $M = 3.56$ on the scale of levels 1 to 5. The book that displays the best comprehension is 'Five Little Monkeys', with an average comprehension of $M = 3.56$, and the book that displays the least comprehension is 'The Queen's Knickers' with an average level of $M = 3.1$. The difference between these books is 0.46. No trend with regard to a decrease or increase in comprehension can be seen in this figure. Although the latter three books were understood slightly better than the first two, the difference is not high and there is a drop in level of comprehension with the book 'Something Good' to 3.22, which is close to $M = 3.1$ of 'Paddington at the Palace'. Each book's average comprehension is therefore somewhere around level 3, partly moving into the direction of level 4.

Overall, the book that was understood best according to the recall and questioning data is 'Five Little Monkeys', but the results here range most with the highest standard deviation of $SD = 1.42$. While Simone showed only very little comprehension of this book and could only reach level 1, Max, Dani and Emil showed a very elaborate understanding and reached level 5. The other learners are found somewhere in between, with no clear trend towards one extreme or the other. The whole range of possible levels is thus covered.

Focusing on the standard deviation, Table 20 shows that it ranges between $SD = 0.83$ for the book 'Something Good' and $SD = 1.42$ for the book 'Five Little Monkeys'. For some books, the standard deviation is actually quite high. This shows that the individual learners' performance and thus comprehension levels on these books vary greatly. Therefore, more attention will be paid to the performance of individual learners in the course of this chapter. Figure 26 shows each learner's comprehension level of each book, as well as the learners' mean value for reading comprehension (black bar). As explained above and indicated by the grey numbers in Table 20, some books were left out for some learners, as the results were possibly not a realistic reflection of their true levels of comprehension.

Figure 26: Comprehension levels of each learner on each book, including each learner's mean values, as indicated by the oral recall and comprehension questions (rated from 1 to 5; 1 being the lowest and 5 the highest possible level).

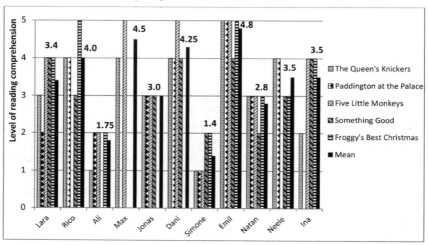

Figure 26 shows that the individual learners' performances are indeed very different, and that the learners themselves also display different results across different books. Some learners' comprehension levels are very high with an average mean that is very close to level 5, the highest possible level; in particular Max with $M = 4.5$ and Emil with $M = 4.8$. Also Rico's and Dani's levels are high, with $M = 4.0$ and $M = 4.25$. All of these four learners had at least one book where they showed a very elaborate and complex degree of comprehension (level 5). In fact, all books were understood at level 4 or 5, with the exception of Rico who once only reached level 3.

Four further learners showed an average comprehension around level 3 and slightly higher; these are Lara ($M = 3.4$), Jonas ($M = 3.0$), Neele ($M = 3.5$) and Ina ($M = 3.5$). Two of these learners show a higher range of $SD = 0.9$ (Lara) and $SD = 1.0$ (Ina), while Jonas' level of comprehension is continuously at level 3 and does not vary at all. One learner, Natan, is very close to level 3, as his average comprehension level is 2.8. He understood four out of five books at level 3, while there is one book, 'Something Good', where he only displayed comprehension at level 2. Therefore, he also does not range much in results.

Only two learners reached lower comprehension levels, namely Ali and Simone. Ali's average comprehension level is $M = 1.75$ ($SD = 0.5$) and Simone's is lower than that with $M = 1.4$ ($SD = 0.55$). Both never appeared to have understood a book better than level 2 and understood at least one book at level 1 only, indicating that almost nothing of that book could be comprehended. Generally, Ali seemed very little interested during the recall and questioning phase and often hardly participated unless he was asked to contribute. Even when asked, he could often not provide the answer as he had not paid attention to what was being talked about. Simone, by contrast, seemed to be concentrating hard and listened carefully to what the others had said, but did not contribute much herself. This got slightly better towards the last books, when Simone contributed more; however, her remarks were mostly about details that were obtained from the visualisations and not structured coherently.

Looking at individual learners, an increase in comprehension levels can partly be seen. Ali's, Lara's, Simone's and Ina's comprehension levels rose in the course of the five books. All four participants advanced to at least one higher level, while Lara and Ina even reached two levels higher. For one learner, Neele, a decrease of one level of reading comprehension was found. She started at level 4 for the first two books, but then fell back to level three for the latter two. None of the remaining learners showed a clear trend in one or the other direction in terms of their levels of reading comprehension.

Lastly, a closer look at the comprehension schemes provides tentative evidence that more detailed aspects of comprehension improve over time. For example, an increase in mentions of important details that were placed in the context of the story was found for Ali, who only offered isolated and redundant statements for the first books. Furthermore, Dani improved her recall in that she followed the books' storyline for all the books but the first. Thus, her ability to follow the logical order of events might have improved. A closer analysis of these detailed aspects of improvement, however, remains a task for future research in focused case-studies.

9.2.2.2 Interpretation and Discussion of Results

Overall, the results to a large extent mirror what had already been found through the learners' self-assessment (Chapter 9.2.1) and also the impression that the learners could cope well with the task of reading (see Chapter 9.1) is supported. All the books were on average understood on more or less similar levels, in that there is no book that a majority of the learners struggled with and also no book that the majority of learners found too easy. Looking at the overview of the comprehension of all the books in Figure 25, a similar average comprehension level ($M = 3.1$ to $M = 3.56$) can be discerned across the board. This shows that the learners on average understood a number of aspects of each book, could extract the global message of a text, mostly understood the book's logical order of events and could extract information from the pictures as well as from the text (see Chapter 4.5.2 for the description of the levels of reading comprehension). That young learners can at least grasp the overall gist of English picture books has also been found by Kolb (2013; see Chapter 5.5.2). She established that many learners in her study understood the overall story but were wrong about some details. For teaching practice this overall result indicates that the selection of the books for the present study seems appropriate with regard to the learners' reading abilities and levels of comprehension. More so, this finding underlines that authentic picture books can be used as reading material in the primary school EFL classroom.

Interestingly, the book that was understood best, 'Five Little Monkeys', also shows the highest standard deviation. The reason clearly is that the learners' comprehension levels range from 1 to 5 for this book, with no clear trend in a certain direction. While some learners must have found this book rather easy to understand and displayed a very elaborate comprehension of it, other learners clearly struggled with it. To a certain extent this finding also holds true for the other books and goes to show the extent to which the comprehension of a book is dependent on factors like the individual learners and their interest in the topic, their previous FL knowledge, their world knowledge concerning that topic, their concentration or their moods. This confirms that learners are different with regard to their levels of competence and thus also display different reading abilities and different prerequisites for reading a certain FL text. The same is also shown by the fact that on all books the individual learners' comprehension varied noticeably; while some learners only understood parts of a story, others understood most or all of it.

Despite the wide variety in results, many learners did not range much across different levels of comprehension, but usually between two levels and sometimes between three. There seems to be a certain level of competence that each learner possesses, and that is either somewhere between levels one and two, or between levels two and four or between levels four and five. While most of the learners are found in the latter two groups, two were found in the first group of comprehending not higher than levels one or two for all five books (Ali and Simone).

This result indicates that despite the factors mentioned in the previous paragraph and despite all differences which might occur, learners still possess a certain level of reading competence and remain at this level regardless of other influencing factors. In order to improve each learner's individual reading ability, all factors that influence their reading thus need to be considered and supported in their development.

Across the books, four learners increased their comprehension levels gradually, six learners did not show any clear decrease or increase in comprehension, and one learner decreased in reading level. Reasons for an increase of reading comprehension may include the influence of a familiarisation effect with regard to the task of reading which enabled the learners to better cope with it (also see Chapter 9.1.2). This might correspond to an increase in reading strategies, as particularly found for Lara (see Chapter 10.1.5). A higher level of confidence, as potentially achieved through familiarisation and through the experience that one can cope with a task, can also lead to better results in comprehension. In addition, more confidence about reading can also allow learners to contribute better and more in a group discussion on content; for example, Simone hardly contributed to the recall for the first books, but offered more information for the last two. With regard to the recall process, the ability to actually recall a book's content more competently might also have improved over time, with regard to the storyline and extracting the global message as well as important detail.

The fact that no clear trend concerning a decrease or increase of reading comprehension occured, as well as the fact that Neele's levels slightly decreased, supports the notion that reading competence is dependent on the a number of different factors. Regular reading in itself and a potential familiarisation effect are not sufficient to enhance all learners' reading abilities of picture books. Apart from that, reading one book in two weeks might not be enough reading practice to show a clear increase in reading comprehension that is general enough to be transferred to different texts.

Some learners' reading comprehension, however, displayed a ceiling effect in that their comprehension levels were high (level 4 or 5) from the beginning of the reading study. As such, there was hardly any room for further improvement for them. More difficult reading texts might be beneficial for such readers in order to progress in FL reading competences and transfer their FL reading abilities to more complex texts.

In a last step, a closer look will be taken at four individual learners. Firstly, the weak readers Simone and Ali, then the strong reader Emil and lastly the average reader Jonas, who revealed some interesting compensation techniques with regard to comprehension.

Ali's weak results and reluctant participation in reading as well as in the recall and questioning phase might indicate that he is caught in a vicious circle of reading (Nuttall, 2005; see Chapter 9.1). Ali generally seemed challenged while reading, occasionally even frustrated about the task, encountered difficulties despite listening to the audio-recording while reading and did not appear to be very interested in the books. Clearly, reading books and being engaged in activities concerned with reading is not everyone's favourite activity and Ali might prefer different means of learning a FL. Nevertheless, frustration and lack of interest in reading might have led to denial, boredom and a lack of concentration. Nuttall (2005: 127), who distinguishes between the vicious circle of the weak reader and the virtuous circle of the good reader, would explain this in terms of the vicious circle of reading. The vicious circle describes the cycle of frustration in that weak readers do not understand much, therefore read slowly, do not enjoy reading and lack practice because they thus do not read much (Nuttall, 2005: 127). Any of these stages can lead to the other and all four influence each other, no matter at what stage a weak reader enters the circle. Ali, obviously, neither enjoyed reading nor did he understand much. Therefore, there is reason to assume that Ali is caught in such a cycle of frustration. Nuttall (2005: 127) explains that such readers should be supported in reaching the virtuous circle of reading, in which those who can be characterised as good readers find themselves in a cycle of growth, in that they enjoy reading, read faster, read more and understand better. At any stage, this virtuous circle can and should be entered by readers, but particularly enjoyment and quantity of reading are key factors to get readers of out the vicious circle (Nuttall, 2005: 128). Thus, Ali should be supported in experiencing the pleasure of reading which could also enhance his reading quantity. This could, in return, enhance his reading quality and allow him to enter the virtuous circle of reading. To enhance Ali's pleasure in reading it might be beneficial for him to practise techniques that help him to follow the book's storyline and to understand the global message of a story instead of sticking to details too much. Also, a reflection on tolerance of ambiguity might be beneficial for him, as well as a gradual decrease in using the audio-recording in favour of reading parts of the text without it. Lastly, Ali might benefit from choosing reading texts that he is interested in instead of having to read FL texts that are given to him by teachers or researchers.

By contrast, the second weak reader, Simone, did not seem unmotivated or frustrated, although she also seemed slightly overtaxed with reading. She concentrated hard and was interested, focused on task and was motivated to master it. Also, she listened carefully during the recall and said she had profited from it, although contributing much to it herself might have been too demanding for her. Therefore, despite her weak FL reading abilities, she was obviously not caught in the vicious circle. At this point teachers need to pay careful attention so that such learners do not enter the vicious circle but continue to enjoy reading and are motivated to practise it.

One learner that would clearly be found in Nuttall's (2005: 127) virtuous circle of reading is Emil. Emil's comprehension of the books was very elaborate and he understood how to summarise a book's content by following its storyline and revealing global information as well as important details. This shows that he had developed summarising skills that helped him to retain important details as well as the global message of the book (see Chapter 4.4.2). According to Westphal Irwin (2007: 194), "good readers select important ideas and summarise as they go. They do not necessarily remember large numbers of details." The fact that Emil understood information that could only be understood from the textual elements shows that his reading comprehension skills were advanced and that he did not always need visual information in order to understand the FL in writing. Overall, Emil could read the authentic picture books well and showed elaborate FL reading skills. Not much development of reading comprehension or recall skills can be seen in Emil's performance, which indicates that his reading skills were already advanced at the beginning of the data collection and that probably a ceiling effect occurred. Thus, maybe more difficult books, for example graphic novels, might be the right reading material for him in order to further develop his FL reading abilities.

For other learners, such as Jonas, the reading material appeared to be just right. Understanding each book at level 3 according to the recall and questioning, Jonas appeared to be fully engaged in the process of developing the competences needed to cope with the task of reading picture books at the time of the study. He could supply a large number of correct content observations, including global as well as detailed ones, but he had not yet managed to understand many aspects that were only presented in the text; he still needed the visualisations for support in comprehension. He could partly follow the storyline of books but seemed to still need some practice in coherently organising the logical order of the events in a book. His strategy of guessing and interpreting a lot seemed to compensate for problems in comprehension and seemed to be an effective way for him to overcome text difficulties. Overall, the task of reading authentic picture books seemed to be just the right activity for him to practise his FL reading skills, as he showed that he had mastered some aspects already but also might need some more practice with others.

Besides the strategy of guessing and interpreting to compensate for comprehension problems, also the factor of world knowledge and previous topic knowledge improved comprehension. It was striking that those three learners who had already been to London could bring in a lot of information that they knew from their trips and could also understand several details of the book 'Paddington at the Palace' better than those who did not know about them; for example, the 'Changing of the Guards'. Therefore, books that contain non-fictional information are potentially understood better when learners already possess some previous knowledge about the topic. In classroom practice, such previous knowledge could be established via carefully selected pre-reading activities that purposefully activate or introduce knowledge that supports the comprehension of a FL text.

In sum, the results of the oral recall and questioning provided interesting detail about the learners' reading comprehension and their ability to cope with the FL texts. It is striking that these results match what had already been found via the self-assessment to a large extent, but that the oral recall and questioning added important details which had not been discernible before. Overall, the impression that the participants could cope with the task of reading FL picture books and understand them at least to a certain extent was confirmed, while some readers even provided evidence that they would have been able to cope with more complex texts.

9.2.3 Comprehension Levels as Indicated in the Written Comprehension Tasks

The level of reading comprehension was also measured by means of the written comprehension tasks (see Chapter 8.2.3). For each book, the learners completed a set of six tasks with a maximum score of 30 points (see Chapter 8.2.3. This subchapter will firstly present and then discuss the results.

9.2.3.1 Presentation of Results

Table 21 shows the results of all children on all six books. Additionally, an average score as well as the standard deviation were calculated for each book (bottom line) as well as for each participant (right column). The average scores per child have to be taken with caution, as the degree of difficulty of the tasks per book can vary from book to book due to potential differences in the books' degrees of difficulty and potential differences in the tasks, although the tasks all followed the same structure (also see Chapter 9.2.1.1). Therefore, the mean only provides an overview of the overall reading comprehension level of all six books and serves to provide a better picture of the participants' overall comprehension performance.

Table 21: Overview of the scores on the written comprehension tasks (max. score 30 points).

	The Queen's Knickers	Paddington at the Palace	Five Little Monkeys	Something Good	Froggy's Best Christmas	Winnie in Winter	Average scores per child
Lara	24	28	25.5	19.5	22	17	$M = 22.67$ $SD = 4.02$
Rico	28	28	26.5	30	25	28	$M = 27.58$ $SD = 1.69$
Ali	17.5	26	16.5	27.5	27	27	$M = 23.58$ $SD = 5.13$
Max	24.5	26	28	27	28	25	$M = 26.42$ $SD = 1.5$
Jonas	18	9	14.5	12.5	18.5	14	$M = 14.42$ $SD = 3.54$
Dani	23	25	26	26	24.5	30	$M = 25.75$ $SD = 2.36$
Simone	11.5	20	18.5	21.5	24	17	$M = 18.75$ $SD = 4.3$
Emil	29.5	27	26.5	28	28	25	$M = 27.33$ $SD = 1.54$
Natan	18	17	15	18.5	18	14	$M = 16.75$ $SD = 1.84$
Neele	29	24	24	27	29	24	$M = 26.17$ $SD = 2.49$
Ina	20	26	22.5	26	23	13	$M = 21.75$ $SD = 4.86$
Average score for each book	$M = 22.09$ $SD = 5.65$	$M = 23.27$ $SD = 5.82$	$M = 22.14$ $SD = 5.07$	$M = 23.95$ $SD = 5.28$	$M = 24.27$ $SD = 3.71$	$M = 21.27$ $SD = 6.33$	

The bottom line displays the average scores that the learners attained on each of the six books. Figure 27 visualises them:

Figure 27: Average scores on the written comprehension tasks of each book.

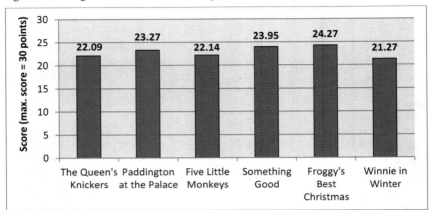

The average scores on each book range from an average of $M = 21.27$ points for 'Winnie in Winter' to an average of $M = 24.27$ points for 'Froggy's Best Christmas'. Thus, according to the results on the written comprehension tasks, the book 'Froggy's Best Christmas' was understood best, while the book 'Winnie in Winter' was understood least. All average scores neither noticeably decrease nor increase over time, but instead seem similar with no big differences across the books. The difference between the lowest and the highest score is about 3 points. Generally, all average scores are quite high, with all of them being in the upper third of possible scores.

As seen in Table 21, the standard deviation is very high for each book. This indicates that the children's individual performances on the tasks differ considerably and that the range of individual scores is high. Therefore, the individual learners will be looked at more closely. Figure 28 shows the average score of each child on all six books.

Figure 28: Average scores of each child on the written comprehension tasks.

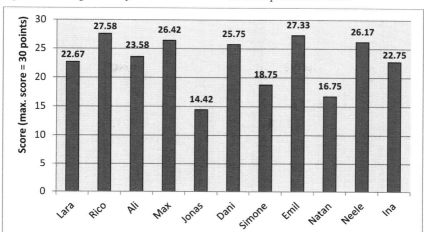

The average scores of the children range noticeably, from 27.58 (Rico) to 14.42 (Jonas) points. There are two children with a very high mean of $M = 27.58$ and $M = 27.33$ (Rico and Emil). Max, Neele and Dani's average scores are also high, ranging from 26.42 to 25.75. All these five learners' scores on the written tasks are high and range in the upper sixth of all possible scores and are hence very close to the maximum score. There is only one child, Jonas, whose performance is under the benchmark of 50 % with a mean of $M = 14.42$. Jonas', as well as Simone's ($M = 18.75$) and Natan's ($M = 16.75$) scores are lower in comparison to most of the other participants'.

As can also be seen in Table 21, the standard deviation of some children is very high, whereas that of others is fairly low. The reason is that some children's scores on the written tasks differ strikingly across different books, whilst other children consistently scored about the same points. Therefore, Figure 29 shows the scores of all the children on all the books in order to see to what extent a possible decrease or increase in scores might have taken place and to what extent the scores differ across the books.

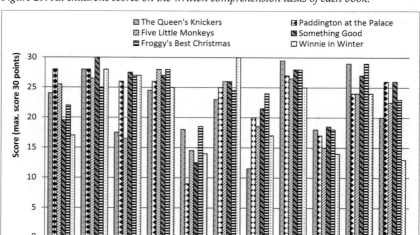

As can be seen in this diagram, four children's scores are very much the same across all books: Rico, Max, Emil and Natan only display a standard deviation of $SD = 1.5$ to 1.84. While the scores of Rico, Max and Emil are very high on the tasks on all the books, ranging from 24.5 to 30 points, Natan's scores are consistently lower. Other learners, namely Ali, Lara, Ina and Simone, differed more across the books. In total, they all scored at a medium level of between 18.75 and 23.58 points, but their scores on each individual book range with a difference of up to 13 points. Likewise, Jonas' range is high, but his average score is lower than that of the latter four learners.

With regard to a possible decrease or increase in scores, which might indicate a decrease or increase in reading comprehension from book to book, Figure 29 does not reveal a clear or continuous trend. Five learners' scores go up and down across the different books without a tendency (Rico, Max, Neele, Natan and Jonas). Jonas and Natan's scores are rather low, while the other learners' scores are rather high. A slightly positive trend, in that the scores mostly increased across the books, is found for Dani, Ali and Simone. Whilst Dani's scores are all fairly high, Simone's scores range considerably but seem to improve. Ali's scores have clearly improved on the last books. A negative trend is found for Emil, Ina and Lara. While Emil's scores still remain high and only slightly decrease, Lara's and particularly Ina's scores started rather high but then decreased drastically from 26 down to 13 points.

One aspect that is striking and where a clear decrease occurred, is the time the children needed to solve the tasks. Figure 30 provides an overview:

Figure 30: Time (in minutes) needed to complete the written comprehension tasks of each book.

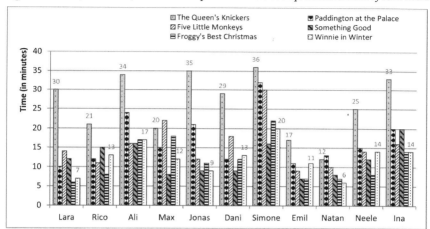

As shown in Figure 30, the time the learners needed to complete the written comprehension tasks reduced noticeably from book to book. While the children needed between 17 and 36 minutes for the set of tasks for the first book 'The Queen's Knickers', they only needed between 6 and 17 minutes for the set of tasks for the last book 'Winnie in Winter'. With the exception of Max, for whom no gradual decrease in time occurred, all other ten learners reduced the time they needed.

When compared to the average scores one can see that across all children, except for Natan and Jonas, there seems to be an increase in time needed to complete the tasks that accompanies a decrease in average scores. Therefore, the more time a learner needed for completing the tasks, the lower the score on the tasks. Conversely, those learners that scored high mostly needed less time.

9.2.3.2 Interpretation and Discussion of Results

Overall, the average scores on the tasks for all books are relatively high. On the one hand this means that the learners could on average cope well with the tasks and could work on them competently as post-reading activities. Additionally, the high scores indicate fairly high comprehension levels of the books. On the other hand, taking into account that the average scores on each book all seem high, a ceiling effect must be assumed. This effect can also be seen when looking at the results of the individual children in Figure 28. Some learners display a very high average score while only a few display a low average score. One could argue that the tasks were too easy and that an increase in task difficulty or also additional and more challenging tasks should have been provided. A similar effect had already been found in the reading tests of the EVENING study and the BIG study (see Chapter 3.4). Both studies found ceiling effects with regard to reading competence as shown on written tests.

Those children with high average scores, and particularly Rico, Emil, Max, Neele and Dani, might have needed more challenging tasks in order to really show what they had understood. Emil actually once voiced this when working on the tasks of the book 'Froggy's Best Christmas'. He said that the tasks were too easy and that he would have liked to have had more difficult ones. More challenging written comprehension tasks, for example more open tasks, might have allowed a closer analysis and given a more differentiated picture of the individual comprehension levels of all the learners, as such tasks might have shown more detailed differences in the individual performance levels between the children. With regard to classroom practice the results underline the importance of individualised reading tasks in order to cater for individual reading competences. Some learners need more challenging tasks, for instance, more open post-reading tasks, than others.

As shown, some children's performances on individual books differed considerably. Chapters 9.2.1.2 and 9.2.2.2. already discussed reasons for such variations in performance, which could be, among others, that the children with a high standard deviation found the level of difficulty of the books very different and that the written tasks indeed displayed their changing abilities with regard to the comprehension of the individual books. It should also be taken into consideration, however, as noted before, that the performance of a learner, particularly of a young learner, can depend on the individual well-being and mood of each day. A low score could simply indicate a bad day. For some children it can also reflect their varying levels of concentration. Jonas in particular had trouble concentrating and his concentration varied on a daily but also hourly basis, which might explain his difference of 9 points between the first and the second book. Also, varying levels of motivation can influence the performance on tasks. Lara's scores, for example, might have been influenced by her lack of motivation (see Chapter 9.1). Moreover, children's interests in different books and topics might vary, so that also the amount of effort they invest regarding a topic and thus a particular book might differ. This can, in return, lead to variations in scores.[188]

For some learners, an increase or decrease in scores could be found. Those children that displayed an increase in scores might have benefited from a familiarisation effect in that they had to get used to the task format in order to successfully complete the written tasks. Other learners' performance actually decreased. Lara's decrease on the last book's tasks ('Winnie in Winter') might be based on the fact that she read this book without the audio-recording, while she had read the previous four books with the recording. This might show that Lara's comprehension with the audio-recording was higher and more elaborate than without it. Overall, however, Lara was one of very few children who did not like reading the books and who consistently lacked motivation. Therefore, it is conceivable that the decrease in scores on the written comprehension tasks is not necessarily based on a decrease in comprehension of the books, but rather a question of motivation and task endurance. Familiarisation with reading tasks can thus have two different effects: On the one hand it can help learners in improving their performance over time, on the other hand it can increase boredom, demotivation and frustration when the task itself is not well-liked by the learner.

Taking into consideration that there was a clear decrease in time needed to solve the tasks for all the learners but Max, again a familiarisation effect may have occurred. By getting used to the tasks' structures, the learners could solve

---

188 Whenever scores might not display a realistic comprehension level, for example due to a lack of motivation, this could lead to possible errors in the results caused by factors that could not be controlled for. Therefore, there is reason to take such results out of the data to get a possibly more realistic picture of the actual comprehension levels (as done with the results on the oral recall and questioning when it was obvious that a result was unrealistic; see Chapter 9.2.2). However, for several reasons the current results were all left in. Firstly, children with varying interests, moods and motivation levels with regard to written tasks mirror a regular classroom situation and provide a realistic picture of the heterogeneity of classes and individual differences amongst learners. Secondly, such results provide interesting insights and valuable information about possible influential factors on reading comprehension and post-reading tasks and should therefore be discussed rather than deleted. Lastly, influential factors were hard to pinpoint clearly for the written tasks, because no direct interaction took place with the learners. The latter was the case with the oral recall and questioning. Finally, the sample was so small that taking children like Lara out would have reduced it to an even lower number. Therefore, I decided not to take out any learners or any results of the written comprehension tasks.

the tasks faster in that they could concentrate on content without having to focus on understanding the task instruction. For classroom practice, this implies that learners might sometimes benefit from familiar task formats. However, this familiarisation effect should not be pushed to the limits, as variation is equally important to provide challenge and prevent boredom.

The results showed that the more time a learner needed to complete the tasks, the lower the average score. Several reasons are imaginable for this effect. One cause could be that those children that needed more time probably found the tasks more difficult than those who completed them faster. However, the time they spent on the tasks did not improve their scores. In contrast, the learners that solved the tasks quickly scored noticeably higher and were hence more successful in completing the tasks. This is not surprising, in that low-performing learners usually need more time than high-performing ones when given the same task (see Bartnitzky, 2009). Still, the latter group usually performs better since their level of competence typically allows them to reach a higher performance level overall. However, it is interesting to see that Natan and Jonas spent little time on solving the tasks for the last books, but at the same time achieved very low scores. This indicates that they might not have concentrated on the tasks very much but just wanted to complete them quickly. Such an effect is found when learners work too quickly and too hastily, which in return leads to mistakes and a lower score than what they might have achieved when working more slowly and with greater concentration.

Taken overall, the results on the written comprehension tasks show that the demands placed on the learners by these tasks were not too high. The tasks were in parts too easy rather than too difficult. Certainly, tasks like these can be used in the classroom as post-reading activities and the children can autonomously work on such tasks when reading books independeltly.[189] The written comprehension tasks also show that the reading comprehension levels are medium to very high. In return, this provides evidence that reading the books was not too challenging for the learners but matched their current proficiency levels. However, some learners should be given more difficult tasks to allow them to show their actual competences and avoid a ceiling effect.

The possible downsides of this task format (see Chapter 8.2.3), which were concerned with a) the uncertainties surrounding the extent to which general reading and writing competence was tested in lieu of the reading comprehension of the books and b) the extent to which the oral recall and questioning that took place

---

189   Clearly, however, more interesting post-reading activities exist (see, e.g., Reckermann & Bechler, 2018).

before solving the written tasks might have influenced the results on the written tasks cannot fully be controlled for. Rather, these drawbacks underline the importance of various measurements for a holistic picture of reading comprehension, since the downsides show how misleading it can be to rely on only one measure, such as written tasks. Therefore, various instruments should be used in order to investigate young learners' FL reading competence reliably. The common practice of using only multiple-choice questions should thus be regarded very critically since they are probably not sufficient to grasp the actual comprehension level of a text.

9.2.4 Summary of Comprehension Levels

This chapter briefly summarises the data collected on the children's level of reading comprehension as measured by the three different instruments. It also compares the results collected from the different instruments and underlines the need for mixed methods in order to investigate reading comprehension.

Firstly, Table 22 gives an overview of the eleven participants and their average performance on the three instruments that investigated their reading comprehension as well as on the average time they needed for reading.

Table 22: Overview of the participants' reading comprehension levels on all three instruments.

Participant	Average level of self-assessment (scale from 1 to 5; with 1 being the lowest and 5 the highest level of comprehension)	Average comprehension level on oral recall and questioning (level 1 to 5; with 1 being the lowest and 5 the highest level of comprehension)	Average score on written comprehension tasks (max. 30 points)	Average time needed for reading
Lara	$M = 3.2; SD = 0.84$	$M = 3.4; SD = 0.9$	$M = 22.67; SD = 4.02$	$M = 8$ min 24 sec
Rico	$M = 4.2; SD = 0.84$	$M = 4.0; SD = 0.82$	$M = 27.58; SD = 1.69$	$M = 5$ min 50 sec
Ali	$M = 3.0; SD = 0.71$	$M = 1.75; SD = 0.5$	$M = 23.58; SD = 5.13$	$M = 8$ min 44 sec
Max	$M = 4.75; SD = 0.5$	$M = 4.5; SD = 0.71$	$M = 26.42; SD = 1.5$	$M = 7$ min 28 sec
Jonas	$M = 4.8; SD = 0.45$	$M = 3.0; SD = 0.0$	$M = 14.42; SD = 3.54$	$M = 8$ min 14 sec
Dani	$M = 3.2; SD = 0.84$	$M = 4.25; SD = 0.5$	$M = 25.75; SD = 2.36$	$M = 10$ min 22 sec
Simone	$M = 2.2; SD = 0.45$	$M = 1.4; SD = 0.55$	$M = 18.75; SD = 4.3$	$M = 13$ min 13 sec
Emil	$M = 4.8; SD = 0.45$	$M = 4.8; SD = 0.45$	$M = 27.33; SD = 1.54$	$M = 4$ min 13 sec
Natan	$M = 2.8; SD = 0.45$	$M = 2.8; SD = 0.45$	$M = 16.75; SD = 1.84$	$M = 5$ min 41 sec
Neele	$M = 4.0; SD = 0.0$	$M = 3.5; SD = 0.58$	$M = 26.17; SD = 2.49$	$M = 6$ min 21 sec
Ina	$M = 3.8; SD = 0.45$	$M = 3.5; SD = 1.0$	$M = 21.75; SD = 4.86$	$M = 9$ min 29 sec

This summary of results shows that for some learners the three different instruments show similar results with regard to their reading comprehension level. Firstly, Rico, Max and Emil all display similar results on all three instruments, and a high level of reading comprehension is shown on all three measures. Therefore, there is reason to assume that these three learners understood all the books well overall and were all able to reach a high level of reading comprehension. Similarly, Neele shows good results that seem to match across all instruments, although her results are not as good as those of the other three. All four learners seem to be aware of their mostly high performance as they realistically self-assessed this high level. Likewise, Lara shows similar results on all instruments, but hers are lower than those of the four participants just mentioned. Lara's comprehension is rather average and found somewhere between the two extremes on each instrument. Her average results are for the most part based on reading while listening to the audio-recording of the particular books and might have been different without this device.

For the other six learners, the results on the three different instruments do not match that well and are occasionally contradictory. For example, Ali's results on the self-assessment and the written comprehension tasks are comparable to those of Lara, but he performed noticeably worse on the oral recall and comprehension questions. A possible reason for this might be that he might not have shown his actual abilities during the recall and questioning and this oral activity might not have appealed to him. Another reason might be that he profited a lot from the group discussion of each book's content in the recall and questioning and could therefore perform considerably better on the written comprehension tasks. In this case, an influence of the oral discussion on the solving of the written tasks cannot be excluded.

Differences in results also hold true for Simone, who scored surprisingly high points on the written tasks in comparison to her rather low performance in terms of her self-assessment and in the oral recall and questioning. Like Ali, the oral discussion might have helped her in understanding the book and this might have supported her work on the written tasks. The fact that she concentrated well during the recall and questioning and mentioned the usefulness of the oral group discussions supports this notion. Thus, for her the written tasks might not necessarily show her individual comprehension level as well.

In contrast to that, Natan and also Ina scored worse on the written tasks than would have been expected. While both participants' self-assessment and performance on the oral recall and questioning seem very similar, their performance on the written tasks appears weaker in contrast. It is particularly noticeable that

Natan scored second lowest on the written tasks, with an average of about half of the maximum points. This might show that Natan benefits from oral discussions of a book and has difficulties with written tasks. In this case, written tasks might not display a realistic picture of his reading comprehension level. With an average of $M = 21.75$ points, Ina's performance on the written task is not as low as Natan's, but still does not fully match the results that she displayed on the other two instruments.

Similarly, Jonas scored even lower on the written tasks than Natan did, after he performed averagely with $M = 3.0$ on the oral recall and questioning. Thus, the same explanation might hold true for him. Interestingly, Jonas' self-assessment does not comply with his performance on the recall and questioning or on the written tasks at all, as he assessed his reading comprehension as being very high with an average of $M = 4.8$. That means that he perceived himself as having almost fully understood all of the books.[190] That this is not the case, which can be seen on the other two instruments, shows that he overestimated his reading comprehension and that his self-assessment is probably not realistic; a difficulty that is often found with young learners (see Chapter 9.2.1.2). Therefore, a reflection is needed which might have helped Jonas in developing more realistic self-assessment abilities. This was not done in the present study, but is recommendable in regular teaching situations in order to avoid such a mismatch. Likewise, Ina and Neele seem to have slightly overestimated their reading abilities, but not to the extent to which Jonas has.

In contrast to that, Dani seems to have underestimated her abilities. While she reached a relatively high average score on the written tasks and also the recall and questioning indicate a high level of reading comprehension, she herself only rated her comprehension as average with $M = 3.2$ on the self-assessment scale. This is interesting, as young learners usually overestimate their abilities. Maybe, however, Dani had very high expectations about reading comprehension based on her experience with reading in her L1, where usually most of a text can be understood. With this expectation she might have rated her comprehension of the English books lower than it actually was, because she possibly encountered gaps and could maybe not fully understand some content. That an incomplete understanding does not necessarily indicate a low level of FL reading comprehension might not be clear to her, and might need to be reflected on in terms of understanding the gist versus understanding details of a text.

---

190   In terms of reading motivation, this should of course be regarded positively.

These overall results allow a tentative division into three groups of readers according to different performance levels.[191]

- Strong FL readers: Rico, Max, Dani, Emil
- Average FL readers: Lara, Neele, Ina, Natan, Jonas
- Weak FL readers: Ali, Simone

There is also reason to group Natan and Jonas as weak readers, but in comparison to Ali and Simone they were noticeably better; therefore, they were grouped as average readers.

Interestingly, some learners that are weak or average FL readers are good or even very good L1 readers according to their L1 reading marks (see Appendix A). For instance, Lara and Neele are both very good L1 readers that were marked with the highest possible mark (1 = *sehr gut*), but they are not as strong L2 readers as other learners in the study are. Also Ali, a weak L2 reader, is a good L1 reader (mark 2 = *gut*). Only Simone, who is a weak L1 reader (mark 4 = *ausreichend*) is also a weak L2 reader. The latter finding seconds Haß' (2006: 83) view that often those pupils who already face great difficulties with reading in their L1 also face similar difficulties when it comes to FL reading. Therefore, advanced L1 reading competence does not necessarily lead to advanced L2 reading competence, while weak L1 reading competence seems to coincide with weak L2 reading competence. A larger sample would be needed to support this hypothesis.

The different measurements for each individual's reading comprehension also allow a distinction with regard to realistic assessment of the level of reading comprehension for most learners:

- Over-assessor: Jonas
- Realistic assessors: Rico, Max, Emil, Lara, Neele
- Under-assessor: Dani
- Unclear: Ali, Simone, Natan, Ina

Because of the low number of participants and the problems of allocating certain learners clearly to any one group, it is impossible to argue which level of comprehension might accompany a certain degree of realistic self-assessment. However, based on the present data, the strong readers in particular could for the most part realistically self-assess their abilities, while the average readers partly had trouble doing this. However, there is reason to assume that not only the level of

---

191 The term 'reader', as in strong, average or weak reader, denotes the level of reading comprehension that a learner attained and does not take into consideration any other factors concerned with reading competence.

reading comprehension influences realistic self-assessment, but also other factors such as emotions and personal expectations with regard to reading comprehension. Exploring these factors remains a task for future research.

In general, self-assessment might have been difficult for the learners, since no expectations with regard to detailed or global comprehension of the book were made transparent. While, for instance, Jonas might have rated his comprehension of the books on the basis of global comprehension, Dani might have used detailed comprehension as a basis for her self-assessment. The reason why I did not mention such expectations to the learners was that this seemed too difficult for them to understand. In follow-up studies, however, it might need to be clarified beforehand what 'no comprehension' or 'full comprehension' mean and refer to.

Lastly, looking at the time needed for reading, which is displayed in the last column of Table 22, one can see that often the shorter the time needed for reading, the better the comprehension, and the longer the time needed for reading, the more the learners struggled with reading and with understanding the books. This confirms Ehlers (2007: 118) statement which argues that reading pace mirrors reading competence. Simone, for example, needed a long period of time and understood little of the books, while Emil needed a very short time to understand almost everything. Therefore, the more fluent a reader is, as indicated by his/her reading pace, the more advanced his/her reading abilities and thus competence with regard to comprehension (also see Chapter 4.1). Ehlers (2007: 119) explains that a slow reading pace makes it difficult to transfer the information as stored in the reader's working memory to the reader's long-term memory for longer retention, because the working memory only has a limited capacity with regard to storage time and storage space. Reading pace thus seems to be an indicator of reading competence. However, a shorter reading time does not always indicate better reading abilities, which can for example be seen with Natan. Similarly to Emil, Natan only needed about five minutes on average to read each book, but in contrast to the other fast readers, Natan's comprehension level was average to weak. Thus, the present study does not show a clear-cut relation between a short reading time and an elaborate reading comprehension. The latter depends rather on the ability to read fluently but grasp meaning at the same time.

Overall, the results on reading comprehension underline the crucial importance of measuring reading via different means. One instrument is not enough to get a clear picture of young learners' reading abilities. Certainly, different instruments make it more difficult to attribute a certain reading competence to a learner, particularly when the results of the different instruments are contradictory, but exactly this finding allows deeper insights into the learners' reading skills and their individual ways of learning.

9.3 The Use of Supportive Devices while Reading

While reading, different supportive devices were available to the participants (see Chapter 8.1.3): picture dictionaries, dictionaries, word lists especially created for each book and MP3-players that contained an audio-recording of each book. Moreover, the children were allowed to work together with their peers if they wanted to. The use of these supportive means was investigated via field notes that I took while the children were reading, a video-recording of the reading process and also semi-structured interviews on reading strategies (see Chapter 8.3.2). In these ways, data on which devices the learners used and also which of the means they deemed as useful for the reading process were collected.[192]

9.3.1 Presentation of Results

Firstly, an overview will be given of which supportive devices were used and how frequently. The frequency was calculated by counting the number of children who used the device for each book. For example, when Lara used the word list several times while reading one book, this was counted as 'one', as she used the word list for comprehension of that particular book. An overview can be seen in Figure 31.

Figure 31: An overview of the use of supportive devices and the frequency with which they were used.

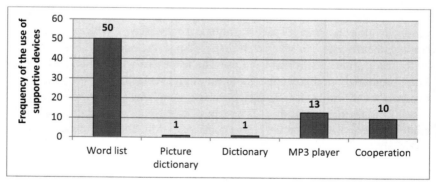

---

192 Using the devices while reading is a reading strategy, thus this chapter overlaps with what is outlined on reading strategies in Chapter 10.

Figure 31 shows which devices the learners used while reading the different books and how often that respective device was used in total. All of the five supportive devices that were offered to the learners were used, but with widely varying frequencies. The word list was used 50 times altogether, and is thus the device that was used most frequently by far. The other four devices were used noticeably less often. The participants used the MP3-player second often, but also with a frequency of only 13 times in total. Likewise, the number of instances of working together with a partner, which overall ten learners did or tried to do, is fairly low. Both dictionaries were only used once during reading all the six books.

Some of the learners partly stated that there was no need for supportive devices for reading the books. For example, Natan argued that the book 'The Queen's Knickers' was too easy for using a supportive device: "*Das Buch war zu einfach dafür*" (Transcript RS QK3 05.09.2014 #30:26). Emil gave the same explanation for the book 'Five Little Monkeys', "*Also, ich *fande das Buch eigentlich/ das konnte man gut lesen und Hilfsmittel brauchte man nicht [sic]*" (Transcript RS FLM3 31.10.2014 #28:31).

To get a closer insight into the different devices and to discover reasons why the learners used some of them more than they used others, the following sections will provide information and more detailed numbers about each device.

Word list

Overall, the word list was used a lot and by far most frequently. Figure 32 provides an overview of how many children used it for each book:

Figure 32: Overview of the number of learners who used the word list, ordered by books.

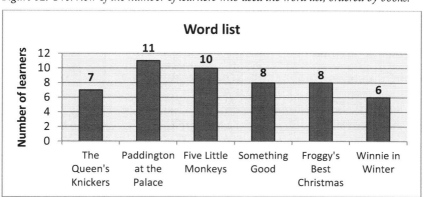

The Figure shows that (almost) all eleven learners used the word list for the second and the third book and that six to eight learners used the word list for the other four books. Therefore, although the numbers vary, the word list was used for each book by at least half of the children. Sometimes, I as the researcher had to remind the learners that they could use the word list if they had vocabulary questions, and as a result the list was usually used more frequently afterwards. For example, following my prompt Max used the word list to look up several words in the book 'Winnie in Winter'.

Taking individual learners into consideration, all of them used the word list for at least two of the six books, and three learners (Emil, Natan and Neele) used it for all six books. However, there is no detectable decrease or increase in use. Interestingly, the use of the list seemed to sometimes depend on what the others in the small reading group did. Only two of the three small groups, namely RG 1 and RG 3, used the word list for reading the first book, 'The Queen's Knickers'. Except for Ina, all the learners in these two groups utilised it, while no learners in the other reading group, RG 2, did.

With a closer look at when the world list was used, it becomes apparent that it was not only used as a while-reading device, but often also looked at either before or after the reading process. Some examples will be provided:

- Max looked at the word list before reading the book 'Paddington at the Palace' (#0:09).
- Simone used the word list twice while reading the book 'Something Good' (#6:50 and #8:45); the first use was initiated by Dani.
- Rico looked at the word list before he started reading the book 'Paddington at the Palace', then used it while reading once (#6:59) and then looked at it again after reading the book.
- After reading the book 'Something Good', Emil looked at the world list and checked one page of the book again (#12:22).

Thus, the word list supported the learners before, during and/or after reading the authentic texts.

During the semi-structured interviews on reading strategies, several learners mentioned that the word list was a useful help for reading the books and a device that supported their reading process (Ina, Lara, Rico and Neele). Neele explained that she could find unknown words on the word list (Transcript RS PP3 30.09.2014 #30:58-31:25):

> **R:** *Was habt ihr denn gemacht, wenn ihr ein Wort beim Lesen nicht verstehen konntet?*
> [...]
> **Neele:** *Ähm, ich habe dann versucht das auf der Wörterliste herauszufinden.*

Rico explained that he tried to figure out the German equivalent of unknown terms with the help of the word list: "*Ich habe mir überlegt, was die deutschen Wörter sein könnten* (points to the word list)" (Transcript RS PP1 29.09.2014 #31:42). Ina emphasised the usefulness of explanations via the pictures on the word lists: "*Also ähm da ähm also da sieht man auch die Bilder und da drunter steht dann, was es dann ist(?) [sic]* " (Transcript RS PP3 30.09.2014 #30:12).

In sum, the word list was thus used by far the most often, either before, while or after reading, and a number of learners could explain its supportive function in reading.

Picture dictionary and dictionary

The picture dictionary as well as the regular dictionary were both only used once and only for the first book 'The Queen's Knickers'. After that, the learners did not try them again.

Lara was the only learner who tried the picture dictionary. On the second page of the book 'The Queen's Knickers' she wanted to look up the word 'smartly' in it. However, after turning pages for some time and not really knowing how to look it up she eventually gave up when she (correctly) concluded that she could not find the word in the picture dictionary.

Similarly, the bilingual dictionary was hardly used at all to look up unknown words. Ali was the only learner who tried to use it once when he also wanted to find a translation for the word 'smartly'. This incident will be described in more detail in order to show the difficulties which he faced. As he had already been unsuccessful in finding the word on the word list and as he saw that Lara did not find 'smartly' in the picture dictionary, Ali took the dictionary for help. It was obvious that he had no idea how to use it and that he had not used such a dictionary before when he started to read the very first page of it word by word. Thus, I tried to explain to him how he would have to look for that word (i.e., by looking at its letters) and also supported him in finding the letter categories in the dictionary. When with help he finally found the word 'smart' he stated that he would still have to keep searching as he needed 'smartly' and not just 'smart': "Smart. *Ja und –ly brauch ich ja auch noch*" (#14:18). After I had explained to him that the translation for both were the same, Ali got stuck at the very first translation that the dictionary offered for the word 'smart', and that was '*klug*'. The trouble was that in the context of the story the translation into '*klug*' did not make sense, but he should have used one of the translation equivalents given further down, which is '*schick*', for that sentence. However, he resisted looking at the other German equivalents and stuck to '*klug*', which hardly helped him in understanding the sentence "The Queen likes to dress smartly" (Allan, 1993).

Despite the difficulties, Ali stated during an interview on reading strategies that the dictionary would help as it supposedly contained a large number of words: *"Also, ähm, weil das dick ist und da kann man dann so reingucken"* (Transcript RS QK1 03.09.2014 #37:52). Similarly, Lara claimed during the first interview on reading strategies that the picture dictionary helped her in understanding the book (Transcript RS QK1 03.09.2014 #37:23). However, she did not explain this any further. This is interesting in that both learners had not really been successful with the dictionaries.

Despite the fact that the learners did not effectively use the dictionaries for reading the books, some nevertheless showed interest in them and wanted to find out about their structure and possibilities. Max, Jonas and Dani, in particular, explored them out of interest and curiosity before or after reading some of the books. But this is not displayed in the figures and numbers, since the children just looked at the dictionaries without the explicit aim of finding an unknown word from the text.

Audio-recording

The audio-recording was used more often and more consistently than the dictionaries. Figure 33 provides an overview:

Figure 33: Overview of the number of learners who used the audio-recording while reading, ordered by books.

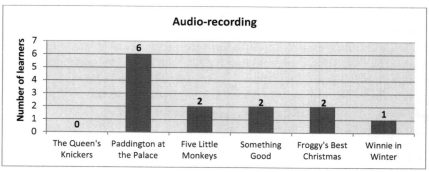

The figure shows that no learner used the audio-recoding for the first book, but yet six of them used it for the book 'Paddington at the Palace'. After that, the number of learners stabilised and one or two used the recording for the last four books. When the audio-recording was used it was always listened to for the whole book and never for only parts of the story. Overall, six different learners listened to the audio-recording of a book while reading it. The other five never used it at all. Two learners used it regularly (Lara and Ali): Lara used it for all the books but the first and the last and Ali used it for all books but the first. The other four learners (Rico, Natan, Neele and Ina) only used it once; all of them for reading the book 'Paddington at the Palace'.

During the interviews, both Lara and Ali mentioned that the audio-recording was very useful for comprehension and both mentioned the recording in four different interviews as the device that allowed them to comprehend the books (e.g., Transcripts RS PP1 29.09.2014 #31:10-31:21 and RS SG1 14.11.2014 #24:07-24:16). Lara explained twice that the audio-recording helped her to read the books because it provided her with the correct pronunciation of words (e.g., Transcript RS FBC1 05.12.2014 #22:47-22:51):

> **R:** *Kannst du noch mal erklären, warum das so gut hilft?*
> **Lara:** *Ja, weil man die Wörter richtig ausgesprochen hört.*

Likewise, Natan, Ina and Neele mentioned it as useful after they had used it once for the book 'Paddington at the Palace' (Transcript RS PP3 30.09.2014 #29:06-29:46, #29:59, #30:47 and #33:04).

The interviews also revealed that the learners read along and did not just listen to the audio-recording without following the text, or at least they stated that this was the case (e.g., Transcript RS PP1 29.09.2014 #32:27-32:31). However, Ali sometimes had trouble reading along and following the recording at the same time. With some books he partly seemed to turn pages randomly and also turned pages back and forward. Thus, I occasionally helped him, particularly with the first books, to find the correct part in the book while reading and listening.

Generally speaking, all the children found the audio-recording, and especially the MP3-player, fascinating and were eager to try it out. When they listened to these audio-recordings, they stated that they found the native speaker voice, and the appealing intonation and onomatopoeia it provided, very fascinating. Particularly when the learners found that other participants in their reading group were reading with the recording, they expressed the wish to listen to it as well, for the sake of the fascination of this device.

Cooperation with a partner

Although the learners could freely choose whether they wanted to work by themselves or with a partner, they usually read the books by themselves. Some children, however, either wanted to or tried to read in cooperation with a partner.

Rico, who was in RG 1, stated that he wanted to read cooperatively for three different books. However, none of the other learners of his reading group were interested in doing so, and therefore Rico also had to read on his own. Similarly, Dani and Max asked their peers about reading the book 'Paddington at the Palace' in cooperation, but without success.

Three times, however, learners found partners for reading cooperatively. For instance, Simone and Dani decided to read the book 'Something Good' in cooperation. However, after a page they gave up on that as their ideas of cooperative reading differed considerably. While Dani wanted to just read the book silently, Simone wanted them to read it out to each other. As this reading aloud was not successful at all and in addition Simone was a lot slower than Dani, Dani took her own book after one page and thus they then worked individually. During the interview afterwards, Dani outlined that she found it difficult to read in cooperation (Transcript RS SG2 12.11.2014 #34:15-34:22):

> **R:** *Ihr habt ja am Anfang erst versucht zusammen zu arbeiten* (addresses Dani and Simone), *das habt ihr ja dann doch nicht mehr ganz gemacht, ne?*
> **Dani:** *Mhm* (affirmative).
> **R:** *Wisst ihr warum nicht?*
> **Dani:** *Äh, weil das irgendwie schwierig ist, finde ich.*

This was the only real attempt at cooperative reading. Two smaller cooperative reading situations could be found with Neele and Natan who briefly read together a small part of 'Something Good' and with Neele and Ina, who read one page of the book 'Paddington at the Palace' together.

9.3.2 Interpretation and Discussion of Results

The present study has conducted exploratory research in an attempt to investigate the use and the success of different devices that potentially support young EFL learners' reading of authentic picture books. The devices were chosen based on previous studies that were either conducted with older learners or conducted with young learners in different settings (see Chapters 6.4 to 6.7). Intentionally, none of the devices was explicitly introduced to the learners prior to the study, in order to mirror daily EFL classroom practice as realistically as possible. For example, a bilingual dictionary would usually not be introduced in the primary school and was thus also not explicitly introduced to the young learners of the present study.

Overall, the devices that proved useful for reading in this study were the word list and the audio-recording. The dictionary and the picture dictionary did not prove to be supportive. Results on cooperative reading are mixed and seem to depend on the chosen setting and the reading context.

The word list, which is the supportive device that was used most frequently and was also used by all the children, appears to be the most useful supportive device by far. The facts that it was used very often, that it was mentioned as a help during the interviews and that its value could be explained, indicates that the word list is a device that effectively and flexibly supports young learners in their individual reading of authentic FL texts. The learners did not have to discover its usefulness over the period of time, but it was used from the very first book on by many children. Its use, however, seems to be partly dependent on the situation, that is, dependent on encouragement from other learners or a teacher. The learners sometimes tended to use it more frequently after someone had reminded them of its function. Given that no guidelines for such word lists existed prior to this study, the criteria for word lists, which were set up in Chapter 6.6.4, seem to be appropriate for young FL learners and word lists can be created for reading authentic English picture books on the basis of these.

The possible reasons why the word list proved to be so successful are manifold. Firstly, the word list was especially created for each book and thus contained words and phrases that were of immediate use for the children. Secondly, it was easy to handle and the children could quickly find lexical items on it. They could place it next to the book while reading and there was no need to turn pages (which is the case with glossaries in many graded readers, see Chapters 5.2.1 and 6.6.4). There was also no need to grab another book, such as a dictionary, and start searching for a word in it. Therefore, it is efficient in terms of time spent and also efficient in problem-solving for a particular lexical issue – at least as long as the lexical item can be found on it. The effort that teachers have to put into creating such world lists for particular books therefore seems worth it.

It is interesting that the learners consulted the word list not only during reading, but often also before or after reading. Looking at it before reading enabled the learners to pre-teach themselves lexical items and can be seen as some sort of individual pre-reading activity. It provides an overview of the lexical load and the words or chunks that the learners can expect in the reading and might allow them to understand a text more easily due to previous language knowledge and previous global content knowledge. Looking at it after the reading process might allow learners to critically question or make sure of their comprehension of a particular part of the text. They might still remember a lexical item that they were insecure about and might want to double-check whether their inferencing of its meaning was correct. The example of Max, who looked at the word list after reading 'Paddington at the Palace' and then checked a page of the book again, could provide evidence for this. Looking at the word list before and after the reading also indicates that the learners found the word list interesting and were keen on getting to know some of the book's lexical items that were potentially new for them. Its use might thus stimulate the purposeful learning of vocabulary out of individual and personal interest.

In contrast to the word list, the picture dictionary as well as the bilingual dictionary did not prove useful for young learners in reading picture books. A big problem of the picture dictionary is certainly that is does not contain all the words found in picture books and that words that the learners might not know and might want to look up cannot be found in them. Lara encountered exactly this problem when attempting to find the word 'smartly'. As already outlined in Chapter 6.6.4, the range of words in picture dictionaries is limited and they might hence not be useful for unknown vocabulary in picture books. This statement could be confirmed in the present study. Moreover, the learners seemed to lack a purposeful and specific introduction to effectively working with picture dictionaries, which probably hindered them in using them competently. As was pointed out in Chapter 6.6.4, it is very important to teach learners (picture) dictionary skills.

The bilingual dictionary did not prove to be a useful supportive device for young learners in reading picture books either, because it was simply too difficult for them. The same has also been observed by Freudenau (2017: 23, 110). The learners were overtaxed in finding words in the dictionary for reasons of language awareness (knowing about the lemmatisation of words), thorough knowledge of the alphabet (which letter comes when), overall reading competence (scanning very small print without getting lost) and knowledge about translation equivalents of words in different contexts. The difficulties which Ali faced when trying to find a translation equivalent for 'smartly' in the dictionary nicely exemplify the need for introducing bilingual dictionaries with great care and preparation. As with the picture dictionary, a targeted introduction to such a device is vitally necessary in order to enable learners to work with it competently. This, however, is not the task of the primary school EFL classroom, as bilingual dictionaries are normally only introduced later in the learning process. The pioneering attempt to use one earlier has shown that the demands this might place on young EFL learners are too high and that it might thus only be appropriate for reading authentic texts at the secondary school level.

Another reason why the dictionaries were hardly used at all might be the following: The learners might simply not want to bother with looking up an unknown word, especially when they have the feeling that they can also proceed without it. This is different when learners look up words which they need so as to produce language and formulate a message which they want to get across. The dictionary might thus be more appealing to them when they want to know the English equivalent of a German word in order to communicate their own thoughts in the FL. Such individual vocabulary might be more interesting for them (also see Freudenau, 2017: 222ff) and trigger the use of dictionaries more than the context of reading FL books does.

In sum, both the picture dictionary and the dictionary were not really useful and cannot be taken as meaningful supportive devices in reading picture books in the primary school EFL classroom, at least not without a purposeful introduction and a reflection on their function in reading. Still, the learners were interested in both dictionaries and were keen on exploring them. This interest shows that even at a young age learners are generally interested in dictionaries and their potential; a factor that should be regarded positively in that it expresses interest in FLL. However, an explicit introduction of dictionaries that demonstrates their supportive function in reading might have to be postponed to the secondary school level.

As neither the picture dictionary nor the dictionary proved supportive for reading authentic English picture books, it remains to hypothesise that an online dictionary might have solved some of the problems that the learners encountered with the other two types of dictionaries. An online dictionary offers the two advantages that it firstly contains a large number of search words and secondly search words just need to be typed in to find them. This is a lot faster than searching for a word in a dictionary. The use of an online dictionary in the primary school EFL classroom has been explored by Freudenau (2017) and offers promising results. Its function in reading, however, still needs to be investigated.

A device that proved useful for reading and supported some learners in their reading process was the audio-recording. This result concurs with what other studies (e.g., Brusch, 2000; Diehr, 2010; Kolb, 2013) have found about the usefulness of an audio-function in FL reading. The present study provides clear evidence of its effectiveness for young EFL learners when reading authentic texts. Particularly Lara and Ali used it continuously. Interestingly, these children were the ones that were not motivated to read the books and that displayed no tolerance of ambiguity and towards unknown words (see Chapter 10.1.1), at least in the initial sessions. The audio-recording seemed to have at least partly helped them to overcome their reading difficulties with regard to ambiguity tolerance as well as possibly fostering their motivation somewhat, and encouraging them to read the books with its help. The listening function might have been a motivator for Lara and Ali that made the reading text accessible to them. Interestingly, Lara did not use the audio-recording for the last book, 'Winnie in Winter', but read that book on her own. This might show that over the course of time her reading competence as well as her confidence in her own reading skills had improved and that she believed that she might be capable of doing it without the recording. The reading of further books might have clarified this hypothesis.

Generally, the use of audio-recordings during reading might help in initial stages, but should gradually be reduced over time in favour of a shift to reading comprehension without the listening function. This could be done by following Metzger's (2010: 79f) suggestion of alternating assisted reading with independent reading, in that for example only every second page of the book is read with the recording. That way, the learners might gradually get used to reading without listening.

The present study has shown that group dynamics can play a role with regard to using devices such as the MP3-player. The fascination and pleasure of listening to a well-read story seemed enhanced when other learners used that device. Thus, it is not surprising that six learners, which was the whole of RG 1 and most of RG 2, read the book 'Paddington at the Palace' with the audio-recording. Some learners might have listened to it only because of fascination and group dynamics, while others might have actually needed it to ease the book's difficulty. However, except for Lara and Ali, none of the four learners who used it for that particular book used it again. They might have found that they did not really need it. In this case it is important to reflect with the learners on when it is necessary to listen while reading and when reading by itself is the appropriate activity for them to meet their current levels of competence.

The frequent and occasional use of the audio-recording demonstrates the usefulness of audio-recordings to make reading texts accessible to all learners. Potential difficulties with regard to clear-cut research on reading comprehension, in that the interplay with listening comprehension cannot be controlled for, must therefore be accepted in favour of methodological advantages with regard to successful participation of all learners (also see Chapter 8.1.3). Nevertheless, the learners claimed that they had still read the text while listening, which shows that the learners were still engaged with reading while listening to the text at the same time. Therefore, the listening-function did not stop them from reading the books in favour of mere listening, but only supported them in reading. Thus, one can assume that at least to a certain extent reading comprehension was tested and that listening comprehension alone did not form the basis of the performance levels outlined in Chapter 9.2.

The last supportive factor that was provided was the option of cooperative reading. Cooperation in reading the picture books seemed to be difficult in the setting chosen and did not prove particularly useful in that context. Some readers who wanted to read in cooperation did not find a partner (e.g., Rico) and thus it remains unclear whether cooperative reading would have been beneficial for them or not. The lack of a suitable reading partner shows the importance of choosing and finding peers to effectively work together with. Reading partners can either be chosen by the learners or be decided on by the teacher; both options have advantages and disadvantages (also see Chapter 6.4).

In practice, the reading setting should be set up in a way that cooperative reading is encouraged. This implies that only one book should be used in a reading team, as for example in Reichart-Wallrabenstein's 2004 study on cooperative FL reading settings, rather than each child having his/her own copy of the book as in the present study. Green and Green (2005: 83) argue that in cooperative settings it is advisable to share material in order to create a positive interdependence of resources, which is a crucial element of cooperative learning. Reading with only one book enables the learners to share the reading text so that they roughly read the same parts at the same time and also discuss what they are currently reading. The present study's setting provided each learner with his/her own copy, which might have hindered the positive interdependence and hence more cooperative reading. Moreover, in the current study the learners could not freely talk to each other when they read with a partner, because the other children around them were reading silently and did not want to be disturbed. In addition, although a weak and a strong reader might benefit from each other (as, e.g., Dani and Simone), learners might find it easier to read together with a similarly capable peer when cooperative reading is initiated. Therefore, the setting that the reading of the books took place in was maybe not ideal for cooperative reading and should be reconsidered in terms of sharing material, choice of a partner and an appropriate place for reading. Also, some guidance by the teacher as well as a reflection on best practice in cooperative reading might be helpful for the learners. This might have been particularly beneficial for Dani and Simone, who soon failed to succeed in their attempt to read together. Thus, young learners should know about techniques for successful cooperative reading to avoid ineffective attempts at reading parts aloud to each other.

However, cooperative reading can also be understood in a broader sense, and cooperatively reading a text does not necessarily imply reading the same pages at a similar reading pace. Cooperative reading can also entail a discussion of the reading text during as well as after reading, occasional questions among peers and comments or negotiations about the text while reading, while everyone reads at his/her own reading pace. This happened frequently in the present study and will further be discussed in Chapter 10.1.3 (social reading strategies). With reference to the idea of 'think-pair-share', Chapter 6.4 explained that in reading, a phase of individual reading might be fruitful for follow-up phases of cooperative reading or discussions of the reading text. Cooperative reading hence does not only include reading the text together word by word, but should be understood in a broader sense that allows individual reading processes while being engaged in cooperative situations when feasible and necessary.

To sum up the results on supportive devices, word lists and audio-recordings proved most useful and thus the present study suggests that a word list that is specifically created for each book as well as an audio-recording of the text of the book are beneficial for supporting reading authentic English picture books in the primary school. The usefulness and supportive character of cooperative reading settings can neither be positively nor negatively shown with the present study. Therefore, it is certainly imaginable that cooperative reading also supports young learners in reading authentic English books, when set up skilfully. Based on the present data, neither of the dictionaries provided can be recommended as a support in reading with young learners, at least not without an explicit introduction. This list of devices, however, is by no means supposed to be exhaustive. The usefulness of an online dictionary, for instance, remains to be explored in further research.

Overall, it proved useful to have a range of supportive devices that the children could choose from depending on their individual needs. While the audio-recording helped, for example, Ali and Lara to read the books, the word lists helped Emil, Natan and Neele with all six books. Therefore, learners should have several devices that they can freely select from according to their individual requirements and preferences. This differentiates the reading process in that it allows the learners to choose devices individually and in accordance with their own competences, which in return allows individual learners to read a book at their individual performance levels.

The extent to which a particular supportive device was actually useful for comprehension and even enhanced a learner's comprehension cannot be investigated through the present data. As there is no data on the level of comprehension that the learner might have reached without the support, it is mere speculation whether and how much the support provided had an influence on comprehension. One has to rely on the children's own perspective and observations on the devices, their choice of devices and their explanation about the devices' usefulness. It is very likely, however, that with the help of supportive devices the comprehension level of a text is higher than without the help.

9.4 Summary of Central Results and Answer to Research Question I

The presentation and interpretation of results on the task of reading, on reading comprehension and on the use of supportive devices while reading has shown that the task of reading is not too demanding for young EFL learners, but that on the contrary all the learners in the study could cope with this task. Therefore, authentic English picture books seem to be suitable reading materials for the primary school EFL classroom and the authenticity of the books and the books' language should not hinder the learners from reading and understanding them.

In view of a development of reading competence over time, some factors such as reading confidence, quality of an oral recall, completion of written comprehension tasks and the skilful use of supportive devices could to a certain extent improve. Maybe further increases in reading abilities could be achieved if reading were practised more frequently, if extensive reading allowed the learners a choice of books or if phases of explicit reading instruction and a reflection on reading skills were integrated into EFL lessons.

With regard to the use of supportive devices, the study has been able to show that the learners profited most from the word list and the audio-recording. Results on cooperative reading are inconclusive. Dictionaries did not prove helpful for the young learners, at least not the two which were used. The results also indicate that it is beneficial to allow learners to freely choose from a range of devices depending on their individual skills and preferences. Again, a reflection on this might be supportive for discussing the advantages and disadvantages.

Overall, the results show that different learners have individual competences and the study underlines the importance of and crucial need for differentiated reading tasks for young learners. This includes teachers allowing individual reading times and having reflected and realistic expectations with regard to reading performance and comprehension levels. Teachers need to understand that some readers might need more support than others and might also need some more guidance in reading. Clearly, the aim of this should not be that all readers reach the same level of comprehension, but more so the aim should be to allow each individual learner to reach his/her best possible performance level in reading. It is also imaginable that explicitly teaching reading (as, e.g., Frisch (2013) has investigated), maybe including reading strategies, would help some learners to enhance their comprehension or at least their perceived understanding of the books. Both remain topics for further research.

In sum, the results allow the following answers to research question I (*To what extent are Year 4 EFL learners capable of reading and understanding authentic English picture books?*):

- Year 4 learners are capable of reading and understanding authentic English picture books.
- The level of comprehension depends on several different factors, including the learners' motivation, the learners' individual reading skills, the learners' background knowledge, the learners' moods and emotional status, the learners' interest in a book and topic and lastly the instrument chosen to investigate comprehension.
- Some learners' comprehension is very elaborate, other learners are still in the process of developing their FL reading abilities. Therefore, differentiated reading tasks and reading texts are needed to cater for individual learners and their individual abilities.
- The learners' L1 reading competence only gives limited information about their L2 reading competence. Strong L1 readers are not necessarily strong L2 readers, but weak L1 readers might be weak L2 readers.
- Mixed methods and the use of different research instruments are crucial in investigating young learners' reading competence.
- Some aspects of reading competence, for example reading confidence, develop over time, which is probably based on a familiarisation effect; more development might be achieved through more focused practice and reflection.
- Supportive devices are useful for some learners, particularly when they can freely choose from a range of different devices.
- A word list and an audio-recording, both specifically created for a particular book, proved to be useful for reading. Dictionaries did not prove useful.
- Cooperation in reading is helpful when defined in a broader sense; in the narrow sense of reading together page by page, the setting needs to be better suited to the activity.

These points provide some initial insight into aspects of research question I and could be understood as hypotheses to further investigate EFL reading comprehension at primary school level in follow-up studies with possibly larger settings.

10. Reading Strategies: Presentation, Interpretation and Discussion of Results for Research Question II

Abstract: This chapter presents, interprets and discusses the study's results on reading strategies. It presents and categorises the different strategies the learners used. After that, the chapter provides details on the development of strategy use, the learners' awareness of strategy use and a connection between strategy use and comprehension.

Research question II focused on the learners' use of reading strategies while they were reading the books. The research question as well as the key aspects investigated are presented in Table 23:

Table 23: Reiteration of research question II including key aspects investigated.

Focus	Research question	Key aspects investigated
II Reading strategies	**(II) Which reading strategies do young EFL learners apply when reading authentic English picture books for understanding?**	→ The description and categorisation of reading strategies → The development of strategy use → The awareness of strategy use → The connection of reading strategies and the level of comprehension

As outlined in Chapter 8.3, data on reading strategies were collected via three different instruments. Firstly, I as the researcher observed the learners while they were reading the different picture books and took field notes during the observation. As it was impossible to spot all their strategies while immersed in the situation, the reading process was video-recorded so that the videos could later on be watched and analysed with regard to more observable strategies. The strategies that I was able to find in the video-recordings were also noted as field notes. Apart from that, semi-structured group interviews were conducted at the end of each first reading session of a book. These interviews were video-recorded for later transcription. As a last instrument, a questionnaire on reading strategies was conducted after the learners had read the last book 'Winnie in Winter'.

Chapter 8.3.4 elaborated on the steps and procedure of organising and analysing the data pool with the help of qualitative content analysis: this included case summaries and a categorisation of the strategies. Chapter 10.1 will present the results of this procedure by providing the categories and an overview of all the strategies that were used by the reading group, including details on and examples of each strategy. Information about a potential development of strategy use over time as well as the young learners' awareness of strategy use will then be given in Chapters 10.2 and 10.3. Lastly, a possible connection between reading comprehension and the use of strategies will be investigated in Chapter 10.4, before an answer to the research question and a final discussion of the results is found in Chapter 10.5.

10.1 Categorisation of Young Learners' Reading Strategies

This Chapter provides an overview of all the reading strategies that were used in the study. As main categories, the strategy categorisation developed by O'Malley and Chamot (1990) and also used by Finkbeiner (2005, 2013) and Pinter (2006) (see Chapter 4.6.5) was used deductively as a basis for strategy classification into the four main categories: cognitive strategies, meta-cognitive strategies, social strategies and affective strategies. All the strategies found in the case summaries were then classified into 29 categories, while eleven of the 29 categories contained two to eight further sub-categories.[193] These categories contain strategies which were deductively inferred from previous research as well as those which could not be deduced from previous research but were identified inductively from the data. The result is found in Table 24, which displays all the reading strategies as used by the young learners in the study.

---

193   The terms 'category' and 'sub-category' are used in accordance with qualitative content analysis. In fact, the categories present strategies, while the sub-categories present sub-strategies that could be assigned to particular strategies.

Table 24: Categorisation of reading strategies: an overview of all reading strategies as used by the young learners in the reading study, ordered by categories. The numbers in brackets indicate how many learners used each respective strategy. The grey font indicates that this strategy or this number of learners was only identified in the questionnaire and not in the observation and interview data.

Main strategy classification (based on O'Malley & Chamot, 1990)	Category (= reading strategy)	Sub-category (= further sub-strategies that could be assigned to a certain reading strategy)
Meta-cognitive reading strategies	Directing attention and cognitive effort (9+1)	
	Turning pages	Turning back a page or more (6+1)
		Turning forward a page or more (6+1)
	Orientation aids	Putting a hand on the page (7)
		Using a pointing finger (3)
		Following the text with a finger (6)
	Self-monitoring (4+5)	
	Tolerance of ambiguity	Tolerating unknown words/phrases (9)
		Keeping reading if anything was unknown/not understood (4+6)
		Skipping parts (1+2)
	Adjusting the reading pace (2)	
	Considering priorities (6)	
	Thinking of and planning support (5)	
Cognitive reading strategies	Getting an overview	Skimming through the book before reading (9+1)
		Skimming through the book after reading (1)
		Looking at the cover before reading (3+3)
		Getting an overview of a page before reading (1)
	Elaboration: using previous knowledge	Previous language experience (1)
		Already known words (3+5)
		Previous reading experience (1)
		Previous knowledge about the book (3+5)
		World knowledge (4)
	Imagery (10)	
	Translating into German (7)	
	Re-reading (3+4)	
	Resourcing	Looking up unknown words (1)
		– Dictionary (1)
		– Picture dictionary (1)
		– Word list (11)
		– Internet (1)
		Audio-recording (6)

347

Main strategy classification (based on O'Malley & Chamot, 1990)	Category (= reading strategy)	Sub-category (= further sub-strategies that could be assigned to a certain reading strategy)
Cognitive reading strategies	Vocalisation	Semi-vocalisation (6+1)
		Sub-vocalisation (3)
		Reading aloud (whole text 1; single words 6)
	Inferencing strategies (to decode unknown words)	Using the context (2+5)
		Using the follow-up sentence/part to decode the previous one (2+6)
		Guessing the meaning of unknown words/parts (2+3)
		Seeking further explanations in the text (1)
		Using L1 similarities (1+1)
		Seeking its auditory representation (3+4)
		Thinking hard about it (4)
		Seeking a part of the word that might be known (4)
		Seeking a repetition of the word in the following text (4)
	Making predictions (1+5)	
	Summarising parts of the book (4)	
	Underlining (2)	
	Dividing the text into sections (1)	
Social reading strategies	Reading cooperatively (5)	
	Questioning for clarification (6+3)	
	Exchange with others	Discussing aspects of the story (4)
		Pointing something out to someone else (7)
	Expressing (mis)-understanding	(Eagerness to) express understanding (4)
		Expressing misunderstanding (2+3)
		Expressing difficulties (1+3)
	Seeking orientation: looking at other children (8)	
Affective reading strategies	Emotional involvement (10)	
	Personal elaboration: projecting oneself into the story	Imitating the story's sounds (and make up new sounds) (2+3)
		Imitating the story's actions (2)
		Identifying with the story's characters (1+4)
	Self-motivation (8+3)	

Table 24 shows all FL reading strategies that were used by the learners. Overall, the learners used 56 different reading strategies, including the sub-strategies. These consist of 13 meta-cognitive strategies (eight main strategies), 30 cognitive strategies (12 main strategies), eight social strategies (five main strategies) and five affective strategies (three main strategies).

As stated above, the number in brackets after each strategy in the table indicates how many learners used this strategy. Such quantification is an essential part of qualitative content analysis (Kuckartz, 2012: 94). Some strategies were only used to a very minimal extent, but are still presented in this chapter because strategy use is highly individual and therefore also strategies that only one learner used might be successful reading strategies. A different or larger group of young EFL learners might reveal different numbers, so that a strategy that was only used once in the present study might be used more often in a different sample.

For reasons of readability and a better overview, Table 24 only contains the categories of the classification system and refrains from providing definitions and examples for each. As the latter is an important step in a qualitative content analysis (Kuckartz, 2012: 84), however, all the strategies will be elaborated on in detail in the following subchapters (10.1.1 to 10.1.4), including a clear description and examples of the use of each strategy. These subchapters are divided into the main classification of meta-cognitive, cognitive, social and affective strategies and linearly follow the strategies as listed in Table 24. Firstly, the different strategies will be presented and explained. Since the presentation of a strategy and a thorough explanation of it are in parts similar to an interpretation, slight overlaps between the presentation and interpretation of each strategy will occur in Chapters 10.1.1 to 10.1.4. For reasons of readability and in order to avoid repetition, the presentation and interpretation of each strategy were hence not clearly separated in these subchapters. An overall interpretation of all strategies used is then found in Chapter 10.1.5.

10.1.1 Meta-cognitive Reading Strategies

Meta-cognitive reading strategies are those that are concerned with organising the reading process and that allow learners to consciously control and coordinate their reading of FL texts (see Chapter 4.6.5). Table 25 firstly provides an overview of the meta-cognitive reading strategies which could be identified in this study, as well as a description of each strategy. Examples will then be given in the detailed explanation of each strategy.

Table 25: Overview of meta-cognitive reading strategies, including a description of each (grey font indicates that this strategy was only identified in the questionnaire).

Meta-cognitive reading strategy	Description
Directing attention and cognitive effort	The learners focus their attention on the reading process and concentrate on it.
Turning pages	During reading, the learners turn pages of the book back or forward. (This turning is different to the actual pace of turning pages while reading.)
Orientation aids	The learners use physical orientation aids, in particular their hands and their fingers, in order to find orientation in the book and in the text.
Self-monitoring	The learners self-question and re-assure their comprehension of a book during the reading process.
Tolerance of ambiguity	The learners tolerate that they do not understand every word or sentence in that they keep reading if anything was not understood and potentially skip difficult parts.
Adjusting the reading pace	The learners adjust the reading pace in that they read slower or faster at particular points in the text.
Considering priorities	The learners consider priorities during reading.
Thinking of and planning support	The learners think about the reading process and plan support that they might need for reading.

Directing attention and cognitive effort

The strategy of directing attention and cognitive effort was applied by ten learners in the present study, who focused on the task of reading and concentrated while doing so. That the learners consciously directed their attention onto the reading task was shown by a number of indicators. Firstly, I could observe that seven learners regularly[194] focused on reading and concentrated well while doing so. Only two learners, Jonas and Simone, were easily distracted, particularly after reading for a longer period of time. However, after a distraction they quickly focused again on the task. Even Simone, who needed a long reading time for all the books (see Figure 21 in Chapter 9.1.1), read all of them to the end, despite difficulties with concentration on the last pages. These observations were underlined

---

194 'Regularly' was defined in Chapter 8.3.4 as those strategies that a learner used at least twice and with at least two different books.

by the questionnaire data, which revealed that the majority of the learners (eight) concentrated hard while reading the books.

Three learners (Ali, Rico and Emil) also mentioned during the interviews that they focused on the task and tried to concentrate on reading, although they had difficulties with verbalising this. By stating that their 'brain' or 'intelligence' helped them with reading, they showed that they were aware of the cognitive effort needed in reading. In return, this shows focused attention and concentration. Rico, for example, explained, "*Also mir hat mein Verstand geholfen*" (Transcript RS SG1 14.11.2014 #24:22; also RS FLM1 31.10.2014 #29:18 and RS FBC1 05.12.2014 #23:44), and likewise Ali refered to his "*Gehirn*" (Transcript RS FLM1 31.10.2014 29:22) when he outlined how he read the book 'Five Little Monkeys'. Emil further explained that he thought hard about some aspects of the book: "*Ich hab habe überlegt und meistens hab/ wenn ich den [sic] darüber nachgedacht habe, habe es [sic] da dann auch verstanden*" (Transcript RS QK3 05.09.2014 #30:53).

Interestingly, Rico explained the use of cognitive effort during the interviews, but then stated in the questionnaire that he did not concentrate hard during reading. This might imply that the books were slightly too easy for him and that he could understand them without focusing and concentrating on the reading process very much. The same holds true for Max, who also read and understood the books with ease.

These results show that the learners, despite their age, were aware of the need for cognitive effort and of the concentration involved in reading and knew that reading needs focused attention. This notion of "paying attention" (Oxford, 1990: 20) is concerned with consciously deciding to direct attention to a learning task and to ignore possible distractions (Brown, 2007: 134). Although previously only described for older learners, the results of the present study show that even young learners are concerned with and aware of this strategy and utilise it regularly and intentionally.

Turning pages

Another meta-cognitive strategy that is used to organise one's own reading process is that of turning pages, both back and forward.[195] In the study, seven learners used the strategy of turning back a page or more. Six were observed to

---

195 This does of course not include the regular turning of pages during reading based on the reading pace.

sometimes[196] do so and in addition Dani reported on doing so in the question-naire. Additionally, seven learners turned a page or more forward, occasionally until the end of the book. I observed two learners (Simone and Dani) to do so regularly, and another four learners to sometimes apply this strategy. Four of these six learners confirmed in the questionnaire that they used this strategy. In addition, the questionnaire revealed that Ali also turned pages forward to see how much was left to read.

Several reasons are imaginable for turning pages back and forward during reading, but none of them were explicitly mentioned by the learners. Firstly, turning pages back allows the reader to check a content or language aspect from a previous page in order to confirm understanding of the present page. Secondly, pages might also be turned back in order to seek a lexical item that was not un-derstood while it was read but might be decoded in retrospect, based on knowl-edge from the ongoing story. Thirdly, if they had problems of comprehension, readers might turn back a page or more to re-read a certain part or to re-read all of the text from that point. Likewise, reasons for turning pages forward are manifold. Getting an overview of how much is left to read, as stated in the cor-responding questionnaire item, allows the reader to get an overview of the num-ber of events that could still happen. More so, the amount of text, number of pages or events still to come show the reader how much time, concentration and endurance is still needed to finish reading the story. In addition, turning pages forward can provide the reader with an idea of what will come next and what can be expected in the course of the story. Furthermore, readers can read a passage ahead which might give them an impression of what will come later and might also help to comprehend what had already been read earlier. However, except for the reason revealed in the questionnaire (see how much is left to read), none of these purposes were mentioned in the present study.

In previous research with young learners, already Reichart-Wallrabenstein (2004: 444) had found that young learners turn pages forward and backward dur-ing cooperative reading in order to figure out the context of a story. Likewise, in the present study more than half of the participants used this strategy. However, the questionnaire revealed that only one learner was aware of turning pages for-ward and only four were aware of turning pages backward. This indicates that the learners might have automatised this strategy already so that it is not necessarily

---

196 'Sometimes' was defined in Chapter 8.3.4 as those strategies that a learner only used once or twice, but with no more than one book.

available to consciousness any longer (see Chapter 4.6.6), since it is also a common strategy in L1 reading.

Orientation aids

Another meta-cognitive reading strategy that could be found in the study is concerned with orientation aids, including the learners' fingers and hands. Three different strategies could be found in this regard: (1) putting a hand on the page that is currently being read, (2) using a pointing finger, (3) following the text with a finger. I could observe these physical orientation aids, but they were only once reported on in the interviews and were not included in a questionnaire item.

Firstly, seven learners regularly put a hand on the page that they were currently reading, without explicitly pointing to any part of that page. This could either serve for orientation in that the learners put the hand on that page that they were currently focusing on, or could be used to smooth the page and to fix the book on the table. The latter would of course not be a reading strategy.

The next strategy was clearer with regard to its purpose of orientation: Three learners used a pointing finger to point to those parts of a page that they were currently reading or looking at. I could observe that Emil and Ina regularly pointed to parts of the pages with their fingers and Simone sometimes did so. Emil, for example, often put a pointing finger under the whole textual element of a page while he was reading it.

The most prominent orientation aid was putting a finger under the text to follow the lines word by word while reading. Six learners did so: Lara and Neele only sometimes used this strategy, Ina, Jonas and Ali regularly used it, and Simone followed the lines with her finger all the time during reading. On my request Ali explained in an interview that he followed the lines with his finger to not get confused: "*Damit man nicht äh durcheinander kommt*" (Transcript RS PP1 29.09.2014 #32:40). Thus, learners use this strategy so as not to lose track of what they are reading and to find orientation in the lines of the text being read.

Ali's explanation for why he followed the lines already indicates the most prominent reason for using physical orientation aids: Pointing ensures that in reading the reader does not get lost on a page and is not distracted from the part that he/she is currently looking at. Particularly when looking back and forth between the text and the pictures, which is typical in reading picture books, a pointing finger can help to fix the part that is currently being read or focused on.

As outlined in Chapter 4.6.5, young learners in particular are trained to use their finger as an orientation aid in primary school, predominantly by following the lines of a text word by word with a finger.[197] Reichart-Wallrabenstein (2004: 491), too, found finger pointing with some of the young EFL learners in her reading study. Possibly it is particularly those readers that have not yet developed strong reading skills that need this strategy in order to read a text, while more advanced readers do not need this orientation aid any longer. This is underscored by the fact that none of the studies on reading strategies conducted with older EFL learners report having observed this strategy. Therefore, physical orientation aids seem to be a strategy that is particularly used by younger learners that have not yet developed advanced FL reading skills.

Self-monitoring

Another reading strategy is self-monitoring, which includes self-questioning and re-assuring oneself of one's own comprehension of a text. This strategy could be found in the observation and questionnaire data of the present study.

In three different situations, four learners used the strategy of self-monitoring during reading. Firstly, Max and Emil counted the monkeys in a picture on a page of the book 'Five Little Monkeys'. By doing so, the two readers could confirm their comprehension of the text, which was mirrored in the picture. Secondly, Emil once checked with his peers[198] if he had understood a textual part correctly: When reading 'Froggy's Best Christmas' he asked whether he had correctly understood a part of the book by asking "*Ist das hier Popcorn?*" (#10:04). Thirdly, Simone was found to double-check her comprehension by looking back and forth between the text and the pictures. This is a strategy that is particularly useful in picture books because of the relation between text and pictures.[199] As such, this strategy has already been reported on in Reichart-Wallrabenstein's (2004: 492) picture book project.

Although the strategy of self-monitoring was hard to observe and only three instances could be detected, the questionnaire data underlined that this strategy was applied by a number of learners. The questionnaires firstly revealed that Emil sometimes posed himself questions about the text. Secondly, seven learners reported that they thought of what they had already understood during reading. In addition, six learners reported in the questionnaire that they considered

---

197 See Chapter 4.6.5 and Nuttall (2005: 58f) for why this should be regarded critically.
198 This overlaps with the social strategy of asking for clarification (see Chapter 10.1.3).
199 This, of course, presupposes that the textual and visual elements of a book are congruent (see Chapters 5.2.3 and 5.3.3), which was the case with the books read in the present study.

how well they had understood the book after reading it. Therefore, the results of the observation and questionnaire overall show that the learners consciously thought about their own understanding, which in return is evidence that they self-monitored their reading comprehension. They were thus involved in a review of the comprehension of information from the text (O'Malley & Chamot, 1990: 46), which on the one hand is a natural part of the reading process (see Chapter 4.4.2), but on the other hand a skill which is rather complex in that it presupposes comprehension at the text level and a purposeful retention and revision of the text and one's own comprehension of it.

Tolerance of ambiguity

Another central meta-cognitive reading strategy is that of tolerance of ambiguity. As already noted in Chapter 6.8, this means tolerating that a word, phrase, sentence or section was not fully understood but still keep reading. Overall, nine learners were found to tolerate ambiguity in comprehension in the present study. Four learners explained in the interviews that they just kept reading when they encountered unknown words or parts. Emil, for example, said simply, *"Ich habe erstmal weitergelesen"* (Transcript RS PP3 30.09.2014 #31:03), and Rico explained that it did not matter if one did not understand all the words and that it was unproblematic to just keep reading: *"Man kommt auch ohne weiter und versteht was. Das geht."* (Transcript RS PP1 29.09.2014 #34:05). Likewise, Max stated that he did not need all the words for comprehending the whole text: *"Also ich habe/ brauche das eigentlich gar nicht. Dann weiß ich es nicht."* (Transcript RS PP2 30.09.2014 #39:48). In addition to that, Ina explained that she could still understand something, even if not everything was understood: *"Ich habe weiter gelesen und dann habe ich ähm hab ich so ein bisschen verstanden"* (Transcript RS FLM3 31.10.2014 #30:01). This practice of keeping reading even if a part was not understood was also mentioned by another six learners in the questionnaire.

These results show that the majority of the young learners have already developed a good understanding of tolerance of ambiguity and its importance in reading. The learners were able to accept that some parts of a text could not be decoded and regarded it as unproblematic to ignore some unknown words or parts of the text for the time being. Some of the statements in the interviews in particular are astonishing, in that they show a deep awareness of ambiguity tolerance as well as indicating that already young learners can give reasons for tolerating ambiguity. The participants already seem to have an understanding of the importance of ambiguity tolerance for developing effective and fluent reading skills and had developed reading practices that meant they did not get stuck at incomprehensible parts of a reading text.

These young learners' tolerance of ambiguity could partly be based on their previous experience in the English classroom, because in a classroom where the FL English is the only or major medium of instruction from the very beginning, it is inevitable that some words or other, maybe larger, elements of the language in the classroom are incomprehensible (see Klippel, 2000: 29; Wessel, 2012: 55ff). As learners thus learn how to follow the classroom discourse without understanding all the words the teacher uses, they also develop a certain degree of ambiguity tolerance in listening that could be transferred to L2 reading. Also, young learners' lower anxiety and inhibitions about FLL (Lightbown & Spada, 2013: 37f) might be an advantage in the early development of ambiguity tolerance, because these characteristics might positively influence it.

The results of the questionnaire present a slightly different picture of ambiguity tolerance, however, from that which has been outlined so far. In contrast to the impression derived from the observation and interview data that most of the learners had a certain level of ambiguity tolerance, seven out of eleven learners stated in the questionnaire that they tried to understand every single word during reading in order to find out what the book was about. Also, only Emil and Simone stated in the questionnaire that they skipped incomprehensible parts while the other nine learners said that they had not done so. Another item of the questionnaire, however, suggested that six learners just kept reading if they encountered a word which they did not understand. There are thus contradictions in the responses to different questionnaire items with regard to ambiguity tolerance, which means that they cannot clearly be analysed. Maybe the learners reported that they wanted to understand every word and did not skip parts, because they assumed that this would be expected of them in school. However, since they explained the opposite during the interviews, it is imaginable that the first two questionnaire items do not reveal the learners' true ambiguity tolerance. This is underscored by the last questionnaire item that showed that six learners just kept reading if they encountered an unknown word.

In previous research, Reichart-Wallrabenstein (2004: 444) found that young EFL learners could occasionally tolerate problems with comprehension in that they postponed and ignored parts that they were uncertain about. Her result, however, is not as clear as the ambiguity tolerance as found in the present study. Still, teachers and researchers should not forget that ambiguity tolerance is only supportive in reading to a certain extent, because too high a level of ambiguity tolerance can lead to miscomprehension of the text as well as to carelessness in reading.

Although, as just noted, there is a limit to the extent to which ambiguity toler-ance is supportive, the limitations imposed by going to the opposite extreme were also found in the present study. Two learners, Ali and Lara, were focused strong-ly on single words and had problems with tolerating ambiguity in that they were very concerned with understanding every word in the texts. Ali explained that he needed to understand every single word in order to make sense of the whole story: *"Weil wenn ein Wort keinen Sinn ergibt, ergibt doch die ganze Geschichte keinen Sinn"* (Transcript RS PP1 29.09.2014 #33:31). As will be seen in Chap-ter 10.2, Lara's tolerance of ambiguity was similarly low in the beginning, but developed in the course of the reading study. Interestingly, Lara and Ali are the learners that used the audio-recording for most of the reading texts. The audio-recording therefore seems to be a supportive device that is beneficial for learners that struggle with ambiguity tolerance. Probably, Lara and Ali also did not know and understand every word of the story that they listened to while reading either, but they could possibly tolerate unknown words that they heard better than writ-ten words they could not decode. A reason for this might be that they were used to aural input that contained unknown words from the regular EFL classroom discourse. Moreover, they probably understood more words while listening than they did when reading, so that through listening a benchmark for the vocabulary knowledge of a text might have been reached which was not reached in reading.

Adjusting the reading pace

The meta-cognitive strategy of adjusting the reading pace[200] was only identified via the questionnaire. Two learners (Dani and Neele) said that they adjusted their reading pace and read more slowly when they encountered a difficult sen-tence. Generally, all readers, even advanced ones, constantly adjust their reading pace depending on what they are reading and depending on the difficulty of certain words or sentences (see Ehlers (2007: 117ff) in Chapter 4.1). Probably, young readers also do so, but only two participants in the present study seemed to be aware of this strategy. A possible reason might be that this strategy is ap-plied unconsciously because it is already well-known from L1 reading and might therefore be automatised and not available to conscious awareness any longer.

---

200   Arguably, this strategy could also be categorised as a cognitive one, particularly since the data suggest that many learners did not consciously adjust their reading pace. However, since adjusting the reading pace is a way of organising one's own reading and often influences the reading style that a reader uses to approach the text based on the reading purpose, the strategy will be classified as meta-cognitive in this study, without denying possible overlaps with cognitive strategies.

Eye-tracking research would provide more reliable data at this point. Interestingly, previous studies on reading strategies hardly report on the adjustment of the reading pace in FL reading either (see Chapter 4.6.5).

Considering priorities

In the questionnaire, the strategy of considering priorities was mentioned as well. In total, five learners revealed that they would think of what was generally important or not during reading. The same five plus one further learner stated that they considered the importance of an unknown word, which is closely connected to tolerance of ambiguity as outlined earlier in this chapter. Previous studies with young EFL learners have not reported on the strategy of considering priorities, which might be due to the fact that with young learners often the teacher provides a clear task instruction and thus sets the priorities. A reflection with the whole class on priorities in reading a book might therefore guide the learners to consciously and more autonomously think of such priorities. These could include considerations about what is most important in a reading task, such as for example reading for gist or reading for details (Finkbeiner, 2005: XXIII).

Thinking of and planning support

Planning support is closely connected to planning for the task of reading and goes back to Oxford's (1990: 20) strategy of planning for a language task. In the present study, I as the researcher provided the task and pre-set the reading environment, so that the only aspect that the learners could plan autonomously was support, which was based on the supportive devices that were provided. In the questionnaire, five learners reported that they thought of and planned support for reading the books. This could, for example, imply that they looked at the word list before reading (see Chapter 9.3). Further data might help to specify the learners' planning process, but is not available because this strategy was not mentioned by the learners during the interviews and was also not observable. However, it is also debatable whether evidence of much planning for support would be found in research with young learners, since they might simply seek support when it is needed. Also, because supportive devices were readily provided for them, there was no need for them to plan support autonomously.

10.1.2 Cognitive Reading Strategies

Cognitive reading strategies were defined in Chapter 4.6.5 as those that require mental processing of the FL and help learners comprehend FL texts by means that are directly related to the FL. Therefore, these strategies are more concerned with the actual process of reading texts written in the FL and less so with the organisation of reading on a meta-level. Table 26 provides an overview of the cognitive reading strategies that were found in the current study, including a description of them.

Table 26: Overview of cognitive reading strategies, including a description of each (grey font indicates that this strategy was only identified in the questionnaire).

Cognitive reading strategy	Description
Getting an overview	The learners get an overview of the whole book by skimming through it before or after reading, carefully looking at its cover page or carefully looking at a page before reading it.
Elaboration: using previous knowledge	The learners use their previous language, reading and world knowledge to understand the reading text.
Imagery	The learners use the visualisations as a means that conveys meaning and supports the comprehension of the text.
Translating into German	The learners translate words or parts of the text into German.
Re-reading	The learners re-read a word, sentence or part of the book.
Resourcing	The learners use resources such as dictionaries or the word list in order to look up unknown parts of the text. Also the use of an audio-recording serves as a resource for FL reading.
Vocalisation	The learners make use of semi- or sub-vocalisation as well as reading aloud for parts of the text.
Inferencing strategies	The learners use various inferencing strategies to decode the meaning of unknown words.
Making predictions	Based on previously read parts or previous knowledge, the learners make predictions about what will come next in the text.
Summarising parts of the book	The learners are engaged in the process of summarisation while reading to ensure that the information is retained.
Underlining	The learners (want to) underline parts of the text.
Dividing the text into sections	The learners (want to) divide the reading text into shorter sections.

Getting an overview

The first cognitive strategy is that of getting an overview. This means that the learners got an overview of what they were about to read before they actually started reading. Three different strategies of getting an overview could be found:

359

skimming through the book before reading, skimming through the book after reading and looking at the cover before reading.

The most prominent strategy for getting an overview was briefly skimming through the whole book before reading. This was done by nine learners who were all observed to start looking into the book and to skim through the pages once they got the books in their hands. Four learners (Ali, Neele, Jonas and Emil) also reported on doing so in the questionnaire. Apart from looking at the whole book before reading, three learners (Emil, Natan and Ina) also carefully looked at the cover before reading the respective book. The questionnaire further revealed that three participants also carefully looked at the title before they started reading.

Skimming through a book before reading provides the readers with an initial overview and impression of the story's content. By doing so, they get an idea of what they can expect to read and how much reading is required. Knowing roughly what to anticipate from a reading text provides valuable advance knowledge about it and might thus aid comprehension processes. The same holds true for looking at a book's cover and/or title, which can also give a first impression of the book's content and often also reveals which characters play a major role in the story. This strategy of getting an overview of a text before reading it has also been reported on by Kolb (2013), who found that the young learners in her picture book project used the books' illustrations to make predictions about the story and to make suggestions about what could happen (Kolb, 2013: 36). Above all, gaining an overview of the book before reading activates previous knowledge and thus allows the learner to connect the story to already existing knowledge; this, in return, supports comprehension. Similarly, discussing the cover of a book is a common pre-listening activity in storytelling (see Chapter 6.5.2) in the primary school EFL classroom and can be transferred to a pre-reading activity as well.

Interestingly, Emil once also skimmed through the book 'Paddington at the Palace' right after reading it. Doing so might have reminded him of the book's overall plot and might also have re-confirmed for him what he had just read. It might thus be a strategy to work out the book's main plot and serve for a final overview of what was read.

Apart from getting an overview of the whole book, Ina as well as Jonas often looked at a whole page before they started reading the respective page and thus got an overview of that page before reading it. Looking at the pictures before starting to read a page is a strategy that allows the learners to get an overview of the page's content and to develop ideas about what to expect in the reading text.

In this way, the visualisations and the text can supplement each other and lead to better comprehension of that page. Kolb (2013: 36) also found in her reading study with young learners that the learners carefully looked at a page before reading it.

Elaboration: using previous knowledge

Getting an overview of a book before reading it, as just outlined, already indicates the benefits of previous knowledge about a book. The strategy of using previous knowledge was used frequently in the present study. Different types of previous knowledge were identified: previous language knowledge, previous knowledge about the book, previous knowledge about reading and previous world knowledge. Using previous knowledge is a strategy that cannot be observed but can only be reported on; therefore, the interviews and questionnaire provided data on this strategy.

Overall, three learners reported in the interviews on having used previous FL knowledge. Rico's use of previous language knowledge is two-fold. On the one hand he explained that his more general previous knowledge of the English language through more or less regular contact with it helped him in reading and understanding the books (see Transcript RS PP1 29.09.2014 #24:44-24:50). On the other hand, he revealed that already known words supported him in reading the books (see Transcript RS QK1 03.09.2014 #39:18-39:28):

R: *Was an dem Buch war einfach zu verstehen? Oder war einfach zu lesen. Ali?*
Ali: *Äh,* knickers. (laughs)
R: *Ok.*
Lara: *Und* Queen.
R: *Ok. Und warum?*
Rico: *Weil wir diese Wörter schon kennen.*

Similar reasons were given by Lara, who said, "*Weil ich manche Wörter verstanden habe*" (Transcript RS QK1 03.09.2014 #37:58) and by Natan, "*Weil ich konnte ein paar Wörter schon. Deswegen war es nicht so schwer*" (Transcript RS QK3 05.09.2014 #29:27). The questionnaire revealed that in addition to the three learners already mentioned, another five learners searched for words and sentences that they already knew in order to read and understand the books. This is a transfer act, in that known linguistic information facilitated the new task or reading an unknown text (O'Malley & Chamot, 1990: 46). Therefore, previous language knowledge and particularly previous knowledge of the books' vocabulary supported the young learners' reading process. The data also show that eight participants were aware of their previous language knowledge and the extent to which this knowledge supported their reading process. The supportive character of previous FL knowledge was also found by Reichart-Wallrabenstein (2004: 443f), who even made a distinction between semantic, orthographic and phonological knowledge. The present data did not provide such a distinction.

Apart from previous FL knowledge, previous reading experience was also mentioned as a supportive strategy in reading.[201] Dani explained that having already read the book 'The Queen's Knickers' helped her in reading the book 'Paddington at the Palace', as it provided her with previous reading experience: "*Und ich glaube das hat auch geholfen von dem letzten Buch was wir gelesen haben. [...] Da habe ich nämlich wesentlich weniger verstanden als da* (points to the current book)" (Transcript RS PP2 30.09.2014 #39:13-39:17). In other words, Dani reported that having read several books was beneficial in that it helped her to gradually understand more from book to book. This indicates that her reading competence developed through reading and that with more books she got increasingly used to the task of reading and worked out strategies for herself to go about this task. This finding supports the notion that learners should be involved in reading regularly to familiarise themselves with the task of reading and supports the claim that reading is learnt through reading (Korte, 2007).

Also, previous knowledge about the books was applied as a strategy, including already knowing something about a book's topic or characters. Three learners (Rico, Ali and Dani) reported that they already knew one of the book's main characters, 'Winnie' from the book 'Winnie in Winter', because the teacher had read out the book 'Winnie the Witch' to the class about a year earlier. In the questionnaire, another five learners reported that previous knowledge about the books' topics helped in reading the book. Four learners (Lara, Natan, Jonas and Neele) even stated in the questionnaire that they consciously thought of and retrieved their previous knowledge about a book's topic. Such previous knowledge of a book helps to activate top-down processes and allows the learners to apply strategies like guessing and hypothesising about the book's content (see Chapter 6.5.2), which in return can ease reading comprehension.

Lastly, also the use of more general world knowledge became apparent. Ali, for example, explained that he had tried 'ginger ale', a grocery item in the book 'Something Good', before and thus knew what it was. Emil, Max and Rico said that they had already been to London and hence knew about the 'Changing of the Guards' and other facts related to 'Buckingham Palace' during the discussion of the book 'Paddington at the Palace'. Also, Jonas related his personal experience

---

201   Oxford (1990: 19) has elaborated on this as (reading) practice.

with Christmas presents to the book 'Froggy's Best Christmas'. Using world knowledge, such as knowledge about the tradition of Christmas presents or factual knowledge about London, is a very common reading strategy and also said to be a major top-down process involved in reading comprehension (see Chapter 4.4.2). The fact that some learners could explain that previous world knowledge helped them to understand some of the words or content aspects of the books shows their awareness of this strategy and the extent to which this knowledge supported their reading process. This had already been found by Reichart-Wallrabenstein (2004: 491), who reports that world knowledge was applied to a great extent by her young learners during reading FL texts and could compensate for their low level of FL competence.

Imagery

Imagery, the use of visual images to understand information (O'Malley & Chamot, 1990: 46; also see Chapters 5.3.3 and 6.5.3), was a very prominent strategy in the present study. Using the visualisations for understanding the books was a strategy applied by ten of the eleven learners. Nine learners mentioned in at least one of the interviews that the visualisations helped comprehension. Dani, for example, explained that the pictures supported the comprehension of the books to a large extent: "*Also mir haben die Bilder da drin ziemlich geholfen, weil wenn ich manchmal was nicht verstanden habe, haben mir die Bilder auch manchmal geholfen dabei ähm das dann zu verstehen*" (Transcript RS PP2 30.09.2014 #39:13). Another example is Emil, who explained that he could understand an announcement of a sales lady in the book 'Five Little Monkeys' with the help of the pictures: "*Ähm, weil/ wegen der Bilder auch. Weil dann hat sie sozusagen eine Durchsage gemacht und dann hat man sie mit dem Mikrophon gesehen*" (Transcript RS FLM3 31.10.2014 #28:41).

In addition, the questionnaire revealed that eight children closely looked at the visualisations. Apart from the explicit evidence from the eight learners who ticked the use of this strategy in the closed statements, the supportive factor of the visuals was also noted in the one open item of the questionnaire by three learners. Firstly, Neele noted that she looked at the pictures in order to understand the book: "*Ich *kucke mir die *bilder genau an [sic]*." The same holds true for Simone, who wrote that she closely looked at what happened in the pictures: "**die *Bilda angeschaut was da passiert [sic]*." Dani explained in more detail that she closely looked at the pictures after reading each written section. She wrote: "*Wenn ich einen Abschnitt gelesen habe gucke ich mir das Bild ganz genau an, das hilft mir meistens. Natürlich hilft es mir nur in Büchern mit Bildern*."

Several learners also mentioned that the visualisations could compensate for a lack of text comprehension and FL knowledge. Dani's utterance above already indicates that the visualisations could support comprehension, even when FL sentences could not be successfully decoded. This was also revealed by Natan and Emil, who said that the pictures could make up for unknown words. Emil explained (Transcript RS QK3 05.09.2014 #31:23-31:56):

> **R:** *Wie ist es denn, wenn man jetzt so ein Wort so gar nicht versteht? Emil, was hast du gemacht?*
> **Emil:** *Ich habe ähm/ also wo ich drauf geguckt habe, haben mir haben mir die Bilder auch geholfen, um das so zu verstehen.*

Still, some learners used the visualisations more than others. Interestingly, Rico is the only learner who did not claim to use the books' visualisations at all. This could be due to the fact that Rico already had advanced FL reading skills and did not need the pictures that much. Possibly, though, he also did not want to admit that he used the pictures for comprehension to show off his reading abilities. In contrast to Rico, other learners might have used the visualisations more than they read the text in that they occasionally seemed to look more at the pictures than to be actually reading. Ina, for example, sometimes looked at the pictures extensively and appeared to turn a few pages too quickly to actually read the whole text.

Generally, reading picture books is an example of multimodal comprehension processes. The extent to which the learners rely on and retrieve information from textual and visual elements respectively often remains unclear, apart from information that can only be depicted by one element or the other. Analysing this issue, Nikolajeva and Scott (2001: 139) found that, for example, elements such as passage of time cannot be directly depicted in images, while details of appearance or setting are much easier shown in them. Apart from such a detailed analysis of each book's text and pictures, also eye-tracking research might give a more detailed insight into the extent that visuals are used for comprehension. As both were not part of the present study, there is only reason to assume that the learners mostly at least tried to read the text and did not only look at the pictures, because the oral recall (see Chapter 9.2.2) indicated that the learners were aware of a large number of content aspects that could not be understood from the illustrations only. Still, this does not exclude the possibility that some learners might have looked at the pictures more extensively from time to time, but based on the observations this did not seem to be the norm.

In general, the supportive function of the books' images is not surprising, since visualisations are an inherent part and crucial component of picture books (see Chapter 5.3.3). Overall, the data suggest that the learners used the pictures very effectively and were also very much aware of the importance of pictures in reading comprehension. In addition, both previous studies conducted with young learners reported that young EFL learners use the visualisations in picture books intensively in order to read them for comprehension (Kolb, 2013; Reichart-Wallrabenstein, 2004). Kolb (2013: 36), for example, found that young learners "often turn[ed] to the illustrations as a support for understanding the story." Carefully using the pictures for comprehension might be an advantage that young learners have over older learners, because the latter might rely more on print.

Translating into German

As outlined in Chapter 4.2, the language aspect plays an important role in FL reading. The strategy of translating while reading plays a particular role in FL reading, since translations into the L1 can be used as a reference in order to understand the FL text (also see Brown, 2007: 135). It is therefore likely that all the learners used translations from English into German as a basis for comprehension in some way. However, translations were difficult to observe, not mentioned in the interviews and only partly investigated via the questionnaire. Therefore, there is only partial evidence for the strategy of translation, particularly verbatim translation, in the study.

The observation data showed that seven children translated words, phrases or larger units, either verbatim or summarised by content. Four learners regularly used this strategy (Ali, Jonas, Emil and Natan), while the other three only did so sometimes. Emil, for example, translated "*einhundert Schokoladentafeln*" (#07:48) verbatim while reading the book 'Something Good'. Jonas translated a section of the book 'Five Little Monkeys' into German by content and summarised, "*Die probieren alle neue Sachen an*" (#09:03). Generally, translations of either words or short sentences were mostly not given word by word, but rather by content. The questionnaire underscores this in that all eleven learners stated that they had not translated the text word by word. Unfortunately, the questionnaire lacked an item that investigated translations by content.

These results are very interesting in that they show that the learners were aware of L1 support, but at the same time all the learners seem to have understood that word by word translations of FL sentences are often not much use. In contrast to this finding, Reichart-Wallrabenstein (2004: 491) found that the group of young learners of her reading study all tried to translate whole sentences of picture books and often attempted to translate word by word. This allows the tentative conclusion that young learners might be more tempted to translate verbatim when reading in groups, as done in Reichart-Wallrabenstein's (2004) study. In the present study, in which the learners mostly read individually (see Chapter 9.3), they seem to have been aware of the problem of verbatim translations while reading silently and constructing meaning for themselves and not aloud in a group situation. It might thus be easier for young learners to construct meaning through translations by content and skilful summarisation when they are not asked to verbalise their comprehension during the actual reading process. Regardless of this speculation it should be regarded as positive that translations, particularly verbatim translations, were hardly found at all in the present study.

Re-reading

As already indicated in the section on meta-cognitive strategies, turning to an earlier page may include re-reading that page or a part of it. Re-reading means going back to a certain point in the text and re-reading it from there. Learners may re-read words, phrases, sentences, sections, pages or even the whole book.

In the present study, the re-reading of a word, sentence or page as well as the re-reading of the whole book could be observed. The questionnaire revealed that three learners (Dani, Lara and Emil) re-read words which they did not understand, and the same three learners plus Ali re-read a whole sentence if they did not understand it. Additionally, I observed that Simone regularly re-read a page, because she always put a finger under the text that she was reading. Moreover, Neele and Ina re-read the whole book 'Paddington at the Palace' with the audio-recording after they had already read a good deal of it without.

The strategy of re-reading enables learners to double-check what they have read and to see if in a second try they potentially understand and/or remember more than beforehand. Already knowing what comes later might facilitate the comprehension of a part that had previously been misunderstood. Re-reading may also take place when learners find that they have lost overall track of the story. In that case, careful re-reading of potentially larger parts is necessary to pick up the story's gist again.[202] For more detailed insight into re-reading, eye-tracking procedures could be used to get a more reliable picture of all the re-reading strategies that

---

202 As such, re-reading could also be classified as a meta-cognitive strategy, because it includes a purposeful decision to start a larger part all over again. However, on a lower level of re-reading words or phrases, it is a cognitive strategy, because it is directly concerned with decoding the FL instead of organising the reading process. Therefore, the strategy of re-reading is categorised as a cognitive one in this study.

learners use. Maybe it is due to the complexities and costs of setting up this kind of research with young learners that re-reading has so far not really been elaborated on in previous studies. Only Finkbeiner (2005: XXVI) mentioned it as part of the strategy of repetition, in that her secondary school learners repeatedly read parts of the text.

Resourcing

Chapter 9.3 has already reported on the use of supportive devices during reading, which is a resourcing strategy. Resourcing means using "reference materials" (Brown, 2007: 134) in order to gain FL comprehension, which in the present study refers to the use of the supportive devices that were provided: the dictionary, the picture dictionary, the word list and the audio-recording. The results (see Chapter 9.3) have shown that above all the audio-recording and the word list were used effectively as resource strategies in the study. Apart from that, Simone suggested the internet as a resource, which could be utilised to look up the meaning of an unknown word: "*Oder wenn man sie zuhause* (inc.) *kein Englischwörterbuch hat, kann man im Internet nachschauen [sic]*" (Transcript RS PP2 30.09.2014 #39:59). Clearly, also previous knowledge, especially world knowledge, is a resource for readers, but has already been reported on earlier in this chapter.

Vocalisation

The next cognitive reading strategy to be addressed is vocalisation, an auditory representation of the FL (see Brown, 2007: 135). As explained in Chapter 4.3.3, the auditory representation of a word, either provided by someone else or semi-vocalised by oneself, supports the retrieval of the meaning of that word from the mental lexicon. In this study, semi-vocalisation, sub-vocalisation as well as reading aloud were found.

Six learners were observed to use semi-vocalisation while reading the books, in that they read aloud or whispered the text or parts of it to themselves. Two learners used semi-vocalisation regularly and with all the books (Simone and Jonas), Ali also used it regularly, but not as continuously as Simone and Jonas, and another three learners (Lara, Max and Ina) sometimes used it.

It is striking that particularly those three learners that were rather weak readers (see Chapter 9.2.4) frequently used semi-vocalisation. This supports the arguments that were outlined in Chapter 4.1, namely that semi-vocalisation indicates that the learners are not yet fluent readers, as they need to decode words letter by letter and cannot recognise their meaning automatically yet.

Frequent semi-vocalisation is thus a strategy that suggests reading difficulties rather than good reading skills. However, the strategy might allow weak readers to gain better access to a reading text and might thus be used successfully by them (see Chapter 4.6.6 on successful strategies). Thus, semi-vocalisation is not a strategy that is deemed ineffective in itself, but only a strategy that, if applied frequently, is indicative of the reader's level of reading competence. Simone and Jonas therefore probably needed this strategy to read the books and to possibly compensate for a lack of automatised reading skills. Ali read all but one book with the help of the audio-recording, so that frequent semi-vocalisation was not necessary for him, since the recording already served as a phonological representation of the text. Those learners that only sometimes used semi-vocalisation were either average or strong readers and probably needed semi-vocalisation for difficult words. As outlined in Chapter 4.3.3, words that are deemed difficult are vocalised by readers in order to decode them in that the readers try to access them via their phonological representation.

Interestingly, in the questionnaire only Lara and Dani stated that they read words aloud to themselves in order to decode them, while the other nine learners said that they had not used this strategy. Therefore, semi-vocalisation seems to be a strategy that is used by young and beginner readers of English, but they are hardly aware of it. However, the learners might also know from their previous experience with English and also written English that the link between the graphological and phonological from of English words is weak because of the non-phonetic spelling of English, and might therefore not deem semi-vocalisation as a strategy worth mentioning. It is certainly difficult for beginner EFL learners to establish the correct pronunciation of English words. Still, the observations have shown that they used this strategy and it thus seems to be important for some learners in FL reading.

In addition to semi-vocalisation, also sub-vocalisation could be detected in parts. In the questionnaire, Jonas and Ali ticked that they imagined someone reading the text aloud to them. For Jonas, this could indicate sub-vocalisation, while Ali probably meant the audio-recordings that he used consistently to read five of the six books. In addition, Ina wrote *"Ich hab es im Kopf gelesen"* on the open item of the questionnaire, which indicates that she sub-vocalised what she read and was even aware of this.

Reading aloud was also found as a strategy in the present study. Only one learner, Simone, preferred reading aloud, though. Simone's idea of cooperative reading, as already discussed in Chapter 9.3, was taking turns in reading aloud the pages to one another: *"Dass man zum Beispiel eine Seite der eine leise vorliest und die andere der andere"* (Transcript RS SG2 12.11.2014 #34:35). Simone also stated in the questionnaire that she read a whole text aloud rather than reading it silently. All other learners stated that they preferred reading silently.

Kolb (2013: 37) had already observed the phenomenon of primary school learners reading a FL text aloud to others in her picture book project. She hypothesised that this might reflect a widespread reading aloud routine in schools (also see Chapter 4.3.2). However, while many children tried this technique in Kolb's (2013) project, only one child suggested it and briefly tried it out in the present study. While reading aloud can on the one hand be too difficult and impose a cognitive overload on beginner readers, on the other hand young EFL learners are, without practice, too inexpert readers for their reading out loud to function as a means of allowing comprehension for listeners.

At the word- and sentence level, six other learners of the present study also read single words or phrases that they came across aloud. Often, these were very prominent words that displayed parts of the text that were for a certain reason of particular interest to the reader. Such words or phrases were mostly not read out monotonously, but rather like an exclamation with an excited voice that made the other learners notice the reader's astonishment. For example, Max read aloud the word "one hundred" when he read the book 'Something Good' (#07:45), and read it out with a loud voice that signalled amazement.[203] Such exclamations, however, probably were not concerned with the role of semi-vocalisation or reading aloud. These words were rather exclaimed in amazement or surprise to make the peers notice something funny or interesting. One can thus assume that exclaiming single words or phrases with an interested intonation is not done to access the mental lexicon by phonologically decoding the word, but rather to gain attention and express one's own opinion on the text (also see Chapter 10.1.4 on affective strategies).

Strategies of semi- and sub-vocalisation as well as reading aloud have only rarely been mentioned in previous studies with older and more advanced learners. Only Finkbeiner (2005: XXIX) mentioned the strategy of auditory elaboration, which means that the learners imagine parts of the text in spoken form (= sub-vocalisation). With regard to the role of vocalisation in reading that was outlined in Chapter 4.3.3, more advanced EFL learners have potentially already reached a stage of sub-vocalisation and developed an inner L2 voice, so that particularly semi-vocalisation and reading aloud are not as prominent any longer as

---

203   Context information: Tyya, a little girl that is the main character of the book, put 100 bars of chocolate into the shopping cart while shopping with her father.

they might be for beginner learners. Semi-vocalisation and reading aloud thus seem to be strategies that are mostly used by young and beginner EFL learners.

Inferencing strategies

Inferencing strategies are those cognitive strategies that the learners used to decode the meaning of unknown words or phrases. One such strategy has already been mentioned in the strategy of imagery, in that the learners used the visualisations of the picture books in order to figure out the meaning of unknown words or parts of the text. However, nine further inferencing strategies were found in the present study and will be elaborated on in the following paragraphs.

Firstly, the learners used the context to work out the meaning of unknown words. Neele and Emil explained their strategy in the interviews. Neele noted that she used her knowledge of other words in order to provide a context for understanding unknown ones: "*Ähm, nee, weil sonst habe ich eben mit anderen Wörtern* (inc.)/ *mit den anderen Wörtern im Zusammenhang* (inc.) [*sic*]" (Transcript RS FLM3 31.10.2014 #29:42). Emil explained that he could guess the meaning of an unknown word from context: "*Weiter gelesen und dann hat man den Zus/ gemerkt, welches Wort das ist*" (Transcript RS FLM3 31.10.2014 #29:51). In the questionnaire, another five learners revealed that they used the words around an unknown word, and thus the context that the word was in, to decode the unknown one. The same five learners plus Neele reported in the questionnaire that they read the whole sentence to see if an unknown word could then be understood in the context of that sentence.

Also, the follow-up sentence or longer part of the text was used to decode a previous sentence. For example, Emil explained that he read the next sentence when a previous sentence contained unknown words (Transcript RS SG3 14.11.2014 #29:30):

R: *Ok. Was hat dir denn geholfen, das dann trotzdem zu verstehen auch wenn du nicht jedes Wort verstanden hast?*
Emil: *Der nächste Satz.*

Including Emil, seven learners reported in the questionnaire that they contemplated whether a sentence that was not completely understood could be understood in the context of the sentences around it.

Another strategy, closely related to 'using the context', is that of guessing the meaning of unknown words. Jonas and Dani reported on doing so in the interviews. Jonas explained: "*Man konnte sich das dann manchmal denken. Dann konnte man alles verstehen*" (Transcript RS PP2 30.09.2014 #40:43). Likewise, Dani argued: "*Dann denkt man sich das so ein bisschen, was das vielleicht bedeuten könnte*"

(Transcript RS PP2 30.09.2014 #40:20). In the questionnaire, three other learners also stated that they guessed the meaning of unknown words.

Another inferencing strategy was only mentioned by one learner, Rico, who said that he explicitly sought further explanations in the text in order to figure out the meaning of an unknown word. The book 'The Queen's Knickers' contained the abbreviation "V.I.P.", which is explained in the book in brackets as "very important pair" (Christelow, 2007). Rico said that this explanation in brackets helped him to understand the abbreviation (Transcript RS QK1 03.09.2014 #38:37 and #41:36).

The next inferencing strategy was that of using L1 similarities, meaning to rely on phonological and graphological similarities between words in both languages. In the present study, the use of this strategy was only identified for one learner, Ali. He, however, did not mention it explicitly, but his exploration of L1 similarities became obvious in vocabulary questions. For example, he asked, "*Was heißt 'smartly'? Heißt das Smarties?*" while reading the book 'The Queen's Knickers' (#13:03). In the questionnaire, one other learner, Natan, specified to consider L1 similarities.

As a further inferencing strategy, seeking an auditory representation of an unknown word, was explicitly suggested by three learners. Ali, for example, explained that he listened to words that he did not understand in order to figure out their meaning (Transcript RS PP1 29.09.2014 #33:07). In the questionnaire, additionally Jonas and Neele stated that they listened to unknown words and Simone and Dani reported that they would ask someone to read the word aloud correctly. This is closely related to listening to the audio-recording (Chapter 9.3) as well as to the role of vocalisation in reading as outlined earlier in this chapter.

Three further inferencing strategies were revealed in the questionnaire. Firstly, four learners stated that they thought hard about words which they did not understand and therefore consciously directed their attention and cognitive effort to such words. This is similar to the meta-cognitive strategy of direction attention in reading, while directing attention to a difficult word is only concerned with single FL words and therefore a cognitive strategy instead. Secondly, four learners reported that they sought a part of the word that they might know in order to decode the rest of the word. Lastly, four learners stated that they sought a repetition of that word in the following parts of the text to see whether meaning could be decoded via the new context.

Overall, this use of nine different inferencing strategies reveals very sophisticated strategy use as well as strategy awareness. A large number of different inferencing strategies allows learners to decode the FL, even if not every word can be understood. This clearly eases the cognitive load imposed by a lack of lexical knowledge and allows learners to approach FL texts skilfully. These results differ from previous reading strategy studies with young learners. First and foremost, previous studies have not found such a high number of inferencing strategies (e.g., Kolb, 2013[204]). Also, the inferencing strategies identified in the present study partly differ from those found in other studies. For instance, Reichart-Wallrabenstein (2004: 493) found that young EFL learners relied a lot on L1 similarities in that many participants assumed that each English word is similar in German. She concluded that a reflection on this phenomenon is necessary in order to raise awareness for possible similarities but also for differences (Reichart-Wallrabenstein, 2004: 493). In the present study, this might have already happened in class, because only Ali, out of all the participants, seemed to rely on L1 similarities a lot. The other learners mostly used different and for the most part more successful strategies in order to decode unknown words.

A possible reason for the differences to the two other studies with young learners might be that the participants in this study had enhanced input in English due to the bilingual programme of the school. Understanding the content matter of, for example, the science or arts class in English might foster inferencing strategies to a greater extent than the regular EFL classroom can achieve, because the learners are, in many situations, required to understand content matter in a FL and therefore need to develop useful inferencing strategies. Thus, learning subject matter through a FL might increase the use and awareness of effective inferencing strategies in young learners.[205]

Making predictions

Making predictions is a strategy of anticipating certain content elements and can support reading comprehension because of the expectations that are built up. It is a strategy that is difficult to observe, so researchers have to rely on reported data. In the present study, only Max reported on making predictions. The book 'Five Little Monkeys' contains several repetitive elements, and Max reported using this repetition to read the book in that he could predict the story's

---

204 Kolb (2013: 38) found the two strategies of using the visualisations and guessing from context.

205 Nevertheless, despite the variety of different inferencing strategies (also see Chapter 6.6.3), which has been interpreted as positive in this section, the meta-cognitive strategy of tolerance of ambiguity is also of significance for successful reading skills (see Chapters 6.8 and 10.1.1) and should not be neglected. Readers do not need to decode and understand each word of a text.

continuation: "*Also ich fand auch das war so geschrieben, dass man sich das vorher erahnen konnte, was als nächstes passiert*" (Transcript RS FLM2 29.10.2014 #35:31). Although only Max mentioned this strategy during the interviews, the questionnaire showed that another five learners also made predictions about what came next in the stories.

Such predictions support learners in anticipating and expecting certain content elements, which can support their reading comprehension. Pinter (2006: 109f) notes that the development of predicting skills is an early strategy that EFL teachers should already encourage in storytelling. Such strategies can then be effectively transferred to FL reading. In fact, the use of pictures for making predictions has already been found to be a prominent strategy for reading picture books by Kolb (2013: 36). She reports that the young learners particularly used the pictures to make predictions about the continuation of the story (Kolb, 2013: 36). Her finding is supported by the present study, even if the strategy was not as prominent here.

Summarising

As outlined in Chapter 4.4.2, summarisation is an important process in reading and refers to the process of synthesising what was read to ensure that the information is retained (O'Malley & Chamot, 1990: 46). In the current study this could be observed in four learners because these four children sometimes (Emil and Natan) or regularly (Rico and Jonas) summarised a part that they understood and then verbalised the result in German. While reading a page of 'Something Good', Rico, for example, summarised, "*Ganz viel Süßkram,*" (#08:54) when the main character put different sweets into the shopping cart. Even though short summaries of pages like this were partly observed in the reading process of some of the learners, the strategy of summarisation was difficult to investigate. The questionnaire did unfortunately not contain an item about summarisation and it was also not reported on during the interviews. Because the learners understood and could retain parts of the books, as outlined in Chapter 9.2.4, presumably more or even all the learners were engaged in ongoing summarisation processes. As a central process in reading, this might be a strategy that has already become automatised from L1 reading and is thus not available to the participants' awareness any longer.[206] The learners had already had three years of practice in L1

---

206 See the process of declarative knowledge becoming automatised and thus less conscious according to information processing theories in Lightbown & Spada (2013: 109); also see Chapter 4.3.2.

reading and the strategy of summarisation is the same or very similar in L1 and FL reading.

Underlining

Underlining and particularly note-taking are common reading strategies for older and more advanced learners (see, e.g., Finkbeiner, 2005: XXVI). In the present study, neither strategy was utilised. Still, underlining was suggested as a reading strategy by Dani and Emil in the questionnaire, in that they ticked that they would like to underline words while reading. The strategy of note-taking while reading was not identified in the questionnaire as having been used or as a strategy they wished to have used by any of the learners.

Oxford (1990: 19) explains that highlighting (which is very similar to underlining) and note-taking support learners in creating structure for input. With picture books, which are on the one hand not very long and on the other hand do not really invite learners to underline words because the text is embedded in illustrations, the strategy of underlining is not really suitable. Moreover, one would not really expect young learners to take notes to a short fictional EFL text, particularly not during their first attempts at reading such books independently. It is therefore not surprising that underlining and note-taking were not found in the present study.

Dividing the text into sections

Similar to the reasons just given for the previous strategy of underlining and note-taking, also dividing a reading text into sections is not really a suitable strategy for picture books, whether it be dividing it before reading, which would be a meta-cognitive strategy, or making one's own divisions based on the language or content during reading (cognitive strategy). Still, dividing the text into sections instead of reading it all at once was identified as a strategy by one learner, Jonas, in the questionnaire. Maybe he would have liked to split the reading into shorter units because this might have enhanced and supported his rather short concentration span (also see Chapter 10.1.1).

10.1.3 Social Reading Strategies

Leaving the stage of cognitive and meta-cognitive strategies, this chapter will go into detail on social reading strategies. These were defined in Chapter 4.6.5 as strategies that help learners to learn through interaction and cooperation with others. Table 31 firstly provides an overview of the social reading strategies which could be identified in the present study, including a description of each strategy. Examples will then be given in the detailed explanation of each strategy.

Table 27: Overview of social reading strategies, including a description of each.

Social reading strategy	Description
Reading cooperatively	A learner reads in cooperation with at least one peer.
Questioning for clarification	The learners ask others, their peers or the teacher, for clarification about an unclear language item, task or situation.
Exchange with others	The learners discuss the book's story in that they talk about the events, pictures, characters, etc. and also point out certain aspects to other readers.
Expressing (mis)-understanding	The learners express their comprehension or express that they have misunderstood a part and have difficulties in that they tell others about it.
Seeking orientation: looking at other children	The learners seek orientation in that they look at what other learners are doing or what the reaction of the peers or teacher is.

Reading cooperatively

Reading in cooperation means reading a book together with a peer. As explained in Chapter 8.1.3, the learners could freely choose whether they wanted to read by themselves or in cooperation with a partner. Reading with a partner was allowed, but not especially encouraged. Still, five of the eleven participants showed interest in cooperative reading. Of those, only Dani ticked in the questionnaire that she would rather read in cooperation than by herself. Overall, cooperative reading as such was thus not used extensively as a strategy by the participants. In both previous studies on young learners' EFL reading, cooperation occurred naturally among the learners because the settings were organised cooperatively (Kolb, 2013; Reichart-Wallrabenstein, 2004). To encourage it, maybe the setting has to be arranged in such a way that cooperative reading is supported to a greater extent, for example by sharing materials. Chapter 9.3 has already provided more details about and a critical discussion of cooperative reading as found in the current study. However, cooperative reading, as already indicated in the aforementioned Chapter 9.3, can also mean cooperation on lower levels and does not necessarily include reading a whole story together page by page. Such social strategies, which are all to a certain extent cooperative, were found in the present study and will be elaborated on the in the following sections.

Questioning for Clarification

A well-known social strategy is asking for clarification. This is a strategy to gain information from others that can guide or support one's own reading process. In school situations, learners can ask peers as well as the teacher. In the current study, also I as the researcher could be asked.

To begin with, three learners sometimes posed questions while reading to gain more general information about the reading task or process. For instance, when Jonas read the book 'Five Little Monkeys', he asked me whether he should also read the numbers on the pages or whether he should only read the actual text (#07:42). For the most part, however, questions for clarification were concerned with vocabulary questions. While reading, four learners (regularly Ali, Lara and Simone; sometimes Max) asked for vocabulary clarification. For instance, when reading the book 'The Queen's Knickers' Lara asked, *"Was heißt smartly?"* (#11:55). In the interviews, Lara then suggested that others could be asked when an unknown word was encountered (Transcript RS PP1 29.09.2014 #34:17). The questionnaire revealed that another three learners would ask someone else if they encountered an unknown word.

During the study, only a few questions were asked in total and these were mostly concerned with unknown vocabulary. Although not many questions were asked, the participants still appear to have been aware of the strategy and the potential benefit of asking for clarification. Not using this strategy regularly might speak for the learners' tolerance of ambiguity (see Chapter 10.1.1) and their individual strategies to decode unknown words (see Chapter 10.1.2).

Exchange with others

The strategy of exchange with others took two specific forms: The learners discussed certain aspects of the stories with their peers and also pointed out certain aspects to others. First of all, two learners (Ali and Jonas) were found to discuss aspects of the story while reading. Jonas in particular did so frequently, as will be explained in more detail later in this subchapter. In the interviews, two other learners (Dani and Simone) mentioned that they found it beneficial to discuss the books' content with the small group after reading (see Chapter 9.2.2 on oral recall and questioning). They both mentioned that talking about the books after reading supported their comprehension. As Simone expressed it, *"Ich fand es auch gut, dass das am Ende zu besprechen war. Das das versteht versteht man mehr/ versteht man, was die anderen so herausgefunden haben dann und dann und dann versteht man das auch, das ganze Buch"* (Transcript RS QK2 05.09.2014 #37:04). Moreover, seven learners, particularly Jonas, were eager to exchange opinions or content aspects with their peers while reading in that they pointed out pictures or certain content, read out single words in amazement or raised the others' attention by expressions like "*Guck mal!*".

One of the major aspects of cooperative reading is a constant exchange with other learners about the story, including its language, pictures, characters, etc. Although the setting of the present study was not truly cooperative (see Chapter 9.3), the learners were still engaged in an exchange with their peers. Such an exchange allows the learners to discuss and compare comprehension of the books. Reichart-Wallrabenstein (2004: 444) already found the strategy of exchange with other learners in her reading study and concluded that it helped the learners to gain confirmation from other group members. Particularly Simone, who did not understand much of the books herself (see Chapter 9.2.2), probably benefited greatly from the oral recall and questioning after reading, in that she could get an idea of the stories' content by means of that procedure. Dani, who was a rather advanced reader, was able to compare her understanding of the story with that of the others to see to what extent possible differences occurred that could be discussed. Pointing out certain aspects of a story to peers and briefly discussing them while reading might lie in the nature of young and beginner learners. Particularly young learners are often eager to express their opinion and emotional reactions like laughter. This helps the learners to share emotions, which can in return lead to a better comprehension of the story because of briefly negotiated opinions of it.

Expressing (mis)understanding

Sharing aspects of the story with others, as just elaborated on, is also a strategy of expressing comprehension. Expressing understanding or also voicing problems or revealing misunderstanding is yet another social strategy. It requires that the learners either express or are eager to express their text comprehension, or reveal that they had difficulties with it.

In the present study, four children were very eager to express what they had understood (particularly Rico, Max and Jonas). I could observe this because those learners could hardly hold back what they had understood once they had read the story and were very eager to talk about it. In contrast to that, only two children mentioned difficulties or said that they misunderstood something (Dani and Neele). For instance, after reading the book 'Something Good', Dani said that there was one sentence that she did not understand (Transcript RS SG2 12.11.2014 #33:35). Also, Neele once mentioned that she found reading the book 'Paddington at the Palace' difficult, in that she determined that it was challenging:

"Das ist schwer!" (#05:36). The questionnaire underscores this impression. Only a minority of four learners (Neele, Natan, Jonas and Lara) ticked that they would tell someone else if they did not understand a book.

The learners' eagerness to express comprehension appears to outweigh the expression of difficulties and may have several reasons. Displaying what they have understood boosts learners' self-confidence because they enjoy the acknowledgement of their peers and of the teacher/researcher. Moreover, expressing understanding might also be a way of re-assuring and checking one's own comprehension in order to see if the meaning one established is correct or contains inconsistencies. The results on expressing difficulties, in contrast, clearly show that the learners rarely admitted or mentioned that something was difficult and that parts of a book were possibly not fully understood. Admitting difficulties is, of course, challenging, because learners usually want to draw level with their peers and do not want to reveal problems. However, mentioning difficulties as Dani did gives learners the opportunity to negotiate about the meaning of a certain part, which can be very beneficial with regard to overall comprehension.

However, the learners' focus on successful comprehension instead of on difficulties can also be evaluated positively because it shows that (young) learners are interested rather in what they understand than in what they do not understand. It thus shows a competence-oriented view of their learning. In contrast to that, more traditional views and some teachers' views are sometimes rather deficit-oriented. A positive and competence-oriented view, though, is more supportive in learning.[207]

Seeking orientation: looking at other children

The last social strategy that could be observed frequently is looking at others for orientation. Looking at others included just briefly looking at them to see what they were doing and then going back to one's own book. Overall, eight learners did this and half of them did so regularly. Particularly Neele often looked at Emil and seemed to sometimes even copy what he was doing. Sometimes, the learners also looked at me, mostly with a questioning face. Particularly Jonas did so in the beginning.

Looking at other learners or also at the teacher for orientation and to see what they are doing is not unusual for (young) learners. They might want confirmation

---

207   The general guidelines for teaching in Bavaria, for example, outline this in detail: http://www.lehrplanplus. bayern.de/leitlinien/grundschule#39206 (last access: 15.05.2017).

that what they are doing is correct or they might want to get an idea of what they should do. While reading, the learners also looked at their peers to see what page they were on. This might have given them an idea about their own reading pace, but might also have allowed them a brief look back or forward in the story. Looking at peers and thereby attracting their attention also allowed the learners to point something out to them or share laughter with them (see the strategy 'exchange with others').

10.1.4 Affective Reading Strategies

As a final main category, the affective reading strategies that were used in the current study will be presented and explained in this section. Affective strategies were defined in Chapter 4.6.5 as those reading strategies that help learners to regulate and control their emotions, motivation and attitudes. More so, they are also concerned with the learners' reaction to such emotions (Böttger, 2005: 150). As such, the social strategies outlined in the previous subchapter already implied some of the affective strategies. Table 28 provides an overview of the affective strategies that were found:

Table 28: Overview of affective reading strategies, including a description of each.

Affective reading strategy	Description
Emotional involvement	The learners are emotionally involved in the reading text in that they show emotional reactions such as laughter or comments that express emotions.
Personal elaboration: projecting oneself into the story	The learners project themselves into the stories and imitate the stories' sounds and actions or identify themselves with the stories' characters.
Self-motivation	The learners are confident and positive about their own reading and have a positive attitude towards the books.

Emotional involvement

The affective strategy of emotional involvement includes using laughter as well as commenting on different aspects of the book and thereby displaying one's opinion or reaction to it. Emotional involvement is firstly shown by laughing or smiling while reading. Eight learners regularly did so, two learners sometimes laughed or smiled (Max and Dani) and only one learner (Simone) did not show any emotional reaction while reading at all.

In addition, the learners supplemented their emotional reaction with comments that somehow displayed emotional involvement. These comments included opinions of the book, comments on content aspects, non-verbal comments and comments on linguistic features. Nine learners regularly commented on the content as well as the pictures. Jonas extensively commented on most of the books and could not help but exclaim at various points while reading, with remarks such as *"Ohhh, wie süß!"* ('Something Good' #06:24 and #14:32). Some learners also commented more directly on a certain content aspect. Ali, for instance, commented on the Queen's big wardrobe in the book 'The Queen's Knickers' and said, *"Der ist echt groß!"* (#14:55). Other comments by the learners more directly revealed the pupils' opinions of the books. Neele, for example, laughed and said *"Hihi, ist das lustig"* when she got the book 'The Queen's Knickers' (#08:15). Jonas expressed the opinion that he sometimes did not like it that some characters of the books were very muddle-headed: *"Ich finde es nicht gut, dass die ganze Zeit/ ähm ich find es nicht so lustig ähm, dass man in manchen Büch/ Büchern alle so schusselig immer sind"* (Transcript RS FLM2 29.10.2014 #34:17). Moreover, non-verbal comments could be identified. For example, Ali nodded his head in agreement with something that he read in the book 'Something Good'. Interestingly, Jonas once also commented on the book's language, and explained that "NNNNO" (Munsch, 1990) in 'Something Good', an onomatopoeic device of the text to express shouting, should not be written with so many letters (#14:04).

These laughs and comments show the learners' spontaneous reaction to the books and seem to be comments that evaluate certain details of the books. They show that the pupils were becoming emotionally attached to and involved in the stories and provide evidence that the learners had opinions about the books' content and could relate to it. Such mostly positive emotional reactions indicate that the participants' attitude towards the books was for the most part positive and also show that the participants looked at the pictures and text very carefully. According to Oxford (1990: 21), using laughter is a strategy for lowering anxiety. However, my impression in the present study is not congruent with this explanation, as the learners did not usually seem overtaxed or even anxious, thus there did not seem to be a reason for lowering anxiety. In the present study, emotional involvement seemed to have had other strategic intentions, such as those given above.

Despite the fact that emotional involvement in the form of laughing or commenting was regularly found in the observation data, the learners seemed unaware of these practices. No learner mentioned it during the interviews and only one learner (Natan) stated in the questionnaire that he commented during reading.

Personal elaboration: projecting oneself into the story

Another partly verbal and partly non-verbal reaction to the book was that some learners projected themselves into the stories and identified with the story's characters or imitated the story's sounds or actions. This strategy was not found frequently, but will still be discussed here as it seems to be a comprehension strategy that is mostly used by young learners. For instance, Finkbeiner's (2005) study with secondary school EFL learners rarely reports this strategy.

Overall, three learners imitated the texts' sounds and actions. Emil once made up a sound for the book 'Something Good' in that he whistled in accordance with one of the actions. Jonas also imitated some sounds found in that book and in addition made up his own sounds. Three learners (Dani, Rico and Ali) reported in the questionnaire that they imagined the sounds of the story in their heads while reading, which goes in the direction of relating to the story's sounds.

Two learners also imitated the books' actions. For example, when Jonas read the book 'Froggy's Best Christmas' he looked up when Froggy looked up, he opened his mouth when Froggy did so and waved his hand when some characters left Froggy's house. Similarly, Natan raised his arms in despair when the Queen's trunk went missing in 'The Queen's Knickers'.

That the learners were often deeply immersed into the story was also shown through identification with the stories' characters. Jonas in particular identified with the book's characters. When he read the book 'Five Little Monkeys', he stated that he was one of the monkeys, "*Ich bin der da* (points to a monkey)!" (#05:59). In the questionnaire, another four learners reported that they identified with the story's characters and empathised with them.

Imitating parts of a story and identifying with its characters shows emotional involvement in a story and might imply that the learners tried to grasp the story's meaning in order to know what happened to the characters. These imitations of the events and sounds of the stories as well as an identification with the characters show that the learners were deeply affected by the stories and somehow wanted to express this in that they tried to bring the story's content out of the book and into their actual surroundings. This might to a certain extent imply that they prefer a kinaesthetic way of learning. Lantolf (2000: 16) states that meaning is only partially constructed through linguistic means, with gesture also playing a significant role. In his context, he was talking about meaning in interaction with others, but this can be transferred to grasping the meaning during interaction with a written text. Gestures and sound effects can help to construct meaning and to comprehend the content of a text.

Self-motivation

In the present study, many learners displayed self-confidence about their own reading as well as a positive attitude towards reading the books, which could both be attributed to the strategy of self-motivation and self-encouragement. This strategy is used by learners to encourage themselves so that a learning activity will be successful (O'Malley & Chamot, 1990: 46; Oxford, 1990: 21).

Firstly, eight learners showed that they were confident about their own reading. This became clear in utterances that they gave about the books and that they made about their own reading. Emil, for example, said that the book 'Five Little Monkeys' was easy for him and that he did not need any additional support: *"Also, ich *fande das Buch eigentlich/ das konnte man gut lesen und Hilfsmittel brauchte man nicht"* (Transcript RS FLM3 31.10.2014 #28:31). Also Max repeatedly expressed the conviction that he did not need any strategies or any support as he could easily read the books on his own by simply reading them. The answers in the questionnaire support the observation and interview data. The majority of ten learners ticked that they believed that they can understand English books and do not consider them to be too difficult. Only Simone indicated that she thought that the books might be too difficult for her. Another item on the questionnaire revealed that eight learners hoped to understand a follow-up part if a previous part was not understood. They thus did not easily give up based on a previous experience of failure or difficulty. Moreover, some learners revealed during the interviews that they found the degree of difficulty of the books suitable and not too difficult. Jonas, for example, explained, *"Ähm, ich fand es war ähm schon einfach, aber nicht, dass man sagen kann sehr einfach"* (Transcript RS QK2 05.09.2014 #36:01).

Besides confidence about the reading skills, all learners somehow also revealed a positive attitude towards the books. Apart from the fact that many learners liked the books and found them funny, as could be seen in the comments that many learners made, they were also happy and excited about new books (particularly Simone, Jonas, Dani and Natan; also see Chapter 9.1). For example, Natan showed enthusiasm and motivation when he encountered new books during the reading sessions and, for instance, exclaimed *"Jaaa!"* in excitement when he first saw the new book 'Paddington at the Palace' (#01:35).

Moreover, in the questionnaire, the majority of eight participants stated that they looked forward to reading a new book. Nine learners also said that they were excited about what would happen in the book. Moreover, ten learners were eager to comprehend the books and ticked in the questionnaire that they would like to understand them, while four learners (Rico, Emil, Max and Simone) also indicated that it did not matter to them too much whether or not they could understand the reading text.

Such attitudes are not really strategies in themselves, but rather underlie the strategy of self-motivation. Without a positive attitude towards reading and understanding the books, motivating and encouraging oneself to reading them is very difficult. A learner's belief or hope to understand a text displays confidence in his/her skills. Generally, having a positive attitude about one's own skills and being self-confident about one's own reading can help in comprehension, as it lowers the affective filter and serves for a relaxed and comfortable reading atmosphere. Having a positive mind-set and being excited about a new book builds up expectations and motivates the reader to find out more about the book's content. When a learner approaches a text with the attitude of 'I can read', the chances are high that that learner does not easily give up and trusts in his/her competences, even when difficulties are encountered. By contrast, a negative mind-set and at worst feelings of frustration or fear might hinder reading and can restrict a reader's motivation. When learners are not confident about their reading skills, as for example in the case of Simone, it is important to support their reading and allow them experiences of success in order to maintain their reading motivation and their self-confidence. Insecure learners in particular might benefit from cooperative reading as well as from teacher guidance in the form of supportive devices as well as strategy training.

With older learners, the strategy of self-talk was found to reduce anxiety (O'Malley & Chamot, 1990: 46). The present study, however, found no evidence that the learners were anxious about reading the books and thus there was also no need to lower anxiety. For young learners, self-motivation might just be needed in order to encourage themselves to focus on a task in order to complete it successfully, but there may be no need to overcome anxiety. Considering that the young EFL learners in the study did not seem to experience anxiety about reading, it is possible that this could be an advantage that young learners have over older ones. If so, starting early with reading activities may be beneficial in that such an approach might encourage competence-oriented reading from the beginning and might reduce potential reading anxiety later on.

Nevertheless, two learners did display a rather negative attitude towards the books and were not very motivated to read them. Neither Lara nor Ali was happy about new books and stated during the reading sessions that they did not enjoy reading them. Contrary to these observations, however, Ali and Lara indicated in the questionnaire that they were looking forward to reading new books and had an interest in comprehending them. Thus, their results on attitudes towards reading the books were mixed. Reading, however, is certainly not everyone's favourite activity and thus it is not surprising that not all learners were enthusiastic about reading and eager to encounter new books. Such a wide range of motivation towards reading and picture books instead displays classroom realities, where teachers find learners that like and prefer different media and different activities. Still, it is desirable to create reading motivation and at best to maintain or increase it, as a positive attitude towards reading and towards books supports young learners in developing reading abilities, understanding English texts and enhancing their FL performance. Teachers should thus take measures that support this, such as allowing the learners to choose their own reading materials.

10.1.5 Interpretation and Discussion of Results on Strategy Use

The previous subchapters have outlined and explained the different reading strategies that were found in the study. Each strategy has been explained in detail, which to a certain extent already included an interpretation of each particular strategy as well as explanations or results as found by other researchers. This chapter will thus only interpret the overall findings with regard to reading strategy use and not go into detail about individual strategies again.

The data have shown that the learners used a wide range of different reading strategies that allowed them to successfully read the authentic picture books. Despite some difficulties with the complex grapheme-phoneme correspondence of English, which made a phonological approach to reading almost impossible, the learners applied a large number of different strategies to overcome this difficulty and these strategies enabled them to read all six different books. Also Reichart-Wallrabenstein (2004: 491) had found earlier that young learners use a wide range of different reading strategies, including bottom-up as well as top-down ones. This could fully be confirmed in the present study, even though in the current study the learners were reading independently and not in a guided reading conference of little groups. In part, the strategies found in the present study even went beyond those recorded in earlier studies and have supplemented the list of possible (successful) reading strategies for (young) EFL learners.

Also, the learners used strategies from all four different categories, with cognitive strategies being the category in which most strategies were found and used. However, a rather large number of meta-cognitive strategies could also be found, although it has often been debated whether young learners can organise and reflect on their learning on a meta-level (see Chapter 4.6.7). The meta-cognitive strategy of using orientation aids indeed even seems unique to FL reading by young readers, because such aids have not been described as reading strategies for older or more advanced FL readers before. Overall, the present study has clearly shown that young learners indeed use meta-cognitive strategies to organise their EFL reading. More details on strategy awareness as found in the present study will be found in Chapter 10.3.

When comparing the strategies used in this study to the table of reading strategies in Chapter 4.6.5, it becomes apparent that many strategies overlap with those that have already been described, particularly for older learners, or are the same. Therefore, young learners seem to already use a great range of reading strategies which are also used by older learners. Taking a closer look at potential differences between younger and older EFL readers, the findings on social reading strategies in particular are very interesting, in that they go beyond the reading strategies that have been described for older, more advanced learners (e.g. by Finkbeiner, 2005). The learners in the present study used a number of social strategies and some learners used these extensively. The notion of reading in cooperation was broadened in that the learners were not concerned with reading a book together page by page, but rather they discussed certain aspects of it, commented on them, compared their reactions, pointed something out to a peer or sought for orientation by looking at others. As such, reading seems to be a much more social activity for children and the notion of reading being interactive (see introduction to Chapter 4) is clearly supported. Young learners seem to have a large repertoire of different social reading strategies that aids them in successfully reading an authentic FL book; given the right setting. Considering this, cooperative reading settings seem to be very beneficial for young learners, even if they do not read together page by page. This is supported by Kolb's (2013: 38) findings, as she found that an adaptation of extensive reading in favour of cooperative instead of individual reading settings seems justified with young and beginner learners of English. Taking individual differences and preferences of learners into consideration, however, a reading setting should be organised in a way that allows both silent reading and various forms of cooperative reading.

Similar to the social strategies of the present study, the current investigation also revealed some affective strategies which had not been classified before (see Chapter 4.6.5). Particularly the idea of commenting on the book while reading as well as projecting oneself into the story and displaying this via actions, sounds or comments have not been described as common reading strategies with older or more advanced learners to the extent they were found in the current study.

Therefore, these could be affective strategies which mostly young learners use and which aid mostly them with approaching a FL reading text.

By contrast, some affective reading strategies which older and more advanced learners commonly apply, such as dealing with anxiety and setting realistic goals, could only partially be identified in the present study. One reason might be that these are too complex for young learners as they require some reflection on one's own emotions, which in turn allows some control over them. On the other hand, it seemed that the learners in the present study did not need to deal with anxiety much, as this seemed to be absent for the most part. A lack of anxiety about FL reading might actually be an advantage that young EFL readers might have over older ones, which indicates that FL reading should be introduced in the early stages of FLL.

Overall, the present study provides evidence that young EFL learners use an impressive number of different reading strategies which support them in successfully reading authentic English texts independently. A potential development of these strategies as well as the learners' awareness of them will be discussed in the following two subchapters.

10.2 Development of Strategy Use

Since the reading study took place over a period of five months that embraced several reading sessions with different books, the question of a possible development in strategy use will be addressed in this subchapter. Development in the use of reading strategies can only be analysed from the observation and interview data, in that a close look is taken at each learner's strategies for each book. The questionnaire data cannot be used to detect strategy development, as this instrument was not used continuously but only at the end of the data collection phase.

10.2.1 Presentation of Results

Regarding development of strategy use, the picture is mixed. Some learners do not seem to have developed with regard to their use of strategies at all, while others changed at least some parts of their strategy use over time. The first group of learners will be presented first and then a closer look will be taken at those strategies and learners that showed some development over time.

Those learners that more or less used the same reading strategies for the six different books were Rico, Max, Dani, Emil, Ina and Simone. For them, no real changes over time and books can be found. Rico, for example, seemed to use the same strategies for all the books. He continuously wanted to read together with a partner (but never found a willing partner), used the word list before, while, and after reading, commented on the book, summarised parts of it and read some words aloud in fascination. He was also always eager to reveal what he had understood. Already in the first reading sessions he was aware of the supportive function of known words and could tolerate ambiguity. This strategy behaviour lasted over all six books. Similarly to Rico, all five other learners mentioned above used their individual strategies that they had used from the very beginning over the whole period of the reading study.

Interestingly, all the strong readers (Rico, Max, Dani, Emil; see Chapter 9.2.4) are part of the group that did not show development in strategy use. Also, one reader categorised as average (Ina) did not really change her reading strategies. These learners' strategies were successful for them, in that they allowed them to become strong or at least average FL readers.

Simone, who was categorised as a weak reader, did not develop her reading strategies either, but in comparison to the effective strategy use of the others her strategy use displayed reading difficulties rather than success or competence in reading (see Chapter 4.6.6). She continuously used the strategies of semi-vocalisation and following the text with a finger, which both show that she had not yet developed advanced FL reading skills. These strategies did not change over the course of time and she applied both of them, plus other strategies such as using the visualisations, from the first to the last book.

Unlike these six learners, the other five learners (Lara, Ali, Neele, Natan and Jonas) showed some development in strategy use, namely with regard to the following strategies:

- Development of knowledge about the usefulness of resourcing strategies: dictionaries (particularly Lara and Ali)
- Development of knowledge about the usefulness of resourcing strategies: audio-recording (particularly Ali and Natan, but also Ina, Neele and Rico)
- Development of social and affective strategies based on reading confidence (particularly Jonas, but also Neele)
- Using the visualisations vs. reading the text (Neele)
- Development of tolerance of ambiguity (Lara)
- Development of the attitude towards reading the books (Lara)
- Development of awareness about the supportive function of the audio-recording (Lara)

The development of the use of these strategies will be dealt with in more detail in the following paragraphs, in which the strategy use of selected participants will also be explored.

Firstly, the learners quickly gained experience about the usefulness of the two different dictionaries as potential resources in reading and soon changed their strategy use with regard to using them after the first book. When trying out the picture dictionary and the bilingual dictionary for the first book, Ali and Lara soon found that neither dictionary was very useful (see Chapter 9.3). They thus quickly understood that the dictionaries were not a successful resourcing strategy for them and decided not to even try using them thereafter but relied on other strategies to decode unknown words. For instance, Lara's and Ali's strategy for decoding unknown words in the reading sessions that followed was to listen to the text via the audio-recording.

Also, the use of the aforementioned audio-recording as a resource developed for some learners. Four participants (Rico, Ina, Neele and Natan)[208] used the audio-recording only for one book, 'Paddington at the Palace', but then found that it was not a useful strategy for them and did not use it again (see Chapter 9.3). As a reason Natan stated that he partly found it difficult to follow the audio-recording's speaker (Transcript RS PP3 30.09.2014 #29:46). After this one attempt, none of the four learners used the strategy of listening to an audio-recording while reading again.

A different development with regard to the audio-recording could be found with Ali, who used it for reading all books but the first. As outlined in Chapter 9.1, he was not keen on FL reading from the very beginning and also slightly overtaxed with reading the books. During the first reading sessions he repeatedly showed that he had no tolerance of ambiguity and that it was important for him to understand all the words (see Chapter 10.1.1). When he found the audio-recording as a useful supportive device for reading the second book, he stuck to using the MP3-player until the end of the reading study. During the interviews, he did not mention anything but the audio-recording as useful in reading. The aspect that developed with regard to Ali's strategy use, however, was his ability to follow the audio-recording. While he had trouble with following the aural storyteller with the first books, which could be seen in that he mostly looked at the pictures and turned pages randomly, this improved with the latter books. With

---

208 Ina and Rico had been mentioned earlier in this Chapter as learners whose strategy use did not develop. Their use of the audio-recording once was not seen as major development, because they did not explain why they did not use it again. They seem to have just tried and rejected this device/strategy.

those, he seemed to be able to better follow the text while listening and he did not appear lost in the book any more.

Some development with regard to social and affective strategies in reading could be detected with Jonas. Jonas overall used a lot of strategies, but not much change in his use of strategies was visible. One development, however, clearly is that his reading confidence increased (see Chapter 9.1). While Jonas was still a bit nervous about reading the first two books, he got more confident in reading the latter ones. What developed along with this confidence was an increase in the use of affective and social strategies, in that he became more outgoing, emotional and active during reading. With the latter books he started to point out funny aspects to his peers, exchanged ideas, continuously commented on the books and gave his own opinion. Therefore, his behaviour during reading changed, from quiet and unsure to rather emotionally involved and outgoing. Similarly, Neele became slightly more outgoing towards the latter books, where she commented more and more on the books and increasingly often pointed out aspects to other learners.

Another development could be detected for Neele. Over time, her reading behaviour changed in that she seemed to increasingly read the text instead of mostly looking at the visualisations. With the first books I had the impression that Neele was not really reading the text but rather looked at the pictures. Her pace of turning pages provided some evidence for this. However, with the latter books, Neele seemed to increasingly read the books' texts. Overall, however, without eye-tracking research it was impossible to clearly detect what parts exactly, the text or the visualisations, she looked at for each book.

Lastly, the most interesting child with regard to development of strategy use is Lara. Her development seemed to depend on several strategies, including tolerance of ambiguity, attitude towards reading and towards the books as well as the use of an audio-recording. Firstly, Lara seemed to have developed tolerance of ambiguity to a certain extent in the course of reading the different books. While she showed no tolerance of ambiguity when reading the first two books (she tried to look up words with all different devices, asked for words, was frustrated to not understand all the words), did still not display much ambiguity tolerance for the middle two books, some statements were made by her that displayed tolerating ambiguity for the last but one book 'Froggy's Best Christmas' (Transcript RS FBC1 05.12.2014 #22:53-23:04). Such a gradual development of ambiguity tolerance is also underscored by the fact that Lara read almost all the books with the help of the audio-recording and was sure that she could not read without it, but did not use the recording when reading the last book, 'Winnie in Winter'. With regard to the audio-recording she also seemed to have developed an understanding of its function in reading, as she could explain during the third and fourth interview that she needed the audio-recording in order to listen to the correct pronunciation of the words so as to understand them (e.g., Transcript RS SG1 14.11.2014 #24:16). In the beginning she had only stated that she needed the recording to understand the books, without any further explanation. What seemed to have developed alongside with this was Lara's attitude towards reading the books. While it worsened from book to book at first, and Lara continuously displayed demotivation about reading, she seemed in a much better mood when she read the last book, 'Winnie in Winter'. In sum, Lara showed strategy development with regard to ambiguity tolerance, the function of the audio-recording and her attitude towards approaching a FL reading text; three strategies which all seem to be interlinked and dependent on each other. Also, the factor of time and continuous reading practice seems important, in that Lara's development took place over the five month course of the reading study.

To sum up the results that were presented with regard to the development of strategy use in this section, none of the four strong readers really showed any change or development in their strategy use over time. By contrast, one weak and four average readers showed change in that they used different strategies for different books and somehow developed their strategy use over the course of the reading study. Overall, the use of seven different reading strategies changed and developed for some of the learners.

10.2.2 Interpretation and Discussion of Results

Looking at the results, there is not one particular strategy that develops over time for all the learners, nor do all the learners show development. This shows how highly individual strategy use as well as the development of reading strategies is. Both depend on the individual learners and their personal experiences with reading.

The data revealed that about half of the learners did not show much development in reading strategy use. These were for the most part the readers that had been categorised as strong FL readers. The most prominent reason might be that all strong readers (Rico, Max, Emil, Dani) used a number of different FL reading strategies from the beginning, which all proved successful and appropriate (also see Chapter 4.6.6). In that case, there was not much need to develop or change their reading strategies. Possibly, they transferred their (successful) L1 reading strategies to reading in the L2. This assumption is supported by the learners' L1 reading marks, which were investigated prior to the data collection (see Chapter

9.2.4 and Appendix A). Their L1 reading was marked as either good or very good,[209] which indicates that they probably already possessed effective L1 reading strategies that could, at least partly, be transferred to L2 reading. Interestingly, however, also other learners' reading marks in German were marked as good or very good (Lara, Neele, Ina, Natan, Ali), but these learners did not prove to be strong FL readers (see Chapter 9.2.4). These readers do not seem to have successfully transferred L1 reading skills to L2 reading to the extent of the strong FL readers. Therefore, the results of the study indicate that advanced L1 reading skills do not necessarily result in strong L2 reading skills for young EFL learners, but some learners still need to develop strategies to read in a FL. They might have to learn to overcome difficulties that FL reading involves (see Chapter 4.2) and develop strategies, such as tolerance of ambiguity, that are needed in L2 but not so much in L1 reading.

Still, reading without any explicit instruction, as in the current study, might not be sufficient to develop FL reading strategies. Simone, who was a weak L1 and also weak L2 reader, did not develop her FL reading strategies over the course of the six books. Generally, weaker readers might not have a large repertoire of different strategies and might therefore need some guidance or explicit instruction in strategy use. This, of course, can also be beneficial for stronger learners and stronger readers. Certainly, there is a limit to the number of reading strategies that can be developed by experience and trial and error (as done in the present study). All learners, but particularly weaker ones or those that do not use a set of adequate and effective reading strategies, might benefit from some explicit reading strategy instruction or a reflection and discussion about possible reading strategies. Several researchers, for example Schick (2016), have suggested teaching certain sets of strategies to young learners in a child-friendly way in order to allow struggling learners in particular to gain a set of different strategies for successful FLL. This seems beneficial for FL reading strategy development as well. Pinter (2006: 104) believes that such reflections on the learning process are a natural part of effective learning. In addition, she suggests that teachers highlight good strategies and discuss good models of strategy use with the whole class in order to support strategy development (Pinter, 2006: 110). In that respect Chamot (2005: 120) found that some teachers found it easier to teach successful FL reading strategies in the learners' native language instead of the FL. Particularly for young EFL learners, these

---

209   In German marks they were 1 (*sehr gut*) or 2 (*gut*), which are the highest possible marks.

suggestions seem a viable way to enhance young EFL learners' reading strategy development and thus support FL reading skills.

Nevertheless, despite a lack of explicit strategy training in the present study, five weak and average FL readers did show some development with regard to their use of FL reading strategies. Some of them tried out different strategies, for example using the audio-recording for one book, in order to find out the extent to which the strategies might be effective or not. It is a sign of effective strategy use if a strategy like using the audio-recording did not prove useful or necessary and is thus rejected again. Rico, a strong reader, probably found that he did not need the recording to understand the books, which is why he only tried it for one book. Using or trying different strategies for different books also indicates that the learners might be able to distinguish which support they needed for which book, which shows that they can use different reading strategies that are suited to different books. Trying out new or alternative strategies, although a learner already has several, shows openness towards strategy use and might allow the learners to develop or confirm their successful use of strategies.

The example of Ali, who gradually learnt to follow the reading text while listening to the audio-recording, shows that learners can also develop within a strategy. It appears that Ali had found the auditory representation of a text to be the device that made it best possible for him to read the FL texts, but over the course of time he learnt to fine-tune this strategy. The more often he read with the help of the audio-recording, the better he became at it. He learnt to find orientation in the reading texts, guided by the audio-recording, and with the latter books no longer got lost while reading and listening. Potentially, he could read further books only partially supported by the audio-recording, and eventually without it, and thereby gradually develop further reading strategies that replace the auditory representation.

A further development in strategy use could be detected with regard to reading confidence and an increase in social and affective strategies. Of all the children, Jonas in particular showed an enhanced use of social and affective strategies after he had developed some reading confidence during the reading of the first two books. This newly gained reading confidence allowed him to make use of more social and affective reading strategies. He did not feel shy and uncertain any longer about exclaiming at funny features, talking to his peers while reading or showing his emotional involvement in the books. This suggests that a certain level of reading confidence might be needed in order to allow various affective and social strategies to develop and come to the surface. Young learners may have to get used to a new situation, such as reading English books, and work out what is viable for them, where they can find help and how they can go about the task. Once confidence has been established, possibly also strategy use can develop in that the learners might feel comfortable to experiment with different strategies.

The most interesting case that showed the most apparent development in FL reading strategy use was that of Lara. Over the course of the six books, Lara seemed to have developed at least some tolerance of ambiguity, which is a very valuable strategy in reading authentic FL texts. Potentially, reading several books helped Lara to develop ambiguity tolerance. Over the course of time, vocabulary questions and understanding every single word seemed to become less important to her as she went from book to book. As she read most of the books, but not the last one, with the audio-recording, she might have found that even when she listened to the text, she still encountered words that were not understood. This might have helped her to gradually gain tolerance of ambiguity and might have enabled her to transfer this experience from listening to reading. Lara obviously got accustomed to reading authentic books over the course of time and gradually developed strategies to tolerate unknown or phonologically difficult words. She might have needed the audio-recording in order to get used to FL reading and familiarise herself with its specific features and characteristics. She was much more at ease and in a better mood when it came to reading the last book, and this seems to be due to this familiarisation and the gradual development of strategies such as tolerance of ambiguity.

Summing up the discussion, some development in strategy use could be found in the study; thus it is clearly not impossible to develop different reading strategies while reading authentic English picture books without explicit instruction. Still, some strategy instruction or some skilful reflection on reading strategies might support learners in developing reading strategies and in trying them out for future books. Encouraging individual learners' independence through a reflection on strategy use is consistent with the principle of catering for individual learner differences, interests and needs (Pinter, 2006: 112). Some learners, however, simply did not need to develop their FL reading strategies or change them over time, as they were successful from the very beginning with the reading strategies they already used. For them, it might be interesting to reflect on their success and find reasons why these reading strategies were effective, which in return might be beneficial for weaker readers or less efficient strategy users. Strong FL readers and successful strategy users might also need more difficult reading texts so that they can transfer their reading strategies to those and develop them by applying them to more challenging material.

10.3 Young Learners' Awareness of Strategy Use

As outlined in Chapter 4.6.7, there is some debate as to whether young learners can approach their learning and working processes on a meta-level and can thus be aware of their strategy use and be able to verbalise and describe their strategy use. Therefore, this chapter will investigate to what extent the data revealed the participants' awareness of FL reading strategies.

10.3.1 Presentation of Results

Strategy awareness can be investigated by looking at the different instruments that revealed the use of a certain strategy. As outlined in Chapter 8.3, observation, interview and questionnaire data provided detailed information about the learners' use of FL reading strategies. Awareness of these strategies can be explored as follows:

When a learner reports on a strategy, either in one of the interviews or in the questionnaire, the learner is aware of having used that strategy. However, a precondition for revealing a consciously used strategy in an interview is that the learner can verbalise the respective strategy. The advantage of the questionnaire thus is that it already verbalises the strategies for the learners and they only need to indicate whether they had used them or not. The questionnaire data therefore counterbalances the problem of verbalisation that the interview might entail and offers a deeper insight into the learners' strategy awareness. By contrast, strategies that a learner used and was not aware of could be identified via the observation data. When a learner was observed using a certain strategy, for example putting a finger under the text, and the learner did not report on that strategy in the interview or questionnaire, that strategy was used without awareness.

Regarding the results on strategy awareness,[210] firstly the learners will be looked at individually, ordered by the classification into weak, average and strong readers (see Chapter 9.2.4). Figure 34 provides an overview of the relation between strategies that each learner was or was not aware of using. Awareness of strategy use is displayed in percentages in order to allow comparisons between the learners, because the total number of strategies detected varied from learner to learner.

---

210 A detailed table which provides an overview of all the strategies used, including the instrument that identified the use of this strategy, is found in Appendix E.7. The data shown in that table form the basis for the results presented in this chapter.

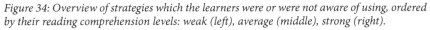

Figure 34: Overview of strategies which the learners were or were not aware of using, ordered by their reading comprehension levels: weak (left), average (middle), strong (right).

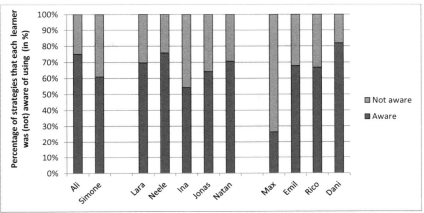

Figure 34 shows that Dani was most aware of her strategy use with about 82 % of her reading strategies being used consciously. Another seven learners can be seen to have used between 60 % and 80 % of their strategies consciously. Slightly below that, Ina was aware of 54 % of her strategies. Max is an exception to all other learners already mentioned, in that he was by far the least aware of his strategies. He only used about 26 % consciously, suggesting he was not aware of 74 % of the reading strategies he applied.

Looking at the grouping of learners into weak, average and strong readers, there is no clear-cut difference between strategy awareness and a certain level of reading comprehension. In each group, at least one learner with a high degree of awareness is found as well as at least one learner with a lower level of awareness. No pattern or clear connection between strategy awareness and level of reading comprehension seems to emerge.

To get a better overview of the strategies that the learners were or were not aware of using, the following sections will explore those strategies that the learners were not aware of. Hereby, not the individual learners but strategy use in general will be looked at. A distinction will be made between a strategy that

- many learners were aware of; meaning that three or more were aware of it
- some learners were aware of; meaning that one or two learners were aware of
- no learner was aware of.

Table 29 is divided by the main classification of strategies into meta-cognitive, cognitive, social and affective reading strategies and shows the number of strategies in each category that were consciously used by many, some or no learners. Those reading strategies that no learner used consciously are listed in the right-hand column.

Table 29: Overview of the number of strategies that many, some or no learners were aware of using, with a focus on those strategies that no learner was aware of. Numbers in brackets behind the strategies that were used without awareness reveal the total number of learners that used that strategy.

Main classification of reading strategies	Number of strategies many learners were aware of using	Number of strategies some learners were aware of using	Number of strategies no learner was aware of using	Actual strategies that no learner was aware of using
Meta-cognitive reading strategies (total: 13)	5	6	2	- Using a pointing finger (3) - Putting a hand on the page (7)
Cognitive reading strategies (total: 30)	17	8	5	- Skimming through the book after reading (1) - Getting an overview of a page before reading (1) - Translating into German (7) - Semi-vocalisation (7) - Summarising parts of the book (4)
Social reading strategies (total: 8)	4	1	3	- Pointing out something to someone else (7) - Expressing understanding (4) - Seeking orientation (8)
Affective reading strategies (total: 5)	3	1	1	- Imitating the stories' actions (2)

Table 29 shows that no learner was aware of two out of 13 meta-cognitive strategies, five out of 30 cognitive strategies, three out of eight social strategies and one out of five affective reading strategies. This shows that overall only eleven reading strategies were used without at least some learners being aware of using them.

Of these eleven strategies, three strategies were only used by one or two learners at all, so that there was no opportunity for a larger number of learners to reveal awareness of them (see numbers in brackets behind the actual strategies). The total of eleven out of 56 strategies that were used without the learners being aware of them only accounts for about one fifth altogether. Many learners (at least three) were aware of using another 29 strategies and some learners (one or two) were aware of using the other 16 strategies. The 45 strategies used with awareness thus make up about four fifths of all strategies. Figure 35 summarises these results and also orders them by the main categories of reading strategies:

Figure 35: Overview of all strategies the learners were or were not aware of using, separated by the main categories of strategy use as well as summarised in the right bar.

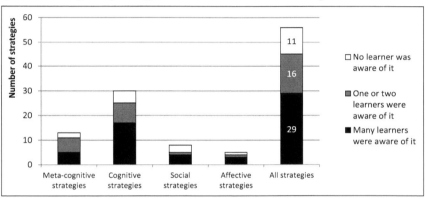

When looking at the 45 strategies that the learners were aware of using, this only indicates that some or many learners were aware of using them, but not all learners. For example, Simone regularly used the strategy of questioning for clarification, but Simone never reported on doing so in the interviews or in the questionnaire. Still, this strategy is listed as one that many learners were aware of, because at least three other learners were aware of using it. The 45 strategies that are claimed as strategies the learners were aware of using were thus only used consciously by a certain number of learners, but not by all of them. A more detailed analysis would have to be done in case studies, but does not serve the purpose of answering the research question of the current study.

Moreover, some results with regard to awareness of strategy use are inconsistent. For instance, Natan reported twice in the interviews that he kept reading when he encountered an unknown word, but he stated that he did not do so in the questionnaire. Again, a detailed analysis of these cases of inconsistencies goes beyond the scope of the book,[211] but this aspect will be taken into consideration for the discussion and interpretation of the results.

One aspect is striking when looking at which instruments revealed awareness of particular strategies, and that is the potential importance of the questionnaire with regard to the learners' awareness. Nine strategies that the learners indicated that they had used in the questionnaire were not shown in the observations or in the interviews at all. Only the questionnaire reported them, as was indicated by the grey font in Table 24. Another eleven strategies were observed and also revealed by the questionnaire, but were not mentioned by the learners in the interviews. When looking at the strategies in the right column of Table 29, which were those that no learner was aware of using, one can see that six of the eleven strategies were not presented as questionnaire items (also see Appendix D.4). The questionnaire thus seems to play an important role in making young learners aware of their strategy use. This, of course, presupposes that the learners were competent in filling in the questionnaire, which the learners in the study seem to have been.[212]

10.3.2 Interpretation and Discussion of Results

Overall, the learners who took part in the study were aware of about four fifths of the reading strategies which they used and so displayed awareness of the majority of their reading strategies. The high degree of overall strategy awareness shows that young learners are able to reflect on and talk about their reading strategies and are able to consciously apply certain strategies when approaching a FL reading task. This finding concurs with what Kolb (2013: 41) has found in her reading study: Young learners are "very able to reflect on their learning experiences and to describe the procedures they used when working with the books." Kolb's results and also those of the present study underline that young learners are very capable of being consciously aware of their reading strategies and are not overtaxed by a reflection on them. Returning to the discussion in Chapter 4.6.7, which noted that some researchers have apprehensions and doubts with regard to young learners' ability to talk about and describe their (reading) strategies, these data suggest that such doubts are unfounded.

---

211 Follow-up one-to-one interviews could be used to research this further.

212 My impression was that the learners were competent in filling in the questionnaire. This impression was confirmed by the fact that the learners ticked the option "do not know" for selected items and thus admitted that they did not know about some strategies. I can hence assume that the questionnaire data revealed a realistic picture of strategy use and provides useful information on the learners' awareness of it.

Of the individual learners, only Max was not aware of roughly 75 % of the reading strategies he applied. Awareness of reading strategies thus seems independent of reading competence, since learners whose reading comprehension was at different levels had very similar awareness levels. Indeed, Max' low awareness level indicates that a low awareness of strategy use can still co-occur with advanced reading skills. The evidence from the study does thus not suggest that weak reading skills are attributable to a lack of strategy awareness, while at the same time strong reading skills are not linked to a high degree of strategy awareness. Hence, strategy awareness does not seem to play a major role in reading competence in this setting; at least it does not appear to be a decisive factor.

Looking at the strategies themselves, those strategies that at least a certain number of learners were aware of can be understood as strategies that are generally not too complex for young learners to reflect on or talk about. Therefore, even if not all the learners were aware of a certain strategy one can assume that a discussion of this strategy in class might be beneficial for young learners, because such a strategy cannot per se be too complex to understand and reflect on.

Generally speaking, a reflection on strategies might support strategy awareness as well as the development of reading strategies (see Chapter 10.2.2): "The often underestimated ability of primary-school children to reflect on their learning (Kolb, 2007) can provide the basis of the discussion of reading strategies and learning outcomes in class in order to further enhance the student's reading competence." (Kolb, 2013: 41). In other words, Kolb's (2013) results as well as those of the present study suggest that a reflection on reading strategies in EFL classrooms with young learners is useful and indicate that such reflections are beneficial for enhancing successful strategy use.

Despite the rather high degree of awareness, the learners still used some reading strategies which they were not aware of. Possibly, some of these strategies were already well-known to the learners from L1 reading, such as 'turning pages' or 'summarising', so that using these strategies might have happened automatically and not have been available to conscious reflection any longer (also see Chapter 10.1.2). However, at least the FL reading strategy of 'translating into German' can clearly not be transferred from L1 reading. Therefore, such strategies really seem to be strategies that the learners were not aware of. At the same time, however, the learners had never been taught this strategy, but nevertheless used it unconsciously. This gives reason to assume that some learners might benefit from explicit teaching of strategies, as such an approach might make the learners more aware of strategies that they use already or those that they could use in future.

Another point with regard to awareness is that some learners were aware of certain strategies which others were not aware of. This goes to show that strategy use and also awareness of strategy use is highly individual and depends on the learners as well as the reading situation. As such, strategy use and the awareness of it might also depend on the individual books. The use of certain strategies might have been more dominant for one book than for another.

Inconsistencies in the data of the interviews and the questionnaire with regard to awareness might indicate that the young learners were at a stage where they started becoming aware of their strategies, but were not constantly aware of them. Particularly in the case of young learners, awareness might depend on factors such as concentration, mood or motivation to participate actively in the reading sessions and in the interviews/questionnaire. Also, as already discussed in Chapter 10.2, strategy use is individual and might change from book to book. Therefore, Natan might have mentioned a strategy in the interviews that he then denied using in the questionnaire because he did not use that strategy for all the books. In that case, inconsistencies between the different sources of data might be based on the fact that the learners did not apply all the strategies universally for all the books, but might have either used or left out certain strategies in specific cases. This should be regarded positively, since selecting strategies depending on the book indicates that the learners can purposefully choose certain strategies for certain reading texts.

When looking at the strategies that the learners were not aware of, there is no clear difference between cognitive, meta-cognitive, social and affective strategies. The number of unconsciously used strategies in each main category is similarly low (between one and five per category), which means that the learners were aware of a wide range of strategies across all the different categories. This complies with what researchers such as Pinter (2006: 112) suggest, in that they recommend that strategy use and awareness in all of these categories should be fostered with young learners in order to raise awareness about the learning process and develop successful language learning strategies.

Still, given the wide consensus that meta-cognition is not fully developed in young learners such as the participants in the study (see Lightbown & Spada, 2013: 36), it is striking that awareness about meta-cognitive reading strategies is not shown by the data to be any lower than awareness about other types of strategies. Maybe meta-cognitive reading strategies that are discussed right after reading a book are more present to young learners than more general meta-cognitive learning strategies that might be discussed without such a specific context. This, in return, indicates that it is beneficial to reflect on meta-cognitive strategies only in specific contexts and always present a certain situation or tasks to the learners when investigating and developing their use of meta-cognitive strategies. Pinter (2006: 100), too, emphasises the importance of having a specific context for meta-cognitive strategies to develop, in that she suggests prompting children to think about meta-cognitive strategies bound to specific tasks and learning experiences; a suggestion which is also applicable to other strategy categories. Nevertheless, it is notable that, going by the data, even young learners show awareness of meta-cognitive reading strategies despite a possible lack of more general meta-cognitive competences.

Taking a closer look at which strategies the learners were not aware of, it is noticeable that six of the eleven unconsciously used strategies were not investigated in the questionnaire. This means that there is a chance that a few or even all six strategies strategies might in fact have been used consciously, but as the questionnaire failed to focus the learners' attention on them, it was not possible to detect the learners' potential awareness of them. It is unfortunate that the learners might not have verbalised these strategies in the interviews because of potential difficulties with expressing them, and at the same time did not have the chance to reveal their awareness in the questionnaire (also see Footnote 213).

Generally, it is worth noting that the questionnaire revealed many strategies that the learners were aware of, while the interview did not offer such insights. Exactly this was the reason for using the questionnaire, which turned out to be an important instrument to complement the data from the observations and the interviews, as it provided data above all on the learners' awareness of strategy use. Since the learners stated in the questionnaire that they used strategies which they had not reported on before, the questionnaire might have played an important role in making young learners aware of certain strategies. Presenting reading strategies to the learners in a questionnaire thus seems linked to raising their awareness of them. Possibly this is due to the fact that the learners simply did not know how to express and verbalise certain strategies and partly might also not have known what strategies in reading really were. This finding seconds what Wendt (1997: 77) stated, namely that strategies which learners were not aware of using might become available to consciousness in retrospect when being asked about them (see Chapter 4.6.6). More so, these findings suggest that there is a fuzzy boundary between awareness and non-awareness of strategies, which is seemingly easy to cross. Despite criticism and doubts about young learners' abilities to reflect on their learning on a meta-level (see Chapter 4.6.7), the use of the questionnaire in the study has proven to be very beneficial in making strategies conscious to young learners and allowing them to reveal their strategy awareness. In follow-up studies it therefore seems advisable to use questionnaires, amongst other instruments, to investigate young learners' (reading) strategy use and awareness.[213]

Overall the results on the learners' awareness of strategy use show that mixed methods and a variety of different instruments are necessary to investigate young learners' use of reading strategies. Firstly, the learners used far more strategies than those that were observable. Therefore, observation data, even when backed up by video data, cannot provide clear insights into all the reading strategies that young learners use. Observation data also do not allow much insight into strategy awareness. The interviews were not fully satisfying either, as already mentioned, in that by means of the interviews it was difficult to find out about certain strategies that the learners might have been aware of, as suggestive questions such as "Did you predict what could come next?" might have led to answers motivated by social acceptability rather than to answers that reported on actual strategy use. Triggering the potentially conscious use of certain strategies in an interview was thus difficult. Therefore, the questionnaire proved to be a useful third instrument in the investigation of strategy use, and particularly the awareness of it. Using the questionnaire before and after the reading study might have given some insight into an increase of strategy use awareness, which was found by Kolb (2013: 41), but could not be investigated in the present study. Still, in sum, the triangulation of observation, interview and questionnaire data provides a detailed picture of young learners' strategy use and is thus recommendable for researching (reading) strategies.

10.4 A Connection between Strategy Use and Reading Comprehension

Chapter 10.3 has already shown that there was no clear-cut connection between the level of reading comprehension and strategy awareness. This chapter investigates a possible connection between the use of certain reading strategies and the level of reading comprehension (see Chapter 9). Instead of presenting detailed strategy profiles for each learner, the categorisation into 'weak', 'average' and 'strong' readers (see Chapter 9.4) will be used to summarise the learners into

---

213 Unfortunately, not all strategies that were used and investigated via observations and interviews prior to conducting the questionnaire were asked about in the questionnaire. The reason is that not all observation and interview data had been analysed by the time the questionnaire was compiled and conducted. Therefore, it remains somewhat unclear which of the observed strategies the learners might have been aware of if explicitly asked about them. In follow-up studies it would be beneficial to investigate all possible reading strategies that were found in the present study via a questionnaire.

groups according to their level of reading comprehension. Chapter 10.4.1 will present several aspects of strategy use that seem to be dependent on a certain level of reading comprehension and Chapter 10.4.2 will offer an interpretation and draw some conclusions.

Because of the small sample of only 11 participants, it was not possible to carry out statistical correlation research with the data. With a larger sample it would be possible to identify statistically significant correlations between a certain level of reading comprehension and the use of certain strategies. However, for the present study the approach to analysing the data will be primarily qualitative, and quantified data will be provided only when possible and only descriptively.

10.4.1 Presentation of Results

When looking at the data on reading comprehension and reading strategies, several aspects are noticeable with regard to a possible connection between the two. Table 30 provides an overview of those strategies that seemed to be connected to a certain level of reading comprehension.

Table 30: Overview of strategies that seem to be connected to a certain level or reading comprehension.

	Weak readers (Ali, Simone)	Average readers (Natan, Jonas, Lara, Neele, Ina)	Strong readers (Rico, Max, Dani, Emil)
Meta-cognitive reading strategies	Following the text with a finger		
Cognitive reading strategies			Getting an overview
		Elaboration: using previous knowledge	
		Resourcing: using the word list	
	Resourcing: audio-recording		
	Semi-vocalisation		
		Decoding an unknown word by its context	
	Decoding an unknown word via L1 similarities		
Social reading strategies	Questioning for clarification		
		Eagerness to express understanding	
		Expressing difficulties	
	Seeking orientation		

On the left side of the table one can see those strategies that tended to be used more by weak readers, on the right side one can see those that were rather used by strong readers.[214] When looking at the classification of these strategies into the four main categories (meta-cognitive, cognitive, social and affective strategies), no clear pattern with regard to a certain strategy category in connection to a level of reading comprehension can be found. However, no affective reading strategy was used more by one group of readers than another. The following paragraphs will firstly present those strategies that were only used by weak and average readers and then continue with those that were mostly used by strong readers.

The weak and partly also the average readers used six strategies that the better readers did not apply. The first one is the meta-cognitive reading strategy of following the text with a finger. This was continuously done by Simone, but also Ali, Jonas and Ina used this strategy regularly. Therefore, both weak and two of the average readers used this strategy, while the strong readers did not.

The same holds true for the cognitive resourcing strategy of listening to an audio-recording while reading, which was regularly done by Lara and Ali who both used the audio-recording for almost all the books. While Ali is a weak reader, Lara was able to improve her reading skills with the audio-recording and was eventually classified as an average reader (see Chapter 10.1.5). Also Natan, Neele, Ina (average readers) and Rico (strong reader), used the audio-recording once but rejected it again. Lara and Ali share another similarity, and that is their difficulty with tolerating ambiguity (see Chapters 10.1.1 and 10.2). Thus, using the audio-recording is not necessarily a strategy chosen by weaker readers, but possibly rather by readers that cannot tolerate ambiguity. In fact, the other weak reader, Simone, never used it.

Another cognitive strategy that is closely connected to the auditory representation of a text is that of semi-vocalisation. This strategy was used continuously by those readers that struggled with reading and that were weak or at most average: Ali, Simone and Jonas. In fact, Simone semi-vocalised every bit of each reading text while Jonas applied semi-vocalisation often, but not continuously. Ali also semi-vocalised regularly, but as he listened to the audio-recording he not did so as much as the other two. More advanced readers only used this strategy for selected and particularly difficult words.

---

214   The strategies listed at both sides of the pole were partly also used by the average readers. But for a comparison of reading comprehension and strategy use it seemed more interesting to look at the extreme sides. However, the average readers were still taken into consideration and will be mentioned in the explanation.

Three further strategies were only applied by weak or average readers. Firstly, the cognitive strategy of using L1 similarities to decode unknown words was only used by Ali (weak reader) and Natan (average reader). Moreover, weaker and occasionally also average readers more frequently asked clarification questions, either general ones or vocabulary questions. Lastly, the social strategy of seeking orientation, in that a reader looked at other readers or me as the researcher, was only done by the weak and average readers.

Two further aspects could only be found with individual readers and were thus not displayed in the table above. Firstly, the weak reader Simone used almost no inferencing strategies while all strong readers used and were aware of a number of them. However, the other weak reader, Ali, also used different inferencing strategies. Thus, a lack of inferencing strategies might be linked to weak reading skills, but not necessarily. Similarly, the weak reader Ali hardly had any tolerance of ambiguity, which most other readers, including the other weak reader Simone, did have. Thus, a lack of ambiguity tolerance might be an indicator of weak reading skills, but is not necessarily one.

Another six strategies were used mostly by the strong readers. Firstly, the weak readers did not really apply any strategies for getting an overview before reading. Simone only once briefly skimmed through a book before reading it and Ali ticked a statement in the questionnaire indicating that he would look at the title of a book before reading it. By contrast, the average and strong readers used a number of different strategies to get an initial overview before they read a book.

Also the strategy of using previous knowledge was used by strong rather than by weak readers. According to the data, strategies of using previous knowledge were consistently applied by the strong readers: Dani, Max, Rico and Emil showed evidence of using their previous knowledge, for example of a trip to London or of reading other books, Likewise, some average readers were found to do so as well. Only once did the weak reader Ali exhibit the use of previous knowledge, which was his explanation for why he knew 'ginger ale' (see Chapter 9.2.2.1).

The word list as a cognitive resourcing strategy, too, was mostly used by the average and stronger readers, and indeed, for the most part by the average readers. By contrast, the weak readers only occasionally looked at it, but did not really use it as a supportive device to compensate for a lack of vocabulary knowledge. The weak reader Simone only used it after Dani, a strong reader, had shown it to her and suggested that she should use it to look up unknown words.

Three further strategies were not used by the weak readers but only by the average and strong ones. Firstly, the decoding strategy of using the context to figure out the meaning of an unknown word was used by all the strong and some average readers, but not by weak readers. Lastly, two social strategies were only used by the average and strong readers, and these were eagerness to express understanding as well as the tendency to express difficulties. The weak readers used neither of these strategies.

In addition to a comparison of strategies that were used more so by one group than another, also a more general picture of the overall number of reading strategies per reader was investigated. Figure 36 provides an overview:

Figure 36: Number of reading strategies used by each learner, divided into the three different groups of comprehension levels: weak (left), average (middle), strong (right).

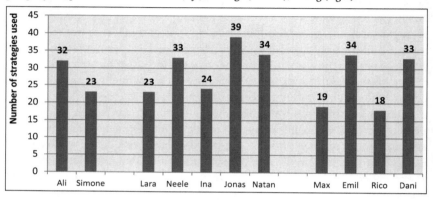

The figure shows the number of reading strategies that were used by the individual learners, categorised into weak, average and strong readers. The overall number of reading strategies ranges from 18 to 39 reading strategies. The weak readers used 23 to 32 strategies, the average readers 23 to 39 and the strong ones between 18 and 34. Therefore, there is no clear pattern with regard to the number of strategies and the level of reading competence. A low number of strategies is found in all three categories, but similarly a high number of strategies is as well. Hence, there is no connection between the number of strategies a learner uses and his/her level of reading comprehension. In other words, the total number of reading strategies is in no way an indicator for the level of reading competence in this study.

Two of the strong FL readers, indeed, seem to not have used many strategies: Rico and Max. Rico only used 18 strategies in total, Max used 19. In the questionnaire, both of them only indicated a very low number, three (Max) and seven (Rico) strategies respectively. Independently of each other, both said that they did not use most of the strategies that were listed in the questionnaire and proudly told me that they did not need all these strategies because they could just read the texts without them. Looking at their strategy awareness, particularly Max, as already indicated in Chapter 10.3.1, was also by far the least aware of his reading strategies.

In a last step, the use of strategies from certain categories was investigated amongst the three different proficiency levels. Figure 37 shows which learners used strategies from which main categories, given in percentages to allow a comparison across the learners and groups.

Figure 37: Percentage of each learner's reading strategies divided by the four main categories of meta-cognitive, cognitive, social and affective strategies as well as the learners' level of reading comprehension: weak (left), average (middle), strong (right).

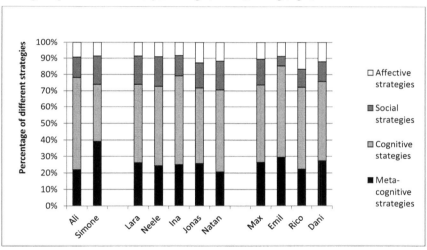

The figure shows that most of the learners used around 25 % meta-cognitive strategies, 50 % cognitive strategies, 10 to 15 % social and 10 to 15 % affective strategies, except for Simone, who used more meta-cognitive strategies than the others and at the same time fewer cognitive ones. Therefore, there seem to be no notable differences between the percentages of strategies of a certain strategy type across the learners, so that there is also no clear pattern in the use of certain types of reading strategies and a low, average or high level or reading comprehension.

10.4.2 Interpretation and Discussion of Results

The weak and partly also average readers displayed some strategies that the strong readers did not really use. When looking at the notion of strategies on a continuum as outlined in Chapter 4.6.6, one can see that many of the strategies that only the weak readers applied were those that display difficulties with reading. This holds true for the strategies of following the text with a finger, listening to an audio-recording while reading and semi-vocalisation. These are still effective strategies, because they allow the weak readers to master the task of reading, but the use of such strategies tells teachers and researchers that the learners still face difficulties with reading and need further support. Asking others for clarification or seeking for orientation by looking at others are strategies, too, that weaker readers need more than stronger ones, as already advanced readers might not have questions or insecurities about reading any longer. Some strategies thus seem more prominent and more important for weaker readers, because stronger readers are more successful at reading and thus do not need certain strategies that tend to occur with still-developing reading skills any longer.

Other strategies were mostly used by strong readers. For example, the weaker readers, in contrast to the stronger ones, were neither eager to express their comprehension nor admitted any difficulties with reading. This might show that the weaker readers were aware of their difficulties but tried to keep them to themselves. By contrast, the stronger readers were eager to express what they had understood and did at the same time not mind mentioning potential difficulties. While it might thus not matter to strong readers to admit slight difficulties, it might be a strategy of weaker learners to keep silent in order to not reveal their problems.

Overall, it would also be interesting to see to what extent explicit training in reading strategies might support reading comprehension and might be beneficial for weaker readers. This notion is supported by the situation of Dani and Simone, where Dani as a strong reader encouraged Simone to use the word list, which she then did a few times. More continuous practice and maybe also some guidance in how to use the word lists might therefore help weaker readers to learn to use this device skilfully. Based on this, some strategies might be worth teaching, particularly to those learners that have not yet developed good FL reading skills. Such strategies could include getting an overview of a text before reading it or making use of previous knowledge. This might seem obvious to already experienced readers, but young readers who are still developing their reading competence might need to be made explicitly aware of such strategies in order to apply them. It would be interesting to know whether less advanced readers already use such strategies in L1 reading, since if not, it might be worth looking at L1 reading strategy use first to facilitate transfer of some universal reading strategies to L2 reading.

However, some strategies which weak readers do not apply yet might be too difficult for them. Chamot (2005: 120) noted that low proficiency learners might need a focus on bottom-up processing strategies instead of more complex top-down strategies. For example, using the context to hypothesise about the meaning of an unknown word might not be applied by weaker readers: Since this group focuses strongly on decoding single words, the demands of looking at the context as well could well be too high, especially as this is a strategy that depends to a certain extent on word decoding skills, fluency and automaticity in reading. Similar difficulties might hold true for using the word list. If too many words are unknown, the word list might not help weaker readers as it only provides information about some of the words. Still, making such strategies explicit to weaker readers might give them an idea of different strategies that can be applied to decode unknown words. Therefore, weaker readers, such as Simone, might need a number of different inferencing and resourcing strategies that can help them to overcome potential language difficulties.

Some strategies that weaker readers were found to use but stronger ones not might be connected to automatisation of reading strategies. The more a skill becomes automatised through practice and experience, the more probable it is that actual knowledge about that skill may be forgotten (Lightbown & Spada, 2013: 109). This might hold true for the strategy of using L1 similarities to decode unknown words, as mostly done by weak readers in the study. Searching for L1 similarities seems a rather basic FL reading strategy that more advanced readers probably use as well, but might not be aware of any longer. However, more advanced readers might also be more experienced with failure in decoding words via L1 similarities and might thus not rely on that strategy too much but instead have developed more successful strategies for decoding the FL. Also the fact that Rico and Max did not use many strategies at all and deliberately ticked most items of the questionnaire as 'not used' might show that they have automatised many of their reading strategies and were not consciously aware of applying them anymore. This is underlined by the fact that they only indicated a very low number of strategies which they used consciously. A similar finding was made by O'Malley and Chamot (1990: 118) in their study on learning strategies with high school learners. They found that beginner level students who were less advanced identified more strategies than more advanced learners. O'Malley and Chamot (1990) speculated that the difficulty of the task might play a role in this respect. It is possible that with more difficult texts, for which strong readers such as Max and Rico might need to apply different strategies more deliberately, the strategy use of these learners would become more apparent. Overall, however, the automatisation of the FL reading strategies of the strong readers is a positive sign, as it provides evidence for their good FL reading abilities.

In any event, the present study has shown that the number of strategies used does not correlate with reading comprehension levels; other factors of strategy use seem to be more important in this regard. This was also established by Fink-beiner et al. (2012: 60), who found that it is neither the total number, nor the va-riety or the frequency of strategies that lead to success, but more so the suitability and the success of the strategies employed. In this respect, Steck (2009: 104) ar-gues that poor readers often do not know how to utilise their reading strategies skilfully for the maximum benefit in the situation and task at hand. Both these findings from previous research are fully corroborated by the evidence from the current study. Still, it is certainly beneficial to have a variety of different reading strategies that can be chosen from, so that, depending on the text or task, learn-ers can apply the strategy or strategies that best support successful reading.

In contrast to O'Malley et al.'s (1985: 37) finding that intermediate level stu-dents used more meta-cognitive strategies than students with beginning level proficiency, the present study has shown that a certain level of comprehension is not linked to the use of certain categories of meta-cognitive, cognitive, social and affective strategies. However, O'Malley et al.'s (1985) study was concerned with learning strategies in general and not bound to reading strategies. Thus, with regard to the FL reading of young learners, other factors apart from the use of strategies from a certain category must play a role in effective FL reading.

10.5 Summary of Central Results and Answer to Research Question II

First of all, the present study has shown the importance of using different in-struments and various measurements, including the observation, the videos, the interviews as well as some back-up data from the questionnaires, in order to thoroughly research young learners' reading strategies. It is difficult to inves-tigate reading strategies, particularly those of young learners, and thus mixed methods and triangulation is needed in order to get a clearer picture of strategy use.

Overall, the learners used a wide range of different strategies. These covered all the categories of meta-cognitive, cognitive, social and affective strategies that had already been described in Chapter 4.6.5. Many of these strategies had al-ready been found in previous studies, particularly with older and more advanced learners, but some strategies seem to be unique to young learners and beginner learners. These include above all certain social and affective strategies such as sharing emotions or seeking orientation, or meta-cognitive strategies such as following the text with a finger.

Development of strategy use could be found to a limited extent in the study. In order to enhance and support this with young learners, some explicit instruction might be necessary, at least for some learners. Because strategy use is highly individual and depends on factors such as the individual learner, the specific task or the setting, it is advisable to offer young EFL learners a broad range of possible strategies in order to allow them to choose the strategies that are most useful for them. However, keeping in mind that it is not the number of different strategies but rather the extent to which they were applied successfully and appropriately, these aspects should be reflected on with the learners. With regard to teaching vocabulary learning strategies to young learners, Schick (2016) suggests referring to them as 'tricks'. This child-friendly approach can also be followed with regard to teaching FL reading strategies. However, careful attention should be paid to the learners' L1 reading strategies, because these might have to be developed prior to a successful transfer to FL reading (also see Chapter 4.2 on the interdependence hypothesis).

Despite the common argument that young learners are not yet able to reflect on their learning on a meta-level and hence apparently have a low level of awareness with regard to strategy use (see Chapter 4.6.7), the learners in the present study were generally aware of a large number of reading strategies. Their awareness seemed to increase by filling out the questionnaire, probably because it listed a number of strategies and thus made them explicit to the learners. Indeed, the participants sometimes showed difficulties with verbalising certain strategies during the interviews. However, as mentioned above, FL learners might become more aware of reading strategies through explicit teaching and through regular reflection phases on these.

Lastly, the study tried to establish a connection between the use of reading strategies and the level of reading comprehension. This was difficult in that the sample was too small to allow for statistical procedures and the data did not always yield discernible patterns. Certainly, the number of strategies does not correlate with success in reading in the study. The same holds true for applying strategies of a certain category. Still, some strategies seemed to be used only by more advanced readers, while others were used more by weaker ones. In order to support the effective strategy use of weaker readers, some explicit teaching as well cooperative reading with a weaker and a stronger reader might be necessary to raise the weaker readers' awareness of different (successful strategies) and to support a critical reflection on effective reading processes. However, in these data there was no evident link between awareness of reading strategies and successful reading comprehension.

Overall, the results allow the following answers to research question II (*Which reading strategies do young EFL learners apply when reading authentic English picture books for understanding?*):

- Year 4 learners use a wide range of different FL reading strategies.
- Young EFL learners apply reading strategies from all different categories; meta-cognitive, cognitive, social and affective strategies, irrespective of their reading comprehension level.
- The use of reading strategies is highly individual and depends on the individual learners as well as the situations and tasks.
- Some strategies have already been described for older or more advanced learners; some seem to be unique to young and beginner learners.
- The number of strategies does not correlate with a certain level of reading comprehension.
- Strategy use developed to a limited extent during the course of the project. Explicit teaching and awareness-raising might be necessary to further enhance the development of FL reading strategies.
- Some learners already possessed an effective set of FL reading strategies; development did not occur, but was also not necessary.
- Some strategies used by advanced FL readers could possibly be taught to weaker FL readers.
- Most learners were aware of a large number of their reading strategies. This was irrespective of their level of reading comprehension.
- Awareness was partly triggered through the questionnaire on reading strategies, which made strategies explicit to the learners, particularly strategies which they might not have been aware of or might not have known how to express before.
- Strategy awareness does not noticeably correlate with FL reading competence.
- Mixed methods are needed to investigate young learners' reading strategies thoroughly.

Apart from answering the research question and related key aspects, these points can also be understood as hypotheses for further investigation in research on young learners' FL reading strategies, with a different and possibly larger sample.

11. FL Performance: Presentation, Interpretation and Discussion of Results for Research Question III

Abstract: This chapter presents, interprets and discusses the study's results for focus III: FL performance. Results are presented as average scores as well as with the scores divided by the three different word categories and by the three areas of language competence. An influence of reading comprehension on these scores is discussed.

The last focus of this study was on FL performance. This was treated as a subsidiary research question and was not investigated in as much detail as research questions I and II. Research question III as well as the key aspect investigated are presented in Table 31:

Table 31: Reiteration of research question III including the investigated key aspect.

Focus	Research question	Key aspect investigated
III FL performance	**(III) To what extent does the reading of authentic English picture books influence the FL performance of EFL learners in Year 4?**	→ FL performance of the reading group compared to that of the control group

The reading group's and the control group's FL performances were measured at three points over the data collection process, after each of the three thematic units: 'London', 'Shopping' and 'Christmas and Winter' (see Chapter 7.3.4). For each topic, a topic-based language test (see Chapter 8.4) investigated the FL performance of both groups. These tests consisted of eight tasks each and covered the language competence areas of orthographic, semantic and syntactic morphemic knowledge (see Chapter 8.4.2). For each task, language items from three different word categories were chosen: category A (topic words used in the EFL classroom), category B (general words most frequent in English books and in English picture books) and category C (the most frequent words from the picture books read with the reading group) (see Chapter 8.4.1). The structure of the tests was the same for all three topics and a maximum score of 44 points could be achieved on each test (see Chapter 8.4.2). A detailed overview of all results including the scoring of each task can be found in Appendix D.6.

Both groups took these tests (see Chapter 7.2.4), but only the reading group had had the weekly reading sessions; the control group had continued with their regular English lessons (see Chapter 7.3.3). Prior to the data collection, the groups had been comparable to a certain extent (see Chapter 7.2).[215] Thus, the test results for the respective groups should indicate whether FL performance on the three topics had been influenced by the reading sessions.

11.1 Presentation of Results

In this subchapter, firstly, both groups' average scores on each test will be presented. After that the results are presented according to the three different word categories (A, B, C) and possible differences between the reading and control group are explored in this regard. Lastly, Chapter 11.1.3 presents both groups' results according to the three different areas of FL competence as investigated via the tests. The results of the tests will all be provided in percentages, as the maximum scores on each word category as well as the maximum scores on each component of FL competence differed slightly.[216] Thus, percentages offer a better overview than raw frequencies.

11.1.1 Average Scores on the Tests

Firstly, Table 32 gives an overview of both groups' overall performance on the tests and provides the average scores as well as their standard deviation.

---

215 The insignificant difference in performance on the YLE test, however, which was about 10 % between the groups, with the reading group scoring higher, might play a role in the results on FL performance as presented in this chapter and will be critically considered in the interpretation and discussion of results. A more general discussion about the value of the results is found in Chapter 12.2.

216 The maximum score on orthography was 17 points, the maximum score on semantic knowledge was 18 points and the maximum score on syntactic morphemic knowledge was 9 points. Also the points per word category differed slightly, as the maximum score in word category A was 15 points, while the maximum scores in word categories B and C were 14.5 points each.

Table 32: Mean and standard deviation of both groups on the three language tests, in raw frequencies and in percent.

	Topic: London (max. score 44 points)	Topic: Shopping (max. score 44 points)	Topic: Christmas & Winter (max. score 44 points)
Reading group	M = 30.5 points (≙ 69.3 %) SD = 8.0 (≙ 18.2 %)	M = 31 points (≙ 70.4 %) SD = 9.0 (≙ 20.5 %)	M = 28.3 points (≙ 64.4 %) SD = 9.0 (≙ 20.5 %)
Control group	M = 25 points (≙ 56.8 %) SD = 8.3 (≙ 18.7 %)	M = 25.9 points (≙ 59 %) SD = 6.6 (≙ 15 %)	M = 22.6 points (≙ 51.4 %) SD = 5.7 (≙ 13 %)

For a better overview, Figure 38 visualises both groups' average scores:

Figure 38: Reading and control group's average scores on the topic-based language tests (in percent and in points).

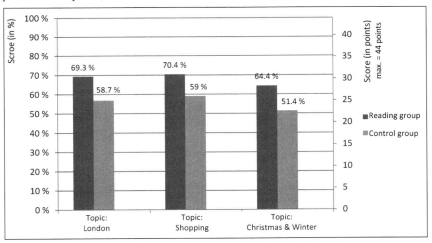

The figure clearly shows that in each test the reading group performed better than the control group. The reading group achieved an average of 69.3 % on the topic 'London', an average of 70.4 % on the topic 'Shopping' and an average of 64.4 % on the topic 'Christmas and Winter'. The control group achieved 10 to 13 % less on each test. Therefore, on all three topics, the reading group was superior to the control group in their performance on the language tests.

Looking back at Table 32, one can see that across the participants the individual performance on the tests differed noticeably, as indicated by the standard deviation of the overall results. The deviation ranges between about 13 and 20 %, with the reading group's results ranging slightly more than those of the control group, particularly on the last two tests. As this suggests that each individual learner's results might add valuable information in terms of understanding the overall results, Figure 39 shows each learner's average result on the three tests.[217]

Figure 39: The reading group learners' average performance on the three topic-based language tests (in %).

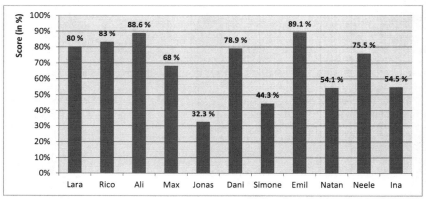

Figure 26 shows that the average scores of the reading group learners range from 32.3 % to 89.1 %, which is a difference of almost 60 %. The learners that scored the lowest are Jonas and Simone, with roughly 32 and 44 % respectively. Natan and Ina's average scores, at only just over 50 %, are also relatively low. All the other learners scored in the region of 70 to 90 %. In view of the differences in these individual average results, the wide range of the reading group's results on the language tests is not surprising.

Summing up these results, the performance of the reading group's participants on the language tests varies slightly more than that of the control group, but still the reading group outperformed the control group on all three tests.

---

217 As the control group did not receive the regular reading sessions, their average results and their range are not as relevant and will thus not be displayed here. However, both are found in Appendix E.8.

11.1.2 Scores Divided by Word Categories

To gain a better insight into the results, Figure 40 shows the results of the tests according to the three different word categories (see above and Chapter 8.4.1).

Figure 40: Average scores (in percent) on all three tests separated by the different word categories.

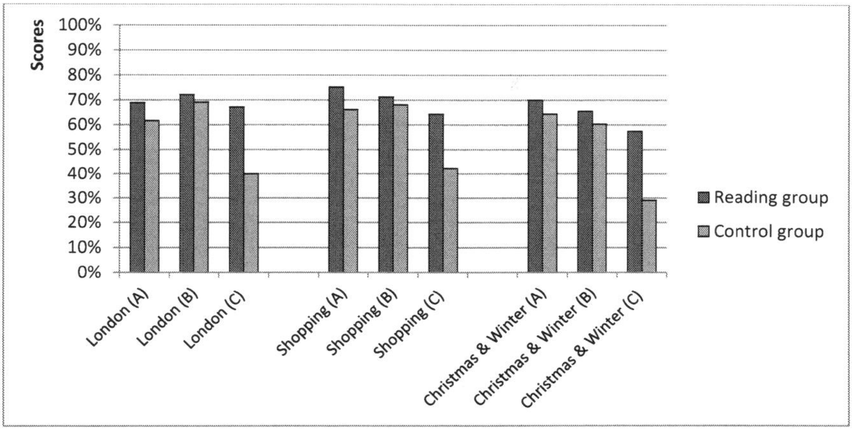

Figure 40 shows that the reading group performed better than the control group on all topics and in all three word categories, but to varying degrees. In word categories A and B, the differences are relatively small. By contrast, though unsurprisingly (see Chapter 11.2), there is a marked difference in the results for word category C;[218] the tasks with words based on the picture books read by the reading group. The reading group was nevertheless also superior to the control group in the other two word categories.

The next subchapter will further investigate the reading group's superior performance to that of the control group, exploring in detail the three different areas of FL competence that were tested alongside the different word categories.

11.1.3 Scores Divided by Areas of FL Competence

The language tests investigated three different areas of FL competence: orthographic, semantic and syntactic morphemic knowledge. For a more detailed insight into

---

218 No t-test analysis was done at this point as, in view of the small sample size, the significance of t-test results would have been questionable. The same holds true for the t-test that was done for the YLE test, as discussed in Chapter 7.2.4.

the differences between the two groups, this subchapter examine the groups' performances in these three different areas of FL competence. This examination also takes into consideration the three different word categories that were used to compile the tests. This differentiation will provide some insight into whether the better performance of the reading group is based on a certain area of FL competence or whether it is more generally found across all areas.

To begin with orthography, Figure 41 displays the results of the participants' performance in this area. The exact percentages can be found in Appendix D.6.

Figure 41: Scores (in percent) in the area of 'orthographic knowledge' on the three topic-based language tests separated by word categories A, B and C.

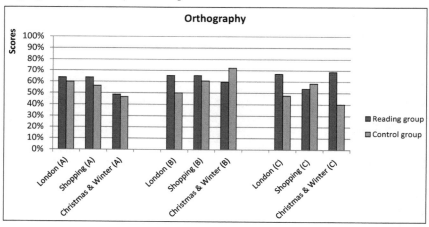

The results for orthographic competence in the different word categories are mixed. In seven cases, the reading group scored better than the control group. In four cases, however, the differences seem minor and the reading group was only slightly better than the control group: 'London (A)', 'Shopping (A)', 'Christmas and Winter (A)' and 'Shopping (B)'. Nevertheless, in the other three cases, the reading group was much better than the control group and showed strikingly better results: 'London (B)', 'London (C)' and particularly 'Christmas and Winter (C)'. At the same time, however, the control group outperformed the reading group in two cases. Firstly, on the 'Christmas and Winter' test (B), the control group was clearly better in the area of orthography. Secondly, in 'Shopping (C)', the control group had slightly better results. Although the difference is not remarkable, the reading group was actually not generally superior to the control group in word category C (see previous subchapter), but the control group outperformed the reading group in the area of orthography on the topic 'Shopping' by about 5 %. In sum, although the results for orthographic knowledge are in some respects inconclusive, in general they tend to be slightly better for the reading group. Nevertheless, the reading group's results are not always noticeably superior; in places they are very close to or worse than the control group's results.

Turning now to semantic knowledge, Figure 42 displays the results for these elements of the tests.

Figure 42: Scores (in percent) in the area of 'semantic knowledge' on the three topic-based language tests separated by word categories A, B and C.

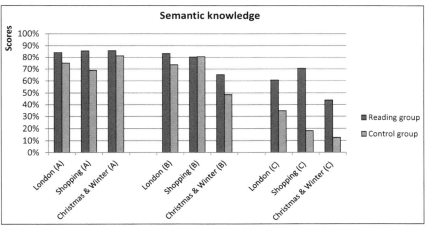

The diagram shows that except for the semantic category 'Shopping (B)', in which the control group was minimally better, the reading group outperformed the control group. In word categories A and B, the differences between the reading and control groups are overall not as slight as the differences in orthographic knowledge were. A noticeable difference between the reading and control group can be seen in word category C, which consisted of the tasks with words taken from the picture books. The learners in the reading group strongly outperformed the control group in semantic knowledge on all three topics. The exact percentages can be found in Appendix D.6.

Finally, the results for syntactic morphemic knowledge are shown in Figure 43.

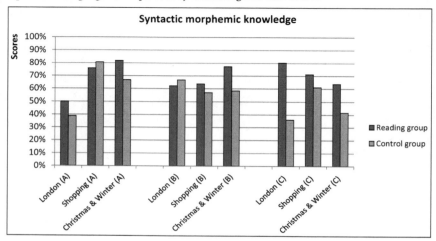

Figure 43: Scores (in percent) in the area of 'syntactic morphemic knowledge' on the three topic-based language tests separated by word categories A, B and C.

Figure 43 shows that the results for syntactic morphemic knowledge are mixed in word categories A and B. While the reading group was better in four parts, the control group was better in the remaining two. Still, the slight difference between the groups appears to be in favour of the reading group, which outperformed the control group more often and more noticeably.

However, category C shows a visible difference between the groups. In word category C, the reading group was clearly superior to the control group on all three topics. Indeed, on the topic 'London', the reading group performed twice as well as the control group. The difference in the topic 'Christmas and Winter' is also clearly noticeable, while the difference in the topic 'Shopping' is not as high as the other two, yet still obvious.

To sum up the results of this chapter, the reading group was superior to the control group in many parts of all three tests. While they outperformed the control group in the areas of semantics and syntactic morphemic knowledge, the results in orthographic competence are less distinct. Overall, this might indicate that reading the picture books had a positive influence on the learners' development of FL competence. This will be discussed in the following subchapter.

11.2 Interpretation and Discussion of Results

Overall, the reading group's performance on the topic-based language tests was better than the control group's performance. The reading group outperformed the control group on all three tests with a better average score of around 10 to 13 % (see Figure 38). This result indicates that the reading group's FL competence and development benefited from the regular reading of picture books and the participants were able to improve their FL performance slightly more than the control group, which was not engaged in regular reading. Thus, this study provides some of the first and tentative evidence that reading can have a positive effect on young learners' EFL development in different areas of language competence, as shown by the topic-based language tests that were used for this study.

This finding partly contradicts Biebricher's (2008: 36) study with Year 8 learners in a German secondary school, which found that 15 minutes of extensive reading per week did not have a clear effect on the learners' FL development. However, her study was conducted with older learners, the approach to reading was different in terms of extent and time, and she used standardised tests and statistical correlations to collect data on FL development; thus, the context and research instrument differed considerably. Be that as it may, in contrast to Biebricher's (2008) study, the present study has been able to show differences in FL performance in favour of the reading group. Potentially, besides factors of context and research design, also the factor of the age of the learners might be a decisive factor in FL development through reading, in that young learners might still be more open towards the FL as well as less reluctant and inhibited in dealing with it (see Saville-Troike, 2006: 82).

The reading group did not only outperform the control group in general, but also outperformed them in all word categories that were used for the tests. In particular, the reading group's FL performance was better than that of the control group in word category C, which consisted of words taken directly from the picture books. This does not seem surprising, because the control group did not read the books. However, the reading group did also not show any deficits in word categories A and B – topic-related words from the classroom and from the topic as such – although they missed one English lesson out of three each week in order to take part in the reading sessions, while the control group had all regular lessons. On the contrary, it appears that in the other two word categories, A and B, the reading group was able to draw level with the control group or even perform slightly better than them.

This finding could suggest that through regular reading, topic-based FL competence can be improved not only as far as the language of the books that were read (category C) is concerned, but also in terms of language that is part of the same thematic area yet infrequent or not existent in the books (categories A and B). The results under discussion thus indicate that words that were neither frequent nor in the texts at all were processed slightly better by the reading group. This is an interesting finding which tentatively suggests that reading not only supports learners' FL knowledge of words related to the books but also of other lexical items. Possibly, topic-based reading coupled with topic-based post-reading activities support the learners' FL acquisition and deepen the topic-related vocabulary that was part of the regular English lessons but not – or not of high-frequency[219] – in the books. It is also conceivable that the extensive use of written language, which is not common in the primary school EFL classroom (see Chapter 3.2) but was focused on in reading the picture books, is generally supportive for young learners' awareness of the target language and, therefore, also supports the learners at a more general level in the acquisition of words. This, however, is speculative and needs further investigation. However, apart from the areas of semantic, orthographic and syntactic morphemic knowledge, other FL competences, such as speaking or listening, were not tested in the present study. These, though, might have been more positively influenced by the regular classroom instead of the reading sessions. While this also requires future reserach, teachers should generally pay careful attention to holistic FL development when introducing enhanced reading activities with young learners, in that the reading and its potential gains should not interfere with the acquisition of other FL skills.

To sum up, regular reading appears not to prevent learners from acquiring the FL knowledge that would be acquired in regular classroom lessons. On the contrary, reading seems to develop the learners' FL knowledge not only in terms of what they acquire from the books, but also in terms of lexis acquired from regular classroom teaching. As such, regular reading seems beneficial for young learners' overall FL development.

---

219 As outlined in Chapter 5.4.3, several researchers have stated that the frequency with which a word occurs in a text is important for remembering that word (e.g., Jenkins et al., 1984: 782; Waring & Takaki, 2003: 150f). In the books used for this study (see Chapter 8.1.1), only about ten words per book show a frequency of ten occurrences or higher (see Chapter 5.4.3 on previous results on word frequency). The number of words with a frequency higher than ten is as follows in each of the books used in the present study: 'The Queen's Knickers': 6 words; 'Paddington at the Palace': 14 words; 'Five Little Monkeys': 10 words; 'Something Good': 18 words; 'Froggy's Best Christmas': 14 words; 'Winnie in Winter': 10 words. Many of these words, however, are words which are probably known to children already, such as 'and', 'of' or 'the'.

If one examines the three different areas of language competence, orthography, semantics and syntactic morphemic knowledge in turn, the results are however more mixed than at a more general level. Orthography, for instance, did not seem to improve through reading as much as semantic and syntactic morphemic knowledge did. In the area of orthography, both groups were more or less comparable. The reading group appeared to be slightly better than the control group at first sight, but in fact, the differences were minimal for the most part. Even the words that came directly from the books were not spelt noticeably better by the reading group. Therefore, the regular reading of picture books did not have a perceptible impact on the learners' orthography in this study. The results do not show a clear trend, either across the topics or when comparing the results by the different word categories. Hence, reading appeared not to influence orthographic skills in this study. This finding supports Lightbown et al.'s (2002: 452) findings, which showed that pupils overlook target language features, such as spelling, while reading for comprehension. At the same time, the finding contradicts Krashen's (1989: 441) claim that more reading is associated with greater competence in spelling (see Chapter 5.4.3). However, it is possible that not enough reading was done to accord with Krashen's ideas.

The process by which good readers approach and read texts (see Chapters 4.1 and 4.4) might also explain why improvement of spelling through reading might be a myth. Advanced readers do not read word for word and do not decode most words letter by letter; instead, their word recognition is automatised so that they read in larger units (saccades) and construct overall text meaning through top-down processes and a constant process of summarisation. Therefore, good readers do not often focus on aspects at the actual linguistic text level, such as orthography, because they focus more on the automatic recognition of words and on constructing overall text meaning. Consequently, developing spelling skills via reading for comprehension seems unrealistic because the focus of reading is not on the exact spelling of words. Thus, orthography might best be practised in other activities in the EFL classroom. Such activities might need a stronger focus on bottom-up processing or linguistic factors at the letter or word level. Nevertheless, regular reading did not have a negative effect on the learners' orthography, which should be regarded as positive in that increased reading activities appear not to lead to deficits in the area of orthography.

In contrast to orthography, the reading group outperformed the control group in semantic knowledge on all three topics. In particular, the reading group appeared to have gained vocabulary from the books that they read, as they performed markedly better in word category C in comparison to the control group.

However, the reading group was also better than the control group in the other two word categories, A and B. Therefore, the results show that through the reading of picture books the vocabulary of the learners improved and they gained more semantic knowledge than the control group did.

This finding supports the common belief that vocabulary is broadened through reading (see Chapter 5.4.3). Hu Hsueh-chao and Nation (2000: 403), for example, hold the view that new words are learnt through reading. Despite critical factors such as frequency, consciousness and reading comprehension (see Chapter 5.4.3), the semantic knowledge of the learners in the present study appears to have benefited from the regular reading.[220] Therefore, Krashen's (1989: 440) idea that learners acquire vocabulary knowledge as a side effect of reading for comprehension can be confirmed by these findings. Future research could show whether vocabulary learning through reading could be improved further when factors such as frequency, consciousness and activities which aim at improving semantic knowledge are taken into consideration in reading settings.

It is interesting to see that the learners not only outperformed the control group in word category C, but the reading group's performance was also better in word categories A and B. In other words, the reading group did not lag behind the control group when it came to lexical items that were not frequent in the books, although they missed every third regular English lesson. This concurs with the finding that the reading group was superior to the control group in all three word categories in general. Potentially, increased reading also supports the acquisition of topic-based vocabulary that was not prominent in the book but could be contextualised via the story because of the shared thematic focus. Clearly, reading did not prevent the reading group from acquiring the vocabulary which they would also have acquired during their regular English lessons; rather, regular reading allowed them to learn these lexical items well, plus add further semantic knowledge from the picture books.

The reading group also outperformed the control group in syntactic morphemic knowledge in word category C. While the reading group mostly performed better in word categories A and B, without spectacularly outperforming the control group, they were undoubtedly better in the syntactic morphemic knowledge of word category C. This provides preliminary evidence that reading

---

220 Unfortunately, the data do not allow an insight into the number of words that was acquired via reading. This question needs to be investigated in a follow-up study with a slightly different research design, including a pre- and post-test vocabulary investigation.

books enhances the syntactic morphemic competence of young FL learners and allows them insight into the language system at the sentence level. The reading group's learners were better able to form syntactically and morphemically correct sentences than the control group, which suggests that the reading supported this area of FL competence. This finding partly opposes Lightbown et al.'s (2002: 452) finding, as their study found that grammatical features are overlooked in reading. Maybe particular grammatical features such as grammatical endings, which the aforementioned study tested, might be overlooked, but the reading group showed that they profited from reading in terms of syntactic morphemic knowledge at a more general level.

Overall, the results as ordered by areas of FL competence confirm that the reading group performed better than the control group, particularly in category C. The reading group clearly gained FL knowledge related to the words that derived from the books. However, the differences in FL performance are mostly found in the areas of semantic and syntactic morphemic knowledge. There are no such clear differences in orthographic knowledge. This provides support for the notion that, in FLL, semantic as well as syntactic morphemic knowledge increases through reading, even at the beginner stage. In addition, orthographic knowledge is not negatively influenced.

To recapitulate, generally speaking the reading group's FL performance was to a certain extent better than that of the control group, although both groups had been more or less comparable prior to the study (see Chapter 7.2.4). However, at this point, one should critically consider the extent to which possible initial differences between the groups might have had an influence on the results at hand.

Looking at Chapter 7.2.4, both groups were comparable in terms of their previous FL knowledge. Nevertheless, the very few and statistically insignificant differences in initial FL performance could still explain differences in topic-based performance on the language tests. When looking in particular at the results of the YLE test, the reading group scored higher than the control group with a difference in means of about 10 %, although a t-test analysis did not reveal a significant difference.[221] Still, the fact remains that the reading group did do slightly better in the preliminary test. Therefore, the advance of the reading group in FL performance in contrast to the control group could possibly be explained by the previous differences between the groups. This would indicate that reading might

---

221 Extreme values like a score of only 1 or of all 40 points were not found; therefore, no calculation excluding any outliers could be done.

in fact not have had the positive influence on FL performance outlined above. However, the YLE test and the topic-based language test tested two different kinds of knowledge; the YLE test investigated the learners' general FL reading and writing competence, while the topic-based language tests investigated three different areas of FL competence based on thematic units and different words. Potential initial differences in topic-based knowledge of different language areas were not investigated prior to the data collection and could, therefore, not be controlled for. Therefore, it cannot be shown clearly whether this prior difference on the YLE test might have had an impact on the results of the topic-based language test, and the possibility of such an influence can neither be fully excluded nor clearly proven. In other words, the results presented in this chapter should be regarded somewhat critically; more research is needed in order to confirm or reject the findings.

Despite their generally promising results, the reading group's participants did not all perform equally well on the topic-based language tests. Their wide range of results (see Figure 39) may have several reasons. First of all, reading is obviously not everybody's favourite activity or preferred way of learning (also see Chapter 9.1). Therefore, the learners might vary in their interest and motivation with regard to reading and activities related to it, which might influence their performance on a certain topic or activity and, thus, the results on the tests. However, one of the learners who did not show much motivation to read was Ali (see Chapter 9), yet, interestingly, Ali's scores on the topic-based FL tests were nevertheless very high (see Figure 39). Therefore, low reading motivation does not seem to necessarily lead to poor results in topic-based FL competence. Thus, reading motivation could, but does not have to, influence FL performance on a certain topic in the context of language gains through reading.

Looking at the wide range in the learners' performance on the tests, one should consider whether a Matthew effect (Merton, 2010) occurred. The Matthew effect explains that

> children at a low initial level of performance for a given skill are hypothesized to remain at a relatively lower level in this skill and other related skills that depend on it. Moreover, their rate of development is slower than the rate of development of children with high initial levels of performance. (Protopapas, Parrila & Simos, 2014: 1)

As such, strong initial learners are hypothesised to profit more from a treatment than others. For the present study, this could mean that those learners who scored high on the language tests might also be those that profited more from the reading sessions. Such an effect is not desirable in teaching because in educational settings a treatment should generally be beneficial for all learners and should support all learners equally in their learning process and progress.[222]

The only result that could back up a Matthew effect is the comparison between the range of the reading group and the control group on average scores on the three tests. Table 32 has shown that there was a difference of up to 7 % in standard deviation between the means of both groups, whereas the reading group had a consistently greater range of scores than the control group. This difference might indicate that in fact some learners in the reading group profited more from the reading treatment than others and, therefore, the reading group learners' scores were slightly more varied than that of the control group. However, this difference does not appear to be considerable, and also there is no data on how the reading group might have ranged on these tests without the reading sessions. In fact, the available data only show that some learners in the reading group scored (considerably) less on the language tests than others; a finding that is not surprising in heterogeneous groups and classrooms (Hermes, 2017: 18). In addition, those learners who scored low on the topic-based language tests might simply not be good at doing (FL) tests; a notion that is not necessarily related to the benefits of regular reading.[223] Lastly, a slight Matthew effect is only assumed on the basis of the learners' performance on written tests. Although they are loosely related to the reading sessions, they should not be taken as the only measure to evaluate them. Other factors such as the learners' comprehension, motivation and development of reading competence (see Chapters 9 and 10) appear to be more important outcomes of the reading study than the learners' ability to improve on written tests.

In sum, the current study has shown that reading picture books can be beneficial for young learners' development of FL competence, particularly in regard to semantic and syntactic morphemic knowledge. In addition, enhanced reading does not lead to deficits in the area of orthography or in the knowledge of

---

222   Such a desirable situation regarding equal benefits from a certain treatment has been referred to as entrainment (McGrath, 1991: 164). Entrainment stands metaphorically for imagining all pupils on a train, and as the train moves forward through a certain treatment, all pupils move forward from their individual position. If a treatment is not beneficial for all, it should be critically questioned and measures of differentiation need to be considered instead.

223   This is underscored when looking at the detailed information on the participants (see Appendix B). One can see that those learners who scored low on the topic-based language tests (Ina, Simone, Jonas and Natan) are also those that initially scored low on the YLE test (see Chapter 7.2.4).

words unrelated to the books. Thus, regular FL reading seems beneficial for all the learners, even though the range of these learners' individual FL competences is and remains wide. The latter, however, is a factor in formal education that is impossible and undesirable to influence or change (also see Reckermann, 2017: 227f).

11.3 An Influence of Reading Comprehension on the Development of FL Performance

After the results on the topic-based language tests have now been looked at in detail and the results for reading comprehension have also been detailed in Chapter 9.2, this chapter will briefly look at a potential connection between a certain level of reading comprehension and the learners' performance on the topic-based language tests. The reason is that research has found that the better the comprehension of a text, the likelier FL knowledge, particularly word knowledge, from that passage will be retained (e.g., Pulido, 2007: 159f as explained in Chapter 5.4.3). Such a comparison should show whether a good result in FL performance might be linked to the level of reading comprehension and thus a certain level of FL reading competence. Because of the small sample, this is not investigated by statistical correlations as could be done with a larger sample, but by rather comparing the results that have already been described.

Figure 44 displays all the learners' average scores on the language tests, categorised by the groups of weak, average and strong readers:

Figure 44: Each learner's average result on the topic-based language tests, ordered by their reading comprehension levels: left (weak), middle (average), right (strong) readers.

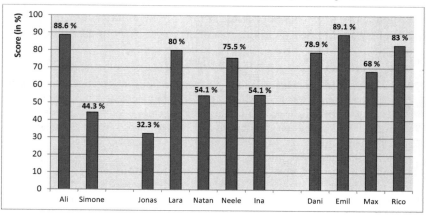

One can see that the weak readers' average scores on the language tests vary considerably with a difference of over 40 %. The same holds true for the average readers, who show a difference of almost 50 % on the language tests. Only the group of strong readers is slightly more homogeneous in that they all reached scores in the upper third, between 68 % and 89 %. Within the group, the strong readers show a difference of only about 20 %, which is less than the large differences in the groups of weak and average readers.

The results do not offer any clear picture as regards a connection between reading competence and FL performance. The strong readers are those who scored best and with the least in-group-variation on the language tests. This indicates that the good readers' FL performance is continuously high. They might have benefited most from regular reading in terms of their FL development, but they already possessed good FL competences before the reading study.[224] Still, some weak and average readers achieved high average scores on the language tests as well. Therefore, other factors besides good reading skills appear to contribute to an advance in FL development through reading, and young learners might still be able to gain FL knowledge from reading texts, even if they do not understand them to high degrees.

Thus reading again appears to be beneficial for all readers, regardless of their level of reading comprehension. At the same time, readers with a high level of reading comprehension seem to show a steadier increase in competence from regular reading than readers with lower comprehension levels.

11.4 Summary of Central Results and Answer to Research Question III

The presentation and interpretation of results has shown that reading authentic English picture books on a regular basis can have a positive influence on the learners' FL performance. In contrast to the control group, the reading group showed a higher level of FL performance in all three topics.

The improvements could be seen mostly in those parts of the tests that were based on word category C, that is, the words that were directly taken from the books. While this might not seem too surprising, the reading group also often outperformed the control group on the other two word categories, but not that noticeably. This indicated that thanks to reading picture books, the learners in

---

224   The strong readers all scored average to high on the YLE test and all had good marks of *sehr gut* [very good] or *gut* [good] in English prior to the onset of the study (see Appendix B).

the reading group did not have any deficits in areas that they might have missed in class, as they were absent from one out of three regular weekly EFL lessons. Therefore, the reading did not negatively influence the reading group's overall FL performance; rather, it appears to have supported it.

Of the different areas of FL competence that were tested, semantic as well as syntactic morphemic knowledge seemed to be those where the learners benefited the most, and both developed through the regular reading of picture books. Orthography appeared not to be influenced noticeably by regular reading.

Overall, the study provides initial evidence that reading is beneficial for the FL development of young EFL learners, in different word categories as well as in different areas of FL competence. If regular reading was implemented in the EFL classroom, one can thus assume that the learners would benefit from such an approach in their EFL development and would, at the same time, not sacrifice content knowledge or language development that they would gain in regular EFL lessons without enhanced reading. This proposes a shift towards more reading in the primary school EFL classroom.

In sum, the results allow the following answers to research question III (*To what extent does the reading of authentic English picture books influence the FL performance of EFL learners in Year 4?*):

- The reading group's FL performance outperforms the control group's performance on the topic-based language tests.
- The reading group's development of FL skills is in many aspects better than that of the control group.
- Learners benefit from regular reading in semantic and syntactic morphemic knowledge; less so in orthographic knowledge.
- Learners develop their skills particularly in the areas of topic-based language that derive directly from the books. At the same time the learners do not show any gaps but rather also development with regard to topic-based language from other sources.
- Regularly reading authentic English picture books in the primary school EFL classroom can have a positive influence on FL development at all ability levels.
- Despite the authenticity of the books and their potential language difficulties, the learners were still able to develop their FL resources by reading them. Thus, the selection of reading material was appropriate.
- Learners with different levels of reading comprehension show good FL competences in the topic-based language test data; however, strong readers in particular seem to gain FL knowledge more consistently from reading.

These initial answers to researching FL development through regular reading in the primary school EFL classroom can be understood as hypotheses that can serve as a basis for future research in this area, possibly with larger samples that allow correlation research. One final remark, however, should be made at this point: Teachers and researchers should be careful not to let the pleasure of reading move too much into the background in favour of pure language learning activities. The latter is less important than the first.

12. Summary, Conclusion and Future Perspectives

Abstract: This chapter contains a summary of the study and its findings and includes the answers to the three research questions. Implications for teaching and some limitations of the study are discussed.

This final chapter will briefly summarise the findings of this study, starting with the answers to the research questions. These answers are linked to impulses for future research; an aspect that is also part of the critical reflection on the research design Chapter 12.2. The latter discusses some limitations of the study and proposes possible ways to overcome the study's shortcomings. Finally, the study's implications for future teaching with a focus on reading in the primary school EFL classroom will be discussed and a final conclusion will be drawn.

12.1 Summary of the Study and its Central Findings: Finding Answers to the Research Questions

This book was concerned with reading authentic English picture books in the primary school EFL classroom and sought to explore this notion from various perspectives. Literacy in the primary school EFL classroom in Germany has been an issue of debate since EFL teaching with young learners started in the 1960s (see Chapter 3.1). Nowadays, teachers and researchers agree on the supportive function of literacy and its place in a holistic and communicative approach to FLL, but the extent to which reading and writing are applied in primary school EFL classrooms still varies and is somewhat unclear (see Chapters 2.4, 3.1 and 3.2). This study focused on reading and sought to explore this skill and its potential for young FL learners in more detail. Reading is a receptive, but nevertheless an active and very complex skill, in which various processes are in constant interaction and readers apply different reading strategies in order to decode a reading text (see Chapters 4.4 and 4.6). Some factors related to FL reading do differ from those which are relevant to L1 reading, but transfer from certain aspects of L1 reading to FL reading certainly takes place (see Chapters 4.1 and 4.2). Bearing in mind that neither the role of reading in FLL nor a FL reading methodology have been clearly defined for the primary school EFL classroom, it is not surprising that there has been very little research so far on whether young EFL learners can read English texts independently, let alone authentic English texts such as picture books (see Chapters 3.4 and 5). This book hypothesised that authentic English picture books as defined in Chapter 5.3 represent suitable reading material for young EFL learners, since such books are already used for storytelling in primary school EFL classes (see Chapter 5.5). Since reading authentic English picture books constitutes an appropriate challenge for young EFL learners, they need support in reading such texts (see Chapter 6).

Given the current lack of research in the area of reading in the primary school EFL classroom and in the light of support for the proposal that authentic English picture books are suitable reading materials for the purpose, this study explored reading authentic picture books in the German primary school EFL classroom. This reading study (see Chapters 7 and 8) included weekly reading sessions with a reading group of eleven Year 4 learners, in which six different authentic English picture books were read and various activities were conducted around this. The study used various different instruments to explore the learners' reading comprehension of the books (see research question I) as well as the reading strategies the learners applied (see research question II). In addition, a quasi-experimental element was embedded into the reading study, in that the reading group as well as a control group ($N = 12$) took a topic-based language test after each of the three thematic units that were covered in class. These tests provided data about the learners' FL performance and could be compared across the groups (see research question III).

In Chapters 9 to 11, the results for the three foci (reading comprehension, reading strategies and FL performance) have been presented and discussed in detail. The following section will summarise these results and provide final answers to the three research questions.

Answer to research question I: To what extent are Year 4 EFL learners capable of reading and understanding authentic English picture books?

This study has shown that Year 4 EFL learners at different levels of EFL proficiency were able to master the task of reading authentic English picture books independently and were not overtaxed by the reading demands. The learners reached varying levels of reading comprehension: Some of them showed a very detailed and thorough comprehension of the books while other learners gained a more basic understanding of the stories (see the levels of reading comprehension in Chapter 4.5.2 for a definition of the varying competence levels). The participants' performance on the three different instruments that explored their reading comprehension allowed a distinction into two weak, five average and four strong FL readers. The data showed that weak L1 readers were also weak L2 readers, while strong L1 readers were not per se strong L2 readers. The data also indicated that the learners' reading comprehension was dependent on factors such as their reading motivation, their previous topic and FL knowledge, their interest in the books as well as their moods. To enable the learners to successfully read the books, the provision of different supportive devices, which the learners could freely choose from, proved to be useful. In the end, a word list that was especially designed for each book to provide vocabulary support for selected lexical items as well as an audio-recording of the books that the learners could listen to while reading proved to be particularly supportive and useful during reading. To a certain extent, (situations of) cooperative reading were also beneficial for the learners, while neither picture-dictionaries nor bilingual dictionaries were found to be supportive. Over the period of five months, the learners developed in some aspects of their reading competence (i.e., reading confidence, completion of post-reading tasks, quality of oral recall, skilful use of supportive devices), although no explicit teaching or targeted reflections on reading competence took place. In sum, Year 4 EFL learners can hence independently read and to varying degrees understand authentic English picture books; a task for which individualised support is useful.

Answer to research question II: Which reading strategies do young EFL learners apply when reading authentic English picture books for understanding?

While reading authentic English picture books, young EFL learners use a wide range of meta-cognitive, cognitive, social as well as affective reading strategies. In total, the learners in the study used 56 different reading strategies which could be classified into 28 main strategies with further sub-strategies. Some of the social and affective strategies seem to be unique to young EFL learners, in that they have not been described for older or more advanced learners before. Generally speaking, the study has shown that young EFL learners' use of reading strategies is highly individual in that the reading strategies that are applied to a certain reading text depend on the individual learners, the context that the reading is embedded into as well as the actual task. Development of strategy use could be detected to a limited extent, in that certain learners seemed to develop or fine-tune their use of certain strategies. However, without explicit strategy training or regular reflections on strategy use – two factors that might help strategy development but were not part of the present study – only minor development of strategy use was found. Nonetheless, two strong readers in particular (see Chapter 9.2.4) already possessed a successful set of reading strategies from the very beginning, so that for them no development took place because it was not necessary for the texts given. In addition, the data have shown that despite the widespread belief among researchers that young learners are not conscious of using strategies, the participants in the study were well aware of a large number of the reading strategies they applied. Although the learners partly had difficulties in verbalising strategies, the questionnaire in particular helped to reveal their awareness of certain strategies. Strategy awareness, however, did not correlate with reading comprehension, because a high degree of strategy awareness was not dependent on the learners' different levels of reading comprehension. In addition, the data could not provide any evidence of a clear-cut connection between the use of a certain set of reading strategies and a certain level of reading comprehension, although some strategies were used more by strong and others used more by weaker readers. Clearly, however, the number of strategies that a learner used did not correlate with a certain level of reading comprehension. In sum, the young EFL learners used a wide range of different reading strategies, which they were mostly aware of and which they were able to develop to a certain extent in the course of the study. The learners' use of reading strategies was highly individual, though neither strategy awareness nor the number of reading strategies correlated with reading comprehension performance; this is apparently influenced by other factors.

Answer to research question III: To what extent does the reading of authentic English picture books influence the FL performance of EFL learners in Year 4?

The study has shown that reading can have a positive effect on young EFL learners' FL development. The reading group outperformed the control group on all three topic-based language tests, although the groups had been comparable prior to the onset of the study (see Chapter 7.2.4 and discussion in Chapter 11.2). The advances of the reading group were most noticeable in those parts of the tests that were based on lexical items taken from the book (one third of the test), while the reading group also drew level with or outperformed the control group on the two thirds of the tests that were independent of the books. Therefore, regular reading of authentic English picture books has a positive influence on young learners' topic-based FL development, in that the learners acquire the same FL knowledge as comparable peers, plus additional FL knowledge from the books. Taking into consideration the three different areas of language competence that were investigated, the data showed that the reading group's advances are found in the areas of semantic as well as syntactic morphemic knowledge. These two areas therefore seem to benefit from regular reading, while orthographic competence appears to be influenced neither positively nor negatively. Furthermore, the data suggest that while all the readers gained FL knowledge through reading, the strong readers did so more consistently. In sum, regular reading of authentic English picture books seems beneficial for Year 4 learners' FL development, particularly in the areas of semantic and syntactic morphemic knowledge.

These results suggest that the following statements or hypotheses should be further investigated by research, ideally with larger samples of young EFL learners and also with learners at primary schools without a bilingual programme.

Reading comprehension

- Weak L1 readers are also weak EFL readers.
- There is no correlation between strong L1 reading skills and FL reading comprehension.
- FL reading comprehension is dependent on the learners' reading motivation, the learners' previous topic knowledge and the learners' interest in the books.
- FL reading competence does develop through regular reading without explicit instruction, but explicit instruction could further FL reading competence even more.
- Cooperative reading situations support FL reading comprehension.

Reading strategies

- Young EFL learners use a wide range of cognitive, meta-cognitive, social and affective FL reading strategies.
- Development of strategy use only partly happens without explicit strategy instruction, but explicit instruction or reflections could promote the development of strategy use.
- Strong FL readers already possess a successful set of reading strategies and only more challenging reading tasks can further develop their use of (FL) reading strategies.
- The level of reading comprehension is not dependent on the awareness of reading strategies.
- The level of reading comprehension is not dependent on a certain number of reading strategies.

- Regular reading in the EFL classroom is beneficial for young learners' FL development.
- Implementing regular reading does not lead to deficits in other areas of FL knowledge dealt with in the regular EFL classroom.
- FL semantic as well as syntactic morphemic knowledge benefit more from implementing regular reading more than orthographic knowledge does.

The final results presented and discussed in this subchapter as well as in Chapters 9 to 11 have so far been offered without many indications of the possible limitations of the study. To this end, the next section will include some reflection on the design of the study and its limitations, and what these imply in terms of regarding the results critically and with caution.

12.2 A Reflection of the Research Design, Limitations of the Study and Implications for Future Research

The mixed methods design of this study was complex and included various qualitative as well as quantitative elements. To recapitulate, this approach has proven to be useful in that particularly Chapters 9 and 10 have repeatedly shown the importance of using mixed methods and triangulation when researching young learners' reading comprehension and strategies. On the other hand, this can be regarded critically from an economic perspective, because the collection and analysis of data in a mixed methods study is very resource-intensive and time-consuming.

Apart from the question of research economy, which can be regarded as minor as long as the results offer viable implications for classroom teaching as well as interesting starting points for future research, further limitations of the study need to be taken into consideration. The following sections will provide a critical reflection on the research design and elaborate on limitations of the study. In doing so, suggestions for future research will implicitly be provided in order to show how possible weaknesses could be overcome.

A reflection on the sample: considerations about generalisability of the study

As outlined in Chapter 7, the study was necessarily concerned with explorative research to the extent that there was virtually no comparable previous research in this area. As such, a mixed methods design that investigated the three different foci of reading comprehension, reading strategies and FL performance was set up in order to get some exploratory but nonetheless detailed insights into the reading of picture books. To do so, qualitative but also quantitative instruments were chosen, and the sample was followed in a longitudinal study over a period of five moths. These factors make the study explorative and the circumstances suggested a small sample with a manageable number of participants (also see Bortz & Döring, 2006: 566).

Because of the small sample size, however, the study's findings are essentially bound to the context this study was conducted in and can only be transferred to other contexts with the greatest of caution. Therefore, the results do not achieve a degree of representativeness and generalisability, but only show possible tendencies concerning reading authentic English picture books. Thus, any sweeping generalisations with regard to the reading of picture books in primary school EFL teaching must be avoided; only tentative conclusions, ideas, first impressions and hypotheses for follow-up studies can be formulated on the basis of the study. Clearly, the results could well have been different with a different group of participants as well as in a different context. This does not, however, limit the validity or justification of the present study, but only acknowledges that learners and classes can be different and that contextual factors can influence the affordances of a certain method.

Besides, a lack of generalisability is not necessarily a problem. Firstly, it is a natural feature of classroom research, and particularly of explorative and qualitatively-oriented approaches (also see Chapter 7.5). Such an approach allows detailed insights into the practice of FLL in a specific context and setting and thus enables teachers and researchers to draw clear-cut conclusions that are useful for exactly that context. Secondly, the lack of generalisability should be seen as an impulse or starting point for further investigations. Conducting the same or a similar study in a different setting, for example a primary school without a bilingual programme (see point below), could supplement the results of this study and subsequently offer more differentiated insights into reading authentic English picture books with young learners. Different studies in different settings will, it is to be hoped, eventually allow more generalisable conclusions.

This lack of generalisability in the findings nevertheless still needs to be examined with regard to all the results and all the implications and conclusions drawn from them. As indicated at the beginning of Part C, this caveat has not been mentioned for every finding, so the remarks on the limitations of the study in this subchapter should serve as a general discussion of the generalisability of the findings that were presented and interpreted in the present study.

Reflection on the setting: choosing a school with a bilingual programme

Chapter 7.2.1 has outlined reasons for why the study took place at a primary school with a bilingual programme. These included remarks on the debate on early biliteracy as well as potential benefits of enhanced FL input for mastering the challenging task of independently reading authentic English texts. The argument was that if learners at a school with enhanced English input could not successfully read the books, learners with only two regular English lessons per week would also very likely not be able to master the task. By contrast, if learners in a bilingual programme could manage the task, a similar study could then be set up with learners who have not had any enhanced input. Since the present study found that learners in a bilingual programme were very well able to read authentic picture books by themselves, even though they reached different comprehension levels, the viability of such a programme could consequently be explored with Year 4 learners at a regular primary school. Although theoretically any school could set up a bilingual programme, for which the results of the present study might then be similar, it appears more realistic to explore the reading of authentic English picture books with learners that have not received enhanced English input.[225]

As suggested here, the choice of setting for this study can be seen as a further limit on its generalisability, in that only tentative conclusions can be drawn with regard to implementing the reading of authentic English picture books in primary schools without a bilingual programme. Still, these results can on the one hand serve as impulses for the development of classroom practice in CLIL[226] and on the other hand can be understood as ground-work for follow-up research in schools without a bilingual programme. In fact, the initial evidence from Kolb's (2013) study indicates that Year 4 learners at regular schools could cope with the task of reading a picture book. Although this was only a small-scale project that provided few deeper insights into reading comprehension or strategies, the fact that the learners were not overtaxed by the task of reading is noteworthy. Also of interest in this regard is an Austrian study conducted with 12-year-old EFL learners which found that global comprehension of FL stories is comparable amongst CLIL and non-CLIL learners (Hüttner & Rieder-Bünemann, 2007).

---

225 Possibly only more advanced learners at a regular school can successfully master the task of independent reading; but this would simply imply that reading texts like authentic picture books could be used as a means of differentiation that supports very skilled EFL learners. However, this requires future research.

226 See Chapters 2.2.2, 3.1.1 and 5.4.2 about a lack of CLIL teaching materials, the importance of reading in CLIL and the potential of picture books for integrating language and content.

Hence, follow-up studies at primary schools without a bilingual programme appear to be possible and might actually produce results that are not too different from the ones presented in this book.

About researching reading comprehension: oral recall and questioning

In order to investigate reading comprehension, oral recall and questioning was used as one instrument (see Chapter 8.2.2). The following paragraphs will reflect on three aspects that are concerned with this instrument: the collection of data in groups instead of individually, the effectiveness of the recall and questioning to investigate reading comprehension and the question of research economy.

Firstly, the recall and questioning procedure was conducted in the small reading groups of three to four learners. From a practical and organisational perspective, this group situation was very convenient, but from a research perspective it entailed some difficulties. One difficulty was already discussed in Chapter 8.2.2, namely that what is said in a group discussion is influenced by what others have said before or might still want to say. Hence, in groups, the reading comprehension of individual children is difficult to measure. This drawback was considered during the data analysis (see Chapters 8.2.2 and 9.2.2). Another weakness was, however, that the learners sometimes got confused about the extent to which they should present information that had already been mentioned. Both drawbacks – the confusion of the learners as well as the limitations in data analysis – could have been solved with an individual recall and questioning phase, which allows learners to recall every aspect and detail that they understood without any peer influence. However, on the one hand this is difficult to coordinate with daily school routines, as it would mean that learners have to be taken out of class individually,[227] and on the other hand a one-to-one situation with the researcher and one learner might put too much pressure on the learners. And besides, a one to one situation is unrealistic in classroom practice, in which group situations are normal procedures. Therefore, although the group situation entails some drawbacks that need to be considered, it is most practical, best fits into school routines and allows realistic implications for classroom teaching.

Secondly, in retrospect the analysis of the oral recall and comprehension questions showed that the recall was a much better instrument to investigate reading comprehension than the questions were. The recall was more open than the

---

227   In the present study, this was the reason why the three small groups were formed and why the groups were only taken out during the English lessons. Other school routines were not to be interrupted.

questioning and allowed the learners to reveal their individual comprehension, based on their perception and their own organisation of ideas and thoughts. Furthermore, the learners had often already provided answers to some of the questions that should have been asked later on, so that some utterances were doubled. In follow-up studies, the questioning could therefore be left out in favour of an extended recall phase and concrete questions might better be asked in written form.

Lastly, analysing the recall and questioning with the analysis scheme was an effective way to attribute comprehension levels to individual learners, but the procedure is very time-consuming. Still, such a qualitative analysis takes into consideration more than just the number of content aspects mentioned by a learner and is thus advisable if researchers are aiming at a holistic picture of reading comprehension. However, it is desirable to have a more economical tool to holistically investigate young learners' reading comprehension, particularly when researching a larger sample. Therefore, future research could aim at developing such a tool.

About the instruments to research reading strategies

Three different instruments – observation data including a video analysis, group interviews and a questionnaire – were used to investigate the learners' reading strategies (see Chapter 8.3). As discussed in Chapter 10.5, this methodological triangulation proved to be necessary to trace as many reading strategies as possible, but still some downsides of the instruments will be reflected on in the following paragraphs.

Like the recall on reading comprehension, which might have benefited from a one-to-one exchange between the researcher and the learner, the interviews on reading strategies might also have profited from such an approach. Instead of group interviews, interviews with single children or pairs might have allowed a deeper insight into their strategy use, as the researcher would have had more time to ask more probing questions and to try to get to the bottom of aspects that the learners mentioned. Another difficulty was that the learners partly repeated a strategy that had already been mentioned by a peer. Due to the group situation it remained unclear whether this strategy was mere repetition of what another learner had said, or whether the learner actually used the strategy him/herself. In addition, the learners might have failed to mention strategies that they had used because a peer had already mentioned that strategy and the learner did not deem it necessary to repeat it. A final weakness regarding the interview was that the learners also often had difficulties with verbalising a certain strategy. Their meta-language and their ability to express working processes might indeed not be advanced enough yet to verbalise a large number of reading strategies. Therefore, in addition to group interviews, other instruments should be used to supplement data on reading strategies.

Another instrument that was used in the study is the questionnaire on reading strategies. The results of this instrument should to a certain extent be viewed cautiously, as research has not yet clearly established whether young learners are fully capable of reliably filling in questionnaires on reading strategies (also see Chapter 4.6.7). Although my impression was that the learners were able to competently fill in the questionnaire (also see Footnote 212), the learners might have just ticked the boxes indiscriminately. However, such behaviour was counterbalanced by the fifth column of answers to choose from, which clearly allowed the learners to indicate that they were uncertain about a strategy. Another difficulty was that whenever the learners ticked 'no', I could not fully be sure whether they really did not use that strategy or were simply not aware of using it. This shortcoming, however, is always found in questionnaire research and hardly confined to young learners. Despite these issues, the questionnaire has proven to be a useful instrument in investigating the learners' reading strategies, also because it was an instrument that appeared to help the learners overcome their problems with verbalising reading strategies and at the same time make them aware of their strategy use; as such, and also because it was filled in individually, it counterbalanced the weaknesses of the interviews. The present study thus suggests the use of a questionnaire, amongst other instruments, to research young learners' FL reading strategies.

Despite the use of three different instruments, some strategies may still remain undetected.[228] In this study, many efforts were made to detect as many strategies as possible. A further potential instrument – not used in this study but that can provide information about reading strategies – is eye-tracking research. However, eye-tracking investigations require profound technical knowledge and it remains questionable whether using more instruments, particularly such complex ones, is necessary and would have a meaningful influence on the final outcome of a study. Therefore, researchers have to be aware of and accept the fact that despite triangulation some strategies might remain unknown, whereas the number of those is improbable to be high.

Lastly, strategy development was one aspect that the present study explored. However, with the data available it was relatively difficult to track. Regular

---

228 Some strategies cannot be observed, for instance, re-reading a word that was not understood. In that case, researchers have to rely on reported data (interview and questionnaire). If a non-observable strategy was not reported on, that strategy might remain undetected.

observation data only offers an insight into the development of those strategies that can be observed. This needs to be supplemented with data on strategies that cannot be observed, for example via interview data, but as outlined above the interview data was not exhaustive. Therefore, the observation and interview data have limitations with regard to investigating any development in strategy use. Possibly, the questionnaire on reading strategies should be conducted before and after the reading study in future studies, in order to gain more detailed insights into a possible development of reading strategies.[229]

About the quasi-experimental study to investigate FL development

For a quasi-experimental study with quantitative data, as used to investigate FL performance with research question III, the sample size was very small. This meant that no correlation research was possible. The data only allowed some insight into the learners' FL competence, as presented via descriptive statistics in Chapter 11. In future research, a larger sample would be needed for further calculations.

Another possible weakness of this part of the study is the sampling procedure. As outlined in Chapter 7.2, convenience sampling was necessary and all efforts were made to ensure that both groups were comparable. However, groups of young learners can never be fully comparable and minor differences cannot be avoided (e.g., the difference of performance on the YLE test as discussed in Chapters 7.2.4 and 11.2). Although this is a natural feature of classroom research, where a laboratory situation is impossible, researchers need to consider such differences, even if small and unavoidable.

Furthermore, no standardised tests were used to investigate the learners' FL performance; instead I, as the researcher, designed the topic-based language tests. The simple reason for this procedure was that hardly any standardised language tests are available to measure young EFL learners' competences, particularly not tests focusing on certain topics. Still, to enhance the validity of possible follow-up studies, researchers could consider the use of standardised tests, even though such tests might not be able to explore minor differences among learners. Teachers and researchers know that assessing and measuring FLL progress can be very difficult, and that small steps and slight progress in selected areas can be particularly hard to trace. Therefore, tests should on the one hand comply with research standards, but on the other hand allow the researcher to actually trace

---

229 This was not done in the present study because the need for a questionnaire only became apparent during the data collection phase (see Chapter 8.3.3).

what may be very small-scale developments and differences in performance, including those differences that might be based on reading.

In exploring the differences between the two groups, this study has only focused on three areas of FL performance: orthography, semantics and syntactic morphemic knowledge. Other competences, such as FL listening or speaking, were not investigated. As such, some aspects that might have been influenced by reading might remain undetected in this study. Evidently, the reading study might have had a positive or negative influence on a number of other areas of FL competence which this study did not investigate. In follow-up studies, further competences could therefore be taken into consideration when exploring FL performance. For instance, a pre- and post-test design with the potential to show to what extent both groups had different types of FL knowledge before and after one group received regular reading would be interesting. These tests must not necessarily be topic-based, but could also be more general in order to investigate a more general change in FL knowledge.

Furthermore, delayed post-tests would be interesting in order to see whether regular reading had a long-term positive effect on the learners' FL competence or whether the effect was bound to the time-frame of the reading study. Looking at the results presented in Chapter 11, it would be interesting to ascertain whether the reading group maintains their advances in semantic and syntactic morphemic knowledge, whether they can increase their lead over the control group or whether the control group catches up in the long run. Such a study would reveal interesting insights into the long-term effects of FL reading on FL performance, but would clearly need a longer time-span.

Another point that deserves consideration is the fact that the variable 'reading sessions' constituted the difference between the reading and control group in the quasi-experimental part. These reading sessions, however, consisted of a number of different activities and materials, the effects of which cannot be separated. Therefore, the analysis of a possible effect of the reading sessions on FL performance can only be attributed to the whole reading study; the results do not allow insights into what parts of the reading sessions might have led to the eventual outcome. For example, the reading group's enhancement in word knowledge may derive from reading the books, but could just as well have come from the word lists that were provided while reading.[230] At this point, further research is needed in order to allow more detailed attributions and conclusions.

---

230   The retention of lexical items that the pupils looked up on the word list is a very interesting topic for follow-up research. As outlined in Chapter 5.4.3, lexical items

In addition, it may be somewhat difficult to clearly attribute the reading group's advance in FL performance to the reading sessions. Other factors, such as potential differences between the groups prior to the study (see above), or also a motivational leap due to a possible psychological effect of being taken out of class, might have led to the better results. In order to avoid the latter, a certain 'special' treatment would have to be given to both groups so that possible psychological effects are balanced. In follow-up studies, for example, a waiting-group design[231] (see Gerken, Natzke, Petermann & Walter, 2002) or a crossover design (see Freudenau, 2017: 141, 144f)[232] could be used to counterbalance a possible effect of excitement or disappointment in both groups. In follow-up studies, one could also consider the regular teacher conducting the reading study with a whole class, so that children do not have to be taken out of class. In that case, a parallel class taught by the same teacher but without a special reading focus would serve as control group. Such a design would ensure that reading is integrated into the regular teaching proceedings, which would on the one hand demand more resources, but on the other hand make a complex sampling procedure dispensable and limit the possible influences of working in small-group situations. All alternative designs, however, entail other advantages and disadvantages and research designs always need to be set up based on the study's context by taking all variables into consideration.

Despite possible shortcomings of the quasi-experimental part of this study as outlined in the previous paragraphs, I still decided to collect and analyse data on FL performance, by seizing the opportunity a longitudinal study offers to collect such data. The results are to be understood as initial insights which need backup from further research in this area.

Considering the multimodal nature of picture books

Picture books constituted the reading material for this study, because their interplay of textual and visual elements seemed appropriate for the participants' language levels. However, the multimodal nature (Lewis, 2001; see Chapter 5.2.3) of such books poses difficulties on researching comprehension, because researchers

---

are learnt best if they are treated consciously and processed at deeper levels. Certain words that the learners looked up might thus be retained better than other words.

231 Translated by the author for '*Wartegruppendesign*'. In a waiting group design, the control group receives the same treatment as the experimental group, but after the regular data collection procedure has finished.

232 In a crossover design, control group and experimental group are alternated several times over the data collection procedure.

can often not be sure to what extent comprehension derived from the textual elements, the visual elements or a combination of both (although the analysis scheme, see Chapter 8.2.2.2, took this notion into consideration). Obtaining more insight into the information-load of the pictures is hence desirable and calls for further investigation. In fact, a model of (FL) reading that encompasses the multimodality of texts that are supplemented by pictures would be an interesting advancement, for example based on the model presented in Chapter 4.4.2.

About the type of reading

In the study, I as the researcher chose the books, organised the reading of the books and planned all the steps of the reading sessions. In contrast to this procedure, extensive reading sessions in which the learners choose their own reading texts, are not engaged in (too many) post-reading activities and are given extended reading time could enhance reading motivation and also lead to a more autonomous approach to FL reading texts. Because the data were collected systematically for the three foci of the current study, however, extensive reading was not possible in this project, but should still be considered with regard to teaching practice and also possible follow-up studies (see Chapter 12.3).

In addition to the ideas for future research which were generated from the critical reflection of the research design in the previous sections, and in addition to the summaries of results which suggested hypotheses for further investigation (see Chapter 12.1), the following aspects might also deserve consideration and could be investigated in follow-up studies on FL reading with young learners:

- **Extending the time-span of the study:** The longitudinal nature of this study could be extended, so that more long-term effects of regular reading in the primary school EFL classroom can be investigated. Possible effects of including more reading activities at the primary school level might, amongst others, be that the learners later have fewer difficulties with FL reading at the secondary school level and that an earlier start with reading FL texts allows them an easier and less inhibited access to FL text in general. However, such effects can only be measured in studies that cover a time-span of at least two or three years.
- **Include reading at text level earlier than Year 4:** Similarly, it would be interesting to include regular reading activities, such as the reading of carefully selected authentic texts, earlier than in Year 4. An early start of FL reading, in a playful way that matches the learners' proficiency levels, might have a positive impact on FLL. Enhanced reading activities in earlier years would probably be found to lead to other beneficial results when researching reading competences in Year 4. However, teachers and researchers should be

careful to not put too much emphasis on reading, because the primacy of spoken language should not be contested.

- **Investigate teaching reading and reading strategies:** Explicitly teaching reading as well as reading strategies to young EFL learners probably influences their reading comprehension and can have a positive impact on their reading competence (see Chapters 9.4 and 10.5). Although the present study has demonstrated that young learners can read picture books without explicit reading instruction, this task might be easier for them if they had some systematic reading training. Particularly for learners that have not been in a bilingual programme, a more explicit approach to reading might be beneficial and allow them to read authentic texts. Previous studies by Jöckel (2016) and Frisch (2013) (see Chapter 3.3) can be taken as the basis for teaching reading skills in the primary school EFL classroom; both have shown that reading skills can be effectively taught to young EFL learners.

- **Further explore a connection between reading strategies and reading comprehension:** Clear-cut evidence of a correlation between a certain set of reading strategies and a certain level of reading comprehension still needs to be investigated in follow-up studies. Larger samples might reveal more insights into possible links, particularly because such samples might allow research based on correlational statistics. However, it should be borne in mind that such a correlation is very difficult or even impossible to find, due to the individual nature of strategy use.

- **Investigate the learners' self-assessment of FL development:** As the learners' self-assessment of reading comprehension was investigated, their self-assessment of perceived FL development can also be researched. This might give interesting insights into their FL development as well as into their own perception of learning a FL through reading, neither of which can be satisfactorily measured by tests.

- **Reading e-texts on digital devices instead of print texts:** The study only investigated reading printed picture books. Given current technologies, reading electronic texts also constitutes an interesting research topic. For example, learners could read picture books as e-texts on electronic devices such as tablets (see Burnett & Merchant, 2013; McMunn Dooley, Martinez & Roser, 2013: 401f). Such devices might even allow learners to read and seek help at the same time, for example by tapping on an unknown word and immediately getting a picture, definition or translation.

- **Learning content aspects through picture books:** Focusing on reading picture books in CLIL and on such books' potential for integrating language and content, research should pay attention to the content aspects of such books. Aristov et al. (2015) provide suggestions for the use of picture books in CLIL science classes; their research could be extended to explore to what extent learners can acquire content knowledge by reading picture books.
- **Finding a threshold for lexical knowledge needed for reading picture books:** As outlined in Chapter 5.4.3, no study has so far suggested a threshold for lexical knowledge when reading authentic L2 picture books. With a focus on previous lexical knowledge, future research could define such a threshold for picture books as texts which contain not only textual but also visual information. For a realistic threshold, the lexical density and the visual-text relationship should be taken into consideration. Nation (2006: 73ff) has proposed a threshold for understanding children's movies and concludes that because of the strong visual support a movie provides there is no need for a large vocabulary size.[233] It is therefore conceivable that a threshold for reading picture books is lower than that for reading texts without visual supplements (see Chapter 6.5.3).
- **Graded readers vs. authentic picture books:** Intentionally, this study investigated authentic picture books (see Chapter 8.1 for reasons). However, graded readers could also be used for reading with young learners (see Bechler & Reckermann, 2018). Follow-up research could compare the potential of both types of reading material and explore whether one type of book is more effective at different stages of FLL or for different learning objectives and purposes.

All these suggestions offer ideas for follow-up studies, because more research on reading and writing in the primary school is clearly needed in order to offer well-grounded proposals for classroom teaching. Certainly, the next step would include a transfer of this study to a primary school without a bilingual programme in order to assess the generalisability of such reading activities to a broader range of primary schools. As for research designs, mixed methods have proven here to be a successful approach to getting a holistic picture of young learners' reading abilities; therefore, mixed methods and triangulation are recommended and appear crucial in investigating aspects of literacy with young FL learners.

---

233   Nation (2006) did not provide a threshold in percentages.

12.3 Implications for Teaching

Despite certain limitations of this study and a need for many further research projects, the results have various implications of relevance to teaching English to young learners. The most obvious implication is that more reading activities can and should be included in primary school EFL classes. Concerns about overtaxing the learners were allayed in the research presented here. As reading materials, carefully selected picture books have proven to be appropriate, but also other (authentic) texts appear suitable. In contrast to what was done in this study, the results indicate that some phases of explicitly teaching reading as well as reflections on reading strategies might be supportive for young learners' FL reading. In addition, explicitly looking at and dealing with aspects of language that can be learnt through picture books seems beneficial, although not crucially necessary. Further ideas and implications for future teaching that derive from this study and are linked to an enhancement of reading activities in the primary school EFL classroom will be elaborated on in the following sections, which include a final conclusion of this book and study.

Generally, learners should be introduced to a variety of books, including FL books, at school. According to Krashen (2013: 20), the use of storybooks at school encourages children to develop good long-term reading habits and increases the likelihood that learners also read books in their free time. Therefore, schools and teachers are responsible for creating a literature-rich environment: in German as the language of schooling as well as in FLs such as English. As such, well-equipped school libraries can contribute to surroundings rich in books and help learners establish beneficial reading habits. Bland (2013b: 3) argues that "without school libraries with a good variety of children's literature, also in the L2, the chances for children to become readers, and all the empowerment that being a reader entails, are extremely unequal, and an extensive reading programme has little chance to be persuasive and successful." Good school libraries allow learners more access to books, which in return results in more reading and hence better reading (Krashen, 2013: 20).

A practical suggestion for a book-friendly environment in the (EFL) classroom is that of topic-based book collections. Such collections contain a pool of different books that all deal with a certain topic, which in turn serves as the common thread of all the books in the collection (see Weerning, 2006: 12; also see Chapter 2.3 on planning units around a theme). Not only different types of German books, but also various books in English or other languages should be part of the collection, in order to include different languages for multiple learning opportunities (also see Massler, 2012a: 15) and embrace the idea of the functional use of at least two languages in FL teaching approaches (see, Butzkamm & Caldwell, 2009; Diehr, 2012). While dealing with a certain topic, such a book collection should be available for the learners at all times (Weerning, 2006: 12) to meet their desire for knowledge, enable them to investigate a topic independently, encourage them to look at and read different books, cater to varying interests in a topic, support an individual choice of reading texts and allow learners to search autonomously for information.

For compiling book collections on a certain topic, a syllabus for the use of books in topic-based teaching would be helpful. Such a syllabus could firstly contain topics that were carefully selected from an analysis of curricula, and then suggest books of different genres and of different languages for these topics. For the topics dealt with in the present study, Appendix E offers some ideas for such a syllabus. In addition, this syllabus could be supplemented with learning objectives, task suggestions and connections to different topics as well as different subjects. Eventually, a syllabus for teaching selected topics either in the EFL classroom or across the curriculum could be designed, which amongst many other aspects includes a collection of different topic-based books.

Bearing in mind that primary school EFL learners can already deal with authentic texts in supportive contexts, the value of EFL course books should be critically reflected on. Teachers might want to consider whether they actually need a course book that contains a collection of carefully created and adapted texts and tasks, or whether other materials such as authentic picture books could not be used as a basis for their teaching. Such an approach might be more interesting for learners as well as teachers and at the same time provide learners with more authentic and richer input. However, such a very general question of planning EFL lessons remains the teacher's choice and is always based on the individual classroom context.

Nevertheless, the results of this study suggest that more reading activities and also more challenging reading tasks than those which are currently found in course books can and should be used with young EFL learners. As shown in this book, learners are very well capable of performing such tasks, and the enhanced reading of picture books does not lead to a shortfall in other FL competences either. On the contrary, the reading group appears to have profited from the reading sessions. This means that reading can well be implemented at primary level to a greater extent than it is at the moment, without risking deficits in other areas and without questioning the primary focus on oral skills.

The enhanced implementation of reading in the primary school EFL classroom with texts such as picture books might not have to be postponed to Year 4 or even secondary school either, but could already be initiated in earlier years. There are numerous different authentic picture books available that vary in their degrees of difficulty; and easier ones could already be used with younger learners. In terms of differentiation, the teacher can also include the reading of picture books for some learners, while for others reading at the text-level might have to be delayed to later stages. Particularly for those learners that are by nature not very open and communicative, reading might be a very suitable task with which to engage in FL communication. In fact, Sambanis (2008: 60) suggests reading activities for learners that are in the silent period, a phase of listening in which some learners are not ready to speak yet, because reading allows them to remain silent but at the same time engages them in FLL.

Generally, differentiation and individual support are key factors in planning learning and teaching and should also be considered in FL reading tasks. The results of this study show that readers differ in many respects and thus also need differentiated reading tasks that cater to their individual needs, abilities and competence levels. The EFL teacher can differentiate FL reading by providing reading texts of varying difficulties, by allowing learners to choose a reading text based on their own interests, by giving a range of supportive devices that learners can choose from, by allowing individual reading time and by setting realistic and individualised expectations (also see Doms, 2012: 61).

The free choice of a reading text, motivated by personal interest, caters to individual interests and competences. This is put into practice through the approach of extensive reading. Extensive reading is characterised by a high reading frequency, longer texts, having free choice from a range of reading material and reading according to one's interests and reading speed (Biebricher, 2008: 39). Another important characteristic of extensive reading is that reading texts should not or at least not primarily serve as a basis for FLL activities (Kolb, 2013: 35; Krashen, 1989: 442). If the learners are given freedom of choice in selecting books and topics according to their interests, different reading materials that match the learners' varying levels of FL competence as well as their interests should be provided, so as to foster the learners' motivation (Deane & Rumlich, 2013: 190; Nuttall, 2005: 131, 141). By increasing the learners' involvement in stories, teachers can positively influence the learners' interest in and enjoyment of reading, which in return can positively influence their FL development (Cameron: 2001: 164; Mason, 2013: 25; Waas, 2016: 36). Given the positive side-effects of extensive reading, such an approach seems highly desirable and is accordingly one of the proposals this book makes for the primary school EFL classroom. In fact, the curriculum of NRW requires teachers to make use of extensive L1 reading (see MSW NRW, 2008b: 23, 26), a requirement that should also be transferred to the English classroom. Book collections or class libraries (see above) that contain a variety of English books can be used as a basis for such an approach. As such, extensive reading and a focus on the pleasure of reading itself seems therefore very suitable for EFL classroom practices and for establishing long-term reading habits.

An enhancement of individualised reading activities with young FL learners can have a number of further advantages that go beyond those already mentioned. Firstly, reading can be used as the bridge to writing. Looking at the order of skills development (see Chapter 2.4.2), writing comes after reading and reading can thus pave the way for developing FL writing skills (also see Waas, 2014b: 35).

Not only that, but reading can enhance learner autonomy. Butzkamm and Caldwell (2009: 183) point out that the threshold where learners can start learning independently from FL texts is crossed once they can read authentic texts on their own: "A real English book ... is the great leap forward." Whittaker (2003: 182f) points out that the autonomous reading of children's literature can pave the way to reading and understanding more complex content-matter texts later on. As outlined in Chapter 1, being able to read is a prerequisite for autonomously gathering information, so that the skill of reading opens up a whole new world of being able to understand and autonomously seek information on a topic. Reading therefore helps learners to become independent and can be an important step in the direction of more open forms of learning in the EFL classroom.

With more focus on written skills already in primary school, the (apparent) gap between the primary and the secondary school could be bridged. Secondary school teachers often complain about the poor literacy skills pupils have after four years of primary school English (see Chapter 3.1.2). Diehr and Frisch (2010b: 145) argue that at the start of secondary school, basic English reading competencies are expected from the learners and English texts are used as a matter of course from the very beginning. Including suitable reading (and writing) activities in primary school and thereby getting learners acquainted with these skills offers a response to this criticism and would be beneficial for both teachers and learners (also see Haß, 2006: 89; Kolb, 2013: 35f). With regard to the materials focused on in this study, Whittaker (2003: 182f) argues that children's literature offers a motivating, encouraging and supportive way of getting accustomed to FL reading. That is not to say that primary school should not maintain its playful methodology and its primary focus on oral skills, in order to meet the young learners' needs. This book only argues that reading (and writing) should be implemented to a greater extent than is currently the case, without contesting the oral focus and child-friendly methodology.

Briefly looking at secondary school EFL classrooms, teachers at this level too should be encouraged to follow the trend towards selecting authentic instead of adapted materials (see Chapter 5.2.2) more courageously, bearing in mind that already at primary school authentic texts can be used. An increased use of authentic texts instead of graded readers would be advantageous for older and more advanced learners as well, as the evidence for the benefits of authenticity as outlined in Chapters 5.1 and 5.2 attests.

In sum, the previous sections have clearly shown that primary school EFL classrooms should increase the use of reading activities and also include more challenging reading activities, such as reading authentic English children's books. Keeping in mind that it is very unlikely that such books are available at schools for every learner in a class (also see Chapter 5.5.1), and also that some learners might benefit more from FL reading than others, the following practical suggestions can be made for the primary (English) classroom. EFL teachers could/should:

- Support the installation of class libraries or topic-based book collections that contain authentic and appealing English children's books.
- Create a book-box or book corner with English books which children can read during breaks, borrow to take home, read in phases of open beginnings, etc.
- Use five minutes or more of every English lesson for free and voluntary extensive reading.
- Encourage fast pupils to choose an authentic English book from the English corner and read it once they finished with the regular tasks.
- Encourage learners to prepare book reports about English books that they liked and present those to class (also see Bechler & Reckermann, 2018).
- Include the reading of an English text in phases of open learning; for example activity corners, work plans, weekly schedules or free work.
- Include phases of learning in which the learners are required to use books or texts to autonomously seek information.
- Differentiate EFL teaching, also with regard to reading, and offer choices of materials and supportive devices, so that every learner is sufficiently challenged and at the same time sufficiently supported in his/her learning process.
- Consider whether an authentic book can serve as the basis for a teaching unit, including an individualised approach to reading the text (see Brewster & Ellis, 2002: 192 on this idea).

In conclusion, this book and its underlying study indicated that young EFL learners can often do more than teachers and researchers expect them to be capable of doing. The results suggest that teachers can place higher task demands on young learners, including, as demonstrated in the study, the use of authentic texts such as picture books for reading activities that provide an enriching experience in the primary school EFL classroom. As shown in the study that was presented in this book, more research is needed in order to explore the potential of FL reading for young learners and in order to investigate the potential of different texts, such as authentic English picture books, for the EFL classroom. No matter what exactly the next steps in empirical research and practical teaching are, it is high time to leave behind the debate on early biliteracy and further explore the extent to which the skill of FL reading can be used effectively and to the benefit of all concerned in teaching FL to young learners.

References

Note: Children's books and teaching materials are listed in separate sections at the end of this chapter.

List of Literature

Afflerbach, P., Pearson, P. D., Paris, S. G. (2008). Clarifying Differences Between Reading Skills and Reading Strategies. *The Reading Teacher, 61*(5), 364–373.

Aguado, K. (2000). Empirische Fremdsprachenerwerbsforschung. Ein Plädoyer für mehr Transparenz. In Aguado, K. (Ed.). *Zur Methodologie in der empirischen Fremdsprachenforschung* (pp. 119–131). Hohengehren: Schneider.

Albers, C. (2014). More than just Fun? Comic Books and Graphic Novels. *Grundschulmagazin Englisch, 12*/2, 7–9.

Alderson, J. C. (2005). The Testing of Reading. In Nuttall, C. (Ed.). *Teaching Reading Skills in a Foreign Language* (pp. 212–228). London: Macmillan.

Alig, F. (1992). Kommunikative Progression als Leitprinzip für Sprachenlernen an Grundschulen – Erste Erfahrungen mit dem Unterrichtswerk *Here we go*. In Gompf, G. (Ed.). *Fremdsprachenbeginn ab Klasse 3. Lernen für Europa* (pp. 7–10). Berlin: Cornelsen.

Alter, G. (2013). Developing Intercultural Competence through First Nations' Children's Literature. In Bland, J. & Lütge, C. (Eds.). *Children's Literature in Second Language Education* (pp. 151–158). London: Bloomsbury.

Appel, J. (2010). Englisch lernen. *Praxis Grundschule, 5*, 4–5.

Appel, J. & Wilson, D. H. (2010). Spracherwerb durch bekannte Inhalte. *Praxis Grundschule, 5*, 7–11.

Aristov, N. & Haudeck, H. (2013). Bilingual Education – Subject Matter(s) – Natural Science. In Elsner, D. & Keßler, J.-U. (Eds.). *Bilingual Education in Primary School. Aspects of Immersion, CLIL and Bilingual Modules* (pp. 42–50). Tübingen: Narr.

Aristov, N., Haudeck, H. & McCafferty, S. (2015). *Chilitex. Children's Literature and Experiments.* Offenburg: Mildenberger.

Artelt, C., Stanat, P., Schneider, W. & Schiefele, U. (2001). Lesekompetenz. Testkonzeption und Ergebnisse. In Baumert, J., Klieme, E., Neubrand, M., Prenzel, M., Schiefele, U., Schneider, W., Stanat, P., Tillmann, K.- J. & Weiß, M. (Eds.). *PISA 2000. Basiskompetenzen von Schülerinnen und Schülern im internationalen Vergleich* (S. 69–137). Opladen: Leske + Budrich.

August, G. (2011). Spelling Facilitates Good ESL Reading Comprehension. *Journal of Developmental Education, 35*(1), 14–24.

Bach, G. (2005). Bilingualer Unterricht. Lernen – Lehren – Forschen. In Bach, G. & Niemeier, S. (Eds.). *Bilingualer Unterricht. Grundlagen, Methoden, Praxis, Perspektiven* (pp. 9–22). 4th edition. Frankfurt a.M.: Peter Lang.

Backes, L. (2014). *Understanding Children's Book Genres.* Retrieved from http://writeforkids.org /2014/02/understanding-childrens-book-genres/ (last access: 15.05.2017).

Bahls, G. (1992). Vergangenheit und Gegenwart des Fremdsprachenunterrichts ab Klasse 3 in den neuen Bundesländern. In Gompf, G. (Ed.). *Fremdsprachenbeginn ab Klasse 3. Lernen für Europa* (pp. 11–16). Berlin: Cornelsen.

Bartnitzky, H. (2009). Kindgemäßheit – und Fördern durch Fordern. In Bartnitzky, H., Brüggelmann, H., Hecker, U., Heinzel, F., Schönknecht, G. & Speck-Hamdan, A. (Eds.). *Kursbuch Grundschule* (pp. 320–323). Frankfurt a.M.: Grundschulverband.

Bartnitzky, H. (2010). Individuell Fördern – Kompetenzen stärken. *Grundschule aktuell, 109,* 6–11.

Bartsch, S. (2014). *Structural and Functional Properties of Collocations in English. A Corpus Study of Lexical and Pragmatic Constraints on Lexical Co-Occurrence.* Tübingen: Narr.

Bassetti, B. (2009). Orthographic Input and Second Language Phonology. In Piske, T. & Young-Scholten, M. (Eds.). *Input Matters in SLA* (pp. 191–206). Bristol: Multilingual Matters.

Bebermeier, H. & Stoll, U. (2008). Soll auch gelesen werden? In Christiani, R. & Cwik, G. (Eds.). *Englisch unterrichten in Klasse 1 und 2* (pp. 78–84). Berlin: Cornelsen.

Bechler, S. & Reckermann, J. (2018). Graded readers for young learners. Passende Lektüren für den Englischunterricht finden. *Grundschulmagazin Englisch, 16*(1), 37–38.

Becker, C. & Roos, J. (2014). What Research Tells us. Bewährte Methoden ade? *Grundschulmagazin Englisch, 12*(3), 37–38.

Beckmann, U. (2006). Frühes Fremdsprachenlernen. Historischer Überblick. In Pienemann, M., Keßler, J.- U. & Roos, E. (Eds.). *Englischerwerb in der Grundschule* (pp. 11–23). Paderborn: Schöningh UTB.

Belgrad, J. & Pfaff, H. (2010). Sachtexte in der Grundschule. In Schulz, G. (Ed.). *Lesen lernen in der Grundschule (pp. 62–74).* Berlin: Cornelsen.

Beyer-Kessling, V., Decke-Cornill, H., MacDevitt, L. & Wandel, R. (1998). *Die Fundgrube für den handlungsorientierten Englisch-Unterricht. Schüleraktivierende Übungen und Spiele.* Berlin: Cornelsen.

Bezirksregierung Detmold (2008). *Didaktisch-methodische Fortbildung Englisch in der Grundschule. Modul 6: Kommunikation – Sprachliches Handeln. Leseverstehen und Schreiben.* PDF retrieved from https://www.schulentwicklung.nrw.de/cms/upload/egs/Modul_6_Leseverstehen_und_Schreiben.pdf (last access: 15.05.2017).

Biebricher, C. (2008). *Lesen in der Fremdsprache. Eine Studie zu Effekten extensiven Lesens.* Tübingen: Narr.

BIG-Kreis – Beratung Information Gespräch Stiftung Lernen (2015). Der Lernstand im Englischunterricht am Ende von Klasse 4. Ergebnisse der BIG-Studie. München: Domino.

Bitchener, J. (2010). *Writing an Applied Linguistics Thesis or Dissertation. A Guide to Presenting Empirical Research.* New York: Palgrave Macmillan.

Bland, J. (2013a). *Children's Literature and Learner Empowerment. Children and Teenagers in English Language Education.* London: Bloomsbury.

Bland, J. (2013b). Introduction. In Bland, J. & Lütge, C. (Eds.). *Children's Literature in Second Language Education* (pp. 1–11). London: Bloomsbury.

Bleyhl, W. (2000a). Empfehlungen zur Verwendung des Schriftlichen im Fremdsprachenerwerb in der Grundschule. In Bleyhl, W. (Ed.). *Fremdsprachen in der Grundschule. Grundlagen und Praxisbeispiele* (pp. 84–91). Hannover: Schroedel.

Bleyhl, W. (2000b). Methodische Konsequenzen aus dem Wissen um das Lernen. In Bleyhl, W. (Ed.). *Fremdsprachen in der Grundschule. Grundlagen und Praxisbeispiele* (pp. 24–30). Hannover: Schroedel.

Bleyhl, W. (2000c). Wie funktioniert das Lernen einer fremden Sprache? In Bleyhl, W. (Ed.). *Fremdsprachen in der Grundschule. Grundlagen und Praxisbeispiele* (pp. 9–23). Hannover: Schroedel.

Bleyhl, W. (2002). *Fremdsprachen in der Grundschule. Geschichten erzählen im Anfangsunterricht. Storytelling.* Hannover: Schroedel.

Bleyhl, W. (2003). Ist früher besser? Die Bedeutung des frühen Lernens. In Edelhoff, C. (Ed.). *Englisch in der Grundschule und darüber hinaus. Eine praxisnahe Orientierungshilfe* (pp. 5–23). Frankfurt a.M.: Diesterweg.

Bleyhl, W. (2007). Schrift im fremdsprachlichen Anfangsunterricht – ein zweischneidiges Schwert. *Take Off!, 1,* 47.

Börner, O. (1997). Zur Akzeptanz von Englisch in der Grundschule. In *English, 3,* 81–83.

Börner, O. (2000). Übergang in die Klasse 5. In Bleyhl, W. (Ed.). *Fremdsprachen in der Grundschule. Grundlagen und Praxisbeispiele* (pp. 99–103). Hannover: Schroedel.

Börner, O. & Brusch, W. (2004). *Die Hamburger Bücherkiste für den Englischunterricht in der Grundschule. Eine Umfrage.* PDF retrieved from http://li.hamburg.de/contentblob/3845872/data/download-pdf-buecherkiste-eng-grundschule-auswertung.pdf (last access: 15.05.2017).

Börner, O., Engel, G. & Groot-Wilken, B. (Eds.) (2013). *Hörverstehen Leseverstehen Sprechen. Diagnose und Förderung von sprachlichen Kompetenzen im Englischunterricht der Primarstufe.* Münster: Waxmann.

Börner, O. & Frisch, S. (2013). Förderung und Erhebung des Lesens im Englischunterricht der Grundschule. In Börner, O., Engel, G. & Groot-Wilken, B. (Eds.). *Hörverstehen, Leseverstehen, Sprechen. Diagnose und Förderung von sprachlichen Kompetenzen im Englischunterricht der Primarstufe* (pp. 71–94). Münster: Waxmann.

Böttger, H. (2005). *Englisch lernen in der Grundschule.* Bad Heilbrunn: Klinkhardt.

Böttger, H. (2009). Von Brücken und Klüften. Der schwierige Übergang in die weiterführenden Schulen im Fach Englisch. *HotSpot – Das Online Magazin zum frühen Fremdsprachenlernen, 5,* 2–6.

Böttger, H. (2012). Learning in Two Languages. A Foreign Language in Primary School Subjects. In Egger, G. & Lechner, C. (Eds.). *Primary CLIL Around Europe. Learning in Two Languages in Primary Education* (pp. 98–116). Marburg: Tectum.

Böttger, H. (2013). Was Kinder wirklich können. Ein Plädoyer für die Entfaltung kindlicher (Sprachen-) Potenziale. *Grundschule Englisch, 43,* 42–44.

Böttger, H. (2014a). Strategisch lesen und schreiben lernen. Erste Lern- und Arbeitstechniken für den frühen Fremdsprachenunterricht. *Grundschule Englisch, 45,* 12–13.

Böttger, H. (2014b). Weil Kinder es können und wollen. Lesen und Schreiben im Englischunterricht der Grundschule. *Grundschule Englisch, 45,* 4–9.

Bortz, J. & Döring, N. (2006). *Forschungsmethoden und Evaluation für Human- und Sozialwissenschaftler.* 4th edition. Heidelberg: Springer.

Bosenius, P. (2009). Content and Language Integrated Learning. A Model for *Multiliteracy?* In Ditze, S.- A. & Halbach, A. (Eds.). *Bilingualer Sachfachunterricht (CLIL) im Kontext von Sprache, Kultur und Multiliteralität* (pp. 15–26). Frankfurt a.M.: Peter Lang.

Braun, D. (2010). *Leseschwierigkeiten erkennen. Schüler individuell fördern.* In Schulz, G. (Ed.). Lesen lernen in der Grundschule (pp. 174–183). Berlin: Cornelsen.

Breen, M. P. (1985). Authenticity in the Language Classroom. *Applied Linguistics, 6*(1), 60–70.

Brewster, J. & Ellis, G. with Girard, D. (2002). *The Primary English Teacher's Guide.* 2ⁿᵈ edition. London: Penguin.

Briner, S. W., Virtue, S. M. & Schutzenhofer, M. C. (2014). Hemispheric Processing of Mental Representations during Text Comprehension. Evidence for Inhibition of Inconsistent Shape Information. *Neuropsychologia, 61*, 96–104.

Brown, H. D. (2007). *Principles of Language Learning and Teaching.* 5ᵗʰ edition. White Plains: Pearson Longman.

Brown, H. D. & Abeywickrama, P. (2010). *Language Assessment. Principles and Classroom Practices.* White Plains: Pearson Longman.

Brown, J.D. (2001). *Using Surveys in Language Programs.* Cambridge, Cambridge University Press.

Brown, J. D. & Rodgers, T. S. (2002). *Doing Second Language Research.* Oxford: Oxford University Press.

Brüning, L. & Saum, T. (2009). *Erfolgreich unterrichten durch Kooperatives Lernen. Strategien zur Schüleraktivierung. Band 1.* Essen: NDS.

Brusch, W. (1994). Erziehung zum Lesen im Englischen durch Klassenbibliotheken. Ein empirisches Unterrichtsprojekt. *Praxis des Neusprachlichen Unterrichts, 41*(1), 17–26.

Brusch, W. (2000). Englisch vom ersten Schultag an. *Grundschule, 6*, 38–42.

Bundesministerium für Unterricht, Kunst und Kultur, Stadtschulrat für Wien, Pädagogisches Institut der Stadt Wien (Eds.) (2008). Leselust statt Lesefrust. Erfolgreich lesen lernen. Ein Leseprojekt speziell für Kinder mit Migrationshintergrund. 2ⁿᵈ edition. Wien: BMUK.

Burmeister, P. & Piske, T. (2008). Schriftlichkeit im fremdsprachlichen Sachfachunterricht an der Grundschule. In Böttger, H. (Ed.). *Fortschritte im frühen Fremdsprachenlernen. Ausgewählte Tagungsbeiträge Nürnberg 2007* (pp. 183–193). München: Domino.

Burnett, C. & Merchant, G. (2013). Learning, Literacies and New Technologies. The Current Context and Future Possibilities. In Larson, J. & Marsh, J. (Eds). *The SAGE Handbook of Early Childhood Literacy* (pp. 575–586). 2ⁿᵈ edition. Los Angeles: Sage.

Burwitz-Melzer, E. (2007). Ein Lesekompetenzmodell für den fremdsprachlichen Literaturunterricht. In Bredella, L. & Hallet, W. (Eds.). *Literaturunterricht, Kompetenzen und Bildung* (pp. 126–157). Trier: Wissenschaftlicher Verlag Trier.

Burwitz-Melzer, E. (2013). Approaching Literary and Language Competence. Picturebooks and Graphic Novels in the EFL Classroom. In Bland, J. & Lütge, C. (Eds.). *Children's Literature in Second Language Education* (pp. 56–70). London: Bloomsbury.

Butzkamm, W. & Caldwell, J. A. W. (2009). *The Bilingual Reform. A Paradigm Shift in Foreign Language Teaching.* Tübingen: Narr.

Bynner, J. (2006). Longitudinal Study. In Jupp, V. (Ed.). *The SAGE Dictionary of Social Research Methods* (pp. 164–165). London. Sage.

Cameron, L. (2001). *Teaching Languages to Young Learners.* Cambridge: Cambridge University Press.

Carrell, P. L. (1988). Introduction. In Carrell, P. L., Devine, J. & Eskey, D. E. (Eds.). *Interactive Approaches to Second Language Reading* (pp. 1–8). New York: Cambridge University Press.

Chamot, A. U. (2005). Language Learning Strategy Instruction. Current Issues and Research. *Annual Review of Applied Linguistics, 25,* 112–130.

Chiu, S.- I., Hong, F. Y. & Hu, H. Y. (2015). The Effects of Family Cultural Capital and Reading Motivation on Reading Behaviour in Elementary School Students. *School Psychology International, 36*(1), 1–15.

Chomsky, C. (1972). Stages in Language Development and Reading Exposure. *Harvard Educational Review, 42*(1), 1–33.

Claire, N. (2013). Acquiring Literacy in the Bilingual Primary School. Paper presented at *Fachtagung Bilinguales Lehren und Lernen – Vertiefende Perspektiven,* University of Hildesheim, 19.01.2013.

Coelho, E. (1992). Cooperative Learning. Foundation for a Communicative Curriculum. In Kessler, C. (Ed.). *Cooperative Language Learning. A Teacher's Resource Book* (pp. 129–152). New York: Prentice Hall.

Coles, G. (2013). Reading Policy. Evidence Versus Power. In Larson, J. & Marsh, J. (Eds). *The SAGE Handbook of Early Childhood Literacy.* (pp. 345–363). 2nd edition. Los Angeles: Sage.

Cook, V. (2008). *Second Language Learning and Language Teaching.* London: Edward Arnold.

Copland, F. & Garton, S. (2014). Key Themes and Future Directions in Teaching English to Young Learners. Introduction to the Special Issue. *ELT Journal, 68*(3), 223–230.

Coyle, D., Hood, P. & Marsh, D. (2010). *CLIL – Content and Language Integrated Learning.* Cambridge: Cambridge University Press.

Creswell, J. W. & Plano Clark, V. L. (2011). *Designing and Conducting Mixed Methods Research.* 2nd edition. Los Angeles: Sage.

Crystal, D. (2003). *English as a Global Language.* 2nd edition. Cambridge: Cambridge University Press.

Cummins, J. (1979). Linguistic Interdependence and the Educational Development of Bilingual Children. *Review of Educational Research, 49*(2), 222–251.

Daneman, M. & Newson, M. (1992). Assessing the Importance of Subvocalization During Normal Silent Reading. *Reading and Writing,* 4(1), 55–77.

Dausend, H. (2014a). *Fremdsprachen transcurricular lehren und lernen. Ein methodischer Ansatz für die Grundschule.* Tübingen: Narr.

Dausend, H. (2014b). Transcurricular unterrichten. A Place Called Home. *Grundschulmagazin Englisch,* 12(5), 31–34.

Davidson, J. (2006a). Non-Probability (Non-Random) Sampling. Jupp, V. (Ed.). *The SAGE Dictionary of Social Research Methods* (pp. 196–197). London: Sage.

Davidson, J. (2006b). Sampling. In Jupp, V. (Ed.). *The SAGE Dictionary of Social Research Methods* (pp. 270–271). London: Sage.

Davies, P. (2006). Exploratory Research. In Jupp, V. (Ed.). *The SAGE Dictionary of Social Research Methods* (pp. 110–111). London: Sage.

Deana, N. & Rumlich, D. (2013). Using Comics in the Classroom – The Obvious Way of Creating a Favourable Learning Environment? In Eisenmann, M., Hempel, M. & Ludwig, C. (Eds.). *Medien und Interkulturalität im Fremdsprachenunterricht: Zwischen Autonomie, Kollaboration und Konstruktion* (pp. 183–203). Duisburg: Universitätsverlag Rhein-Ruhr.

Decke-Cornill, H. (2003). 'We would have to Invent the Language we are Supposed to Teach': The Issue of English as a Lingua Franca in Language Education in Germany. In Byram, M. & Grundy, P. (Eds.). *Conext and Culture in Language Teaching and Learning* (pp. 59–71). Clevedon: Multilingual Matters.

Decke-Cornill, H. & Küster, L. (2010). *Fremdsprachendidaktik. Eine Einführung.* Tübingen: Narr.

Dehaene, S. (2010). *Lesen. Die größte Erfindung der Menschheit und was dabei in unseren Köpfen passiert* (trans. H. Reuter). München: Knaus.

DeKeyser, R.M. (1998). Beyond Focus on Form. Cognitive Perspectives on Learning and Practicing Second Language Grammar. In Doughty C. J. & Williams, J. (Eds.). *Focus on Form in Classroom Second Language Acquisition* (pp. 42–63). Cambridge: Cambridge University Press.

DeKeyser, R.M. (2001). Automaticity and Automatization. In P. Robinson (Ed.). *Cognition and Second Language Instruction* (pp. 125–151). Cambridge: Cambridge University Press.

Denzin, N. K. (1970). *The Research Act. A Theoretical Introduction to Sociological Methods.* New York: McGraw-Hill.

Denzin, N.K. (1978). *The Research Act. A Theoretical Introduction to Sociological Methods.* 2nd edition. New York: McGraw-Hill.

DeVaus, D. (2006). Experiment. In Jupp, V. (Ed.). *The SAGE Dictionary of Social Research Methods* (pp. 106–108). London: Sage.

Diehr, B. (2010). Research into Reading in the Primary School. A Fresh Look at the Use of Written English with Young Learners of English as a Foreign Language. In Diehr, B. & Rymarczyk, J. (Eds.). *Researching Literacy in a Foreign Language among Primary School Learners. Forschung zum Schrifterwerb in der Fremdsprache bei Grundschülern* (pp. 51–68). Frankfurt a.M.: Peter Lang.

Diehr, B. (2012). What's in a Name? Terminologische, typologische und programmatische Überlegungen zum Verhältnis der Sprachen im Bilingualen Unterricht. In Diehr, B. & Schmelter, L. (Eds.). *Bilingualen Unterricht weiterdenken. Programme, Positionen, Perspektiven* (pp. 17–36). Frankfurt a.M.: Peter Lang.

Diehr, B. & Frisch, S. (2010a). A Roadmap to Reading. Bewusstmachende Verfahren im Umgang mit der englischen Schriftsprache. *Grundschule, 9*, 26–28.

Diehr, B. & Frisch, S. (2010b). Lesen sie doch? Fragen an die LiPs-Studie (Lesen im Englischunterricht auf der Primarstufe). *IMIS Beiträge – Institut für Migrationsforschung und Interkulturelle Studien, 37*, 143–163.

Diehr, B. & Frisch, S. (2011). Take Heart and Read. Vorschläge zum systematischen Aufbau der Lesefertigkeiten. *Grundschule Englisch, 37*, 42–44.

Diehr, B. & Rymarczyk, J. (2008). „Ich weiß es, weil ich es so spreche". Zur Basis von Lese- und Schreibversuchen in Klasse 1 und 2. *Grundschulmagazin Englisch, 6*(1), 6–8.

Diehr, B. & Rymarczyk, J. (Eds.) (2010). *Researching Literacy in a Foreign Language among Primary School Learners. Forschung zum Schrifterwerb in der Fremdsprache bei Grundschülern.* Frankfurt a.M.: Peter Lang.

Dines, P. (2000). Themenorientierter Fremdsprachenunterricht in der Grundschule. In Bleyhl, W. (Ed.). *Fremdsprachen in der Grundschule. Grundlagen und Praxisbeispiele* (pp. 72–80). Hannover: Schroedel.

Doms, C. (2010). Lost in Transition? Herausforderungen des Übergangs bewältigen. *Grundschulmagazin Englisch, 8*(4), 7–8.

Doms, C. (2012). Differenzieren und Individualisieren. In Böttger, H. (Ed.). *Englisch. Didaktik für die Grundschule* (pp. 60–77). Berlin: Cornelsen.

Dörnyei, Z. (2007). *Research Methods in Applied Linguistics.* Oxford: Oxford University Press.

Doyé, P. (1993). Fremdsprachenerziehung in der Grundschule. *Zeitschrift für Fremdsprachenforschung, 4*(1), 48–90.

Doyé, P. & Lüttge, D. (1977). *Untersuchungen zum Englischunterricht in der Grundschule. Bericht über das Forschungsprojekt FEU.* Braunschweig: Westermann.

Dresing, T. & Pehl, P. (2013). *Praxisbuch Interview, Transkription & Analyse. Anleitungen und Regelsysteme für die qualitative Forschende.* 5th edition. PDF retrieved from http://www.audio transkription.de/download/praxisbuch_transkription.pdf?q=Praxisbuch-Transkription.pdf (last access: 15.05.2017).

Drew, I. (2009). Reading and Writing in Norwegian Primary EFL Education and How it Compares with the Netherlands. In Engel, G., Groot-Wilken, B. & Thürmann, E. (Eds.). *Englisch in der Primarstufe – Chancen und Herausforderungen. Evaluation und Erfahrungen aus der Praxis* (pp. 101–110). Berlin: Cornelsen.

Duchowski, A.T. (2007). Eye Tracking Methodology. Theory and Practice. 2nd edition. London: Springer.

Dunn, O. (2006). Do Boys as Young Learners of English Need Different Language Learning Opportunities from Girls? Can Authentic Picture Books Help? In Enever, J. & Schmid-Schönbein, G. (Eds.). *Picture Books and Young Learners of English* (pp. 115–121). Berlin: Langenscheidt.

Duscha, M. (2007). *Der Einfluss der Schrift auf das Fremdsprachenlernen in der Grundschule. Dargestellt am Beispiel des Englischunterrichts in Niedersachsen.* PDF retrieved from https:// publikationsserver.tu-braunschweig.de/receive/ dbbs_mods_00021088 (last access: 15.05.2017).

Edelhoff, C. (2003). Fremdsprachen in der Grundschule. Herausforderung und Wagnis. In Edelhoff, C. (Ed.). *Englisch in der Grundschule und darüber hinaus. Eine praxisnahe Orientierungshilfe* (pp. 143–149). Frankfurt a.M.: Diesterweg.

Egger, G., Lechner, C. & Ward, S. (2012). Introduction. In Egger, G. & Lechner. C. (Eds). *Primary CLIL Around Europe. Learning in Two Languages in Primary Education* (pp. 11–12). Marburg: Tectum.

Egger, G. (2012). Rethinking Teacher Education. Sprachausbildung von Grundschullehrerinnen. Primary Language Teacher Education. In Egger, G. & Lechner, C. (Eds). *Primary CLIL Around Europe. Learning in Two Languages in Primary Education* (pp. 229–261). Marburg: Tectum.

Ehlers, S. (1998). Lesetheorie und fremdsprachliche Lesepraxis aus der Perspektive des Deutschen als Fremdsprache. Tübingen: Narr.

Ehlers, S. (2007). Lesetheorien, Lesekompetenz und Narrative. In Bredella, L. & Hallet, W. (Eds.). *Literaturunterricht, Kompetenzen und Bildung* (pp. 107–126). Trier: Wissenschaftlicher Verlag Trier.

Eisenberg, P. & Fuhrhop, N. (2007). Schulorthographie und Graphematik. *Zeitschrift für Sprachwissenschaft, 6,* 15–41.

Ellis, G. & Brewster, J. (2014). *Tell it Again. The Storytelling Handbook for Primary English Language Teachers. British Council.* PDF retrieved from https:// www.teachingenglish.org.uk/sites/teacheng/files/D467_Storytelling_hand book_FINAL_web.pdf (last access: 15.05.2017).

Ellis, N. C. (2005). At the Interface. Dynamic Interactions of Explicit and Implicit Language Knowledge. *Studies in Second Language Acquisition, 27*, 305–352.

Elsner, D. (2010). *Englisch in der Grundschule unterrichten. Grundlagen, Methoden, Praxisbeispiele*. München: Oldenbourg.

Elsner, D. & Keßler, J.- U. (2013a). Bilingual Approaches to Foreign Language Education in Primary School. In Elsner, D. & Keßler, J.U. (Eds). *Bilingual Education in Primary School. Aspects of Immersion, CLIL, and Bilingual Modules* (pp. 16–27). Tübingen: Narr.

Elsner, D. & Keßler, J.- U. (2013b). Aspects of Immersion, CLIL, and Bilingual Modules: Bilingual Education in Primary School. In Elsner, D. & Keßler, J.U. (Eds.). *Bilingual Education in Primary School. Aspects of Immersion, CLIL, and Bilingual Modules* (pp. 1–6). Tübingen: Narr.

Enever, J. (Ed.) (2011a). *ELLiE. Early Language Learning in Europe*. London: British Council.

Enever, J. (2011b). Policy. In Enever, J. (Ed.). *ELLiE. Early Language Learning in Europe* (pp. 23–42). London: British Council.

Engel, G. (2009). EVENING – Konsequenzen für die Weiterentwicklung des Englischunterrichts in der Grundschule. In Engel, G., Groot-Wilken, B. & Thürmann, E. (Eds.). *Englisch in der Primarstufe – Chancen und Herausforderungen. Evaluation und Erfahrungen aus der Praxis* (pp. 197–215). Berlin: Cornelsen.

Engel, G., Groot-Wilken, B. & Thürmann, E. (Eds.) (2009). *Englisch in der Primarstufe – Chancen und Herausforderungen. Evaluation und Erfahrungen aus der Praxis*. Berlin: Cornelsen.

Erten, I. H. & Razi, S. (2009). The Effects of Cultural Familiarity on Reading Comprehension. *Reading in a Foreign Language, 21*(1), 60–77.

European Commission (1995). *White Paper on Education and Training – Teaching and Learning: Towards the Learning Society*. PDF retrieved from http://europa.eu/documents/comm/white_papers/pdf/com95_590_en.pdf (last access: 15.05.2017).

European Commision (2006). *Special Eurobarometer 243. Europeans and Their Languages*. PDF retrieved from http://ec.europa.eu/commfrontoffice/publicopinion/archives/ebs/ebs_243_en. Pdf (last access: 15.05.2017).

European Commission (2008). Erschließung des Rates vom 21.November 2008 zu einer europäischen Strategie für Mehrsprachigkeit. *Amtsblatt, Nr. C320 (16.12.2008)*, 1–3.

European Commission (2012). *Special Eurobarometer 386. Europeans and Their Languages.* Report. PDF retrieved from http://ec.europa.eu/commfrontoffice/publicopinion/archives/ebs/ ebs_386_en.pdf (last access: 15.05.2017).

Eurydice – The Information Network on Education in Europe (2006). *Content and Language Integrated Learning (CLIL) at School in Europe.* Brussels: Eurydice.

Fay, G. & Hellwig, K. (1971). *Englischunterricht in der Grundschule.* Hannover: Schroedel.

Finck, K. & Schulz, C. (2008). Fremdsprachen von Anfang an. Das Konzept der Integrierten Fremdsprachenarbeit (IFA) in der rheinland-pfälzischen Primarstufe. In Böttger, H. (Ed.). *Fortschritte im frühen Fremdsprachenlernen. Ausgewählte Tagungsbeiträge Nürnberg 2007* (pp. 35–41). München: Domino.

Finkbeiner, C. (2005). *Interessen und Strategien beim fremdsprachlichen Lesen. Wie Schülerinnen und Schüler englische Texte lesen und verstehen.* Tübingen: Narr.

Finkbeiner, C. (2013). Lernstrategien und Lerntechniken im Kontext neuer Unterrichtsaufgaben. In Bach, G. & Timm, J.P. (Eds.). *Englischunterricht* (pp. 230–255). 5th edition. Tübingen: UTB.

Finkbeiner, C., Knierim, M., Smasal, M. & Ludwig, P.H. (2012). Self-Regulated Cooperative EFL Reading Tasks. Students' Strategy Use and Teachers' Support. *Language Awareness, 21*(1–2), 57–83.

Finkbeiner. C., Ludwig, P.H., Wilden, E. & Knierim, M. (2006). Forschungsprojekt ADEQUA. Bericht über ein DFG-Forschungsprojekt zur Förderung von Lernstrategien im Englischunterricht. *Zeitschrift für Fremdsprachenforschung, 17*(2), 257–274.

Flick, U. (2006). Triangulation. In Jupp, V. (Ed.). *The SAGE Dictionary of Social Research Methods* (305–306). London: Sage.

Flick, U. (2011). Triangulation. *Eine Einführung.* 3rd edition. Wiesbaden: VS Verlag.

FMKS – Frühe Mehrsprachigkeit an Kindertageseinrichtungen und Schulen FMKS e.V. (2014). *Bilinguale Grundschulen in Deutschland 2014.* PDF retrieved from http://www.fmks-online.de/download.html (last access: 15.05.2017).

Freeman, D. (1998). *Doing Teacher Research. From Inquiry to Understanding.* Boston: Heinle and Heinle.

Freudenau, T. (2012). Multimedia Dictionaries in the Primary School. In Lennon, P. (Ed.). *Learner Autonomy in the English Classroom. Empirical Studies and Ideas for Teachers* (pp. 95–122). Frankfurt a.M.: Peter Lang.

Freudenau, T. (2017). *Wortschatzarbeit im Englischunterricht der Grundschule. Eine Studie zum autonomen Lernen mit Online-Wörterbüchern.* Frankfurt a.m.: Peter Lang.

Frisch, S. (2010). Bewusstmachende Verfahren beim Umgang mit dem Schriftbild im Englischunterricht der Primarstufe. Erste Ergebnisse der LiPs Studie. In Diehr, B. & Rymarczyk, J. (Eds.). *Researching Literacy in a Foreign Language Among Primary School Learners. Forschung zum Schriftspracherwerb in der Fremdsprache bei Grundschülern* (pp. 107–130). Frankfurt a.m.: Peter Lang.

Frisch, S. (2011). Explizites und implizites Lernen beim Einsatz der englischen Schrift in der Grundschule. In Kötter, M. & Rymarczyk, J. (Eds.). *Fremdsprachunterricht in der Grundschule. Forschungsergebnisse und Vorschläge zu seiner weiteren Entwicklung* (pp. 69–88). Frankfurt a.m.: Peter Lang.

Frisch, S. (2013). *Lesen im Englischunterricht der Grundschule. Eine Vergleichsstudie zur Wirksamkeit zweier Leselehrverfahren.* Tübingen: Narr.

Frisch, S. (2014a). Can You See...? Lesetexte im Anfangsunterricht. *Grundschule Englisch, 49,* 14–16.

Frisch, S. (2014b). I Can Read English! Mit *Phonics Readers* das Lesen fördern. *Grundschulmagazin Englisch, 12*(4), 29–32.

Frisch, S. (2014c). Moving On. Herausforderungen des Englischunterrichts am Übergang der Grundschule zur weiterführenden Schule am Beispiel des Lernbereichs Lesen. Keynote presentation presented at *3. Bielefelder Grundschultag Englisch,* Bielefelder Spinnerei, 12.11.2014.

Frisch, S. (2014d). Reading Revisited. Der bewusste Umgang mit dem Schriftbild. *Grundschulmagazin Englisch, 12*(4), 33–34.

Frisch, S. (2015). Eckpunkte einer theoretisch und empirisch basierten Lesedidaktik für den Englischunterricht der Grundschule. In Kötter, M. & Rymarczyk, J. (Eds.). *Englischunterricht auf der Primarstufe. Neue Forschungen – weitere Entwicklungen* (pp. 15–34). Frankfurt a.m.: Peter Lang.

Frisch, S. & Holberg, S. (2015). Read it out Loud! Mit motivierenden Aufgaben zum sinngebenden Vorlesen. *Grundschule Englisch, 51,* 38–41.

Frith, U. (1985). Beneath the Surface of Developmental Dyslexia. In Patterson, K. E., Marshall, J. C. & Coltheart, M. (Eds.). *Surface Dyslexia. Cognitive and Neuropsychological Studies of Phonological Reading* (pp. 301–330). Hillsdale: Erlbaum.

Fröhlich-Ward, L. (1999). Ways to Successful Foreign Language Teaching in the Primary School. In Hermann-Brennecke, G. (Ed.). *Frühes schulisches Fremdsprachenlernen zwischen Empirie und Theorie* (pp. 55–72). Münster: Lit Verlag.

Fuchs, S. & Tippelt, R. (2012). Bereichsübergreifende Kooperationen als Notwendigkeit für erfolgreiche Übergänge im Bildungssystem. In Berkemeyer, N., Beutel, S.- I., Järvinnen, H. & Van Ophuysen, S. (Eds.). *Übergänge bilden. Lernen in der Grund- und weiterführenden Schule* (pp. 73–97). Köln: Carl Link.

Gailberger, S. (2011). *Lesen durch Hören. Leseförderung in der Sek. I mit Hörbüchern und neuen Lesestrategien.* Weinheim: Beltz.

Ganzeboom, H. B. G., DeGraaf, P. M., Treimann, D. J. & DeLeeuw, J. (1992). A Standard International Socio-Economic Index of Occupational Status. *Social Science Research, 21,* 1–56.

Garbe, C. (2010). Wie werden Kinder zu Lesern? In Schulz, G. (Ed.). *Lesen lernen in der Grundschule* (pp. 9–23). Berlin: Cornelsen.

Gebauer, S. K., Zaunbauer, A. C. M. & Möller, J. (2012). Erstsprachliche Leistungsentwicklung im Immersionsunterricht. Vorteile trotz Unterrichts in einer Fremdsprache? *Zeitschrift für Pädagogische Psychologie, 26*(3), 183–196.

Gehring, W. (2004). *Englische Fachdidaktik. Eine Einführung.* 2nd edition. Berlin: Erich Schmidt Verlag.

Gehring, W. & Stinshoff, E. (Eds.) (2010). *Außerschulische Lernorte des Fremdsprachenunterrichts.* Braunschweig: Klinkhardt.

Geisler, U. (1985). *Faktoren der Verständlichkeit von Texten für Kinder. Kinder und Medien – ein Interaktions-Modell.* München: Causa.

Genesee, F. (1987). *Learning Through Two Languages. Studies of Immersion and Bilingual Education.* Cambridge: Newbury House Publishers.

Gerken, N., Natzke, H., Petermann, F. & Walter, H.- J. (2002). Verhaltenstraining für Schulanfänger. Ein Programm zur Primärprävention von aggressivem und unaufmerksamen Verhalten. *Kindheit und Entwicklung, 11*(2), 119–128.

Gerngroß, G. & Diekmann, A. (2003). Englischsprachige Kinderbücher im Anfangsunterricht. To Simplify, or Not to Simplify. That is the Question. *Fremdsprachenunterricht, 47*(1), 20–23.

Gompf, G. (1992). *Fremdsprachenbeginn ab Klasse 3. Lernen für Europa.* Berlin: Cornelsen.

Gompf, G. (2002a). Auswertende Zusammenfassung der bundesweiten Untersuchung. In Gompf, G. (Ed.). *Fremdsprachenunterricht beginnt in der Grundschule. Jahrbuch 2002 Kinder lernen europäische Sprachen e.V.* (pp. 92–109). Leipzig: Klett.

Gompf, G. (2002b). Länderspezifische Darstellung der Reform des Fremdsprachenbeginns. In Gompf, G. (Ed.). *Fremdsprachenunterricht beginnt in der Grundschule. Jahrbuch 2002 Kinder lernen europäische Sprachen e.V.* (pp. 7–91). Leipzig: Klett.

Goodman, K. (1988). The Reading Process. In Carrell, P. L., Devine, J. & Eskey, D. E. (Eds.). *Interactive Approaches to Second Language Reading* (pp. 11–21). New York: Cambridge University Press.

Gorsuch, G. & Taguchi, E. (2010). Developing Reading Fluency and Comprehension Using Repeated Reading. Evidence from Longitudinal Student Reports. *Language Teaching Research, 14*(1), 27–59.

Gramley, V. (2008). Bilingualism. In Gramley, S. & Gramley, V. (Eds.). *Bielefeld Introduction to Applied Linguistics. A Course Book* (pp. 301–311). Bielefeld: Aisthesis Verlag.

Green, N. & Green, K. (2005). *Kooperatives Lernen im Klassenraum und im Kollegium. Das Trainingsbuch.* Seelze: Klett Kallmeyer.

Greene, J. C., Caracelli, V. J. & Graham, W. F. (1989). Toward a Conceptual Framework for Mixed-Method Evaluation Designs. *Educational Evaluation and Policy Analysis, 11*(3), 255–274.

Grellet, F. (1986). *Developing Reading Skills.* Cambridge: Cambridge University Press.

Groot-Wilken, B. (2009). Design, Struktur und Durchführung der Evaluationsstudie EVENING in Nordrhein-Westfalen. In Engel, G., Groot-Wilken, B. & Thürmann, E. (Eds.). *Englisch in der Primarstufe – Chancen und Herausforderungen* (pp. 124–157). Berlin: Cornelsen.

Groot-Wilken, B. & Husfeldt, V. (2013). Die Testinstrumente und –verfahren des EVENING-Projekts. Eine empirische Betrachtungsweise. In Börner, O., Engel, G. & Groot-Wilken, B. (Eds.). *Hörverstehen Leseverstehen Sprechen. Diagnose und Förderung von sprachlichen Kompetenzen im Englischunterricht der Primarstufe* (pp. 121–140). Münster: Waxmann.

Grosjean, F. (1992). Another View of Bilingualism. In Harris, R. J. (Ed.). *Cognitive Processing in Bilinguals. Advances in Psychology* (pp. 51–62). Amsterdam: Elsevier.

Guariento, W. & Morley, J. (2001). Text and Task Authenticity in the EFL classroom. *English Language Teaching, 55*(4), 347–353.

Häuptle-Barceló, M. & Willerich-Tocha, M. (2008). Sprachliches und literarisches Lernen mit Bilderbüchern. Ein interdisziplinärer Ansatz Englisch – Deutsch. In Böttger, H. (Ed.). *Fortschritte im frühen Fremdsprachenlernen. Ausgewählte Tagungsbeiträge Nürnberg 2007* (pp. 103–112). Müchen: Domino.

Haines, S. (1995). For and Against Authentic Materials. *Modern English Teacher, 4*(3), 60–64.

Hall, K. (2013). Effective Literacy Teaching in the Early Years of School. A Review of Evidence. In Larson, J. & Marsh, J. (Eds). *The SAGE Handbook of Early Childhood Literacy.* (pp. 523–540). 2nd edition. Los Angeles: Sage.

Hallet, W. (2010). Fremdsprachliche Literacies. In Hallet, W. & Königs, F. G. (Eds.). *Handbuch Fremdsprachendidaktik* (pp. 66–70). Seelze-Velber: Kallmeyer.

Hamers, J. G. & Blanc, M. H. A. (2000). *Bilinguality and Bilingualism.* 2nd edition. New York: Cambridge University Press.

Harmer, J. (2007). *The Practice of English Language Teaching.* 4th edition. Harlow: Pearson Longman.

Haß, F. (Ed.) (2006). *Fachdidaktik Englisch. Innovation – Tradition – Praxis.* Stuttgart: Klett.

Haudeck, H. (2011). Lernstrategien und Lerntechniken im schulischen Fremdsprachenunterricht. In Reinfried, M. & Rück, N. (Eds.). *Innovative Entwicklungen beim Lehren und Lernen von Fremdsprachen. Festschrift für Inez De Florio-Hansen* (pp. 269–286). Tübingen: Narr.

Hecht, K. & Waas, L. (1980). *Englischunterricht Konkret. Linguistische und didaktische Grundlagen, Stundentypen, Übungsformen.* Donauwörth: Auer.

Heckt, D.H. (Ed.) (2010). *Praxis Grundschule, 5,* cover.

Hedge, T. (2000). *Teaching and Learning in the Language Classroom.* Oxford: Oxford University Press.

Helfrich, H. (1992). Englisch im 3. Schuljahr: Modellversuch in Rheinland-Pfalz. In Gompf, G. (Ed.). *Fremdsprachenbeginn ab Klasse 3. Lernen für Europa* (pp. 32–37). Berlin: Cornelsen.

Hellwig, K. (1992). Fremdsprachen in der Grundschule zwischen Spielen und Lernen. In Gompf, G. (Ed.). *Fremdsprachenbeginn ab Klasse 3. Lernen für Europa* (pp. 38–50). Berlin: Cornelsen.

Hellwig, K. (1995). *Fremdsprachen an Grundschulen als Spielen und Lernen. Dargestellt am Beispiel Englisch.* Ismaning: Max Hueber Verlag.

Henrici, G. (2001). Zur Forschungsmethodologie. *Zeitschrift für Fremdsprachenforschung, 12*(2), 33–40.

Henseler, R. & Surkamp, C. (2010). Lesen und Leseverstehen. In Hallet, W. & Königs, F. G. (Eds.). *Handbuch Fremdsprachendidaktik* (pp. 87–92). Seelze-Velber: Kallmeyer.

Hermann-Brennecke, G. (1994). Affektive und kognitive Flexibilität durch Fremdsprachenvielfalt auf der Primarstufe. *Zeitschrift für Fremdsprachenforschung, 5*(2), 1–21.

Hermann-Brennecke, G. (1998). Die affektive Seite des Fremdsprachenlernens. In Timm, J.- P. (Ed.). *Englisch lernen und lehren. Didaktik des Englischunterrichts* (pp. 53–59). Berlin: Cornelsen.

Hermes, L. (2017). Heterogenität damals und heute – wie können wir mit Heterogenität im Englischunterricht umgehen? In Chilla, S. & Vogt, K. (Eds.). *Heterogenität und Diversität im Englischunterricht. Fachdidaktische Perspektiven* (pp. 13–32). Frankfurt a.m.: Peter Lang.

Holderried, A., Lücke, B. & Müller, A. (2012). Vom Nutzen der Schulbibliothek für die Schule und die Schüler. In Holderried, A. & Lücke, B. (Eds.). *Handbuch Schulbibliothek. Planung – Betrieb – Nutzung* (pp. 11–31). Schwalbach: Dehus Pädagogik.

Holle, K. (2010). Strukturen von erzählenden Texten. Zum didaktischen Nutzen von Story Grammars. In Albers, C. & Saupe, A. (Eds.). *Vom Sinn des Erzählens. Geschichte, Theorie, Didaktik* (pp. 141–177). Frankfurt a.m.: Peter Lang.

Hollingshead, A.B. (2011). Four Factor Index of Social Status. *Yale Journal of Sociology, 8*, 21–51.

Hopkins, D. (2008). *A Teacher's Guide to Classroom Research.* 4th edition. Maidenhead: Mc Graw Hill Open University Press.

Howatt, A. P. R. (1984). *A History of English Language Teaching.* Oxford: Oxford University Press.

Hüttner, J. & Rieder-Büneman, A. (2007). The Effect of CLIL Instruction on Children's Narrative Competence. *Vienna English Working Papers (Special Issue: Current Research on CLIL 2), 16*(3), 20–27.

Hu Hsueh-chao, M. & Nation, P. (2000). Unknown Vocabulary Density and Reading Comprehension. *Reading in a Foreign Language, 13*(1), 403–430.

Hulstijn, J. H. (2001). Intentional and Incidental Second Language Vocabulary Learning. A Reappraisal of Elaboration, Rehearsal and Automaticity. In Robinson, P. (Ed.). *Cognition and Second Language Instruction* (pp. 258–286). Cambridge: Cambridge University Press.

Hulstijn, J. H. & Laufer, B. (2001). Some Empirical Evidence for the Involvement Load Hypothesis in Vocabulary Acquisition. *Language Learning, 51*(3), 539–558.

Husfeld, V. & Bader-Lehmann, U. (2009). *Englisch an der Primarschule. Lernstandserhebung im Kanton Aargau.* PDF retrieved from http://sprachenunterricht.ch/sites/default/files/E_Bericht _090108_0.pdf (last access: 15.05.2017).

IEA – The International Association for the Evaluation of Educational Achievement – TIMSS & PIRLS International Study Center (2011a). *PIRLS & TIMSS 2011 Elternfragebogen. Im Auftrag des BMUKK.* PDF retrieved from https://www.bifie.at/system/files/dl/Elternfragebogen.pdf (last access: 15.05.2017).

IEA – The International Association for the Evaluation of Educational Achieve-ment – TIMSS & PIRLS International Study Center (2011b). *PIRLS & TIMSS 2011 Schülerfragebogen. Im Auftrag des BMUKK.* PDF retrieved from https://www.bifie.at/system/files/dl/Sch%C3%BClerfragebogen.pdf (last access: 15.05.2017).

Jäger, A. (2012). Scaffolding. Gerüste für den Englischunterricht. In Böttger, H. (Ed.). *Englisch. Didaktik für die Grundschule* (pp. 209–216). Berlin: Cornelsen.

Janesick, V. J. (1994). The Dance of Qualitative Research Design: Metaphor, Methodology, and Meaning. In Denzin, N. K. & Lincoln, Y. S. (Eds.). *Handbook of Qualitative Research* (pp. 209–219). Thousand Oaks: Sage.

Jenkins, J. R., Stein, M. L. & Wysocky, K. (1984). Learning Vocabulary through Reading. *American Educational Research Journal, 21*(4), 767–787.

Jiménez Catalán, R. M., Ruiz de Zarobe, Y. & Cenoz, J. (2006). Vocabulary Profiles of English Foreign Language Learners in English as a Subject and as a Vehicular Language. *Vienna English Working Papers (Special Issue: Current Research on CLIL), 15*(3), 23–27.

Jöckel, A. (2016). Lesen und Schreiben im Englischunterricht der Grundschule. In Böttger, H. & Schlüter, N. (Eds.). *Fortschritte im frühen Fremdsprachen-lernen. Tagungsband zur 4. FFF-Konferenz* (pp. 134–142). Braunschweig: Westermann.

Johannsen, S. (2014). The English Corner. Eine schülerorientierte Lernumge-bung gestalten. *Grundschulmagazin Englisch, 12*(5), 25–27.

Johnson, B. & Gray, R. (2010). A History of Philosophical and Theoretical Is-sues for Mixed Methods Research. In Tashakkori, A. & Teddlie, C. (Eds.). *Sage Handbook of Mixed Methods in Social and Behavioral Research* (pp. 69–94). 2nd edition. Los Angeles: Sage.

Johnson, R. B., Onwuegbuzie, A. J. & Turner, L. A. (2007). Toward a Defini-tion of Mixed Methods Research. *Journal of Mixed Methods Research, 1*(2), 112–133.

Johnston, R. & Watson, J. (2007). *Teaching Synthetic Phonics.* Exeter: Learning Matters Ltd.

Johnstone, R. (2000). Context-Sensitive Assessment of Modern Languages in Primary (Elementary) and Early Secondary Education. Scotland and the Eu-ropean Experience. *Language Testing, 17*(2), 123–143.

Jupp, V. (2006). Validity. In Jupp, V. (Ed.). *The Sage Dictionary of Social Research Methods* (p. 311). London: Sage.

Kamitz, M. (2015). Get the Party Started! Projektorientiertes Arbeiten beim Planen einer Party. *Grundschule Englisch, 50,* 8–9.

Kennedy, E. (2013). Creating Positive Literacy Learning Environments in Early Childhood. Engaging Classrooms, Creating Lifelong Readers, Writers and Thinkers. In Larson, J. & Marsh, J. (Eds). *The SAGE Handbook of Early Childhood Literacy* (pp. 541–560). 2nd edition. Los Angeles: Sage.

Keßler, J.- U. (2009). Zum mündlichen englischen Sprachgebrauch von Grundschulkindern in Nordrhein-Westfalen am Ende des 4. Schuljahres. In Engel, G., Groot-Wilken, B. & Thürmann, E. (Eds.). *Englisch in der Primarstufe. Chancen und Herausforderungen. Evaluation und Erfahrungen aus der Praxis* (pp. 158–178). Berlin: Cornelsen.

Kierepka, A. (2010). Historischer Blick auf den Fremdsprachenunterricht in der Grundschule. *IMIS Beiträge – Institut für Migrationsforschung und Interkulturelle Studien, 37,* 83–97.

Kindt, W. (2002). Pragmatik. Die handlungstheoretische Begründung der Linguistik. In Müller, H. M. (Ed.). *Arbeitsbuch Linguistik.* Paderborn: Schöningh UTB.

Kintsch, W. (1998). *Comprehension. A Paradigm for Cognition.* Cambridge: Cambridge University Press.

Klieme, E. (2008). Systemmonitoring für den Sprachunterricht. In DESI-Konsortium (Eds.). *Unterricht und Kompetenzerwerb in Deutsch und Englisch. Ergebnisse der DESI-Studie* (pp. 1–10). Weinheim: Beltz.

Klippel, F. (2000). *Englisch in der Grundschule.* Berlin: Cornelsen.

Klippel, F. & Doff, S. (2007). *Englisch Didaktik. Praxishandbuch für die Sekundarstufe I und II.* Berlin: Cornelsen.

Klippert, H. (2010). *Heterogenität im Klassenzimmer. Wie Lehrkräfte effektiv und zeitsparend damit umgehen können.* Weinheim: Beltz.

Kloth, M. (2007). *Sputnik Schock. Roter Mond über America.* Retrieved from http://www.spiegel. de/einestages/sputnik-schock-a-947992.html (last access: 15.05.2017).

KMK – Kultusministerkonferenz (2010). *Glossary on Education. Institutions, Examinations, Qualifications, Titles and Other Specialist Terms.* PDF retrieved from https://www.kmk. org/fileadmin/Dateien/pdf/Eurydice/Glossary_dt_engl.pdf (last access: 15.05.2017).

KMK – Kultusministerkonferenz (2013). *Bericht Fremdsprachen in der Grundschule – Sachstand und Konzeptionen 2013.* PDF retrieved from http://www.kmk. org/fileadmin/Dateien/veroeffentlichungen_beschluesse/2013/2013_10_17-Fremdsprachen-in-der-Grundschule.pdf (last access 15.05.2017).

Kobela, S. (2008). Neue Möglichkeiten für den Einsatz von Bilderbüchern und Storytelling. Das "Add-to-it"-Konzept Revisited. In Böttger, H. (Ed.).

Fortschritte im frühen Fremdsprachenlernen. Ausgewählte Tagungsbeiträge Nürnberg 2007 (pp. 113–121). München: Domino.

Koda, K. (2004). *Insights into Second Language Reading. A Cross-Linguistic Approach.* Cambridge: Cambridge University Press.

Koda, K. (2007). Reading and Language Learning. Crosslinguistic Constraints on Second Language Reading Development. In Koda, K. (Ed.). *Reading and Language Learning* (pp. 1–44). Malden: Blackwell.

Kolb, A. (2007). *Portfolioarbeit. Wie Grundschulkinder ihr Sprachenlernen reflektieren.* Tübingen: Narr.

Kolb, A. (2008). Task-Based Language Learning. Impulse für den Fremdsprachunterricht der Grundschule. In Böttger, H. (Ed.). *Fortschritte im frühen Fremdsprachenlernen. Ausgewählte Tagungsbeiträge Nürnberg 2007* (pp. 61–69). München: Domino.

Kolb, A. (2013). Extensive Reading of Picturebooks in Primary EFL. In Bland, J. & Lütge, C. (Eds.). *Children's Literature in Second Language Education* (pp. 33–43). London: Bloomsbury.

Korte, J. (2007). *Lesen lernt man nur durch Lesen! Ein Programm zur intensiven Leseförderung in der Sekundarschule.* Donauwörth: Auer.

Krashen, S. (1981). *Second Language Acquisition and Second Language Learning.* Oxford: Pergamon.

Krashen, S. (1982). *Principles and Practice in Second Language Acquisition.* New York: Pergamon.

Krashen, S. (1989). We Acquire Vocabulary and Spelling by Reading: Additional Evidence for the Input Hypothesis. *Modern Language Journal, 73*(4), 440–464.

Krashen, S. (2013). Free Reading. Still a Great Idea. In Bland, J. & Lütge, C. (Eds.). *Children's Literature in Second Language Education* (pp. 15–24). London: Bloomsbury.

Krechel, H.- L. (2003). Bilingual Modules. Flexible Formen bilingualen Lehrens und Lernens. In Wildhage, M. & Otten, E. (Eds.). *Praxis des bilingualen Unterrichts* (pp. 194–216). Berlin: Cornelsen.

Krügel, A. (2014). *Eye Movement Control During Reading: Factors and Principles of Computing the Word Center for Saccade Planning.* PDF retrieved from https://publishup.uni-potsdam.de/opus4-ubp/frontdoor/index/index/year/2015/docId/7018 (last access: 15.05.2017).

Krüger, R. (2011). Sachfachinhalte im Fremdsprachenunterricht der Grundschule – eine Möglichkeit zum fächerverbindenden Arbeiten. In Reinfried, M. & Rück, N. (Eds.). *Innovative Entwicklungen beim Lehren und Lernen von Fremdsprachen. Festschrift für Inez De Florio-Hansen* (pp. 345–362). Tübingen: Narr.

Krüsmann, G. (2003). Eigenständiges Lesen im Englischunterricht der Grundschule. It's Fun Reading. *Grundschulmagazin, 1*(1), 49–56.

Kubanek-German, A. (1994). Der frühe Fremdsprachenunterricht und sein Kanon – einige Anmerkungen. *Zeitschrift für Fremdsprachenforschung, 5*(2), 22–31.

Kubanek-German, A. (1999). Frühes Fremdsprachenlernen in Europa. In Hermann-Brennecke, G. (Ed.). *Frühes schulisches Fremdsprachenlernen zwischen Empirie und Theorie* (pp. 155–176). Münster: Lit Verlag.

Kuckartz, U. (2012). *Qualitative Inhaltsanalyse. Methoden, Praxis, Computerunterstützung.* Weinheim: Beltz Juventa.

Kuckartz, U. (2014). *Mixed Methods. Methodologie, Forschungsdesigns und Analyseverfahren.* Wiesbaden: Springer.

Kuckartz, U., Dresing, T., Rädiker, S. & Stefer, C. (2008). Qualitative Evaluation in sieben Schritten. In Kuckartz, U., Dresing, T., Rädiker, S. & Claus, S. (Eds.). *Qualitative Evaluation – Der Einstieg in die Praxis* (pp. 15–57). Wiesbaden: Verlag der Wissenschaften.

Külekci, E. (2014). Authenticity in English Language Classrooms. Paper presented at *LIF2014 – Language in Focus*, Antalya, Turkey, 27.03.2014.

Kuhn, T. (2006). *Grammatik im Englischunterricht der Primarstufe. Theoretische Grundlagen und praktische Unterrichtsvorschläge.* Heidelberg: Winter.

Labov, W. (1972). *Sociolinguistic Patterns.* Philadelphia: University of Pennsylvania Press.

Lantolf, J. P. (2000). Introducing Sociocultural Theory. In Lantolf J.P. (Ed.). *Sociocultural Theory and Second Language Learning* (pp. 1–26). Oxford: Oxford University Press.

Lantolf, J. P. & Poehner, M. E. (2014). *Sociocultural Theory and the Pedagogical Imperative in L2 Education. Vygotskian Praxis and the Research/Practice Divide.* New York: Routledge.

Lasagabaster, D. & Sierra, J. M. (2010). Immersion and CLIL in English: More Differences than Similarities?. *ELT Journal, 64*(4), 367–375.

Laufer, B. (2013). Lexical Thresholds for Reading Comprehension. What They Are and How They Can Be Used for Teaching Purposes. *TESOL Quaterly, 47*(4), 867–872.

Lauströer, M. (2013). Writing is Fun! Motivierende und herausfordernde Schreibaufgaben im Englischunterricht der Grundschule. *Grundschule Englisch, 45*, 32–35.

Lázaro Ibarrola, A. (2010). English Phonics for Spanish Children. Adapting to New English as a Foreign Language Classrooms. In Diehr, B. & Rymarczyk,

J. (Eds.). *Researching Literacy in a Foreign Language among Primary School Learners. Forschung zum Schrifterwerb in der Fremdsprache bei Grundschülern* (pp. 89–106). Frankfurt a.m.: Peter Lang.

Leeck, P. (2012). Some Possibilities for Implementing and Increasing Learner Autonomy in the English Lesson. In Lennon, P. (2012). *Learner Autonomy in the English Classroom. Empirical Studies and Ideas for Teachers* (pp. 65–94). Frankfurt a.m.: Peter Lang.

Leeck, P. (2014). *Portfolioarbeit und ihre Auswirkung auf das Hörverstehen sehr junger Englischlerner.* Aachen: Shaker.

Legutke, M. K., Müller-Hartmann, A. & Schocker-v. Ditfurth, M. (2009). *Teaching English in the Primary School.* Stuttgart: Klett.

Lennon, P. (2008). Second Language Acquisition Studies. In Gramley, S. & Gramley, V. (Eds.). *Bielefeld Introduction to Applied Linguistics. A Course Book* (pp. 91–102). Bielefeld: Aisthesis.

Lennon. P. (2012a). Introduction. In Lennon, P. (2012). *Learner Autonomy in the English Classroom. Empirical Studies and Ideas for Teachers* (pp. 9–18). Frankfurt a.m.: Peter Lang.

Lennon. P. (2012b). The Story of Learner Autonomy: From Self-Access to Social Learning. In Lennon, P. (2012). *Learner Autonomy in the English Classroom. Empirical Studies and Ideas for Teachers* (pp. 19–64). Frankfurt a.m.: Peter Lang.

Leopold-Mudrack, A. (1998). *Fremdsprachenerziehung in der Primarstufe. Voraussetzungen, Konzept, Realisierungen.* Münster: Waxmann.

Lewis, D. (2001). *Reading Contemporary Picturebooks.* London: Routledge.

Lightbown, P. M. & Spada, N. (2013). *How Languages are Learned.* 4th edition. Oxford: Oxford University Press.

Lightbown, P. M., Halter, R. H., White, J. L. & Horst, M. (2002). Comprehension-Based Learning. The Limits of "Do it Yourself". *The Canadian Modern Language Review, 58*(3), 427–464.

Lincoln, Y. & Guba, E. (1985). *Naturalistic Inquiry.* Beverly Hills: Sage.

Lipka, O. & Siegel, L. S. (2011). The Development of Reading Comprehension Skills in Children Learning English as a Second Language. *Reading and Writing, 25*(8), 1873–1898.

Little, D. (1999). Learner Autonomy is More than a Western Cultural Construct. In Cotterall, S. & Crabbe, D. (Eds.). *Learner Autonomy in Language Learning. Defining the Field and Effecting Change* (pp. 11–18). Frankfurt a.m.: Peter Lang.

LSW NRW – Landesinstitut für Schule und Weiterbildung – Lehrerfortbildung in Nordrhein-Westfalen (2001). *Qualitätsentwicklung und Qualitätssicherung von Unterricht in der Sekundarstufe I. Englisch. Materialien zu dem Themenbereich Arbeiten mit dem Wörterbuch. Erprobungsfassung.* PDF retrieved from https://www.schulentwicklung.nrw.de/cms/upload/ue-englisch/weitere_materialien/e-umgangwbuch.pdf (last access: 15.05.2017).

Ludwig, P. H. (2012). Thesen zur Debatte um Gütestandards in der qualitativen Bildungsforschung – eine integrative Position. In Gläser-Zikuda, M., Seidel, T., Rohlfs, C., Gröschner, A. & Ziegelbauer, S. (Eds.). *Mixed Methods in der empirischen Bildungsforschung* (pp. 79–89). Münster: Waxmann.

Lütge, C. (2013). Otherness in Children's Literature. Perspectives for the EFL Classroom. In Bland, J. & Lütge, C. (Eds.). *Children's Literature in Second Language Education* (pp. 97–106). London: Bloomsbury.

Lyster, R. (1987). Speaking Immersion. *Canadian Modern Language Review, 43*(4), 701–717.

Ma, A. (2014). Review on Children's Literature in Second Language Education. *English Language Teaching, 68*(3), 352–355.

Macaro, E. (2001). *Learning Strategies in Foreign and Second Language Classrooms.* New York: Continuum.

Macaro, E. & Erler, L. (2008). Raising the Achievement of Young-Beginner Readers of French through Strategy Instruction. *Applied Linguistics, 29*(1), 90–119.

Marschollek, A. (2005). Phonetische Umschrift. Schon in der Grundschule? *Grundschulmagazin Englisch, 3*(2), Fachbeilage Primary English.

Mason, B. (2013). Efficient Use of Literature in Second Language Education. Free Reading and Listening to Stories. In Bland, J. & Lütge, C. (Eds.). *Children's Literature in Second Language Education* (pp. 25–32). London: Bloomsbury.

Massler, U. (2012a). CLIL-Sachunterricht in Stationenarbeit. Let's Explore the Moon. *Grundschulmagazin Englisch, 10*(4), 13–17.

Massler, U. (2012b). Primary CLIL and its Stakeholders. What Children, Parents and Teacher Think of the Potential Merits and Pitfalls of CLIL Modules in Primary Teaching. *International CLIL Research Journal, 1*(4), 36–46.

Massler, U. & Ioannou-Georgiou, S. (2010). Best Practice. How CLIL Works. In Massler, U. & Burmeister, P. (Eds.). *CLIL und Immersion. Fremdsprachlicher Sachfachunterricht in der Grundschule* (pp. 61–75). Braunschweig: Westermann.

Massler, U. & Steiert, C. (2010). Implementierung von CLIL-Modulen – die Perspektive von Lehrenden, Kindern, Eltern. In Massler, U. & Burmeister,

P. (Eds.). *CLIL und Immersion. Fremdsprachlicher Sachfachunterricht in der Grundschule* (pp. 11–29). Braunschweig: Westermann.

Massler, U. & Burmeister, P. (Eds.) (2010). *CLIL und Immersion. Fremdsprachlicher Sachfachunterricht in der Grundschule.* Braunschweig: Westermann.

Matloff, N. (n.d.). *From Algorithms to Z-Scores: Probabilistic and Statistical Modeling in Computer Science.* PDF retrieved from http://heather.cs.ucdavis.edu/~matloff/132/PLN/ProbStatBook.pdf (last access: 15.05.2017).

Mayer, N. (2013). Comics & Co – More than Pictures. Sprachenlernen und Leseförderung mit Comics und Graphic Novels. *Take Off!, 3,* 24–27.

Mayring, P. (2012). Mixed Methods – ein Plädoyer für gemeinsame Forschungsstandards qualitativer und quantitativer Methoden. In Gläser-Zikuda, M., Seidel, T., Rohlfs, C., Gröschner, A. & Ziegelbauer, S. (Eds.). *Mixed Methods in der empirischen Bildungsforschung* (pp. 287–300). Münster: Waxmann.

McCarthy, M. (1990). *Vocabulary.* Oxford: Oxford University Press.

McElvany, N., Becker, M. & Lüdtke, O. (2009). Die Bedeutung familiärer Merkmale für Lesekompetenz, Wortschatz, Lesemotivation und Leseverhalten. *Zeitschrift für Entwicklungspsychologie und Pädagogische Psychologie, 41*(3), 121–131.

McGrath, J.E. (1991). Time, Interaction, and Performance (TIP). A Theory of Groups. *Small Group Research, 22*(2), 147–174.

McKay, S.L. (2006). *Researching Second Language Classrooms.* London: Lawrence Erlbaum.

McLaughlin, B. (1987). *Theories of Second-Language Learning.* London: Edward Arnold.

McMunn Dooley, C., Martinez, M. & Roser N. L. (2013). Young Children's Literary Meaning Making. A Decade of Research 2000 – 2010. In Larson, J. & Marsh, J. (Eds). *The SAGE Handbook of Early Childhood Literacy* (pp. 395–408). 2nd edition. Los Angeles: Sage.

Meendermann, M. (2014). Schrifteinsatz im Englischunterricht der Grundschule: Lernhilfe oder Gefahr? In Böttger, H. (Ed.). *Englisch. Didaktik für die Grundschule* (pp. 141–153). Berlin: Cornelsen.

Mehisto, P. Marsh, D. & Frigols, M. J. (2008). *Uncovering CLIL. Content and Language Integrated Learning in Bilingual and Multilingual Education.* Oxford: Macmillan.

Meister. T. (2012). Authentic Texts as a Basis for Autonomous Learning. In Lennon, P. (Ed.). *Learner Autonomy in the English Classroom. Empirical Studies and Ideas for Teachers* (pp. 273–297). Frankfurt a.M.: Peter Lang.

Merton, R. K. (2010). Der Matthäus-Effekt in der Wissenschaft, II. Kumulativer Vorteil und der Symbolismus des intellektuellen Eigentums. *Berliner Journal für Soziologie, 20,* 285–308.

Metzger, K. (2010). Lesen im medialen Umfeld. In Schulz, G. (Ed.). *Lesen lernen in der Grundschule* (pp. 75–82). Berlin: Cornelsen.

Meyer, E. (1992). Es muß nicht immer Englisch sein. Ein Plädoyer für Französisch in der Grundschule. In Gompf, G. (Ed.). *Fremdsprachenbeginn ab Klasse 3. Lernen für Europa* (pp. 62–74). Berlin: Cornelsen.

Meyer, H. (2004). *Was ist guter Unterricht.* Berlin: Cornelsen.

Meyer, M. (2005). *English and American Literatures.* 2nd edition. Tübingen: UTB.

Meyer, O. (2010). Towards Quality-CLIL. Successful Planning and Teaching Strategies. *Pulso: Revista de Educación, 33,* 11–29.

Mihaljević Djigunović, J. & Lopriore, L. (2011). The Learner. Do Individual Differences Matter? In Enever, J. (Ed.). *ELLiE. Early Language Learning in Europe* (pp. 43–59). London: British Council.

Mihara, K. (2011). Effects of Pre-Reading Strategies on EFL/ESL Reading Comprehension. *TESL Canada Journal, 25*(2), 51–73.

Mindt, D. (2007). Fortschritte im frühen Fremdsprachenlernen von 2000 bis heute und Perspektiven für die Zukunft. In Böttger, H. (Ed.). *Fortschritte im frühen Fremdsprachenlernen. Ausgewählte Tagungsbeiträge Nürnberg 2007* (pp. 12–22). München: Domino.

Mindt, D. & Schlüter, N. (2007). *Ergebnisorientierter Englischunterricht. Für das 3. und 4. Schuljahr.* Berlin: Cornelsen.

Mishan, F. (2005). *Designing Authenticity into Language Learning Materials.* Bristol: Intellect.

MKJS BW – Ministerium für Kultus, Jugend und Sport Baden-Württemberg (2004). *Bildungsplan Grundschule.* Stuttgart: Neckar-Verlag.

MKJS BW – Ministerium für Kultus, Jugend und Sport Baden-Württemberg (2016). *Bildungsplan 2016, Allgemein bildende Schulen, Grundschule, Endfassung Englisch.* PDF retrieved from http://www.bildungsplaene-bw.de/site/bildungsplan/get/documents/lsbw/export-pdf/depot-pdf/ALLG/BP2016BW_ALLG_GS_E.pdf (last access 15.05.2017).

Möller, C. (2009). The History and Future of Bilingual Education. Immersion Teaching in Germany and its Canadian Origins. *Cross/Cultures: Translation of Cultures, 106,* 235–254.

Möller, C. (2013). Zur Geschichte und Zukunft des bilingualen Unterrichts. In Steinlen, A. K. & Rohde, A. (Eds.). *Mehrsprachigkeit in bilingualen*

Kindertagsstätten und Schulen. Voraussetzungen – Methoden – Erfolge (pp. 14–30). Berlin: DVB.

Morris, C. D., Bransford, J. D. & Franks, F. J. (1977). Levels of Processing Versus Transfer Appropriate Processing. *Journal of Verbal Learning and Verbal Behavior, 16*, 519–533.

Morse, J. (2010). Procedures and Practice of Mixed Method Design. Maintaining Control, Rigor, and Complexity. In Tashakkori, A. & Teddlie, C. (Eds.). *SAGE Handbook of Mixed Methods in Social and Behavioral Research* (pp. 339–352). 2nd edition. Los Angeles: Sage.

Mourão, S. (2013). Picturebook. Object of Discovery. In Bland, J. & Lütge, C. (Eds.). *Children's Literature in Second Language Education* (pp. 71–84). London: Bloomsbury.

MSW NRW – Ministerium für Schule und Weiterbildung des Landes Nordrhein-Westfalens (2007). *Kernlehrplan für den verkürzten Bildungsgang des Gymnasium – Sekundarstufe I (G8) in Nordrhein-Westfalen. Englisch.* Frechen: Ritterbach.

MSW NRW – Ministerium für Schule und Weiterbildung des Landes Nordrhein-Westfalens (2008a). *Kompetenzorientierung. Eine veränderte Sichtweise auf das Lehren und Lernen in der Grundschule. Handreichung.* Frechen: Ritterbach.

MSW NRW – Ministerium für Schule und Weiterbildung des Landes Nordrhein-Westfalens (2008b). *Richtlinien und Lehrpläne für die Grundschule in Nordrhein-Westfalen.* Frechen: Ritterbach.

MSW NRW – Ministerium für Schule und Weiterbildung des Landes Nordrhein-Westfalens (2011). *Kernlehrplan für die Hauptschule in Nordrhein-Westfalen. Englisch.* Frechen: Ritterbach.

Müller, H. M. (Ed.) (2002). *Arbeitsbuch Linguistik.* Paderborn: Schöningh UTB.

Müller-Hartmann, A. & Schocker-v. Ditfurth, M. (2014). *Introduction to English Language Teaching.* Stuttgart: Klett.

Muñoz, C. & Lindgren, E. (2011). Out-of-School Factors. The Home. In Enever, J. (Ed.). *ELLiE. Early Language Learning in Europe* (pp. 103–123). London: British Council.

Nampaktai, P. Kaewsombut, R., Akwaree, S., Wongwayrote, U. & Sameepet, B. (2013). Using Story Grammar to Enhance Reading Comprehension. *International Forum of Teaching and Studies, 9*(1), 35–38.

Nassaji, H. (2007). Schema Theory and Knowledge-Based Processes in Second Language Reading Comprehension. A Need for Alternative Perspectives. In Koda, K. (Ed.). *Reading and Language Learning* (pp. 79–113). Malden: Blackwell.

Nastasi, B. K., Hitchcock, J. H. & Brown, L. M. (2010). An Inclusive Framework for Conceptualizing Mixed Methods Design Typologies. Moving Toward Fully Integrated Synergistic Research Models. In Tashakkori, A. & Teddlie, C. (Eds.). *Sage Handbook of Mixed Methods in Social and Behavioral Research* (pp. 305–338). 2nd edition. Los Angleles: Sage.

Nation, I. S. P. (2006). How Large a Vocabulary is Needed for Reading and Listening? *The Canadian Modern Language Review, 63*(1), 59–82.

Navés, T. (2011). How Promising are the Results of Integrating Content and Language for EFL Writing and Overall EFL Proficiency? In Ruiz de Zarobe, Y., Sierra, J. M. & Gallardo del Puerto, F. (Eds.). *Content and Foreign Language Integrated Learning. Contributions to Multilingualism in European Contexts* (pp. 155–186). Bern: Peter Lang.

Nikolajeva, M. (2005). *Aesthetic Approaches to Children's Literature.* Lanham: Scarecrow Press.

Nikolajeva, M. & Scott, C. (2000). The Dynamics of Picturebook Communication. *Children's Literature in Education, 31*(4), 225–239.

Nikolajeva, M. & Scott, C. (2001). *How Picturebooks Work.* New York: Garland Publishing.

Nold, G. & Rossa, H. (2007). Leseverstehen. In Beck, B. & Klieme, E. (Eds.). *Sprachliche Kompetenzen. Konzepte und Messung. DESI-Studie* (pp. 197–211). Weinheim: Beltz.

Nold, G., Rossa, H. & Chatzivassiliadou, K. (2008). Leseverstehen Englisch. In DESI-Konsortium (Eds.). *Unterricht und Kompetenzerwerb in Deutsch und Englisch. Ergebnisse der DESI-Studie* (pp. 130–138). Weinheim: Beltz.

Nunan, D. (2004). *Task-Based Language Teaching.* Cambridge: Cambridge University Press.

Nunan, D. & Lamb, C. (1996). *The Self-Directed Teacher.* Cambridge: Cambridge University Press.

Nuttall, C. (2005). *Teaching Reading Skills in a Foreign Language.* London: Macmillan.

O'Cathain, A. (2010). Assessing the Quality of Mixed Methods Research. Toward a Comprehensive Framework. In Tashakkori, A. & Teddlie, C. (Eds.). *SAGE Handbook of Mixed Methods in Social and Behavioral Research* (pp. 531–555). Los Angeles: Sage.

O'Malley, J. M. & Chamot, A. U. (1990). *Learning Strategies in Second Language Acquisition.* New York: Cambridge University Press.

O'Malley, J. M., Chamot, A. U., Stewner-Marzanares, G., Kupper, L. & Russo, R. P. (1985). Learning Strategies Used by Beginning and Intermediate ESL students. *Language Learning, 35*(1), 21–46.

Ortlieb, E. (2013). Using Anticipatory Reading Guides to Improve Elementary Students' Comprehension. *International Journal of Instruction, 6*(2), 145–162.

Otten, E. & Wildhage, M. (2003). Content and Language Integrated Learning. Eckpunkte einer "kleinen" Didaktik des bilingualen Sachfachunterrichts. In Wildhage, M. & Otten, E. (Eds.). *Praxis des bilingualen Unterrichts* (pp. 12–45). Berlin: Cornelsen.

Oxford, R. L. (1990). *Language Learning Strategies. What Every Teacher Should Know.* New York: Harper Collins.

Oxford, R. L. (2011). *Teaching and Researching Language Learning Strategies.* Harlow: Pearson.

Park, G.- P. (2013). Relations Among L1 Reading, L2 Knowledge, and L2 Reading. Revisiting the Threshold Hypothesis. *English Language Teaching, 6*(12), 38–47.

Paulick, C. & Groot-Wilken, B. (2009). Rezeptive Fähigkeiten und Fertigkeiten am Ende der 4. Klasse unter besonderer Berücksichtigung der sprachlichen Schülerbiographien. In Engel, G., Groot-Wilken, B. & Thürmann, E. (Eds.). *Englisch in der Primarstufe – Chancen und Herausforderungen. Evaluation und Erfahrungen aus der Praxis* (pp. 179–196). Berlin: Cornelsen.

Peterßen, W. H. (2000). *Fächerverbindender Unterricht. Begriff, Konzept, Planung, Beispiele.* München: Oldenbourg.

Phillipson, R. (2007). English, No Longer a Foreign Language in Europe? In Cummins, J. & Davison, C. (Eds.). *International Handbook of English Language Teaching* (pp. 123–136). New York: Springer.

Piepho, H.- E. (2000). Story Telling. Which, When, Why. In Bleyhl, W. *Fremdsprachen in der Grundschule. Grundlagen und Praxisbeispiele* (pp. 43–55). Hannover: Schroedel.

Piepho, H.- E. (2003). Individuelle Lernfortschritte beim Englischlernen in der Grundschule. In Edelhoff, C. (Ed.). *Englisch in der Grundschule und darüber hinaus. Eine praxisnahe Orientierungshilfe* (pp. 24–33). Frankfurt a.M.: Diesterweg.

Pinner, R. (2013). Authenticity and CLIL. Examining Authenticity from an International CLIL Perspective. *International CLIL Research Journal, 2*(1), 44–54.

Pinter, A. (2006). *Teaching Young Language Learners.* Oxford: Oxford University Press.

Piske, T. (2007). Pro & Kontra. Die Einführung der Schrift im fremdsprachlichen Anfangsunterricht. *Take Off!, 1*, 46–47.

Piske, T. (2010). Positive and Negative Effects of Exposure to L2 Orthographic Input in the Early Phases of Foreign Language Learning. A Review. In Diehr,

B. & Rymarczyk, J. (Eds). *Researching Literacy in a Foreign Language among Primary School Learners. Forschung zum Schrifterwerb in der Fremdsprache bei Grundschülern* (pp. 37–50). Frankfurt a.M.: Peter Lang.

Protopapas, A., Parrila, R. & Simos, P. G. (2014). *In Search of Matthew Effects in Reading.* PDF retrieved from http://ldx.sagepub.com/content/early/2014/11/26/0022219414559974.full.pdf +html (last access 15.05.2017).

Pulido, D. (2007). The Relationship between Text Comprehension and Second Language Incidental Vocabulary Acquisition: A Matter of Topic Familiarity? In Koda, K. (Ed.). *Reading and Language Learning* (pp. 155–199). Malden: Blackwell.

Rasinski, T.V. (2010). *The Fluent Reader. Oral & Silent Reading Strategies for Building Fluency, Word Recognition & Comprehension.* New York: Scholastic.

Rasinski, T. V., Rupley, W. H., Paige, D. D. & Dee Nicholas, W. (2016). Alternative Text Types to Improve Reading Fluency for Competent to Struggling Readers. *International Journal of Instruction, 9*(1), 163–178.

Rayner, K. (1998). Eye Movements in Reading and Information Processing: 20 Years of Research. *Psychological Bulletin, 124*(3), 372–422.

Reckermann, J. (2014). As Fast as a Hare. Einen eigenen Popsong texten. *Grundschulmagazin Englisch, 12*(1), 29–34.

Reckermann, J. (2016a). I Can Read an English Book. "The Queen's Knickers" eigenständig lesen. *Grundschulmagazin Englisch, 14*(2), 24–26.

Reckermann, J. (2016b). My Dream House Has Got. In Kunst gestalten und auf Englisch beschreiben. *Grundschulmagazin Englisch, 14*(3), 15–19.

Reckermann, J. (2017). Eine Aufgabe – 25 richtige Lösungen: Das Potential offener Lernaufgaben für den inklusiven Englischunterricht in der Grundschule. In Chilla, S. & Vogt, K. (Eds.). *Heterogenität und Diversität im Englischunterricht. Fachdidaktische Perspektiven* (pp. 205–233). Frankfurt a.M.: Peter Lang.

Reckermann, J. & Bechler, S. (2018). I Can Read it By Myself. Selbstständiges und gemeinsames Lesen fördern. *Grundschulmagazin Englisch, 16*(1), 19–22.

Reichart-Wallrabenstein, M. (2004). *Kinder und Schrift im Englischunterricht der Grundschule. Eine theorie- und empiriegeleitete Studie zur Diskussion um die Integration von Schriftlichkeit. Band 1.* Berlin: Dissertation.de – Verlag im Internet.

Reichen, J. (1988). *Lesen durch Schreiben. Wie Kinder selbstgesteuert Lesen lernen. Heft 1.* Zürich: Sabe.

Reichl, S. (2013). Doing Identity, Doing Culture. Transcultural Learning through Young Adult Fiction. In Bland, J. & Lütge, C. (Eds.). *Children's Literature in Second Language Education* (pp. 107–117). London: Bloomsbury.

Reisener, H. (1999). Motivation und Authentizität. *Der Fremdsprachliche Unterricht Englisch, 41,* 11–18.

Reisener, H. (2008). Mit Übungsspaß zu Lernerfolgen. In Böttger, H. (Ed.). *Fortschritte im frühen Fremdsprachenlernen. Ausgewählte Tagungsbeiträge Nürnberg 2007* (pp. 148–160). München: Domino.

Richards, J. C. & Rodgers, T. S. (2014). *Approaches and Methods in Language Teaching.* 3rd edition. Cambridge: Cambridge University Press.

Rittersbacher, C. (2009). Literalität im multifokalen Unterricht. Die Beachtung sprachlicher Phänomene als Katalysator bei sachfachlichem Lernen. In Ditze, S.- A. & Halbach, A. (Eds.). *Bilingualer Sachfachunterricht (CLIL) im Kontext von Sprache, Kultur und Multiliteralität* (pp. 75–90). Frankfurt a.M.: Peter Lang.

Roche, J. (2008). *Fremdsprachenerwerb Fremdsprachendidaktik.* 2nd edition. Tübingen: UTB.

Roschlaub, C. (2012). *Textverständlichkeit und Textverstehen. Ein System zur Analyse von Textschwierigkeiten im Hinblick auf ihre Funktion als Prädiktoren von Verstehensleistung in der Grundschule.* Saarbrücken: Akademikerverlag.

Rosenzweig, E. Q. & Wigfield, A. (2017). What If Reading is Easy But Unimportant? How Students' Patterns of Affirming and Undermining Motivation for Reading Information Texts Predict Different Reading Outcomes. *Contemporary Educational Psychology, 48,* 133–141.

Ruiz de Zarobe, Y. (2011). Which Language Competencies Benefit from CLIL? An Insight into Applied Linguistics Research. In Ruiz de Zarobe, Y., Sierra, J. M. & Gallardo del Puerto, F. (Eds.). *Content and Foreign Language Integrated Learning. Contributions to Multilingualism in European Contexts* (pp. 129–153). Bern: Peter Lang.

Ruiz de Zarobe, Y. (2015). Metacognitive Strategy Training in a CLIL Context. Effects on Reading and Listening Skills. Paper presented at *Language in Focus 2015,* Cappadocia, Turkey, 05.03.2015.

Ruiz de Zarobe, Y. & Zenotz, V. (2015). Reading Strategies and CLIL. The Effect of Training in Formal Instruction. *The Language Learning Journal, 43*(3), 319–333.

Rumlich, D. (2016). *Evaluating Bilingual Education in Germany. CLIL Students' General English Proficiency, EFL Self-Concept and Interest.* Frankfurt a.M.: Peter Lang.

Rymarczyk, J. (2008). Früher oder Später? Zur Einführung des Schriftbildes in der Grundschule. In Böttger, H. (Ed.). *Fortschritte im frühen Fremdsprachenlernen. Ausgewählte Tagungsbeiträge Nürnberg 2007* (pp. 170–182). München: Domino.

Rymarczyk, J. (2010). Bilderbücher und Grammatik. Die Lektüre anspruchsvoller Bilderbücher – mit Hilfe von Grammatik möglich machen. *Grundschule, 9*, 33–37.

Rymarczyk, J. & Musall, A. (2010). Reading Skills of First Graders Who Learn to Read and Write in German and English. In Diehr, B. & Rymarczyk, J. (Eds.). *Researching Literacy in a Foreign Language among Primary School Learners. Forschung zum Schrifterwerb in der Fremdsprache bei Grundschülern* (pp. 69–88). Frankfurt a.M.: Peter Lang.

Sächsisches Staatsministerium für Kultus (2009). *Lehrplan Grundschule Englisch.* PDF retrieved from http://www.schule.sachsen.de/lpdb/web/downloads/lp_gs_englisch_2009.pdf?v2 (last access: 15.05.2017).

Sambanis, M. (2008). Sprechen im Anfangsunterricht oder ist Schweigen Gold? In Christiani, R. & Cwik, G. (Eds.). *Englisch unterrichten in Klasse 1 und 2* (pp. 54–67). Berlin: Cornelsen.

Sarter, H. (1997). *Fremdsprachenarbeit in der Grundschule. Neue Wege, neue Ziele.* Darmstadt: Wissenschaftliche Buchgesellschaft.

Sauer, H. (2000). *Fremdsprachenlernen in Grundschulen. Der Weg ins 21. Jahrhundert. Eine annotierte Bibliographie und das Beispiel Nordrhein-Westfalen.* Leipzig: Klett.

Saville-Troike, M. (2006). *Introducing Second Language Acquisition.* Cambridge: Cambridge University Press.

Saville-Troike, M. (2012). *Introducing Second Language Acquisition.* 2nd edition. Cambridge: Cambridge University Press.

Scharer, P. L. & Zutell, J. (2013). The Development of Spelling. In Larson, J. & Marsh, J. (Eds). *The SAGE Handbook of Early Childhood Literacy* (pp. 448–481). 2nd edition. Los Angeles: Sage.

Schick, K. (2016). English All Inclusive? Wortschatzstrategien im inklusiven Englischunterricht. *Grundschulmagazin Englisch, 14*(2), 31–34.

Schmid-Schönbein, G. (2001). *Didaktik: Grundschulenglisch.* Berlin: Cornelsen.

Schmid-Schönbein, G. (2008). *Didaktik und Methodik für den Englischunterricht.* Berlin: Cornelsen.

Schmidt, K. (2016). Immersion für alle? Zur Entwicklung von Kindern mit besonderen Bedarfen in bilingualen Programmen. In Böttger, H. & Schlüter, N. (Eds.). *Fortschritte im frühen Fremdsprachenlernen. Tagungsband zur 4. FFF-Konferenz* (pp. 252–260). Braunschweig: Westermann.

Schmidt, R. (2001). Attention. In Robinson, P. (Ed.). *Cognition and Second Language Instruction* (pp. 3–32). Cambridge: Cambridge University Press.

Schmidt, R. W. (1990). The Role of Consciousness in Second Language Learning. *Applied Linguistics, 11*(2), 129–158.

Schnaitmann, G. W. (1996). Analyse subjektiver Lernkonzepte. Methodologische Überlegungen bei der Erforschung von Lernstrategien. In Treumann, K.- P., Neubauer, G., Möller, R. & Abel, J. (Eds.). *Methoden und Anwendungen empirischer pädagogischer Forschung* (pp. 130–144). Münster: Waxmann.

Schulz, G. (2010). Vorwort. In Schulz, G. (Ed.). *Lesen lernen in der Grundschule* (pp. 7–8). Berlin: Cornelsen.

Schwab, G., Keßler, J.- U. & Hollm, J. (2014). CLIL Goes Hauptschule. Chancen und Herausforderungen bilingualen Unterrichts an einer Hauptschule. Zentrale Ergebnisse einer Longitudinalstudie. *Zeitschrift für Fremdsprachenforschung, 25*(1), 3–37.

Segalowitz, N. (2003). Automaticity and Second Languages. In Doughty, C. J. & Long, M. H. (Eds.). *The Handbook of Second Language Acquisition* (pp. 382–408). Malden: Blackwell.

Seidlhofer, B. (2011). *Understanding English as a Lingua Franca.* Oxford: Oxford University Press.

Sharwood Smith, M. (1993). Input Enhancement in Instructed SLA. Theoretical Bases. *Studies in Second Language Acquisition, 15*(2), 165–179.

Skehan, P. (1998). *A Cognitive Approach to Language Learning.* Oxford: Oxford University Press.

Skorge, P. N. (2006). *The Affordances of Visuals in Materials for Foreign Language Learning and Teaching. Perspectives from Theory and Research.* Bielefeld: Bielefeld University.

Snow, M. A., Met, M. & Genesee, F. (1989). A Conceptual Framework for the Integration of Language and Content in Second/Foreign Language Instruction. *TESOL Quarterly, 23*(2), 201–207.

Spada, N. (2007). Communicative Language Teaching. Current Status and Future Prospects. In Cummins, J. & Davison, C. (Eds.). *International Handbook of English Language Teaching Part I* (pp. 271–288). New York: Springer.

Spiegel, H & Selter, C. (2003). *Kinder & Mathematik. Was Erwachsene wissen sollten.* Seelze-Velber: Kallmeyer.

Spinner, K. H. (2006). Literarisches Lernen. *Praxis Deutsch, 200,* 6–17.

Spinner, K. H. (2010). Lesekompetenz ausbilden, Lesestandards erfüllen. In Schulz, G. (Ed.). *Lesen lernen in der Grundschule* (pp. 48–61). Berlin: Cornelsen.

Standardsicherung Englisch NRW (2010). *Merkmale guten Englischunterrichts.* PDF retrieved from https://www.schulentwicklung.nrw.de/cms/angebote/egs/angebot-home/index.html (last access: 15.05.2017).

Steck, A. (2009). *Förderung des Leseverstehens in der Grundschule. Fortbildungsbausteine für Lehrkräfte.* Baltmannsweiler: Schneider Verlag Hohengehren GmbH.

Steiert, C. (2010). Unterrichtsmaterialien für CLIL – CLIL in Unterrichtsmaterialien. In Massler, U. & Burmeister, P. (Eds.). *CLIL und Immersion. Fremdsprachlicher Sachfachunterricht in der Grundschule* (pp. 119–130). Braunschweig: Westermann.

Stork, A. (2010). Integrated Skills. In Hallet, W. & Königs, F.G. (Eds.). *Handbuch Fremdsprachendidaktik* (pp. 100–103). Seelze-Velber: Kallmeyer.

Sumner, M. (2006). Qualitative Research. In Jupp, V. (Ed.). *The SAGE Dictionary of Social Research Methods* (248–249). London: Sage.

Swain, M. (2000). The Output Hypothesis and Beyond. Mediating Acquisition through Collaborative Dialogue. Lantolf, J. P. (Ed.). *Sociocultural Theory and Second Language Learning* (pp. 97–114). Oxford: Oxford University Press.

Swain, M., Kinnear, P. & Steinmann, L. (2011). *Sociocultural Theory in Second Language Education. An Introduction through Narratives.* Bristol: Multilingual Matters.

Swain, M. & Lapkin, S. (1982). *Evaluating Bilingual Education. A Canadian Case Study.* Clevedon: Multilingual Matters.

Swain, M. & Lapkin, S. (2005). The Evolving Sociopolitical Context of Immersion Education in Canada. Some Implications for Program Development. *International Journal of Applied Linguistics, 15*(2), 169–186.

Swann, J. (2001). Recording and Transcribing Talk in Educational Settings. In Candlin, C. N. & Mercer, N. (Eds.). *English Language Teaching in its Social Context* (pp. 323–344). London: Routledge.

Szpotowicz, M. & Lindgren, E. (2011). Language Achievements. A Longitudinal Perspective. In Enever, J. (Ed.). *ELLiE. Early Language Learning in Europe* (pp. 125–142). London: British Council.

Tarone, E., Bigelow, M. & Hansen, K. (2009). *Literacy and Second Language Oracy.* Oxford: Oxford University Press.

Taylor, D. (1994). Inauthentic Authenticity or Authentic Inauthenticity. *Teaching English as a Second or Foreign Language, 1*(2), 1–12.

Teddlie, C. & Tashakkori, A. (2010). Overview of Contemporary Issues in Mixed Methods Research. In Tashakkori, A. & Teddlie, C. (Eds.). *SAGE Handbook of Mixed Methods in Social and Behavioral Research* (pp. 1–41). 2nd edition. Los Angeles: Sage.

Thürmann, E. (2005). Eine eigenständige Methodik für den bilingualen Sachfachunterricht? In Bach, G. & Niemeier, S. (Eds.). *Bilingualer Unterricht.*

Grundlagen, Methoden, Praxis, Perspektiven (pp. 71–89). 4th edition. Frankfurt a.m.: Peter Lang.

Thürmann, E. (2013). Sprachtests im Englischunterricht der Grundschule. Orientierungen auf dem Weg von Behauptungen zu Gewissenheiten. In Börner, O., Engel, G. & Groot-Wilken, B. (Eds.). *Hörverstehen, Leseverstehen, Sprechen. Diagnose und Förderung von sprachlichen Kompetenzen im Englischunterricht der Primarstufe* (pp. 11–41). Münster: Waxmann.

Timm, J.- P. (2013). Lernorientierter Fremdsprachenunterricht: Förderung systemisch-konstruktiver Lernprozesse. In Bach, G. & Timm, J.- P. (Eds.). *Englischunterricht* (pp. 43–60). 5th edition. Tübingen: Francke UTB.

Todtenhaupt-Duscha, K. & Duscha, M. (2008). Methoden und Medien. In Christiani, R. & Cwik, G. (Eds.). *Englisch unterrichten in Klasse 1 und 2* (pp. 16–42). Berlin: Cornelsen.

Traverso, P. (2013). Enhancing Self-Esteem and Positive Attitudes through Children's Literature. In Bland, J. & Lütke, C. (Eds.). *Children's Literature in Second Language Education* (pp. 183–194). London: Bloomsbury.

Trofimovich, P., Lightbown, P. M., Halter, R. H., & Song, H. (2009). Comprehension-Based Practice. The Development of L2 Pronunciation in a Listening and Reading Program. *Studies in Second Language Acquisition, 31*(4), 609–639.

Ushioda, E. (2011). Motivating Learners to Speak as Themselves. In Murray, G., Gao, X. & Lamb T. (Eds.). *Identity, Motivation and Autonomy in Language Learning* (pp. 11–24). Bristol: Multilingual Matters.

Van Lier, L. (1996). *Interaction in the Language Curriculum. Awareness, Autonomy & Authenticity.* Harlow: Longman.

VanPatten, B. & Benati, A.G. (2010). *Key Terms in Second Language Acquisition.* London: Continuum.

Vollmuth, I. (2004). *Englisch an der Grundschule. Wie Handreichungen den Frühbeginn sehen. Eine didaktisch-methodische Analyse.* Heidelberg: Universitätsverlag Winter.

Vygotsky, L. S. (1978). *Mind in Society. The Development of Higher Psychological Processes.* London: Harvard University Press.

Waas, L. (2014a). Auf dem Weg zu kommunikativen Fähigkeiten. Songs, Rhymes and Then? *Grundschulmagazin Englisch, 12*(1), 35–36.

Waas, L. (2014b). Take Your Pen. Schreiben – aber richtig. *Grundschulmagazin Englisch, 12*(4), 35–36.

Waas, L. (2016). The Two Faces of Reading. Sinnentnehmendes Lesen. *Grundschulmagazin Englisch 14*(2), 36–36.

Wagner, U. (2009). Übergang Englisch – Fallanalysen zum Wechsel von der Grundschule zur weiterführenden Schule. Tübingen: Narr.

Waring, R. & Takaki, M. (2003). At What Rate Do Learners Learn and Retain New Vocabulary from Reading a Graded Reader? *Reading in a Foreign Language, 15*(2), 130–163.

Waschk, K. (2008). *Öffnung des Englischunterrichts in der Grundschule. Studien zur Wahlfreiheit und Lernerautonomie.* Duisburg: UVRR.

Weerning, C. (2006). Kinder entwickeln Theaterspiele im fächerübergreifenden Unterricht von Kunst und Deutsch. E-book retrieved from http://www.buch.de/shop/home/rubrikartikel/ID30600618.html?ProvID=10905481&iapkpmtrack=9-83538353132363231313 03-103-100101#kinder-entwickeln-theaterspiele-im-faecheruebergreifenden-unterricht-von-kunst-und-deutsch (last access: 15.05.2017).

Wendt, M. (1997). Strategien und Strategieebenen am Beispiel von Lernaktivitäten im Spanischunterricht. In Rampillon, R. & Zimmermann, G. (Eds.). *Strategien und Techniken beim Erwerb fremder Sprachen* (pp. 77–94). Ismaning: Max Huber.

Werner, B. (2007). Entwicklungen und aktuelle Zahlen bilingualen Unterrichts in Deutschland und Berlin. In Caspari, D., Hallet, W., Wegner, A. & Zydatis, W. (Eds.). *Bilingualer Unterricht macht Schule. Beiträge aus der Praxisforschung* (pp. 19–28). Frankfurt a.M.: Peter Lang.

Wessel, F. (2012). Nur Englisch sprechen?. In Böttger, H. (Ed.). *Englisch Didaktik für die Grundschule* (pp. 49–59). Berlin: Cornelsen.

Westphal Irwin, J. (2007). *Teaching Reading Comprehension Processes.* 3rd edition. Boston: Pearson.

Whittaker, M. (2003). Getting Ready. Der erweiterte Englischunterricht im Vorlauf zum bilingualen Sachfachunterricht. In Wildhagen, M. & Otten, E. (Eds.) *Praxis des bilingualen Unterrichts* (pp. 170–193). Berlin: Cornelsen.

Widdowson, H.G. (1978). *Teaching Language as Communication.* Oxford: Oxford University Press.

Wilden, E. (2008). *Selbst- und Fremdwahrnehmung in der interkulturellen Onlinekommunikation. Das Modell der ABC's of Cultural Understanding and Communication Online.* Frankfurt a.M.: Peter Lang.

Wilden, E., Porsch, R. & Ritter, M. (2013). Je früher desto besser? Frühbeginnender Englischunterricht ab Klasse 1 oder 3 und seine Auswirkungen auf das Hör- und Leseverstehen. *Zeitschrift für Fremdsprachenforschung, 24*(2), 171–201.

Wilden, E. & Porsch, R. (2015). Die Hör- und Leseverstehensleistungen im Fach Englisch von Kindern am Ende der Grundschulzeit unter besonderer

Berücksichtigung lebensweltlicher Ein- und Mehrsprachigkeit. In Kötter, M. & Rymarczyk, J. (Eds.). *Englischunterricht auf der Primarstufe. Neue Forschungen – weitere Entwicklungen* (pp. 59–80). Frankfurt a.M.: Peter Lang.

Willgerodt, U. (2003). Kinderbücher im Englischunterricht der Grundschule. Fremdsprachenlernen in Niedersachsen. In Edelhoff, C. (Ed.). *Englisch in der Grundschule und darüber hinaus. Eine praxisnahe Orientierungshilfe* (pp. 50–59). Frankfurt am Main: Moritz Diesterweg.

Willis, J. (1996). *A Framework for Task-Based Learning.* New York: Longman.

Wode, H. (2009). *Frühes Fremdsprachenlernen in bilingualen Kindergärten und Grundschulen.* Braunschweig: Westermann.

Wolff, D. (1998). Lernerstrategien beim Fremdsprachenlernen. In Timm, J. P. (Ed.). *Englisch lernen und lehren* (pp. 70–77). Berlin: Cornelsen.

Wolff, D. (2007). Bilingualer Sachfachunterricht in Europa. Versuch eines systematischen Überblicks. *Fremdsprachen Lehren und Lernen, 36,* 13–29.

Wolff, D. (2013). CLIL als europäisches Konzept. In Hallet, W. & Königs, F. G. (Eds.). *Handbuch Bilingualer Unterricht. Content and Language Integrated Learning* (pp. 18–26). Seelze: Klett Kallmeyer.

Wood, D., Bruner, J.S. & Ross, G. (1976). The Role of Tutoring in Problem Solving. *Journal of Child Psychology and Psychiatry, 17,* 89–100.

Wright, A. (1995). *Storytelling with Children.* Oxford. Oxford University Press.

Wysocki, K. (2010). *Kooperatives Lernen im Englischunterricht. Die Kommunikationsfähigkeit fördern – vom ersten Schuljahr an.* Essen: NDS.

Young, D. J. (1993). Processing Strategies of Foreign Language Readers. Authentic and Edited Input. *Foreign Language Annals, 26*(4), 451–468.

Yule, G. (2006). *The Study of Language.* 3rd edition. Cambridge: Cambridge University Press.

Zaunbauer, A. C. M. (2007). Lesen und Schreiben in der Fremdsprache – von Anfang an. *Take Off!, 1,* 46.

Zaunbauer, A. & Möller, J. (2007). Schulleistungen monolingual und immersiv unterrichteter Kinder am Ende des ersten Schuljahres. *Zeitschrift für Entwicklungspsychologie und Pädagogische Psychologie, 39*(3), 141–153.

List of Children's Books

Allan, N. (1993). *The Queen's Knickers.* London: Red Fox.

Allan, N. (2009). *Father Christmas Needs a Wee!* London: Red Fox.

Arengo, S. & Robert, B. (2011). *The Little Red Hen. Classic Tales Level 1.* Oxford: Oxford University Press.

Barry, R. (1991). *Mr. Willowby's Christmas Tree*. New York: Random House.

Bond, M. (2007). *Paddington. The Original Story of the Bear from Peru*. London: HarperCollins.

Bond, M. (2010). *Paddington at the Palace*. London: HarperCollins.

Bond, M. (2011). *Paddington at the Tower*. London: HarperCollins.

Browne, E. (1994). *Handa's Surprise*. London: Walker Books.

Briggs, R. (1973). *Father Christmas*. London: Penguin.

Buehner, C. & Buehner, M. (2005). *Snowmen at Christmas*. New York: Dial.

Burningham, J. (1980). *The Shopping Basket*. London: Red Fox.

Christelow, E. (2007). *Five Little Monkeys Go Shopping*. Boston: Sandpiper.

Donaldson, J. & Scheffler, A. (1999). *The Gruffalo*. London: Macmillan.

Dr. Suess (1985). *How the Grinch Stole Christmas*. New York: Haper Collins.

Dumbleton, M. & Jellett, T. (2013). *Santa's Secret*. Sydney: Random House.

Laidlaw, C. & Williams, M. (Eds.) (2013). *Animal Camouflage*. London: Penguin Kids.

London, J. & Remkiewicz, F. (1996). *Froggy Goes to School*. New York: Puffin Books.

London, J. & Remkiewicz, F. (2000). *Froggy's Best Christmas*. New York: Puffin Books.

Martin, B. & Carle, E. (1999). *Brown Bear, Brown Bear, What Do You See?* New York: Macmillan.

Mayhew, J. (2003). *Katie in London*. London: Orchard Books.

Moore, C. C. & Harness, C. (1989). *The Night Before Christmas*. New York: Random House.

Munsch, R. (1990). *Something Good*. Toronto: Annick Press.

Murphy, J. (2007). Peace at Last. London: Macmillan.

Rosen, M. & Langley, J. (1998). Snore. London: Haper Collins.

Ross, T. & Oram, H. (1995). *A Message for Santa*. London: Andersen.

Sharratt, N. (1994). *Mrs Pirate*. London: Walker Books.

Taylor, N. & Williams, M. (Ed.) (2013). *A World of Homes*. London: Penguin Kids.

Thomas, V. & Paul, K. (1987). *Winnie the Witch*. Oxford: Oxford University Press.

Thomas, V. & Paul, K. (1996). *Winnie in Winter*. Oxford: Oxford University Press.

Wells, R. E. (1993). *Is a Blue Whale the Biggest Thing There Is?* Morton Grove: Albert Whitman & Co.

Rosen, M. & Oxenbury, H. (1989). *We're Going on a Bear Hunt.* London: Walker Books.

List of Teaching Material

Cornelsen (2009a). *Ginger. Handreichungen für den Unterricht 3. Early Start Edition Class 3.* Berlin: Cornelsen.

Cornelsen (2009b). *Ginger. Handreichungen für den Unterricht 4. Early Start Edition Class 4.* Berlin: Cornelsen.

Elsner, D., Kühl, S., Leonhardt-Holloh, U., Spangenberg, A. & Wolfram, J. (2004). *Findefix Englisch. Wörterbuch für die Grundschule.* München: Oldenbourg.

Ernst Klett Sprachen GmbH (2007a). *ELI illustrierter Wortschatz Englisch.* Stuttgart: Klett.

Ernst Klett Sprachen GmbH (2007b). *PONS. Englischwörterbuch für Grundschulkinder.* Stuttgart: Klett.

Gehring, W. (2013). *Ginger – Fit for Five.* Berlin: Cornelsen.

Gerngross, G. & Puchta, H. (2009). *Playway 4.* Stuttgart: Klett.

Klett (2014). *Lesen! English. Alle Lektüren für Ihren Unterricht.* Stuttgart: Klett.

Langenscheid Collins (2007). *Großes Schulwörterbuch Englisch – Deutsch.* Berlin: Langenscheidt.

McCafferty, S. & Kresse, T. (2011). *Let's Read and Write… That's it!* Offenburg: Mildenberger.

Mildenberger (2006). *Time for Stories.* Offenburg: Mildenberger.

Oldenbourg (2009a). *Sally 3. Lehrermaterialien. Ausgabe D/E.* München: Oldenbourg.

Oldenbourg (2009b). *Sally 4. Lehrermaterialien. Ausgabe D/E.* München: Oldenbourg.

University of Cambridge (n.d.). *Cambridge Young Learners English Tests. Sample Papers. Starters. Movers. Flyers.* Handed out from Englisches Institut Köln.

Westermann (2008). *Discovery 3. Teacher's Guide.* Braunschweig: Westermann.

Westermann (2009). *Discovery 4. Teacher's Guide.* Braunschweig: Westermann.

Index

Appendix (Online)

This work contains additional information as attachments. These can be downloaded from our website:
http://dx.doi.org/10.3726/b14360
Please enter the following activation code: PL18Dx9D

The online appendix contains the following contents:

Fremdsprachendidaktik / Foreign Language Pedagogy
inhalts- und lernerorientiert / content- and learner-oriented

Herausgegeben von / Edited by Gabriele Blell und Rita Kupetz
Mitbegründet von / Co-founded by Karlheinz Hellwig

Band 26 Rita Kupetz / Carmen Becker (eds): Content and Language Integrated Learning by Interaction. 2014.

Band 27 Hannah Ruhm: Narrative Kompetenz in der Fremdsprache Englisch. Eine empirische Studie zur Ausprägung mündlicher Erzählfertigkeiten am Ende der Sekundarstufe I. 2014.

Band 28 Ivana Marenzi: Multiliteracies and e-learning2.0. 2014.

Band 29 Gabriela Fellmann: Schüleraustausch und interkulturelle Kompetenz: Modelle, Prinzipien und Aufgabenformate. 2015.

Band 30 Heike Niesen: The impact of socio-cultural learning tasks on students' foreign grammatical language awareness. A study conducted in German post-DESI EFL classrooms. 2015.

Band 31 Jenny Jakisch: Mehrsprachigkeit und Englischunterricht. Fachdidaktische Perspektiven, schulpraktische Sichtweisen. 2015.

Band 32 Carmen Becker / Gabriele Blell / Andrea Rössler (Hrsg.): Web 2.0 und komplexe Kompetenzaufgaben im Fremdsprachenunterricht. 2016.

Band 33 Tanja Freudenau: Wortschatzarbeit im Englischunterricht der Grundschule. Eine Studie zum autonomen Lernen mit Online-Wörterbüchern. 2017.

Band 34 Gabriele Blell / Gabriela Fellmann / Stefanie Fuchs (Hrsg.): Die Sprachlernklasse(n) im Fokus. Deutsch als Zweitsprache und Englischunterricht. 2017.

Band 35 Claudia Müller: Serious Games for Global Education. Digital Game-Based Learning in the English as a Foreign Language (EFL) Classroom. 2017.

Band 36 Claudia Müller: Sichtweisen auf den Englischunterricht. 2018.

Band 37 Julia Reckermann: Reading Authentic English Picture Books in the Primary School EFL Classroom. 2018.

www.peterlang.com